Embargo
Apartheid's Oil Secrets Reveal

Embargo
Apartheid's Oil Secrets Revealed

Shipping Research Bureau
edited by Richard Hengeveld and Jaap Rodenburg

AMSTERDAM UNIVERSITY PRESS

Cover design: Pro Studio, Ferry Lindeman. For counterfeit stamps reproduced on cover, see page 118.
Typesetting: A-zet, Leiden

ISBN 90 5356 135 8

© Amsterdam University Press, Amsterdam 1995

Acknowledgements – We are grateful to the following for their assistance: Martin Bailey, David Craine, Kevin Davie, Frene Ginwala and ANC Johannesburg Research staff, John van Schaik, Øystein Gudim, H., Tom de Quaasteniet, Paul Gabriner, Huguette Mackay, Iris Maher, Liesbeth Poortman, Peter Sluiter, Erik van den Bergh and Carry van Lakerveld. Special thanks go to Keith Pieterse who assisted the editors and provided translations.

We thank the author and Faber and Faber Ltd Publishers (London) for their permission to include a quote from André Brink's novel *States of Emergency* on page 106.

This publication was made possible through the support of the funding partners of the Shipping Research Bureau (page 375) and the Association of European Parliamentarians for (Southern) Africa (AWEPA).

Interviews – The following list includes persons quoted in the first part of this book, except for those who wished to remain anonymous. Members and former members of the Shipping Research Bureau board and staff as well as Martin Bailey (London) and Bernard Rivers (New York) have been quoted on the basis of correspondence and discussions over several years. Interviews were conducted by the SRB in the places listed, unless otherwise indicated. Henrik Berlau, Amsterdam 26 January 1994; Kevin Davie, Johannesburg 6 June 1994; Frene Ginwala, London 8 June 1993, Johannesburg 9 June 1994; Aboobaker Ismail, Johannesburg 7 June 1994, telephone (Pretoria/Johannesburg) 22 December 1994 and 29 January 1995; Brian Lapping, telephone (London) 18 November 1994; Gwen Lister, letter 23 November 1993 and telephone (Windhoek) 3 December 1993; Zolile Magugu, Amsterdam 30 September 1992; John Malcomess, Amsterdam 14 May 1994; David Moisi, November 1993 [Cape Town, by Richard Blake/Carry van Lakerveld], Johannesburg 11 June 1994, telephone (Cape Town) 19 October 1994; Per Anders Nordengen, January 1995 [Oslo, by Øystein Gudim]; Aziz Pahad, Pretoria 9 June 1994; Joe Slovo, written interview (Pretoria) 7 November 1994; Jacob Zuma, Durban 10 June 1994. Tapes/transcripts are kept in the SRB archives (Amsterdam). Copies of the video registration of the Moisi interview by Blake and Van Lakerveld are kept at the Mayibuye Centre (Cape Town) and the Amsterdam Historical Museum.

Illustrations and Picture Credits – The responsibility for the selection of illustrations used in this book rests with the editors. Picture credits: American Labor Education Center 331; Christien Boeles 27, 248; Kare Bondesen/Aftenposten 286; Stefano Cagnoni/Report 107; Financial Times 68; Frank Greiner 23; Hans Hoffmann/FNV Magazine 49; Donna Katzin 328; The Mercury 85, 252; Kok Nam/AIM 236; Richard Hengeveld 133; Mark Peters/The Star 34; Jan Stegeman 46, 108, 317; United Nations/SRB XII; Arend van Dam 19; Ronny Willems 148; Bert Zijlma 58.

Contents

Preface by President Nelson Mandela

The awareness of history is critical in managing the present and in building the future. The year 1994 witnessed the end of the evil system of apartheid, institutional racism and white minority rule. South Africans have embarked on a course towards the reconstruction of a damaged society and national reconciliation. However, to heal the wounds of the past, that past has to be known. Apartheid has gone, but its legacy is still with us. The authors of this book help us to address one aspect of our past.

Oil is a strategic commodity, and the ability to import crude oil was vital for the survival of apartheid. Without adequate supplies, apartheid's aggressive and repressive military and security system could not function. Imports of oil were also necessary to maintain the South African economy. Rich as South Africa is in natural resources, the failure to find local oil deposits was the Achilles heel of apartheid:

The oil embargo was thus one of the most important sanctions against the apartheid regime. This book is the first one to bring out the seminal role of the ANC and particularly the late President Oliver Tambo in promoting this campaign. At the height of the sanctions movement in 1986, Tambo said in a speech to the Royal Commonwealth Society in London: 'We believe that the time has come for an end to the interminable debate about the effectiveness or non-effectiveness of sanctions. Practice itself has answered this question.'

The book before us comes straight from the heart of the international campaign for the oil embargo, with contributions from the Shipping Research Bureau, the United Nations and several other quarters that have for many years been dedicated to the embargo. It proves that oil sanctions helped tremendously in the efforts to end apartheid. It also allows an insight into the detrimental effects of decades of apartheid management of the energy sector. I believe that this book is a useful input to the 'interminable debate' on sanctions as an instrument of peaceful international pressure.

This experience, therefore, has had an impact beyond the boundaries of South Africa. But I do not regard this as merely a scholarly exercise. It is my firm conviction that a book such as this is important. For it tells the story of the tireless efforts to expose the clandestine oil trade to South Africa, and of the sacrifices by South African combatants in their missions against strategic oil installations – a story that has hitherto remained largely untold. It is also a good story.

Nelson Mandela
President of the Republic of South Africa

Glossary and Abbreviations

1 billion = 1,000 million

$ = US dollar, unless otherwise stated

R = South African rand; R1 (commercial rate) dropped from $1.28 in 1980 to $0.45 in 1985 and below $0.40 in 1989

ton = metric ton (1,000 kilos or 2,205 lbs); 1 long ton = 1.016 mt; 1 mt of crude oil (average gravity) = 7.33 barrels of 159 litres

AAPSO	Afro-Asian People's Solidarity Organisation
AFL-CIO	American Federation of Labor and Congress of Industrial Organizations
ANC	African National Congress of South Africa
AVU	Afrikaner Volksunie
AWEPAA	Association of West European Parliamentarians for Action Against Apartheid – now AWEPA European Parliamentarians for (Southern) Africa
b/d	barrels per day
B/L	Bill of Lading: receipt for goods shipped on board a vessel
b/o	bulk/oil carrier (see OBO)
BOSS	Bureau of State Security
CEF	Central Energy Fund
COCOM	Co-ordinating Committee (regarding export restrictions on strategic goods to East bloc countries)
COSATU	Congress of South African Trade Unions
CP	Communist Party
CWIU	Chemical Workers Industrial Union
DP	Democratic Party
dwt	deadweight tonnage: weight in metric tons that a ship can carry; 90–95 per cent of this is the actual cargo capacity, the remainder is accounted for by bunker fuel, stores, etc.
EC	European Community
ECOSOC	United Nations Economic and Social Council
ETA	expected time of arrival
Foc	flag of convenience
FRELIMO	Frente da Libertação de Moçambique: Mozambican Liberation Front
GATT	General Agreement on Tariffs and Trade
HCSA	Holland Committee on Southern Africa (Komitee Zuidelijk Afrika, KZA)
ICCR	Interfaith Center on Corporate Responsibility
ICFTU	International Confederation of Free Trade Unions
IEA	International Energy Agency
ILO	International Labour Organisation
ITF	International Transport Workers' Federation

LO	Landsorganisasjonen i Norge (Norwegian Federation of Trade Unions)
LPG	liquefied petroleum gas
MK	Umkhonto weSizwe
MNAOA	Merchant Navy and Airline Officers' Association – now National Union of Marine, Aviation and Shipping Transport Officers (NUMAST)
MUAA	Maritime Unions Against Apartheid
NGO	non-governmental organisation
NIOC	National Iranian Oil Company
NIS	(1) National Intelligence Service (South Africa) (2) Norwegian International Ship Register
NOCOSA	Norwegian Council for Southern Africa (Fellesrådet for det sørlige Afrika)
NP	National Party
NRP	New Republic Party
NSA	Norwegian Shipowners' Association
NUM	National Union of Mineworkers (South Africa)
NUS	National Union of Seamen (UK)
OAPEC	Organization of Arab Petroleum Exporting Countries
OATUU	Organization of African Trade Union Unity
OAU	Organization of African Unity
OBO	ore/bulk/oil carrier (combined carrier): vessel designed to carry either dry or liquid cargoes
OECD	Organisation for Economic Co-operation and Development
o/o	ore/oil carrier (see OBO)
OPEC	Organization of the Petroleum Exporting Countries
PAC	Pan Africanist Congress of Azania
p.c.	part cargo
PFP	Progressive Federal Party
RPG	rocket-propelled grenade
SACTU	South African Congress of Trade Unions
SADF	South African Defence Force
Sasol	South African Coal, Oil and Gas Corporation
SBM	single buoy mooring
SFF	Strategic Fuel Fund Association
Soekor	Southern Oil Exploration Corporation
Swakor	South West Africa Oil Exploration Corporation
SWAPO	South West Africa People's Organisation of Namibia
t/c	time charter: charter for a specified period of time
t/s	transhipment or ship-to-ship transfer
UDF	United Democratic Front
ULCC	ultra large crude carrier (300,000 dwt and over)
UMWA	United Mine Workers of America
UNCTAD	UN Conference on Trade and Development
UNGA	United Nations General Assembly
v/c	voyage charter: charter for one voyage
VLCC	very large crude carrier (200,000 dwt and over)
WCC	World Council of Churches
WFTU	World Federation of Trade Unions

South African Oil/Fuel Infrastructure

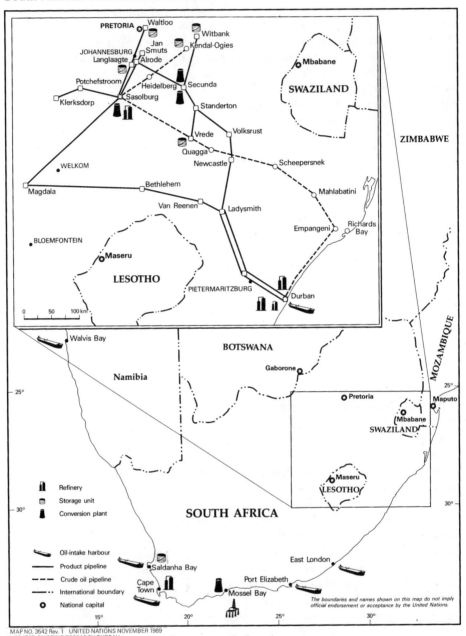

Refinery

Storage unit

Conversion plant

Oil-intake harbour

Product pipeline

Crude oil pipeline

International boundary

National capital

The boundaries and names shown on this map do not imply official endorsement or acceptance by the United Nations.

South Africa's crude oil refineries (capacity estimates late-1980s)[1]

SAPREF (1963) Durban *Shell/BP*	200,000 b/d
CALREF (1966) Milnerton, Cape Town *Caltex (Socal/Texaco)*	90,000 b/d
NATREF (1971) Sasolburg *Total/Sasol/NIOC*[2]	78,500 b/d
MOREF/GENREF (1953) Wentworth, Durban *Mobil*[3]	65,000 b/d

1   (a) Sources differed in their estimates during the sanctions years; (b) due to Sasol, the actual production was considerably lower than the above figures would suggest.
2   NIOC withdrew in the 1980s.
3   Sold to Engen (Gencor) in 1989.

Introduction

Iraq, Serbia, Haiti, Libya: by the 1990s, oil sanctions had become a fashionable weapon in international politics. But when they were tried against apartheid in South Africa over the preceding decades, they met with considerably less enthusiasm among the very governments who are today's champions of sanctions.

'Oil is the one vital raw material which South Africa does not possess,' the late Ruth First wrote in 1972 when discussing oil as *'the Achilles heel'* of the white minority regime.[1] The phrase was repeated in numerous studies, articles and speeches during the years that followed. Hardly a report would be published by the oil embargo watchdog, the Shipping Research Bureau, set up in Amsterdam in 1980, without some variation on the same theme.

This book tells the story of the international oil embargo against South Africa. From the first call for oil sanctions against the apartheid state in 1960 to their final lifting by the UN at the end of 1993, it describes how the oil embargo was steered through the intricacies of international diplomacy and pursued in spite of strong economic interests. The book provides an inside view of the secret oil trade and how it was revealed, showing how the embargo eventually proved that economic sanctions could work after all.

Contributions have been elicited from authors who have been closely involved in the embargo. The Shipping Research Bureau felt it important to record the experience of 20 years of sanctions monitoring and campaigning. Part A is written by the Bureau's last researcher, Richard Hengeveld, and constitutes its final publication. It not only gives a full account of the findings from 15 years of monitoring oil embargo violations, but also reveals important information which could not be told when apartheid was in place and the embargo in force. This part aims not only at 'revealing apartheid's oil secrets', but also at showing *how* these secrets were revealed. It is partly based on interviews with representatives from the ANC, the South African parliamentary opposition and anti-apartheid supporters outside South Africa; key figures of the South African energy sector, such as leading executives of Sasol, SFF and CEF, kept their doors shut. Although it was to be expected that paper shredders were put to work as apartheid drew to a close, the Shipping Research Bureau managed to lay its hands on several important confidential documents from within South Africa. Some of these arrived in time to be included in this book.

The operations of *Umkhonto weSizwe* against strategic oil installations in South Africa are chronicled in the chapter entitled 'The Spear of the Nation'. The June 1980 attack on the Sasol refineries became a legend in the story of the armed resistance against apartheid. This book is the first to present an account of the attack and later armed actions against

Sasol and other oil installations, based on interviews with the key militants involved, including the late Joe Slovo, who granted an interview a few months before his death.

The principal aim of the Shipping Research Bureau was to promote the oil embargo against South Africa with research findings on sanctions busting. In its series of reports, the names of countries and companies were listed in detailed tables, so that readers could single out the data that interested them. For this final publication, the Bureau has updated its database on oil embargo violations during the period 1979–93, which are summarised in a 16-page table.

Part B of this book comprises contributions by 11 authors, most of whom were intimately involved with the campaigning for and monitoring of the oil embargo.

The oil embargo against Rhodesia (1965–80) preceded that against South Africa. The British journalist *Martin Bailey*, who was actively engaged in research and writing on the Rhodesian and South African sanctions in the 1970s and 1980s, compares the two embargoes.

As a Senior Political Affairs Officer at the UN, the Iraqi *Amer Araim* was at the centre of the UN's involvement over sanctions, and he reflects on its role.

When George S. Bartlett, the last Minister of Mineral and Energy Affairs of the National Party era, wrote: 'The sanctions era demanded that government place a blanket of secrecy over our liquid fuel industry to ensure the supply of the energy lifeblood to our economy. Regrettably, this resulted in much public ignorance...',[2] not all were impressed by his crocodile tears. Two South Africans give their critical verdict on the government's energy policies under apartheid. Journalist *Kevin Davie* discusses the excessive burden placed on the economy by the policy of energy self-sufficiency, and he denounces the interventionist policies of the South African government. *Clive Scholtz* gives a first-hand account of the scandal which blew up around South Africa's secret oil contracts in the early 1980s. His story is the first to shed light on the identity of the *'anonymous gossip'*[3] who sparked off the scandal.

The question of why large volumes of oil continued to flow to South Africa from the Arab countries and Iran is addressed by two Dutch researchers on the Middle East, *Tom de Quaasteniet* and *Paul Aarts*. They analyse differences between Saudi Arabia, the main supplier during the early 1980s, and Kuwait, the 'cleanest' of the major oil exporters.

Øystein Gudim, Norway's principal oil embargo activist, tells how a broad anti-apartheid coalition was able to bring about the introduction of a statutory ban on oil transportations to South Africa in the face of a powerful shipping industry lobby. The role of seafarers' unions is dealt with by *Henrik Berlau*, president of the Danish Seamen's Union and one of the leaders of the Maritime Unions Against Apartheid initiative of the mid-1980s.

As this example of trade union action shows, oil sanctions against South Africa were not simply a matter of official embargoes. Individuals, action groups, unions, churches, local authorities and others participated in a worldwide campaign against the involvement of Royal Dutch/Shell in South Africa. Its successes and failures are discussed by *Erik van den Bergh*, who focuses on the Netherlands, home of Royal Dutch Petroleum Co., where the campaign started, and *Donna Katzin*, who presents a critical assessment of the American experience.

In the final contribution, Dutch economist *Peter van Bergeijk* attempts to bridge the existing gap between the academic debate on sanctions and the world of practical research and action. Van Bergeijk discusses academic theorising on the application and effectiveness of economic sanctions in the light of the experience of the oil embargo against South Africa.

PART A

Embargo
Apartheid's Oil Secrets Revealed

Oslo, September 1990 – 'Didn't you know NRK regulations do not allow video copies of news broadcasts to be given to third parties – not even to our friends of the Shipping Research Bureau?' Indeed, the Bureau's researcher knew that, but did the reporter realise that the Shipping Research Bureau would consider presenting his employer, the Norwegian State Broadcasting Corporation, with a steep bill for broadcasting, a few days earlier, a series of colour slides that had been shot in the Amsterdam harbour and had been passed off on unsuspecting viewers as original NRK material, in another of these celebrated Norwegian television reports that portrayed the latest violations of the oil embargo against South Africa by Norwegian tankers?

While his friend left the room with a brand new video cassette on his way to committing another violation of the rules, the Dutch researcher thought, 'Thank heavens, the Norwegians *had* jumped at the suggestion to use our slides...' His thoughts were interrupted by the unexpected appearance of yet another reporter, whose face lit up at the encounter which carried him back to the year before, when it had been his turn to get his teeth into embargo-busting shipping companies: 'You know, for me these days it's only opening nights at the theatre and that sort of thing. Never before or after have I seen anything like what we did in Amsterdam'.

Amsterdam, 8 November 1989 – This was exactly what the Shipping Research Bureau's researcher realised on his way to the port of Amsterdam: that he had never seen anything like this. He had managed to do his job for five years without ever having set foot on board an oil tanker.

One telephone call from the Bureau – 'Don't ask us how we know that the ship that has just docked in Amsterdam is loading for South Africa; all we can say is that our source seems reliable' – had sufficed for the NRK reporter to catch a flight to Amsterdam. A few days earlier, a man, who was subsequently code-named 'Forum', had called the Bureau with some really interesting information. Paradoxically, the most convincing aspect of his tip, that 'the *Höegh Foam* is currently loading some 65,000 tons of petrol in Amsterdam for South Africa on Marc Rich's orders, and will be taking coal from South Africa next', was *that it was not true*: there was no sign of the ship in Amsterdam at all – but four days later she showed up. 'Forum' must have had access to inside information. And he must have had a motive to blow the whistle. Speculating about the sources' motives is an interesting pastime for investigators; what really matters, however, is whether their information is correct.

On that November morning, when the researcher was en route to the vessel, a visit which he had made to Rotterdam the previous year came to mind. He had participated in an informative boat trip in which local politicians were introduced to the shadier sides of their harbour. He had felt quite at home seeing all the familiar names of tankers docked at the port, and it had taken some time for him to realise that never before had he set an eye on the ships themselves. ('Your work is exposing oil tankers to South Africa? So you must be strolling around the ports all day with raincoat-and-binoculars?')

It was amazing to see how easy it was to talk the watchman into raising the boom at the entrance to the dock area and reach the gangway unattended. The dyed-in-the-wool Dutch cameraman had taken over the reins in view of the slight apprehension which had taken hold of the NRK reporter: 'Just tell him you're a Norwegian and would like to see the captain'. The running camera swayed in the hand of the cameraman as he and his colleague followed the reporter up the gangway onto the deck of the tanker, and to the captain's cabin. Behind them, an unnamed assistant trailed along.

It was not clear whether the captain had his misgivings as to why a Norwegian television reporter had chosen *Amsterdam* of all places to make a documentary on 'The Current Boom in Norwegian Shipping'. Maybe he was a bit flattered anyway. While the camera crew patiently awaited the outcome of the deliberations, the reporter's 'assistant', who had not until then been quizzed as to the reasons for his presence, was trying hard, though not unsuccessfully, to adjust himself to the demands of a new day in the life of an SRB researcher. He was practising the trick of feigning a casual glance while making the most of this exciting extension of the Bureau's research routine. Indeed, just before the start of the interview he managed to whisper to the Norwegian reporter that from the documents scattered around, it was as clear as daylight that the ship had just returned to Europe *from South Africa*.

It was only when the interviewer brought the innocent conversation round to the question of which were the more popular routes for Norwegian shipping nowadays, and the captain was asked what, for example, had been his ship's last voyage and what would be her next destination, that the latter began to smell a rat. No, he didn't have the remotest idea, as he had just relieved his predecessor in Zeebrugge in Belgium a few days ago. And your next trip? 'We only get our orders once we leave port'. But what about the suggestion, by one of your crew, that it might be *South Africa*? The captain had some difficulty in maintaining his composure during the rest of the interview. The camera had hardly stopped shooting when the captain jumped up: '*Who* told you about South Africa? I want to consult my company in Oslo... I don't want you to broadcast that part of the interview...'

And so, while the camera crew swiftly disembarked in order to safeguard their recording from possible far-reaching second thoughts, the negotiations continued on the bridge. The shipping company, which had meanwhile been contacted by radio, did not have any objections, but the captain was adamant in demanding that this part of the interview not be broadcast. As for the Dutch assistant – well, he assumed that perhaps his presence was not really required in the ensuing Norwegian quarrel, and he was quite certain that it would be far more rewarding to discreetly withdraw to the officers' coffee lobby, where he would be able to steal a glance at a few Höegh ships' position lists lying about on the reading table. While remaining on the alert for Norwegian officers who occasionally walked in (he was kindly offered coffee by one of them), he managed to run through some of the lists and take some stealthy notes. This was really excellent material! It was going to serve as a basis for much further research, as ammunition for a media campaign exposing a sudden increase of refined petroleum shipments to South Africa by Norwegian vessels, and for a lobby and public campaign aimed, ultimately, at the tightening of oil sanctions against South Africa. It was clear that Amsterdam's own tarnishing of its self-proclaimed image as an 'anti-apartheid city' would have to be exposed; that the Norwegian oil shipping ban was being undermined; that Romanian oil embargo regulations and Danish and Swedish export bans had been broken. This would certainly stir up interest at the United Nations, which was about to draft a new report on the oil embargo. Just that week, indications were reaching the outside world that the South African government had finally admitted that sanctions could no longer be brushed aside as irrelevant; international pressure was having the intended effect.

The day after, the Berlin wall fell. This event, which sparked off a series of global developments whose outcome was to have far-reaching consequences for the apartheid regime, pre-empted Dutch media interest in a ship which was loading petrol in the port of Amsterdam and which would sail 'for Gibraltar' a few hours after the fall of the wall. The NRK, however, went on to broadcast its scoop, and to confront the Chief Executive Officer of the Höegh shipping company and the State Secretary of Foreign Affairs in the Norwegian government with the latest, alarming findings of the 'highly reputable Amsterdam Shipping Research Bureau'.

'The Last Peaceful Weapon'

It had been tried before. When the idea first surfaced with regard to South Africa during the early decades of apartheid rule, no one seemed to have enthusiastic recollections of the previous attempt to implement an oil embargo. In a conference convened in 1964 to discuss economic sanctions against South Africa, participants were told: 'To very many people "sanctions" means something that somebody tried, or did not really try, to do to Italy about Ethiopia in the 1930s; and failed'.[1] The course of that chapter of history, thus far the 'most celebrated attempt to apply sanctions in modern international politics',[2] did not inspire much confidence in the practicality of the oil embargo as an instrument. Anglo-French *raisons d'état* had blocked the intervention by the League of Nations under the provisions of its Covenant when Mussolini threatened to annex Ethiopia in the course of 1935. When the attack came in October, the League voted for half-hearted economic sanctions against Italy; however, oil and coal – 'the two products that might have thwarted Italy's attack'[3] – were not included. The British kept the vital Suez Canal route open for Italian shipping, and the USA and Germany, not members of the League, were not bound by the decision. The US government tried to dissuade oil companies from trading with Italy, and it was generally expected that the international sanctions would still be extended to include oil. In early 1936, the new British Foreign Secretary, Anthony Eden, advocated oil sanctions on the condition that everybody joined in order to make them effective, 'but it was clear that the condition negated the promise and made it an empty one'.[4] Hitler's occupation of the Rhineland (March 1936), the rapid Italian victory in Ethiopia (May 1936), and the onset of Franco's insurrection against the Spanish government (July 1936) were the final death knell for the unfortunate experiment. At the end of June 1936, only two nations voted in favour of the continuation of the League's sanctions programme: New Zealand and *South Africa*.

First steps

The first steps en route to economic sanctions against South Africa had a unilateral character. A decision to consider the imposition of economic sanctions as a result of the treatment of citizens of Indian origin in South Africa was taken by India as early as November 1944. When the measures came into effect in July 1946, India was the first country to institute a total ban on exports to and imports from South Africa (India did not export oil). India was also the first country which put the matter on the agenda of the United Nations.[5] In the UN, the issue soon merged with the broader question of apartheid as such, which first appeared on the agenda of the General Assembly at the request of 13 Afro-Asian states in 1952.[6] Meanwhile, South Africa's conduct towards the mandated territory of South-West Africa was another bone of contention between the international community and South Africa. Initially, recommendations and requests were directed at the South African government, and there was much legal haggling about the UN's power to institute sanctions.

'Economic boycott is one way in which the world at large can bring home to the South African authorities that they must either mend their ways or suffer from them'. A landmark in the growth of the movement for sanctions against the apartheid regime was the call which the later Nobel Peace Prize laureate, Chief Albert Luthuli, made in 1959 in his capacity as President of the African National Congress, together with the leaders of the South African Indian Congress and the Liberal Party.[7]

The Sharpeville massacre, 21 March 1960, in which 69 peaceful anti-pass protesters were killed and 180 wounded, marked the end of the non-violent phase of the struggle against apartheid. The ANC and the Pan Africanist Congress (PAC) were forced to pursue their activities underground. Meanwhile, abroad, support was mounting in favour of Luthuli's call for the economic isolation of South Africa. Oliver Tambo, who later became Luthuli's successor, fled the country five days after Sharpeville and became one of the leading figures in the 'South African Unity Front' which was formed in June 1960 and included members of both ANC and PAC. Until its demise in early 1962, the SAUF was engaged in a concerted campaign for an economic boycott. It was then that oil reappeared on the agenda.

Boycotts & Embargoes

Towards the end of the 16th century, the English borrowed a word from their Spanish enemies ('embargar': to arrest or restrain) and spoke of the 'embargement' of ships, merchants and goods. They started using the term *embargo* when referring to a prohibitory order, often issued in anticipation of war, by which ships of a foreign power were prohibited from entering or leaving English ports, or native ships from proceeding to (anticipated) enemy ports. The use of the word has since been extended to include the prohibition of trade in certain products or goods in general, imposed by a government or an international organisation.

The word *boycott* was coined in more recent times. The English estate manager Charles C. Boycott (1832–97), who achieved notoriety for his harsh collection of land rents in the face of demands by the Irish Land League for a rent reduction when harvests were bad, was the first to be subjected to a successful tactic of total isolation by his Irish tenants in the autumn of 1880. The term "Boycotting" was immediately adopted by newspapers in many languages as a generic term describing concerted plans of deliberate non-violent isolation of persons. In commerce, the term came to refer to the organised refusal by a group of persons to have dealings with a person, a firm or a country. The ultimate aim of a boycott in this sense – the word soon lost its capital B and inverted commas – is to exert pressure on the target.

Strictly speaking, an embargo such as one on oil sales to South Africa is established by an explicit legal undertaking on a government level. The word 'boycott' more loosely applies to all sorts of actions with the aim of isolating and influencing the targeted party – the apartheid government, or oil companies which refused to stop sales to or investments in South Africa.

In practice, the term 'oil boycott' was often used where 'oil embargo' would have been more appropriate. Most people didn't bother about the terminology and regarded 'oil embargo', 'oil boycott' and 'oil ban' as more or less interchangeable terms. The movement for oil sanctions – a convenient umbrella term – was a broad one and was not centered around government policy only. Local authorities, companies, concerned organisations and individuals all participated as they saw fit.

The first recorded call for sanctions specifically regarding oil can be traced to the Second Conference of Independent African States, held in Addis Ababa in June 1960. The conference 'invited the Arab states to approach all petroleum companies with a view to preventing Arab oil from being sold to the Union of South Africa' and recommended that African states 'refuse any concession to any company which continues to sell petroleum to the Union of South Africa'.[8] A few years later, at the July 1964 summit of the Organization of African Unity (OAU), founded in 1963 by the newly independent African states, a resolution was passed 'to appeal to all oil producing countries to cease as a matter of urgency their supply of oil and petroleum products to South Africa'.[9] Hardly any oil-exporting country heeded the call; one of the exceptions was Kuwait which had already banned exports of its oil to South Africa in the early 1960s. It was only in 1973 that the Arab states responded to the OAU's request, in their attempt to strike an alliance with the African states against Israel.

From the mid-1970s onwards, the oil embargo came to occupy a prominent position on the UN agenda regarding international sanctions policy. Dr Amer Araim, who for many years was closely involved in the UN oil embargo, tells the story in his contribution. However, the ball only started rolling slowly. When the newly appointed Pakistani director of the United Nations Centre against Apartheid, Assistant Secretary-General Iqbal Akhund, visited the Shipping Research Bureau in Amsterdam in 1985, he proudly recalled the fact that he had been a member of the Pakistani delegation which had been the first to plead for an oil embargo against South Africa. On 13 November 1961, Pakistan introduced an amendment to a draft resolution on apartheid calling upon all UN member states to refrain from exporting petroleum to South Africa; the amendment failed to obtain the required two-thirds majority.[10] Exactly two years after the Pakistani initiative, on 13 November 1963, a General Assembly resolution in connection with South Africa's policies on Namibia did include a once-only call for oil sanctions against South Africa. The USA, supported by 21 other countries, had tried in vain to prevent the clause from being included in the resolution; the opponents included the parent countries of all the world's major oil companies.[11] During the 1960s, oil sanctions were conspicuous by their absence from the resolutions of the General Assembly and the Security Council dealing with the issue of apartheid in South Africa, including those in which calls were made or decisions taken to implement punitive measures.[12]

1964: A pioneering conference

In its first report to the General Assembly after its establishment in 1963, the United Nations Special Committee against Apartheid recommended a study of the means to ensure an effective embargo on the supply of petroleum to South Africa.[13] At that time, such a study, though not connected with the UN recommendation, was already being undertaken by a group of British 'Young Fabians'.

In March 1960, following the announcement that the ANC was to be banned, the South African journalist Ronald Segal smuggled Oliver Tambo out of the country in his car. Four years later, Segal convened an *International Conference on Economic Sanctions against South Africa*, which was held in London from 14–17 April 1964 under the patronage of 11 heads of government from Africa and Asia. Proponents of economic sanctions and their opposite numbers had until then been involved in a debate on the issue described by Segal as 'a dialogue of pulpits, with the phrases of revelation'. The aim of the conference was 'to root the whole issue in reality'; it was 'essential to discover just how practical a proposition sanctions were if successful agitation for their employment against South Africa was ever to be mounted'.[14] Segal commissioned a number of experts to cover all the main problems of sanctions in a series of papers. The collected writings, including the conclusions and recommendations, were published under the title *Sanctions against South Africa* and were a pioneering achievement in the field.

The chairman, Tunisia's Foreign Minister Mongi Slim, told the conference: 'Economic sanctions are the last possible way of defeating *apartheid* peacefully'. The conference papers provided the participants with the evidence supporting the conclusion that 'total economic sanctions against South Africa, internationally organized, are necessary, legal, practical, enforceable, and much less costly ... than has previously been assumed'. However, they were 'likely to succeed only with the full cooperation of Britain and the United States'; with prophetic vision, a problem was laid bare which would remain during the decades to come, namely, 'How the Governments of those two countries are to be drawn from their present policy of profitable neglect – under which they do nothing calculated to disturb white supremacy while allowing their trade and the investments of their citizens in South Africa to grow'.[15]

Oil was briefly touched upon in several conference papers, but thoroughly explored in a paper by Brian Lapping, entitled 'Oil sanctions against South Africa'.

'We were passionate young men, just graduated from university at the end of the 1950s. As a budding journalist, I would often write on South Africa at a time when the Defence and Aid Fund and the Anti-Apartheid Movement were founded,' Brian Lapping recalls more than 30 years later. 'I had the simple-minded view that the apartheid regime embodied wickedness. I intensely hated them, and even seriously thought about finding a way to obtain a bomb and throw it into the South African embassy in London... A number of sensible friends convinced me that there were better ways, and with a group of young members of the Fabian Society we started to look into the viability of economic sanctions against South Africa.'

The members of the group (all 'rather more expert than me,' according to Lapping) came to the conclusion that the only sort of sanctions that might be viable would be oil sanctions. 'Ronald Segal somehow got to know about our group, and I wrote up a paper for the conference, which was partly based on the work that we had done.'

Despite the basic premise of Lapping's paper, 'that the withholding of oil is the one action which might be expected to be as damaging as total sanctions,'[16] his conclusions were not overly enthusiastic: unless the British and the Americans would wholeheartedly blockade the shores of South Africa, an embargo could not be enforced. Lapping says that he lost his belief in the viability of oil sanctions in the decades which followed: 'I actually reached the conclusion that economic sanctions per se would not work – until I was persuaded that I had been wrong when the measures taken by the international banks made the South African government change its tune in the mid-1980s.'

In the beginning of the 1960s, South Africa imported most of its requirements of crude oil, petrol and paraffin from *Iran*.[17] Iran prohibited trade with South Africa – except for petroleum. At a UN meeting held in 1963, an Iranian delegate said that his country was not prepared to stop its sales as long as South Africa was certain to get the oil from another source. Collective measures, he said, would willingly be accepted by Iran; a decade later, Iran had apparently forgotten this declaration of intent.[18] For Lapping and other participants in the 1964 conference, speculation about the possibility that British-ruled Southern Rhodesia and the Portuguese colonies in Africa could eventually become alternative sources in the case of an embargo still made sense. Angola was an exporter of crude oil, Mozambique had its Matola refinery, and a Shell–BP refinery was being set up in Umtali in Southern Rhodesia. The end of white rule in those countries was still in the lap of the gods.

There were other strategies which would enable the South African government to counter a possible oil cut-off. With reference to the government-owned Sasol corporation, which extracted oil from coal, one speaker said: 'The weakness here is recognized and action with a tinge of desperation is evident in this field'.[19] Lapping wrote that the process 'would be hopelessly uneconomic elsewhere', but was 'just able to pay in South Africa, thanks to a duty on imported natural oil, and exceptionally cheap coal, even by South African standards, which has been made available to the oil-from-coal organization'.[20] Nevertheless, the potential to rapidly raise Sasol's production capacity in the event of an embargo was considered to be negligible. The only South African crude oil refinery in operation at the start of the 1960s was the Mobil refinery in Durban. The much larger Shell–BP refinery in Durban and the smaller Caltex refinery near Cape Town came on stream in October 1963 and 1966, respectively. The accumulation of oil stocks (Lapping wrote that disused mines could be adapted for storing crude oil) was also discussed as a way by which South Africa could circumvent the effects of an embargo; therefore, 'Only an embargo with a clear prospect of outlasting South Africa's stocks would be worth attempting.'[21]

Although the problem of applying economic sanctions against South Africa was to a large extent defined at the conference in terms of 'total sanctions', the enforcement of which was thought to be synonymous with applying a blockade, there was also a feeling that total sanctions and a totally effective blockade were not required in order to obtain the intended result. In this connection, oil was singled out as a key strategic material; South Africa was most vulnerable to its shortage. The conference commission which addressed the question of oil sanctions agreed that 'although oil sanctions would not by themselves be enough, an effectively policed system would play an important role in a programme of total sanctions';[22] the withholding of oil would seriously affect the agricultural sector, private transport, and above all the mobile defence and security forces.

As early as 1964, Brian Lapping saw that embargoes, including an oil embargo against South Africa, were not foolproof. His judgement reads as a foreboding of many of the problems which were to beset the implementation of the international oil embargo in the following decades: 'Unless it is backed by a blockade, an embargo could be rendered ineffective if one Western government decided not to break it, not even to encourage companies to break it, but merely to allow some trifling inefficiencies of administration occasionally to hamper the free movement of the embargo inspectors sent by the United

Nations, or regularly, but always accidentally, to fail to stop sales of oil to independent businessmen, for whose subsequent use of the oil the government concerned could not be held responsible ... Thus it can be seen that an oil embargo requires the active cooperation of the powerful countries of the West ... Such cooperation will never be obtained by exhortation...'[23]

Calm before the storm

Brian Lapping admits that he was 'quite flattered when some professor in reviewing Segal's book in the South African Anglo American Corp. magazine *Optima* said the only really valuable and well-researched paper was mine,' but says that his paper 'was a pebble in the pond...'

After the discussion on the above-mentioned November 1963 resolution, the UN Special Committee against Apartheid wrote to OPEC seeking advice on the operation of an oil embargo.[24] OPEC as such never took up the idea. Araim shows that all the suggestions regarding the oil embargo which were aired within the UN during the 1960s came to nothing. If there was a body which kept the notion of an oil embargo alive during those years, then it was the OAU which consistently pleaded for comprehensive sanctions. But more was needed for the actual action which followed. The first impulse was provided by a development which started in 1965; the second by one which took place in 1973.

At the opening session of the 1964 London conference, a message was read from the Leader of the Opposition, Labour leader Harold Wilson, who, in the words of Ronald Segal, 'expressed opposition to economic sanctions but did so with such finesse as to allow almost limitless room for subsequent manoeuvre'.[25] This room was just what Wilson as Prime Minister needed when Rhodesia's white minority government led by Ian Smith proclaimed its unilateral declaration of independence (UDI) on 11 November 1965.

Britain had threatened Smith with an oil embargo but did not implement the measure following UDI. It failed to take any steps when the Security Council called upon UN member states to institute oil sanctions against the breakaway regime. When it was put under pressure by the OAU, it eventually implemented an oil embargo on 17 December 1965 – meanwhile doing nothing to prevent its oil companies from violating it. The oil embargo (mandatory since 1966) remained in effect until Zimbabwe gained its independence in April 1980. Thanks to its white neighbours – Portuguese-administered Mozambique until 1975, and South Africa – and the complicity of the international oil companies, Rhodesia's oil lifeline was not cut off. It took more than a decade of UDI rule before two British researchers, Bernard Rivers and Martin Bailey, broke the story of the scandal of the officially condoned busting of British and UN oil sanctions against Rhodesia, which won them more than one 'Journalist of the Year' award in 1978. A brief chronicle of the Rhodesian oil embargo, which hardly does justice to all the fascinating details of his book *Oilgate* (1979), can be found in Bailey's contribution, in which he makes a comparison between the Rhodesian and the South African embargoes.

Closing the net

The emerging role of South Africa in the sustenance of the Rhodesian regime by means of shrewdly arranged oil supplies was to provide a new argument in favour of and renewed interest with regard to oil sanctions against the former. But first, another development gave an impulse to the use of the oil weapon against South Africa. In their contribution, De Quaasteniet and Aarts show how in November 1973 the African states finally succeeded in persuading the Arab oil-producing countries to proclaim an oil embargo against South Africa.

They also relate, however, how the oil continued to flow, as Iran did not follow the example set by the Arab states. Soon after 1973 Iran had, to all appearances, taken over as a virtual monopolist supplier of oil to the embargoed apartheid state.[26] Yet the measures taken by the Arab states, and the ensuing activity at the UN and elsewhere, served to heighten South Africa's awareness of its vulnerability, and various measures were taken to counter the threat.

It is common practice for countries to have a strategic oil reserve in order to cope with irregularities in the supply. In South Africa this practice was given a new significance in the 1960s in view of the need to defend the apartheid system from the hostile outside world; a South African newspaper commented: 'It is believed that the Government plans to maintain a perpetual stock of oil and vital goods no matter what the outcome of the Rhodesian and South West Africa issues are, so that the policy of separate development is assured of unimpeded progress over an indefinite period'.[27] In 1964, the *Strategic Fuel Fund* was established as a government organisation to control the stockpiling programme. Storage tanks were built at the refineries, and from 1967 onwards disused coal mines were employed for storing crude oil. When the Arab countries cut off supplies in 1973, South Africa was able to absorb the shock by drawing upon the reserves. In the years that followed it transpired that South Africa had increased the rate at which it added to the volume of its oil stockpile; however, exact figures were not disclosed.

Introducing austerity measures was another policy. Within days of the announcement of the Arab embargo, the government decided to limit the trading hours for service stations, lower speed limits and take other steps aimed at reducing fuel consumption. Ration coupons were printed, but in the end rationing was not actually introduced.[28]

Further attempts were made in order to tap alternative sources. This did not primarily mean that a search was on for other friendly suppliers, although one was found in the tiny Far Eastern sultanate of Brunei; from 1975 onward a rising percentage of its oil production was shipped to South Africa.[29] After the imposition of the Arab embargo, the search continued for oil and gas deposits in South Africa as well as in occupied Namibia. Soekor, the government-controlled oil exploration corporation which had been set up in 1965, and its South-West African subsidiary, Swakor, had had little success until then. The most significant development which was triggered by the 1973 embargo was the decision, taken in December 1974, to build another oil-from-coal factory, much larger than the existing plant in Sasolburg. Sasol 2 was built, at an enormous cost, in Secunda in the Eastern Transvaal and was to increase the production of synthetic fuel seven- to tenfold. As usual, the exact figures were kept secret.

Reinforcing the secrecy surrounding energy-related matters was another reaction to the embargo. From late 1973 onwards, the publication of oil import and export statistics was suspended indefinitely. In the years which followed, the clauses relating to secrecy in the National Supplies Procurement Act of 1970 were tightened with regard to oil-related matters in the Petroleum Products Act of 1977. Heightened official secrecy was but one of the methods used by the government to enhance its control of the energy sector to ensure that the foreign-owned oil companies operating in South Africa continued to serve the national interest. The National Supplies Procurement Act made it an offence for oil companies operating in South Africa to refuse to supply any customer – read: army and police. The government was able to order oil companies to produce specialised oil products for strategic reasons, irrespective of commercial potential. When these measures were tightened even further in 1977 as a result of the United Nations' proclamation of a mandatory arms embargo against South Africa, the Minister of Economic Affairs explained that the aim was to prevent foreign parent companies from prohibiting – under pressure from their own governments or anti-apartheid pressure groups – their subsidiaries from producing certain strategic goods.[30] This very conveniently provided the international oil companies with an alibi; they seemed far from unwilling to satisfy the wishes of the South African government.[31] The oil majors controlled a global 'pool' of oil, into which embargoed as well as non-embargoed oil was fed, and they were able to keep supplying South Africa from that pool, by diverting Iranian oil to South Africa while shipping more Arab – embargoed – oil to 'neutral' destinations. The compliance of the oil companies was apparently achieved by means of a combination of compulsion and incentives. The oil companies were, for example, forced to foot part of the bill arising from the buildup of strategic stocks, in exchange for the franchise given to them to build or expand their refineries. Back in the 1960s the threat of forced nationalisation of shareholdings in South African refineries had been used in order to obtain guarantees from parent companies that they would not stop the flow of oil to the country. At the end of 1973, the government raised fuel prices; in the official South African Yearbook for 1974 there was speculation concerning the motives: 'Nobody was saying so, but it ... seemed clear that, by ensuring that South Africa remained one of the most profitable and attractive of the world's smaller oil markets, the government was helping to secure maximum cooperation from the international oil companies in the difficult days ahead'.[32]

Indeed, there were difficult times ahead. The Arab embargo served to focus the attention of the UN Special Committee against Apartheid on the oil embargo.[33] In December 1975, after preparatory activities of the Committee (two years may seem a long time, but UN activity has a momentum of its own, often related to the schedule of annual sessions), the General Assembly adopted a resolution on the 'situation in South Africa' which included an appeal to all states concerned to impose an oil embargo. From that moment on, during almost two decades, not a single session was to pass without the oil embargo featuring in the resolutions of the General Assembly on South Africa.

Developments within South Africa added fuel to the fire. More intergovernmental organisations joined the call for an oil embargo. Uprisings began in Soweto in June 1976. Two months later the 86 members of the Non-Aligned Movement unanimously issued a call for oil sanctions; the Commonwealth was also taking up the issue, and so did the UN Economic and Social Council.[34]

During this period, the UN Special Committee against Apartheid consulted with and appealed to various other organisations which were of relevance to the issue or had al-

ready started their own programmes to promote oil sanctions, among them the League of
Arab States (1976), the OAU (1977) and OPEC (1977). In the December 1977 resolution
of the General Assembly, the OAU was singled out as the appropriate organisation for the
Special Committee to cooperate with in promoting the oil embargo. In July 1977, the
OAU had established a Committee of Seven on Oil Sanctions to visit oil-exporting states.

The action on the part of official bodies got a further impetus from two developments on
the 'private' scene.

Firstly, in various quarters, individuals and organisations concerned about developments in South Africa started to highlight the role of *transnational oil companies* in up-
holding apartheid. In his contribution to this book, Van den Bergh describes how, prior to
the Arab embargo in 1973, a small Dutch Christian group took an initiative which went on
to become a worldwide campaign against the presence of Shell in South Africa. Cor
Groenendijk, then chairman of the 'Working Group Kairos', says that the group 'soon
realised that our aim could not be attained through action in one country only. That is why
we soon decided to make contact with churches abroad.' Some church groups and anti-
apartheid organisations in Britain, the USA and elsewhere had already started to take
action against companies with investments in South Africa, in some cases acting independently, in other cases in unison with their colleagues in other countries, and gradually,
oil companies came to be singled out as major targets. In Britain the first ripples were felt
when Kairos translated its study on *Shell in South Africa* (June 1976). In the USA the
Interfaith Center on Corporate Responsibility and others had developed a strong movement on the issue of business ethics, which was also directed against the involvement of
oil companies such as Mobil and Texaco in South Africa, and against the role of Fluor
Corporation as the principal contractor on the Sasol 2 project. An example of an early
interest taken in the issue by trade unions is provided by oil workers in Trinidad who
initiated actions in 1977 to stop oil and other trade with South Africa.[35]

In a second, independent development, the aforementioned English economist
Bernard Rivers had begun an investigation into the failure of Rhodesian oil sanctions. In
1974 Rivers got in touch with someone who had worked for Mobil in Rhodesia, and after
a series of secret meetings, always at different locations in London, he managed to persuade 'Oliver' to hand over 95 pages of documentation which had been secretly copied in
Mobil's office in the Rhodesian capital, Salisbury, to a South African exile in London.
Thanks to his relations with the ANC, the South African could guarantee that the highly
revealing and incriminating material would be exposed to maximum effect. This did not
get Rivers any further, as he was not allowed to inspect the papers. Before long, things
began to go wrong for Okhela – the secret organisation of which the South African, as it
turned out, had actually been a member. Rivers had to wait until May 1976, when he was
eventually asked to prepare a publication on the basis of the documents, which had by
then been transferred to New York. He was astonished when he set eye on them for the
first time. The papers confirmed in considerable detail that Mobil subsidiaries had been
deeply involved in a scheme to supply Rhodesia, and moreover showed that the arrangements had been set up with the deliberate intention of concealing Mobil's involvement in
sanctions busting.[36]

Two lines of approach – the Rhodesian one in Rivers' *The Oil Conspiracy*, and the
South African one in the Dutch *Shell in South Africa* – converged when both reports were

by chance released within days of each other, which happened to be just after the start of the Soweto uprisings. Interest in the role of oil companies in Southern Africa was aroused, and more publications followed, such as one by Rivers' friend Martin Bailey on *Shell and BP in South Africa*, which drew extensively on the Dutch report and was published in London in March 1977 by the Haslemere Group, a Third World research group, and the Anti-Apartheid Movement. Bailey summarised his message as follows: 'Shell and BP – together with the three other major international petroleum companies operating in South Africa (Mobil, Caltex and Total) – have played a crucial role in helping to break the oil embargo', while he struck a rather more activist tone in his conclusion: 'Shell and BP, by operating in South Africa, have been helping to prop up – and profit from – the apartheid system. While the two petroleum companies continue to do business in South Africa they are oiling the wheels of apartheid. Shell and BP have now become an integral part of the repressive apartheid system'.[37] It is interesting to note that the publishers thanked the International University Exchange Fund, 'which financed the printing costs of this pamphlet'. The Fund's deputy director, a South African exile called Craig Williamson, wrote on 23 September 1977 to offer his congratulations: 'I have been most impressed by the entire campaign which has developed around the oil issue'. At this point anti-apartheid movements had no suspicion that Williamson was not a committed supporter, and it came as a shock when in 1980 he was exposed as a South African spy. We will meet him later on in this book.

At this stage, official and private initiatives were beginning to merge. The Bingham Inquiry on Rhodesian sanctions busting, discussed in Bailey's contribution to this book, was triggered by *Shell and BP in South Africa*. Rivers and Bailey were subsequently invited to act as consultants to the Commonwealth and the United Nations.

Oil Sanctions against South Africa by Bailey and Rivers, a 90-page report published by the United Nations Centre against Apartheid in June 1978, was the first study of the feasibility of an oil embargo against South Africa to appear after Brian Lapping's 1964 paper. South Africa's oil consumption had meanwhile risen sharply, the political map of Southern Africa had drastically changed, and the OAU mission to oil-producing countries of 1977 had established that all the non-Arab members of OPEC, excluding Iran, had joined the Arab members in subscribing to the oil embargo. According to Bailey and Rivers, if the UN were to make the oil embargo mandatory, then the most important loopholes would disappear: Iran would presumably be willing to participate, and oil companies would no longer be able to channel oil from their 'pool' to South Africa.

A naval blockade was no longer seen as necessary by Bailey and Rivers. Much simpler, but effective, methods could be devised, such as a Security Council measure which would make it possible to seize tankers after a delivery to South Africa, or to withdraw national registration facilities to such tankers. There were no insurmountable problems in determining which ships had delivered oil to South Africa, according to Bailey and Rivers, who had experimented with the monitoring of tanker movements on the basis of data from Lloyd's, the British insurance giant which has a worldwide network of agents, through which it gathers information on shipping movements. 'The scheme we have outlined, if implemented, could not guarantee that no tanker ever delivered oil to South Africa. *But it would mean that it would become extremely difficult – and very expensive – for South Africa to obtain transport facilities for importing oil*'; the costs to the international

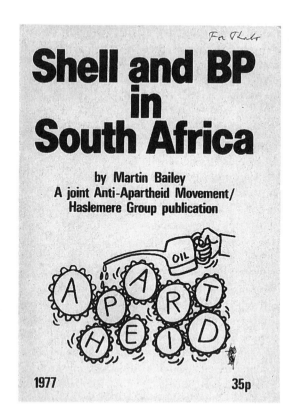

community would be relatively small, which led Bailey and Rivers to conclude that an oil embargo was 'one of the most cost-effective forms of pressure'.[38]

But the principal part of the report addressed technical, not political, issues. A lot of attention was given to South Africa's extreme dependence on imported oil and its vulnerability to an effective embargo, and to the question of how long it would be able to survive the effects of an embargo. Even with regard to the implementation of its counter-strategy, South Africa was critically dependent on foreign capital and technology. Referring to the Sasol 2 coal liquefaction project, Sasol's chairman in 1977 said that 'Foreign purchases and contracts are concerned mainly with specialized and proprietary equipment not manufactured or normally obtainable in the Republic'; Bailey and Rivers cited a figure of 43 per cent of the estimated cost of Sasol 2, or some $1.2 billion, that would be incurred from goods and services from abroad.[39] At that time, prior to the completion of the Sasol 2

'A petty example of Shell's acceptance of apartheid was shown by the company's proud announcement that 25 luxury toilets had been installed in their service stations for "whites only". Shell's Public Relations Officer pointed out that "when we find that the non-whites have proved that they are capable of looking after and keeping their present toilets clean, the new luxury restrooms would be made available to them".'

From: M. Bailey, *Shell and BP in South Africa*, 1977, 22-24 (quoting *The Leader*, 14 January 1972)

plant, 99 per cent of the liquid fuel needs had to be imported. Prospects of finding domestic oil appeared to be minimal, and in any event commercial exploitation would take many years. Although oil provided only about a fifth of the country's domestic needs, this did represent 'an almost irreducible minimum ... Certain sectors of the economy which are currently dependent on oil cannot convert to other energy sources; others could only do so at considerable expense'.[40]

Bailey and Rivers used an incident which had taken place in November 1973 to illustrate South Africa's *military* dependence on imported oil. A tanker carrying aviation gasoline to South Africa was delayed for a few weeks in the Middle East. This fuel was not produced by a single South African refinery, and since stocks were limited, privately owned light aircraft throughout the country were grounded until the tanker arrived. Thousands of these aircraft were involved in the Air Commando system and formed a vital element in the government's 'counter-subversion' measures.[41]

It was estimated that by the time Sasol 2 came on stream, the two oil-from-coal plants would provide only 13 per cent of the country's oil needs. Suggestions that a third Sasol plant be built were dismissed by the Minister of Economic Affairs who in February 1978 announced that 'capital expenditure and manpower requirements for such a project are vast, and we are not at this moment planning the construction of a further Sasol'.[42]

Bailey and Rivers estimated that South Africa could theoretically survive a cut-off of all oil imports for two years at most even after Sasol 2 came on stream, during which time there would be enormous economic and social disruption. According to Bailey and Rivers, 'To suggest, as some South African sources have done, that oil stocks could keep the country going until Sasol II starts full production in 1982, and that the two Sasol plants could then somehow provide most of their needs, is clearly not based on an accurate evaluation of the situation'. They concluded that South Africa remained vulnerable, but even quite apart from the threat of a UN embargo, it had 'considerable cause to worry at its dependence on the continued support from Iran. No Government likes to know that 90 per cent of its oil comes from a single supplier'.[43]

'Imperial Majesty, will South Africa get oil?' On a wide marble verandah overlooking the Caspian Sea, Roelof 'Pik' Botha put this question to the Shah of Iran. The year was 1977. Prime Minister Vorster had sent his young, newly appointed Minister of Foreign Affairs on a highly secretive mission. Botha had been picked up at the Waterkloof Air Force base by a Boeing 747 with an Iranian crew sent by the Shah. The aircraft took off in the dark, and around daybreak it was approaching Yemen, which was in the throes of a civil war. A number of MiG fighter aircraft of the People's Democratic Republic of Yemen surrounded the 747. While Botha and the other passengers were in suspense inside the plane, the pilot was engaged in a lengthy explanation to his pursuers, who eventually allowed him to continue unimpeded to Iran, where Botha was awaited by a lonely and fearful Shah. Just before the two men had lunch at the Shah's palace on the Caspian Sea, Botha took the bull by the horns: 'We are vulnerable in a number of areas, especially oil. My Prime Minister would like to know whether, in the event of an oil embargo against South Africa, we can rely on continued supplies from Iran.' The Shah stared out to sea in contemplation. After some time he said: 'You know that if things get out of hand in my country, it will be over within a couple of weeks not months.' – Botha knew that he had to warn Vorster that the time had come to find other sources of supply.[44]

A unique opportunity

In September 1978, Iranian workers in the Ahwaz oilfields went on strike, later followed by Abadan refinery workers and staff employees in the Ahwaz oilfields. The opposition to the Shah's regime mounted; a nationwide general strike of oil workers started on 4 December. On 23 November and 3 December, the exiled Ayatollah Khomeini urged a halt to all oil exports and endorsed the strike in the oil industry. Oil production and exports fell to less than a quarter by late December. On 13 December Khomeini warned that states supporting the Shah would get no oil when his movement came to power. On 11 January 1979, five days before the Shah left Iran, his new Prime Minister, Bakhtiar, announced that no further sales of oil would be made to South Africa; the strike had, however, already effectively stopped supplies. Khomeini returned to Tehran, Bakhtiar resigned on 11 February, and the new revolutionary regime pledged to join the oil embargo.[45]

'The cut-off of Iranian oil has created an important new situation ... This situation offers a unique opportunity for the international community to put pressure on the South African Government', Martin Bailey said in a statement made before the UN Special Committee against Apartheid on 8 June 1979.[46] Not a single OPEC country openly sold oil to South Africa; the time had come for a mandatory oil embargo to succeed. In January 1979 the General Assembly had subscribed to the same view in a resolution, the first to be solely concerned with the oil embargo.

The Special Committee stepped up its efforts concerning the embargo and, after being requested by the Assembly in December 1979 to promote the organisation of conferences and seminars in cooperation with governments and non-governmental organisations, took the decision to sponsor a seminar to specifically address the question of the oil embargo.

Meanwhile, the South African government had been forced into taking measures in order to adapt to the new situation. 'One Sunday morning in November 1978,' a former South African oil director recalls, 'Chris Heunis, then Minister of Economic Affairs, called a meeting with the managing directors of the oil companies. He met with them in alphabetical order. First with BP, then with Caltex, Mobil, Sasol, Shell and Total, in that order. Heunis repeated the same story to each in turn. He said, "Our petrol pumps must stay wet". Each managing director was asked: "Can you import crude oil, and do you want to import crude oil?" Eventually three companies said they were able and willing to provide oil: Sasol, Shell and Total.'[47] The Strategic Fuel Fund Association (SFF) was given a new role. After the discussions between Heunis and the oil companies, an 'Equalisation Fund' was established on 1 January 1979 to compensate the subsidiaries of Western oil companies refining oil in South Africa for their abnormal costs of crude oil purchases. The SFF, managed by Sasol, administered the Equalisation Fund, and effectively became the state procurement agency for South Africa's crude oil purchases from abroad. (It was only towards the end of 1993, when the secrecy surrounding oil affairs was lifted, that the then Energy Minister, George Bartlett, revealed that during the period in which the SFF purchased crude oil on behalf of those companies that could no longer be supplied by their parent companies, Shell SA and Total SA were the exceptions and obtained their own crude oil.[48])

Former opposition MP and energy spokesman John Malcomess recalls: 'When we lost Iranian supplies, I think Heunis lost his head to a certain extent: he was prepared to pay *any* price as long as we got fuel.' According to SFF chairman Danie Vorster many years later, joint purchases via the SFF made it possible for South Africa to sign more favourable long-term contracts despite its weak position.[49] The available evidence – see for example Scholtz's contribution – indicates that the terms offered were much less favourable than suggested and that South Africa had to pay extra premiums in its scramble for oil after the fall of the Shah. Heunis himself was quoted as saying that his country had to pay premiums as high as 70 per cent on the world oil price in open-market purchases.[50] In December 1978, the South African *Financial Mail* predicted that 'If Iran joins the boycotters, SA will have to resort to unorthodox methods of acquisition'.[51] Heunis, who had his portfolio changed to Transport Affairs in June 1979, admitted later that the 'acquisition of oil was more difficult than arms', and that the oil embargo 'could have destroyed this country'. Pietie du Plessis, who became Energy Minister in August 1980, once claimed his purchasing officials spent their time abroad 'endangering their lives'.[52]

South Africa went to great lengths to find alternatives to make up for the loss of Iranian oil. In one bizarre scheme, it tried to secretly finance the building of a refinery on the Caribbean island of Dominica, in exchange for future oil supplies, but when news of the scheme was leaked, the resulting scandal was one of the factors which led to the fall of the Dominican government.[53] In South Africa, Soekor redoubled its efforts, and on 22 February 1979, Heunis announced that yet another Sasol plant would be built, doubling the capacity of the Sasol 2 plant which was still under construction. In May 1979, Heunis was asked why the oil companies had been allocated such a large proportion of the quota for South African coal exports. He replied that the quotas for the companies had been 'subjected to the condition that they continue to fulfil their obligations in supplying liquid petroleum fuels'; if the oil tap was shut, their quotas would be 'reviewed'.[54]

Monitoring oil embargo violations

In their 1978 report to the United Nations, Bailey and Rivers toyed with the idea of a 'clearing house' under the aegis of the UN into which information – ranging from Lloyd's shipping data to data obtained by aerial reconnaissance – could be fed, in order to establish which tankers had violated the embargo. The Organization of African Unity took up the idea in July 1979, when its Council of Ministers passed a resolution in which it advocated steps towards 'the creation of an appropriate machinery to monitor oil shipments to South Africa'.[55]

The call was echoed in the final declaration of the UN co-sponsored *International Seminar on an Oil Embargo against South Africa*, held in Amsterdam from 14–16 March 1980, which stated that 'an essential component of an effective oil embargo against South Africa is the creation of a machinery to monitor all shipments of oil to South Africa'. The seminar was organised by two Dutch anti-apartheid organisations, the Working Group Kairos and the Holland Committee on Southern Africa. Martin Bailey and Bernard Rivers attended the seminar as key experts. Participants discussed concrete actions such as those already being taken by Nigeria, and explored possibilities for further action to make companies and governments stop 'Fuelling Apartheid' (the title of the contribution by the ANC). In his address, the chairman of the UN Special Committee, the Nigerian ambassador to the UN, Mr B. Akporode Clark, said that 'the big oil companies have resorted to unscrupulous treachery to defeat the policy objectives of those countries which produce the oil ... [They] have gone to elaborate lengths to perfect oil swapping arrangements, cooking of the books regarding the movements of tankers and to stage manage the Rotterdam oil spot market'.[56]

A mind-boggling scheme to break the embargo had come to light less than two months before and was the topic of the day. The case of the tanker *Salem* – which soon became known as the 'Fraud of the Century' – epitomised the devious lengths South Africa went to in its 'unorthodox methods of acquisition'. On 17 January 1980, crew members of the tanker *British Trident*, sailing off Senegal, witnessed the mysterious sinking of an allegedly fully laden tanker. The rescued crew of the *Salem* climbed calmly aboard the *British Trident* carrying packed suitcases and freshly cut sandwiches, but surprisingly, they hadn't had enough time to save the ship's log. 'If this was scuttling, then it was king-sized. A ship more than three football fields in length ... cannot lose itself beneath the ocean without causing speculation'; what unfolded was a 'saga of mystery and intrigue, setting in motion a mass of speculation concerning piracy, sanctions busting and documentary fraud'.[57] It soon filtered through that most of the *Salem* cargo had been discharged in South Africa, where the ship had called under a false name; the SFF had bought the oil from a group of fraudsters who had themselves stolen the oil in the first place and had put a 'captain' on the ship who held no proper certificate and whose name was linked to an earlier maritime fraud involving the scuttling of a ship. Court cases ensued in various countries, and some of the key players were brought to justice – although one of them,

Oil embargo seminar, Amsterdam 14 March 1980. Left to right: Ambassador Clark (UN Special Committee against Apartheid), Cor Groenendijk (Kairos), Ambassador Sahnoun (Algeria), Sam Nujoma (SWAPO), Jan Nico Scholten MP (Netherlands)

Frederick Soudan, who received a sentence of 35 years in the US for his part in the fraud, managed to escape from jail after less than three years, and the case against the Dutchman Anton Reidel was dropped in 1987 after a lengthy legal wrangle.

The first book devoted in its entirety to the *Salem* affair has already been written,[58] while the *Salem* also features prominently in other books on maritime fraud, such as those written by Barbara Conway, the journalist who broke the story, and Eric Ellen, the director of the International Chamber of Commerce's International Maritime Bureau, a maritime fraud watchdog founded in 1981 in the wake of the *Salem* affair.[59] More revelations are expected from a number of South Africans who have been closely involved in the issue and who are able to give their version of the events, now that apartheid's official oil secrets are gradually being uncovered. A start has been made in this book by Clive Scholtz, but a lot remains to be told, for example, on the role of Shell in the affair, or who the real masterminds behind the *Salem* fraud were – Reidel, Soudan, or perhaps the Greeks Mitakis and company?

For the first time, the SRB is able to record an earlier oil delivery to South Africa, made by the *Salem* under her former name, *South Sun*, in March 1979.

The Amsterdam seminar was held a year after the flow of Iranian oil to South Africa stopped. In the media, there had been reports such as those on the *Salem*, on swaps approved by the British government involving North Sea oil in exchange for embargoed oil, and on transhipment of oil in the Caribbean. There was now clearly a need for more comprehensive information on how South Africa still managed to obtain oil. The seminar paved the way for the establishment of the first full-time professional institution for the monitoring of South Africa's oil supplies, parented by the two Dutch organising committees.

Thus, the director of the UN Centre against Apartheid, Mr E.S. Reddy, was informed by the director designate of the 'oil and shipping research desk' in Amsterdam (officially established as the *Shipping Research Bureau* on 11 July 1980), that the die had been cast, and investigations were to commence shortly. The letter from Amsterdam was dated *June 2nd, 1980*; there is nothing to show that the researcher, while writing it, was aware of a sensational event which had taken place in South Africa that very day.

The Spear of the Nation

'Talk to David Moisi. He was actually roasted on a spit...' *Roasted on a spit?* It sounds like quite an extraordinary variation of the traditional Afrikaner *braai*, held in store for those who in June 1980 had the nerve to aim right at the heart of the apartheid economy, when they blew up the Sasol fuel-from-coal plants that were the technological pride of white South Africa and the very symbol of its defiance of the outside world.

> *They treated me very badly. They beat us up a lot and they used fire, burnt me under-neath the feet, from there put my feet in these small very short leg-irons, they put some sort of a string through the holes of the chains of these leg-irons, and swung me upside down and hung me up there, put a mask over my face, a bag made of chamois – they put that chamois into water and then they put it onto my face, put my head through like this, and then it sticks to your face, you can't breathe... They hit me like a punching-bag, I hung there like a punching-bag in between those poles, and they hit me, hit me... I make myself loose from the start, and then when I feel it's really tough for me I pretend to be dying and then I'd stiffen my body up, they'd loosen me, keep on asking me these questions. Then blisters developed underneath my feet from the fire, then they stood us on a mat, a mat made out of wire, like a very tough doormat. Now, they make you stand for hours on that mat. Now what happens if you have those blisters with water inside, the mat tears the blisters and then the blood starts flowing out of the wounds... That's the type of torture they subjected us to; beating us, kicking faces, everything. They're bloody ruthless I must say.*

On 19 August 1981 Umkhonto guerrilla David Moisi (25) was sentenced to death by the Pretoria Supreme Court. But he survived the sentence, two years on death row and eight years on Robben Island and now lives in a liberated South Africa in which he is able to relate his story.

The MK combatant

Umkhonto weSizwe ('the Spear of the Nation' in Zulu and Xhosa), or MK for short, was formed as the armed wing of the ANC in 1961; its first commander-in-chief was Nelson Mandela. During the first decade and a half MK tried to put pressure on the white minority government by rather modest acts of sabotage. The government responded with increased repression. On 16 June 1976 the outburst came in Soweto, when police opened fire on a peaceful demonstration of high school students, which triggered a lengthy period of insur-rection.

'No Mum, I'm not going to the military', said Soweto student activist David Moisi, in an attempt to comfort his mother when he said goodbye to her in January 1978. A few months earlier, in September 1977, he returned home bruised and swollen following his umpteenth detention by the security police after attending Steve Biko's funeral. This was the last straw. In his heart of hearts, David knew he was not telling his mother the truth. 'Most of us couldn't stand the harassment of the police. It was virtually impossible to continue a normal life under the circumstances. If you were detained, you ran the risk of being killed in detention, like Biko. Most of the students felt that the military might of the government could not be countered with stones. So we decided to go for military training.' The objective was no longer limited to a protest against the use of Afrikaans in education. 'The actual reason for leaving the country was to get a military training in order to overthrow the apartheid regime.'

Whilst there were some who, in their desperation to leave the country, undertook the dangerous border crossing on their own, David Moisi was able to contact a member of the ANC underground and left the country 'the well-organised way.' Together with a companion, he boarded a train in Johannesburg which took them in an easterly direction. They jumped off the train in the open *veld* near Piet Retief, where an experienced ANC member showed them the way to the Swazi border, which they reached jumping fences and evading the jeeps used by the border guards. After a long and risky journey on foot and by bus, they eventually arrived in the Swazi town of Manzini. It was impossible to avoid being questioned by the police. 'We were forced to tell them everything. Some of these policemen were earning two salaries, one from their own government and one from Pretoria. So, even if you'd left successfully, the regime would instantly know; they even took our photographs. But one sympathetic policeman whispered to us where we could find the local ANC representative.'

The following day, on the border with Mozambique, they met a woman who didn't quite look the underground-type to Moisi, 'but she was!' Lindiwe turned out to be the daughter of Walter and Albertina Sisulu. More than ever before, he felt he 'needed to go for military training urgently – and be like her!' Having crossed the border into Mozambique, Moisi saw 'for the first time in my life a people who had come to power by force of arms.' His impatience to start training soared.

By then MK training camps had been moved to Angola. Moisi's group of aspirant-trainees were sent to Novo Katenga, Portuguese for New Katenga, 'but there was nothing *novo* there – except the military life which one wasn't used to!' Basic training was given by ANC and Cuban instructors, until the camp was destroyed in a bombing raid by the South African Air Force in March 1979. Moisi, known to his comrades in arms as 'Shadrack Moloi', resumed his training in Pango and Quibaxe, and from July to December 1979 he was in the German Democratic Republic. For Moisi's group, the East German course concentrated on the sabotage of strategic targets. 'We were made to believe we were a special group.' Back in Angola, in the Funda camp, 'everything we did was orientated towards the frontline now.'

The commander of Special Operations

'We had perhaps the most steeled comrades but unfortunately most of the comrades that were involved in Special Operations died in action. In fact, when I think of it, of the original Sasol group, only five have survived; that's including myself.'

Most people know the former commander of Special Operations by his *nom de guerre*, Rashid Patel, or just Rashid. His real name is Aboobaker Ismail. 'Now everybody knows it; and the regime... uh, the former regime knows it.' Fifteen years separate the distinguished 40-year-old military man, who was to be promoted to major-general in the South African National Defence Force soon after our interview, from the lanky deputy commander from the mud of the Angolan training camps – 'Do you see, all those grey hairs... it takes its toll at the end of the day.'

'Towards the end of 1979, we received an instruction from the high command to start training a special group of people. As the ammunitions expert within MK, I was given the task to instruct people in the sabotage of strategic targets. An élite team was formed from amongst the best of the comrades. At a special base area in Funda, we took people through a "survival training" course, in which they were prepared for survival under any condi-

Aboobaker Ismail ('Rashid'),
Pretoria 1994

tions. The resourcefulness of some of these people actually led to the success of the operations.'

'Of course, in choosing a special group out of the hundreds that were in the camps there was the danger of élitism, which had to be avoided. In later years this became quite a problem; it was virtually everybody's dream to become a member of Special Operations.'

A final selection of 14 was made. MK commander Joe Slovo met with the group, and told them that as members of the *Solomon Mahlangu Squad* they were soon to undertake a number of special missions. The guerrillas were excited when told that they were to leave for Mozambique the following day. The details of their missions were to be made known in a briefing soon after their arrival in Maputo. Rashid was to accompany the team as their political *commissar*. The rank of commissar, according to Ronnie Kasrils in his autobiography,[1] originated in the Russian Red Army from the time of the Civil War. The commissar had to ensure that the commander (often a former Czarist officer) adhered to the new Party line. It was also his task to ensure that the commander did not behave despotically. Motso Mokgabudi or 'Obadi', the Funda commander who became the leader of the squad in Maputo, certainly did not fit this category.

The strategists

In 1979, only a select group knew what the ANC had in mind for the ensuing decade. One of them was Jacob Zuma, former Robben Island prisoner based in Maputo, who welcomed the new squad.

A new military strategy against selected targets was adopted – but why at that particular point in time? Today, in his modest Durban office, the present KwaZulu/Natal ANC leader brushes the question aside: 'You could ask why the ANC at a certain time wrote the Freedom Charter, or adopted the armed struggle. I think everything had its own time. The basic question was how to bring the day of the destruction of apartheid closer.' As the 1950s drew to a close, it became clear that the peaceful means of struggle had passed its zenith. Zuma says that by then it was already clear to him that the armed struggle had become inevitable. 'From its inception in 1961, the armed struggle was aimed at increasing the pressure on the government. The strategy during the first phase was to avoid the loss of life. A new phase started after 1976, when sabotage per se was no longer sufficient, because the repression had intensified. Given the dynamics of the struggle throughout southern Africa, our armed struggle had to be adapted. Army units and the police force became legitimate targets. We had reached a stage where the guerrilla war could no longer avoid loss of life. In the process of developing this strategy, we could no longer say that we merely wanted to pressurise the government into accepting change. Our objective was to *hit* the regime; to defeat it. Not by sabotaging a pylon or a railway line somewhere but by hitting at the actual power of the government. In the late 1970s, early 1980s, there were several raids on police stations. But if you wanted to hit so as to reduce the power of the South African regime, *energy* became the objective. Power stations would certainly become a target, but so would fuel. There was an embargo, but we were aware of the smuggling of oil, and the development of Sasol. Oil is a very strategic commodity. It was therefore important to hit it – something that would be felt immediately, in that it would indeed reduce the capacity of the economy of this country. It was the view of the ANC that the more South Africa was isolated and the economic fabric weakened, the weaker the regime would be. Our regular guerrilla activity was not capable of implementing this type of strategy. Sensitive operations had to be handled by the president of the organisation himself. We therefore created a parallel structure, which would not be subjected to the usual bureaucratic procedures. This is what, for lack of a better name, later came to be called the "Special Operations Department".'

Terror Nest

Zuma, though not a member of the command of the special operations, was nevertheless involved. He was a member of the National Executive Committee (NEC) of the ANC and head of the regional politico-military command, known in Maputo as the 'Senior Organ'; later he became the ANC's Chief Representative in Mozambique as well. Joe Slovo was also based in Maputo and a member of the Senior Organ. He was appointed by the president of the ANC to run Special Operations.

In Mozambique MK had safe houses, but no training camps. The double-storey residence where Obadi, Rashid and their squad – the forerunners of the new strategy – were housed was located in the quiet suburb of Matola on the outskirts of Maputo. David Moisi, renamed 'Lots' – in MK, name changes were part of the normal routine – says that the house was a 'Terror Nest' as far as the South African regime was concerned, but the guerrillas soon adopted the name as their own. 'Our training period had ended. We now operated in units of three or four, preparing, meeting Slovo and the others, looking at the prospects, getting briefings about the nature of the installations and how the oil-from-coal plants were different from the international oil refineries, discussing the politics, putting in perspective why we were supposed to attack this particular installation at this point in time.' Members of the various units were not allowed to discuss their orders 'but we are humans. We told each other of our excitement at being part of a highly select team. We did not know on what grounds we had been selected. "Why entrust *us* with this task, why put so much confidence in *us*?" What we did know was that it was quite a privilege to be part of such a historical unit in our army.' The Solomon Mahlangu Squad had, of course, been named after the famous freedom fighter, the first ANC guerrilla to be sentenced to death and executed in April 1979.

Spying missions

'The stationing of Mr Slovo in Maputo is part of a well conceived communist and ANC plan to place him as close as possible to South Africa. This is to enable him to exercise easier control over trained terrorists infiltrating into South Africa. He is also much closer and much more accessible to people who enter South Africa on spying missions and then leave it to make reports. He is specifically there to coordinate and plan their action.' This statement by the Minister of Police, Louis le Grange, appeared in the South African press on 3 June 1980, one day after the sensational attack on Sasol. Discounting the familiar rhetoric, the South African government's intelligence could surely have been worse. Yet they had not been aware of the planned attack.

Neither were the 'terrorists' themselves aware of it when they were sent on their first 'spying missions' in January–February 1980. Rashid's task was to brief one or two people from each of the units who were subsequently sent into the country to do the initial reconnaissance. One person was sent to do reconnaissance around Secunda, two went to Sasolburg, and Rashid himself went to Durban. Their instructions were to gather information, leave the country and report back to the command. 'They were not told the real reasons for their reconnaissance work.'

Who was selected for missions into the country? Rashid: 'Before people were given any tasks, they were always checked to see that they had the means, be it family or friends, to survive inside the country. Contact with immediate family had to be avoided – we knew that the police had set up quite a network of informers. The important thing was that they had to show some kind of resourcefulness in solving their problems. In those early days, we didn't yet have such a developed network amongst the population. In the Western Transvaal, one of the people who was part of the Special Operations group had once been involved in combat with the police after the local people had informed the police. People thought they were cattle-rustlers – they weren't expecting that guerrillas were coming into the country to carry out operations.'

The cadres were given small amounts of money; the group's resources were limited. 'Some wanted to come in with weapons. We told them: no, your best method of survival is to be like Mao's fish in the water, try to melt away amongst the people. There are searches being conducted on the trains, on the buses. Policemen can stop you and ask for your reference book. We convinced our people not to travel with weapons, and this worked very well. When Barney Molokoane had been doing some reconnaissance on Sasol 1 the year before, there was an attack on a police station not too far away from where he was. Out of curiosity he went there the next day, but the police rounded up all the youth who were hanging around, checked reference books (which he had), put down names, searched them – but they had nothing to go on. A number of such incidents also taught us that the police had no inkling of the possibility that such attacks were to take place.'

The route into the country always went via Swaziland. In those days the South African border guards were still rather relaxed: 'We were actually in a position to jump the border fences even during the day; we knew the patrols, their patterns. In the border areas, we would move with the local population who often crossed the fences. In fact, in later years we were able to get across some of the fences which they considered to be high-security. We knew that once it got dark, the border guards stationed along the fence became scared, and we would move in. Come eight o'clock, we used to say: "The night time is ours"...'

The scouts were instructed to check on the conditions during the day and at night, and to 'look at the feasibility to carry out an attack, either from outside or preferably to get inside the installation. Our ideal was to be able to strike exactly at the right point.' Rashid himself spent about a month inside the country, doing the reconnaissance for the Mobil refinery in Durban. There is a hill overlooking the refinery, and he rented a room from a woman, introducing himself as a student looking for a place to stay. 'So I was living in a house right at the front. I had a view of the entire plant. It was a cushy job; all I had to do was sit there. At night I would observe the activity at the plant, and during the day I took walks around it.'

David Moisi had bigger problems to deal with. He and Richard 'Barney' Molokoane were on the Sasolburg mission, and Moisi soon realised that the Vaal area was not a good area for him to work in. As a former activist, he ran the risk of being identified. 'Everywhere I went during the day, I saw people I knew. I often found myself unnecessarily tying my shoelaces.' This resulted in Moisi's transfer to the Secunda unit. Once during their reconnaissance mission the two men had a narrow escape when they were saved by Moisi's greater fluency in Afrikaans. Police threatened to arrest the two: 'They suspected almost everyone who was from Johannesburg (according to our reference books that was our place of residence). The white officer who was questioning Barney said, *Hierdie donners is van Johannesburg, ag ja...* – those bastards are from Johannesburg! The young black policeman who searched me must have noticed my new raincoat from Swaziland, and even a face cloth that I had bought back in the GDR. But he just told the other one that he had found nothing. Had it been another guy... When Barney was trying to say in Afrikaans "Yes, my Boss" – remember the time – he erred and said, *"my broer"*, my brother... The white policeman really got annoyed; he felt he couldn't be the brother to a black man! I was able to save the situation saying that he was not very fluent in Afrikaans, that he wanted to say "my Baas"... We were ordered to get out of the area immediately and stay out of it.'

Fairly detailed information was obtained on some of the targets and, in most cases, the reports were positive. Not so for Natal. Rashid had informed the command that 'it was dead easy to carry out the attack. But the problem with Durban was that a housing area surrounded the refinery. We had determined that we wanted to hit the fractionating towers, but realised that an escaping gas cloud could explode over a suburb. It would create havoc amongst the population, and that was something we did not accept.' After hearing and discussing the report, Slovo and Obadi decided to skip Durban. Rashid was then put onto the command structure with them.

The command now concentrated on the planning of the actual operations – i.e. the overall planning. Rashid: 'It was extremely important that the operational units felt comfortable doing the job themselves, and did not feel that somebody had drawn up a plan which they merely had to execute. When people went in, they would only be able to adapt a plan if they had been involved in drawing it up. They had to feel confident that their operation would succeed.' It was only at this stage that the individual teams gradually were informed of what it was they were going to do. 'One could feel the rising nervous tension in the group.'

   In the meantime the command had the responsibility of getting the necessary equipment inside the country. As a brand-new structure, it had some assistance from the existing Front Commands, which operated from the various frontline states, each with its own 'territory' in South Africa. The ordnance department of MK would take the equipment to the frontline states, and each of the operational units was then responsible for moving its own equipment inside the country. 'The stuff was prepared, we packed it, sealed it, then sent it in, and it was hidden in arms caches we called DLBs, for "Dead Letter Boxes". Once people were inside the country they would dig it up.' These experiences certainly contributed to Rashid's later promotion to Ordnance Chief of MK in 1987.

The equipment chosen for the attacks was the *limpet mine*. David Moisi: 'Normally limpets are meant for sinking ships. Joe Slovo and the others wanted to try and use them for other purposes, like burning down installations, something which I daresay had not been tried before. The experiment proved a success! So we kept on using them, to the extent that they became sort of fashionable.' The limpets were opened, and thermite was added to them, an idea which Rashid says he had learnt during his training in East Germany. 'Thermite is a mixture of iron oxide and aluminium which doesn't ignite very easily. You need a special ignition mechanism for it or you can ignite it with explosives, but once it is ignited, it burns at 2000 degrees. So even if they had a very thick steel plate on the fractionating towers we were sure that it would penetrate it and melt through the thing and ignite the fuel within.'

Technical questions such as these influenced the planning. The ANC had originally hoped to carry out the operations by March, but as it turned out, they were postponed to May. Joe Slovo tells us that 'the Sasol actions were planned over a very long period. The attack was not initially timed to coincide with any other event, but as the time came closer for the attack, we tried to link it to the international oil embargo conference.' Rashid says that the original plan was to carry out the operation on the night of 20 March, i.e. the night before Sharpeville Day, a few days after the UN oil embargo seminar in Amsterdam, but that plan had to be abandoned. On 20 May, designated 'International Day for an Oil Embargo against South Africa' by the United Nations, ANC President Oliver Tambo was to make a statement on the oil embargo to the international community; the operations were supposed to coincide with that, according to David Moisi's recollection. 'We as MK cadres were very conscious of the contribution of the international community to our struggle. We felt it was our duty to reciprocate in kind. We wanted to express our appreciation of their support and show them what we were capable of doing towards our own liberation.'

Finally, the command planned the attack for the night of 30 May, the eve of 'Republic Day', the day on which white South Africa celebrated its unilateral declaration of independence in 1961. The message to the regime, which habitually displayed its military force on Republic Day, was that it was vulnerable. Rashid: 'But we felt that the night of 31 May or 1 June would also be adequate.'

'Sasol Inferno'

The news headlines which appeared in the South African newspapers on Monday, 2 June 1980, were bigger than usual. The public saw photographs of the blazing Sasol 1 plant in Sasolburg: 'The biggest fire known in South Africa'. The attack on Sasol 1 coincided with an attack on the Natref refinery, a few kilometres away and almost coincided with an attack on Sasol 2 in Secunda. The next day, it became clear that the offices of Sasol contractor Fluor had also been a target.

Until the very last moment the guerrillas were not aware that they were involved in a synchronised attack. Just before they entered the country, they were ordered to carry out their attack on a specific night. When asked what the reason was, Rashid told his men: 'Let me just say to you that it's a coordinated attack. You must remember not to go in too early or too late because one area could alert the other.'

It was the coordinated nature of the attack which, together with the gigantic column of smoke, left a strong impression. Thus, F.W. de Klerk, then Minister of Mineral and Energy Affairs, in a first reaction on 2 June stated that it was clear that the attacks on Sasol installations were of a sophisticated nature, 'evidenced by the fact that there were three separate attacks on three separate installations almost simultaneously'.

This is not to say that the entire operation went without a hitch. According to commander Rashid two very significant events serve to 'highlight the tenacity of the comrades involved in the entire Sasol story. After the men had crossed the border fence, they were picked up by people in cars, one of which capsized. They had to abandon it and eleven of them piled into one small car. They continued their journey, dropping off people at various points. The group which was heading for Sasol 1 managed to reach Sasolburg on time. On their arrival, they discovered that some of the conditions had changed since the earlier reconnaissance. 'They couldn't find places to stay for all of the unit. On the day before the operation, after doing the last reconnaissance, four of the unit members (Barney, Faku, Solly Mayona and Jackie) went to the Sasolburg police station, because they did not want to be arrested for loitering. They gave their reference books – which were all false – to the police officers, and told them that they were looking for work. They then asked for a place to spend the night and were given an open cell. So those who provided the base for those people were the South African police!'

Sasolburg, Sunday night, 1 June 1980 – Guerrillas wearing white overalls and helmets cut their way through the fence and entered the terrain of the Sasol 1 plant. Cutters, limpets and weapons were hidden in their overalls. The ANC had managed to get identity cards and had produced some kind of card that looked fairly similar to it. Once inside, the intruders resembled workers at the plant.

The factory was fully operational, people were moving around, so the attackers decided not to go for the fractionating towers themselves. Their cover would have made that possible but hitting the towers would have resulted in casualties. The guards were too late in discovering the holes in the security fence; their investigation was soon interrupted at 11.40 p.m. when the first of a series of relatively small explosions ignited a storage tank. Within minutes a series of thunderous explosions set off other tanks filled with petrol. 'It was like watching a nuclear bomb going off in the movies,' according to someone who had been taking a midnight walk. People in the nearby township of Zamdela told the press the next day they had been terrified: 'It was a tremendous explosion which even rocked my bed. Everything in the house was shaking.' Some ran into the *veld*, others fled by car. People far from the plant could feel the intensity of the heat. Red flames, hundreds of metres high, were soaring to the sky for hours after the blaze started.

Events had not proceeded this far when four kilometres away, at the Natref refinery, the only casualty occurred. A member of the MK squad had been left to guard a hole in the fence. A security guard who was patrolling on a bicycle saw the hole, dismounted to investigate and to his surprise a man wearing a black balaclava and dark jacket took out a pistol and fired at him. The guard was hit in the shoulder; all the guerrillas got away safely. It was reported later that the first Natref storage tank, containing semi-refined aviation fuel, exploded moments after a policeman investigating the shooting had climbed down from the tank. The tank went up only five minutes after the first blast at Sasol 1. More aviation fuel tanks exploded later.

2 June 1980: Flames and smoke rising from Sasol oil installations at Sasolburg after the attack

At Secunda, about 135 km from Sasolburg, the Sasol 2 plant had only just come on stream, having started the production of synthetic fuels less than three months before. Within an hour of the first explosions in Sasolburg, the plant was hit by the other MK unit which included David Moisi, Mabena, Mochudi and 'the old man' Victor. Moisi recalls that 'Mabena was supposed to be the commander, and Victor the commissar, but the first didn't really live up to the expectations of a commander. He had a problem of nerves, the usual problem especially if you're getting into action for the first time. Victor had more or less taken over before we got into place.'

The unit at Secunda was much more successful than that at Sasolburg in getting right into the processing unit. And yet a tinge of disappointment can be heard in the words of commander Rashid: 'It didn't look all that spectacular. They were still building up the place; unfortunately there was no fuel in those things.' But he claims that some very expensive pieces of equipment had been hit. David Moisi: 'What happened is that as we were moving right inside the target, we hadn't expected that the process was so terribly noisy. There were some people there, who probably wondered what these "engineers" were doing there, walking on these stairs without earplugs. Victor was just about to leave his limpet mines inside the fractionating tower, but the other comrade whose task it was to secure them couldn't reach that place anymore as we had been spotted. It was impossible to talk, but I then signalled to Victor – fortunately he was looking at me – and he took them out, and we retreated to where some drums were standing. Victor decided to go back and put one on a different target, some pipe, where it caused a lot of damage.'

Spokesmen for Sasol quoted by the press appeared less convinced. Seven explosions were heard in quick succession at Sasol 2 at 20 minutes past midnight, 'but caused no significant damage'. Explosives had been attached to 220-litre drums of chemicals and, 200 metres away, to a pipe carrying reactor gas. 'If a nearby transformer kiosk had been eliminated, production would have come to a complete standstill.' The 'abortive sabotage attempt' resulted in a few damaged drums; the saboteurs had 'probably thought the drums contained inflammable material' – indeed, they had.

A year later, one member of the squad would be sentenced to death for having caused this 'insignificant damage'.

'No smoking beyond the fence' – The explosions in Sasolburg were spectacular. Hours after the blasts, while firemen were desperately trying to put out the blaze, another tank filled with butadiene exploded, sending flames high into the sky. By daybreak, reporters of *The Star* confirmed that the saboteurs had not heeded the 'no smoking' sign: 'Immediately behind the wire fence, acrid, heavy black smoke billowed sluggishly skyward. Its darkness accentuated by licking mod-orange tongues of flame...' Of eight tanks that had been ignited either by the explosives or secondary explosions, seven were still burning after dawn, and huge plumes of dark smoke were visible for miles. Smoke drifted more than 80 km to Soweto and the southern suburbs of Johannesburg. At Natref one diesel fire had been put out, but the investigation, there and at Sasol, was hampered by the intense heat from the fires which were still raging.

The press said that it was 'remarkable' that 'although all the plants are manned 24 hours a day', the only injury was to the guard at Natref. However, it was in line with MK policy. It was a deliberate decision to hit the 'tank farms' in Sasolburg rather than the processing units. It was the hit on the storage tanks that resulted in the tremendous blaze during the June 1980 action which became the trademark of Umkhonto.

The fourth attack of the coordinated MK action followed later during the day. A one-man 'unit' planted three bombs at the old Town Hall in Springs, which housed the offices of the American company Fluor, chief contractors for the building of Sasol 2 and 3. The bombs were discovered before they were due to explode, and the following day dramatic reports appeared in the press, telling how hundreds of people were watching with 'their hearts in their mouths' when the bombs were defused.

While the tanks were still blazing, Sasol estimated the direct damage at approximately R6 million (mainly lost aviation fuel and petrol). A definite figure for the direct and consequential costs was never revealed. Later, independent estimates ranged as high as R60–70 million.

'We did it'

It was the combination of the enormous pillar of smoke which remained visible for days, the element of complete surprise and the coordinated character which has made the Sasol attack go down in the history of South Africa as one of the most spectacular features of the armed struggle against apartheid.

Within the ANC, there is a marked consensus regarding the importance of 2 June 1980. Joe Slovo, the former enemy of the state who became a respected member of the South African government in May 1994, says that 'the impact of the Sasol attack was phenomenal. It was the first major action against a strategic target and sent a very strong message to the other side.' Frene Ginwala, who was appointed Speaker of the South African Parliament in 1994, and who spent her exile years in London closely involved in work on the oil embargo, also emphasises the importance of the first strike. 'It was tremendously important. Firstly, an oil fire is very spectacular, physically. For miles away the enormous column of smoke was visible. It wasn't something they could hide. Secondly, the regime had made *so* much about Sasol... – it was very important, psychologically. Nobody could deny or downplay the action. It shattered the myth of white invulnerability. It was not about a quantity of oil that was lost by sabotage; it was that column of smoke that was important. Sasol was a symbol of power.' Commander of Special Operations Rashid: 'The impact that it had inside the country and throughout the world was just amazing. And the ANC... all we had to say was: *we* did it.' In the morning of 2 June, the African National Congress issued a statement in London claiming full responsibility for the attacks. There was perhaps no comment as succinct and to the point as that of the British *Financial Times*, which wrote two days later that the bomb attacks 'showed that time is not on the side of the existing system'.

All of a sudden many people declared that they had been expecting such an attack. Prof. Mike Louw, former director of Pretoria University's Institute for Strategic Studies, said he had 'expected this a long time ago. Oil refineries are seen as perhaps the most vulnerable of industrial and strategic targets. So they would be among the first one would expect

> Share prices on the Johannesburg Stock Exchange were hardly influenced by the Sasol attack, stockbrokers said this morning, though Sasol shares lost 20c each.
>
> Stock market news, 2 June 1980

would come under attack.' Sasol employees were quoted in the press as saying they had been expecting an attack on the installations, especially in view of their critical importance to South Africa since Iran joined the oil embargo. A Sasol engineer told the *Rand Daily Mail*: 'We knew it was only a matter of time before the terrorists attacked us.'

KwaZulu's Chief Minister, Gatsha Buthelezi, said he had not been surprised when he heard of the Sasol blasts. Speaking in the Assembly in Ulundi on 2 June, he said he had had information over the weekend that 'today there was going to be lots of fires. It is no coincidence that there were fires at Sasolburg and Secunda.' In the same statement he expressed the view that the time had come for the creation of armed black vigilante groups who were to 'shoot to kill' when they saw people tampering with buildings. The deteriorating relationship between the ANC and Buthelezi sunk to an all time low after the Sasol attack. ANC Secretary-General Alfred Nzo, speaking in London later that month, bitterly attacked Buthelezi. At a press conference held in Lusaka in July, Oliver Tambo said Buthelezi had 'emerged on the side of the enemy against the people'.

On 2 June Police Minister Le Grange stated that the ANC's claim that it was responsible for the Sasol attack came as no surprise to the South African Police. Newspaper headings such as *'Slovo, Ginwala behind anti-SA activities'* reflected the minister's statement. Joe Slovo was pinpointed as the mastermind behind the attacks, while Frene Ginwala was said to have actively assisted the 'communist onslaught' of the Kremlin in southern Africa. Ginwala: 'The regime could not accept that blacks were able to carry out such attacks, and so it tried to blame the Soviet Embassy in Lusaka...' Slovo discerns 'an element of racism on the part of the regime in selecting me as the bogeyman. They couldn't (or didn't want to) believe that strategically planned acts which damaged them very publicly could have been conceived by anyone other than a white man – which was nonsense, of course, as many people of all ethnic origins were involved in the planning and execution of the attacks.'

Despite all the 'forecasts' and bold words, no one had been capable of predicting, let alone preventing, the attack.

It so happened that the Second Police Amendment Bill, which was designed to increase censorship with regard to police anti-terrorist activities, was to be debated in parliament on the evening of 2 June. During the day press reports carrying headlines such as *'Bill could gag Press over Sasol'* stated that there was 'already speculation among MPs that police follow-up operations following last night's Sasol blasts would have been veiled in secrecy if the Bill were law.' The following day, *The Star* described the debate as follows: 'Seldom is a security debate in Parliament illuminated by anything as spectacular as the burning fuel dumps at Sasolburg ... Things became so heated across the floor in the Assembly last night that Mr Speaker eventually ruled that he would have all references to "snakes and baboons" excised from the Hansard record. The MPs involved were talking about one another, not the people who placed the explosive charges at the Sasol installations.'

The honourable member for Hillbrow (Progressive Federal Party, PFP) asked: 'If the Bill were already law, would South Africans have been forced to rely on overseas broadcasts to find out about the Sasol attacks?' In contrast, the New Republic Party (NRP) spokesman on police matters applauded the Bill; referring to Sasol, he asked 'why details should be splashed in the Press? What country at war advertised its troop movements in the daily Press?'

Country at war

Energy Minister F.W. de Klerk, who made a special visit to Sasolburg on 2 June, said he hoped the incident would put beyond doubt the fact that South Africa had to face an organised assault aimed at causing damage and disrupting stability and order. Later the same day, this statement was endorsed by the country's new security chief, Dr Niël Barnard. On his first day in office as head of National Security, the 30-year-old warned his audience that the attacks 'should not be regarded as isolated incidents, but in the context of a broader revolutionary strategy'.

The government came under fire from members of the white opposition. The leader of the NRP, Mr Vause Raw, said it was unforgivable that the sabotage had come after the warning South Africa had received from the attack on fuel installations in Rhodesia in December 1978. Mr John Malcomess, spokesman for the PFP, stated that 'The fact that people could break into three major fuel installations on the same night was indicative of inadequate security arrangements. One successful attempt could be written off as bad luck but three successful attempts could only mean bad security.'

Minister De Klerk rejected charges of negligence and said urgent attention was being given to improving existing security arrangements. That the government was indeed pre-

---

John Malcomess, former South African MP and spokesman on energy matters of the Progressive Federal Party, 1994:

'Sasol in June 1980 was the only successful act of industrial terrorism that the ANC achieved. The extent of the damage? You must not forget that under P.W. Botha we had a "total onslaught" mentality in South Africa. It was considered that the public should know nothing. There was an obsession with secrecy about absolutely everything. So, I never did know those figures. In fact, it's only since the end of apartheid that we begin to realise how serious a fire it actually was and how serious an act of terrorism. The press were muzzled, don't ever forget that. I certainly gained more of a sense of how serious it was in the last couple of years, than I did at the time it happened. The event didn't go unnoticed, but it was played down. As an MP I used to get ten newspapers every day, but I don't believe any of us actually realised what a major thing it was. We thought that maybe a few storage tanks had gone up and that's it. And sure, it makes a lovely spectacular blaze, and sure it has cost us money, but tanks are not difficult to replace and refill with fuel... It's only since we've started caring a bit more that I begin to wonder how much the government covered up as to the extent of the damage. I don't know; maybe it wasn't as serious as the ANC think it was. Certainly, it is sure that they would consider it a success. But I'm not in favour of terrorism, not in any shape. And I consider that what the ANC was doing... some would call it liberation struggle, I call it straight terrorism.'

National Key Points Act

Sasol had been regarded a 'key point' of the South African economy before the adoption of the National Key Points Act in 1980. In August 1979, *Paratus*, the journal of the South African armed forces, explained the role of the 'Sasol Commando', a unit comprised of Sasol employees responsible for the protection of their installations:

> *When the men of the Sasol Commando change their white coats for the uniform of the South African Defence Force they become members of a specialised unit, which in times of war will defend two key points of the South African nation. The Sasol factory ... and the Natref Refinery are two of the most important installations in the country. The importance of the task which the Sasol Commandos have in defending these two key points cannot be overemphasised.*

The National Key Points Act gave the government sweeping powers to compel owners of strategic installations to enforce security measures. Under the Act, the government could take over company facilities and place military personnel on the premises during emergencies. The Act empowered the Minister of Defence to declare any place or area which was of strategic importance to the functioning of the South African state a national key point; less sensitive points could be designated as 'essential operating sites'. Release of information on key points was severely restricted – there were heavy penalties for even disclosing that a given plant or installation had been designated a key point – and their owners were instructed how to deal with the press in the event of sabotage attacks and other emergencies. Companies were required to organise their employees into militia, to finance and provide military training for them, to facilitate the storage of arms on their premises, and to integrate their installations into regional defence plans. Foreign companies were not always happy about the duties placed on them. Oil companies were reported to have been reluctant to arm their guards; their objections were overcome by hiring guards from outside the company (*Financial Times*, 13 July 1982).

In the course of her work on oil in the ANC's London office in the early 1980s, Frene Ginwala was 'finding out a lot about the National Key Points Act, about the ways companies were being used to support the apartheid structures. In every country, in times of war, industry is mobilised to support the war. In South Africa, all this legislation was used for a war against its own people. Once we found that out, we started using it. There was so much secrecy; we started feeding that information to the unions inside the country, telling them how companies were being used. We were able to give the companies in Europe pictures of their plants which had been declared "key points".' Oliver Tambo explained the workings of the Act to businessmen in London in May 1987, concluding that 'we believe that statements rejecting apartheid must be accompanied by concrete action which visibly breaks the intimacy that characterises the relationship between international business and the apartheid state and economy. The cooperation that exists in relation to the repressive machinery of the State tends to be ignored by those who justify their refusal to disinvest on the grounds that by their presence they are helping to bring about change in the interests of the black man'.

Ginwala: 'You were not allowed to photograph a national key point. So when the press in South Africa wanted to know, "How can we know whether we are breaking the law or not?", they were confidentially given the information as to what a key point would look like. They had certain types of fences, certain types of watchtowers; it's a very particular structure. They're now deserted.'

paring nothing less than a war effort became clear on 11 June, when it introduced the 'National Key Points Bill' in Parliament. The Bill, which laid down rules for the protection of strategic installations, had been in preparation for some time, but work had been speeded up as a result of the attacks. The National Key Points Act was approved shortly afterwards (see Box). Not unexpectedly, one of the purposes of the legislation was again to prohibit the publication of information on guerrilla assaults on classified installations.

Additional legislation was not needed to stop ANC President Oliver Tambo from being quoted in the South African press on 3 June: 'Tambo is quoted in the British press in an interview in Dar-es-Salaam today ... His statement may not be published.' *What* South Africans were not able to read was that Tambo had known in advance of the attacks; that they were directed against these installations 'because of their strategic positioning in the South African economy'; and that the action 'was in pursuit of the aims of peace': a peaceful settlement could 'only come with the demolition of the structures of apartheid domination'. What Tambo wisely remained discreet about was the organisation of the attacks; he said these 'were planned and executed by guerrilla units inside the country', and he made light of the role played by Joe Slovo in Mozambique which had been singled out in the South African government's comments.

'Hotstuff'

After placing the charges, the guerrillas from Sasolburg had immediately driven back. Rashid and some others were waiting for them on the border: 'We lifted the fence and they drove across.' The following day the press was told by the police that they had 'thrown in every available man to hunt the saboteurs,' but policemen and army commandos patrolling the region and manning roadblocks were withdrawn by lunchtime. The MK units from Secunda and Springs also retreated safely to their base in Matola.

Some observers have said that the success of the attacks in June 1980 was evidence of the ANC's inside contacts in these closely guarded facilities, and that MK had succeeded in infiltrating the work force at the plants. David Moisi dismisses the idea: 'We carried out the attacks ourselves. But it is true, Slovo and the others had their men everywhere!' Commander Rashid admits: 'We had some people who had been providing some intelligence from within the targets. For instance, in some places they had huge files in which they actually laid out the processes etcetera. But the regime just couldn't believe that units of MK could have carried out the attacks without assistance from within the installations. At Secunda they rounded up the entire workforce and went through them. One chap of Mozambican origin who had been working in Secunda for years happened to be on leave at the time; he was arrested and tortured on his return. The only effect being that after he was released from detention, he came out and joined the ANC. We used to call him "Hotstuff". It is to his credit that we carried out more attacks on Secunda! And he wasn't the only one. The ripple effect of the attacks was just enormous. We've had lots of other people who subsequently came to join MK because of these attacks.'

The ANC on everybody's lips

After the attacks the people were dancing and singing in the MK training camps. Kasrils recalls how the chants were added to the new craze of the toyi-toyi: '... *Hup hup hup, guerrillas coming, AK's talking, Sasol's burning ...*' Rashid's Matola group was euphoric: 'The guys were walking on air, having been involved in these operations.' But also as a member of the command, he had every reason to be satisfied. Joe Slovo says that the June 1980 attacks 'were not to test the water, but already part of the full-blown Special Ops programme as it had been developed from the beginning.' The outcome was nevertheless important, according to Rashid: 'The original mandate was to carry out the Sasol operation. Given success, that would then be widened to deal with all the strategic installations, and people in uniform. It was only after June 1980 that the National Executive Committee of the ANC agreed to give the President the mandate to continue. There's nothing like success to get the kind of mandate you want. Here it was proven that it was possible to carry out operations successfully by entering the country in small groups. It wasn't very expensive to carry out the entire operation, and at the end of the day, all the cadres returned to base.'

As an NEC member, Jacob Zuma had some knowledge of Special Operations after the Sasol attack, but as he says now: 'It became an adopted policy and it worked, we did not even worry – that was the baby of the President! He had to deal with it; he provided the National Executive Committee with global reports and we never questioned details.' And Oliver Tambo left the details to the squad. According to David Moisi, even Joe Slovo himself wasn't involved in much of the detailed planning of attacks on 'secondary targets', except for giving the cadres the go-ahead to reconnoitre and plan the attacks on their own.

Contrary to the normal front commands of MK, the Special Operations Command was involved in operations throughout South Africa. Rashid concedes that this setup sometimes created problems, 'because some then said that it was impossible to proceed with their own operations if they did not know what others were doing in their area. Special Operations became the culprit because it was operating all over the show.' However, he is convinced that 'in the overall thinking, the Special Operations group became the prime runner in terms of MK strategy. The attacks had an immense propagandistic impact. They put South Africa and the armed struggle on the international agenda, but I believe it had the greatest impact *within* South Africa. After Sasol it was as if people started to realise that for the South African regime the writing was on the wall. From this attack on Sasol to the next attacks by Special Operations, it became an unstoppable flood. All the other military units in MK felt they had to make their mark. The terrain made a classical border war impossible. We felt our strength lay in being amongst the population. Within two to three years the entire population had been mobilised and it was precisely because of these kinds of attacks which took place. In early 1981 we started to hit the power stations; in August 1981 we hit Voortrekkerhoogte. A whole spate of major operations followed. At the time, 1983–84, ANC and MK were on everybody's lips.'

One of the issues with regard to which the policies of the ANC and the *Pan Africanist Congress* (PAC) diverged at the time was how the organisations assessed the importance of these operations. 'In discussions with both leaders and the cadres of the PAC', *Africa Now* wrote in July 1981, 'it becomes clear that ... they do not support the tactic of carrying out spectacular acts of sabotaging installations such as those of SASOL at this stage. There is little doubt that the ANC-CP alliance has gained considerable influence following their sabotage of the SASOL installations and even inside the PAC there are those who express admiration for the sophisticated planning and execution of that mission.' However, *Africa Now* quoted PAC leader Nyathi Pokela as saying that the line of the PAC was that of 'mobilising the people; it is slow and painful ... It does not lend itself to spectacular publicity. But if you are with the people, the victory is yours'. According to Rashid, 'Many PAC members joined MK after these attacks...'

Retaliation

After June 1980, the South African government became obsessed with retaliatory action. Rashid says ANC intelligence had information from within the country that 'the enemy had vowed they were going to wipe out the entire group that had been involved in the Sasol operation'.

Already two days after the attacks, a revenge assassination mission was undertaken by a security police death squad led by Captain Dirk Coetzee, who later blew the whistle on atrocities carried out by the South African security forces. The suspicion was that the guerrillas had infiltrated South Africa through Swaziland, which resulted in the death squad bombing two ANC transit houses in Manzini, killing a nine-year-old boy and one ANC member. On his return to South Africa after the raid (his first), Coetzee was told not to worry about the child; sooner or later he would have become a terrorist himself.

Four months after the Sasol attacks, the security police were given their long-awaited first opportunity.

On 26 October 1980, four members of the Special Operations squad entered the country for reconnaissance as part of the planning of a new coordinated action. David Moisi and Norman Yengeni were on their way to Cape Town – one of the targets there being the Caltex refinery – whilst two others were going for the Alberton oil storage depot in the East Rand. (Later, on Robben Island, Moisi realised that, had the raid on the Caltex refinery been successful, the incarcerated ANC leadership on the nearby island would have got their share of the pleasure out of the flames. Caltex was never attacked; in Alberton, an attempt was still made in 1981, but the four had been behind bars for some time by then.)

The main thing for Moisi and his three companions after crossing the South African border was to evacuate that area as soon as possible. 'But we were sold out by a taxi man. We wanted to get into the interior, to Witbank or even to Springs. In the border area one was easily exposed. The taxi driver probably suspected us of being guerrillas. He told us that he had to report to his firm in order to inform them that he was leaving the area. Instead, we were taken to a police station, where we were arrested.'

The identities of some of the Sasol saboteurs had in the interim become known to the police. Ellis and Sechaba relate that a few months after June 1980, commander Obadi was

'detained in a swoop by security men in Swaziland, who held some suspected ANC operatives without knowing exactly who they were. Only when Pretoria learned of the arrest,
and offered the Swazi government a R1 million ransom for Obadi, did the Swazis realise
that they had detained someone too hot for comfort. Fearing the ANC's possible reaction,
they panicked and handed Obadi back to the ANC in Maputo.' However, in October it
took some time before it dawned on the South Africans that one of the four arrested men
was not just another fledgling guerrilla. In the police station, Moisi and his companions
were beaten during the interrogation which followed their arrest. 'They wanted me to say
who we were, what we were up to and what we had done in the past. Fortunately, neither
Norman nor I revealed the other target we were supposed to go for – it became a success
later! – so they only managed to get Caltex out of us. But in the meantime they had found
out about me. A policeman confronted me with details of the operation, about how the
commander of our unit got scared, etcetera. It was then that I realised that they really knew
a *lot* about me. But I now knew the source of their information, and I decided not to reveal
more than the source was able to tell them. They treated me very badly... Even black
policemen beat me up, swearing you've attacked Sasol, you... – as though they were fight-
ing for what belonged to their fathers!'

The Matola raid

The police did not get more out of Moisi. They had to wait until an event took place which
was to become one of the most notorious examples of South Africa's aggression against
its neighbouring states. In January 1981, just ten days after a new president of the United
States was sworn in, SADF Special Forces hit the capital of Mozambique in South Africa's first official cross-border raid after its involvement in Angola. The 'Matola raid' was
the start of the hard line of destabilisation. The new Reagan government failed to condemn the incursion – indeed, unconfirmed reports have it that Washington had approved it
in advance. Similar raids were carried out in the years that followed.

A few hours prior to the attack, SADF commandos crossed the Mozambique border
without hindrance. The initial report of the incursion was blocked by a high official in the
Mozambican army who was subsequently unmasked as a South African agent. The commandos drove the 70 kilometres to Matola and located their target, three residences, which
were attacked at around 2 a.m., 30 January 1981.

The following day, SADF Chief General Constand Viljoen stated that the three houses
contained the 'planning and control headquarters of the ANC in Mozambique'. He said he
had 'irrefutable information from sources close to the ANC that the Sasol attacks and
several other ANC operations had been planned in the three houses.' Indeed, the commandos were acting on the basis of information supplied by *askaris*, former guerrillas who had
stayed in Matola before being arrested and 'turned'. One of the three houses was the
residence of Obadi's Special Operations group; another, known as the 'Castle', was used
by MK's Natal operatives; but the third residence had nothing to do with MK; it belonged
to the trade union SACTU.

At the house used by Special Operations, a number of SADF commandos – dressed in
FRELIMO uniforms and speaking Portuguese – were able to approach Obadi, who had
just come back from Angola that afternoon, and a few others. Kasrils writes: 'Weapons

were suddenly pointed, and the occupants ordered out of the house and lined up against a garden wall. The enemy opened fire and several comrades died on the spot. Obadi staggered away with his guts ripped open. An MK comrade, posted in the loft of the house, opened fire and hit several of the attackers.' Zuma was in a late-night meeting in Maputo, until he was told about the attack in a telephone call immediately after it had taken place. He says the raiders suffered severe casualties. 'We counted about five or six rifles that were left behind by them as they were leaving, and there were a lot of syringes, which indicated that people had been given treatment on the spot.' Two commandos were killed; one was identified as a British mercenary who had previously served in the Rhodesian SAS. He was wearing a helmet painted with swastikas and the slogan 'Sieg Heil!'.

All in all, 11 occupants were reported to have died in the attack on the three houses. Several guerrillas, including Mabena who had been a member of the unit which attacked Sasol 2 in June 1980, were wounded but recovered later. Mabena was the one who had managed to fight back during the raid. His colleague Mochudi was one of those killed by the commandos. Obadi died in hospital a week later. Zuma: 'It was a big loss, he was a very effective commander. But if anything, the raid added more anger and determination to escalate the struggle.' The South African forces were satisfied despite their initial claim to have killed 30 terrorists ('all armed'), and although their jubilation subsided when it became clear that their main victim was not Joe Slovo. They had, instead, killed a passing-by Portuguese electricity technician who bore a striking physical resemblance to Joe Slovo.

In fact, Slovo was out of harm's way in Maputo. He tells: 'I had been in the house attacked in the Matola raid until some hours before the attack. I left at about 7 or 8 in the evening, and the raid took place several hours later.' After Obadi's demise Slovo saw to it, in consultation with Tambo, that Rashid – who had left for Swaziland the night before the attack took place – was appointed Obadi's successor as commander of Special Operations. When Slovo later became Chief-of-Staff of MK and went over to Lusaka, Rashid took over his role as the overall commander. It was then decided that the command should no longer operate just under Tambo, but that it should come under the military headquarters, where Slovo would still be the one responsible for Special Operations. However, as the latter says, 'Special Ops continued to have a direct line to the President and to be autonomous of other military structures.'

Three guerrillas had been abducted by the commandos in the Matola raid, taken to South Africa and secretly held at an army base. It was only after several weeks during which there was an international uproar about the raid and the kidnappings that the three men were handed over to the police, and formally detained. Their detention was then publicly confirmed by the police who said they were investigating a possible connection between the three and the June 1980 sabotage attack on Sasol.

What the police probably meant was that they were trying to 'turn' the kidnapped guerrillas. During the interrogation, one of the captives, Vuyani Mavuso, admitted that he was a member of MK, but he refused to become an *askari*. His refusal was to cost him his life. Lacking sufficient evidence to charge him and not wanting to release him either, the police decided to get rid of him. Dirk Coetzee has told how his death squad shot and burnt Mavuso in October 1981 and disposed of his remains in the Komati river.

In a number of areas across the country, the authorities invoked the 'Riotous Assemblies Act' and forbade memorial services for the ANC members who died in the Matola raid. Yet they could not entirely prevent these from taking place, for instance when residents of Soweto organised a memorial service at Regina Mundi Cathedral, which was attended by thousands of people later in February.

'Boys of Umkhonto Are Fighting for the Liberation of Their Country'

After weeks of interrogation, one of the kidnapped men succumbed. Motibe Ntshekang – the police had disclosed his name before he started to talk – revealed what he, a member of the Solomon Mahlangu Squad, knew about the operations which had been carried out from Matola, and about the guerrillas who had been arrested on their way to the fuel depot in Alberton and the Caltex refinery. Most importantly, the authorities could now bring charges against David Moisi for his role in the Sasol attack. Ntshekang testified against Moisi as state witness. 'Motibe, or "Ghost" as we used to call him, was my former colleague, he used to be my close friend... He once gave me a shirt to which he was very attached and which he had brought from South Africa when he fled into exile. He gave it to me in Maputo as a present. The next present I got from him was the death sentence!' The ANC defector eventually became an informer and was sent on missions to kill ANC people – in order to make it impossible for him to change sides once again.

The three who had been arrested with Moisi had a separate trial. They were charged with joining the ANC, receiving military training and returning to reconnoitre oil facilities, and were sentenced to 10 years each. Moisi, on the other hand, was charged with two others who had not been involved in the Sasol operation. Bobby Tsotsobe had been involved in a rocket attack on Booysens police station in Johannesburg; Johannes Shabangu had attacked the house of a policeman. 'They brought us together for what they called "common purpose", because we were involved in "operations to overthrow the state".'

In April 1981, five and a half months after his arrest, David Moisi appeared for the first time in the Pretoria Magistrates Court. Johannes Shabangu had spent 252 days in his cell waiting for this day to arrive. The three men had to plead to charges for more than one and a half hours without benefit of defence counsel. In June they appeared before the Pretoria Supreme Court. Here Ntshekang testified that he had seen Moisi in Mozambique during his report-back session after the sabotage mission.

All three accused were found guilty of high treason on 18 August 1981 and sentenced to death the next day. When the news of the men's conviction reached the crowd which had gathered outside the court on 18 August, a demonstration started in which people chanted and raised clenched fists; six were arrested. The next day, as soon as the sentences had been pronounced and the condemned men heard that they would be *'hanged by your necks until you are dead'*, the packed spectators' gallery saw Moisi turn towards them, raising his arm in a clenched-fist salute. As Judge C. Theron left the courtroom, the three started singing a freedom song in Zulu; fortunately for the policemen, they were unable to understand its message.

More than a decade later Moisi says, 'It wasn't a shock as such to hear the death sentence being passed. There were others before us like Solomon Mahlangu who had been executed and others who had been sentenced to death, some of whom were still on death row. We knew the South African law says that the maximum sentence for high treason is the death sentence, and all the racist judges saw to it that they made use of that privilige afforded to them by the apartheid laws.'

The three men were sent to death row in Pretoria Central Prison. They lodged an appeal, but it was turned down by the Bloemfontein Appeal Court on 26 November 1982. The only possibility to escape the hangman's noose was for the men to ask the State President for clemency. After his release in November 1982, a political prisoner informed the outside world that the morale of the condemned men – the 'Sasol-Booysens 3' and the 'Moroka 3' who had joined them after a year – was high. Every night the six led the other prisoners in chanting freedom songs and political slogans. Moisi: 'The struggle doesn't end outside prison. It continues even when you are on death row. We were defiant, we wouldn't listen to what they told us. Initially, we didn't have any access to newspapers. We protested and in the end they gave in. To be able to read about the political developments such as the formation of the UDF kept our morale high. What especially lifted our spirits was to see progress being made by our fellow combatants inside the country. We also came to know of United Nations resolutions and other actions internationally and inside South Africa, calling for our release.'

On Monday morning, 6 June 1983, Moisi, Shabangu and Tsotsobe were taken from their cells. 'Normally, they didn't take you out on Monday mornings. We were convinced that we were going to be executed. In the administration office we found the sheriff waiting for us; he was the man who announced the death warrants. Never in my life have I been shocked by words as such, least of all by syllables. But that morning, when the sheriff

Amsterdam 18 December 1982

said, *"The State President has decided to ex..."* – I was already expecting: *"...execute you..."*. I really felt shocked by the prospect. But he was actually saying that "The State President has decided to *extend mercy to you...*".'

The three men were taken off death row, but their comrades were executed three days later.

Welcome to Robben Island

About a month after his sentence had been commuted to life imprisonment, David Moisi was transferred to Robben Island. The journey, in leg-irons, was rather uncomfortable, but he is now able to look back on his arrival with a note of irony in his voice: 'When we arrived on Robben Island, there was a sign saying "Welcome to Robben Island!", as though we were tourists... Our expectations were very high because we knew that was where political prisoners were being kept. We felt that political prisoners had privileges! We arrived at about lunchtime. When food was given to us, we thought that due to our late arrival, we were just having left-overs. We were given what they called soup, but we felt, OK, we'd rather eat this now; we thought that perhaps we would be given better food at a later stage – only to find out that this was the normal prison fare on Robben Island...'

David Moisi was to spend eight years of his life on Robben Island. He was released in the beginning of May 1991, more than a year after the release of Nelson Mandela and the unbanning of the ANC. His release and that of 200 other political prisoners required a hunger strike to force President De Klerk to keep his promise that all political prisoners would be set free.

Obadi, Barney, Victor and others of the Sasol group of 1980 did not survive the struggle. There were those who, even after the period of transition had started, still believed that the survivors had escaped due punishment. In May 1992 the South African *Weekly Mail* published the hitlist of a covert police operation linked to the assassination of ANC members in the Vaal; a number of known ANC members had already mysteriously been killed. The one on top of the list: David Moisi.

Invincible fortresses

Killing and kidnapping MK members in Matola; arresting and sentencing to death one of the Sasol guerrillas; adopting legislation allowing the militarisation of strategic installations – these were some of the events which constituted the regime's 'total strategy' against the ANC and its armed struggle. Nevertheless, the armed struggle was not to be stopped. In addition to the attacks on power stations and key military targets, Special Operations, or the 'Solomon Mahlangu Squad' – the names were used interchangeably – continued to deal with oil installations.

All ANC and MK sources confirm that there was a direct link with the ANC's international policy in which the outside world was requested to diplomatically and economically isolate South Africa. Rashid points to the information gathered from anti-apartheid sources overseas on oil and oil shipping, which had been instrumental in identifying fuel as a key issue; this preceded the founding of the Shipping Research Bureau. Joe Slovo says that 'the importance of oil sanctions in the battle against apartheid undoubtedly played a role in identifying Sasol as a strategic target.' It did not end with Sasol. Jacob Zuma: 'We looked at special operations against fuel installations as a complement to the oil embargo. This could also involve installations of foreign companies; we were not selective.' In the words of David Moisi: 'The Western oil companies realised that apartheid was an evil system, but they were not prepared to sacrifice their profits. Our message was: if you don't want to disinvest from South Africa, you're going to see your money go up in flames.' This was not the private opinion of a few combatants; it was pronounced in public by the ANC. Speaking in Tanzania in March 1982, ANC representative Masondo warned that oil installations of Western countries which broke UN sanctions were a legitimate target: 'We shall keep on visiting oil installations. That is in our interests.' It is perhaps interesting to note that the initial 'Sasol' attacks were in fact not only directed against Sasol. It was coincidental that the flames at Sasol 1 were brighter than those at Natref (partly foreign-, partly Sasol-owned) or Fluor (a US company, albeit with Sasol links), and that the original plan to also hit the US-owned Mobil refinery was dropped.

In June 1980, the guerrillas had overcome the supposedly best developed security system in the country. Soon afterwards, the oil installations were turned into actual fortresses. Six weeks after the attacks, unrest broke out at Sasol 3 as a result of the stricter security measures that had been implemented. Workers said they were being harassed by military personnel, who were even accused of having shot one worker. When David Moisi was taken to Secunda after his arrest, he saw the difference: 'We had been able to choose a convenient spot in between the watchtowers, which had always been there. Now the security had been visibly reinforced. But despite the additional measures, I felt that we could still hit the installation. I was itching to relay this information to the people in Maputo!' According to Rashid, the new measures were partly based on information regarding MK's methods which the police had managed to wring from the guerrillas in detention. 'At first there was a single diamond-mesh fence, made of soft wire; you cut it and walked in. They eventually installed triple layers of fencing and put up high walls to prevent our people from firing artillery rockets at the targets.' The areas surrounding the installation were defoliated to keep attackers at a distance. One such 'buffer zone', surrounding the Natref refinery, was fit to be converted into a game reserve stocked with ostriches and zebras in 1994.

South African newspapers were absolutely forbidden to publish photographs of these fortresses. The outside world was given a glimpse when a Dutch journalist visited South Africa. He was on a mission to discover 'the truth about Shell in South Africa' and had been advised by the Shipping Research Bureau to have a look at the extraordinary security surrounding the Shell/BP refinery in Durban, and if possible, to defy the law which prohibited the taking of photographs. He took a number of photographs from a car and when he described the facilities, he was evidently astounded:

Durban 1986

The storage tanks near the Durban harbour and the Shell/BP refinery – South Africa's
biggest – are enormous, almost invincible fortresses ... The several lines of defence
against unwelcome visitors can be clearly seen from the motorway which runs on
higher terrain. First a strip of grassland, then a fence of steelnetting, another strip of
grassland, another fence rather higher this time, grass again, then a concrete wall and
finally an electrified iron curtain of at least thirty metres high. At intervals of a hundred metres there were heavily armed watchtowers, with sloping green windows of
bullet-proof glass. Highly mounted, high-powered floodlights illuminated the walls
and fences. The storage tanks at the harbour lacked the electrified fence, but were
instead surrounded by three concrete walls topped by razor wire as a defence line.
Here, too, watchtowers, military patrols armed to the teeth, and watchdogs.

But even these measures proved inadequate to keep out the Special Operations group,
which after the Matola raid was led by Rashid. 'Although we were restricted as a result of
the security measures around the refineries, we kept carrying out lots of other attacks on
oil installations, and also on smaller targets such as fuel depots and pipelines. Special
Operations also tried several times to sever the rail link with Richards Bay, in order to
disrupt coal exports via that port. We encouraged other commands to even carry out attacks on petrol filling stations – the idea simply was: go wherever the oil goes – but that
didn't take place as much as we would have liked. Our comrade "Hotstuff" went back to
Secunda, on a solo mission. He knew the way there. His plan was to creep through the
manholes into the plant and then strike it from inside. But unfortunately they had put up
new fencing, so he then placed the charge on the pipe itself. Unfortunately for him, there
were two pipelines there; one was a fuel line, but he chose the other one, which was a
water line...'

Attacks on fuel installations

The following list – which is far from comprehensive – has been derived from a variety of sources. The ANC/MK have not claimed the responsibility for all the actions listed. Except for the August 1993 attack in East London, no sabotage action in this field could be identified as having been claimed by the PAC/APLA.

1/2 Jne 80	Sasolburg	Sasol 1	synchronised action
1/2 Jne 80	Sasolburg	Natref refinery	
2 Jne 80	Secunda	Sasol 2	
2 Jne 80	Springs	Fluor HQs	
Jne 81	Alberton (E.Rand)	Shell fuel depot	limpet mine discovered and defused
22 Oct 81	Secunda	Sasol	water pipeline slightly damaged
28 May 82	Hectorspruit (E.Transvaal)	BP fuel depot	limpet mines; a number of fuel tanks, a grease and oil store, and the cabin of a fuel tanker caught fire
3 Jne 82	Paulpietersburg (N.Natal)	Total fuel depot	seven tankers and storage tank destroyed by bomb explosions
28 Jne 82	Scheepersnek (N.Natal)	oil pipeline from Durban to Reef	pipeline damaged, lubrication pump destroyed, railway depot and pump station damaged by two massive bomb blasts
8 Nov 82	Mkuze (N.Natal)	Mobil petrol storage depot	heavily damaged by bombs and ensuing fire
20 Jly 83	Secunda	Sasol	abortive rocket attack; 'minor damage'
10 Oct 83	Warmbaths	fuel depot	six petrol storage tanks exploded, 2 railroad tankers and a road tanker badly damaged by limpet mines and ensuing fire
11 Mar 84	Ermelo (E.Transvaal)	Mobil fuel depot	limpet mines; five tanks extensively damaged by series of bomb blasts and 8-hour fire; nearby Shell and Caltex fuel depots saved by firefighters
13 May 84	Durban	Mobil refinery	abortive attack with RPGs causing fire and damaging some installations
6 Jne 85	Mobeni (Durban)	railway tankers	five empty railway tankers damaged by limpet mines

26 Jne 85	Umtata (Transkei)	fuel depot	limpet mine explosion and huge fire destroyed Transkei Development Corporation's bulk fuel depot
28 Nov 85	Secunda	Sasol	assault on two Sasol plants with number of 122-mm rockets, missing their targets
22 Jne 86	Merebank (Durban)	oil pipeline	Mobeni pipeline between Mobil refinery and Sapref; explosion causing leakage and fires lasting for several hours
mid-May 88	Luipaardsvallei	Shell depot	limpet mine
24 May 90	Louis Trichardt (N. Transvaal)	BP & Shell petrol depot	limpet mines gutting four petrol storage tanks and four petrol tankers; considerable damage
19 Aug 93	East London	Engen oil depot	RPG attack, hit top of empty tank [APLA]

The group used various types of equipment. 'At some stage we were even considering using anti-aircraft guns to fire into the refineries, applying armour-piercing incendiary round, so that the armour-piercing would go through the tanks and the incendiary would then ignite the fuel. But we abandoned the idea, and started using artillery, also in Secunda. There were two attacks with artillery on Sasol.'

On 'Kruger Day', 10 October 1983, an attack with limpet mines was made on a fuel depot at Warmbaths, two days before Prime Minister P.W. Botha was to visit the town. In a retaliatory action an ANC office in Maputo was bombed a week later by South African commandos, including a man called Wynand Petrus du Toit, who was caught in May 1985 trying to blow up fuel tanks in Angola.

No bases in Mozambique?

An ongoing 'war of words' accompanied the conflict between the ANC and the South African regime. Subsequent to signing treaties with some of the frontline states, the South African government jubilantly announced that the ANC was going to find itself in hot water; without bases in these countries, it would be impossible to launch further attacks. A few months after South Africa's signing of the *Nkomati accord* with Mozambique on 16 March 1984, the head of the security police, General Steenkamp, described the ANC as probably one of the 'least successful' insurgency organisations in operation. In June 1984, *The Citizen* newspaper published an interview with a former member of Special Operations, who had handed himself over to the police. The unnamed former guerrilla ('John X') told of how the ANC's crack unit under the command of Slovo and "Rashid" had had to take 'desperate' action to offset Nkomati.

Victor: Trampolining over the Apartheid Barriers

Rashid Patel: 'We had an old man called Victor, who knew the Sasol area very well. He had a criminal sort of history. The regime had recruited him to assassinate some of our comrades outside the country. But he went straight to our Chief Representative: I am so and so, I have been sent by the regime, here's the pistol that they gave me; they released me from prison to carry out this game – just to show the criminality on their part. Before he was taken into the Special Operations team, he was sent on a special mission to deal with some enemy agents. That was his ticket in. He was an amazing chap. For years we depended on him, for the movement of people inside. His dream was always to flatten Sasol 2. He died in November 1985, together with Barney, after carrying out our last attack on Secunda. Barney was the commander during that attack; he had often been a unit commander, as for instance at Sasol 1 in June 1980. They were on their way back when they were involved in a gun battle with the enemy forces near the Swazi border.' – Barney's biography says that three MK combatants were intercepted near Piet Retief, and that the three were reported by local residents to have killed a large number of SADF troops before finally losing their own lives.

David Moisi: 'When Victor left the "assassination machinery" to join us, he confided some details about the new operation to some of the comrades. Later, when they got into the country and got arrested, they were beaten up because the Boers thought those were the guys who were involved in Sasol. So they had to prove that they were not, and they told them who were involved. That's how they first found out about us...'

Rashid: 'Once Victor came back from a reconnaissance mission in Natal, to the Mobil refinery, and he said, I think I can do it. So we said, how are you going to cut through these electrified fences? I'll use a trampoline, he said... I'll trampoline in, I'll tie everything, the weapons and so on, to my body and jump and get in, and then, once the thing goes off, there will be chaos all around. If we set off a small explosion somewhere, there'll be chaos, everybody will abandon the place because of the security regulations, you then run and the big explosions will go off... – It was this kind of thinking. It was like some people thought: I'm gonna make it my life's work to destroy this sort of thing!'

The timing of the attack by Special Operations on a fuel depot in Ermelo, a few days before Nkomati, was to make it clear that the ANC did not fear the accord. Neither were the claims of the South African security police borne out by the subsequent developments. Rashid: 'I would not say that the reaction was desperate, but rather that the accord strengthened the will on the part of the unit not to be thwarted. Part of Special Operations continued to operate from Swaziland; the bulk of it moved to the western front in Botswana.' Joe Slovo says that MK did try to continue Special Operations from Swaziland and Mozambique after Nkomati, but he admits that 'the facilities were no longer the same.'

It seems clear that the question of bases in neighbouring countries *was* a sensitive issue for the ANC. Contemporary news reports reflecting the state of knowledge on the part of the security forces (based as it was on information obtained from captured or defected guerrillas, or by infiltration) are more often than not confirmed today by insiders. At the time, however, ANC spokespersons discussed this issue in guarded terms in public statements. As we saw before, the 1980 attacks on Sasol were described as having been 'planned by units inside the country'. When interviewed by the Mozambique Press Agency (AIM) in 1983, Tambo's replies were in part influenced by the official Mozambican view implied by the reporter ('*Since the ANC has no bases in Mozambique,* where then does it have its bases?'); Tambo rightly pointed out that it had always been 'part of the regime's defence strategy to suggest that within South Africa everybody is satisfied with everything: the only trouble comes from outside...' However, he went as far as to dispel as a 'myth' the view that there were bases in the neighbouring countries, saying, 'Any such bases are inside South Africa.' Rashid still prefers to talk about 'transit areas, not "bases",' when referring to the neighbouring states. Slovo emphasises that 'there was a need to protect our host countries, which made us disinclined to talk too much about bases in the frontline states.'

Front-page news once again

Not long after Nkomati, Special Operations planned an attack on a refinery in Durban. The group decided upon an attack with rocket-propelled grenades on Mobil's Wentworth plant – the one that had been scrapped from the programme in 1980 – and not on the nearby Sapref refinery of Shell/BP. According to Rashid, 'It was an easier target. There was more security around Sapref, because of the airport there and also because the Air Force used that place. In addition, the huge fences made it an impenetrable fortress. Sapref had a very narrow access route; from the sea it was also fenced off.' Four MK guerrillas, Clifford Brown ('Alf Sigale'), Vuyisile Matroos ('Johnny'), Mzwakhe Mthwebana and Vuyisile de Vos ('Abel'), were selected to carry out the attack. It was certainly spectacular, but the outcome was calamitous for those involved.

None of the unit members lived to tell the tale. The author of a book on MK entitled *Apartheid's Rebels* therefore based his version of the events on a few newspaper reports:

> Darkness and thick brush along the ridge above Durban's Mobil oil refinery complex must have seemed welcome protection to the guerrillas silently assembling a rocket launcher and automatic weapons on the night of May 13. Ordered to hit the petroleum facility, one of the nation's largest, the unit had probably scouted the area in advance for the best firing position offering the greatest chance of escape. At 10:22 P.M., they launched a brief attack with a rocket bombardment and blasts of gunfire. One missile whistled narrowly over a large oil tank but slammed into a smaller one, causing explosions and a spectacular fire. For the next two hours security forces combed the area, later claiming to have killed four "terrorists" in a gun battle. But it may never be known whether these victims had been involved in the operations ... The bold Durban raid made front-page news throughout the country the next morning.

What is reasonably sure is that *these victims* did not view themselves as such, neither did the ANC in Lusaka in its statement on the attack, nor the thousands of mourners who attended the funerals of their freedom fighters. Other newspapers gave more detailed accounts of the aftermath. After firing three RPG rockets at the refinery, the four made a getaway by car. They succeeded in stopping a pursuing police van by gunfire, and escaped a roadblock by throwing a hand grenade at the police. Another police vehicle gave chase and its occupants punctured the tyres of the escape car. The four jumped out and took shelter in a construction company yard; a fierce shootout with the police ensued, in which the guerrillas fought to the death. Four hours had elapsed since the firing of the rockets. In addition to a number of wounded police officers, three persons sleeping in a nearby paint storage shed died when the shed caught fire during the shooting.

An activist from nearby Merebank has been quoted as expressing his anger at the leadership of the ANC: 'They used comrades from Port Elizabeth for the attack! They didn't know their way around in Merebank and were caught and shot. They should have contacted us; we were all keen to see the refinery go up in smoke.' Rashid's dry comment: 'No, people always say that... They could have come out and volunteered.'

Two of the four guerrillas took their secret to their grave; a secret which their commander, Rashid, is now prepared to reveal. In line with the strategy to complement the pressure caused by sanctions, Special Operations had also started investigating how the existing strategic oil reserves could be exhausted, and what the possibilities were to hit *tankers* which brought in the oil. 'We had obtained information about mines being used for stockpiling oil, and were trying to find ways to get into these mines. We had been studying the reports published by the Shipping Research Bureau, and from them we knew which ships were involved in the deliveries. We had started training divers. In fact, two of the people that were killed in Durban, comrade Alf Sigale and comrade Abel, were divers. They had been sent in partly to do reconnaissance around the ships that were unloading oil in Durban. We wanted to hit a ship while it was unloading oil. The idea was that the ensuing blaze would be disastrous for the tanker as well as for the storage tank. The comrades we had trained for the job were very keen on getting into action – they were awaiting the necessary equipment from our command – but that was not to be after their unsuccessful escape following the attack on Mobil.'

The state imposed tight restrictions on the funeral arrangements for the four guerrillas. By then, funerals of political activists had become anti-apartheid rallies. The restrictions on the funerals of the four stipulated that they could not take place on a weekend or a public holiday, that the services had to take place within a building, that the coffins and the mourners had to be transported to the graveyards by vehicle, that the funerals were to take place between 8 a.m. and 2 p.m., that the funeral procession had to take the shortest route between mortuary and church and between church and cemetery, and that there were to be no posters, placards, pamphlets or singing of freedom songs at the burials.

The mourners ignored many of the imposed regulations. Nearly 3000 students attended a memorial meeting for Brown at the University of the Western Cape. In Port Elizabeth about 5000 people attended the funeral of Matroos and De Vos, whose coffins were draped with ANC flags; a UDF banner was displayed before the coffins were lowered into the graves.

Lights at the end of the tunnel

The defiance expressed by the mourners was indicative of how special operations organised outside the country served to enhance the internal resistance against apartheid.

On 1 June 1984, four years after the Sasol attack, an editorial appeared in the British *Guardian*, saying, '"Armed propaganda" has had considerable success both in worrying the regime, and in raising the morale of thousands of Africans, who have seen from it that apartheid is not totally impregnable. The flames of the refineries in Sasolburg and Durban are lights at the end of the tunnel.'

When asked about their views on the impact of Special Operations, those involved express a balanced opinion. Looking back, Rashid is mildly self-critical, saying that 'to some extent, we should perhaps have concentrated on certain areas. We tried to do too much with too small an infrastructure. We were aware of this, but the need for secrecy also influenced our decisions. At the same time, it should be borne in mind that secrecy and a narrow command structure were the very key to our success. Naturally, our actions didn't always turn out the way we intended; when you have an enemy, he also leaves his mark on the development. We suffered casualties... But the fact that we were able to carry out such massive operations is stunning.'

Jacob Zuma is convinced that the Sasol attacks and other special operations 'did go a long way to shake the South African situation. Those actions had more impact than the ordinary classic guerrilla kind of activity. That's when the business community actually began to say to the government, until when are we going to have this unbearable situation? Until when is our economy going to be the subject of sanctions and sabotage? Botha himself began to have major conferences with business leaders and started announcing reforms. This was certainly part of the impact we were making. I think it was in 1980 that our intelligence sources informed us that there were serious discussions about the possibility of negotiations.'

'Eventually,' says Rashid, 'there was no longer a sharp differentiation between people who had been conventionally trained outside the country, and people inside. Armed actions became a spur for action on the part of the people. By 1983, it really started becoming a people's war. By 1987, we were considering the possibility of setting up all operational units inside the country, in what was known as "Operation Vula". It was certainly no surprise when the regime announced it had decided to opt for negotiations.'

The former commander of Special Operations concludes by adding that for a long time people were very critical of MK: 'It is as if in their mind, MK should have marched in with tanks and taken Pretoria... But at no stage in our strategy did we say we were going to defeat the regime militarily. I think we were able to target the soft underbelly. The one thing they were not prepared to sustain was the loss of white life. They had to deploy tens of thousands of people throughout the country. All these call-ups put an enormous toll on the economy. I think we succeeded. Our objective was always to bring the regime down. That objective has succeeded; today the difficult task of rebuilding has begun.'

First Steps of the Shipping Research Bureau

Canonical historiography on the Shipping Research Bureau has it that the founding of the Bureau was a direct sequel to the UN-sponsored Amsterdam oil embargo seminar of March 1980. After all, didn't the seminar's final document state that 'an essential component of an effective oil embargo ... is the creation of a machinery to monitor all shipments of oil to South Africa'? Preparations for the founding of such a machinery were already well on their way since the year before, however, and the recommendation of the seminar's final declaration only formalised an already existing intention of the Dutch anti-apartheid movement. Its activists had, in fact, done their best to elicit just such a convenient official endorsement of their own plans.[1]

A former colleague of the Holland Committee on Southern Africa (HCSA) was considered to be the best candidate for the job: Mr Frank Janzen was already listed among the participants in the UN report on the seminar as a representative of the *'Oil and Shipping Monitoring Bureau'*. Janzen: 'It was actually little more than a continuation of my work for the Holland Committee in a more study-like direction. A committee member is more or less forced to be busy with twelve things at the same time; this was a nice, concrete issue. Maybe for someone else the work offered too little scope for action, because we were always busy with data and minutiae. But for me it was much more attractive, and, like an industrious ant, I put myself into the study of this "terra incognita", the world of shipping and oil... Bernard Rivers and Martin Bailey had already built up a fund of experience, and the Dutch committees had enjoyed contact with them for some time.' Bailey and Rivers had come together in the beginning of 1979 with the American Mike Tanzer and the Canadian Terisa Turner, in an ad hoc 'Sanctions Working Group' to address the question of oil and South Africa. Janzen remembers how he applied himself to studying the papers which this group had produced, and how he felt somewhat uncertain when he came to reflect on all of their ideas concerning the operations of a worldwide 'central clearing house' for the monitoring of the embargo. 'The involvement on our side was considerably less ambitious, and we also had fewer international pretensions. Of course, our activity here in the Netherlands was for the most part directed toward the discovery of evidence for the involvement of Shell and Rotterdam in embargo breaking; that the tropical islands of the Dutch empire in the Caribbean also had to be looked into had already become clear the year before.'

In June 1979 the Dutch weekly *Vrij Nederland* had published a lengthy article entitled 'South African oil boycott broken from the Netherlands Antilles'.[2] The names of some of the tankers involved were actually mentioned, and the Dutch Kairos and HCSA committees had moved into action by asking the Antillean government to take those steps necessary to put an end to the 'oil-running' practice that was using their harbours. The primary association brought to mind when looking at oil in connection with the Antilles was: *Shell*. The Dutch anti-apartheid activists were very anxious to be able to unearth hard evidence that could be used in their campaign against the Anglo-Dutch oil giant.

The ideas developed by the Sanctions Working Group assumed that the 'clearing house' would collate information on tanker movements and transmit it to the participating countries, especially to those in the OPEC group. The clearing house that was envisioned would be provided with a computer, an enormous budget (needed, among other things, for the 'fairly generous rewards' that would have to be disbursed for paying off informants), a headquarters in one of the oil-exporting countries and offices in New York, London and Rotterdam.[3] It soon became evident that a more modest set-up would have to suffice. The Sanctions Working Group, moreover, did not long continue to exist in the same form. Janzen remembers a number of 'somewhat difficult talks' in Tripoli, Libya, shortly after the Amsterdam seminar, between the initiators of the Dutch monitoring bureau, the English branch of the group and the New York branch; all of these representatives had been invited ('at Ghaddafi's cost') to participate in an 'Oil Workers' World Antimonopolist Conference'. Rivers and Bailey saw more value in the Dutch initiative and turned away from the American branch of the Sanctions Working Group. 'Bernard began to work for our Bureau immediately, in the capacity of a consultant. We did the first report together – my part therein was more or less that of an apprentice. Martin remained at a somewhat greater distance, but still closely involved as an advisor and a source of information.'

Looking at the initial phase of things, one might well ask how it came to pass that this small Dutch group eventually surfaced as the internationally recognised authority on the subject of embargo monitoring ('the well-known oil embargo watchdog'), and not the Sanctions Working Group with its longer standing. The aims of the latter did not, after all, seem to differ very widely from those of the nascent SRB.[4]

One of the differences between both groups was that the Dutch committees and the British researchers thought it very important to plan new activities in cooperation with the ANC and SWAPO; the New York branch appeared to be more interested in cultivating its connections with the Organization of African Trade Union Unity (OATUU). The contacts of the Sanctions Working Group and its successor – the International Oil Working Group (IOWG), centred around the person of Terisa Turner – with the United Nations Centre against Apartheid and the UN Council for Namibia were not always smooth. In later years the Shipping Research Bureau would regularly be asked if it 'had anything to do with the IOWG,' or what it thought of that group. Year in, year out, the IOWG would reappear with a plan to produce a 'Workers' Action Handbook' for the oil embargo. Sometimes the group would seem to have disappeared from the face of the earth, and then it would suddenly approach the SRB with proposals for cooperation and joint publications – proposals that the SRB greeted with a goodly dose of reserve, since it seemed preferable to keep a healthy degree of distance. Only once did the IOWG appear with independent research results concerning embargo violations in the form of a list of tankers thought to have delivered oil to South Africa in 1982. The group continued to distribute this list for years, despite its apparent inaccuracies and the availability of more reliable information from the SRB. When the list was distributed again at the 'Maritime Unions Against Apartheid' conference in October 1985,[5] the SRB decided that it would be a good idea to warn the unions and the OATUU against their using such information which, because of its manifest unreliability, could all too easily make them vulnerable to hostile criticism.[6]

Getting down to work

At the time that the Bureau began its work, the question as to the international 'market' for the research results that were produced was not yet an object. Such, at least, is the way the first research director, Frank Janzen, remembers things. 'I imagine that the Dutch committees felt a certain satisfaction when the UN gave its blessing in March 1980, and when they were able to attach the English, who were then the world's monitoring experts, to their own initiative, and that they would have seen the work of the Bureau as a prestigious extension of the work they were engaged in. But for the time being I had few pretensions about the international impact that our future research results might have. We were primarily busy with the slow building up of a feeling for what we were doing – it was really work for monks! What would be *done* with our results was another question. Time would tell.'

In fact, the organisational structure had been so designed that the parent committees, which were already busy campaigning for the oil embargo and for Shell's withdrawal from South Africa, retained the responsibility for any action that might be undertaken on the basis of the SRB's research results. It was only the actual research work itself which was made independent of them. The governing body was made up of activists of the Holland Committee and Kairos, organisations whose primary work was done at the national level, but who also remained the negotiating partners for the United Nations, the

Demonstration in Amsterdam 24 June 1980: Stop the Terror of the Apartheid Regime – Oil Boycott Now

ANC and other international organisations. Janzen did accompany the board members on one occasion, in May 1980, when they went over to London to visit the ANC office. 'We were assured that the ANC found our initiative an important one; they congratulated us for our willingness to take it on. In a certain sense, what we were doing took on an international allure that the other work being done by the committees did not enjoy: the ANC had connections with the OAU, with the UN... It actually seemed that they found monitoring the oil embargo somewhat more important than all kinds of other anti-apartheid work.'

Letters announcing the formation of the SRB were sent out in the beginning of June 1980, to the sanctions bureau of the OAU, OAPEC, OPEC, SWAPO, the UN Centre against Apartheid, and to a number of foreign solidarity groups. This was done not only to keep everyone well-informed, Janzen relates, but also in the hope that a network would hereby be created through which information on the oil connection with South Africa and especially on breaches of the embargo would begin to funnel onto the Bureau's desk.

In the beginning, the Bureau's short-term aims were formulated for internal use: the publication of comprehensive lists of oil tankers which had visited South African ports during at least 24 hours in 1979 and 1980, together with their owners, flags and cargo capacities; the publication of a black list of shipping companies and ships (especially those of the major oil companies) which had made themselves guilty of shipping oil to South Africa; the extension of this basic data with the 'voyage histories' of the tankers in question, with the specific goal of determining whether a pattern of any kind could be elucidated from the data respecting the origin of the oil and the various detours and tricks of the embargo-breaking trade by means of which the oil eventually wound up in South Africa (swap arrangements, transhipments in Rotterdam, the Netherlands Antilles, Singapore). 'A lot of essential questions will remain unanswered, such as who is responsible for having chartered a particular tanker, who the owner is of a particular cargo of oil, how negligent which authorities are in which of the oil-producing countries, etc.,' the memorandum stated. It was decided that more ambitious research, such as that concerning itself with the geographical distribution of refinery capacity, the world of shipping insurance, the role of the spot market and supplies of refined oil products – all of it necessary in order to put together a really complete picture – would have to wait.

As things progressed, the intensity with which the various research directions could be pursued and the internal order of priority among them kept on changing. In the first months Janzen (in Amsterdam) and Rivers (who had taken up residence in New York) analysed computer printouts of tanker arrivals at Durban and Cape Town in 1979. The printouts were obtained from a company which preferred that any credit given to the origin of the data be made no more specific than 'reliable international shipping publications'. Rivers had already experimented with this type of printout in the work he had done, together with Bailey, for the United Nations; Lloyd's of London had proved an excellent source of information on shipping movements. Janzen and Rivers obtained further information from a variety of sources about the tankers under investigation, which primarily dealt with who owned, managed and chartered the tankers in question, as well as where they had travelled before and after their call at South Africa. This kind of data was often only available in somewhat private reports produced by consultancy companies; the costs of some of these publications were prohibitively high, and, moreover, not all companies proved particularly eager to make their publications available at all, so the Bureau sometimes had to resort to more devious methods in order to acquire the information it wanted.

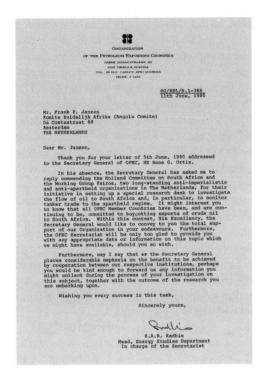

Finally, Rivers and Janzen attempted to ascertain for every vessel whether or not she offloaded crude oil, and if so, where that crude had originated. In so doing, they also developed research methods which would help them to learn which other tankers had delivered crude oil to South Africa, even though Lloyd's had not reported them as calling there – Lloyd's proved to be less and less informative with regard to calls of tankers at South African ports.

The interested reader is directed to read the story of the tanker *Mobil Hawk*, which is related later on in this book,[7] in order to get some impression of the research difficulties attendant on unravelling each separate detail of what was going on. Thereby, it is necessary to note that the clarifying sources which became available in later years were not yet there in 1980. In the first main report which the SRB published, covering the period between 1 January 1979 and 31 March 1980, 23 of the 150 tankers listed were 'considered most likely to have delivered crude oil when they called at South Africa'. In an update published in 1985, the Bureau listed 61 apparent oil deliveries, and the list of the Bureau's 'definitive' results as these are published in the present book even contain 67 identified deliveries for the same five quarters. The later staff of the SRB got into the habit of saying that its first report was out of print, for too many 'childhood' diseases of one kind or another had affected it; at the same time, however, they could not look back upon their predecessors in the Bureau without a feeling of awe, considering that so strong a foundation had been laid by pioneers on ground that, before their time, had been almost wholly unexplored.

A remarkable feature of the first SRB report, including the section that announces the direction of 'Future Research', is the emphasis that is placed on the shipping side of

things. This is not to say that it did not succeed in exposing to public scrutiny the significant role in embargo breaking that was played by Shell, in its capacity as tanker owner but
also as oil company. Yet, characteristic of the report was that oil companies only appeared
in their role as owners or charterers of tankers – the category 'owners of the oil cargo on
board the tanker' did not yet exist. And now that a new problem was becoming apparent,
namely the fact that tanker calls were no longer being reported at all, and that the emphasis
of the research had therefore to shift to what the Bureau began to call 'gap tankers' (tankers showing what appeared to be inexplicable gaps in their reported movements), this
could easily have the effect of confining the scope of the Bureau's work once more to the
monitoring of shipping alone, as opposed to the monitoring of both 'oil and shipping'.[8]
Nevertheless, it appears from documents in the SRB archive that already around November 1980, that is, before the already completed research work had led to any publications,
discussions in the Bureau were shifting away from shipping alone to include the whole
subject of oil. Rivers philosophised that the Bureau should be in a position to extend its
knowledge of tanker movements, and that this, together with a study of oil trade statistics,
could be used to build up a clear overall picture that would show which oil-exporting
countries and oil-transhipping countries, and which companies, were involved (and to
what degree) in the supply of crude oil to South Africa; he imagined that his colleagues in
the SRB would agree that 'our ultimate objective' should be to produce a report of this
kind.

A glance over the border

It was not quite true that the Bureau's work in the beginning completely took place within
the confines of the study, or that everything it did was restricted inside the borders of the
Netherlands. The campaigns being waged by the parent organisations were not only directed against Shell and the achieving of a unilateral Dutch oil embargo; the Dutch government would also have to exert pressure at the international level in order to bring about
a mandatory international embargo. And there was no reason why the oil embargo activists on the committees and the SRB would have to restrain themselves from glancing
across the national border. So a careful note was made of which relevant organisations
were scheduled to hold international conferences, where it was felt that lobbying could get
the embargo on the agenda if it was not listed as such already, and where resolutions
seemed likely to be passed in which the embargo should not be forgotten. Such conferences would soon enough become part of the Bureau's fixed routine; members of the
board and/or the staff attended them, whether or not they had been spontaneously invited.
It was always possible to try and elicit a request for a paper from the organisers. Participating as a 'journalist' for an anti-apartheid paper was one of the other possibilities, while in
some cases, conference participants from the ANC or the United Nations could be found
who were willing to lend an ear to the Bureau.

As the moment approached when the Bureau was ready to publish its first research
findings, attention was also paid to international developments. Was it a good idea to
allow publication to coincide with the debate in the Dutch parliament on the subject of the
oil embargo? Was it likely that a new oil embargo resolution would be voted on in the UN
General Assembly more or less at the same time – if so, then the report should be simulta-

neously released both in the Netherlands and in New York. Best would be if the release could be timed to coincide with some major international meeting, such as that of the UN Conference on Trade and Development (UNCTAD), where the problem of 'flags of convenience' was supposed to be discussed. But that meeting was postponed. Perhaps the conference in Kuwait where OAPEC was scheduled to discuss the supply of oil to South Africa? But there the SRB was not welcome; yet, it was decided, in close counsel with Frene Ginwala of the ANC, that the OAPEC ministers should at least be made aware of the SRB's research findings – a delegation sympathetic to the Bureau's work should confidentially receive the material before it was scheduled to be published (we may guess that a likely candidate was the chairman of the Amsterdam seminar and later UN ambassador from Algeria, Mr Mohamed Sahnoun).

The ANC, meanwhile, had already made itself familiar with the raw material of the pre-publication findings, for that had been the agreement: it would be apprised at an early stage of all relevant findings, it would be allowed to give its advice as to the way of publishing the findings, and to make use of pre-publication material at the diplomatic level. It was Frene Ginwala, too, who insisted that an earlier 'mini-report' be brought out based on the large numbers of Norwegian tankers in the report. She had been to Norway and Denmark for discussions on the oil issue, was convinced that Norwegian public opinion was interested in the issue, and that the Norwegian government might be inclined to take some kind of action if there would only be enough of the right kind of publicity concerning the involvement in embargo-breaking shipments of Norwegian tankers. The release of a special 'Norway report' before the publication of the general report would give the Norwegians the chance to concentrate on their own involvement, and would have the effect of lessening counter-arguments that all sorts of ships and other countries were also involved.

That Norwegian shipping companies were deeply involved was already clear from a number of incidents, but the SRB special report provided the first indication of how extensive that involvement was. Norwegian concern was well-known. If the SRB was ever successful in its cementing of relations with foreign contacts, this was never more so than with the Norwegians, whose own press had already exposed the involvement of Norwegian shipping companies in the breaking of the oil embargo, and where the anti-apartheid movement had succeeded in sparking off a growing interest in the whole subject. That part of the story can be read elsewhere in this book in the contribution of Øystein Gudim, a one-time anti-apartheid activist and researcher who at times must have felt himself to be 'our man in Oslo' for the Shipping Research Bureau.

The special Norway report was presented as the Bureau's first publication in Oslo on 3 December 1980. The history and movements of the Norwegian tanker *Havdrott* was its central publicity feature. The principle underlying the SRB research was its intended limitation to those tanker calls at South Africa ports which had been publicly reported; at the time, these calls provided enough material for the production of a sizeable report. But in the case of the *Havdrott*, the first cracks were showing up in that principle. In the period of time covered by the report the ship had only made two reported calls, whereas research unmistakably indicated that the ship was engaged in a veritable shuttle operation between the Persian Gulf and South Africa: as many as 12 further possible trips over a somewhat longer period (January 1979–October 1980) were identified, which simply had not been disclosed to the international shipping press (read: Lloyd's).[9] The Bureau could not avoid

concluding that its research scope would have to be widened to include unreported epi-
sodes such as these.

The Norway report was the first of many SRB reports which continued to provide new
impulses to the public debate on the embargo in the Norwegian media and parliament. The
SRB could only applaud the fact that, as reported from Norway, the shipowners had felt
constrained to prepare their own 'counter-report' which maintained that not all the listed
ships had actually delivered oil: the Bureau welcomed such reactions 'which effectively
admitted that the embargo was being breached'![10]

What could be achieved in Norway could also be achieved back home. The comprehensive general report, when it was published, would show that tankers owned or chartered by Shell (the largest company in the Netherlands), plus tankers sailing from the
Netherlands or the Netherlands Antilles, had played a larger role in delivering crude oil to
South Africa than had tankers connected with any other country. This would be the subject of a second partial report that would be accorded priority publication.

The Antilles connection

On 16 December 1980, the consultant to the Shipping Research Bureau, Bernard Rivers,
arrived in the Netherlands Antilles, with some busy days lying ahead of him. On 8 December, Rivers and SRB board member De Jong had met the envoy of the Netherlands Antilles in The Hague, Mr Ronald Casseres, to discuss evidence gathered by the Bureau with
regard to tankers sailing from his country to South Africa. The first person Rivers contacted by telephone after his arrival at Curaçao was Mr Franco, a member of the island
government, who had been present at the meeting in The Hague. Now, Franco refused to
meet Rivers, claiming that he was too busy and that anyway this was a matter for the
national government of the Netherlands Antilles, not for the Curaçao island government
(which Rivers thought was true enough).

Rivers then learned that subsequent to the The Hague meeting and a consequent telex
from De Jong which the envoy had sent onward to his government, a special, small group
of civil servants had been set up to look into the matter and to report to Don Martina, the
Prime Minister, who would then decide what, if anything, to do.

Rivers tried to meet the advisor on oil to the Prime Minister, whom he had been recommended to see by Casseres. The advisor decided, despite Rivers' pleading, that since the
problem was already being dealt with by a special group, and that since he, the advisor,
was not a member of that group, it would not be correct for him to meet the Shipping
Research Bureau. Rivers was more successful in arranging meetings with the Deputy
Harbour Master of Curaçao, with the Lloyd's agent, with Shell Curaçao, and with two
members of the special group.

The leader of the group, Mr Ter Haar from the Ministry of Foreign Affairs, and the main
other member, Mr Wellen from the Ministry of Economic Affairs, met with Rivers two or
three times between 19 and 24 December. They told him, in response to his request to
meet Don Martina, that the Prime Minister was too busy to see him, but that what he said
to them would be relayed to Martina.

The meetings were stiff and difficult. Rivers got the impression that the gentlemen he was dealing with genuinely hadn't known about these tanker trips to South Africa, but also that they didn't really *want* to know about them: 'They seemed to find me and my message what might be called an "embarrassing inconvenience".' Ter Haar and Wellen were particularly upset at the 'judgements' they felt the Bureau was making in the draft report (which Rivers had handed them at their first meeting), which they considered to be based on insufficiently detailed information that was also insufficiently accurate. At the second meeting, on 23 December, Rivers gave them a specially prepared memo containing additional details on each of the tankers featured in the report. Wellen took the list, and contacted the harbour masters on the three islands, Curaçao, Bonaire and Aruba. On the 24th, he told Rivers that on the basis of a preliminary investigation, he considered that several of these tankers had not been to the Antilles at or near the time the SRB said they were there. This shocked Rivers, since the SRB list was based on published data from Lloyd's, who obtained most or all of its information from their agents in the Antilles and other ports, while the Antilles Lloyd's agent had told him that he acquired all his data directly from the Antilles harbour masters...

Ter Haar and Wellen were very nervous about the SRB report. They didn't accept that all the tankers had come to the Antilles in the first place; and for those that did, the Antilles government had no idea that they then went to South Africa. Therefore, they argued, the whole tone of the report was unfair to the Antilles, which did not know and was not responsible for what these ships did.

Rivers also phoned the top official at the Curaçao Oil Terminal (COT), the Shell-controlled crude oil transhipment terminal – the largest in the Western world – from whence a considerable number of the 19 listed tankers had sailed, to ask if he could meet him to discuss the issue. His respondent, Mr Howard, said that since Rivers' arrival in Curaçao he had been approached by the government about the allegations and added that 'all activities of the terminal are confidential, as I mentioned to the government here.' (Rivers wondered: confidential from the government also?) Howard said that rather than seeing him, Rivers should see Robert de Vos, chief executive of Shell Curaçao. So a meeting was set up on 24 December, during which De Vos told Rivers that the Shell Group very strictly obeyed destination restrictions imposed by oil-exporting countries, and 'We at Shell Curaçao and COT ensure to the very best of our ability that those to whom we sell embargoed oil themselves respect these embargo conditions.' He refused to confirm whether any particular Shell tanker had come to the Netherlands Antilles, or where it went later: 'That is confidential,' he said. And he told Rivers that most or all oil at COT was, in fact, owned by non-Shell companies.

Afterwards, Rivers realised that if the last statement was true, De Vos's first two statements were not very relevant. Presumably, if some independent 'Company X' paid COT to store some of its oil, that company could supply vast amounts of embargoed oil to South Africa via COT, and even via Shell tankers if it would pay Shell to carry a certain amount of Company X oil to South Africa while (say) these tankers were on their way back to the Persian Gulf, and then, strictly speaking, De Vos's denials would still remain true. And if all that was the case, then what was to stop Shell from finding some Company X to do all of this on Shell's behalf? After all, one only had to remember the key role played by the independent company, Freight Services Ltd, in getting oil from Shell South Africa to Rhodesia.[11]

The Shell Curaçao public relations man who had sat in on the meeting told Rivers that he should feel free to phone or telex him if he had further questions, and he would reply 'within 24 hours'. So on 29 December Rivers sent a few questions by telex from New York, among which: 'Is it possible for crude oil owned by a non-Shell-Group company to be carried to or from COT in a tanker owned or chartered by a Shell-Group company?' and: 'Mr. De Vos explained that it is against Shell policy for oil originating in a country which embargoes South Africa to be delivered from COT to South Africa if the oil is owned by a Shell-Group company. Does that restriction apply if that oil is owned by a non-Shell company?'.

On 31 December, De Vos sent his reply: 'After the discussion held on Wednesday 24th December 1980 we are of the opinion that a clear insight has been given in the principles by which Shell Curacao N.V. and Curacao Oil Terminal N.V. are guided in the handling of their business. Therefore we do not intend to further elaborate on the supplementary questions you have raised in your telex of 29 December 1980.' Bernard Rivers: 'I must say that I found that an interesting reply. It suggested to me that maybe my telexed questions had touched a sensitive point...'

When Rivers phoned Wellen from New York in the first days of the New Year, the latter told him that his government had just issued a press statement in response to the SRB's information. This was no cause for unalloyed joy for the Shipping Research Bureau, since it had been planning to announce its research results at its own press conference to be held later in January 1981. When Rivers asked if the SRB could at least be sent a copy of the press statement, Wellen replied that the Prime Minister would have to be consulted first. Rivers remembers that he considered this reply to be 'one of the most remarkable statements I had ever heard from a bureaucrat.'

In the press statement which, after a week or more of effort, the SRB finally obtained, it was stoutly maintained that eight of the 19 tankers cited by the SRB had not called at the Netherlands Antilles at all,[12] and that of the remaining 11, only three had departed the Antilles with 'South Africa' as their destination, of which two had done nothing more than take on bunker fuel. Six of the 19 ships were loaded at the Netherlands Antilles and then left with destinations other than South Africa. 'This information,' the statement read, 'is in accordance with information obtained from the oil companies which are domiciled in the Netherlands Antilles. The government of the Netherlands Antilles is of the opinion that the important role that has purportedly been played by the Netherlands Antilles in the supply of oil to South Africa has been proved untrue. Considering the total oil imports of South Africa, the Netherlands Antilles is not an important supplier of oil to South Africa.' The press statement added that the Antilles government strongly condemned the apartheid regime in South Africa, and would carefully follow all further developments related to the case.

The SRB's first report

The Antillean episode taught the relative value of 'painstaking research' that was sponsored by the governments of those very countries which themselves, whether wittingly or unwittingly, played a role in the traffic of oil to South Africa.[13] It also showed how much weight could be attached to the veracity of a tanker's destination as reported on leaving the harbour. What is more, the list in question had only mentioned those tankers whose calls at South Africa had been reported; however, 'Increasing numbers of tankers are now calling at South Africa *secretly*, and we are already aware of some Shell tankers and some tankers sailing from the Netherlands Antilles which have arrived in South Africa in recent months but whose arrival there was not reported by the standard shipping publications,' the Bureau observed in its report on *Oil Supplies to South Africa: The Role of Tankers Connected with the Netherlands and the Netherlands Antilles*, which it released at a press conference on 13 January 1981.

Meanwhile, Martin Bailey, as a British journalist, had expressed his interest in the *Oman* angle of the report that was to be published on 13 January: five of the identified tankers had sailed to South Africa directly from Oman, an Arab country (with an embargo on South Africa) in which Shell was the principal international oil company. He could already see the headline in front of him: 'Shell breaks South African oil sanctions', a headline which, as he told the SRB, would sound like the Rhodesian scandal all over again, including the same old situation of Shell impressing public opinion with false 'assurances' that none of its oil was being sold to South Africa. As opposed to other journalists, Bailey already knew what the Shipping Research Bureau's report would reveal, and the Bureau was not unwilling in principle to let him have a 'scoop' in exchange for services rendered, at least so long as doing so would not interfere with its own plans for making public the role being played by Shell and the Netherlands Antilles. The technique of paying for valuable information by privileging the journalist in question with that most highly prized journalistic currency, the 'scoop', was one that would be repeated on many occasions in years to come. Yet, the Bureau had to weigh its fear that journalists would lose their interest in the matter if a colleague had been given an advantage, against the possible boost that an article in an authoritative foreign newspaper – proving that the issue was important – might give to the interest from the media. In Martin Bailey's case, the fear prevailed this time. Almost immediately, however, new information came to the Bureau's attention that was too recent to be published in the first report. An obscure oil-trading company named Transworld Oil (TWO), which the Bureau originally thought was based in the United States, turned out to be managed by a *Dutchman*, John Deuss, and one of its head offices was actually located in the eastern part of the Netherlands. In a very short time, this company's star in the Bureau's embargo research made a meteoric rise that put it almost in the same league with Shell itself, especially when it was discovered that the 'shuttle tanker' *Havdrott* had all the time been sailing on time charter to Transworld. Journalists were apprised of the role being played by TWO at the press conference that was held in January 1981, and Martin Bailey had the scoop in the form of a detailed article that was published a few days later.[14]

By coincidence, in the very same weekend that Bailey's piece appeared, news leaked out in Norway about one of TWO's planned transports – an embarrassment for the Norwegian government, which only four days earlier had informed the United Nations that it had 'taken steps to ascertain that oil produced on the Norwegian continental shelf is not exported to South Africa'.[15] The Norwegian tanker *Jane Stove* was on her way to Durban with a cargo of 125,000 tons of crude oil taken from the Norwegian Ekofisk field. The oil had been sold by Norske Fina, a subsidiary of the Belgian oil company Petrofina, on the understanding that it was destined for the Caribbean; the sale included the usual clause forbidding the transport of oil to South Africa. When, just before the cargo was about to be discharged, the news somehow leaked out to the press that the buyer (which was quickly enough identified as TWO) had indeed sent the tanker to South Africa, the Norwegian government moved to halt the operation.[16]

The SRB's revelations were making their claim on public attention in the Netherlands as well. The TWO affair, the dominant role being played by Shell in the breaking of the embargo, and the large numbers of tanker departures from the Netherlands Antilles as well as some from Rotterdam brought Dutch parliamentarians to the conclusion that an oil embargo, imposed under the Dutch Sanctions Law, would considerably hamper the existing pattern of oil supply to South Africa and would certainly not be an action of the token variety, which was what the Dutch government had always claimed. Every so often, the SRB and its parent committees would tell the world that such reactions were proof of the 'strong impact' which the publication of its first report had had in the Netherlands. In reality, however, the fire of parliamentary debate on the subject had subsided since the time, in June 1980, when the then government had almost fallen over the issue.

In spite of its first director's professed modesty, the SRB's international ambitions were certainly not set too low. The main report, *Oil Tankers to South Africa*, was eventually released in New York, where SRB chairman Cor Groenendijk, in the company of Bernard Rivers, put it into the hands of the chairman of the UN Special Committee against Apartheid, and at simultaneously held press conferences in both New York and London on 11 March 1981. In London the press conference was held jointly with the British Anti-Apartheid Movement, which also released its own report on the subject of Britain's role in supplying oil to South Africa.[17] On the same day press communiqués were issued in Norway, Denmark (where the role of the major shipping company A.P. Møller in supplying oil to South Africa had become evident), Sweden and Germany (where the role of German companies in Sasol had already been a focal point of criticism); in all these places the communiqués were issued in cooperation with the respective national anti-apartheid movements. The Arab oil world was not forgotten either: summaries of the report and of the press releases were translated into Arabic and widely distributed. Frank Janzen, who had meanwhile left his position as SRB director but was still involved in its research, remembers the enormous publicity: 'Our research findings were widely covered by the international press, but also, where we had hoped they would be, in oil and shipping trade journals.[18] We were certainly a little bit proud that we had proven ourselves capable of delivering work that was so solid it could not easily be called into question as mere campaign propaganda. And there was, unexpectedly, an enormous market for it, too, so that a reprint was necessary within a very short time. On the other hand, as an activist I also knew that the publicity which the report generated was one thing, but that finally what really mattered was whether it would lead to the taking of really effective action.' Janzen could have added that the two founding committees in any case had achieved exactly what they were aiming to achieve when the Bureau was first started: Shell could now be tackled with even harder facts than heretofore had been available, and the national as well as international campaign for a more effective oil embargo had had new weapons thrust into its hands. As Chairman Clark of the UN Special Committee against Apartheid said, 'The Bureau has already, within its first year, fully justified its existence.'

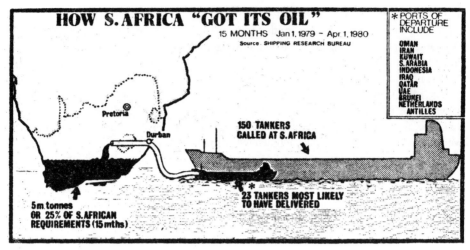

From a review of the SRB's first report in the British *Financial Times*, 12 March 1981

Later on, the daughter would slowly but surely begin to function more independently from her parents, from whom it was harder to demand continuous concentration, year in, year out, on the one theme of the oil embargo than was the case with the daughter with her 'one-track' mind. An increasingly important customer of the SRB's research findings was the United Nations, which later on even began to contribute to the funding of the SRB's work (the fact that the SRB staff gradually began to take over the responsibility for the Bureau's own funding from the parent committees was another sign of its coming of age). At the Bureau's founding, a conscious choice had been made to keep the relation between the SRB and the UN an informal one, in order to exempt the former as much as possible from too much bureaucratic and diplomatic involvement in its affairs. In the first years even a UN decision to provide the Bureau with financial support other than its ordering of a reasonable number of the Bureau's publications would have required a too complicated diplomatic decision process.

The organising of simultaneous releases in different countries, mostly in cooperation with the local anti-apartheid movement, remained standard practice for all of the main reports the Bureau had yet to issue, which began to see the light of day at the rate of about once every two years. In the course of time the committees stopped playing a central role in making known the Bureau's research findings; the SRB began to take upon itself the organising of its own press conferences. The parent committees continued to run the Bureau via the governing body and kept their original hold on questions of policy. As time went on, however, the Bureau's staff to all intents and purposes lost the feeling that they were working 'for the committees'; since the work was done in the name of the *international oil embargo*, the latter would even have to be 'defended', if need be, against what was sometimes felt to be the capriciousness of the committee bosses who were above them, some of whom would every now and then come up with plans which the staff considered to be incompatible with an adequate performance of the Bureau's job of embargo monitoring.

A mounting tide

The data which the Shipping Research Bureau produced were having a visible impact in more than one place, and the Bureau never tired of publicising the most noteworthy examples – in part in order to demonstrate that it was fulfilling a useful service and thus deserving financial support, but also in part in order to demonstrate that monitoring was not only feasible, but also 'that such an exercise can help countries to render the embargo more effective'. Examples were continually being repeated and added to in the Bureau's subsequent reports, in conference papers, subsidy applications, etc.[19]

The SRB did its best to publicise the oil embargo, but Amsterdam was not the only place where embargo work was being done. In the USA the *Sanctions Working Group* was active preparing papers for sanctions conferences, was engaged in advisory work and in publishing material setting forth the various ways and means by which the embargo could be enforced. In Africa the veteran champion of sanctions against South Africa, the *Organization of African Unity*, had set up its own Standing Committee on Sanctions. The OAU, which had a few years before given sanctions on oil pride of place in its policy list, issued a statement on 21 May 1980 in which it called for a mandatory oil embargo on South Africa to help ensure that apartheid 'will not roll on into the 21st century'.[20] At its meeting in Freetown, Sierra Leone, in June 1980, the OAU Council of Ministers discussed the impact of an oil embargo on South Africa's neighbouring states and adopted a 'Resolution on Sanctions' that was almost totally devoted to the subject of the oil embargo.[21]

By the time the OAU Chief of Sanctions, Dr Solomon Gomez, found the first SRB report about Norway on his desk in Addis Ababa, he had already been apprised of the situation by an article on the shuttle tanker *Havdrott*, which had appeared in *The Observer*. He told the SRB, in a letter of 16 December 1980, that the OAU had immediately despatched a note to the OAPEC countries appealing for their support in blacklisting the *Havdrott*. In the meantime, Bernard Rivers was engaged in discussions about the possibility of his being retained by the OAU as a part-time consultant on all matters concerning the oil embargo. At the end of January 1981 Gomez and representatives of the SRB met each other in Brussels. Among the topics on their discussion agenda was the desirability of an international monitoring office in which the OAU and OAPEC would cooperate.

Subsequently, Gomez invited the SRB to a week-long closed meeting of the OAU Sanctions Committee in Arusha, Tanzania, in March 1981, which was to deal with the oil embargo and with its effect on South Africa's neighbouring states. Martin Bailey, who had also been invited as an expert, addressed the meeting on the latter subject. The main report of the Shipping Research Bureau, which had just come out, was presented to the meeting by Bernard Rivers, whose testimony formed the basis for a discussion on how the oil embargo could be made more effective; the recommendations which the meeting produced were later adopted by the OAU Heads of State.

The above-mentioned discussions in Brussels had taken place during a *Conference of West European Parliamentarians on an Oil Embargo Against South Africa*, which was a sequel to the Amsterdam seminar of March 1980; it, too, was conceived of as a part of the preparations that were being laid for the major UN/OAU Sanctions Conference, to be held in Paris in May 1981. The chairman of the parliamentarians' organising committee was Jan Nico Scholten, the initiator of the oil embargo motion that was submitted in the Dutch parliament in November 1979, and adopted against the wishes of the government with a three-quarters' majority; Scholten was also the driving spirit behind the above-mentioned debate that was held in June 1980. He later became president of the Association of West European Parliamentarians for Action against Apartheid (AWEPAA). In his opening address to the Brussels conference, Scholten highlighted the results of the recent investigations undertaken by the Shipping Research Bureau and expressed the opinion that since oil supplies to South Africa were largely in Western hands, Western governments should be the first ones to put their houses in order.

In the Arab world a Boycott Bureau was in existence which also concerned itself with South Africa, but which was, in fact, preoccupied with measures to be taken against Israel.[22] In *OAPEC* there was more attention being paid to the oil embargo against South Africa as well. The organisation was busy preparing a resolution that was partly modelled on similar measures being taken elsewhere and probably also partly modelled on existing boycott measures which were in force against Israel; the resolution was passed in a Council of Ministers meeting on 6 May 1981. In it, OAPEC member countries committed themselves to improving the existing embargo legislation and monitoring procedures (detailed recommendations were set forth with respect to the more effective control of tankers' discharge certificates given at ports of destination), and clear penalties were laid down to be imposed upon embargo breakers. The recommendations would certainly have made all the difference, provided that they had been rigorously put into force. The OAPEC resolution was favourably received in the United Nations[23] and cited as an exemplary case of 'how it should be done' in diverse publications relating to the oil embargo. But not all OAPEC member states were equally interested in a rigorous enforcement of their embargoes.[24]

The *United Nations General Assembly* had repeatedly called for a mandatory oil embargo to be imposed by the UN Security Council, and in 1980 the call was again heard on 16 December with 123 votes for and 7 votes against (there were 13 abstentions). Previous attempts by the General Assembly and others such as the OAU and the *Non-Aligned Movement* had always been defeated by the vetoes of some of the Security Council's permanent members, who were now also among those who had cast their votes against the General Assembly resolution, namely the US, the UK and France.[25] But the *UN Special Committee against Apartheid* received a mandate from the General Assembly to continue and extend its work on the oil embargo. The administrative machinery of the Special Committee, the *UN Centre against Apartheid*, under its then director, E.S. Reddy, already closely followed and in its own turn stimulated all further initiatives in the same field; for this reason, it was logical that the Centre and the Shipping Research Bureau should express a mutual desire to maintain their working relationship after the Amsterdam seminar. When the SRB report on *Oil Tankers to South Africa* was completed in December 1980, 50 advance copies were sent to Ambassador Clark, chairman of the Special Committee and ambassador of Nigeria to the UN. Clark sent these copies, in confidence, to the governments of countries which supported the embargo but which were also, for whatever reason, mentioned in the report. On the occasion of the testimony of SRB chairman Groenendijk before the Special Committee on 11 March 1981, Clark released the responses which he had thus far received from the governments concerned; these were later published by the UN.[26] Among the responding countries were some which promised their

own investigations; others were prompted by the report's findings to sharpen their embargo legislation or to impose penalties in the concrete cases which the report had mentioned; a typical shipping country like Norway denied the responsibility of owners in the
first place by referring to the decisive role being played by the charterers of tankers ('these
countries appear not to have taken note of the possibility that any owner can insert clauses
into charter-parties forbidding the use of their ships in the South African oil trade,' the
SRB commented in a letter sent to Ambassador Clark).

The kind of impact at the diplomatic level which the Bureau was able to achieve via the
United Nations enhanced the wish to continue working together. But things would have to
be done differently next time, Reddy told the Bureau. Some countries, linked by name in
the report to tankers which had gone to South Africa but in many cases had not offloaded
any oil there, had been very embarrassed. A different procedure was agreed upon: preliminary findings for the following reports would be shown to the countries named beforehand
for their commentary and possible corrections that could then be taken into account when
writing the definitive report. In 1982, at the time of the second main report, the Centre
against Apartheid submitted memoranda which had been prepared by the SRB; in later
years, the Bureau itself would directly send its 'Summary Data Sheets' to the UN ambassadors of all relevant countries, whereby the United Nations would receive its own copies
simultaneously, so as to be enabled to undertake any action it thought necessary. The UN
wished to keep itself at some visible distance from any allegations which the SRB might
find it necessary to make regarding the involvement of certain member states; in 1982 it,
for example, no longer included a request to governments to set up their own investigations in the letters by which it submitted the preliminary data.

Could things have taken a different course? Would it have been possible for existing plans
– or at least calls for action – for the setting up of an official monitoring centre associated
with bodies such as the OAU or UNCTAD to have been realised? Or, alternatively, could
the SRB have developed into such a centre, primarily serving, for example, the OAU? As
things turned out, the Bureau continued to operate independently, and its principal international partners remained the ANC and the UN Centre against Apartheid[27] (incidentally,
the ANC also ran into unexpected diplomatic problems with regard to its association with
the Dutch research bureau after the publication of *Oil Tankers to South Africa* – about
which more later).

After the first SRB report appeared, Ambassador Clark sent an open letter to the board
of the SRB saying that the Bureau's work must continue and be extended until there was
'an effective international machinery to monitor the oil embargo and punish the culprits'.
When the OAU came up with the idea of a joint OAU/OAPEC monitoring office, and the
Paris Sanctions Conference subsequently declared in May 1981 that it 'welcomes with
appreciation their [i.e. the oil-producing States] intention to consider establishing a
mechanism, including a monitoring agency, to ensure that their oil embargo is effectively
and scrupulously respected,' the Shipping Research Bureau, which had no wish to detract
from the importance of realising initiatives on the official level, still had the feeling that
the need for some 'monitoring of the monitors' by means of an autonomous institution
such as itself would continue.

After some time, the idea began to be heard less often in international forums. This
may perhaps have been owing to the fact that a general satisfaction was felt with the work

that the Bureau was doing. Insofar as OAPEC is concerned, the idea's fading away could have been due to the embarrassment that rigorous monitoring by the countries themselves would have meant to some of its own members. During a visit of the SRB to the *League of Arab States* in 1985, monitoring still came up as a subject for discussion. The Bureau was sounded out on its possible willingness to extend its monitoring activities into 'other' fields – a proposal which only confused the inexperienced SRB researcher, but which his companion and dyed-in-the-wool predecessor seemed able, in terms no less diplomatic, to effectively brush aside. 'He was referring to Israel,' was what the surprised novice heard, once they were both again walking down the street. At about this time, the OAU had not yet completely given up the idea of setting up its own monitoring office, witness the request of Dr Gomez, its Chief of Sanctions, to come to Amsterdam in order to work as a trainee under the SRB's supervision; two new researchers who had just joined the Bureau in 1985 and had their hands full learning the job themselves were not at all dismayed when the idea was eventually abandoned.

It was only as of 1986–87 that a monitoring centre was established at the official level in the form of an Intergovernmental Group of the United Nations. By then, however, there was no catching up with the Shipping Research Bureau's lead on investigatory experience.

Secrecy Is Essential

When Gwen Lister, then political reporter of the independent Namibian weekly the *Windhoek Observer*, landed at Johannesburg's Jan Smuts airport on 1 May 1983, she was detained by the South African Security Police for several hours. Her luggage was turned inside out and her offence quickly established. As well as a package of other papers she had been given at a UN conference on Namibia in Paris which she had covered for her newspaper, Ms Lister carried with her a 104-page report published in 1982 on *Oil Tankers to South Africa 1980–1981*. The various documents were considered by the authorities to be *prejudicial to the safety of the state*.

'As a matter of fact, none of these publications were banned at the time of my arrival,' Lister says. They were nevertheless not returned. It was only a matter of weeks before the *Government Gazette* on 27 May 1983 published new banning orders including No. P83/5/51, which declared the importing and distributing of the Shipping Research Bureau report

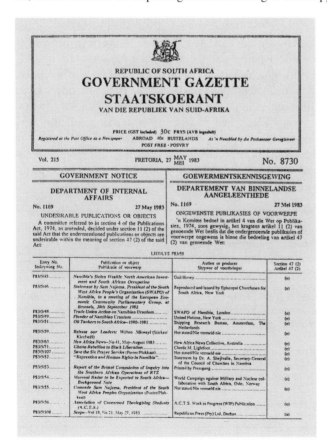

'undesirable within the meaning of section 47 (2) of the Publications Act, 1974'. Lister: 'The confiscated publications were banned some weeks later, with retroactive effect, which then enabled the authorities to charge me under the Internal Security Act, Customs and Excise Act, and Publications Act. This was a crucial and costly court case in Johannesburg, crucial because I could not have started my own newspaper, *The Namibian*, with a conviction under the Internal Security Act, and had to raise funds abroad for my defence.' Gwen Lister was finally acquitted on all charges.

What was considered so detrimental to the safety of the state about a report published by a tiny research institute located almost ten thousand kilometres away? '[The] crux of the matter is not what is said overseas but what we say in South Africa,' parliament was told in 1985 by the Minister of Mineral and Energy Affairs,[1] in defence of the government's muzzling of the press regarding the suppliers of South Africa's oil. Oil merchants were concerned about the coupling of their names with South Africa: 'They made it very clear that, if we did not put an immediate end to the publication of their name in our newspapers, they would discontinue their oil supply to us ... [If] we in South Africa were to confirm for one moment that we were buying oil from country A or undertaking B, we would lose our oil supplies from those sources as surely as we are all sitting in this House.'[2]

Artfully applying the Publications Act was only one of the methods in the arsenal which the state had at its disposal to enforce the intended total clampdown on all oil-related matters. The possibilities provided by the *National Key Points Act* were described earlier in this book. The core item in the legislation was the *Petroleum Products Act* of 1977 (further tightened in 1979 and 1985), which strictly prohibited the disclosure of any information on oil matters. Since the amendment made to the Act in 1979, offenders faced penalties of up to seven years imprisonment and/or fines up to R7000. The Act also applied 'in the territory of South West Africa', and it had extraterritorial jurisdiction: any contravention committed outside the country was deemed to have been committed in South Africa, which prevented foreign correspondents from sending out reports prohibited in South Africa. The press reported that the clauses even applied to suggested petroleum substitutes such as sunflower seed oil.[3]

'The Minister may ... regulate in such manner as he may deem fit, or prohibit, the publication, releasing, announcement, disclosure or conveyance to any person of information or the making of comment regarding (a) *the source, manufacture, transportation, destination, storage, consumption, quantity or stock level of any petroleum product* [i.e. incl. crude oil] *acquired or manufactured or being acquired or manufactured for or in the Republic;* (b) *the taking place and particulars of negotiations in respect of the acquisition of petroleum products for the Republic and the transportation or consumption thereof, or of any other business transaction in connection with any such petroleum product.*

Any person [contravening such prohibition or regulation] *shall be guilty of an offence and liable on conviction to a fine not exceeding seven thousand rand or to imprisonment for a period not exceeding seven years or to both such fine and such imprisonment'.*

From: South African *Petroleum Products Act* 1977 as amended in 1979 and 1985

Minister Steyn smugly told MPs about his meetings with oil suppliers 'in my office up-stairs': '[E]very offer contains the clause: We will give you oil but nobody must know about it.' He once gave two examples: 'The one offer reads as follows:

The conditions made by both Governments that company A...

I am not going to disclose the name of the company:

...must solely operate within this very closed orbit and that no activity in oil trading should be associated with its name.

That is the requirement, otherwise they do not want to sell oil to us ... I come now to the second offer:

At the same time Mr X of company B must enjoy protection in order to prevent any exposure.

That is how simple it is, Sir. These people will supply oil to South Africa but they refuse to have their names made known.'[4]

Firing shots in the dark

A recurring theme in the debates on secrecy was that of the boycotteers and the 'overseas shipwatchers'. As Minister Steyn phrased it in March 1985: 'To tell the truth, I think that the efforts since 1979 to cut off South Africa's oil resources have increased ... [The shipping companies] are being watched 24 hours a day and 365 days a year, and not for nothing. A definite and deliberate attempt is being made to influence shipping companies in this way'.[5] Two years earlier, F.W. de Klerk, who was one of Steyn's predecessors as Energy Minister, had been more specific, saying: 'The struggle against boycotts is by no means over. UN attempts to prevent crude oil deliveries to South Africa continue. Active groups such as Kairos and the Amsterdam Shipping Bureau are attempting to embarrass South Africa. The latter attempting to monitor ships plying around the Cape in order to determine which of them deliver oil here. At the moment they are firing shots in the dark as long as it is only speculations and rumours in the outside world. Any relaxation in respect of secrecy, however, can help to spotlight the target and enable our enemies to identify our friends and partners who deliver to us. Secrecy is essential...'[6]

The media were imbued with the need for secrecy; the argument that South Africa's oil supply had to be ensured at all costs was blindly accepted by large sections of the press as a reason for restraint. Self-censorship was rife, not only on oil-related matters: 'Pretoria's campaign to co-opt the media was sophisticated in that it preserved some of the forms of a free press. Legislation was so broad and ill-defined that editors themselves carried the burden of exercising censorship. The government had only to initiate token criminal cases against newspapers or reporters and maintain a steady rhetorical offensive based on implicit threats. Proprietors of the nation's papers, fearful of further legislation and costly court defenses, pressed editors to conform to wide and safe definitions of the law'.[7] Minister Steyn self-assuredly told parliament that 'The Press discontinued the publication of the names [of oil traders] after we had held consultations with their editors.'[8] The South African journalist Kevin Davie recalls how well self-censorship worked: 'The basic rule for editors was: on oil we do not write. And in the mid-1980s there *were* surely more important matters: the townships were in flames, and the press censorship linked to that...'

A tanker once got water from a South African Prisons Service craft off Cape Town: 'Ironically, the *Blouberg*, which delivered the water, serves Robben Island where incarceration of so-called political prisoners has contributed to the tanker boycott of South African ports and offlimits services. At risk of yet again raising the ire of overseas shipwatchers ... we refrain from naming the tanker for fear of causing problems for her owners,' the *South African Shipping News & Fishing Industry Review* wrote in December 1988. In this specialised shipping magazine one was able to find monthly statistics of port traffic but 'Petroleum products are excluded' – the sword of Damocles hung over the editors. In 1982, a South African newspaper was reprimanded for publishing an aerial photograph of the Richards Bay harbour, the main coal export harbour, which had apparently been declared a 'national key point'.[9] The editor of *The Star* was prosecuted in 1983 for allowing a report to be published in his newspaper concerning fuel supplies to Zimbabwe, allegedly in contravention of the Petroleum Products Act.[10]

Sometimes names appeared in articles on tankers making 'innocent' calls or tankers which had run into problems off South Africa; in many cases the editors dutifully asked for permission.[11] Only once did an innocent-looking press report about a tanker lying idly off Cape Town escape the sharp eyes of the censor and provide the Shipping Research Bureau with a welcome clue. When the cargo of a damaged tanker had to be transferred, her owners were said to have insisted on 'using their own choice of tanker and turned down the Indiana' which was awaiting orders off Cape Town. Here was the proof that the report on the Greek supertanker *Indiana* which said that she was lying at anchor in the Middle East had been false.[12]

Overseas monitors were denied information; on the other side, South Africans were unable to read what was being published overseas by the Bureau and others. It was clear for all to see that press reports were censored. In an article which appeared on 23 January 1981, the *Cape Times* wrote that the Norwegian Energy Minister had called in oil companies for a meeting on shipments to South Africa after an unspecified 'recent incident', details of which could not be disclosed 'because of prohibitions under the Petroleum Products Act' (readers are referred to page 66-67 for the solution to this riddle). When *Southern Africa Report* reviewed the third SRB main report, it added a 'Footnote': 'Details of the report were given in a Press release. South Africa's Petroleum Products Act prevents publication of further information.'[13] The *Rand Daily Mail* preferred a more

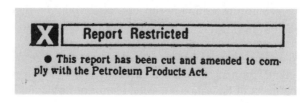

Report Restricted

● This report has been cut and amended to comply with the Petroleum Products Act.

positive formulation, when it quoted a Sapa-Reuter report from Oslo which said that 'Norway has emerged as a centre for exporting oil to South Africa – a trade shrouded in secrecy because of the risk of the country being seen to be propping up apartheid'; readers were told that the Dutch Shipping Research Bureau had accused Norwegian shipping companies of supplying about 35 per cent of South Africa's needs and were given a curious picture of the Bureau's work: 'Anti-apartheid groups monitor the movement of vessels near SA ports, so the vessels often near their destination at night, unlit, with the ship's name painted out.' To all this, the paper added in bold print: 'The Director-General of Mineral and Energy Affairs has cleared this report for publication.'[14]

In parliament government officials remained tight-lipped on oil-related matters if it was deemed expedient. In February 1984 the Minister of Transport invoked the Petroleum Products Act when he refused to answer questions about a new pipeline that was being planned – a refusal later labelled 'ridiculous' by opposition spokesman John Malcomess as 'hundreds and possibly thousands of people must be aware from seeing the work going on that a pipeline is being built.'[15]

In 1982–83 the role of the exuberant Italian *Marino Chiavelli* had been the subject of stormy debates. Was the refusal to cancel his a residence permit by Minister of Internal Affairs F.W. de Klerk based on improper grounds? Had Chiavelli accumulated his fortune as a mastermind behind Saudi oil deliveries to South Africa? Was he given protection because of his generous contributions towards National Party funds? In March 1982 De Klerk told parliament that any comment on Chiavelli's involvement in South Africa's oil supplies would be against the law. When in August 1982 the chairman of Soekor, Dawid de Villiers, said on a radio programme that there was too much secrecy on oil – 'It does create rumours. For instance Chiavelli is continuously mentioned as a person supplying oil to South Africa and he's never supplied oil to South Africa. Not at all, I can assure you' – this earned him the wrath of the then Energy Minister, Pietie du Plessis. The latter expressed the view that 'the laws concerning the acquisition of crude oil should be complied with'; De Villiers, though, claimed the legal right to make comments, as it was sometimes necessary to deny 'untrue reports' when they posed a danger to the interests of South Africa's oil situation.[16] At about the same time, the British *Observer* published a juicy story on the 'billionaire oil baron', which said that 'When opposition MPs asked questions in the South African Parliament earlier this year about Chiavelli's source of funds, they were warned they "had never been closer to treason".'[17]

Inevitably, suspicions arose as to what the opposition had labelled the government's 'obsession with secrecy'. Minister De Klerk repaid in kind on 3 May 1984 when he announced a statement on Mr Chiavelli, 'the person with whom the hon member for Port Elizabeth Central seems to have an obsession'.[18]

'Sheer stupidity'

The honourable member for Port Elizabeth Central (November 1977–September 1989) was John Malcomess, a South African businessman-turned-politician, who started in the United Party and left its successor, the New Republic Party, to become a member of the Progressive Federal Party (PFP), which later joined with others to form the Democratic Party. As the opposition spokesman for Mineral and Energy Affairs, Malcomess had a keen interest in oil matters, but he soon found himself up against a wall: 'They tried to bottle everything up, often not to protect their sources of supply, but to stop the South African public from knowing what *they* were doing. The *Salem* case was a classic example of a government obsessed with secrecy, trying to keep a thing quiet when the whole world knew about what had happened. When I raised it in parliament in 1983, three years after the event, the government was absolutely furious with me: the main reason being that the newspapers were then able to print the story. They threatened to do away with parliamentary privilege. They knew that the whole world knew; there had been court cases in London, and the whole file was available worldwide. I had gotten copies from a solicitor friend in England. But nobody in South Africa was able to print it, until I made the speech in parliament. The story immediately became headline news.' Malcomess has a cartoon at home 'with my neck on the chopping block and Pietie du Plessis who was the responsible minister at the time, with a big axe ready to chop my head off...'

For Malcomess the *Salem* affair was just one example of 'sheer stupidity' with disastrous economic effects: 'A lot of people were given prison sentences in other countries as a result, including a South African schoolfriend of mine, Jim Shorrock, who was put behind bars in America. For several years afterwards I kept asking the question in parliament: "Has anybody in South Africa been charged? Has there been any police investigation?" South Africa lost millions of rands of the taxpayers' money, and yet nobody in South Africa had to pay any sort of penalty.' The purchasing of oil was done by Sasol and the Strategic Fuel Fund Association (SFF). Malcomess is convinced that 'people with more commercial experience could have gotten the oil much cheaper despite sanctions.' The people who bought the *Salem* oil 'were buying stolen oil, so there could not have been valid Bills of Lading or invoices. Now if you buy something, even if you're going to buy it "under the counter", you should make sure that whoever you're buying from is entitled to sell. That wouldn't have been very difficult... This case made headlines but I'm absolutely convinced that over the many decades of apartheid there were many instances of this nature, which were kept quiet by the government and which cost the South African taxpayer lots of money. This is probably one of the reasons why South Africa is as broke as it is today, and why something like 50–60 per cent of the black population is unemployed.'

As a member of the Committee for Public Accounts, the parliamentary watchdog which ensures that State funds are properly spent, Malcomess saw things go 'terribly wrong' when in 1978, the Information affair (the 'Muldergate' scandal) hit the headlines: 'The prevalent type of secrecy in accounts obviously makes it a lot easier if you are crooked to siphon some money off into your own pocket. The more secrecy, the more chance there is of something going wrong. I think we could have built a lot of black houses, for the amount of money we spent over the odds on this sort of thing. But then blacks didn't have the vote, so you didn't need to spend money on them...'

The debate flared up on various occasions. The government, angered by the moves of Malcomess and other MPs, wanted to tighten the laws; various proposals were discussed from March 1984 onwards and eventually, in May–June 1985, the Petroleum Products Act was amended. Around that time, questions were also asked about two court cases which could have provided answers to the opposition's queries on oil deals: Fontana (Taki Xenopoulos) v. Chiavelli, and Sellier c.a. v. Sasol c.a.; the plaintiffs in both cases were claiming that 'respondents fiddled them out of their rightful cut' (*Financial Mail*). However, the two cases were held *in camera*, once again with reference to the secrecy laws relating to oil.[19] Another incident which sparked off a major debate involved a parcel of documents pertaining to South Africa's oil deals which had been passed on to the PFP. 'Oil scandal clouds FW's future', was a caption on the front page of the *Sunday Express* on 29 April 1984: 'The political career of the Transvaal leader of the National Party, Mr F W de Klerk, has been put on the line by the oil scandal which blew up in Parliament this week. The ambitious Mr de Klerk is tipped to become the chairman of the House ... but his chances could be harmed if evidence emerges that oil procurement was mishandled while he was Minister of Mineral and Energy Affairs.' Part of the ensuing story can be gleaned from newspapers and minutes of parliamentary sessions at the time (April–July 1984); here we allow John Malcomess to give his account of the events, ten years after the debate:

'Somebody anonymously sent a lot of information to our party, suggesting that South Africa paid too much for its oil, and that some South Africans were enriching themselves in oil deals. At that stage, I personally was in favour of standing up and speaking about this, because to me, the documentation and the evidence seemed remarkably strong that somebody was creaming off money at the top. However, the leader of my party, Dr Van Zyl Slabbert, rejected the idea of making it public in parliament, saying that it should be handed to the Advocate-General, who had been appointed by the South African government and whose job was to investigate corruption. I didn't believe we would get any joy out of that, and in fact we didn't. Slabbert's reasoning was that South Africa's oil supply should not be endangered even if it meant doing business under the counter. My view was that if in doing this there were people who were costing the South African taxpayer extra money by creaming off something for themselves, they should be found out and dealt with. The documentary evidence seemed to indicate that there were such people among those who were responsible for procuring oil.'

The PFP was repeatedly reproached for not revealing the identity of the source of the 'anonymous' parcel. John Malcomess says: 'We had absolutely no idea who the source was. I do not believe for instance that it was Xenopoulos. I think it was someone within the SFF, a civil servant, who either had a grudge against somebody, or who was a genuinely honest man, unhappy about the fact that these things were happening.'

John Malcomess says he plans to write a book based on his experiences. Soon after interviewing him in Amsterdam in May 1994, researchers of the Shipping Research Bureau travelled to South Africa and met someone who had also been directly involved in this episode. Having read Scholtz's contribution, Malcomess will be able to include the long overdue answer to the question who the source of the documents was in his book.

The whole world knows

On 27 June 1984 Advocate-General Piet van der Walt presented his report to parliament.[20] MPs were given a version which had been censored by a Select Committee, and the press was even more limited in its ability to gain an insight into the contents; it was only able to give an account of the debate, which took no longer than one and a half hours, a substantial part of which was taken up by the usual amount of cursing and 'points of order'. The

The House of Assembly debating the pressing question of South Africa's oil procurement (Hansard 9 July 1984, col. 11003-11008):

Mr H J TEMPEL: [...] This whole scandal-mongering story – it was a story after all, and it has been proved to be such – has exploded very badly in the face of the hon the Leader of the Official Opposition, as well as that of his party by the publication of this report. In view of this report, he and his party owe the country and this House quite a number of answers. We can assure them that we are going to ask them for those answers. They will have to give us those answers. [Interjections.]

Mr H E J VAN RENSBURG: Not to a Government with such a record of corruption!

Mr F J LE ROUX: Mr Speaker, I should like to associate myself with the thanks and appreciation conveyed by the hon member for Ermelo to...

Mr A VAN BREDA: Mr Speaker, on a point of order: May the hon member for Bryanston say "Not a Government with such a record of corruption"? Can he refer to the Government in that way, Mr Speaker?

The DEPUTY SPEAKER: Order! Did the hon member for Bryanston utter those words?

Mr H E J VAN RENSBURG: Yes, Mr Speaker.

The DEPUTY SPEAKER: What did the hon member mean?

Mr H E J VAN RENSBURG: Mr Speaker, I meant that the record of this Government included a great many examples of corruption. That is on record, and they know it, too. [Interjections.]

[...]

The DEPUTY SPEAKER: It has been ruled in the past that hon members may refer to "the Government" in terms which, if applied to an hon member, would be unparliamentary. I do not necessarily agree with that. Personally, I think it was a mistake, but this has been ruled in the past.

The LEADER OF THE HOUSE: Mr Speaker, may I then say that the official Opposition are sly?

The DEPUTY SPEAKER: Yes.

The LEADER OF THE HOUSE: They are sly. [Interjections.]

The MINISTER OF COMMUNITY DEVELOPMENT: Mr Speaker, does your ruling mean that I can say that the Opposition are a lot of crooks? [Interjections.]

The DEPUTY SPEAKER: Order! [...]

[...]

Mr H E J VAN RENSBURG: Mr Speaker, I said that the record of this Government include a great many examples...

HON MEMBERS: No!

Mr H E J VAN RENSBURG: ...of corruption. [Interjections.] The record of the Government is a record of corruption. [Interjections.]

The DEPUTY SPEAKER: Order! Hon members must afford the hon member for Bryanston an opportunity to provide an explanation.

Mr H E J VAN RENSBURG: To support my standpoint I could mention that the Government has dismissed several Cabinet Ministers due to corrupt dealings in the past. In the course of the Information Scandal the Minister of Internal Affairs was dismissed for corruption.

[...]

The DEPUTY SPEAKER: Order! The hon member must withdraw those words.

Mr H E J VAN RENSBURG: Mr Speaker, may I address you in this regard?

The DEPUTY SPEAKER: The hon member may address me, but my ruling is that the hon member must withdraw those words. [Interjections.]

Mr G S BARTLETT: You should take your medicine like a man.

Mr H E J VAN RENSBURG: Shut up, you idiot.

[...]

The DEPUTY SPEAKER: Order! I stand by my ruling that the hon member for Bryanston must withdraw his allegation.

Mr H E J VAN RENSBURG: Sir, I am not prepared to withdraw it.

The DEPUTY SPEAKER: Order! Because the hon member disregarded the authority of the Chair, I must order him to withdraw from the House for the remainder of the day's sitting.
    (Whereupon the hon member withdrew from the Chamber.)

censored report was leaked. Frene Ginwala of the ANC in London had it ('Everybody had it,' she says), and the Shipping Research Bureau soon had it (although none of those involved can remember who had smuggled it into its hands or when). However much seemed to have been covered up by the Advocate-General, it was absolutely fascinating for the embargo watchers to obtain so much detailed information from an unimpeachable source, confirming suspicions concerning certain oil traders, and providing proof (despite the censor's efforts) of the involvement of certain oil-producing countries. But the documents which had led to the investigation remained inaccessible. Ginwala: 'There was the odd document floating around, but at that time I was trying desperately to get the documents which Van Zyl Slabbert had handed over; I didn't succeed.' Soon afterwards Martin Bailey did meet with someone who showed him certain documents. The Shipping Research Bureau was approached by Bailey with questions relating to shipments which apparently concerned Chiavelli, and, in retrospect, could only have been based on a brief glance at the document, the first page of which has been reproduced on page 82.
    On the front page of *The Observer* of 5 August 1984, Martin Bailey and David Leigh set out to 'reveal a censored South African report' in a large 'World exclusive' article. The *Rand Daily Mail* Ombudsman, commenting on the refusal of the Department of Mineral

SUMMARY OF DATA IN POSSESSION ... OF THE DEPARTMENT OF MINERAL AND ENERGY AFFAIRS RELATING TO CRUDE OIL, EMANATING FROM SAUDI ARABIA, WHICH, BY REASON OF INFORMATION APPEARING ON RELEVANT DOCUMENTS, OR BY REASON OF ALTERATIONS IN OR DELETIONS FROM DOCUMENTS (OR BY REASON OF OFFICIAL BILLS OF LADING NOT BEING AVAILABLE), COULD POSSIBLY REFER TO CRUDE OIL SHIPPED BY CENTRAL PETROLEUM & MINERAL ORGANIZATION, THAIRAN (PETERMIN) OR CRUDE OIL SHIPPED INTO SUMMIT INDUSTRIAL CORPORATION (PANAMA) DURING 1979, 1980, 1981 and 1982.

SUPPLIER	SHIP	DATE LOADED	VOLUME IN BARRELS AND TYPE	PRICE PER BARREL IN USD	INVOICE AMOUNT IN USD	SHIPPER	CONSIGNEE	DESTINATION
Liquin (X1)	Violande	5. 5.1979 5. 5.1979	1 102 194 AL 500 000 AH	33.00 32.50	36 372 402.00 16 250 000.00	Deleted	To order To order	Freeport, Bahamas Freeport, Bahamas
Liquin (X2)	Mobil Hawk	12. 5.1979 12. 5.1979	596 326 AL 602 791 AM 604 772 AH	33.00 33.50 32.50	19 612 758.00 19 892 101.00 19 655 090.00	Deleted Deleted Deleted	Deleted Deleted Deleted	Singapore Singapore Singapore
Liquin (X3)	Velma	22. 5.1979	498 419 AL	100 000.00x33	3 300 000.00	Deleted	Deleted	Algerian Smtn
Liquin (X4)	Sylvania	13. 6.1979 13. 6.1979 13. 6.1979	678 558 AL) 245 000 AL) 495 711 AM	33.00	30 477 414.00 16 391 463.00	Deleted Deleted Deleted	Deleted Deleted Deleted	Caracao Netherlands Antilles Remato
Liquin (X5)	Energy Determination	24. 6.1979	287 750 AM) 326 039 AL) 198 624 AM	33.85 21.372 & 33.972 33.85	9 495 750.00 14 199 733.31 6 554 592.00	Deleted	Deleted	Curacao
Liquin (X6)	Ryuko Maru	25. 6.1979 25. 6.1979 25. 6.1979 25. 6.1979	189 291 AM) 444 841 AM) 118 624 AM) 396 782 AL)	767 780.33x32.85 319 850.67x34.00 61 133x33.996	25 221 583.84 10 874 922.78 2 077 666.14	Deleted Deleted Deleted Deleted	Deleted Deleted Deleted Deleted	Curacao Curacao Curacao Curacao
Mimil (X7)	Nicos I. Vardinoyannis	21. 4.1979	404 796 AL	22.75	9 209 109.00	Deleted	Deleted	Freeport, Bahamas
Mimil (X8)	Manarix	1. 5.1979	1 489 337 AL	23.20 17.3404	27 609 693.60 3 189 337.46	Deleted	Deleted	Singapore
Mimil (X9)	Manarix	24. 3.1979	1 113 835 AM 1 145 002 ALB	368 677.22x21.85 342 292.23x23.85 763 509x23.85 744 358x21.85	8 035 597.23 9 117 669.68 18 209 704.01 16 264 239.34	Deleted Deleted	Deleted Deleted	Singapore Deleted
Mimil (X10)	South Sun	27. 2.1979	1 496 737 AL	808 702.10x23.991 298 054.9 x23.991 300 000 x13.999	19 401 372.08 7 150 635.10 4 199 880.00	Deleted	Deleted	Singapore
Liquin (X11)	Schelderix	30. 7.1979	446 576 AL 593 931 AL	1029 303x33 595 931x33	33 066 999.00 19 645 723.00	Deleted Deleted	Deleted Deleted	Singapore Singapore
Lucina (X12)	Irenes Serenade	9. 2.1979	90 000 AL	24.70	2 223 000	Transworld	Lucina	
Liquin (X13)	Prijan I	8. 9.1979	642 440 AL	21.8376	14 029 367.74	Deleted	Deleted	Deleted
Liquin (X14)	Laura Prima	13.10.1979	281 461 372 437	21.8368 24.036R	6 145 644.64 8 951 445.81	No Bill of Lading found		Singapore
Liquin (X15)	Manarix	3.11.1979	1 577 697	40.50	63 896 728.50	No Bill of Lading found		
Transworld (X16)	Humboldt	26.11.1979	544 445	34.00	18 511 130	No Bill of Lading found		

and Energy Affairs to allow newspapers to reproduce the British report, concluded that 'if the information was harmful, the harm was done by its publication in the Observer, with its world-wide circulation. To shut the stable-door now is to treat South African citizens like children and to give rumours a chance to grow.'[21]

Oil: What THEY know about what WE may not know – SA supply 'secrets' are common knowledge overseas: '... It is one of the worst-kept secrets of the decade as published lists of companies and tankers breaking United Nations sanctions against selling oil to South Africa are widely available overseas.' This outcry in the *Sunday Express* of 18 March 1984 was echoed by several other newspapers at the time. The *Rand Daily Mail* wrote on 20 March 1984 that 'it is open to argument as to how much is actually hidden from the world's gaze: details about purchases and shipments are regularly published abroad; indeed some individuals and organisations devote a great deal of time to ferreting out such information and making it public.' Three months later, *The Star* of 16 July 1984 wrote that 'our secrets don't seem to be very secret in the international oil-dealing community. As with so many areas of the Government's "security" obsessions, such as defence, the people left most in the dark are those with the most valid right to know – the South African taxpayers.'

The argument was always the same: the whole world knows what is going on – *The Observer* writes about it, the Shipping Research Bureau publishes reports on it... In 1984 the SRB decided to add the word *secret* to the title of its main report on oil deliveries to South Africa; it had long become impossible to compile tanker lists on the basis of reported tanker calls. It took some time for the researchers to understand that if a South African newspaper added inverted commas to the word 'secret' when referring to an SRB report, there was no sarcasm implied; the inverted commas reflected the light-years between the SRB researchers who were hampered by a lack of information, and South Africans who had no information *at all*.

But there was a sequel to the argument. 'Oil men are linked with Swiss banks' – in its headline of 30 April 1984 *The Star Weekly* certainly did not refer to the Swiss operations of foreign traders such as Rich and Deuss: '...the Leader of the Opposition, Dr F Van Zyl Slabbert, told the Prime Minister and Parliament that Opposition MPs had received anonymous telephone calls claiming that certain civil servants had opened Swiss bank accounts.' In the context of secrecy, rumours and speculations were rife. The *Financial Mail* was rather cautious at first: '[In] the light of the *Salem* case and of talk surrounding the court cases, there is inevitably the suspicion that secrecy is cloaking inefficiency – or worse' (16 March 1984). In a later editorial it was more explicit, saying: 'If, behind this cloak of secrecy, some official, or politician, was enriching himself, the sense of betrayal would be particularly intense – and the political consequences for the Botha administration would be disastrous' (11 May 1984).

The Advocate-General was brief: '14.4 Swiss bank accounts, a fertile source of imaginative and incontestable rumours, have been mentioned. No evidence in this regard was placed before me'. He had slightly more to say on 'The Possibility That Officials of the State or Officials of Sasol/SFF Have Been Improperly Enriched at the Expense of the State in Connection with Crude Oil Purchases': '11.1 No grounds for such allegation have been placed before me and with all the available documents and information I could find no grounds whatever for such allegations. [...] 11.3 The only possibility of such an enrichment would be if the supplier paid the officials amounts as bribes or as remuneration. Having regard to the calibre of the officials of the State and Sasol whom I interviewed, I would regard any suggestion to this effect as a gross insult to their high integrity as persons and as officials. They are people who have with great success and ability performed a most difficult and sensitive task on behalf of the State and in the national interest'. It might not come as a surprise that after this flag-waving, many South Africans felt that a number of questions remained unanswered.

John Malcomess: 'There is no doubt, from my own personal experience, that there were many, many suppliers of oil who wanted to do business with the South African government and were able to supply cheaper oil. On many occasions I, as the spokesman for the official Opposition, was approached by people from outside the country, telling me what they had to offer, including bribes, if I could get their oil accepted.'

In his last year as an MP, Malcomess, in a speech to parliament, said: 'The potential for corruption in this area is absolutely colossal ... I would be highly surprised if [the former Minister of Mineral and Energy Affairs] were not offered some commissions on oil purchases by various persons in the international oil business. I say that, because I was offered these commissions myself ... I would not have accepted, but the temptations for those in positions of power, particularly in view of our secrecy provisions, must have been enormous'.[22]

The 1990s: Testing the law

The parliamentary opposition and certain newspapers remained an ineffectual lot and could no more than rehash the same arguments. In the early 1990s the government's policy showed signs of changing in that the authorities were less stringent in their application of the clauses under the Petroleum Products Act, except for the strict policy of 'no comment' which they stuck to in parliament and vis-à-vis the press. When Kevin Davie, then editor of *The Executive* magazine, published the first of a series of articles on oil in its August 1991 issue ('Confidential – How South Africa Gets Its Oil'), he says 'this was still testing the law. You never knew how they would react.' Davie wrote that, with hindsight, the system of laws designed to keep South Africa's energy affairs secret appeared to 'have little to do with protecting the oil lifeline and everything with hiding the massive costs which apartheid has added to our energy bills. Why else keep from South Africans what is public knowledge overseas?'

The *Weekly Mail* had preceded Davie in November 1990, when it reviewed the SRB report which had appeared in September of that year. Headlines on the front page echoed those of six years earlier: *What they don't tell us about oil (but the whole world knows)*. This time the paper went further than the press had in 1984:

> We are not supposed to tell you, but Swiss-based commodity trading company Marc Rich is the main supplier of petroleum products to South Africa.
>
> We can't say South Africa gets a large proportion of its oil from the United Arab Emirates, as well as, among others, Egypt, Saudi Arabia, Oman, Iran, and Qatar.
>
> We cannot reveal that Norwegian shipping companies, banned from delivering oil to South Africa, have taken advantage of a loophole in Norwegian law to deliver refined petroleum products to South Africa.

We are not allowed to tell you these things because Minister of Mineral and Energy Affairs Dawie de Villiers believes it may still be used by the country's "enemies" – the sanctions lobby.

However, the sanctions lobby knows all this already. The Dutch pressure group which monitors the oil-embargo against South Africa, the Shipping Research Bureau, has published it in a 100-page report on oil supplies to South Africa, distributed world-wide.[23]

In January 1992 the Shipping Research Bureau was in the process of producing an up-dated report which spanned January 1989–July 1991. The purpose of keeping up the work was no longer to campaign for additional embargo measures, but to support the demand that the oil embargo be maintained in order to keep the pressure on the negotiations. The previous two reports had been released in Greece (1988) and Norway (1990) as part of a campaign to influence legislation in these countries. The Bureau was faced with the question of what added value could be given to the presentation of a report during the last stages of the embargo. Supporting the above-mentioned attempts by the South African press to rid itself of the yoke of censorship seemed a worthy cause. Moreover, the re-

On 19 March 1993, at a time when the government was gradually lifting the clampdown on energy matters, with the exception of all data on the supply of oil to the country, *The Natal Mercury* was the first newspaper to publish this picture of a tanker discharging oil off Reunion Rocks, Durban. The Single Buoy Mooring to which the vessel's bow was attached (to the right of the photograph) is located approx. 2.5 kms offshore; the first SBM was put into use in 1970 by a consortium of Sapref (Shell/BP), Mobil and Sasol. The names on the ship's bow and stern were removed to avoid detection by those who were able to watch the offloading operation from the shore. The SRB was none-theless able to identify the tanker as the *Assos Bay*, which made a secret call at Durban (13–16 March) to unload crude oil from Egypt. Under her former name *British Trident*, the tanker picked up the crew of the sinking *Salem* in 1980.

searchers were tempted by the thought of striking the final blow in the lion's den. The Bureau set its sights on the *Weekly Mail* ('What they don't tell us...') for the scoop. The newspaper indicated that it fell in with the idea. January 24, the day of the opening session of the South African parliament, was regarded an opportune moment for maximum publicity. The SRB staff spent hours faxing the text and tables to Johannesburg, while an international press release was drafted in which the emphasis fell on the fact that for the first time since the introduction of the oil embargo, the findings were released in the press within the country itself, at a time when newspapers in South Africa were still 'liable to prosecution' for publishing such reports.

Instead of it being an opportune moment, the opening of the parliamentary session monopolised the attention of the local press; the research findings of the SRB were tucked away in a piece of 300 words on page two of the *Weekly Mail*...

South Africa's Lifeline

In the concluding section of his confidential report of 27 June 1984, the South African Advocate-General wrote that he was of the opinion 'that the publication of the full contents of this report will not be in the interest of the security of the State'; only two paragraphs were made public. When, nevertheless, a copy was leaked and ended up abroad, it became clear that publication would not be in the interest of certain oil-exporting countries either.

The leaked copy had been censored, though. The parliamentary Select Committee which saw the full report before it was tabled in parliament decided that, amongst others, all references to countries of origin of South Africa's oil had to be removed. Names were erased and replaced by various codes. Readers were left with passages which for instance read that 'negotiations on TYPE 1 crude had been held directly with the Y people in   Z country', and 'The Z people have again emphasized that these transactions must be kept absolutely secret'.

As soon as they laid their hands on a copy of the report, the researchers of the Shipping Research Bureau set out upon a painstaking reconstruction of what the censor had attempted to conceal. A major section in the report dealt with the large 'Z contract' between the SFF and John Deuss. On the basis of the number of letters which had been erased, it seemed plausible that the 'Z country' might be *Saudi Arabia* and that the 'Z people' – always squeezed into a small space – were most likely 'Saudis'. The censor had apparently not thought of a more intelligent way of performing his job, but then, in paragraph 6.4.20, he let slip that *'it was a ministerial decision to take only 4 instead of 6 m.p.a. from SA through Deuss initially'*. On another page, in a fairly innocent context, 'SA' replaced

> The memorandum put it clearly that the Z people were aware of the fact that the oil was destined for South Africa.
>
> 6.4.6 On 10 July 1980 Deuss telephoned Mr Wiggett from New York, as a result of which the latter wrote a long office memo. Concerning the
>
> ---
>
> 6.4.1L1 The concluding paragraphs of the memo read *Inter alia* as follows:
>
> "The Z people have again emphasized that these transactions must be kept absolutely secret.
>
> ---
>
> offset the disadvantage of 'having all the eggs in one basket'. We have asked Deuss for an extension up to Thursday and have asked Mr U for prices so that we can weigh up the one against the other. We however feel strongly that the Minister should be consulted in the matter since it was a ministerial decision to take only 4 instead of 6 m.p.a. from SA through Deuss initial-

'Saudi Arabia' (South Africa was abbreviated with 'RSA'), and moreover, elsewhere the Deuss contract was said to involve 4 million tons per year from 'Z country'. On top of all this, considerations in the report about market developments and about changes in the official selling price of 'Z crude' on specified dates made the conclusion inevitable: *Z country was Saudi Arabia.*

For quite some time, it had been clear that large quantities of Saudi Arabian oil were being delivered to South Africa, but only now had proof been obtained from an unsuspected quarter – from South Africa itself – that these deliveries were based on a long-term contract. The SRB now had splendid documentary evidence in its possession, but it was hampered in its ability to publish 'accusations' against individual oil-exporting countries in its own reports. At the time, the Bureau was preparing to launch a Newsletter on the oil embargo, which would serve not only as an outlet for more up-to-date research findings but also as a compilation of various reports on South Africa and oil which had appeared in the media. Thus, if a newspaper had published a report, it meant it was in the public domain anyhow, and the SRB was able to reproduce it without fear of having to bear responsibility for its contents.

The next step was to find a newspaper which had competent investigative journalists on its payroll of whom no one would have second thoughts if they were to decipher and reveal a secret report. In the Netherlands there was such a paper, the weekly *Vrij Nederland*, where journalists were not at all adverse to finding an interesting South African report on their desks – including the key needed to decipher the codes... And thus it happened that the SRB Newsletter in its second issue carried a front page article entitled: *A John Deuss contract: oil from Saudi Arabia?* – quoting the revelations from *Vrij Nederland*. And thus it happened that two Dutch journalists were to go down in history as those who had deciphered this 'piece of shoddy proofreading by an inept South African censor'.[1]

Main suppliers

Until well into the 1980s, Saudi Arabia topped the SRB list of producer countries connected with oil supplies to South Africa. This was not merely due to the Deuss contract; Marc Rich and others also delivered Saudi crude. Between the last quarter of 1979 and mid-1985, *30 per cent* of the total volume identified by the SRB was shipped by tankers that had called at Saudi Arabia before sailing to South Africa. From the second half of 1985 onwards, the *United Arab Emirates* took over the role of the main supplier from Saudi Arabia in the SRB findings. Only 13 of the Saudi Arabian total of 134 deliveries took place during 1986–88 and none after May 1988, while the UAE, which had accounted for only relatively small numbers of deliveries during the previous years, jumped to a share of no less than 54 per cent of the total volume in 1986 (27 out of the 61 deliveries identified in that year). Yet, so large was Saudi Arabia's lead in the overall list that it had to yield pride of place to the UAE only in October 1989, when the SRB recorded the 135th shipment from the latter country.

The figures in Table 1 do not cover all identified shipments of oil originating from the countries mentioned. The table lists *sailings from* the various countries. On the one hand, oil which reached South Africa after having been temporarily stored in third countries is only included under the names of the latter. The figure for Saudi Arabia, for instance, would have been considerably higher than 134 if it had been possible to take all instances in which Saudi oil was delivered to South Africa from storage in the Caribbean or Rotterdam into account. Only if it was possible to establish the provenance of an oil cargo on account of the fact that it was transferred directly from one ship to another, has such a shipment been added (as indicated in the table).[2] On the other hand, some ships may have sailed from the countries indicated without having collected oil there. This is especially true for those ships which called at more than one port before sailing to South Africa. Often, the aim of this practice of 'multi-porting' was to load part cargoes of oil in all ports of call; sometimes, however, ships may have collected an oil cargo in one port, and called at another one for different purposes, such as loading bunker fuel for her own propulsion or picking up crew members. In a small number of cases there was the, mainly theoretical, possibility that (part of) the cargo loaded in a certain port was unloaded in the subsequent port of call, before the ship sailed on to deliver oil to South Africa; this was another reason for the SRB to stick to the formulation that ships 'sailed from' a country X, so as not to point its finger at X as the presumed country of origin of the oil sold to South Africa.

865 oil deliveries – 180 million tons of oil

Over the period January 1979–December 1993, the Shipping Research Bureau identified *865* oil deliveries by vessels of 50,000 tons deadweight and over. The total cargo capacity of the 865 tankers was *180 million tons*. During the 15 years in question, South Africa's crude oil import needs (stockpiling included) was estimated by the SRB to amount to 223 million tons. If each of the 865 tankers delivered a full cargo of crude oil to South Africa, the volume delivered covered 81 per cent of the country's crude oil import needs.[3]

Table 2 gives a breakdown of the SRB's findings per year. To the extent that the Bureau can be assumed to have covered a fairly constant percentage of the actual imports (an assumption which is, however, difficult to verify), fluctuations in the figures listed are largely attributable to manipulation of the strategic stockpile of oil.

Changing patterns

The number of countries or areas from whence ships sailed to South Africa decreased considerably over the years.

During 1979–80, more than 29 per cent of the tonnage identified was accounted for by ships sailing to South Africa from *transhipment ports* in the Netherlands and the Netherlands Antilles. Since 1981, the role of these ports diminished rapidly. While according to the Bureau's findings, in 1979 and 1980 no less than 23 and 27 per cent, respectively, of South Africa's estimated crude oil import needs were met from Rotterdam and the Netherlands Antilles, this figure fell to 11 per cent in 1981 and 4 per cent in 1982. Only one shipment was detected in each of the years 1983, 1984 and 1985, and none since mid-1985.

The importance of the *Persian Gulf* as a source of oil for South Africa increased accordingly. This area accounted for 53 per cent of the tonnage identified in 1979,[4] 61 in

Table 1 The regions/countries from whence the 865 tankers sailed to South Africa

country/region	number of cases	dwt tonnage
United Arab Emirates	213[*]	54,026,747
Saudi Arabia	134[*+1,2]	31,581,732[*1,2]
Iran	115[*3]	30,335,970[*3]
Oman	91[*]	22,241,313[*]
Qatar	31[*4]	8,037,016[*4]
Kuwait	6[*+]	1,224,510[*]
Bahrain	5[*+]	468,832[*]
Iraq	2[*]	414,706[*]
unknown countries in the Persian Gulf[5]	125	31,698,629
Persian Gulf	**602**	**149,332,760**
Egypt	37[*2,3]	8,652,941[*2]
South Yemen/Yemen	5[+]	372,355
Saudi Arabia	1[*2]	—
Red Sea	**41**	**9,025,296**
Unknown countries in the Middle East[5]	28	6,776,386
Middle East	**671**	**165,134,442**
Brunei	70	8,644,024
Malaysia	2	199,469
Indonesia	2	130,483
Singapore	2[+1]	86,408
Australia	1[+]	80,945
unknown countries in the Far East	1	249,223
Far East and Australia	**77**	**9,390,552**
Unknown Middle East or Far East	**4**	**899,837**
Netherlands	43[*+6,7]	7,130,320[*6,7]
United Kingdom	11[*7,8,9]	1,327,524[*7,9]
Norway	4[8,9]	645,348[8,9]
Spain	4[*9]	441,543[*]
Finland	2[+]	173,434
Sweden	1[*+]	78,488[*]
Portugal	1[*+]	77,673[*]
Algeria	5[9,10]	725,185[9,10]
Greece	4[+]	659,243[+]
France	4[+11,12]	550,160[12]
Soviet Union	3[*+11]	252,784[*11]

country/region	number of cases	dwt tonnage
Italy	3 *+	238,172 *
Malta	3 *+	218,491 *
Libya	1	136,100
Romania	1 +	78,571
Tunisia	2 +10	78,075
Europe, Mediterranean and Black Sea	**76**	**11,498,846**
Netherlands Antilles	25 +13	6,142,668 13
Ecuador	2	240,625
Canada	2 +	119,300
USA	1	50,967
Caribbean, South & North America	**30**	**6,553,560**
West Africa: Gabon	**2**	**342,204**
Unknown countries or transhipment	**5**	**1,220,996**
TOTAL	**865**	**195,040,437**

* Including multi-porting.
+ Including refined petroleum products.

This table summarises the 'final' table of SRB findings on pp. 206-21. Included in the figures for each country are known cases of ship-to-ship ('board/board') transfer of oil originating from the country in question; these cases are indicated in footnotes. Not included are known cases of transhipment via temporary onshore storage (see, e.g., notes 6 and 13); cf. the remark in note 2, page 353.

1   Including ship-to-ship transfer of Saudi crude in Singapore (1 case); not included in the total figure for the Far East.
2   Including one tanker which had loaded crude oil in Egypt and a Saudi Arabian Red Sea port; subsumed under the figure for Saudi Arabia under the heading 'Persian Gulf'.
3   Including ship-to-ship transfer of Iranian crude in the Gulf of Suez (1 case).
4   Including ship-to-ship transfer of crude from Qatar off South Africa (1 case).
5   Persian Gulf/Middle East, or (most) probably Persian Gulf/Middle East; country or countries of loading unknown. For some of the vessels in the large table, the Persian Gulf or the Middle East are indicated as the most likely regions from which the vessels sailed. In these cases, clear information on the loading region is lacking. However, in a typical case, a vessel would deliver oil on South Africa's east coast, depart northwards in ballast, and return from the north one month later with another cargo. In such a case, the second cargo was apparently collected in an oil-exporting region located at some two weeks sailing to the north of South Africa, or, most likely, in the Middle East.
6   *1979–85*: 28 vessels delivering crude oil or mixed crude oil (originating, e.g., from the Persian Gulf, the UK, Norway, the Soviet Union and Libya, but probably not from the Dutch part of the North Sea) from bonded storage in Rotterdam (see also note 7). *1989 and onwards*: 15 vessels delivering refined petroleum products, mostly from Amsterdam.
7   Including ship-to-ship transfer (1 part cargo) of British gasoil in Rotterdam.
8   Including Norwegian North Sea oil loaded from a terminal in the UK (3 cases).
9   Including ship-to-ship transfer of crude from the UK, Norway and Algeria in Bilbao (1 case).
10 Including Algerian crude oil loaded from a terminal in Tunisia (1 case).
11 Including ship-to-ship transfer of fuel oil from the Soviet Union in Port de Bouc (1 case).
12 Mediterranean and N.W. French ports.
13 *1979–84*: 24 vessels delivering oil transhipped in the Netherlands Antilles (one of these vessels sailed to South Africa via St. Lucia). *1992*: 1 vessel delivering refined petroleum products.

Various types of crude oil were blended and in other cases crude was 'spiked' with refined products. This, together with the fact that the oil was channelled through ports such as Rotterdam and ship-to-ship transfer on the high seas, made it difficult to trace the countries of origin. Two photographs printed here were taken by a crew member in May 1980. The Danish tanker *Karoline Mærsk* had loaded a part cargo in Saudi Arabia, and next anchored off Bahrain. The first photograph shows the *Havdrott*, riding high after the transfer of her cargo of Saudi and UAE oil to the *Karoline Mærsk*. In the second photograph, the *Havdrott* leaves the scene while the Danish vessel sets course for South Africa. The photographs offer a unique view of the devious ways by which oil was channelled to South Africa, and were therefore often used in press reports during the embargo years. An example of a more complex mixing operation off Bahrain, involving the *Karen Mærsk* (South Africa September 1980), the *Fleurtje*, the *Havdrott* and an unidentified Chinese tanker, was discussed on page 14 of the SRB's 1985 survey on A.P. Møller; three photographs of that operation were printed in *Land og Folk* (Denmark) on 11 March 1981.

Table 2 SRB findings on oil shipments to South Africa by vessels of 50,000 dwt and more

	number of deliveries	*total deadweight*
1979	53	11,590,321
1980	79	17,872,255
1981	78	15,584,308
1982	72	14,684,379
1983	67	14,023,211
1984	52	11,401,439
1985	58	12,595,112
1986	61	13,452,532
1987	52	13,489,996
1988	53	13,840,158
1989	59	13,335,887
1990	44	9,997,420
1991	43	10,392,964
1992	49	10,691,080
1993	45	12,089,375
Total	**865**	**195,040,437**

1980, 70 in 1981, while the 80 per cent mark was passed in 1982. At the end of 1986, supplies from the Far Eastern sultanate of *Brunei*, which accounted for almost 8 per cent of the tonnage identified in the period 1979–86,[5] dried up. Already in 1986, shipments from the Middle East accounted for *more than 90 per cent* of the total tonnage, a percentage which rose to over 98 in 1987. As noted earlier, Saudi Arabia was prominent in the first half of the 1980s, while the UAE came to the fore as the principal source of oil from 1985–86 onwards. *Iran* ranks third in the SRB's findings. It joined the embargo in early 1979; yet, four shipments are listed which date back to that same year, and many more in the subsequent years. In another chapter, we will see that the role of Iran is probably underrated in the list of the SRB's findings. *Oman*, ranked fourth, was important until the mid-1980s.

There were only two significant additions to the list of supplier countries after the mid-1980s. One was *Egypt*, which emerged as a regular source of crude oil from January 1988 onwards; until the lifting of the embargo, it supplied South Africa with almost 10 per cent of its annual import needs. The other was *the Netherlands*, which was prominent among a number of mainly West-European countries as a source of refined oil products as of mid-1989. Between mid-1989 and late 1992, fifteen larger vessels of 60–120,000 tons dwt and at least five smaller ones of 35–50,000 dwt transported approx. 1.4 million tons of oil products from the Netherlands.[6]

At the time the first SRB report was being prepared for publication, Bernard Rivers wrote to the board of the Bureau: 'I imagine that certain oil-exporting countries will be quite upset – either because they had no idea that their oil might be getting to South Africa, or because they had known, and are worried about the publicity. You will notice that I have focused quite a bit on Saudi Arabia. I think that's totally justified. Other research we have done, and some rumours I have heard, make me feel that if anything, Saudi Arabia is *more* involved than this report suggests.'

Oil-exporting countries were indeed upset when their names appeared in a report of the Shipping Research Bureau. However, the United Nations and the ANC, not the Shipping Research Bureau, were the first to come under fire.

The ANC, the Oil Embargo and the SRB

From 1959 onwards the African National Congress, headed by Albert Luthuli, called for the isolation of South Africa. Three years later, the UN acted upon that request, and thus on 7 November 1962, on the last day of his trial, Nelson Mandela was able to declare: 'South Africa is out of step with the rest of the civilised world, as is shown by the resolution adopted last night by the General Assembly of the United Nations Organisation which decided to impose diplomatic and economic sanctions.'[1]

After the Sharpeville massacre of 21 March 1960, Mandela's companion Oliver Tambo had left the country in order to head the planned external mission of the ANC. Amongst those who joined him was Frene Ginwala. The promotion of international sanctions became an important part of her work. Twenty-six years later, in a lecture at the University of Cambridge, Ginwala explained that sanctions 'were a weapon that would complement our people's efforts, not be *a substitute* for them ... We are engaged in the mobilisation of the entire population and its organisation into mass political action, which is being complemented and reinforced by armed struggle. Within this strategy we still see the need for international sanctions – even more urgently than before.' Because 'the length of the struggle, the economic cost, the destruction of the infrastructure of the country, the agony of our people, the loss of life – all these can be minimised by sanctions.'[2]

The ANC's oil unit

In late 1978, President O.R. Tambo took the initiative to form an 'oil unit' within the ANC in London. Frene Ginwala: 'The aim was to stop oil from going to South Africa, but to first find out what was going on. We had been given papers exposing the role of Mobil in Rhodesia, we had been working with Kairos on Shell. Others had been working on the oil embargo, but what was new was that the ANC was taking a direct and deliberate interest in it.' Ginwala was 'brought into this' on account of her earlier research work on nuclear issues and military collaboration.

Tambo brought a variety of people together; Ginwala became the coordinator. 'You had people who were full-time officials of the ANC, which meant it was your job, and in most cases your life. Then you had members who were students or were employed elsewhere, some of whom were very active. The 'oil unit' included Abdul Bham, who occasionally did a lot of work for the ANC; M.D. Naidoo, who was a full-time ANC official (but only involved in the oil embargo on a part-time basis); Francis Meli, the editor of *Sechaba*; Billy Nannan, a long-time ANC activist and among the UK leadership; and Herbie Pillay, a psychotherapist. They had been selected in their personal capacity, whereas the Chief Representative – the first being Cap Zungu before he left for the United Nations – was an ex officio member. The unit was essentially a discussion and planning group. Thus, it was not standard procedure for the unit to be involved in everything, nor did all the participants have access to all the details and sources of information. Some things were dealt with by Tambo himself, and when Ginwala provided the SRB with information it did not necessarily mean that all the members of the oil unit were informed accordingly.

The unit remained in existence in principle, but after a while it was felt that it was not necessary to meet on a regular basis. Ginwala: 'The UN and other organisations took up the oil embargo. I remained the key figure in the ANC work on the oil embargo, and if I needed to consult with the other members, I convened a meeting. Basically, I worked with the President or with the Chief Representatives. There were also other people working on it in the ANC; I was the liaison for everyone.'

The group was not purely a research unit. It was also supposed to initiate action. One of the first steps undertaken by Ginwala was travelling to Iran, soon after the revolution. 'Alfred Nzo and I went there, primarily to address the question of oil. The American hostages had just been taken. It was a time of great turmoil, and a lot of the people we met were subsequently killed or exiled. We met the then Foreign Minister, who was obviously more worried about the hostages, and the main political advisor to the government, who was later killed. I think that the only one alive today is the son of Ayatollah Khomeini. We were too early in order to develop the ties we had hoped for. But we were assured that they had decided to stop oil to South Africa from that very point onwards.'

In 1980 Frene Ginwala was a key expert in the Amsterdam oil embargo seminar, and the author of the ANC seminar paper, *Fuelling Apartheid*. About six months later, she was a member of a delegation which toured the Scandinavian countries, Denmark, Sweden and Norway. 'Denmark had just stopped or was about to stop its tankers. We were particularly anxious to persuade Norway, to no avail. We spoke to the Foreign Minister, and told him we didn't believe that the promises made by the companies, that no Norwegian oil would go to South Africa, would be sufficient. What we wanted was legislation. He insisted that no oil would reach South Africa. Meanwhile they didn't mind if Norwegian tankers transported non-Norwegian oil. Soon afterwards there was the incident with the *Jane Stove*. In another incident, the ANC was able to confirm the delivery of a consignment of Norwegian Ekofisk oil on the basis of information from inside South Africa. I then gave the date and the name of the ship to the Shipping Research Bureau which delved into the matter. We subsequently used it in our attempts to apply diplomatic pressure on the Norwegian government. Eventually the embargo was announced.'

During this period, the ANC also focussed on the use of *flags of convenience* (Foc) in breaches of the oil and arms embargoes. In September 1980 Ginwala addressed a meeting of the Shipping Committee of UNCTAD which was held in Geneva. 'We used the flag of convenience debate to promote the South African issue. On its own, you would often have less success with the South African issue than if you were able to put it into the slipstream of some other big issue. The debate on flags of convenience was a big issue: many countries were keen to break open the use of the "runaway" registers. We supplied them with the argument that unless they had some control over these ships, the whole sanctions machinery of the UN would break down.' The issue remained on the agenda in later years; in April 1982 the British *Guardian* wrote on 'UNCTAD's new campaign against abuses of the "open registry" – a fight it cannot win': 'Finally, there are those politicos who see the writing on the wall for Sergeant Doe's open registry fleet. The OAU is increasingly irate at the way Liberian ships (actually owned by Western oil companies) are carrying oil to South Africa in defiance of the UN embargo.'[3] Representatives of the World Council of Churches – Barbara Rogers in 1980, Prexy Nesbitt in 1981 – also made statements on the issue at UNCTAD sessions. In 1981, Nesbitt drafted his statement in close consultation with the SRB researcher[4] who was also present and who seized the opportunity – in line with the approach advocated by Ginwala – to try and get a foothold with the seafarers' unions protesting against the open registries.

Naming names versus silent diplomacy

The Shipping Research Bureau was set up in close consultation with the London office of the ANC. Within less than a fortnight of the Amsterdam seminar, Cap Zungu received a letter from the Netherlands in which he was informed of the decision to form the SRB; the organisers requested that a meeting be held in order to discuss the future working relationship. The two parties agreed upon a mutual cooperation whilst at the same time maintaining their autonomy. It was a source of some amusement when *Gulf News* later quoted Tambo as having said that 'the ANC had set up monitoring units in Holland and London to trace the movement of crude oil...'[5] In any event, a high level of cooperation developed on various issues. When the Bureau and its parent committees had any queries, they contacted Frene Ginwala, who had contacts both inside and outside South Africa. She offered suggestions on how the Bureau should present the research findings ('Stress the military use of oil'); advised on how to approach certain governments ('Contact embassies in the Netherlands instead of relying too heavily on UN missions'); and gave her assessment of international developments to which she had access on account of her diplomatic contacts ('Do not focus your activities too much on the proposed international conference of oil-exporting and shipping states, because there is another deadlock'; or, in confidence: 'It has been said that Rich and Deuss are no longer welcome in Venezuela'). Fortunately for the Bureau, its parent committees – responsible for the 'political line' – gave it more autonomy and the line with London became more direct over the years. (Some of the SRB researchers recall their frustration with the fact that when the Bureau invited Ginwala to the Netherlands for regular consultations, various committees used to overcrowd the agenda with non-oil issues.)

But it was not to be a smooth passage. When the UN Special Committee against Apartheid and the ANC got into trouble because of the SRB's first main report, it was the reaction of the ANC which carried the most weight with the Dutch researchers.

The SRB was an offshoot of the activist community in the Western world, with its traditional focus on the collaboration of Western companies and governments with the apartheid regime. Now facts were emerging about oil supplies originating in oil-producing countries which were regarded as belonging in the ranks of the ANC's allies and who had shown – as opposed to a number of Western powers – their support for the oil embargo. From the founding of the Bureau, the dilemma of 'silent diplomacy' versus publicity and campaigning was the subject of many discussions between the UN Special Committee and the ANC on the one hand, and the Bureau and its parent committees on the other. Should the oil-exporting countries (i.e. those countries which had endorsed the embargo) be treated in the same manner in the reports as those whose oil and shipping companies were delivering embargoed oil to South Africa, or were the latter the real culprits? If the ANC wished to pursue a policy of cautiously reminding its allies that they had a responsibility to enforce the embargo, then it meant that revelations in the media, such as the naming of these countries in reports, would not be greeted with enthusiasm. Behind the closed doors of diplomacy, both the ANC and the UN were faced with the embarrassment of various countries.

To what extent did the research have to be in line with the wishes of the South African liberation movement? To what extent did researchers and activists have to leave the matter in the hands of the UN and the ANC, who both preferred 'silent diplomacy'? Was the Bureau at liberty to publish the names of individual non-Western oil-exporting nations? This issue became the most important dilemma in the years that followed the publication of the first report. It was a clear illustration of the political dimension of this type of research.

The Bureau's second director, Janwillem Rouweler (late 1980–early 1985) recalls one of his first meetings with an ANC delegation which took place a few months after the preliminary findings of the second SRB report had been handed to Oliver Tambo, personally, during a visit to the Netherlands. 'We had made an appointment to meet with an ANC delegation in an hotel in London because of its proximity to the venue for a demonstration. While we were meeting there, a bomb went off at the ANC office... Meanwhile in the hotel, Alfred Nzo fumed that we had brought some of the ANC's allies into discredit by having published their names in the first report. I was very happy that the chairman of our board was present, and, moreover, I was able to play the innocent, well-intentioned newcomer who was going to be the proverbial new broom.' An agreement was reached: in the forthcoming report the research findings would be presented in a manner as to 'avoid the impression' of blaming the oil-producing countries primarily and to 'stress the responsibility of companies,' as the Dutch committees put it in a letter sent to Comrade Jele at the ANC Headquarters in Lusaka. The names of certain countries within certain regions from which tankers sailed to South Africa would no longer be specified.

Today, Frene Ginwala says: 'After the first few years we didn't mind if others revealed details, but initially we were very cautious, mainly because we felt the focus shouldn't shift from where it really belonged. So we asked the SRB not to reveal the names of certain countries, partly to give us time to try and put pressure on them. After some time we did not intervene in that manner any more. One should take the political dilemmas which faced us at the time into account. Many countries were engaged in breaking *all* the sanctions, including those on oil. The main collaborators with the apartheid regime were Britain, the US, France and Germany. The ANC could not afford to view the oil embargo as an isolated issue. If we focussed on one group of countries, then the others would use that group as a scapegoat in order to absolve themselves. The Norwegians repeatedly told us that the oil came from the Middle East and that we had to focus on that angle. The Arab countries were part of the Third World and members of the Non-Aligned Movement, and we regarded them as our allies. In our dealings with them we could not exclusively deal with oil matters but had to include the broad political context. We had to ensure we didn't disrupt our relations with those who supported us, and this affected the embargo.'[6]

Within the ANC an additional factor played a part. Initially, the relations between the

ANC office and both the Shipping Research Bureau and its parent committees 'were not entirely clear,' as Ginwala puts it. 'The oil unit operated directly under Tambo. Inevitably, when you form specialised units such as that, people start worrying about what's taking place without their knowledge. In addition, in the Netherlands you had a Holland Committee on Southern Africa *and* an Anti-Apartheid Movement which both played a role from slightly different political angles. Some within the ANC, who were used to working with the Dutch AAM, were suspicious about the Holland Committee. There were also differences of opinion as to what attitude to adopt towards solidarity movements. My own view was that very often a solidarity movement helped the ANC tremendously by putting pressure on a national government. It was a great advantage not to have the responsibility for the Bureau's information!'

On several occasions members of the ANC oil unit visited the embassies of Middle Eastern countries in order to discuss the matter. On these visits Frene Ginwala was accompanied by the Chief Representative ('That's when we needed the Chief Rep'). In these talks she faced an additional problem: 'The Shipping Research Bureau was based in the Netherlands, which was seen as pro-Israel. The Arab countries easily dismissed the reports as, *ag*, it's Israeli propaganda. There was nothing we could do. If somebody, supposedly your friend, looks you straight in the eyes and tells you that these allegations are just not true, what more can one do? They always promised to investigate it; by then two years had elapsed and other items were high on the agenda. It was a balancing act; the political context restricted what we were able to do. The *talks* would always be very pleasant, but I do not know of any cases where we got the results we had hoped for. We subsequently lost our scruples against the SRB taking steps to put pressure on these governments.'

Cor Groenendijk, chairman of the SRB from its inception to its demise, says that at no stage were there any doubts as to the orientation on the ANC, but he recalls how 'the Bureau had to claim its independence in order to avoid becoming a bureau "of" the ANC, which produced reports "for" the ANC which ran the risk of eventually gathering dust in a drawer if they were not top priority at the time of their completion, thereby being inaccessible to others who might want to *do* something with their contents.'

Agreement was reached at the request of the ANC and the UN Centre against Apartheid regarding the focus (on companies rather than countries) of the second report; furthermore, it was agreed that the report should be prepared for political use rather than for campaining and actions – which to a certain extent paralysed the researchers and the anti-apartheid movements. However, the Bureau made no secret of its opinion. After the publication of the report, the ANC and the UN were told that it was now up to them to use the report in their diplomatic work. In August 1982 a meeting took place between the Dutch and Josiah Jele and Billy Nannan of the ANC, in which the latter mentioned Tambo's 'careful first visits' to oil-producing countries which had a 'good position on oil', but whose oil 'was nevertheless being shipped to South Africa by companies – so concentrate on *them*!' It was pointed out to the ANC delegation, however, that the countries in question could do much more; there were some, such as Kuwait, Libya and Algeria, which had managed to prevent their oil from flowing to South Africa. It was important for countries to monitor and demand adequate discharge documentation. If tankers 'shuttle' to and from South Africa, countries must be aware and should act, the ANC was told. At a meeting which took place a few months later, the SRB and the committees raised the dilemma that the 'enhanced reputation in oil-producing countries' was at the expense of its 'credibility in Western political circles'.

As a matter of fact, after reaching an agreement regarding the diplomatic approach, the Bureau did not refrain from sending the unpublished details on identified deliveries in confidential memoranda to the countries concerned '...so that they may initiate any investigations and actions deemed to be necessary'[7] – in other words, 'We are watching you.' And in all the diplomatic activity at the UN as well as that undertaken by the ANC, it was clear to everyone that the data used were a product of the research undertaken by the Shipping Research Bureau.

For a few years the ANC feared a Bureau which could possibly thwart its diplomatic efforts. During this period the SRB informed the ANC of intended steps in a manner which can broadly be described as 'seeking its approval' as opposed to later when it became a matter of keeping the ANC abreast of developments and seeking its esteemed advice. The change had not yet taken place in 1982–83, when an idea emerged which as a matter of standard practice was put before and discussed with the ANC. The workload had become too much for the only researcher of the SRB, while the parent committees increasingly let their traditional follow-up task of publicity and lobbying on the oil issue slide; the committees therefore considered recruiting a second staff member for the SRB in order to increase the impact of its research findings. But when the time came for the plan to be implemented, the Chief Representative in London, Ruth Mompati, expressed her 'serious concern' in a letter to the SRB: 'It has been brought to our attention that the Bureau appears to have now appointed personnel for the main purpose of campaigning internationally on the oil issue ... It has always been our understanding that the Bureau is a research unit, and that the material it produced was then available as the basis of campaigns by other groups, including our organisation ... It has also been our understanding that there would be consultations between us in matters of such a nature.'[8] But consultations had taken place, at a very early stage; Mompati was given the assurance that the envisaged steps should not be viewed as a shift in policy. The new staff member was appointed and eventually became an important link between the Dutch groups and the ANC on the oil issue.

The conscience of a research organisation

In its main report dated June 1982 on *Oil Tankers to South Africa 1980–1981*, the Shipping Research Bureau did not allow itself to be deterred from providing *some* insight into the oil-exporting and transhipment regions from whence oil went to South Africa. Twenty-eight of the 52 'most likely' shipments during a period of 18 months had originated in the 'Arabian Gulf' region. Nobody objected to the fact that in the case of ten other shipments the report did not mention the 'Far East' but Brunei, a country which had not endorsed the embargo and whose foreign relations were controlled by the United Kingdom.

The decision to not mention *individual* states in the Middle East was a compound one. On the one hand, the decision, insofar as it was based on political and diplomatic considerations, naturally went against the grain of any conscientious researcher. On the other hand, a number of research-related aspects made it easier to reconcile the SRB researcher with the adopted policy. Despite a healthy professional distrust (and quite a bit of evidence...) which led it to assume that things might in fact be a bit different, the Bureau was not very reluctant – for the time being – to defend the position that in the absence of convincing evidence to the contrary, it must be assumed that ships sailing to South Africa in violation of stated policies of the countries of origin of the oil did so against the will of these countries. Of the oil and shipping companies involved it could be stated with a greater amount of certainty that they had knowingly violated embargo policies.

The technical arguments for the policy arose from factors which have previously been mentioned. 'Multi-porting', transhipment practices and the lack of information on ships calling at some of the Middle Eastern oil-loading terminals often made detection of the country or countries where oil cargoes originated from very difficult.[9] All the shipping press said of many ships was that they had been in the 'Persian Gulf'; therefore, even in this book, which is published long after the SRB abandoned its cautious policy as regards the names of individual countries, there are still many cases in which vague indications such as 'Persian Gulf' or 'Middle East' are used. There was even an *advantage* to the veiled style of reporting used between 1981 and 1985: laborious formulations relating to the question whether ships 'sailed from' certain countries or whether the oil 'originated from' these countries were avoided. In 1986, for once, the SRB had detailed information on what a ship had done in particular countries (the *Manhattan Viscount* which 'sailed from' Qatar and Saudi Arabia[10]), only to discover that she had only called at Saudi Arabia in order to load bunker fuel.

Nevertheless, the Bureau felt that it could not permanently be satisfied with the policy. It persisted in presenting the UN and the ANC with nagging questions. From which countries did South Africa's oil come, and why did these countries appear not to bother? Had the moment not arrived to reconsider what information had to remain confidential and what had to be disclosed? For how long should the findings be kept confidential before the confidentiality became counter-productive? With the release of each new publication, the SRB was asked: Why do you only publish a part of your findings? Why do we no longer read reports about retaliatory measures by the governments of the oil-exporting countries? The Bureau could do no more than hint that the lack of determination to make the embargo work was concentrated in only a few oil-exporting countries, while the others appeared to be successful in stopping their oil from going to South Africa – but it was unable to give names. The credibility of the SRB ('our single most important weapon!') was at stake. Jaap Woldendorp, SRB director from 1985–91, says in no uncertain terms: 'It was, and I still think it is, a serious blot on our otherwise unblemished record. I felt we could not go on like this. Certainly not when both the 1984 report of the South African Advocate-General and our past correspondence with governments of oil-exporting countries made it abundantly clear that they were not merely innocent victims of Western companies.' Over the years the SRB had brought a large number of embargo violations to the attention of the oil-exporting countries, making it impossible for the latter to maintain that they were unaware that certain clients were selling their oil to South Africa; conversely, the line of reasoning according to which these countries were being 'cheated by Western companies' was increasingly losing its plausibility.

Pressure came from persistent journalists and from government representatives of shipping nations who reproached the Bureau for publishing 'biased' reports, something which became more and more difficult to dismiss. Increasingly, journalists were able to divulge more details in their newspapers regarding the origin of the oil than one was able to glean from the Bureau's reports. True enough, they were often able to do so on the basis of information which the Bureau had given to them in an attempt to escape the confines of its straitjacket: see the example of the Advocate-General's 'Z people'.[11]

A related problem was the issue of oil from *socialist countries*. The ANC followed the same policy as that towards the countries in the Middle East. Frene Ginwala: 'When I came across cases where the Soviet Union or another socialist country was involved in breaches of embargoes – nuclear, mining technology... – I treated them in the same manner. I would document the cases, and would then present the material to Mr Tambo. I know of a number of occasions in which he or the Chief Representatives in London took it up with these countries. The reaction was similar to that in the Middle East: they always started by saying it didn't happen. You *knew* there was an agreement about the sale of diamonds, you knew there was cooperation in the sale of gold – but "It didn't happen". The ANC didn't make a fuss because our main aim was to not let the main culprits off the hook.'

Information on oil from socialist countries did reach the Shipping Research Bureau: a small number of deliveries of Soviet oil (6 over the period 1979–83) were identified, albeit a few years after they had happened. All the oil had reached South Africa indirectly, via transhipment; therefore, the question whether the information should be published could easily be answered using the same arguments as those which applied to the Middle East. In this case, it was even easier to maintain that the oil-exporting country could not be held responsible for what happened to the cargoes when transhipped; also in known cases of transhipment of Kuwaiti, Saudi, Libyan, Iranian and Iraqi oil via Rotterdam, the Bureau did not add these to the 'score' of the countries of origin. (In some other cases, involving the transhipment of *English* or *Norwegian* North Sea oil in Rotterdam and Bilbao, it didn't, for one moment, occur to the SRB to refrain from bringing the information into the open, which is saying something about the extent to which these Western countries were felt to be responsible for such transports.) An independent reason which influenced the policy in the cases which involved Soviet oil was the legitimate fear that the Bureau's source could easily be traced.

In the words of Ronnie Kasrils, the ANC view at the time was that 'While the West offered only pious statements about apartheid's evils, the Soviet Union gave practical support.'[12] In a sense, this was exactly why anti-apartheid activists were keen on doing something about embargo violations involving Soviet oil. The trickle of Soviet oil paled into insignificance when compared to the large quantities reaching South Africa from the Middle East (which could have served to justify a decision to pay only little attention to it), but it was felt that every drop of oil from an ally of the liberation movement was one too many, and in any event that it would have been improper for the Soviet Union not to take action.[13] Thus, a Shipping Research Bureau delegation went to the Soviet consulate in Amsterdam – the year was 1984 – with information on various cases of transhipment in Rotterdam. The response of the twelve-strong Soviet delegation: 'Without additional proof, we can't be sure it happens'...

When asked by journalists whether there were known cases of Soviet oil reaching South Africa, the SRB researchers were only too happy to offer them the standard reply. Soviet oil is being transhipped in Rotterdam; until 1982–83 oil from Rotterdam was delivered to South Africa, for example, on orders of the oil-trading company Marimpex, which is known to deal in Soviet oil. In short, it would not *surprise* us... (and why not delve into it yourself?). Of course, no one ever delved into it, but depending on the political inclination of the person the Bureau was speaking to, these stories tended to lead a life of their own. In 1987, the American trade union federation AFL-CIO wrote a letter to the Bureau concerning an 'important issue': 'It has been known for some time that the Soviet Union and many of its client states are actively involved in the trade of oil ... with the apartheid regime in South Africa. An article to this effect was published in the "Reformatorisch Dagblad"...'[14] When the SRB found out about the article in this tiny Dutch newspaper (its author had not been very forthcoming regarding his credentials when he called the Bureau), it saw that the paper had carefully phrased its theories in hypothetical terms: 'One cannot dismiss the possibility that the Soviet Union sells part of its oil surplus to South Africa at an exorbitant price.' The paper quoted SRB researcher Woldendorp ('who is very careful in his choice of words') who put forward the Rotterdam/Marimpex hypothesis, adding: 'It is indeed possible that [the SRB] is unaware of possible Russian oil deliveries. However, it is also quite conceivable, though difficult to prove, that the Bureau has access to information but has decided not to release it for political reasons. If such a country were to violate the oil embargo against South Africa, and this were to become known, the consequences could be highly unpalatable.'

It has to be said that no other newspaper has ever come so close to hitting the nail on the head.[15] However, the transhipment of Soviet oil in Rotterdam had ceased several years earlier. Moreover, the Bureau objected to the author's lack of interest in where South Africa really got its oil from, and the fact that he had ascribed the wrong *motive* to the SRB, the predominant motive being the protection of the Bureau's sources. As soon as the first direct delivery of Soviet oil (the *Dagli* shipment of fuel oil in October 1988) was uncovered, the Bureau did all it could to ensure that the matter was given as much publicity as possible, just as in the event of identified shipments from the Soviet Union and Romania which took place at a later stage. And, in fairness to the former Soviet Union, its authorities were very cooperative when an investigation was launched in order to ascertain how the (second) buyer of the *Dagli* cargo had managed to circumvent the embargo.[16]

The most conspicuous war of words in which the SRB got mixed up was one in which the *Israeli mission to the United Nations* played a key role. In August 1984, Associated Press reported on a survey released by the American Israel Public Affairs Committee (AIPAC), 'the leading pro-Israel lobby', which had compared the data in the first and third reports of the Bureau, and cross-referenced the information with *Lloyd's Voyage Record*. AP said that AIPAC had concluded that 'Arab countries evading the embargo have increased their share of the South African market in two years to an "abnormally large" share.' 'What is clear is that the Arab posture at the U.N., where they pose as great friends of black Africa and spread gross exaggerations and distortions about Israel's relations with South Africa, is a sham,' according to AP quoting the AIPAC statement.[17] Saudi Arabia – singled out as the most important supplier – was swift to hit back: its Foreign Ministry declared that the Saudi Government adhered in full to the boycott of South Africa, and 'there was no better proof of the falsehood of the report than the source which the agency [AP] had cited.'[18]

A year later, the eloquent Israeli ambassador to the UN, Benjamin Netanyahu, raised the issue in a speech to the General Assembly, now also referring to the latest SRB publication. 'Curiously – or not so curiously – the Bureau ... systematically conceals the countries of origin of the oil,' but a combination of data from the SRB with that of Lloyd's had made it possible to obtain 'striking' findings, in which the new data showed a continuation of the trend.[19] Curiously, the ambassador's research staff had overlooked the fact that in the latest SRB publication the names of the countries from which tankers had sailed to South Africa had been added.

When in April 1985, during a meeting between the SRB and the director of the UN Centre against Apartheid, Iqbal Akhund, the SRB raised the possibility of publishing an updated list of shipments under UN auspices, a remarkable reversal of expectations took place. Akhund – who promised to enquire to what extent the list could be accorded the same status as that of the existing UN register of sports contacts and blacklist of artists – said that he envisaged one problem: the list might be considered by some as not sufficiently comprehensive if the names of the countries in the Persian Gulf were omitted... Two months later the Bureau tentatively submitted the idea of 'naming names' to Frene Ginwala – only to discover that she didn't consider it an issue any more. During a meeting with the SRB in Amsterdam in September 1985, Johnny Makatini, then ANC Permanent Representative to the UN, was informed of the rather cautious modification of policy that had meanwhile been implemented. Makatini expressed his doubts ('Frene isn't the ANC!'), but the SRB stood its ground in a lengthy letter ('None of the countries mentioned in our two "pilot" surveys have objected to the contents...'), and was pleased to notice that Makatini left it unanswered. Woldendorp: 'After much debate within the board and with various ANC representatives, we started to mention individual oil-exporting countries. Quite inobtrusively in our 1985 surveys on Mærsk and Bergesen; then openly in our main report of 1986. I think this was the right decision, although it should have been taken much earlier than 1985.'

    Whether the shift had taken place too late or not, the Bureau's credibility had not suffered. And *Israel* no longer saw any harm in the SRB lists; it continued its attacks on the Arab policy, but now the arguments were based on 'irrefutable' data of the 'highly reputable, non-political' Shipping Research Bureau, an 'independent agency' of 'impeccable repute', whose information was 'beyond reproach'.[20] The Bureau was not very selective in its choice of friends in the process of furthering the goal of the oil embargo, but it couldn't help feeling that the time had come for it to somewhat distance itself from this unwanted partnership. The SRB Newsletter of January 1987 scrutinised the material which had been disseminated by the Israeli mission and concluded that 'compared with published findings by the SRB the Israeli list shows a large number of misrepresentations and inaccuracies' – the 'Arab' oil trade with South Africa was for instance 'exposed' by adding a considerable number of vessels which had delivered Brunei or other oil to South Africa and had *subsequently* headed for the Persian Gulf. That the Newsletter had an attentive readership was borne out later by the annual war of words in the General Assembly. In 1988 Ms Nabeela Al-Mulla of the Kuwaiti mission said: 'The reference which the Israeli delegation made to the question of an oil embargo lacks both accuracy and sincerity. That delegation alleges that its information on oil shipments to South Africa is based on data provided by the Shipping Research Bureau. The last time the Israeli delegation prepared a report on the subject, the Shipping Research Bureau found fault with it. The Israeli delegation might explain to the Assembly why the Bureau concluded that the report "shows a large number of misrepresentations and inaccuracies". True to its distorted view of the struggle against *apartheid*, the position of the Israeli delegation lacks sincerity. If it is so concerned about the ability of South Africa to obtain oil, it might explain ... why it chose to abstain on draft resolution A/43/L.41.'[21] By then, *Saudi Arabia* was less enthusiastic about the SRB's publications. Spurred by the publicity which followed the report of the Advocate-General (with its 'Z people') and subsequent speculation on a Saudi and South African oil link in the 'Iran-Contra Affair', the SRB published summaries of its research findings dating back to 1979 in its Newsletter. The Saudis responded by saying that these were 'unauthenticated' rumours and allegations – which in turn prompted the SRB to produce even more elaborate overviews for the period 1979–87 with dozens of shipments listed in extenso.[22]

March 1985: Call for an Oil Embargo

In the early 1980s it appeared as if the movement for an oil embargo which had gotten off to an enthusiastic start in 1979–80 was somewhat losing its momentum. The OAPEC resolution of 1981 was a paper tiger in view of the manner in which the monitoring system was enforced in practice. At a UN level, attempts to get the oil-producing and shipping states to reach consensus by means of a 'group of experts' and to organise an international conference in which both groups participated were unsuccessful. After 1983 no separate resolutions on the oil embargo were tabled in the General Assembly. Within the ranks of the anti-apartheid movement, there was a split as to whether the protracted attention given to such major issues was warranted; Shell showed no signs of disinvesting in South Africa, and a watertight oil embargo appeared to be out of the question. At the beginning of 1983, the Shipping Research Bureau was told by one of its parent committees that the oil issue was 'no longer a matter of top priority'.

As always, the Bureau was able to rely on its old advisors, such as Abdul Minty, whose organisation, the 'World Campaign against Military and Nuclear Collaboration with South Africa', monitored the mandatory arms embargo. Minty, the rapporteur at the Amsterdam oil embargo seminar in 1980, now expressed his doubts about the usefulness of publishing yet another report listing embargo violations, if there was to be no effective political follow-up: 'Wouldn't that demotivate people?' Martin Bailey's advice was to continue the efforts concerning the oil issue, but he warned that the umpteenth main report would be less warmly welcomed by the international press; instead, he suggested topical reports and the publication of a regular newsletter which could serve as a source of up-to-date information for journalists and other interested parties.

But the movement did not bleed to death. Amongst others, maritime unions were preparing an international initiative,[23] and the ANC in London continued to develop its own plans. Together with Peter Manning of SWAPO, Frene Ginwala organised consultative conferences for European anti-apartheid movements in March and November 1984. The consultations resulted in a joint *Call for an Oil Embargo* by the ANC and SWAPO, signed in Lusaka on 7 March 1985 by the Presidents, O.R. Tambo and Sam Nujoma. The call was accompanied by an ANC press statement, entitled 'Oil Fuels Apartheid', which included a black list of 'shipping companies and traders known to have been involved in supply and transport of oil to South Africa since 1979' – its author, of course, was Frene Ginwala, who had been closely assisted by the Shipping Research Bureau. A week later, demonstrations were held in various European countries, among them Spain (against the tranship-ment of oil in Bilbao), Switzerland (against the involvement of Swiss banks in the South African oil trade), and the Netherlands (where a symbolic tanker was burned in a demon-stration outside the offices of Transworld Oil, and demonstrations were organised outside the premises of Vitol and Shell).[24] The joint meetings initiated by the ANC served as a contributing factor to the birth of the international campaign against Shell in 1985.

When the fourth main SRB report was released in September 1986, the fears that the press would no longer be interested were conclusively disproved – but by then the situation regarding sanctions against South Africa had altered dramatically.

South Africa back in the headlines

In the midst of all this upheaval great expectations were raised for a speech by the state president on August the fifteenth, which however turned out to be a pathetic anticlimax. In about sixty minutes this gentleman brought the country's economy to its knees, caused the collapse of the currency and destroyed most of what remained of South Africa's credibility in the Western world: an act of political, economic and moral devastation which, if committed by anyone else, might well have resulted in a charge of high treason.
André Brink, *States of Emergency*. London: Faber and Faber, 1988, 160.

P.W. Botha's 'Rubicon' speech of 15 August 1985 did little to stem the tide which had been rising since August 1983, when the United Democratic Front had been founded, and was heading towards a final contest between the liberation movements and the system of apartheid and its proponents. At the beginning of September 1984, triggered by the se-verely boycotted elections for the 'coloured' and Indian houses of the new Tricameral Parliament, the townships flared up in a revolt which was to culminate in the demise of apartheid. Leaders of the UDF were arrested, and on 20 July 1985 the state of emergency was proclaimed in various parts of the country. International banks froze new credit to South Africa in the midst of the political and economic turbulence. In September a group of South African businessmen and newspaper editors visited the exiled ANC leadership in Lusaka. In November COSATU, the new South African trade union federation, was founded; its programme included the call for international sanctions against South Africa. On 12 June 1986, the South African government imposed a second, more stringent and comprehensive state of emergency. South Africa reappeared in the headlines of the inter-national media, which resulted in an unprecedented upswing of the sanctions movement – also of the oil embargo. A spate of actions followed.

In November 1984 the Association of West European Parliamentarians for Action against Apartheid (AWEPAA) was established during a conference in Copenhagen; a plan of action for oil embargo legislation in the European and various national parliaments was adopted as part of its programme. In December 1984, the City of Rotterdam commis-sioned an investigation on the role of its harbour in oil supplies to South Africa. In early 1985, an international campaign against Shell and its involvement in South Africa was launched. The European Community agreed to an (albeit limited) oil embargo on 10 Sep-

London 30 October 1985. Left to right: Ambassador Garba (UN Special Committee against Apartheid), Aracelly Santana (UN Centre against Apartheid), Preben Møller Hansen (Danish Seamen's Union), Neil Kinnock MP (UK), Oliver R. Tambo (ANC)

tember 1985, a few weeks after the 'Rubicon' speech. At the Commonwealth summit, held in Nassau, the Bahamas, in October 1985, member states agreed to a ban on oil sales. In the same month, maritime unions convened a conference on the oil embargo, co-sponsored by the United Nations. The UN also co-organised an oil embargo conference in Oslo and a large sanctions conference in Paris in June 1986. In 1986, the oil embargo reappeared as the subject of a separate UN resolution, which led to the UN General Assembly forming an Intergovernmental Group on the oil embargo (December 1986). Individual countries took unilateral measures with regard to oil sanctions, e.g. Denmark (legal ban on all shipping of and trade in oil, May 1986) and Norway (voluntary registration of oil transports, April 1986; legal ban on oil exports, June 1986; transport ban, July 1987), and the USA banned oil exports in its Comprehensive Anti-Apartheid Act of 1986.

By the second half of the 1980s, Frene Ginwala says she was no longer working full-time on the oil issue: 'I still kept an overall interest in it and still did the work, such as was necessary. But part of the job had been achieved; it was now on the international agenda, and a lot of the work was being done by the solidarity movements. When the Oslo conference took place in June 1986, I was no longer involved in any particular role. Often, as in Oslo, the ANC was invited to attend while the solidarity movements were not. I did the work inside, having been invited to participate on the grounds that I was an "expert"; from time to time I would leave the meeting in order to consult with the SRB and Norwegian anti-apartheid activists, who were outside, presumably because they were not experts...' Ginwala was often to be found in the drafting group for resolutions and conference declarations, together with Nabeela Al-Mulla, who went on to play a significant role in the UN oil embargo monitoring group from 1987 onwards: 'If we were at a large conference and we needed a country to push something through, we could always go to her. She was very articulate and very committed to the oil embargo.' In Oslo and in Paris (both in June 1986) the Shipping Research Bureau also had extensive consultations with Al-Mulla, and even put out a feeler about the possibility of presenting its forthcoming main report in September 1986 in *Kuwait* – in the midst of the Arab world. Not only was it an unprecedented idea, but it was positively welcomed, too. However, in the end it did not materialise. One of the unresolved items which remained on the agenda of the Bureau until the end was its goal to 'win over' the Arab world.

Go Well, Go Shell

During the second half of the 1980s, the ANC supported the international campaign against Shell; Frene Ginwala was the face of the ANC in the campaign.[25] 'We worked actively with the solidarity workers, and we never hid that. But one of the difficulties in an

Frene Ginwala at a Shell campaign press conference in The Hague, 21 March 1986

embargo campaign is always the targetting of *one* company. When Shell complained, "Why us?", they were right. On the other hand, one needed a focus, and Shell was an obvious choice in Holland as well as for the US mine workers... It meant that companies like BP got off relatively easily. From our own point of view, it wasn't a problem. Multi-nationals are vulnerable in that way, and as far as I am concerned they have no right to complain. But for the ANC it was nonetheless important not to emphasise Shell's role to the extent that it would amount to saying that the other companies were OK. So in *our* statements we always said "the international oil companies", and then we used Shell as the example. At the same time, we worked with the French anti-apartheid movement on To-tal.'

Whilst the anti-apartheid activists in many countries were waging their campaign against Shell, the ANC was also dealing with the oil majors on yet another level. 'As early as 1984–85 we started to hold *talks* with a number of companies. The general issue was disinvestment, but we always made it clear that the oil companies were strategic and therefore had a particular role. Part of my own work in London involved talking to the companies; it was done informally, but certainly very secretly. We were meeting "person-ally", somebody would invite me for lunch and they would invite somebody else for lunch – but they knew who I reported to... The American companies openly admitted to meeting with us much earlier than others. With Shell I was meeting at a very senior level in the later years. Essentially they were trying to find out what the bottom line was whereby the ANC would stop the campaign. My answer was: If you stay there, you support apartheid. We had frequent talks with representatives from British Petroleum as well, who took great pains to emphasise their social responsibility programme. We responded by saying, that's fine, but we stressed the fact that their political support was essential; whatever else they did didn't cancel that out.'

With Shell 'it wasn't a lot of meetings,' Ginwala says, but when asked to name her interlocutor(s), she prefers to remain silent: 'You should look at the pretty highest level...'[26]

In 1991 the ANC purchased a Shell building in Johannesburg which it intended to use as its headquarters. Within the ranks of the solidarity movement, there were those who were able to see the funny side of it, there were hilarious commentaries in some of the Western media, but there were also anti-Shell campaigners who felt they had been left in the lurch and were no longer able to convince the public that Shell had to be boycotted in order to support the ANC. Frene Ginwala believes that the decision whether to purchase the build-ing or not was not one on which the ANC's overseas supporters should have been con-sulted (and she emphasises that the deal did not reflect any special relationship between Shell and the ANC). Ginwala adds that things would have worked out differently had the building been located in London instead of Johannesburg: 'After 1990 the awareness of sanctions did not exist within the country that much – we were into a different scenario.' Now, a few years have passed, and the building is still known as 'Shell House', also within the ANC: 'All the taxi drivers still know it as Shell House. Ironically, it is *Shell* which is upset that the place is still being referred to that way...'

In April 1991 Frene Ginwala travelled to the Netherlands in order to take leave of the Working Group Kairos, the Holland Committee on Southern Africa and the Shipping Research Bureau, prior to finally returning to South Africa. Her new job was going to be in Mandela's office ...at 'Shell House'. She told her friends that she had already asked her future colleagues to ensure that the Shell emblem was removed, '...or you will find me outside not inside!' – The emblem was gone by the time she arrived.

Lifting the oil embargo: Mixed signals

In October 1989 Thabo Mbeki, ANC secretary for international affairs, visited the Commonwealth summit in Malaysia. In an interview with the *International Herald Tribune*, he said he had been telling Commonwealth leaders that 'additional trade sanctions are important. The Commonwealth should ask the United Nations Security Council to make its voluntary oil embargo mandatory.'[27] After Nelson Mandela was released a few months later and negotiations got under way, ANC watchers were looking to see whether a shift would take place in the ANC's position on the question of sanctions. At the Shipping Research Bureau there were speculations as to whether it would have to shut its doors by the end of that year. An internal discussion was started in which the staff had to resolve the question of whether to continue their activities or not. Meanwhile, journalists approached the Bureau, asking whether it was 'getting mixed signals from the ANC'. It soon became clear that the dismantling of apartheid would take longer than expected, and the ANC – followed by the UN – formulated a policy of negotiations-cum-pressure in which the gradual lifting of various categories of sanctions became the modus operandi. The oil embargo remained a matter of top priority; if there were mixed signals, they were the result of the fact that it was not always clear who within the ANC put which sanctions into which category and which events would serve to indicate the transition from one phase to the next. However, the official policy was clear: during a conference in December 1990, the ANC resolved that 'the oil embargo should remain'. In October 1991 the policy was made more explicit. As a first step, 'people-to-people' sanctions had to be lifted; sanctions (excluding the military and oil embargo) had to be lifted after the installation of an Interim Government; the military and oil embargo had to be lifted after the installation of a democratic government. In February 1993 the National Executive Committee of the ANC adjusted the plans slighty; the international allies were now requested to adhere strictly to the arms and oil embargoes until democratic elections had taken place. Thabo Mbeki had previously told the Shipping Research Bureau, during a meeting in Geneva in November 1991, that the oil embargo was primarily a 'psychological' element during the transition phase. According to Mbeki, South Africa no longer had oil problems: it was even selling off its strategic reserves (well, partly in order to finance that other expensive apartheid project, Mossgas, he was told); yet he asked the SRB to 'sustain the pressure through your work, but bear in mind that everything is in a state of flux. Don't be surprised if there is a transitional government within six months, which will mean the end of the last "heavy" sanctions...'

It was to take longer than foreseen. Expectations rose during 1993 prior to Nelson Mandela's address to the United Nations in September: was he going to tell the international community when the oil embargo could be lifted? In his contribution to this book, Amer Araim quotes Mandela – who left it up to the United Nations... When the South African Transitional Executive Council came into office in December 1993, and the Norwegians decided to lift the remaining clauses on oil embargo legislation in accordance with the decision taken by the UN, there still appeared to be some confusion left within the ANC. The press quoted ANC spokesman Carl Niehaus' disappointment when he said: 'The ANC would have preferred a lifting of the oil embargo after the first democratic elections scheduled for April 1994.'[28]

'We could have done more'

The Shipping Research Bureau's contacts with the ANC on oil were not limited to those with the 'insiders' of the London unit. Its research findings were studied and used by more people than it was aware of. At the ANC solidarity conference in Johannesburg in February 1993, SRB board member Frank Hendriks glowed with pride on being told by the former Chief Representative in Italy: 'Your reports were our Bible!' Sometimes the Bureau had a specific request for a local ANC office, hoping that it would be able to exert pressure in a given situation. For example, in 1991 letters were sent to the ANC office in Cairo. Zolile Magugu, who had been stationed in Cairo at an earlier stage, tells of his being 'glued' to the SRB reports that came in on Egyptian oil to South Africa: 'We approached the Egyptian Foreign Affairs department, to no avail. Everyone there knew it happened, but you see, business is business. I also took it up with people in the United Arab Emirates – not on an official level – but the only response I got was a smile.' Sometimes the fact that its research findings influenced others went entirely unnoticed by the SRB; a unit of *Umkhonto weSizwe* used the lists of tankers in order to prepare an attack on oil-discharging facilities – a story which reached the Bureau only ten years after the fact.

According to Frene Ginwala, it was not possible to dictate to ANC members that they actively engage in promoting the oil embargo, although anti-apartheid activists, who sometimes wanted the ANC to set the example, seemed to think that London had that power. At the aforementioned meeting of European anti-apartheid movements, convened by the ANC and SWAPO in London in March 1984, the ANC announced that whilst the meeting was in session MK had launched an attack on oil storage tanks in South Africa. Ginwala: 'But that was just a happy accident! We didn't have the authority to tell them: Do it now... The ANC's way of functioning did not allow for a decision to be made which said, now, let us focus on oil, and everybody would follow suit. We were a unit in President Tambo's office, but we didn't have authority over the whole of the ANC, and Tambo himself had too many things to do. So, at a certain stage, when the focus of the oil embargo had shifted to the United Nations, the work was to a large extent left to our people in New York. We asked the Shipping Research Bureau to send its information to our office at the UN, but very little was being done there. The ANC would take action at the level of UN resolutions, but the rest was now being left to the UN itself, rather than that the ANC went to see the various ambassadors and so on.' Jaap Woldendorp chuckles as he recalls how he and his colleague, Huguette Mackay, were warmly welcomed in the ANC office in New York towards the end of 1987; while there, they were shown a large pile of envelopes bearing the SRB logo stashed between two filing cabinets: 'Look, that's you, that's the oil embargo!' Towards the end of the 1980s, the SRB learned little more from the ANC office in New York than the names of subsequent ANC observers which appeared in the records of the UN oil embargo monitoring group, where they fortunately came up with good proposals once in a while; but in the words of Ginwala, 'For them, it was just another routine meeting.'

Frene Ginwala sums up: 'Unfortunately – I want to be honest about this – the ANC didn't do its work. We could have done much more. Partly, we were too busy and partly, a lot of people didn't appreciate the significance of the embargo. We could have applied much more pressure which for various reasons we didn't. That is a major failure with the ANC. I think that had we, in that first year and a half, acted with great political resolve and determination... – we only realised much later how vulnerable South Africa was then. I regret very much that we did not act very early on at the political level. It might well have made a major difference had we done so.'

Ginwala does not need much time to reflect when asked what she liked best about the work on the oil embargo: 'Frankly, the people in the Dutch committees and particularly in the Shipping Research Bureau. It was great to find people who were so enthusiastic and spent so much time and effort. It was very important! And very often I used to feel bad, almost as if I were letting them down because the ANC wasn't able to deliver as much as it should have. Our job should have been to use the information more effectively. I could not instruct other sections of the ANC; the President could have, but you couldn't go to the President for every little thing. I could make certain suggestions to other sections of the ANC, I could state my requests, and that was all. Whereas the London Chief Representatives were very supportive, they also lacked the power to instruct anybody else. This was the way the ANC was structured.'

Monitoring Invisible Trade

'Spy network plan to cut off SA oil' – On 7 October 1984 the South African *Sunday Express* reported that maritime trade unions were planning to launch a network of seafarers and dockworkers on the oil embargo. According to the newspaper, the plan would result in a 'spy network' which was 'to provide the ammunition for unprecedented action to complicate supplies of South Africa's most vital commodity. Anti-apartheid leaders see the mobilisation of the seamen's spy campaign as potentially one of their greatest boycott success stories. They say that for the first time they will have organised individuals acting for them wherever oil is moved or traded.' The newspaper wrote: 'The network is already receiving the first of what will become a regular supply of circulars advising on what clandestine action to take. All information will go to the Shipping Research Bureau, a highly sophisticated wing of the European anti-apartheid movement, based in the Netherlands. It has already produced several detailed and embarrassing reports on South Africa's oil trade...'

The newspaper referred to the *Maritime Unions Against Apartheid* (MUAA) initiative, about which more is told in this book by one of its protagonists, Henrik Berlau, who was General Secretary of the Danish Seamen's Union at the time. It is beyond doubt that the much-publicised trade unions' initiative, the broad support it met with, the boost it gave to the sanctions movement in general, in addition to a number of actions undertaken by the participating unions in order to impede oil shipments to South Africa, succeeded in getting on some people's nerves. But did the intended flow of information on oil shipments from seafarers to the SRB materialise, either through the MUAA or through the simultaneous initiative of the International Transport Workers' Federation (ITF) or that of the UK Merchant Navy and Airline Officers' Association (MNAOA)?

The general public may tend to picture the essential type of research needed for the monitoring of clandestine and criminal activities as one of spies, informers and undercover agents. Admittedly, at the time the unions came up with their plan, the Shipping Research Bureau's researchers were also tempted by the prospects of gaining much more direct access to information from those who were working *where it all happened*: at the loading terminals, and on board the tankers.

> 'Amsterdam, 18 Nov 85 – Dear Jim and Phil, Last week we received the following information: On 5 Nov 85, a tanker of more than 200,000 tons was seen sailing abt 2 miles off Mossel Bay, apparently to be discharged in that region. First letters of call sign EL (Echo Lima). Name of tanker invisible but the following description may help to identify ship: grey hull, white superstructure, blue funnel with black top and white diamond in which black letter. Please send any information you have which could help to identify ship or company.'

'Nov 85 – Confidential note to NUS ... The voyage record for the Marimpex tanker MIRAFIORI shows vessel anchored off Oman since prev Dec 15, 1984, ostensibly awaiting orders. However, on 24 Aug 85 a charter for the MIRAFIORI was reported. – What did vessel do between Dec 15, 1984 and present?'

'London 1 May 1986 – Dear Jaap, Pat Geraghty has checked out the "Botany Trouba-dour" and its recent trips to South Africa. The information is that the ship carried a cargo of tallow in February and soybean oil in April. The company have re-confirmed the agreement not to be involved in the oil trade. The transformer oil on "Botany Triad" came from Sea Coast Petroleum Inc., a subsidiary of Vitol S.A. Inc., of Connecticut, USA.'

'London 3rd Feb '88 – Dear Jaap, Our N.U.Seamen contact has passed on the following information which I promised I would ask you to check out. He is sure the following company runs into South Africa: Beta Maritime, Conduit Street...'

In a regular exchange of tips and requests for information which was set up between the Shipping Research Bureau and the MUAA unions, the Bureau started bombarding Jim Slater and Phil Heaton of the National Union of Seamen, MUAA's 'clearing house', with questions, and passing on vague tips for further checking and possible follow-up action; conversely, the SRB went out of its way to check even the smallest piece of information passed on to it by the unions. The Bureau hoped that the MUAA initiative would become a duplication, on a broader scale, of the excellent cooperation it had experienced a few years before with the Danish Seamen's Union in exposing the role of the Mærsk tankers. Meanwhile, the MNAOA was also asked for help – on a smaller scale – in compiling evidence; its secretary general supported the request, saying: 'Where you get shady operations you get shady operators ... The owner that defies a UN ban today is the owner who reneges on crew wages tomorrow and operates an unsafe ship the day after.'[1]

In the event, the experiment did not prove entirely satisfactory. Henrik Berlau: 'I do understand this is a sore point with the SRB, but we lacked the resources to turn the exchange of information into a core MUAA activity. All publicity on this so-called "High Seas Spying" operation was very much a part of the show – aimed at striking fear into the enemy. The fact of the matter was that our own members were increasingly being pushed out of their jobs.' Danish seafarers, who had supplied so much detailed information on trips to South Africa in the early 1980s, were rapidly losing their jobs to their poorly paid colleagues from Third World countries on ships flying 'flags of convenience'.

It was difficult, anyway, to demand that seamen put their jobs in jeopardy by blowing the whistle. In actual fact, many seafarers were not averse to making voyages to South Africa. A crew member of a Danish tanker once said that 'the crews are really enthusiastic about calling at South Africa. There's plenty of provisioning there.'[2] It was a place where the crew obtained new video films (at a certain stage, lists of films which had been rented and returned to the Norwegian Welfare Service for seafarers were used by the press[3] and the SRB in order to identify visits of Norwegian tankers to South Africa), and where the facilities were in many ways much better than at some of the outposts used for the loading and unloading of oil tankers.

Courage was needed for seafarers to speak out. They would give their tips to the media anonymously, or the newspapers would omit their names 'at their own request and because they are seeking employment in their sector.'[4] Once in 1987, the Shipping Research Bureau was called in by the ITF when the master of a tanker had sought help from his union, which in turn had contacted the ITF; the case had to be handled with the utmost care because the captain feared reprisals. The tip was, however, valuable in that it enabled the Bureau to verify yet other secret shipments to South Africa.

A variety of sources

November 1989 – A Swedish radio-reporter[5] interviews director Belck-Olsen of the Norwegian company Leif Höegh: *In a recent news broadcast on Norwegian television, a map was displayed showing six voyages undertaken by Höegh vessels to South Africa. Have you been able to confirm these voyages?* 'No; and I don't know where they got their information.' *Don't you have any idea where the information comes from?* 'Uh... I suspect it comes from the bureau in Holland which studies these transports to South Africa. But where *it* gets its information, I wouldn't know.'

The first thing people always wanted to know from SRB researchers was: But how on earth do you *know* all this? If 'spies' were not the main source of information for embargo monitors (or satellites – preferably Russian, as some newspapers were fond of speculating[6]), what then?

In fact, *informers and eyewitnesses* were most definitely an important source of information, although various categories of informers each provided the researchers with specific problems. Informers, even those with fair access to information, are not necessarily reliable. The SRB invested much time and effort in order to verify a crew member's testimony on the *Athene*, only to discover that it was impossible for the vessel to have made a delivery to South Africa. On this occasion, the researchers benevolently concluded that the man must have confused names and dates. Some eyewitnesses reported that they had definitely seen 'a large tanker called *X*' off Cape Town. When seen through a porthole, small bulk carriers can easily take on the shape of a VLCC. (It was only in mid-1994 that the SRB met some Dutch members of the guild of experienced 'shipwatchers' who know all about the appearance of ships – funnel markings, colour of hull, etc. – and who could have been consulted in order to verify information provided by eyewitnesses.)

Sometimes sources presented imaginative schemes, such as the doctor in Singapore who offered to question seafarers who came to his surgery for examinations – mostly for venereal diseases – on possible visits to South Africa. The 'deep throats' within companies (one SRB researcher would often not know the other's informers) were more useful; often they were able to provide information on their competitors as well as their own companies. There was the mysterious caller with a distinctive voice who on account of his usual introduction was referred to internally as 'It's me', and who had access to information on tanker charters and oil deals which time and again proved to be highly reliable. But also this information had to be verified. It sometimes happened that tankers mentioned by such informers did *not* visit South African ports; had a vessel been chartered and the order subsequently annulled? It was just as well the SRB didn't worry too much about the possible motives of an informer – was he or she, anonymous or otherwise, genuinely concerned about apartheid in South Africa or was it perhaps a disgruntled businessman wanting to play a dirty trick on a former associate? The danger of disinformation always lurked in the background.

The most enigmatic telex ever to reach the SRB served as a unique means, not used by any other anonymous informer in the history of the Bureau, to give a hint (and a highly reliable one at that, as it appeared later): *'yr tlx re neptune pavo dated* [...] *noted with thanks regards'*. The Bureau had not sent any telexes on the date indicated; certainly not its former director, to whom the 'reply' was addressed, as he had left the Bureau months before. Research later showed that on the date in question the *Neptune Pavo* had been en route to the port from which the enigmatic telex was transmitted, *after a secret call at South Africa*.

Only after many years, was the Bureau able to gain access to radio messages between ships and shore stations in South Africa, a manner of 'spying' which the authorities had anticipated years before and which had resulted in their insistence on radio silence as a standard precaution. The messages were, generally speaking, limited in their content and never contained the 'true' names nor call signs of the tankers. For example, when the *Kiko Maru* transmitted the following message, 'ETA Durban 181000' (Expected Time of Arrival 18 March), via Durban Radio on 16 March 1989, the Bureau was able to reconstruct – much later – that 'Kiko Maru' was the code-name for the tanker *World Hitachi Zosen*, which was to unload approximately 250,100 tons of oil in Durban on 18–20 March.

Initially, transparent code-names were chosen to 'disguise' visiting tankers. 'Scooter' was the Italian tanker *Nai Rocco Piaggio*; a Norwegian tanker, the *Norborn*, was dubbed 'Viking'. Later, only neutral letters and numbers or mock names that bore no relation to the ships' actual names were used.

The pitfalls of documentary evidence

What served as a more important source of information was – tedious if you hate it – *paperwork*. The basis for the research methodology of the SRB, laid down by Bailey and Rivers in their study undertaken in 1977–78 for the United Nations,[7] was the analysis of the published movements of the world's tanker fleet. Initially, this involved the investigation of tankers reporting calls at South Africa, but when it became clear that the South African authorities had prohibited the public disclosure of tanker calls some time during 1979, the Bureau started to concentrate on tankers whose movements aroused suspicion, on account of the fact that they sometimes 'disappeared' under circumstances suggesting that they might have called at South Africa during gaps in their published voyage records. In the early 1980s there were more than 2000 tankers with a deadweight tonnage exceeding 50,000 tons. Those vessels which were, for instance, exclusively deployed in North and South American waters or the North Sea could be ignored. But South Africa was within reach of many other tankers, and the route around the Cape is used by hundreds of vessels whose voyage patterns had to be studied.

Information on shipping movements can be obtained from a number of published sources such as newspapers which list the arrival of vessels in the national ports and the movements of the national merchant fleet; however, the Bureau's most important source was the databases of Lloyd's in London, the insurance company with a number of departments for maritime information. Extracts from Lloyd's databases are published but can also be tailored to the wishes of the client, who may be particularly interested in specific information on certain classes of ships, harbours, companies, etc. The emerging 'on-line' facilities proved not only too costly for the SRB but also of limited use; printed historical data had the advantage of 'fixing' the facts for later analysis, while today's on-line information is forever lost tomorrow (that a ship had ever been reported as heading for destination X could be quite revealing).

A large variety of sources provided information on other subjects such as the maximum size of a vessel allowed into a specific harbour and, especially, on the ships themselves: their technical specifications and data relating to their owners, managers and charterers. However, most sources were not very informative as regards ownership links. Many shipowners hid behind companies in Panama, Liberia and other flag of convenience (Foc) countries. SRB researcher Janwillem Rouweler recalls how, during a visit to an UNCTAD conference in Geneva which was part of a campaign against Foc registries, he discovered a priceless volume of documentation on Foc ships and shipowners which had most probably cost UNCTAD a fortune, quit the conference, and spent hours at a deserted UNCTAD office photocopying documents until well into the night.

Over the years the mountain of documentation at the Shipping Research Bureau grew at a relentless rate. At the same time the shoestring budget prevented the Bureau from acquiring large quantities of expensive oil and shipping publications. Sometimes, this was overcome by regular visits to libraries and on other occasions sympathetic individuals would donate documents to the Bureau. On one hilarious occasion the Bureau hired a car, after a tip, in order to collect an enormous collection of the trade journal *Oil World* – only to find out that this journal dealt with the world of soybean and palm oil.[8]

It was absolutely essential to compile information from a large variety of sources. Verifying that a tanker had called at South Africa was not tantamount to proving that the vessel had also delivered oil. Once a delivery had been identified, two questions remained, namely, where did the oil originate from[9] and who had authorised the transport. But there were also other more fundamental reasons why all the information had to be cross-referenced. One such reason was the aforementioned unreliability of oral evidence. Another was that printed and documentary evidence, as was abundantly shown by this field of investigation, could be as unreliable. This varied from the most blatant falsification of documents – a very popular practice in this secretive branch – to errors in what was assumed to be the highest authority: Lloyd's data on shipping movements. With regard to the latter, human error could be a cause (confusion resulting from ships bearing similar names could lead to a rather fantastic voyage pattern for a certain tanker), but also certain structural factors, the worst of which was that Lloyd's did not have an agent on-the-spot at certain harbours and oil terminals.[10] Finally, Lloyd's was sometimes *deliberately* fed with false information on which it based its 'voyage records'.

The structural problem relating to the fact that not all terminals were covered does affect the scope of the findings of the Shipping Research Bureau. In the table on page 90 the United Arab Emirates heads the list, whereas Iran is ranked third. To a certain extent this tells us more about the quality of the information passed on to Lloyd's from the two

---

The forging machinery

In October 1983, the British captain of the tanker *Ardmore* (chartered by oil trader Marcotrade, part of the Gokal brothers' Gulf International group, to deliver South African oil products to Tanzania) was offered a bribe in Cape Town to falsify his log book – but rejected it. Later, after unloading had begun in Dar-es-Salaam, the captain discovered that documents bearing his forged signature had been produced to suggest that the cargo had originated in Singapore (*The Observer*, 20 November 1983).

A rather inconspicuous but, on closer inspection, fascinating document was once passed on to the Shipping Research Bureau. It consisted of a few sheets of paper, bearing a variety of stamps, some in blue, others in black ink. The stamps were those of port authorities, customs, agents, etc. in various ports of the world, such as Rotterdam, Abidjan and Marseilles. The only peculiarity was that stamps from various countries are never found on the same sheet of paper. But these sheets came from within South Africa. They supported what the Bureau had been told earlier by confidential informers: that old documents bearing stamps were taken from ships during their calls at South Africa and copied; subsequently, rubber stamps were made which were then used to produce forged documents. South Africa was said to provide its suppliers with complete sets of forged documentation including, if necessary, receipts for towage in ports where the tanker had not been. (Counterfeit stamps from these sheets are reproduced on the cover of this book.)

---

countries than about the actual share of each country in South Africa's oil supply. The information on other oil-producing countries might not be impeccable either, and the same reservation can therefore be made regarding *all* SRB data; however, in the case of Iran, the SRB is thoroughly convinced that its findings considerably underestimate the role Iran played as a country of origin for oil to South Africa since 1979.[11]

An innovation in the field of deception which baffled SRB researchers for some time was one whereby certain shipowners began to furnish Lloyd's with false information on their ships' calls at *Ain Sukhna*, a terminal – not covered by Lloyd's – in the Red Sea, located at approximately the same distance from the Persian Gulf as South Africa. Precise dates of purported calls at the terminal were reported to Lloyd's, which made the movement records published by Lloyd's look more convincing than those undated cases in which Lloyd's had apparently inferred that a call must have been made. It was only when the riddle of the *Fortuneship L.* (see the 'Celina' story on pp. 131-2) was solved – she completed the discharge of her cargo in Durban on the day of her purported arrival at Ain Sukhna – that the extent of the deception became clear.

Letting companies and governments talk

The Bureau developed a sixth sense for identifying 'Iranian cases' even when Lloyd's offered no clues; in such instances it resorted to bluffing. The method was brought to bear when dealing with the third source of information besides paperwork and informers, namely, *correspondence with companies and governments*. Reactions of companies and governments to the preliminary findings submitted to them by the SRB as a matter of standard procedure could serve to confirm, refute or amplify the Bureau's data. It always came in handy if a company's answer was written in a manner suggesting, 'We didn't do it; *he* did it.'[12] This procedure enabled the Bureau to put out an occasional feeler. It would submit an unconfirmed case to, say, Iran – if the ship in question was suspected to have called there – and ten to one, Iran would respond by saying that according to the information at its disposal, the cargo had been discharged 'in Rotterdam', or some other place to which the ship could never have sailed in the time unaccounted for. Two birds with one stone: an indirect proof that the oil had been delivered to South Africa, and the confirmation that Iran had been the country of origin.

Often, an evasive answer or a company's failure to respond could justify the addition of a case to the list. However, if a company was adamant in its denial, the Bureau did not have a leg to stand on and could therefore not promote the case to the class of 'identified cases' – although the suspicions persisted. What could the Bureau do if a published charter report said that Vitol had chartered a tanker for a voyage 'ARA to Durban' (ARA: Antwerp-Rotterdam-Amsterdam), whereas the company responded with a flat denial?[13] In another instance, the Bureau had received the very first tip-off in which a shipment was linked to a company of which it had heard rumours for some time indicating that it had been set up by John Deuss in order to continue his oil deliveries to South Africa;[14] the contents of the SRB's letter were emphatically denied, leaving the Bureau with no other choice that to label the shipment 'Oil company unknown'. The underlying problem: *one* tip (or even a published charter report) relating to *one* shipment was just not good enough, especially when the Bureau had to identify an *oil trader*. It was easier to ascertain whether a *vessel* could have been to South Africa or not; in such cases even categorical denials by the shipowner did not soften the heart of the researcher, especially when the shipments fitted into a regular pattern.

A similar mechanism was visible with regard to the reactions of governments. It would have been relatively easy for the SRB to ignore a denial from the United Arab Emirates – if the latter would still have bothered to reply to correspondence from the Bureau. The same was not true when, in an unclear case of ships that were reported to have called at Nigeria – a country not known for oil deliveries in contravention of the embargo – the Nigerian authorities were none too happy when the Bureau didn't stop sending requests for an additional investigation which might shed some light on the matter. When the SRB received a letter in which it was requested 'to accept this statement as final',[15] what else could it do?

'we do hope that you get your record straight and this vessel is not erroneously reported which of course would not only involve legal implications but would most certainly damage the repute of your bureau. '

in reply to your new enquiry we have nothing more to add other than to say stop chasing ghosts.

we are certain there are more productive things that you can engage yourselves into and fail to understand your persistance over a subject that has been exhausted.

to recap and refresh your memory we can repeat that the vessel you refering to michael ¿ has never called in s. africa and as for the cargo owners we cannot be concerned or aware of same as you will appreciate these days this instrument may change 93 times (actual number) title.

we do wish you every success with your investigations but do hope that this was the last time we heard from you.'

Laurel Sea Transport Ltd, Greece, telex to SRB, 16 April 1986

2nd tx   13 Dec 86

Lies on a sliding scale

Deceit and fraud are more easily detected if the deceiver leaves a 'fingerprint'. After some time the SRB had almost come to the point of automatically including each and every tanker on its list which had on departing from the Persian Gulf stated its destination as being 'Port de Bouc' (a subport of Marseilles). 'Singapore' also used to be a popular 'destination', later replaced by 'Ain Sukhna'. It was a constant battle between embargo monitors and violators in which they did their utmost to outwit each other.

Sometimes, the discovery of a pattern in the lies used by companies gave the Bureau an edge on the embargo violators. An illustrative example is that of a series of refined oil transports involving the Turkish shipping company Martı. Just as with many comparable transports originating in the Netherlands during 1989–91 – most of which were confirmed by the companies involved – the destination given was 'Australia', but the Turkish transports were purportedly the only ones which did *not* terminate in South Africa... The company wrote a lengthy letter to the Bureau denying that any of its combined carriers had discharged in South Africa. It provided a series of details which were in part rather vague, in part unverifiable by other sources, and in part in clear contradiction to information from independent sources. Martı would for instance claim that all cargoes, officially destined for Australia, had been rerouted at the request of the charterers to 'off shore Madagascar' or 'Mozambique', and that the cargoes were discharged accordingly before the vessels collected cargoes of coal or iron ore in South Africa. A spokesperson for Martı told the Bureau that her company had 'nothing to hide'. Yet, 'the company has declined to react to several subsequent requests for a clarification of these and other inconsistencies and inaccuracies' – a variation of the standard formulation pertaining to cases of 'silence implies consent' which the SRB thought it wise to add to its March 1992 report. Of course, the upshot of it all was that all Martı OBOs *had* delivered oil cargoes. The Bureau could have said so straight away if only it had had access to documentation which it only got months later and which proved that a delivery by one of the Martı OBOs was incontestable. Having exposed one lie was sufficient to make all the other statements less bothersome for the researchers. This time, the conclusive evidence reached the Bureau straight from South Africa.

In the lion's den

The second thing people always wanted to know from SRB researchers was: Surely you get most of your information from South Africa, don't you? Do you have people with binoculars roaming Cape Town harbour? Have you been to South Africa yourselves?

The apartheid laws ensured that staff and members of the board of the SRB were unwelcome; it was only in 1991 that the first board member visited South Africa, followed by the first staff member three years later. On the odd occasion when staff members felt the temptation to make contact with possible informers inside the country, they were reminded of the fate that awaited someone who merely had an SRB publication in his or her possession (Gwen Lister!). For the citizens of South Africa, the consequences were more far-reaching than for foreigners.

At the same time this did not make research work impossible; one could as well have considered the possibility of renting a boat and looking about in the Persian Gulf. In fact, the Bureau would have given a great deal to gain access to those places *outside* South Africa where all the information was available, such as the offices of the shipping companies, brokers, bankers and insurance companies. Yet it remained a tantalising thought that valuable information was in South Africa and that *if* the Bureau could get at it... Sometimes the ANC passed bits of information on to the Bureau where the researchers painstakingly matched it with other data. Researchers recall weeks of laborious reconstruction which involved the deciphering of codes, approximate dates of unloading and types of oil. But they knew the ultimate source of information, i.e. the complete, uncoded lists, had to be lying in a drawer somewhere in South Africa. They were.

Somewhat more limited sources had already been tapped, especially by the Norwegian press and anti-apartheid movement (and, through them, by the SRB). One source – he has never gone public on this – was the Norwegian priest and anti-apartheid activist Per Anders Nordengen, who as a missionary in Durban (1985–87) had many contacts with Norwegian sailors and other compatriots who had knowledge about Norwegian tanker calls. He would for instance get information on hospitalised seamen with the names of their ships. But he knew he had to be careful. Once, having seen the names of a few tankers, he remembers going into a pub in order to phone the Church of Norway in Oslo. Having made the call, he immediately paid for his drink and walked out before anybody could have traced him.

However, 'the real stuff' only became available towards the end of the embargo period, when a few individuals in South Africa decided that there was no use in sitting on a mountain of information which people abroad might be willing to pay for. The Shipping Research Bureau directly and indirectly got offers and had to explain that the possibility that the press might be willing to pay vast amounts of money for an item which was slowly fading into the annals of history was fairly remote. At the same time it had to hint that it was itself interested in all the information it could lay its hands on, even historical data. And that's how David Craine, the 'Embargo' worker from London, was sent to southern Africa as a go-between for a face-to-face meeting with one of the potential sources. Negotiations were conducted in between visits to game parks and places of historical interest and later continued in London. Eventually, a deal was struck, and the Bureau became the proud owner of a large amount of absolutely fascinating material. When the Bureau presented its updated findings on 1989–91, it was able to state that 'The findings ... reflect a considerably *improved monitoring effort.*' The list of identified tankers for 1989 covered almost 85 per cent of the estimated oil imports as opposed to the usual 50–60 per cent. An unsuspected source, David Hitchman, Durban branch manager for World Wide Maritime, which acts as port agent for visiting tankers, confirmed that the lists of the SRB were now 'very accurate'.[16]

In the meantime, a new mission travelled to South Africa for a meeting with source no. 2. The chairman of the board of the SRB was delegated to defy the Petroleum Products Act and to evaluate the material which the source had to offer. The possibility had to be taken into account that it was a trap. The chairman, therefore, contacted comrades of the unbanned ANC for advice, protection and a crash course in counter-surveillance. From the outset, things appeared to be heading towards disaster when the chairman's ANC contact discovered that they were definitely being followed, but it appeared that the police officers were under the impression that they were on to a *drugs* deal. The process got going; people trained in intelligence work checked the credentials of 'Mr X' and devised a plan on how to approach him. In the meantime, the intending buyer moved from one hotel to another; he did not want to stay with friends and endanger them by using their homes as a base. He was sore about the fact that he was unable to attend ANC meetings during his first visit to the country. His ANC visitors did not say a word before thoroughly searching the room for listening devices; cars were switched in parking garages, and the homefront in Amsterdam was kept up to date by means of cryptic messages from public call-boxes. While he spent many lonely hours in his hotel room, the first meeting went amiss when Mr X's housemate became suspicious after an unknown person had made enquiries about him. The chairman then decided to undertake the second attempt himself: for him, as a foreigner, it was less risky. At last, a meeting was set up in a reasonably filled bar. Mr X spread the documents (which he produced from a file conspicuously marked 'Shipping Research Bureau') on the table – the material was breathtaking indeed... An agreement was reached on the price as well as the manner in which the documents were to be forwarded (there was one thing the prospective buyer could not do, namely, leave the bar with the material in his possession). The chairman heaved a sigh of relief. 'Well, do you know how many people were covering me inside the bar? *Four!* And outside? *Six!*'

It was a extraordinary experience for the SRB staff two years later, after the government of national unity had taken office under Mandela, when they again met with former enemies of the state who now held senior positions in Johannesburg, Durban and Pretoria ('If you people are going to keep us on our toes like in the old oil days... We know you guys, when you start moving there's no way of getting round it,' said the new Deputy Minister of Foreign Affairs in the subdued atmosphere of his spacious office in the Union Buildings) and were able to safely walk down the road with briefcases filled with what would formerly have been labelled 'subversive documents'.

The abundance of South African material from these various sources made it possible to boost the list of identified shipments by a few hundred. Many had been suspected in the past but not confirmed, and a number of cases had even been referred to in old reports in which readers had been asked – mostly in vain – to provide additional confirmation.[17] It appeared that the Bureau had been more cautious than was strictly necessary. At the same time, the more classified information the researchers managed to uncover for publication in this book, the more they realised that it would be impossible to tell the full story: documents in which columns had been blanked out[18] brought home what the Bureau still did not know – and what it would never get to know.

Research as a weapon

'It is, of course, the element of secrecy that makes it so hard to confirm or refute the SRB's findings. As might be expected, previous reports from the bureau have not proven totally reliable and the tanker "selection procedure" remains inevitably open-ended. The "main reasons" for selecting the 57 as vessels which probably delivered crude oil include confirmation from owners, managers or charterers but that is a rare occurrence indeed. A large number have been so classified simply because they "sailed from an oil-exporting country (or area) straight to S.Africa, and then immediately returned to the same oil exporting country". For 14 of the 57, this is the sole reason given ... The problem is that, in a majority of the cases, there is unlikely to be anything more to go on.'[19]

The author of this review of the third SRB main report addressed the crux of the matter, namely, the reasons why it was so difficult to get all the facts above board – or, put differently, why an institute such as the SRB was necessary.

How serious was the possibility that there were mistakes in the report? The cautious policy of the SRB was based on the view that a single erroneous case could destroy the reputation which it had painstakingly built up. It was convinced that an occasional error would inevitably creep into its reports, but it comforted itself with the thought that if in *this* specific case the cargo had been wrongly attributed to Transworld Oil, there were at least 40 other cases in which TWO was involved but not named. The Bureau was also convinced that it was being saved by the silence of the companies: often, to deny one delivery would have been tantamount to admitting to a host of others. Yet a small mistake could have unpleasant consequences: companies could have an interest in forcing the Bureau to concern itself with trivial details.[20]

There were mistakes in the SRB reports. The same could be said of publications used as source material – to err is human. A careful comparison between the findings in this book and old reports will show a few deletions, as a number of 'identified' deliveries or links with countries were later shown to have been based upon a mistake.[21] The Bureau did not have too many qualms about this; for example, it discovered that it had erroneously linked a shipment to Qatar, whilst at the same time unveiling another shipment from the Emirate.

A more important matter of principle was that it was imperative to work with a certain margin of uncertainty when determining 'identified deliveries'. To insist (if that could be done in any research project) that there be no margin of error with regard to each of the *individual cases*[22] would have defeated the aim of getting a reasonably accurate *overall* view of the oil trade with South Africa. By working the way it did, the SRB was able to outline the overall picture, identifying who the main parties involved were, which would have been impossible had it concentrated on the legal tenability of each and every statement. In other words, if the Bureau had been much more rigid in its criteria for establishing conclusive evidence, the reports would have been much slimmer, to the satisfaction of South Africa's rulers.

There was very little 'scientific' criticism of the Bureau's work – chiefly because it was not in any way related to the academic community and *vice versa*. On one rare occasion, a statistician of the Port of Rotterdam claimed to have discovered a fundamental flaw in a report made by the SRB on the role of the Rotterdam harbour in oil supplies to South Africa. The Bureau had not mentioned its *sources* when it referred to tankers departing from Rotterdam with a cargo of oil for South Africa; according to the critic, this meant that the investigation did not meet the scientific criterion of repeatability. Even now, the researchers will not reveal the names of many informers for fear that the latter will lose their jobs. What the critic mainly showed was that he had difficulty interpreting his academic textbook lessons in a creative manner. Of course the study was repeatable! He was advised to have a go at it himself and was given the assurance that he would come to the same conclusions. When the same SRB report was discussed by the city council of Rotterdam, one of the councillors tried to dismiss it by saying that 'one could not expect objective research' from a research organisation which was 'based on the political premise that "It is generally acknowledged that in order for the peoples in the whole of southern Africa to gain true liberation and independence, apartheid will have to be dismantled" and that

"Economic sanctions are effective and peaceful and therefore the most appropriate methods".' The next day, one newspaper commented: 'The attempt failed when SRB researcher R. Hengeveld pointed out to Baggerman that the latter was quoting a passage from the research proposal of the municipality and not the report itself'[23] (the researcher preferred to leave unsaid that the text of the research proposal, attached as an annex to the report, had been drafted by the very anti-apartheid groups which had for years urged the council to take measures and to have a study undertaken...).

Different brands of journalism

Bad results are not a corollary to goal-oriented research; the latter will, however, inevitably lead to debates. One debate which permeated the work of the Shipping Research Bureau during the first years was not related to the fear that the Bureau's publications would contain *errors*, but rather whether the Bureau should publish the *truth* regarding the large amount of oil flowing to South Africa from the Middle East.[24] Another, equally important, ongoing internal debate was based on the reproach that it was difficult to campaign using the 'outdated' research findings of the SRB. The usual counter-argument was that no one in the world had more recent and comprehensive information; in actual fact, each report was given extensive coverage in the media as reflecting 'the latest information from the SRB'. Moreover, the Bureau was able to include an increasing number of 'preliminary' fairly up-to-date overviews in its later reports. Insofar as there was a problem, it was the inevitable consequence of the SRB's basic methodology which had been developed over time, namely, the systematic research on tankers based on paperwork, followed by the time-consuming procedure of presenting the preliminary findings to companies and governments. This raised another question: to what extent was a more *journalistic* approach needed in order to complement the Bureau's research work? In his review of Klinghoffer's *Oiling the Wheels of Apartheid*, Martin Bailey addressed a similar question: 'There is little evidence that Klinghoffer has developed contacts with oil traders, shippers or insurers, who could have provided an "inside" view of the trade. The authentic detail that might have been gained over a few beers with an oil trader involved in setting up a clandestine sanctions-busting deal would have given Klinghoffer's study a deeper insight.'[25]

The SRB's research routine was not confined to the basic paperwork on tankers, however. Firstly, the Bureau maintained fruitful contacts with professional journalists; the favourite method of 'creating sources' has been touched upon earlier. Indeed, when the Bureau's aforementioned report was presented to the city council of Rotterdam, its recommendations were greatly enhanced by an article that had appeared in a newspaper the same day in which it was revealed that not long before a tanker had once again left Rotterdam bound for South Africa. Soon after the discovery, the SRB had given the basic information to a journalist who, moving much faster than the Bureau could, was able to finish off the story by making a few telephone calls to shipping agents and the shipowner; the Bureau's modus operandi just did not include directly calling a shipowner... The Bureau did not envy the journalist credit for the 'discovery'.[26] Some journalists – such as the Swedish reporter who had 'never dreamed of being the source of an international research institute...' – were rather impressed when they realised they had information which was useful for the Bureau instead of merely the other way round.

```
        A T T E S T A T I O N
        =-=-=-=-=-=-=-=-=-=
        certificate of discharge

     JE SOUSSIGNE RECEVEUR DES DOUANES DE :   VERDON
     I undersigned Head of Customs at

CERTIFIE QUE LA CARGAISON TOTALE DU NAVIRE PETROLIER ;
certify that the entire cargo of the tanker    CAST PUFFIN

ARRIVE LE    21 sep '80 A  VERDON    EN PROVENANCE DE SEAL SANDS
arrived on the        at            coming from

AVEC ;                LONGTONS D'HUILE MINERALE BRUTE, A ETE DECHARGE
       81.695,936
with                  longtons of crude oil, was discharged

DANS CE PORT
                     23 SEP 1980
at this port

        FAIT A  VERDON    LE   24 SEP 1980
        issued at         on the

        PR. LE RECEVEUR DES DOUANES
        for and on behalf of head of Customs
```

```
                    PORT AUTONOME DE BORDEAUX

                                                      SHIPPING RESEARCH BUREAU
                    LE DIRECTEUR                       P.O. BOX 11898

                                                       1001 GW AMSTERDAM

                           15-03-1984                          EC p.tél. 182

Escale au VERDON de 2 tankers                            27 MARS 1984
anglais.



                                    Monsieur,

                                        En réponse à votre lettre de référence,
                               j'ai l'honneur de vous informer que les deux pétroliers anglais
                               "CAST PUFFIN" et "SPEY BRIDGE" n'ont jamais fait escale au
                               VERDON.

                                        Je vous prie, Monsieur, de croire à ma
                               considération distinguée.

                                                                   VALLS
```

False French customs documents were submitted to the Norwegian Ministry of Oil and Energy in order to make it appear that the embargo on North Sea oil to South Africa had been duly observed. French port and customs authorities confirmed that the tankers in question had *not* called at the port indicated by the falsified certificate of discharge (see also: *John Deuss/Transworld Oil*, SRB survey, January 1985).

Secondly, the Shipping Research Bureau slowly developed direct contact with sources outside the framework of the original paperwork. Contacts with various kinds of informers (over a few drinks of *akvavit*, too) have already been mentioned. In addition, from the beginning, the Bureau made occasional contacts with 'official' sources of information: port and customs authorities were asked to confirm that discharge documents bearing their stamps had been tampered with (see the example of the *Cast Puffin*). It took some time before it became standard procedure for the Bureau to turn to port captains and agents in various ports in order to complement the data published by Lloyd's and to test various hypotheses ('Did the vessel sail in ballast, and if not, what type of cargo was loaded?'). For some agents it was simply a paid commission: it was rare for people to question the motives for the request made by the neutral-sounding 'Shipping Research Bureau', and quite often agents just sent the information requested together with an invoice. The first group of the Bureau's favourites were those employees who never failed to provide the relevant information and who perhaps had no idea as to their contribution towards a useful goal (the Bureau let sleeping dogs lie...). Exposing the 'Amsterdam connection', i.e. the spate of refined product shipments that left the port for South Africa in 1989–90, was only possible thanks to the loyal Port Office employee who never tired of searching the files for information. Perhaps such information was not 'classified', but it is not hard to imagine how public information can easily become less public if the authorities are reluctant to release it. The other favourites were the white ravens amongst the port captains who were always prepared to assist the researchers when called upon to do so, even after they had been briefed on the Bureau's aims.

In a later chapter a Norwegian shipowner is quoted as saying that 'the Chinese' had taken over the route to South Africa after the oil transport ban came into effect in Norway. For months the SRB was puzzled and had no idea which Chinese companies and tankers were implicated; it seemed too far-fetched. After months of painstaking research and the occasional tip, the researchers began to see the growing role of World-Wide tankers from Hong Kong; it had not occurred to them that there were Chinese shipping companies outside the People's Republic of China... But making a telephone call to the Norwegian shipowner had not even been considered.

For quite some time, the SRB felt that information of a 'journalistic' nature was insufficiently solid to base its research publications upon, in other words, that reports which were not supported by results based on the usual methods would not meet its standards of reliability. The ideal situation was to integrate both methods, but the Bureau lacked the funds, employees, time – and maybe the fantasy. In the internal debate it was felt that the 'early-warning' approach lacked some of the advantages of the laborious method. Attempts to shorten the distance between research and action and – in the manner of the *Jane Stove* case – to take the motto 'Stop oil to South Africa' literally, often turned out badly. The Iranian government would for instance be informed per telex that according to reliable sources, tanker X was on her way to Durban with a cargo of Iranian oil. But what if the tanker did not arrive in South Africa? Had the 'warning' been effective? Or had it been either a false tip, or a correct tip but had the trader changed his plan? How many excuses had to be sent to Iran, while the SRB was left without a single scrap of evidence which could be used in a publication?[27]

In a field of research where political and economic interests prevailed, one could not rule out the possibility of *disinformation* in publications, and even more so in contacts of a 'journalistic' nature. Tips and allegations which were well nigh impossible to verify could serve various goals; there was always the fear that attempts would be made to trip the researchers into making mistakes in their publications, to distract their attention by giving them irrelevant leads, to involve the Bureau in political games and alternately, by maintaining cordial relations with the Bureau, to stay informed as to what the Bureau was working on and how much information it had at its disposal. It was not easy to determine whether a contact had a hidden agenda or not. The fact that the SRB was unable to verify the recurrent rumour on the role of the *Seychelles* in oil sanctions busting (in which the leading players were the trading company of an Italian millionaire called Giovanni Mario Ricci, who headed a fake 'Sovereign Order of the Coptic Catholic Knights of Malta', and South African master spy turned business consultant Craig Williamson) did not necessarily mean that there were hidden agendas involved in this case.[28] The chance that there were was far greater in the case of persistent rumours regarding Nigerian oil to South Africa, to which the Bureau could not say much except that it had never identified any shipments.[29]

And what was this 'Dr' François Cornish up to, the scientific researcher and director of the International Energy Commission (U.K.), who contacted the SRB expressing an inter-

A 'journalist' unmasked

1.3.78 | de DPF.—; Copie d'une lettre de +Cons. *gén*. Johannesbourg du 8.2.78 et du 3.2.78 concernant Conrad Meier, 41, qui doit être membre du service secret du Premier-Ministre Jan Smith de Rhodésie. GERBER Conrad était en 1976 Président du M., section romande. Diverses annexes.

1.3.78 from DPF.-; Copy of a letter from Cons. Gen. Johannesburg of 8.2.78 and of 3.2.78 concerning Conrad GERBER, 41, who is probably a member of the secret service of prime minister Jan Smith of Rhodesia. In 1976 GERBER Conrad was president of the French-speaking section of the M[ovement]. Various annexes.

Filing card on Swiss Anti-Apartheid Movement in the archives of the Swiss Bureau for Internal Security. The card was reproduced in: *Anti-Apartheid-Nachrichten* 16(2), April 1992.

UNCLASSIFIED   392

Who is this answering this back?

A   That's a fellow in Geneva who does checks for me, that works for me.

Q   Who is he?

A   Well, his name is Gerber, Conrad Gerber.

Q   Did you ever find out, to the contrary?

A   To the contrary, what?

Q   Did you ever find out that Gerber is wrong about this, and Ghorbanifar was involved in crude oil deals?

A   No.

Q   So if he was dabbling oil and his real business is arms --

A   I don't know what his real business is, because he did not introduce himself to me as an arms dealer, and I think if you read through those memos, you know that my inquiries about him show that the people I talked to certainly did not know him as an arms dealer.

Q   Did you ever confirm that Ghorbanifar had worked for SAVAK?

A   Yes.

UNCLASSIFIED

From: U.S. Congress, *Report of the Congressional Committees Investigating the Iran-Contra Affair*, Appendix B: Volume 25, Deposition of Theodore G. Shackley, 21 September 1987. Washington: U.S. Government Printing Office, 1988, 392. Shackley, a former associate director of the CIA, was present at the very first secret meeting, held in a Hamburg hotel in 1984, between Americans and Iranians, which led to the Iran-Contra Affair. He was there on the expense of 'Dois' [sic] (15 September 1987, 144); Shackley's risk analysis company RAI had 'primarily one client ... The client is Trans-World Oil' (idem, 20-1).

est in its reports and hinted that he had 'quite a bit of information that is not in your booklets'; who 'really wanted to halt these deliveries down South' and was convinced that monitoring was not very difficult ('If we have the finance, I can have a person sitting in Durban watching the buoy and reporting on every ship coming in and offloading'); who was planning to 'teach' all the culprits – from Xenopoulos and Chiavelli to Yamani and Taher – 'a lesson' ('We firmly believe that they will come up with some sort of muting offer, in which case we've caught them. As soon as they do, we're going to splash it...'); who, having been advised by the SRB that it would be useful for him to contact Martin Bailey in England, came back wondering whether there might be two Martin Baileys with *The Observer*, because the one he had spoken to 'knew nothing'; who promised to send the Bureau an uncensored copy of the Advocate-General's report, and whose next visit was to the ANC in London, where he told Frene Ginwala that he found the SRB 'old-fashioned' and 'inefficient', and asked her for ...an uncensored copy of the report of the Advocate-General; and who was exposed in the British press a few months later as the 'director' of a non-existent organisation and the ultimate candidate for the Nobel Prize in physics for his achievement, 'so stunning – and so far reaching in its implications – that one day the names of Archimedes, Newton and Einstein will be joined by F.P. Cornish. *He has invented a car which runs on water.*'[30]

Sometimes journalists called: 'Is this the Shipping Research Bureau? Could you please send me whatever you have on company X? *It is said to be involved in oil to South Africa...*' Being asked to act as unpaid consultant on matters unrelated to South Africa was only a mild form of being 'used' for extraneous aims. On other more interesting occasions the queries *did* involve oil to South Africa. The Bureau would often be called by lawyers who wanted as much information as they could get their hands on, but who, 'as the Bureau could understand', were unable to say anything on the grounds that their cases were still pending, but who would definitely give the Bureau interesting material at a later stage – never to be heard of again. One occasion, however, was remarkable. The Bureau was asked to appear in court on behalf of one of the parties in a lawsuit involving Brunei oil to South Africa. The SRB hoped to gain access to detailed information – altough it was asked to give an undertaking (which it turned down) that it would not write about the case afterwards – in return for its expert opinion in court stating that it was quite usual for Brunei oil to reach South Africa in contravention of destination clauses. An article in the oil journal *Platt's Week* which dealt with a court case in Hong Kong involving other parties, in which the Brunei-linked company Saberu sued a subsidiary of Marubeni (the next link in a chain of oil from Brunei Shell Petroleum via Saberu, Marubeni and Marc Rich to South Africa), stated that 'the case may be significant for setting a legal precedent for bringing secretive oil movements [to South Africa] into the open,' but it dryly added that 'if the trend to legal action does continue, it will be motivated more by commercial, competitive consideration than because of a new found desire to comply with selling restrictions.'[31] It was by no means clear that it would be wise for the Bureau to use its expertise to the benefit of companies who, to put it simply, were out to get a slice of the cake in an embargo-busting exercise.

UN monitoring: A balancing act

In his contribution to this book, Amer Araim describes the activities of the *Intergovern-mental Group to Monitor the Supply and Shipping of Oil and Petroleum Products to South Africa*, of which he was the secretary from the beginning until the end. In its first reports to the General Assembly, the Group made veiled references to the extent of its dependence on input from the Shipping Research Bureau, without ever mentioning it by name. For the first time ever, oil-producing countries and shipping states had been brought together in this Group in a lasting cooperation on the issue of the oil embargo. However, the old differences remained, and the role of the SRB was an obvious bone of contention. As in the past, some of the Bureau's findings were contested by one country or a group of countries, other findings by another. Although the Group (or some of its members) may have felt pressurised by the SRB, the actual pressure was caused by the Group's mandate, namely, monitoring the supply and shipping of oil to South Africa – which was impossible without the contribution of the SRB. The Group decided that it could not rely too heavily on one source, and that therefore, in addition to the flow of information from the SRB[32] (basically consisting of the complete sets of preliminary findings on suspected deliveries as presented to companies and governments, of which the UN Centre against Apartheid had received copies all along), a parallel source of information had to be developed in the form of lists of ships for which calls at South African ports had been recorded.

The same lists were also used by the SRB; consequently, there was an overlap between the two sets of information handled by the UN Group. A small number of vessels – mostly combined carriers (OBOs) – whose calls at South Africa had been recorded and which were assumed by the SRB to have delivered oil appeared in both sets. In contrast to em-bargo-breaking oil tankers, OBOs stood a chance of being registered by Lloyd's if, after having discharged their cargo of oil, they took on a load of dry cargo in South Africa. This amounted to an exception to the rule that calls involving oil deliveries were not recorded, while conversely, recorded calls were 'innocent' calls. The lists of recorded calls also covered a further category of vessels, consisting of smaller product and chemical tankers, which were not investigated by the SRB. On the one hand, the above-mentioned rule regarding 'innocent' calls also applied to these vessels; on the other hand, the SRB had in years gone by tried to tackle this category as well – only to discover that it was very difficult to determine in which harbour a small vessel had taken on a cargo, where a cargo had been unloaded, and also to determine what type of cargo was on board (petroleum products, or edible oil, phosphoric acid, molasses, ammonia or other non-petroleum prod-ucts). In comparison, monitoring large crude oil tankers with their straightforward trading patterns was much easier. It probably suited some of the members of the Group that the attention was sometimes diverted from crude oil. This did not apply to Norway: an excep-tionally large number of vessels which featured on the list of 'port calls' were Norwegian-controlled. But from a distance the SRB noted how vast the workload was which the Group had taken upon itself, and how it was running into the all too familiar problems arising from this type of research. Yet, the Bureau felt it was its duty to provide assistance with the research when requested to do so by the secretariat, and it submitted lengthy memos in which it gave assessments of specific cases which the Bureau itself, with its acquired sixth sense for innocent cases (or cases which would never be solved), would not have even bothered to investigate.

The work of the SRB for the UN Group could not avoid the tension between research and politics. When the Group was formed, the Bureau was quick to provide the Special Committee against Apartheid with advice, whether or not on request, and it continued to offer its 'assistance' – a known euphemism for keeping up the pressure – because it felt that it was important that the United Nations had seriously taken up the issue of the oil embargo. For its own work, however, there was a drawback. Saudi Arabia used the founding of the Group as an excuse for not keeping its promise to send copies of discharge documents to the Bureau; in general, most governments no longer felt the urge to provide a small non-governmental organisation with information they had already made available to the United Nations. What in certain cases must have played a part was that the UN Group, as opposed to the SRB, was naturally inclined to accept all the answers at face value; the rules governing UN diplomacy did not include antagonising member states,[33] and thus every statement made by a member state was final. The Bureau had been through all this before: some cases were removed from the Group's list because the only harbour listed as the one prior to South Africa was an anchorage in the UAE, one which the UAE correctly claimed was not used for the loading of oil. Other cases were removed from the list on the grounds that the oil-exporting country involved had stated that according to its information, the oil had been delivered to Rotterdam. The SRB kept telling the Group that it could not base its decisions on these answers only: 'Deleting this case from the list would disregard the practice of "multi-porting" (and non-reporting of calls) in the Persian Gulf area,' or 'In fact, the ship had already returned to the Persian Gulf on the date indicated,' etc. Slowly but surely, the policy of the Group became more stringent; ships were included in the list until such time that copies of discharge documents were made available. A next step was now undertaken by the SRB: 'Clearly, the case of tanker X cannot be deleted on the basis of the "documentation" submitted by the government of country Y. The documents have clearly been forged.' When the Group presented its second report to the General Assembly in 1988, the words of the rapporteur reflected the fact that the Group was moving towards a tougher line: 'Governments concerned should scrutinize the authenticity of the documentation presented and be more vigilant than in the past in order to prevent oil and shipping companies from forging such documentation'; in the meantime, 'We prefer to err on the side of leniency in order to continue the present high degree of co-operation and trust the Group enjoys from Governments.'[34] But the Group was running into difficulties in the event of two governments giving the Group conflicting answers regarding the same case. Time and again, the SRB discussed specific cases in its memoranda to the Group as well as in its Newsletter.[35] Meanwhile, the Group's cooperation with some governments left much to be desired, as was indicated in 1989 by the Group's chairman, the Norwegian ambassador Tom Vraalsen: 'It is difficult for us to go beyond what we are doing. There are certain governments which for their own reasons do not respond to our communications.'[36] Six months later it was the Norwegian government, through its Minister of Development Aid, Tom Vraalsen, which indicated it had its own reasons...[37]

Mobil Arma

Covering ships' names with tarpaulins was not always effective. The SRB often received reports from eyewitnesses who had been able to identify tankers despite such a precaution. A
raging gale hampered the discharging of the cargo of the *World Symphony* at the Durban
offshore oil buoy from 29–31 October 1986. The ship's name and port of registration had been
covered by tarpaulins but the wind moved the covers and even blew one into the sea, which
enabled an eyewitness to identify the ship before her name was covered again. A few weeks
later, on 15 December at 11 a.m., a southwesterly wind blew away the white sheet which
covered the stern of the *World NKK*, thus exposing her name and port in clear white letters.
The crew of the brand new *Sala* just postponed painting the names on the ship until after her
maiden voyage from the UAE to South Africa (March 1993). The most effective method was
set out in instructions transmitted to tankers by the shipping agent on their approach to South
Africa, as shown in one of the examples below. The first is the text of part of a telex message
to the captain of the *Fortuneship L.*, which sailed from Iran and discharged her crude oil cargo
of 242,205 tons at the SBM on 10–12 August 1989. The tanker called at Durban under the
code-name 'Celina'. Ten days later, on 21 August, the same ship called again at the SBM, this
time under the name of 'Jaguar', discharging 174,000 tons.

TO : MASTER 'CELINA'
FM : WORLD WIDE MARITIME DBN *[Durban]*

03 AUG 89
REF : 2181

PLEASE ADVISE:
   1) MASTERS FULL NAMES/ NUMBER OF CREW
   2) B/L FIGS – PLS QUOTE API MT LT BBLS ONLY – NO CARGO NAMES TO BE
      MENTIONED *[Bill of Lading figures, API gravity of oil, metric tons, long tons, bar-
      rels]*
   3) VESSELS PREFERRED DISCHARGE SEQUENCE
   4) ALL VESSELS HUSBANDRY REQUIREMENTS
   5) ETA *[Expected Time of Arrival]*

FYG PLSE NOTE:

111) CONFIDENTIALITY
     AA COMMUNICATION:
     IN ALL COMMUNICATIONS THE VESSELS NAME 'CELINA' SHOULD BE
     USED. THIS APPLIES TO TELEXES, CABLES AND VHF CALLS. FOR CABLES
     VIA S A COASTAL STATIONS, USE 'CELINA' AS VESSELS NAME AND CALL
     SIGN I.E.: 'CELINA/CELINA/DURBANRADIO...ETC'
     DO NOT DISCLOSE VESSELS ACTUAL CALLSIGN TO COASTAL STATIONS
     WHEN REQUESTED TO DO SO. ALSO DO NOT SEND RADIOMARITIME
     DOCUMENTS (RETURNS) TO VSLS RADIOMARITIME ACCOUNTING AU-
     THORITY FOR CALLS MADE VIA SOUTH AFRICAN COASTAL STATIONS.
     AS FAR AS POSSIBLE VESSEL TO AVOID USE OF SOUTH AFRICAN
     COASTAL STATIONS.

     BB DOCUMENTATION
     ALL DOCS – NOR, SOF, PUMPING LOG ETC TO RECORD VESSELS NAME
     'CELINA' AND PORT SBM. VESSEL TO PROTEST AND REFUSE TO SIGN
     SURVEYOR DOCUMENTS WHICH BEAR ACTUAL DISPORT NAME AND

STYLE. *[NOR: Notice Of Readiness, SOF: Statement Of Facts, Disport is port of discharge]*

CC CLEARANCE/PRATIQUE.
PLS SEND PRATIQUE MESSAGE TO AGENTS TLX APPROX 72HRS PRIOR ARRIVAL. FOR CLEARANCE, FOUR CREWLISTS, BEARING VESSELS NAME 'CELINA' IS ALL THAT IS REQUIRED. (NIL CUSTOMS DECLARATION)

DD VESSELS NAME ON SHIPSIDE AND AFT.
VESSEL NAME MUST BE OBSCURED/DELETED. THIS CAN EASILY BE DONE BY USING GREASE (MOBIL ARMA, USUALLY EMPLOYED FOR WIRE ROPES OR OPEN GEARS). A DEGREASER WILL EASILY REMOVE SAME AFTER DEPARTURE. BRIDGE NAME BOARDS TO BE TAKEN DOWN.

EE STORES/HUSBANDRY/MAIL/SPARES.
DO NOT ORDER FROM CHANDLER DIRECT. DO NOT TLX/FAX VARIOUS CHANDLERS FOR QUOTES. SHOULD YOU WISH TO ASK FOR QUOTES, PLS TLX/FAX DETAILS OF PROVISIONS REQUIRED TO AGENTS, AND THE QUOTES WILL THEN BE REQUESTED. ALTERNATIVELY, ADVISE AGENT OF THE NAME OF YOUR PREFFERED SUPPLIER.
VIDEO EXCHANGE – NOT PERMITTED DUE TO VESSELS NAME RECORDED ON EXCHAGE DOCUMENTS.
SHORELEAVE – NIL SHORELEAVE PERMITTED (EXCEPT IN CASE OF MEDICAL EMERGENCY)

FF LOADPORT DOCUMENTS:
ALL DOCUMENTS TO BE HANDED TO AGENT ONLY. THE SURVEYOR MAY REQUIRE TO SEE FOLLOWING DOCUMENTS:
–ULLAGE REPORTS
–OBQ/SLOP CERT *[OBQ: On Board Quantity]*
–VSLS EXPERIENCE FACTOR
–PROTESTS AFFECTING MEASUREMENT (FREE WATER, DIFF IN FIGS..ETC)
ABOVE ONLY TO BE GIVEN WITH FOLL DELETED: 1) VESSELS NAME 2) LOADPORT NAME 3) CARGO NAME (USE GRADE A, GRADE B)

The bulk/oil carrier *Höegh Foam* arrived at the port of Durban on 4 October 1989. The vessel was small enough to enter the harbour in order to discharge her cargo of 45,048 tons of petrol and 15,093 tons of gasoil from Romania. A few days before arrival the captain received the following instruction.

TO : MASTER MARY
FM : WORLD WIDE MARITIME DB

28 SEPT 89
REF : 2812

WE WISH TO ADVISE A FEW NOTES ON CONFIDENTIAL PROCEDURE, WHICH PLEASE CONFIRM / ADVISE IF ANY QUERIES:

1) ARRIVAL / FORMALITIES ONE HOUR PRIOR TO ARRIVAL AT PILOT STATION, PLEASE CALL 'DURBAN HARBOUR RADIO' ON VHF16 ADVISING ETA. VESSELS

NAME 'MARY' ONLY TO BE USED. DURBAN HARBOUR RADIO WILL ADVISE PROSPECTS FOR PILOT. OFFICIALS: CUSTOMS REQUIRES THE USUAL CREW DECLARATIONS, CREWLISTS,ETC. PLEASE USE VESSELS NAME 'MARY' ON ALL FORMS. ADVISE THEM THAT THE LAST PORT WAS HIGH SEAS.

2) LOADPORT DOCUMENTS: ALL, REPEAT ALL LOADPORT DOCUMENTS SHOULD BE HANDED TO THE AGENT (ADRIAN MAASDORP) ONLY. THIS IN-CLUDES MASTER/SHIPS COPY. PLEASE PREPARE ONE COPY OF DOCUMENTS TO BE USED FOR URVEY/MEASUREMENT (ULLAGE REPORT,TANK CLEANLINESS, APPLICABLE PROTESTS, EXPERIENCE FACTOR, ETC) PLEASE ENSURE THAT THESE DOCUMENTS (FOR SURVEYORS USE) HAVE THE FOLLOWING INFO DE-LETED/OBSCURED: AA LOADPORT BB TERMINAL CC SHIPSNAME.
IT IS IMPORTANT THAT LOCAL SURVEYORS/TERMINAL DO NOT AQUIRE THIS INFO

WE WILL ASSIST WITH THE PREPARATION OF SURVEYORS DOCS ONARRIVAL, IF NECESSARY.

PLEASE CONFIRM AGREEABLE/INORDER

KIND REGARDS

After her call at Durban as 'Mary', the *Höegh Foam* delivered South African coal in Belgium, and sailed to the Netherlands. Here she is shown loading another cargo of 65,000 tons of petrol for Marc Rich (6–10 November 1989), once again destined for delivery to South Africa (Amerikahaven jetty, Amsterdam 8 November 1989).

Pidgin Italian

Two 'certificates' reproduced here were presented to the Bahrain National Oil Company by *Total International* (France), the purchaser of a number of gasoil cargoes which were delivered to South Africa. A cursory investigation of such documents would have led to the conclusion that they had been faked.

The *Biscaya*, a bulk/oil carrier and not a 'motor tanker' as she is called in the document, was shown to have discharged her cargo not in South Africa but in Trieste and on a date which would not have allowed the ship to return to the Persian Gulf, as she did, on 6 June 1986, even if she had sailed at maximum speed. (On departure from the Persian Gulf, as well as on her return, the *Biscaya* maintained that she had sailed to *Rotterdam*; she could never have made this voyage within 33 days. Equally conspicuous was the absence of reports of this vessel calling at Trieste or passing through the Suez Canal.)

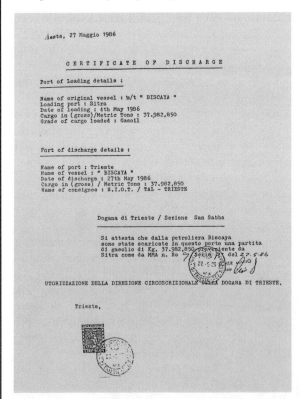

The document shown for the *Singa Star* is peculiar indeed. This vessel sailed from Bahrain (a place the 'certificate' situates in Saudi Arabia) and Kuwait mid-September 1986, again purportedly 'for Rotterdam'. On 20 October 1986, after having discreetly discharged her cargo in South Africa, she emerged in the Persian Gulf. However, according to the document submitted to Bahrain, the cargo had been transferred on 20 September, at a non-specified place, into the *Archontissa Katingo*. This 'motor tanker' was supposed to have discharged the oil in Trieste on 11 October 1986. At the purported date of transhipment, no *Archontissa Katingo* existed. A bulk/oil carrier bearing that name had been renamed *Archontissa* quite some time before the date mentioned in the document. Even so, the *Archontissa* was nowhere near the Persian Gulf nor Italy on 20 September 1986, but in Japan.

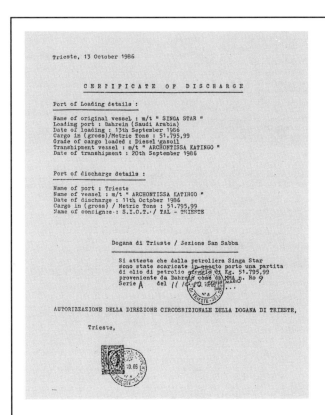

```
                Trieste, 13 October 1986



                       C E R T I F I C A T E   O F   D I S C H A R G E


           Port of Loading details :

           Name of original vessel : m/t " SINGA STAR "
           Loading port : Bahrein (Saudi Arabia)
           Date of loading : 13th September 1986
           Cargo in (gross)/Metric tons : 51.795,99
           Grade of cargo loaded : Diesel gasoil
           Transhipment vessel : m/t " ARCHONTISSA KATINGO "
           Date of transhipment : 20th September 1986



           Port of discharge details :

           Name of port : Trieste
           Name of vessel : m/t " ARCHONTISSA KATINGO "
           Date of discharge : 11th October 1986
           Cargo in (gross) / Metric Tons : 51.795,99
           Name of consignee : S.I.C.T. / TAL - TRIESTE



                    Dogana di Trieste / Sezione San Sabba


                    Si attesta che dalla petroliera Singa Star
                    sono state scaricate in questo porto una partita
                    di olio di petrolio greggio di Kg. 51.795,99
                    proveniente da Bahrein come da MMA S. Ro 9
                    Serie A    del ( ( ( . . .


           AUTORIZZAZIONE DELLA DIREZIONE CIRCOSRIZIONALE DELLA DOGANA DI TRIESTE,


                Trieste,
```

A document regarding the tanker *Beatrice* presents another interesting case. This vessel sailed from Yemen in May 1986, loaded with fuel oil for NIOC. The oil had been refined at the Aden Refinery, which was informed that the cargo was destined for Genoa. On 20 June 1986, after having delivered her cargo to South Africa, the *Beatrice* arrived at Jeddah in the Red Sea, reporting 'Singapore' as her last port of call. No calls were reported at Genoa or Singapore, neither had the vessel passed through the Suez Canal; afterwards, shipowner Ugland felt no qualms about confirming the voyage to South Africa to the SRB. In the document presented by the buyer, Genoa was chosen as the purported port of discharge. However, while adapting the document (which is in all respects similar to the two Trieste 'certificates') to this particular case, the falsifiers forgot that 'Section San Sabba' is the oil terminal area in the port of *Trieste*.

The wording of the 'Italian' documents also gives rise to considerable doubts concerning their producers' mastery of the Italian language. E.g., the *Beatrice* document 'testifies' something to the effect that *'in this port a cargo are discharged tanker Beatrice'*...

Outsmarting the embargo monitors

When it became clear that the above-mentioned tricks were too transparent, new methods were devised to hoodwink the embargo monitors. In April 1987 the Bergesen tanker *Berge Enterprise* collected part cargoes of crude oil in Saudi Arabia, Qatar and the UAE and purportedly sailed 'for Singapore'. When in 1988 the government of Saudi Arabia set out to investigate where their oil had gone, it was first presented with information apparently confirming that the cargo of Arabian Medium crude had been delivered to Singapore, although there were no independent reports to confirm this. The government was later provided with a return copy of the 'Oil Export Declaration' issued by its own Customs Department, from which it now ap-

```
Genova, 30 Maggio 1986


               C E R T I F I C A T E   O F   D I S C H A R G E

    Port of Loading details :


    Name of original vessel : m/t " BEATRICE "
    Loading port : Aden
    Date of loading : 16th May 1986
    Cargo in (gross)/Metric Tons : 49.881,96
    Grade of cargo loaded : Straight Run Fuel Oil



    Port of discharge details :


    Name of port : Genova
    Name of vessel : m/t " BEATRICE "
    Date of discharge : 30th May 1986
    Cargo in (gross)/Metric Tons : 49.881,96
    Name of consignee : To Order



              Dogana di Genova / Sezione  San Sabba
              ------------------------------------------

              Si attesta che petroliera Beatrice
              sono state scaricate in questo porto una partita
              di olio combustibile da distillazione primaria
              di Kg. 49.881,96 proveniente da Aden come da
              MMA n. Ro 9  Serie A del 30.5.86


    AUTORIZZAZIONE DELLA DIREZIONE CIRCOSCRIZIONALE DELLA DOGANA DI GENOVA,


        Genova,
```

peared that the cargo had been discharged at *Ain Sukhna* (Egypt – Red Sea) and transferred to the Mediterranean via the Arab Petroleum Pipeline. According to the document, the cargo had then been transferred to the tanker *Elbe Maru* on 30 April 1987, and discharged at *Fos-sur-Mer*. Stamps and signatures, apparently in use by the Arab Petroleum Pipeline and the French Customs, were used to authenticate the document.

It was a rather clever cover-up at first sight. The Japanese tanker *Elbe Maru* had indeed discharged an oil cargo of approximately the same volume as the *Berge Enterprise* cargo at Fos, on 3 May 1987. However, not only was the exact volume of the cargo different from the original cargo, it also contained a mixture of *Iranian and* Arabian *Heavy* crude rather than Arabian Medium Crude. What was more, the *Elbe Maru* could never have covered the distance between the Mediterranean outlet of the pipeline at Sidi Kerir (Egypt) to Fos (France) in the time indicated.

A final touch of implausibility was added when the government of *Qatar* was presented with a certificate of discharge 'proving' that the Norwegian tanker had discharged her part cargo of Qatar crude in *Singapore*, on exactly the same date that the ship had purportedly delivered her cargo of Saudi crude to Ain Sukhna...

The pipeline trick gained popularity. The SRB was led to conclude that the falsifiers subscribed to *Lloyd's Voyage Record* in order to identify tankers that had loaded oil at Sidi Kerir. Many tankers which made cross-Mediterranean voyages were mentioned in certificates as having taken over cargoes of oil which were suspected to have ended up in South Africa; when the SRB had no independent information confirming a delivery to South Africa, it was only when the owners of such 'innocent' tankers were willing to provide the SRB with data on their ships' actual voyages that proof was obtained that a certificate had been forged. Even more ingenious methods were later used. Harder to crack than forged documents and stamps are genuine ones. A new type of discharge certificate came into vogue relating to tankers which had indeed delivered Middle East oil from Sidi Kerir to Constantza in *Romania*. Rumour had it that the Romanians, at a fee, furnished these documents in which correct data on cargoes from Sidi Kerir were coupled with incorrect information on the ships which had purportedly brought the oil to the Red Sea. The authenticity of the Mediterranean 'leg' of such documents was thus watertight. When for instance a document submitted to Iran showed that the *Agip Marche* and the *Hansa Visby* had between them shipped 255,400 tons of Iranian crude to Romania in August 1988, all the available data appeared to corroborate this information. Only much later, information obtained from within South Africa led to the exposure of the only weak link in the authentic though deceitful document. The oil could not have originated from the *World Champion*: on 19–23 August 1988, this vessel (posing as 'RB1') discharged her cargo of 257,058 tons of Iranian oil in Durban by order of Marc Rich.

Marc Rich: Fuel for Apartheid

Marc never once reflected on the moral implications of a deal. Doing business with corrupt societies was exactly the same as doing business with anyone else. I don't know if that's right or wrong. What I am sure of is that it's business.[1]

As far back as the mid-1970s, the oil-trading company of Marc Rich was already selling cargoes of crude oil to South Africa, in violation of embargoes imposed by the countries of origin. Referring to a shipment of Nigerian crude oil in 1978, a trader employed by Marc Rich was quoted by the author of a book on Rich as saying: 'We told the Nigerians that their oil had been going to Spain, and one day they followed our ship twenty-five miles out of port and saw it hang a left instead of a right. A lot of the Nigerian oil had been sold to South Africa at a huge profit to us, and when the Nigerians found out they cancelled the contract. It cost us a million chocolates to get the contract back.'[2]

Marc Rich 'has a soft spot for commodity-dependent countries in trouble, whether it be in the form of internationally-imposed sanctions or domestic mismanagement,' the South African magazine *The Executive* said of him in its September 1991 issue. In 1979 South Africa – scrambling for oil as a result of the Iranian embargo – and Marc Rich were natural business partners. Rich was able to deliver high-priced spot cargoes, and South Africa's first known term contract for oil was the one it signed with Rich on 12 April 1979, whereby the latter committed himself to supplying oil for at least one year.

Unveiling Marc Rich

Already in its first main report, the Shipping Research Bureau included the name of Marc Rich, albeit in connection with a tanker for which there was insufficient evidence to substantiate the claim that she had delivered oil during her call at South Africa. Whereas in the ensuing years, the slightest indication that Marc Rich was involved set off the alarms at the Bureau, here he remained relegated to the small print.

But did the name, Marc Rich, not ring a bell? In retrospect, it is rather easy to suggest that the SRB should well have known – or at least have remembered – that the name had come up in connection with oil supplies to South Africa. However, during its first year, the Shipping Research Bureau literally lived up to its name: the study of which oil companies were involved in the transport (except for some of the oil majors) was not yet high on the agenda.

When in April 1984 the portrait of *'the mysterious Mr Rich who made a killing from SA deals'* appeared out of the blue in the South African press, this proved to the oil embargo watchers overseas that they had been on the right track for some time. The hints and indications that Rich was involved, the tips on probable shipments and finally hard evidence regarding a number of cargoes had been mounting over the years.

In its third main report, which the SRB published in June 1984, a few weeks before the South African Advocate-General was to present his report on oil deals with Marc Rich and others, the latter featured prominently under the heading 'main companies involved since 1979', partly as a result of the reports in the South African press. To a certain extent this was a novelty in SRB terms, since a mere three ships identified as having delivered oil in 1979–80 in themselves hardly warranted the promotion of Rich to the league of 'main companies'.[3]

In addition to the three identified Rich vessels, one tanker which had *not* called at South Africa was nonetheless named in the 1984 report as connected with Rich. Three days after loading crude oil in the Netherlands Antilles in July 1979, the *Aegean Captain* collided with another supertanker, resulting in the deaths of 36 seafarers, the loss of the two ships, and one of the biggest oil spills in history. Soon afterwards there were rumours in the oil industry that the vessel had not been en route 'to Singapore' at all; a few days after the accident, Martin Bailey wrote an article about it: *Was mystery tanker bound for South Africa?*[4] The speculations were about the destination of the oil cargo; the company which had authorised the shipment was not discussed at the time. It was only in 1982[5] that Bailey was able to reveal whose oil had disappeared beneath the waves. In August 1981 he had managed to gain access to the loading papers of the *Aegean Captain* which showed that most of the cargo was owned by Marc Rich and Company. 'This was the first time I saw actual evidence of the involvement of Rich in supplies of oil to South Africa,' says Bailey. But he was left with yet another puzzle: who was *Minoil Inc.* referred to in the documents as the owner of the rest of the cargo?

Bailey used to share his puzzles with the Shipping Research Bureau as well as with his former colleague and co-author, Bernard Rivers, who worked as a consultant to the Bureau. The Bureau and Rivers contributed their research capacity, while Bailey's journalistic approach provided many tips and leads. With regard to the latter, a convenient mechanism could be discerned, in that publication tended to draw new leads; thus, Bailey was able to capitalise on his reputation as the journalist who exposed the shady oil trade with South Africa. In later years, the SRB would increasingly benefit from the same mechanism.

Thus, the Shipping Research Bureau was informed of the suspected link between Marc Rich and Minoil which Bailey had discovered – as usual 'in confidence', without the source being named and with the usual request for 'any further details'. Additional evidence was delivered when an insider, prompted by a number of articles in which Bailey had discussed the Bureau's first main report, provided him with a fascinating list of names and details pertaining to companies most deeply involved in supplying South Africa. The pieces were falling into place.

The information provided by Bailey's source confirmed the suspicions which Bailey and Rivers had harboured regarding Rich since March 1979, when a small article appeared in the *Journal of Commerce* in which the reporter stated that Rich had chartered the tanker *Moscliff* for a voyage from Saudi Arabia to South Africa. Rich denied the report, and according to Lloyd's, the ship had sailed to the Red Sea, to the pipeline carrying oil to the Mediterranean – case closed. But a few months later, another journalist told Bailey of the

rumour that Rich had transhipped Iranian oil from the Mediterranean to South Africa...
When the Shipping Research Bureau was formed in April 1980, coached by Bailey and
Rivers, the former summarised his findings in a number of lengthy memoranda. In his
very first memorandum, dated 30 April 1980, the Dutch researcher was able to read,
amidst a host of other details, leads and suspicions from many years of research: '*13. I
think that Marc Rich may well be involved in spot sales to SA*'.

As fate would have it, information of this nature often ended up hidden in one of the
Bureau's research files. The importance of a detailed filing system which kept track of all
these various hints and leads, as well as possible connections, only dawned upon the SRB
staff later. But thanks to the *Aegean Captain* and the new information received in 1981,
Marc Rich emerged from his dusty hiding place in the Bureau's files. Bailey got to hear
more about Rich's deals, the SRB checked shipping movements, and in mid-1983 the
Bureau obtained information from its own sources enabling it to at last link two VLCC
shipments from Rotterdam in 1979 to Marc Rich. More than four years had passed since
the implementation of the Iranian embargo. No other significant oil trader involved in
supplying South Africa had been as successful in hiding his involvement.

In September 1983 – months before Rich made headlines in South Africa – Bailey
suggested an innovative approach: the SRB might consider *a special report* on Marc Rich.
The reason was that by then, the latter had made headlines in connection with quite another matter.

Fraudulent mastermind

Marc Rich, who started his career with the US commodity-trading group Phillip Brothers
(Phibro), founded his own company in New York in 1973 after a dispute about his annual
bonus. His company, with its headquarters in Zug, Switzerland, grew into prominence in
oil, metals and ore trading.

From 1981 onwards, Marc Rich became the subject of large-scale investigations by the
US authorities into 'the largest tax evasion scheme ever prosecuted' (US District Attorney
Rudolph Giuliani) and other charges including 'racketeering, fraud, ... and trading with
the enemy'.[6] The enemy referred to was Iran at the time of the American hostage crisis. On
7 April 1980 President Carter had announced a trade embargo against Iran. In the case of
the United States of America v. Marc Rich, his companies and co-defendants, the indictment from September 1983 stated that Rich had violated the embargo by entering into
contracts with the National Iranian Oil Company in order to purchase Iranian crude oil
and fuel oil. 'To further the scheme, in or about July 1980, the defendants and their co-
racketeers devised a secret code for interoffice cable communications when referring to
the illegal Iranian transactions, in order to disguise the participation of NIOC.' But the
prosecutor was able to decode documents packed in two steamer trunks which US federal
agents had seized minutes before a Swiss jetliner took off on a flight to Switzerland. The
indictment included, amongst others, a list of tankers which had been deployed for Iranian
oil transports during the embargo as well as data relating to money transfers.

The precise details listed in the indictment (in which South Africa was not mentioned)
did not appear in the press, and it was not until the early 1990s that the Shipping Research
Bureau was to have access to the document. Yet a few references to South Africa were

being made in the media in connection with the Marc Rich case. Marc Rich and his partner, Pincus Green, had fled the USA seeking refuge in the headquarters of their company; the Swiss authorities treated the case in the time-honoured Swiss tradition. Invoking regulations which prohibited the disclosure of 'business secrets' to a foreign government, they forbade Rich to surrender documents to the USA for the trial. The public prosecutor of Zug used the following arguments in support of the Swiss position in the Rich case:

> The defendant ... trades ... in and with countries which are from a political aspect extremely sensitive ... In addition, the trade goods, in particular crude oil and its products, ... are of high political significance. It is not difficult to understand under these circumstances that especially governments or state-operated trading companies prefer to use intermediary trade (such as, for instance, through the petitioner) for trading with other countries. The reasons for this are many: especially the wish to keep the purchase and sales strategies for certain trade goods secret, [or] to cover up contradictions between economic and political actions ... A disclosure of such transactions and their details would have considerable and very disadvantageous consequences for all participants.[7]

A number of press reports hinted at the identities of these participants. On 17–18 September 1983, the *International Herald Tribune*, quoting Swiss press reports, said: 'The documents sought by U.S. authorities would reveal Marc Rich's role as go-between in crude-oil shipments from Soviet bloc nations to South Africa.' On 1 October 1983, *Arab Oil & Gas* asserted that 'Mr. Marc Rich is notorious for the key role he played in channelling Russian and African oil to South Africa.'[8]

While the charges against Marc Rich's company were settled at a huge cost when it pleaded guilty on a number of counts in October 1984, those against Marc Rich personally were not withdrawn. The settlement served to lift the restrictions on Marc Rich's US operations. But Marc Rich has not been able to legally set foot on US soil since, nor in any other country where tax evasion is an extraditable offence. To this very day, his Spanish passport provides him with a safe haven in Spain and in his 'gilded cage' in Switzerland.

In South Africa, meanwhile, there was something brewing. The ANC in exile sometimes obtained information from within the country. A note in the SRB's files, dated 1 October 1983, clearly shows that Frene Ginwala of the London office (the note is in her handwriting) was aware at that time that South African oil contracts – apparently quite often – contained the name Minoil Inc. She was even able to provide addresses and telephone numbers in Switzerland but that was all ('Probably S.A. cover,' she assumed).

The name Minoil was not mentioned when the matter erupted in the South African parliament during the debate on oil deals in 1984, whereas Marc Rich featured prominently. On 4 May 1984, Progressive Federal Party spokesman on Mineral and Energy Affairs Brian Goodall threw foreign press reports on Rich into the fray. He gave an exposé of the sins of the American-Swiss-Spanish fugitive oil dealer, including all violations of US controls on oil prices, trading with the enemy, and tax evasion ('It seems a matter of principle for oil traders not to pay tax,' Goodall said). The aim of quoting all of this from *Fortune* magazine, Goodall told his fellow MPs, was that 'an obsession with secrecy can become counterproductive because it can create the environment in which those who want to operate illegally ... can do so.'[9]

Did any *details* emerge relating to the deals between Rich and South Africa? The small part of the Advocate-General's report which was cleared for publication told nothing whatsoever. The classified section of the report which was leaked at a later stage indicated that during the first year of the contract signed in April 1979 between Marc Rich and the Strategic Fuel Fund, 17 consignments of crude oil were delivered, and the name under which Rich operated was none other than *Minoil*. The suspected connection was thus confirmed. However, even the classified section of the report did not include the names of the vessels involved and other relevant data.

It was only years later that the Shipping Reseach Bureau was able to fill in the gaps on the basis of classified documents which had come into its possession and which had supplied the basis of the Advocate-General's investigation. Yet even the definitive list which appears in this book does not include the 17 cargoes. One explanation is fairly simple. The document listing shipments under the Minoil contract was *censored*: a number of columns, including the one with the names of the vessels, were blanked out. The types of oil are still legible: Saudi and Iranian oil and a few cargoes from Ecuador; the SRB has, however, not located any oil tankers from Ecuador during this period. But a second factor explains why the Middle East oil cargoes also do not appear in the Bureau's list. Article 4.1 of his contract with the SFF empowered Marc Rich to squeeze extra payments from his client for oil delivered via a *detour* – a 'costly, yet realistic method under the present circumstances,' according to Sasol manager Wiggett in a telex to the Department of Industry in which he requested the go-ahead for the signing of the contract with 'Company X'.

> 4.1 The SELLER shall ship the applicable crude oils from origin to a South African port of BUYER's nomination (hereafter referred to as destination). If, in the opinion of the SELLER, shipping of such crude oil directly from origin to destination shall be risky or impractical the SELLER shall inform the BUYER and if the BUYER agrees the crude oil shall be shipped from origin to an agreed terminal where it shall be transshipped or stored and then shipped to destination. The costs of freight, terminal throughput and losses not covered by insurance shall be for the BUYER's account. The BUYER shall have the right to demand proof of all such extra costs.

Identifying an oil delivery: A time-consuming effort

This, after all, seemed to be a cut-and-dried case. In 1992, almost 13 years after the event, the Shipping Research Bureau obtained a copy of an invoice dated 4 June 1979, which showed that the South Africans had bought a cargo of Saudi crude which had been taken on board the tanker 'M.H.' on or around 11 May 1979. Before the copy reached the Bureau, it had gathered dust in an unspecified place, after having somehow escaped from the official South African file where it belonged.

'M.H.', a poor attempt at camouflage: good enough in the early days. During May 1979, a vessel aptly named *Violando* was chartered to carry the first embargo-violating shipment of Saudi crude under the same brand new term contract; the corresponding invoice listed the tanker as 'V.I.'. The 'M.H.', which had collected 1.8 million barrels of Saudi Arabian crude at Ras Tanura, was the tanker *Mobil Hawk*. When preparing its first

```
S.F.F.Association
P O Box 11437
BRAAMFONTEIN
2017


INVOICE NO. 57922                              4th June 1979


Re:   ONE/ONE, ONE/TWO, ONE/FOUR CRUDE OIL PER TANKER "M.H."
      B/L ORIGINAL LOADPORT 11TH MAY 1979
      ─────────────────────────────────────────────────────

Loaded Details :  ONE/ONE :  594'326    bbls
                  (API 33.4°) 79'621.85 L.T.
                  ONE/TWO :  602'791    bbls
                  (API 31.2°) 81'846.96 L.T.       auc 744,64
                  ONE/FOUR   604'772    bbls
                  (API 27.8°) 83'875.83 L.T.

For Crude :

ONE/ONE
594'326 bbls at US$ 33.00/bbl                 US$  19'612'756.00
ONE/TWO
602'791 bbls at US$ 33.00/bbl                 US$  19'892'103.00
ONE/FOUR
604'772 bbls at US$ 32.50/bbl                 US$  19'655'090.00
120 1229                                      US$  59'159'951.00
For Freight
245'344.64 L.T. at US$ 15.86 at WS 48         US$   1'567'759.67
          TOTAL INVOICE AMOUNT                US$  61'027'710.67

Delivery  :  Terminalling throughput cost plus onward freight charges
             to be invoiced separately.
Payment   :  By TT within 30 days from B/L date (i.e. for value 8th June 7
             in immediately available funds (FEDERAL FUNDS in USA) into
             Acc. of Liquin Resources Corp., with United Overseas Bank,
             11 Quai des Bergues, Geneva, Att. Mr.J.Nussbaumer, via their
             correspondents Bank of America, New York, with tested telex
             confirmation of remittance two business days prior to pay-
             ment due date directly from your Bankers to our Bankers.


                                   LIQUIN RESOURCES CORP.

                                     SCHERLY
```

report, the Shipping Research Bureau had indeed come across this vessel, which had made a reported call at a South African port on 30 May 1979 after sailing from Saudi Arabia on 12 May. It had established that a company named Marc Rich had chartered the vessel for a voyage from the Persian Gulf to either Europe or the Far East. What raised the suspicions of the researchers was the fact that the tanker had instead sailed to South Africa and then on to the Caribbean. On the one hand, the possibility that the oil had been discharged during the ship's lengthy stay in the Netherlands Antilles could not be ruled out; it takes days, not hours, to unload a tanker with the capacity of the *Mobil Hawk*. On the other hand, the reports on tankers discharging oil at South African ports had become rather imperfect at the time – who knows what the Mobil Hawk had done during the 18 days prior to its reported stay of less than one day in Table Bay? There had been ample time for a secret stop at the oil buoy off Durban.

At the time, however, nobody except those directly involved in the transaction knew of any invoices or any term contract. The call of the *Mobil Hawk* at a South African port was not included in the Shipping Research Bureau's report, but it was filed along with many others under the heading 'identified call – delivery not confirmed'.

1992 – The Shipping Research Bureau matched the invoice which had just surfaced with another leaked document, the most sensitive document to have come into its possession from South Africa. The full meaning of the document (reproduced on page 82) had eluded the researchers when it was given to them in 1985. It appeared fairly straightforward: Arabian oil carried by the *Mobil Hawk* (delivery 'X2' in the document) had reached South Africa. The identified call most certainly involved the unloading of an oil cargo. Liquin Resources Corp., the company name listed on the invoice, was one of Marc Rich's companies, a fact known from the Advocate-General's report as well as Copetas' book on Rich.[10] Could a number of shipments ('X1' to 'X6') now be included in the category 'identified call – delivery confirmed'? The *Mobil Hawk* most certainly could: the vessel's Bill of Lading deceptively listed 'Singapore' as destination instead of South Africa – an all too familiar ploy. But after a careful study of the movements of the *Energy Determination* and *Ryuko Maru* some doubts persisted; these vessels listed their official destination as being Curaçao, and indeed, according to Lloyd's, they had sailed there. What had they done on passing the Cape? How was it possible that their cargoes appeared in South African documents? The final blow for the assumption that these tankers might have discharged their oil in South Africa seemed to be that Marc Rich had *openly chartered* four of the six vessels concerned – in later years the clearest indication that a tanker was not meant to go to South Africa.

Various hypotheses were developed in order to explain the apparent anomaly. Had the buyer (SFF) sold part of the oil on to the Caribbean, possibly after having the ships unload part cargoes in South Africa? This would explain the characteristic voyage pattern but was hardly what one expected at a time of acute shortage. Had Lloyd's been given false reports regarding calls at the Netherlands Antilles (as in later years when Lloyd's was often 'misused' in order to disguise trips to South Africa)? Was there a fixed routine by which ships secretly delivered Middle East oil to South Africa, sailed in ballast to the Caribbean where a second cargo was taken on board, which was then delivered during another unlisted call at a South African port? The companies involved in violations of the oil embargo were surely capable of deploying such inventive schemes. One last hypothesis seemed too farfetched. Was it possible that in an attempt to cover up oil deliveries from the Persian Gulf to South Africa, ships were sailing *directly* to the Caribbean instead of stopping at Durban or Cape Town, after which the oil was taken back to South Africa, either by the same vessels or by other tankers? This did not seem a suitable explanation, especially in view of the fact that around the same time other ships – e.g. 'X7' and 'X8' from the same list – were able to sail directly to South Africa from the Persian Gulf without having made the detour.

Whatever the outcome of these considerations regarding the other ships, the SRB was loath to just let the *Mobil Hawk* off the hook on the grounds that various possible explanations could account for her movements, while the weight of the documentation seemed to argue in favour of the conclusion that she *had* delivered oil.

Shipping and oil companies could not be expected to show much interest when confronted with events dating back 15 years, but the Shipping Research Bureau persevered in submitting cases of suspected deliveries to the companies prior to publishing its findings.[11] In two lengthy letters which President Gerhard Kurz of the Mobil Shipping and Transportation Company sent to the Bureau in 1994, he stated that the sole reason for the *Mobil*

Hawk to have stopped off Cape Town in May 1979 was that a Japanese engineer aboard the vessel had been injured and had to be evacuated by helicopter. Kurz wrote he was 'disturbed' that the SRB continued 'to erroneously conclude that the Mobil Hawk was involved in a violation of the South African oil embargo in May 1979.' He was keen to clear the company name, and Mobil spent 'extremely time consuming' efforts to prove once and for all, on the basis of the vessel's surviving official Engineer's Log Book, that the *Mobil Hawk* was 'of no relevance to your proposed publication'.

Such a categorical, and clearly substantiated, refutation forced the Bureau to bury any hopes of upgrading the status of the case to that of 'identified delivery'. But could Kurz be helpful in unravelling the mystery of the pretty convincing evidence that the oil had been purchased by South Africa? Although the SRB was shrewd enough not to mention this in the ensuing correspondence for the time being, honesty demands that it be admitted that Kurz's first emphatic denial had prompted the Bureau to once again carefully scrutinise the *Mobil Hawk* invoice as well as the contract between South Africa and Marc Rich/ Minoil, especially Article 4.1 – and its conclusion was that the hypothesis which until then had seemed the most far-fetched was yet the correct one! The previously overlooked lines in the invoice, *'Terminalling costs and onward freight charges to be invoiced separately'*, indicated that the oil shipments had indeed made the costly detour via a transhipment terminal in the Caribbean.

Article 4.1 of the Minoil contract suggests that it was inevitable that the seller (Marc Rich) make use of the terminal detour; in the aforementioned telex of SFF/Sasol to the government, Wiggett wrote that this procedure was needed 'for security reasons'. The buyer (South Africa) had to foot the bill; this certainly reflected its position as a pariah plagued by embargoes. But the example demonstrates an interesting aspect of the *mechanism* whereby such extra costs are imposed on the victim of an embargo. The fact that, in the two weeks preceding the start of the term contract, the tankers *Nicos I. Vardinoyannis* and *Maasrix* were able to load oil for Marc Rich at the same Saudi terminal and sail directly to South Africa casts serious doubt on the 'inevitability' of the rounda-bout way. Did Rich let the *Maasrix* sail directly to South Africa four days prior to the *Violando* just because the contract regarding the former did not entitle him to an addi-tional revenue from a Caribbean masquerade? Some might find it a discomforting thought that the pain resulting from embargo measures is thus inflicted not by noble souls acting in the cause of humanity but rather by greedy profiteers.

Is it cynical to say that were it not for the greed, or call it the business acumen, of Marc Rich, the ill-fated *Aegean Captain* would not have been at that spot off Tobago in July 1979 and 36 sailors would not have lost their lives in a collision between two tankers, one bound for South Africa?

The SRB's No. 1 embargo buster

In the definitive list of oil deliveries, there are numerous tankers which delivered oil di-rectly to South Africa by orders of Marc Rich during 1979–93. Rich heads the rankings. Of the 865 identified deliveries by tankers in excess of 50,000 tons, 149 have been linked to Marc Rich. Of the total tonnage uncovered, 15 per cent (approx. 26.2 million tons of oil) can be attributed to Marc Rich. However, additional deliveries are most likely hidden

under the names of front companies – more about this later. The number 2, John Deuss'
Transworld Oil, follows with 108 shipments and an estimated 13 per cent.

Why then did the title of one of the Bureau's publications in 1985 not refer to Rich but
instead to Deuss as 'South Africa's main oil supplier'? According to the SRB's estimate,
Deuss had provided South Africa with more than 25 per cent of its oil needs between 1979
and 1983. Rich had his 17 'Minoil' shipments, but for Deuss the Advocate-General mentioned a figure of 69 'Lucina' deliveries; many of these were not identified by the Shipping Research Bureau, yet they served to boost his percentage. It is quite likely that Rich's
ranking is due to the fact that he overtook Deuss at a later stage,[12] although it is also clear
that the Advocate-General did not do justice to Rich's role.[13]

It was not always an easy task for the SRB to explain the relativity of its percentages
and rankings. Often the world press would write: 'The SRB says Rich supplied South
Africa with 8 per cent of its oil needs.' This usually amounted to an incorrect interpreta-
tion of either of two statements: that the Bureau had been able to link Rich to 8 per cent of
the total *import tonnage identified* during a certain period, or that the identified deliveries
by Rich covered 8 per cent of South Africa's *estimated average import needs*. Neither of
the two meant that Rich supplied 8 per cent of South Africa's *oil imports* nor, for that
matter, that supplies from Rich covered 8 per cent of the country's *fuel consumption*.
Imports accounted for only part of South Africa's fuel consumption; in any given year,
imports would deviate from the average, which was a 'guesstimate' anyway; often the
actual amount of oil carried by a tanker was a calculated guess, and it goes without saying
that the SRB never managed to identify each and every incoming tanker.

What can be stated though is that the secretive Mr Rich was more skilful in covering
his tracks than John Deuss. With regard to the latter, the SRB was perhaps helped by the
proximity of Amsterdam to his Dutch headquarters; most definitely, however, the fact that
the two traders differed in their methods played a part. It was fairly easy to link a series of
deliveries by certain tankers to John Deuss once the Bureau had established that he had
taken them on time charter or, in the case of one tanker which maintained a 'shuttle service' to South Africa, that Transworld was the owner. Marc Rich apparently gave prefer-
ence to concluding single-voyage charters, and he must have been relatively successful in
ensuring a high level of confidentiality.

The list of SRB findings in this book testifies to the role of Marc Rich as a loyal oil
supplier to apartheid South Africa even more forcefully than did the Bureau's former
reports. Since the last update which the SRB published of its findings, the score for Marc
Rich has more than doubled.

For many years, Marc Rich was the enigmatic trader whom many knew to be the big
fish in the South African oil trade, but one who was able to escape the net. A previous
sudden increase in the number of shipments ascribed to Marc Rich was prompted by the
unravelling of a scheme whereby Brunei oil was channelled to South Africa through Rich.
When the Bureau published its findings on Rich in 1988, his Brunei shipments (i.e. those
which had been identified thus far) accounted for more than half of all the shipments
ascribed to him since 1979. For the first time, Rich topped the list in a main report. In the
years that followed, the Bureau felt increasingly sure of its ground, and it began to experiment with formulations which in a traditional sense were not always supported by its own
findings ('Marc Rich is responsible for only five of the shipments identified, but most

Transworld Oil/John Deuss

On 13 October 1987, an oil-trading company which the Shipping Research Bureau had ranked as 'South Africa's main supplier of crude oil' made a surprising public announcement. *Transworld Oil* (TWO), owned by *John Deuss*, issued a statement to the effect that 'the company and its affiliates are no longer engaged in the supply of oil to South Africa. The company's decision to withdraw from the business is based upon an assessment of the economic, social and political environment.' It added that oil shipments to South Africa had accounted historically for only a 'minor portion' of Transworld Oil's total revenues.[1] Whether the last claim was justified or not, the fact of the matter is that far more than a 'minor portion' of South Africa's crude oil imports was shipped to the country by companies associated with TWO since 1979.

The Shipping Research Bureau and other observers were puzzled, to say the least. What on earth would have made John Deuss issue such a statement? Were some oil-producing countries becoming increasingly embarrassed, as was suggested in an SRB report? What about the rumour that Oman had put pressure on its large client?[2] Much less likely was the possibility that Mana Oteiba, the oil minister of the UAE, who had been photographed with his friend, Deuss, during a reception on the occasion of the purchase by TWO of a refinery and service stations in the USA in 1985, had raised the alarm – the UAE had become the largest source of oil for South Africa by then. Possible reasons were sought in the new legislation of the United States; the considerable investments made by Deuss urged him to pay due attention to the US anti-apartheid laws. In an interview with the Bermuda *Royal Gazette*, Deuss himself referred to the Commonwealth sanctions policy. He told the newspaper that the cut-off was the result of a review started in August 1986 because of growing international opposition to Transworld Oil's South Africa ties and limited sanctions imposed by Commonwealth nations (Bermuda, where Transworld Oil Ltd was domiciled, was a British dependency). However, 'We are not caving to external pressure,' Deuss said.[3]

In April 1982 a Netherlands-based South African journalist planned to write an article on Deuss, who had made headlines in South Africa, not because of any connection with oil but because he had bought South African golfing idol, Gary Player's, luxury mansion in Honeydew, north-west of Johannesburg. The reporter had a great deal of additional information regarding this 'Chiavelli No. 2': about his background as a bankrupt car salesman, the fortunes he made by dealing in Soviet oil and not paying for it, and – had his paper been allowed to print anything on that subject – about his role in oil deals with South Africa. The journalist was briefed by the director of the SRB, who gave him copies of articles and reports. The next day he called the SRB: 'My newspaper was phoned by BOSS this morning, and asked what they were going to print about Deuss!' He had told his newspaper that he was working on Deuss only the day before. During his call to South Africa, the line was disconnected at least six times, he told the SRB's researcher. At one point it was even disconnected after another voice on the line said 'sorry'. The researcher was quick to conclude that Transworld Oil was hot stuff...

Two years later, his conclusion was confirmed by the Advocate-General's report, which stated that no less than 69 cargoes had been delivered from 'Z country' by Deuss' front 'Lucina' between January 1981 and March 1983. In its special survey on TWO, the SRB added its own findings and concluded that Deuss had supplied South Africa with about *one quarter* of its import needs in the period 1979–83. A calculation on the basis of the Bureau's 'final' list of findings only, leaving the Advocate-General's figure outside of account notwithstanding the fact that the list contains a 'mere' 53 shipments between January 1981 and March 1983, yields an even higher percentage of almost 30 for that period. This still underestimates the role of Deuss in those years. South African documents obtained by the SRB after it had finalised the list of shipments for this book show that Deuss supplied South Africa with 8 million tons per year or *57 per cent* of the country's imports by 1981.

In January 1985, a group calling itself 'Pyromaniacs Against Apartheid' firebombed Deuss' Dutch villa in Berg en Dal because of his oil deals with South Africa. The villa, which is located near TWO's Computer Centre, was badly damaged. The picture shows a peaceful demonstration held outside the building on 13 March 1985.

In its sparse correspondence with the SRB, the company always denied any involvement in secret oil deliveries in defiance of an embargo against South Africa. In most cases, however, the company did not respond when requested to comment on the Bureau's findings.

In October 1985, when interviewed on the occasion of his refinery deal, John Deuss for the first time publicly admitted that one of his companies supplied oil to South Africa; he pointed out, however, that this trade did not create problems in doing business with oil-producing countries.[4] Since then, he made brief statements on the odd occasion when prodded by journalists. 'I disagree with apartheid. At the same time, I maintain that a refusal to supply oil to South Africa is counterproductive to correcting the sociopolitical problems of that country,' Deuss told *Business Week*.[5] 'Sanctions don't work, as Rhodesia showed,' he said in an interview with Martin Bailey. 'Oil is essential, and I don't see anything wrong in selling to the South Africans'; asked about official embargoes by countries like Saudi Arabia and Oman, Deuss replied: 'I don't regard the oil I send as embargoed oil. If you have questions about their oil, ask them about it ... I don't do anything illegal. We do not falsify documents.'[6] Bailey interviewed Deuss on the occasion of the latter's appearance as a speaker at an oil conference in London; the SRB, assisted by anti-apartheid groups in England and Norway, had drawn the attention of journalists to the event.[7] The BBC made the only known television interview with the 'mystery man', when they blocked his path on his way out of the conference room. 'We do not break any laws in any of the countries in which we operate. Using false documents, that I call illegal. But covering up a ship's name? Well, I'm not so sure... I mean, if you have a boat in your backyard and you cover up its name, is that illegal?' BBC: So, it has happened? 'I'm not saying that, I'm asking you a question. See, this is the problem of talking to the press. You're making your own interpretations of what I'm saying...'[8]

1   Press statement TWO, Hamilton, Bermuda, and London, 13 October 1987.
2   True enough, of the 91 shipments from Oman which the SRB has identified, only 10 were delivered to South Africa after mid-1987.

3 *Royal Gazette*, Bermuda, 14 October 1987; UPI.
4 *Daily News*, New York, 14 October 1985; *Algemeen Dagblad*, Netherlands, 2 October 1985.
5 *Business Week*, 30 June 1986.
6 Deuss here referred to the case of falsified French customs documents (reproduced on page 125). M. Bailey, 'Top oilman fuels apartheid', *The Observer*, 26 October 1986. Deuss did not deny reports that his tankers had hidden their names when they entered Durban, Bailey added. See also, e.g., *Dagbladet*, Norway, 25 October 1986; *International Herald Tribune*, 1 December 1986.
7 Official delegations were also informed about the antecedents of the key-note speaker. Norwegian government representatives and civil servants were said to have received a semi-official request 'to be otherwise engaged'; none of them attended Deuss' speech (*Aftenposten*, 25 October 1986).
8 BBC recording at International Herald Tribune/The Oil Daily conference 'Oil & Money in the Eighties – The Third Era', London, 24 October 1986. The BBC never broadcast the interview; the tape was used in a Dutch TV programme despite attempts by Deuss to prevent this (VPRO TV, 'Gouden Bergen', 10 September 1989).

likely for a far greater number of shipments now hidden under the heading "oil company unknown" or under the names of other companies').

Rich's score was boosted in the SRB's final list to a large extent due to the fact that during the last years of its existence, the Bureau gained access to important confidential sources. An organisation such as the SRB first has to establish its reputation over a lengthy period before such information starts to flow in; and processing the information once it has been obtained (e.g. unravelling the identities of front men) is a laborious task. In the list, the name of Rich is unevenly spread over the years. Three main sources covered relatively limited time-spans, which led to a clustering of the findings in three periods: the document on page 82 concerns deliveries around 1980; between March 1981 and September 1984, 35 shipments by Rich from Brunei were identified but only one shipment of Middle Eastern oil; the documents obtained by the chairman of the SRB in a bar in South Africa only covered the period until 1989. In the ensuing years, the Bureau was only able to identify a handful of Rich shipments.

Yet the Bureau still maintains that Rich is most likely linked to a far greater number of shipments for which no oil company could be found, or which are hidden under the names of other oil companies...

What lurks behind the façade

The SFF concluded its April 1979 contract with *Minoil* (Switzerland); invoices were issued by *Liquin* (Panama). The Bill of Lading for the Minoil cargo on board the *Aegean Captain* had been signed by *Intel Inc.* and *Narvell Capital Holdings Inc.* Marc Rich used a whole series of, sometimes short-lived, companies in various countries in order to hide his involvement in oil deliveries to South Africa from the outside world. In the case of the tanker *Dagli*, the Bureau initially only had information that the British company *Hollywell Shipping Ltd* was involved; part of the communication between the captain and the shore was relayed through Hollywell. When the SRB discovered that negotiations for the purchase of the Soviet oil on board the *Dagli* had been undertaken by the Madrid office of Marc Rich, this served to confirm growing suspicions that a whole group of companies centered around the British firms *East Coast Group Ltd (Eastco)* and Hollywell were working closely with Rich in oil supplies to South Africa. From a document connected

> When the *Dagli* sailed from Odessa in the Black Sea on 21 September 1988, the oil aboard the tanker was supposedly destined for Italy. As a matter of standard procedure, delivery or resale to South Africa was explicitly excluded in the contract.
>
> However, the Greek company purchasing the Soviet oil had sold it on to a Swiss company called *Manpétrole*, which in turn had resold it to a British firm called *Falcrest Commodities*. The British firm resold the oil to another Swiss-registered company, *Baltic Chartering*. Only after the ship had left port, the authorities in the Soviet Union were asked permission for the oil to be redirected to the USA. In fact, the whole masquerade had been set up by the real buyer, *Marc Rich*, who made use of a company which soon after ceased operating (Manpétrole) and to which therefore no official questions could be asked, and another company belonging to his empire (Baltic Chartering) of which no traces are left at all.

with the ill-fated voyage of the *Aegean Captain*, which was clearly not intended for the SRB researchers to set their eyes on, the latter had learned of Eastco's claim that 'Narvell Capital Holdings ... appointed us to act in all matters concerning transportation of their cargoes.' During the 1980s more tips on embargo-breaking deliveries reached the Bureau which pointed in the direction of the Eastco 'conglomerate', some even linking it to Marc Rich. Thus, the Bureau could write in the small print in its publications that 'according to sources within the oil and shipping industry,' Eastco was the company which always acted on behalf of *Rainbow Line Ltd* (Hong Kong) – another Marc Rich front, involved in deliveries such as those by the *Brali* and the *Probo Gull*.

By the time the *Dagli* story broke in 1989, Eastco had stopped responding to the letters and telexes of the SRB.[14] At that time, the Bureau was moving towards the next step: to linking *all* shipments to Marc Rich, not only those for which independent evidence showed that the latter had been involved alongside Eastco *et al*. The 1990 report made the step in a rather cautious manner;[15] further investigations provided the Bureau with more information to verify the link. In similar vein, the Bureau would have liked to ascribe all the shipments to Rich when there was a sudden surge of refined petroleum shipments to South Africa from Amsterdam. In this case it didn't dare to go beyond writing that Marc Rich reportedly had a standing contract with one or two storage companies in Amsterdam for the blending of petrol from various sources – the 'translation' of unverifiable tips, the gist of which was that *all* the blending done in Amsterdam was on Rich's orders.

Disentangling company links – or simply finding out where a company is based – is not always easy. Sometimes the SRB could only solve the problem after months of speculation, when it initially only had a name to go by, such as in the case of the *Intercontinental Transportation Corp.*, a company to which several shipments were linked in previous SRB reports. Once it had been established that the company was registered in the Cayman Islands and not Liberia as previously thought, there was nothing in the Certificate of Incorporation to indicate who the owner was.[16] In the list in this book, the name cannot be found any longer: the company fronted for Marc Rich. In some cases, a careful investigation into the personal and other connections between nominally independent firms can provide one with sufficient clues as to who controls whom. However, some 'oil companies' of which the researcher feels in his bones that they were owned by or in cahoots with Rich, but for which the decisive evidence was lacking to substantiate the connection, are still listed in this book. *Latourag SA* and *Montfort Trading SA* are two such companies to which the SRB has attributed a number of shipments during 1981–82. Both were located c/o the same address in Switzerland, and when one examines the list of directors and administrators, all signs point in the direction of links with Rich. One such spider in the web of companies involved in the oil trade was a Dr Erich Gayler; the Swiss Register of Companies linked his name to more than one hundred companies, including Marc Rich & Co. AG, Marc Rich & Co. International AG and Marc Rich & Co. FE AG, all located in Zug, as well as Euravia AG and Beets Trading AG (both also Zug). *Euravia* has been identified as having been involved in a number of oil shipments, also linked to Marc Rich. This begs the question of whether it can be safely assumed that in *all* cases involving Euravia, the company was in fact acting as a front for Marc Rich. Needless to say, Euravia never replied to the SRB's requests for information. The suspected link between Rich and *Beets Trading*, the Anton Reidel company, poses an intriguing new question regarding the *Salem* affair.

A distinction should be made between cases in which the name of a company does not betray the identity of its owner, others in which a company uses another, independent company as a front, and finally, normal trade between independent companies in which case one cannot speak of 'fronts'. Someone with Marc Rich's reputation could have several reasons for choosing to deal through an intermediary when dealing with an oil-exporting country. South African sanctions monitors had to suppress their natural inclination to regard everything as an attempt to conceal embargo-busting shipments from the public eye; various commercial and tax reasons also played a role in certain secretive schemes.

In each case where the SRB established that a cargo had reached South Africa via a chain of companies and that other companies alongside Rich had been involved, it was faced with the dilemma of whose names were to be linked to the cargo in its reports. In this book, the names of Mark Wolman, Euravia, African Middle East and Derby Resources[17] appear in combinations with Rich, whereas in cases in which the latter was the second or third buyer of consignments of oil from companies such as Marubeni, Neste or BP, the names of these companies have been left out.

A favourite argument used by companies in order to exonerate themselves or to substantiate their claim that they were unable to ascertain the real destinations of their oil was

---

In 1989 rumours that a company named *Alandis (London) Ltd* was the main shipper of oil to South Africa reached the Shipping Research Bureau. Only much later, hard evidence surfaced which showed that the rumours had been rather close to the truth. A long list of shipments – as many as *43* in the short period from March 1988 until October 1989, plus a few in the previous years – could be linked to Alandis, and there was no reason to believe that the company had ceased its activities.

Yet the nature of the company's involvement remained unclear. Alandis seemed to act *on behalf of* traders rather than as an oil-trading company in its own right. In response to a letter, one of the directors of Alandis called the SRB. His name sounded familiar to the researcher, who had come across it in tips and during subsequent investigations into the connections between various firms. Conversations with executives of sanctions-busting companies were rare. Yet there was a familiar ring to the voice which said: 'I think it would be nice if we met, OK? What if I ask you if you would very kindly consider coming to London – I'll entice you with a show or something, you stay one night... Are you married? But you should know that we have *never ever* been cargo owners...'

that cargoes are traded, sometimes through a chain of companies, and even when a tanker is already on the high seas; far too often, this was an eyewash.[18] However, in every specific case the question remained as to the role of the original owner. Shouldn't Neste Oy have been named as the original consignee of the oil on board the *Manhattan Viscount*? The question was whether Neste – which had sold the oil to Derby, which in turn had sold it to Intercontinental Transportation Corp. – was aware of or could be held reponsible for the fact that it had been dealing with a company which in this case was clearly acting as a front for Marc Rich. And secondly, whether Neste, if it had recognised its ultimate client, could have known that Rich intended to sell the oil to South Africa, which was only one of Rich's many clients. The SRB was simply not adequately equipped to ascertain to what extent all the parties in each case had knowingly and wilfully participated in violations of the embargo.[19] Things were different in the case of companies which the Bureau knew had repeatedly been involved in such deals (irrespective of their relationship to Rich); their names were published together with that of Rich, if only to raise the question of whether these companies had also worked for Rich on other occasions. *African Middle East Petroleum* (AMP) always categorically denied any involvement of its company in supplies of Egyptian oil to South Africa. Couldn't this be an example of a company which quite rightly claimed not to have delivered oil to South Africa – because *their client* had...? When asked whether it had resold the oil, AMP was unwilling to provide an answer. The first Egyptian shipment to become known in which *Marc Rich* was also involved came as a godsend – eventually three cases were identified, in two of which AMP was found to be the first buyer. Indeed, the SRB had eventually all but reached the stage whereby it ascribed *all* Egyptian deliveries to Rich.[20]

Tackling Marc Rich

During the embargo years, Marc Rich's involvement with South Africa was not limited to that of oil supplier. Rich was also mentioned as one of those involved in marketing oil from the South African strategic stockpile to Europe in late 1990;[21] he most likely continued to be a channel for sales from the stockpile in subsequent years.[22] When his former employer, Phibro, stopped trading with South Africa in 1985 under pressure from the anti-

What follows is a copy of a telex, presumably from early 1988, about a row between Marc Rich ('MR') and Mark Wolman related to South African deals. The *Lucerna*, a product tanker mentioned in the telex, delivered petrol from Greece to South Africa in January/February 1988. In a letter from London bearing the letterhead Tiger Petroleum (Netherlands Antilles) to the SRB dated 9 March 1990, Wolman wrote that 'this company used to trade on occasions with Marc Rich & Co. until it was involved in a dispute involving shipping with them in 1987. Because of their alleged involvement with business in South Africa, our name has been tangled with theirs and consequently speculation has led to a belief that we are some type of "co-conspirator". THIS IS UNTRUE! We further confirm to you *irrevocably* [underlined by M.W.] that we have no dealings with them whatsoever and are definitely NOT INVOLVED DIRECTLY OR INDIRECTLY in supplies of petroleum or any other commodity to South Africa' – perhaps Wolman was indeed no longer involved by the time he wrote this? See also *Private Eye* (UK), 17 February 1989 ('Sanction-busting: Rich pickings').

"'WORLD BERMUDA!! - COMMOIL

I SAW WOLMAN TODAY REGARDING THE JOHANNESBURG ATTACHMENT IN
RESPONSE TO HIS OFFER ON FRIDAY AFTERNOON TO DEMONSTRATE THAT WE
ARE NOT ENTITLED TO MAINTAIN IT. I WAS GIVEN A SELECTIVE VIEW OF
A FILE WHICH WAS OBVIOUSLY HIS PERSONAL FILE ON THE TRANSACTION.
CHRONOLOGICALLY, THIS STARTS WITH THE CONTRACT BETWEEN COMMERCIAL
OIL AND REFINING AND GAZELLE DATED 20TH DECEMBER. THERE IS THEN A
CONTRACT BETWEEN TIGER PETROLEUM CORPORATION N.V. AS SELLER AND
COMMERCIAL OIL AND REFINING DATED 22ND DECEMBER, AND THE MR -
COMMOIL CONTRACT OF 29TH DECEMBER.

WOLMAN CONCEDED THAT HE NOW CONTROLS COMMOIL, TIGER, AND
COMMERCIAL OIL AND REFINING, BUT INSISTS THAT ALL COIR CONTRACTS
ARE OFF SHORE, WITH NO CONTRACTUAL OR OPERATIONAL TELEXES TO OR
FROM LONDON. CONTRACTUAL TELEXES ORIGINATE FROM THE NETHERLANDS
ANTILLES OFFICE WHICH IS PERMANENTLY MANNED, AND OPERATIONS ARE
DEALT WITH BY HIS RESIDENT AGENT IN RAND INTERNATIONAL'S OFFICE.
HE SAYS THAT COIR IS USED FOR SOUTH AFRICAN DEALS TO PROTECT THE
MORE SUBSTANTIAL COMPANIES, IN PARTICULAR, TIGER PETROLEUM AND
THAT COMMOIL IS A RELATIVELY INSUBSTANTIAL COMPANY USED, FOR
HISTORICAL REASONS ONLY, FOR ORIENTE DEALS AND FOR MARC RICH
JOINT VENTURES. OTHER COMPANIES SUCH AS CLARK OIL HAVE REFUSED TO
DEAL WITH COMMOIL BUT WILL CONTRACT WITH TIGER. HE SAID THAT ''WE''
(THE WORD HE USED THROUGHOUT FOR HIS GROUP OPERATIONS) THEREFORE
NORMALLY BUY, FOR EXAMPLE ORIENTE, IN THE NAME OF COMMOIL AND
SELL AS TIGER, WHICH WOULD HAVE BEEN SELLER OF THE ''LUCERNA''
CARGO BUT FOR THE SOUTH AFRICAN CONNECTION. TIGER WAS USED TO
FUND THE PURCHASE FROM MR BECAUSE IT HAD A CREDIT LINE WHICH
COMMOIL DID NOT. PARIBAS REGARDED THE FINANCE AS A LOAN TO TIGER,
AND TOOK AN ASSIGNMENT FROM TIGER (AND COIR) OF THE RECEIVABLES.
NOTICE OF THE ASSIGNMENT WAS GIVEN BY PARIBAS TO GAZELLE ON 8TH
FEBRUARY AND TIGER AND COIR CONFIRMED THE ASSIGNMENT BY TELEX TO
PARIBAS ON 19TH FEBRUARY. THESE TELEXES WERE CLEARLY DRAFTED BY
PARIBAS LAWYERS. HE WENT ON TO SAY THAT AFTER FUNDS ARE RECEIVED
FROM GAZELLE INTO COIR'S ACCOUNT, PARIBAS WILL CREDIT TIGER'S
ACCOUNT.

WITH REGARD TO THE APPARENT ABSENCE OF ANY CONTRACTUAL LINK
BETWEEN COMMOIL AND TIGER, HE SAID THAT COMMOIL ASSIGNED ALL
RIGHTS AND OBLIGATIONS TO TIGER, BUT THAT HE DID NOT HAVE A COPY
OF ANY WRITTEN ASSIGNMENT. IN GENERAL, THIS HOUSE OF CARDS SEEMED
FAIRLY CAREFULLY CONSTRUCTED, AND ANYWAY IT IS SAFE TO ASSUME
THAT IF THIS ASSIGNMENT DOES NOT YET EXIST, IT WILL BE PRODUCED
WHENEVER NECESSARY

HE DECLINED TO LET ME HAVE COPIES OF ALL THE RELEVANT
CONTRACTS/ASSIGNMENTS ETC., BUT DID SUPPLY SOME COIR/GAZELLE
ITEMS, THE MOST SIGNIFICANT OF WHICH WE HAVE ALREADY SEEN. HE
SAID THAT IF WE WANTED COPIES OF THE DOCUMENTS I WAS SHOWN, HE
WOULD HAVE TO ASK HIS SOUTH AFRICAN LAWYERS.

IT SEEMS TO ME THAT THIS INFORMATION CONFIRMS AT LEAST SOME OF
OUR SUSPICIONS, AND DOES NOT ENABLE US TO TAKE AN INSTANT
DECISION TO LIFT THE ATTACHMENT AS HE HAS ASKED. THERE ARE
SEVERAL WAYS IN WHICH THIS ARRANGEMENT COULD BE CONSTRUED, FOR
EXAMPLE THAT TIGER PETROLEUM, NOT COMMOIL OR COIR, IS THE PARTY
WITH THE SUBSTANTIVE INTEREST IN THE TRANSACTION, OR THAT IF THE
COIR CORPORATE VEIL IS TO BE LIFTED, IT WOULD NOT BE COMMOIL BUT
WOLMAN HIMSELF WHO WOULD BE EXPOSED. I SHALL HAVE TO DISCUSS WITH
OUR JOHANNESBURG LAWYERS HOW THE COURT THERE IS LIKELY TO
APPROACH THIS PROBLEM, BUT IN ANY EVENT I THINK WE SHOULD ASK
WOLMAN FOR COPIES OF AT LEAST THE DOCUMENTS I WAS SHOWN TODAY. I
HAVE TELEXED HIM ACCORDINGLY.

I ALSO RAISED THE QUESTION OF THE PAYMENT OF THE FIRST INSTALMENT
DUE TOMORROW. AT FIRST, HE SAID THAT IF THE ATTACHMENT WERE
LIFTED, TIGER'S LIQUIDITY WOULD BE RESTORED AND IT WOULD BE
POSSIBLE TO PAY THIS INSTALMENT WITHIN A COUPLE OF DAYS. I ASKED
WHETHER PARIBAS OR SOMEOTHER THIRD PARTY COULD CONFIRM THIS. HE
THEN WENT INTO A NERVOUS RIGMAROLE ABOUT HIS FINANCIAL POSITION
BUT THE CONCLUSION WAS THAT THERE CAN BE NO GUARANTEE OF PAYMENT
EVEN IF THE ATTACHMENT IS LIFTED.

I SHALL CONTACT YOU AGAIN AS SOON AS I KNOW WHETHER WOLMAN WILL
SUPPLY THE DOCUMENTS REFERRED TO, AND I HAVE HEARD FROM DENEYS
REITZ.

apartheid movement in the USA, Rich stepped in, replacing Phibro as the exclusive sales agent for a giant South African lead mine.[23] Reports in the South African press in December 1990 had it that Rich was building a stake in De Beers, the diamond company within the Anglo/De Beers group.[24] A year later there were reports that Marc Rich was supplying alumina to and 'from time to time' buying aluminium from the South African Alusaf concern. In the late 1980s Rich was also involved in some new developments in the South African mining industry, providing financial support for a ferrochrome smelter and a vanadium pentoxide plant.[25]

But most significantly, by the end of the 1980s Rich had reputedly become the largest trader in South African *coal*, selling the commodity to various countries, including Chile, the People's Republic of China, Hong Kong, Portugal, Romania, Spain and Turkey. Rich's coal division also supplied coking coal from Australia and New Zealand *to* South Africa in 1991. After the lifting of the French and Danish import restrictions in March 1992, Marc Rich was soon contracted to supply South African coal.[26]

Like most traders, Marc Rich shunned publicity and avoided having to respond to allegations that he was a sanctions buster. He never replied to letters from the Shipping Research Bureau.

On the rare occasions that he consented to an interview, some journalists had the nerve to ask Rich whether the allegations were true but were so awestruck by the fact that the great man had agreed to see them that they did not even notice that he gave no reply. Rich refused to meet with journalists of *Forbes* magazine, on the grounds that they had 'consistently written hurtfully' in the past about the fugitive tax evader and sharp dealer; 'He didn't intend that as a compliment, but we take it as one,' the magazine commented.[27] When questioned by a Swiss journalist soon after the appearance of yet another SRB report, a spokesperson for the company said the company did not wish to deny or to confirm 'these assertions': 'Marc Rich has been involved in the crude oil business for seventeen years now and we cannot give any clarification. Also we do not wish any business publicity.'[28] Only on one occasion did Marc Rich himself make a statement. In an interview with the *Financial Times*, he dismissed charges that his group was breaking international embargoes: 'Our policy is that we obey laws, and we comply with embargoes wherever they are. At the same time, I am a believer in free trade, and I believe that people who are affected by embargoes always find ways around them.'[29]

There are firms whose business it is to provide companies with appraisals of yet other companies; their clients might for instance wish to know whether an intended trading partner has a reputation for paying on time. In the case of Marc Rich, a trading partner could fear that Rich's tarnished image as a white-collar criminal in the US might reflect badly on his reputation. Some time during the second half of the 1980s, the Shipping Research Bureau received such a report on Rich from an anonymous source with all fax numbers and other identification marks removed. The authors of the report, who had spoken to many traders in different parts of the world, gave their impression of the general opinion on Marc Rich. The company itself was inaccessible; the report described it as an utterly secretive company which never revealed any details of its business voluntarily. It reputedly had made profits of $200-400m a year since the mid-1970s and was worth billions, from deals both shady and legitimate. According to the report, the company was still regarded as financially undoubted and very liquid, and was treated as a top-class company and performer. A living legend both feared and admired, Marc Rich, despite scandals, had kept market confidence and was considered to retain great worth. Some areas of activity had been affected by the American tax scandal, but in most cases, the report said, customers and sellers seemed to shrug their shoulders and hinted that Rich did nothing many others hadn't done – only more of it. Rich had always paid its often huge bills on time and used reputable banks, and no problems were expected in substantial dealings with the group.[30]

Some remained unfavourably disposed to such dealings though. As a result of the legal proceedings against Marc Rich, the Pentagon debarred Marc Rich & Co. AG (located in Zug) and three of its subsidiaries in early 1985 from doing further business with the US government for three years, and in 1989 Richco Grain was disqualified as an 'unfit' recipient of further subsidies from Washington for grain sales to the Soviet Union.[31] Time and again, Marc Rich was the subject of controversy when commodity deals were discussed, also outside the USA. In 1989, a storm blew up in *Jamaica* regarding a government alumina contract with Rich. The new Manley government was severely criticised for not breaking its ties with the notorious oil sanctions breaker. In 1992, when the government of independent *Namibia* signed an agreement with a Dubai-based consortium called International Development Corporation (IDC) with a view to developing an aluminium smelter in Namibia, eyebrows were raised when it became known that Rich was a prominent partner in the consortium. Later in 1992, during the mandatory UN embargo on *Iraq*, there was a hue and cry at the United Nations when it was proposed that Rich, the major sanctions buster of the other UN embargo, be placed on a list which contained the names of candidates for trading Iraqi oil that was due to be sold in order to pay for war reparations.[32] During that year Rich was in the news when telexes and telefaxes dating from 1991 and originating from his Madrid office were leaked. The documents indicated that Rich had offered to purchase Iraqi oil.[33] When the names of the companies which had successfully applied for term contracts with *Nigeria* in 1994 became known, *Africa Confidential* wrote that commentators were amazed to find that large quantities had been awarded to companies linked to Marc Rich 'who has consistently broken the United Nations' oil sanctions against South Africa over the past 15 years.' Later in 1994 the magazine wrote that the 'near-monopoly position of Rich's *Glencore* company in the allocation of short-term contracts to lift Nigerian crude' had caused concern within the oil industry. A Glencore official in London was quoted as saying: 'We have got 80 per cent of Nigeria, now we are going for the rest.' The article noticed 'growing resentment' by Nigerians 'and questions why Rich, best known for his breaking of oil sanctions against apartheid South Africa, should be handed the Nigerian market.'[34]

Rich's cultural and social sponsoring activities were often viewed in the light of his supposed interest 'in cleaning up his tarnished image', as was speculated when Rich donated *The Marc Rich Collection* of photographs to the Zurich Kunsthaus (Switzerland). When his company contributed 100 million Swiss Francs to the building of the International Red Cross Museum, the beneficiaries were asked if they did not have scruples in accepting a donation from a man supplying oil to South Africa, a country refusing the International Red Cross permission to visit most of its political detainees?[35]

Was Rich's name tainted? In too many cases it was not. If his embargo violations had not yet been drawn into the debate or if the press did not refer to the matter, then anti-apartheid campaigners – or whoever stood to gain by throwing the book at Rich – ensured that this aspect of his business ethics was highlighted. The London-based oil embargo campaigning organisation *Embargo* took the Manley government to task in letters and press briefings for claiming that it had no knowledge of Marc Rich's South African dealings. Later in 1989, the ambassador of *Algeria* in London was questioned when his country, a member of the UN oil embargo monitoring group, planned an alumina processing deal with Rich. The Shipping Research Bureau, though not a campaigning organisation, wrote a letter of concern to the Namibian Representative to the UN when the deal with IDC/Rich became known ('...Therefore, Marc Rich is also to blame directly for having enabled South Africa to continue for many years its occupation of Namibia...'). The Bureau had its own methods to ensure that all such matters remained in the public eye through the global distribution of its Newsletter.

The Swiss anti-apartheid movement was also an active campaigner. In September 1985 a demonstration was organised along the 'Zug Apartheid Track', starting at Baarerstrasse 37, the head offices of Marc Rich & Co. Jo Lang, member of the city council of Zug, Paul Rechsteiner, Swiss MP, and others tabled questions on Rich's oil embargo violations and spoke of the damage to Zug's reputation on account of the fact that the revelations by the SRB were appearing in the press worldwide. But little success was achieved with the Swiss authorities.[36] According to rumours which reached the Bureau, Switzerland had proposed that Rich's name be put on the UN list for Iraqi oil sales.

Over the years many similarities emerged in the campaign material and the arguments of all those who had a bone to pick with Marc Rich; all his sins were put on display for all the world to see. Editors were afforded a golden opportunity: *How to get Rich in aluminium*, or *How Rich got rich*, or the eternal *Rich pickings*... A global network of 'Rich watchers' developed, consisting of oil embargo monitors and campaigners, a number of journalists and television reporters, trade unionists, private investigators, law-enforcement officials and the odd disgruntled businessman. For the SRB this meant that Rich's activities and misdemeanours – even those not related to South Africa and oil – were monitored much more closely than those of other companies; an ongoing exchange of information developed between the media, other interested parties and the Bureau. Had Rich's wife started divorce proceedings? From all corners of the world people called the SRB to enquire whether it had more information and asked for its opinion on speculations that this could become an existential financial challenge for the Rich empire. More than one caller suggested the possibility that a journalist might try to elicit 'some dirt on South Africa' from Denise (safely back in the USA). The Bureau got other peculiar tips and suggestions. Did you know that Mr Du Plessis, who is responsible for South Africa's oil procurement, is currently travelling through Europe, and rumour has it that he is being *wined and dined* by Marc Rich? His superiors, who seem intent at keeping Rich at arm's length after all the scandals, are not aware of his narrow links with Rich. Why don't you send a telex to Sasol and to the SFF to inform them that you are watching Du Plessis closely during his Rich-sponsored visit? On another occasion the SRB received a tip-off that Rich was going to spend a few days in Sun City, in the South African 'homeland' of Boputhatswana; couldn't the Bureau arrange for a journalist to be present on his arrival?

Things were pushed rather far on one occasion in 1991, when a press campaign was started in *Finland* against the collaboration of the state oil company, Neste Oy, and Rich in trading oil to South Africa. In Finland, Rich was persona non grata. By the end of September 1991 word got around that the FBI had requested the Finnish police to arrest and extradite him if he should set foot on Finnish soil. On 19 or 20 September, he was expected to arrive in Finland on a private jet of the Italian firm Olivetti, as a guest of Neste. However, the Finnish police was not able to trace him. Too late, it became known that on 19 September a foreign private jet had landed in Rovaniemi, far to the north of Helsinki, possibly carrying Marc Rich. Neste denied the rumours that the company had invited Rich: 'Rich is not one of our main trading partners, we deal with him on an irregular basis only,' the press was told. Neste added that although the company knew of Rich's involvement with regard to the supply of oil to South Africa, this did not deter it from dealing with him. Later, an internal SRB memo on shipping movements was splashed in the Finnish press. The newspaper wanted to create the impression that the Bureau had substantial 'evidence' of Neste's connivance in Rich's South African trade – something the Bureau would certainly not have published without tangible proof.[37] At the same time, the Bureau was offered the wildest stories about Rich more or less usurping the Neste organisation. The stories were fantastic indeed; however, the Bureau had heard fantastic stories before.

The most-publicised fight against Marc Rich had its beginnings in the USA in October 1990, when the management of the *Ravenswood Aluminium Corp.* (RAC) in Ravenswood, West Virginia, locked out 1800 trade union members, replacing them with non-unionised workers. The ensuing action by the United Steelworkers of America (USWA) put Marc Rich back in the US public eye in a manner which was most probably more damaging than anything which had preceded it. The Rich watchers' network proved invaluable when the USWA got wind of the fact that the 'shadowy influence behind RAC' was none other than 'the billionaire fugitive from justice who had found refuge in Switzerland'. One of the travels by a private investigator, hired by the USWA to look into RAC's ownership, took him to Amsterdam, where he visited the Shipping Research Bureau. As always, the Bureau was delighted to supply interested parties with information – in return for which it hoped to be rewarded with useful tips on oil shipments and South African contracts. The Americans rounded off their investigations after subsequent visits to Zug. In mid-1991 they staged a protest in Zug's main street and marched into the ground floor of Rich's headquarters, demanding to meet with Rich – he refused. The USWA invited Jo Lang to West Virginia in order to testify before the state senate in February 1992. The trade union also prompted a congressional investigation into Rich's continuing US government contracts, led by Congressman Bob Wise. He revealed that Rich's US operation (Clarendon) had sold millions of dollars worth of copper, zinc and nickel to the US Mint; the action led Clarendon to announce that it was withdrawing from tendering for Mint business. The USWA distributed *Wanted: Marc Rich* leaflets in eight countries and in at least six languages and was able to persuade governments to reconsider contracts with Marc Rich and, most important of all, succeeded in thwarting attempts by Rich to reach an agreement with the US that would allow him to return home without having to serve a prison sentence. Rich had been unable to attend his father's funeral; it was clear that he longed to return to the USA. The *Institutional Investor* ('Smoking out Marc Rich') commented that 'nothing could suit Rich more than to gradually fade from the memories of U.S. law-enforcement officials and the public in general. And had it not been for Ravenswood, this may well have happened.'[38] The USA appeared to become more active in pressing, amongst others, former East bloc states to apprehend Marc Rich should he venture onto their territory. Furthermore, there was speculation that South Africa, too, in the dying days of apartheid, would incur the wrath of Washington if it continued to do business with Rich.[39] In the meantime the USWA scored a victory: in July 1992 the locked-out union members were reinstated. In an affidavit, former RAC chief executive Emmett Boyle declared: 'I believe that, as part of his effort to regain entry into this country, Rich ... wishes to "buy off" the United Steelworkers so that it will withdraw its strenuous opposition to such reentry and [also withdraw] pressure on his business ventures in Central Europe, Jamaica, South Africa and Eastern Europe.'[40]

Rich unwelcome in post-apartheid South Africa?

In 1993, Marc Rich announced that he would hand over the day-to-day control of his company and reduce his share in the company's capital to 27.5 per cent. The company was still considered the world's second largest commodity trader after Cargill. Its position as South Africa's main supplier of oil had become subject to erosion. In 1992, a manager of one of the London-based subsidiaries of Metalgesellschaft AG was quoted as saying: 'When there was an embargo on South Africa, Rich provided them with oil, and they paid handsomely for that. Now that the embargo is being lifted, the margins are slimmer.'[41] The meaning was clear: more suppliers had arrived on the scene.

The embargo was lifted in December 1993. There is no one left to investigate whether Marc Rich's company (under its new name Glencore, or in the guise of a front) is still involved in oil deliveries to South Africa under the new democratic government; the SRB has closed its doors. Privately though, the researchers have retained their curiosity.

Will the role of a sanctions buster such as Marc Rich be remembered in post-apartheid South Africa? One individual has a clear response to this question. Frene Ginwala, who during her years in exile was involved in unmasking Rich as a supporter of the apartheid regime, says: 'If I have my way, the answer is yes... There may have been other companies whom we would have liked to see disinvest from South Africa but instead remained in the country. But I want to distinguish these from people like Rich who were purely speculators and profiteers, who broke laws and violated sanctions, and whom I personally would very much want to see treated like criminals and pirates. But what I would like is one thing, what actually happens may be another. To a certain extent, as Speaker of the House, I am gagged. But if South Africa awards a big contract to Marc Rich, I am still able to write to the press and speak out against it.'

Shipping Companies

A matter of routine, taking place all too often during the embargo years: a tanker discharging oil at the offshore oil buoy near Durban. A simple detail of interest to embargo monitors: which shipping company is involved? This is not always an easy question to answer: a great number of companies from as many countries can be involved. Establishing the identity of the ultimate *owner* (in the jargon of the Shipping Research Bureau's reports: the 'apparent beneficial owner') of a tanker can be a headache for those policing maritime fraud, a seamen's union or an embargo researcher. It is easy enough to obtain the name and address of the 'registered owner', i.e. the company which is at least the nominal owner of a ship. The problem here is that a ship often has a registered owner whose total assets consist only of the ship in question. The company may well be owned by another company which also owns a number of other 'single-ship companies'. That company may in turn be owned by yet another company. It is often difficult to identify the company which is at the end of the chain of owners.[1] Such hidden ownership is particularly prevalent with ships flying 'flags of convenience'. Then, the 'ultimate' shipowning company does not have to concern itself with the actual *management* of the ship. Certain owners manage their own vessel(s), but in other cases other companies are contracted to act as technical and/or commercial managers. A ship can also be chartered, or subchartered, under a variety of conditions; for instance, the charterer may or may not be responsible for the crew and the maintenance of the vessel. The charterer of a tanker can be an oil company, or a shipping company which sails for oil companies. In order to simplify matters, the large table in the Annex links each delivery to a single shipping company.

A succession of players

Over the years, the identities of the shipping companies involved in oil transports to South Africa changed to a greater extent than did the identities of the oil companies. Broadly speaking, during the first years of its existence the Shipping Research Bureau identified many *Norwegian* tankers (the Bureau's very first publication was dedicated to this group). Initially, Shell and the Danish shipping company A.P. Møller rivalled the Norwegian companies.

Norwegian shipowners remained in the forefront until 1987 when their involvement in crude oil transports to South Africa was banned by law. Between January 1979 and June 1987 the Bureau identified 232 deliveries by tankers owned, chartered and/or managed by Norwegian shipowners, which together covered at least 40 per cent of South Africa's oil import needs. 'At least', because the Bureau was not able to identify each and every shipment. Not included in this estimate of the Norwegian involvement are those Norwegian shipowners who had long moved their operations abroad.[2] The names of Norwegian companies which did not own the tankers in question but acted as *managers* for foreign owners do not appear in the SRB's list; their role has been discounted in the above figure though. First and foremost was the Oslo-based company Fearnley & Eger A/S, which was responsible for the technical management of a number of Marimpex-owned tankers until this arrangement had to be terminated as a result of the introduction of Norwegian legislation.[3]

After the success attained in Norway when the transport ban was introduced in mid-1987, there was no longer any point in releasing the SRB's 1988 bi-annual report over the period 1985–87 in Oslo, even though Norwegian tankers still headed the list in the report. Attention was turned towards the *Greeks*. Greek tankers had been active during the 1970s but the impression was that they now saw a golden opportunity to fill the gap left by the Norwegian tankers. The first press conference held in Greece in September 1988 resulted in a lot of publicity, but this did not lead to any concrete measures, and the attempt was never repeated. The Greek shipping companies continued to play a major role after the Norwegians left the stage.

What the SRB did not know in 1988 was that the presentation of its report should have been held in *Hong Kong* instead of in Athens. The company which profited most as a result of the Norwegian ban was the Hong Kong-based World-Wide Shipping Group. Within a few years, this shipping company (which appeared to have been hitherto hardly involved) was already accounting for more deliveries than its largest Norwegian counterpart over the entire period 1979–87. World-Wide heads the list in this book by a wide margin: 150 deliveries as opposed to less than 50 each for the No. 1 Norwegian and Greek companies.

In this chapter, a number of shipping companies will be discussed which were particularly active. Although the Bureau always took pains to present its preliminary findings to managing companies as well as shipowners, the SRB's publications have always paid more attention to the latter. The role of companies such as Denholm,[4] Wallem and Barber, which were involved as ships' managers in a large number of shipments to South Africa, mostly remained hidden in the small print in the Bureau's reports and is not evident from the list of findings in this book.

Rather good business

During the embargo years there was a clear distinction between those companies which refrained from South African shipments, others that were heavily involved, and a number of companies which undertook the odd shipment. We refer the reader to the various publications of the Shipping Research Bureau which contain details about most shipping companies named in the list but not discussed in this chapter.

Many companies have at a certain point in time attracted the attention of the SRB researchers. In the early 1980s, these included a Dutch joint-venture which owned the *Schelderix* and the *Maasrix*. The ships were exploited by *Rijn-Schelde-Verolme* (a company which had made headlines and landed the government into trouble in 1975–76 over the intended production of a nuclear reactor for South Africa) together with the energy

Excerpts from: letter of D.F. Mostert of SFF/Sasol to the Director General, Ministry of Mineral and Energy Affairs, 15 May 1981 ('VERTROULIK EN PERSOONLIK' – Private and Confidential). In an attempt to reduce the SFF's dependence on the existing term contracts with John Deuss, Mostert visited New York (Marc Rich) and Hamburg (Marimpex) in early May, and he informed the ministry on the offers made to him. One of the issues discussed was shipping:

```
4.1  Aangesien die vervoer van olie na die RSA een van die
     mees kritieke faktore van die hele proses van
     olievoorsiening aan die RSA is, is heelwat tyd
     hieraan spandeer.

     Weens die onwilligheid van baie skeepseienaars om die
     risiko van 'n assosiasie met Suid-Afrika te loop,
     asook die volgehoue pogings van verskillende
     drukgroepe om enige olieverskeping na Suid-Afrika
     bloot te stel, is dit nodig dat aandag gegee word aan
     verskillende aspekte, soos diversifisering, sekuriteit
     en kontinuïteit, terwyl die ekonomie van verskeping
     nie buite rekening gelaat kan word nie.
```

Marimpex had suggested a cooperation with the German shipping company Essberger. Mostert saw two problems in Essberger's offer:

```
4.2.1     Hulle beplan om van slegs twee skepe
          gebruik te maak waarvan die name van tyd
          tot tyd verander sal word en wat by
          alternatiewe hawens in die Midde-Ooste sal
          laai. Ons gevoel is dat hierdie metode te
          maklik 'n patroon kan skep wat deur die
          anti-Suid-Afrikaanse groepe raakgesien en
          blootgelê kan word en 'n groter mate van
          diversiteit van skepe is dus nodig.
```

The second point raised by Mostert was that the costs of transport could be considerably reduced if the SFF would use its own ships. However:

```
4.4  Die vraag ontstaan onmiddellik: Wat word van
     sekuriteit as SFF sy eie identifiseerbare skepe sou
     finansier? Die oplossing lê egter daarin dat SFF dit
     nie in isolasie doen nie, maar in vennootskap met
     Marimpex en/of Marc Rich en in samewerking met 'n
     bestaande skeepseienaar of -eienaars waar die so
     verkrygde tonnemaat gedurig uitgeruil en verwissel
     word. In die finale instansie kan 'n skip wat so
     verkry en gefinansier is, ook op die opemark verkoop
     en 'n ander een gekoop word indien publisiteit sy
     verdere gebruik te riskant sou maak.
```

Translation: 4.1 Quite some time was spent on discussing the transport of oil to SA as this is one of the most critical factors of the entire oil procurement process. Because of the reluctance of many shipowners to risk being associated with South Africa and persistent attempts by various pressure groups to expose oil shipments to South Africa, due attention has to be given to different aspects, such as diversification, security and continuity, whilst the question of the economics of shipping also has to be taken into consideration.

4.2.1 They intend to use only two ships whose names will be changed from time to time and which will load at various ports in the Middle East. We feel that this method can easily create a pattern that can be detected and exposed by the anti-South African groups; therefore, a greater diversity of ships is necessary.

4.4 This immediately poses the question of what will happen to the security if SFF were to finance its own identifiable ships. The solution is that SFF should not do this on its own, but jointly with Marimpex and/or Marc Rich and in cooperation with an existing shipowner or shipowners who will repeatedly replace and exchange the tonnage thus obtained. Eventually, a vessel thus obtained and financed can also be sold on the open market and another purchased if her continued use would enhance the risk due to the ensuing publicity.

and trading multinational *SHV* (also involved in South African coal and in the Makro supermarket chain which later withdrew from South Africa after violent actions by the Dutch 'Revolutionary Anti-Racist Action' group). Other shipping companies attracting early attention from the SRB, the Norwegian press and the Norwegian anti-apartheid movement included the Norwegian companies *Hansen-Tangen*, *Helmer Staubo* and *Havtor*. In 1984 Mr Tore Staubo confirmed allegations by the SRB that his company's vessel *Staland* had made eight deliveries in 1981–82, although 'the number of calls is incorrect'.[5] This was the typical response given by companies who wished to hide the fact that the real number of calls was higher. The *Staland*, with its 18 recorded voyages between August 1979 and January 1983 is third in the SRB list of 'shuttle tankers'. The Havtor-owned *Havdrott* is in seventh position with 14 identified shipments (January 1979–March 1981; all commissioned by TWO). Shipowner Hans Hansen-Tangen told a radio reporter that 'We sail to wherever the law entitles us to ... I find it unreasonable to expect a private businessman to involve himself in foreign policy.'[6] Shipments involving his tankers *Regina* and *Adna* also caused commotion in the Swedish press and parliament: at some stage the Swedish state had ownership interests in the vessels.[7]

Other Norwegian shipowners were also in the spotlight. One of them was *John Fredriksen* (18 deliveries; see Box). The involvement of another shipowner was hardly as great, but attracted attention due to his public stature. In March 1986 a newspaper revealed that the tanker *Janniche*, owned by Mr Trygve Hegnar, was en route to South Africa. Hegnar confirmed the report ('I reckon this shipment is rather good business'), adding that there was nothing he could do since it was the charterer who had decided upon the ship's destination, but he would certainly reconsider whether it would happen again.[8] Years later, the Shipping Research Bureau was able to ascertain that it *had* happened again, three months after the previous transport.[9] Shipowner and businessman Terje Mikalsen – reportedly the wealthiest man in Norway at the time – also became implicated when a delivery by the *Mospoint*, owned by *Mosvolds Rederi* in Farsund, of which he was the managing director, was divulged by a Norwegian newspaper, which gave a detailed description of how a false destination, 'Singapore', had been used in order to hide the transport. Mikalsen said his company regretted the 'accident': 'It is the first drop of oil we have transported to South Africa during my term in this company. The decision was taken abroad, without [my] knowledge.' A week after the delivery was made public, the company decided to withdraw its three ships from the 'Shipping list' in the Norwegian shipping press, because of the fact that the list had been used to expose a false destination...[10] A Mosvold vessel, the *South Breeze*, was the first Norwegian tanker to discharge a cargo of oil in Durban after the lifting of the Norwegian ban on transports in March 1993.

A 'Norwegian-born Cypriot shipowner'

John Fredriksen was so controversial that his fellow Norwegian shipowners preferred to refer to him as a 'Norwegian-born Cypriot shipowner' after he had transferred part of his operations to Limassol. In 1986, Fredriksen and employees of his Oslo company Marine Management were for some time jailed in Norway, suspected of major insurance fraud. The story of the *Cougar*, which sailed the Persian Gulf 'for Singapore' in November 1983, offers a colourful example of the practices her owner was accused of.

On the way to South Africa, about 1,200 tons of the oil cargo were pumped into the *Cougar*'s bunkers by means of a 'Greek Bend' – a specially devised pipe linking several tanks – and used as fuel for her propulsion, and then 1,000 tons were hidden away in a separate tank. Seawater was pumped into the cargo tanks to 'compensate' for the loss of cargo. When the ship arrived in Durban on 12 December, the South African cargo inspector soon sensed that something was wrong. Insisting that the contents of the ship's bunkers be checked, he found the level of one tank in order, but forgot to measure the other one in which the 1,000 tons had been stored. One of the ship's officers willingly offered to take a sample of the bunker fuel, which the too well-dressed inspector could not do himself. Instead of a sample (of fuel mixed with crude oil) from the bunkers, however, the inspector was handed an old sample of real bunker fuel. When, during the discharging, it dawned on him that he had forgotten one tank, he was persuaded to postpone the measuring until the next morning after the completion of the discharge operation. That night, the inspector and others from ashore were treated to a huge drinking bout aboard the ship. The poor man, not able to get out of his bed early enough to put his plans into effect, saw the ship ready for sailing by the time he awoke.

The Norwegian shipping company *Leif Höegh & Co. A/S*, which between 1980 and 1984 had been involved in crude oil shipments from Rotterdam and Brunei, came to the fore in the last years preceding the lifting of the embargo as one of several companies which exploited a loophole in the Norwegian legislation forbidding crude oil but not product transports. Product transports were not, traditionally speaking, the Bureau's primary field of investigation, but they became a matter of interest when relatively large vessels were used for them.[11] An explanation for the surge in refined product shipments since mid-1989 was sought in fires which had plagued the Sasol oil-from-coal plants; however, at a later stage, the SRB expressed its doubts as to whether South Africa's need for imported petrol and other oil products was a temporary one indeed.

Among the rather mysterious companies was *Palm Shipping*. It chartered tankers on a fairly large scale, and initially, it was not even clear whether it was in fact an oil company or a shipping company. Rumour was rife; the *Albahaa B.*, which disappeared below the waves after discharging a cargo of oil in South Africa just two months after the *Salem* incident, was a Palm vessel. Four years after the last of the Palm shipments which the Bureau uncovered in the period 1980–83, two more followed by an OBO owned by an affiliated company, *Teekay Shipping*. For quite some time, a somewhat obscure source kept feeding the SRB with information pertaining to Palm charters, without the investigation of these tips ever bearing fruit; inevitably, the suspicion of 'disinformation' reared its head. The exact nature of the relationship between the Danish-born owner of Teekay and the company owned by the Danish arms embargo buster Anders Jensen[12] remained a matter of speculation with few firm conclusions.

4 NEWS

Bank that backed Third World countries helped bust sanctions, writes **Nick Fielding**

BCCI broke S Africa oil embargo

STEVE MORGAN

THE BANK of Credit and Commerce International, which before its closure this year had built its reputation on standing up for the countries of the Third World, was closely involved in transporting oil to South Africa in the face of an embargo by the Organisation of Petroleum   Exporting Countries.

One of its principal shareholders in the late Seventies also played a big part in the "Muldergate"   scandal, the name given to an attempt by BOSS, South Africa's intelligence agency, to buy several newspapers in South Africa and other countries to promote the government's   views   on apartheid.

The sanctions breaking can be traced to November 1981, when Attock Oil, a BCCI-owned company, sold a cargo of fuel oil at Karachi, reportedly for Singapore. The oil was loaded on to the 69,000-tonne tanker Cherry Park which was then diverted to South Africa, according to the Amsterdam-based research organisation Shipping Research Bureau.

Lloyds Data, the shipping register, shows a gap in its records for the Cherry Park from 3 October in Karachi, until it showed up again in Trinco-

Friends of BCCI's founder borrowed to ship oil to S Africa. Security was a dozen rusty ships

malee in Sri Lanka on 28 February 1982.

Far more extensively involved in sanctions busting, says the bureau, were the numerous shipping companies owned by the three Gokal brothers, Abbas, Murtaza and Mustafa. The Gokals were long-standing partners and friends of BCCI founder Agha Hasan Abedi. In 1976 they tried to buy New York's Chelsea National Bank on behalf of BCCI, but were turned down.

The Bank of England's section 41 inquiry into BCCI, which led to the Arab bank's closure in July, has a chapter on the Gokal's Gulf Shipping Group which shows that the companies it controlled owed BCCI more than $750m. The security for loans they received from BCCI consisted primarily of a dozen rusting ships.

Typical of the trades involving Gulf group companies was a shipment which went from Saudi Arabia to South Africa in October 1981 on the 80,000 tonne tanker Norse Falcon, a Norwe-

gian tanker flying a Bahamas flag. According to information from the bureau, the tanker was operated by Tradinaft, a Gokal-owned company registered in Switzerland, where Abbas Gokal has a home.

The Gokal shipping empire is now in tatters. Two days before BCCI was closed down on 5 July, Gulf International Holdings SA, the main holding company based in Luxembourg, applied for "controlled management" — effectively administration.

BCCI's links with South Africa were more direct through its connection with Thesaurus Continental Securities Corpo-

ration. Thesaurus is a holding company of Union Bank of Switzerland and its board comprises senior UBS personnel.

In 1976, UBS sold the Banque de Commerce et Placements in Geneva to BCCI, retaining a 15 per cent shareholding which was held by Thesaurus. Thesaurus also became a major BCCI shareholder, according to bank documents.

Among the revelations which sprang from the Muldergate scandal of 1978 — in which South Africa's information minister Dr Connie Mulder and his assistant Dr Eschel Rhoodie were accused of using secret government funds to buy the Johannesburg-based *Citizen* newspaper — it emerged that more than R12m (£2.5m at current exchange rates) had been sent from Switzerland in late 1976 and early 1977 to a company called Thor Communicators in Pretoria to help with the purchases.

The origin of the funds was traced to Thesaurus in Zurich. At the time, UBS refused to comment on the story, but the bank was known for its contacts with South Africa.

The Erasmus Commission, set up to investigate Muldergate, also reported that in 1974 an attempt was made to buy newspapers in America. More than $10m was sent to Michigan publisher John McGoff to finance the purchases. That money too came from South Africa via Thesaurus.

The Independent on Sunday, 13 October 1991

A.P. Møller to the rescue

The honour of being the first shipping company to come to the fore as a worthy subject for a special SRB survey goes to the largest Danish shipping company, A.P. Møller. The year was 1983; there was every reason for the Bureau to consider devoting a special report to Møller. In the course of the Bureau's research on the previous period, it became clear that the company had been the single most active transporter of oil to South Africa for some time (that the involvement of Møller-operated ships had meanwhile dwindled to a large degree was not yet known). A series of 'Mærsk' tankers owned by A.P. Møller had during a short period – between October 1979 and February 1981 – supplied South Africa with at least 19 shipments of oil, meeting approximately *one fifth* of its crude oil import needs, 'thus enabling the South African government to overcome the disruption of its crude oil imports after the fall of the Shah of Iran,' as the Bureau wrote later.[13] Only when taken as a group, the Norwegians were more important; during the same period the SRB identified 27 tankers controlled by various Norwegian shipping companies. The estimated volume of oil shipped by Møller, on the basis of the Bureau's findings, amounts to 5.0 million tons.[14]

In 1980–81, before the SRB published anything on the Mærsk tankers, their involvement had been discussed in the Danish press and parliament, resulting in calls for the implementation of an oil embargo. The media continued to show an interest in the matter, for instance, when the telegrams which can be found elsewhere in this book surfaced and provided new evidence. In the debate, the fear was expressed that Møller, which also had vested interests in oil from the Danish part of the North Sea, was selling this oil to South Africa.[15] When the Danish parliament resolved on 28 May 1984 to inform oil and shipping companies 'that it is contrary to Danish commercial and foreign policy to sell or transport oil to South Africa,'[16] the shoe appeared to fit A.P. Møller in the first place.

The SRB has never been able to locate any evidence for Møller's involvement in oil sales to South Africa beyond his role as a transporter, but that it possibly went much

---

AIDE MEMOIRE OF DISCUSSION BETWEEN A P MöLLER AND SFF ON MONDAY, FEBRUARY 11, 1980 IN CONNECTION WITH CHARTER PARTY FOR DIRCH MAERSK

PRESENT   Mr H Schmidt   –   A P Moller

               Messrs H R Wiggett
                     S P Naude   –   S F F
                     J Bredenkamp
                     R Hugo

– – – –

After extensive discussions held in a very amiable atmosphere the parties reached agreement on the following points:

1   If the charter party for the Dirch Maersk were to be cancelled outright a cancellation fee of $ 3,25 million would be payable by SFF to A P Möller.

2   A P Moller is not convinced that the circumstances surrounding the cancellation of the Semafor/SFF crude oil supply agreement, entitles SFF to exercise the option to purchase the Dirch Maersk in terms of clause 19 of the charter party. [...]

3   Irrespective of whether SFF has an option to purchase the Dirch Maersk the parties agreed that notwithstanding anything contained in the charter party the demurrage payable by SFF to A P Moller in respect of the Dirch Maersk would, for the period 30 January 1980 at 15h00 to 12 April 1980 at 15h00 be calculated at an all inclusive rate of $ 22 943 per day [...].

   3.1 Should SFF find employment for the Dirch Maersk during the aforesaid period SFF shall be entitled to sub-let the ship to any third party provided that in respect of cargoes loaded at Saudi Arabian ports the bills of lading are marked to order. [...]

4   SFF indicated that they are very likely to be involved in the conclusion of a contract for the long term supply of oil in the near future. The parties agreed in principle that subject to the country of origin giving an indication that the Maersk lines/tankers will not be victimised for transporting the oil in question to South African ports, they would negotiate direct with each other with a view to concluding a contract of afreightment or other suitable contract in respect of the transportation of the said oil. [...]

               [signed H C Schmidt
               H R Wiggett]

further than the Bureau suspected at the time is suggested by a leaked internal memorandum ('aide-mémoire') emanating from the files of the South African Strategic Fuel Fund Association, parts of which have been reproduced here. A Mærsk vessel was used to ship oil from Oman to South Africa in accordance with an oil sales contract which had been signed on 12 June 1979 by the SFF and the Swiss company Semafor. The latter was represented by Helge Storch-Nielsen, a Danish national living in South Africa (he named another company after himself, 'Hestonie'). In his contribution, Scholtz describes how the contract soon turned sour. Curiously, the 'aide-mémoire' offers proof that its termination was not discussed between the SFF and Storch-Nielsen but between the former and a representative of A.P. Møller. The company apparently had a direct contractual relationship with the South Africans which he would not have had in his capacity of owner of a ship chartered for these transports by a trader. It has never become clear to what extent Møller had business ties with Storch-Nielsen, nor to what extent Møller had dealings with South Africa in the capacity of *oil* company.

Some interesting remarks in the memorandum seem to indicate that there was a certain amount of fear of retaliatory measures if the involvement of Mærsk tankers was made public, particularly in connection with Saudi Arabia. Indeed, rumours about such measures could be heard from time to time, and on more than one occasion the Saudi Arabian government declared that it would take such steps in the event of violations of the embargo clauses, but in view of the large number of tankers which continued to transport Saudi crude to South Africa, it remains unclear whether, in reality, any steps were ever taken.[17]

The SRB survey *Oil Shipments to South Africa on Maersk Tankers: The Role of A.P. Møller of Denmark* eventually appeared in print in September 1985. It was an excellent example of what cooperation between the Bureau and a seafarers' union could yield; the research had been done in cooperation with the Danish Seamen's Union. Many statements made by crew members appear in the report and give a vivid account of the various methods used to conceal South African transports. The SRB's data had already somehow been leaked to Danish television in January 1985; in an ensuing parliamentary debate Søren Riishøj, a prominent Danish member of AWEPAA, asked the government whether it had responded when it was contacted in 1983 by both the SRB and the UN. A few newspapers appeared to be irritated and said that the television station had 'rehashed' old news, although none expressed sympathy with A.P. Møller – the storm surrounding its activities was the 'price for its arrogance'.[18] The Bureau's researchers had experienced the shipowner's arrogance as well when they received a terse reply in which Møller said that 'it is not our practice to provide information on our vessel activities.'[19] The Danish churches were even less fortunate and did not get any reply at all.[20]

In 1983–84 the *Matterhorn*, formerly known as *Robert Mærsk*, made at least two trips to South Africa. Møller had sold the ship 'to foreign buyers', i.e. a company in Switzerland, and stated that it was therefore not the apparent beneficial owner. The *Matterhorn* shipments seem to have been the last attempts undertaken by Møller to circumvent Danish legislation. Even prior to the implementation in May 1986 of the law which made it a criminal offence to transport oil to South Africa, *Lloyd's List* was able to report that 'Møller "ends oil voyages to S. Africa" – Danish shipowner AP Møller has stopped carrying oil to South Africa, sources within the company said yesterday ... Increasing pressure within Denmark and from abroad appears to have persuaded Møller not to tender its ships for voyages carrying oil to South Africa.'[21]

Mosvold Shipping: Shuttle service

'Our business is shipping, not politics. To survive in a volatile market, we cannot say "no" to cargoes for South Africa,' said shipowner Karl Mosvold when interviewed after the Norwegian Council for Southern Africa (NOCOSA) had exposed the role of Mosvold Shipping Co. A/S as one of the main Norwegian transporters of oil to South Africa.[22] Since November 1981, the company had often said 'yes' when it concerned the transport of cargoes to South Africa. The No. 1 shuttle tanker identified by the SRB was the Mosvold-operated *Moscliff* (approx. 5.6 million tons of oil), which was 'flagged out' to Liberia and sailed under its new name, *Actor*, from mid-1985. The Transworld-owned tanker *Fleurtje* (formerly *Humboldt*) made 23 trips to South Africa, one more than the Mosvold vessel, but ranks second in terms of volume.

At a press conference in Oslo on 3 June 1986, held the day before the opening of the UN oil embargo seminar, NOCOSA revealed that the tanker used the code-name 'Victor' plus a number when secretly calling at Durban. It was only much later that the SRB was able to establish that the *Moscliff* had indeed called at South Africa as 'V 73' in March 1983; other code-names, such as 'L 50' in April 1984 and 'W 45' in July 1984, had been assigned to the ship on subsequent visits, though.

On the day the SRB report *South Africa's Lifeline* was released in Oslo, Mr Mosvold was quoted by one newspaper as saying that his vessels no longer travelled to South Africa: 'It is tempting to do so when one looks at the rates, but we also take the views of the authorities into account. For the company, this is regrettable.' The next day, the Norwegian press agency NTB gave a completely different version, one in which Mosvold was quoted as saying: 'We have drawn our own conclusions and we have decided we will continue'...[23]

'Bare tull!' – Thor Dahl tankers in dubious waters

Mosvold had only one tanker afloat; other Norwegian shipping companies had more, which explains why they are ranked higher on the SRB's list. With 28 identified shipments (estimated volume: 6.3 million tons) A/S Thor Dahl was Norway's No. 2 transporter of oil to South Africa during 1981–85.

On 10 December 1984, Bishop Tutu was awarded the Nobel Peace Prize in Oslo. The very next day during a parliamentary debate, the Norwegian Minister of Commerce and Shipping announced that, according to his information, no Norwegian tankers had shipped crude oil to South Africa during the third quarter of that year. A week later the minister most probably regretted ever having said this when the SRB presented the results of a special survey on the Dahl tankers *Thorsaga* and *Thorsholm* during a NOCOSA press conference. The Bureau had traced three shipments which had taken place in the third quarter, while the press added one more, by the Thor Dahl-operated Hong Kong tanker *Eirama*.[24]

'Guess who was on our plane?', the SRB's researchers were asked by their Norwegian visitors, who had come to Amsterdam for an interview on Norwegian shipping and South Africa: *'Desmond Tutu'*. The Norwegian journalist and his photographer had informed their travelling companion about the purpose of their journey to Amsterdam. Thus, on 2 April 1986 *Verdens Gang* published the SRB interview alongside the comments they had elicited from the bishop. Tutu – who in 1979 had caused a stir by publicly declaring that Denmark should boycott South African coal – made an urgent call upon Norwegian shipowners and politicians to stop oil transports to South Africa. 'Without oil and petrol, the military machinery will come to a halt and the chances for a solution without bloodshed and violence increases,' the bishop said. He was glad that Norwegian politicians wanted to stop the sale of oil to South Africa, but he said he hadn't noticed 'any effect of this attitude so far,' and in a carefully worded statement he added that he had 'the impression that Norwegian ships participated in the oil transports.'

Director Øystein Bøe said his company had 'voluntarily reduced the number of oil transports.'[25] Indeed, the relatively high number of ten deliveries in 1984 was not equalled in 1985. When the newspaper *Dagbladet* revealed a list of Norwegian vessels that had visited South Africa in 1985, Bøe said: 'It's high time you stopped writing nonsense about secret calls at South Africa. It is completely crazy ... You can get the positions of our vessels every Wednesday.' *But according to the list, the 'Thorsholm' called at Durban in March...* – 'Bare tull! Sheer nonsense, that one is so big she can't dock in the harbour.' *But did she perhaps discharge offshore?* – 'No ... the "Thorsholm" was in altogether different waters at the time.'[26] – Perhaps Mr Bøe might find it useful to know that the *Thorsholm* arrived at the oil buoy off Durban on 1 March 1985 and departed soon after midnight on 4 March having discharged her load of Saudi oil. Bøe had difficulty discerning true from false: after the publication of the SRB's main report in 1986, he said that the *Thorsaga* and the *Thorsholm* had been sold in the interim and that the company 'no longer had any trading connections with South Africa whatsoever.'[27] Despite this claim, the company's vessels *Thor I* and *Thorscape* kept calling at South African ports very frequently; both vessels were engaged in shipping Namibian uranium to Canada in violation of *Decree Number One* of the United Nations Council for Namibia.[28]

Towards the end of 1994, the director of Thor Dahl stated that 'at times it was quite burdensome to engage in lawful shipping to South Africa.' There were now possibilities, the Norwegian magazine *Skip & Sjø* was told by Bøe, 'who was himself in the country while history was being made when Mandela was elected president.'[29]

Bergesen: A Norwegian mammoth

In his contribution to this book, Øystein Gudim describes how, at a time when the oil embargo had not yet become one of the focal points of Norwegian anti-apartheid activity, NOCOSA more or less accidentally became interested when two transports were discovered involving one of the world's largest tanker owners, Sig. Bergesen d.y. & Co. Prior to mid-1987 this Norwegian company, later Bergesen d.y. A/S, rose to the top, with 44 shipments identified by the SRB, equivalent to at least 11.5 million tons of oil, or 23 per cent of all the oil transports involving Norwegian companies, and at least 9.4 per cent of South Africa's estimated crude oil imports over the $8\frac{1}{2}$-year period in question. Between them, Bergesen and Dahl – the two foremost Norwegian embargo busters, both subjects of special publications by the SRB and targeted by the Norwegian anti-apartheid movement – supplied at least 72 shipments or 17.8 million tons of oil, most of which was delivered during 1982–85.

Bergesen's director Petter Sundt 'was up in arms on the South African issue',[30] and not without reason. Just before parliament adopted the sanctions law, Sundt said: '...we are being discriminated against by parliament through the oil boycott against South Africa. Our ships account for at least half of the Norwegian-owned crude oil tanker fleet, and so the boycott affects primarily us.' Two months later, when interviewed by the same newspaper, he said: 'In reality, it is an anti-Bergesen law'; he added that management had considered moving its headquarters abroad, one of the reasons being the South African boycott.[31]

Indeed, in order to circumvent the law, the only effective means would have been to move the company headquarters. Earlier, Bergesen availed itself of a method the result of which was that the official registration of oil deliveries to South Africa no longer applied to three of its vessels – which in turn meant that the registration system failed to adequately reflect the involvement of Norwegian companies. Thus, in a quarter showing no shipments by Norwegian-owned tankers (see Table 1 in Gudim's contribution), a vessel which Bergesen had nominally sold to a foreign company but immediately chartered back ('with repurchase option') made one delivery; another made two additional deliveries between April and June 1987.[32]

In 1986–87 the number of deliveries by Bergesen tankers declined; however, during the last four months before the introduction of the Norwegian transport ban, the company seemed to thumb its nose at the authorities: six deliveries by Bergesen tankers supplied South Africa with *more than a third* of its needs for imported oil. And afterwards? Well, the damage wasn't all that significant, if we are to believe Sundt's own statements as cited by Gudim.[33]

Bergesen combined carriers continued to call at South Africa to collect cargoes of coal. The company kept hoping that the law would be repealed; in May 1991 its assistant director said: '...we are prepared to go to South Africa at ten minutes' notice on the day that the boycott is lifted.'[34] In fact, Bergesen tankers did not immediately resume their voyages to South Africa once it was no longer an offence. According to eyewitnesses, 'trial runs' were undertaken by the *Berge Fister*, which was sighted in Durban in June and again in July 1994 – but the SRB, which had by then concluded its monitoring activities, was not able to assess the accuracy of these observations.

World-Wide Shipping: The major oil transporter to South Africa

> *Oil deliveries by World-Wide tankers to South Africa are nothing secret and form part of the company's international business ... Any ship that is fixed to charter can take goods anywhere in the world. There is nothing underhand about us shipping oil to South Africa ... If the charterer sends us to South Africa, that's where we will go.*[35]

This statement, made by Mr R.J. Allen of the World-Wide Shipping Group when the massive scale of his company's involvement since 1986 was exposed in a Shipping Research Bureau survey published in April 1989, was one of the rare public statements the company made on the issue. The Bureau responded to Allen's statement by posing the all too familiar question: 'If there is "*nothing underhand*" about deliveries by World-Wide tankers to South Africa, why, one might ask, has the company always observed the *strictest secrecy*? The deliveries have always been subject to elaborate measures aimed at hiding them from being detected.'[36]

In fact, these measures had been so successful that in early 1988 – almost one and a half years after the World-Wide Shipping Group took the field by storm after it became clear that Norwegian companies would have to step aside before long – the SRB did not have a clue as to what Mr Sundt of the Bergesen Group meant when during an interview on the 'reflagging' of his tankers from Liberia to the new Norwegian NIS register, he said: 'Decidedly the greatest weakness of the Norwegian International Ship Register is the prohibition against sailing to South Africa. Today foreigners – *first and foremost Chinese* – have taken over that part of the trade in which we used to be involved.'[37] World-Wide came to the fore as a prime example of a profiteer from bans imposed by shipping nations whose companies used to be heavily involved in oil transports to South Africa.

HK shipper defends oil ban busting

By LULU YU

AN executive of Hongkong shipping magnate Sir Yue-kong Pao's World-Wide Shipping Agency last night defended sanction-busting and said the firm would continue to ship oil to South Africa.

He shrugged off claims made by a Dutch monitoring group that World-Wide had given false information on the oil's destinations to avoid embargoes against South Africa by oil producers.

"By shipping oil to South Africa, World-Wide . . . has deliberately violated the oil embargo policies of oil exporting countries from where its tankers sailed to South Africa," said the Shipping Research Bureau, a non-government body that monitors Pretoria's oil imports, in a report released in The Hague.

But Mr R. J. Allen, a senior official of the Y.K. Pao group, said oil deliveries by World-Wide tankers to South Africa were nothing secret and formed part of the company's international business.

"Any ship that is fixed to charter can take goods to anywhere in the world. There is nothing underhand about us shipping oil to South Africa.

"We have probably the biggest independent fleet of tankers in the world and if the charterer sends us to South Africa, that's where we'll go," he said.

On providing false information to the monitoring group, Mr Allen said: "We've never provided anyone with any information. How can it be incomplete or incorrect?"

Saying the World-Wide group was the world's leading

□ Sir Y. K. Pao

oil shipper to South African, the Dutch bureau said the group made at least 19 "secret deliveries" to South Africa between October 1986 and the end of 1988.

"Of the 19 voyages identified since October 1986, 17 were made from the Persian Gulf area. One country, the United Arab Emirates, accounted for the majority of these cases. Thirteen tankers sailed to South Africa after having called at the United Arab Emirates," said the Dutch report.

It added that World-Wide increased deliveries after Norwegian and Danish firms were banned by their governments from continuing shipments.

It also accused World-Wide of repeatedly ignoring its requests to comment on the deliveries.

A spokesman for the Trade Department said he had not seen the report of the Dutch monitoring group and was not aware of any other accusations against the World-Wide group regarding oil deliveries to South Africa.

The monitoring group's accusations came nearly two years after a United Nations report struck Sir Yue-kong's shipping empire off a list of Hongkong companies that continued to have trading and economic links with South Africa.

World-Wide Shipping had been named in a 1985 report of the UN Human Rights Commission, but was excluded from the Commission's 1987 report, leading to belief that the firm no longer dealt with South Africa.

Mr Allen said World-Wide had no "trading and economic" links with South Africa unless chartering operations were considered an economic link.

"Shipping is a commercial business. People are not understanding what the real world of shipping is," said Mr Allen.

"We know the destinations of our ships but we can't control them," he said.

The UN had called on 33 national governments, including Hongkong, to act against companies fostering trade links in the "racist and colonialist regime of South Africa" and for profiting from operations which "enhance and sustain the activities of the corrupt and illegal system."

In late 1986 the Hongkong Government introduced sanctions, including a ban on the import of gold coins, iron and steel, a voluntary ban on investment and loans, and a policy of discouraging tourism to South Africa.

South China Morning Post, Hong Kong, 2 April 1989

One should certainly not think of an embargo-breaking company such as World-Wide as a pack of wheeler-dealers who shun the light. World-Wide Shipping is one of the world's leading tanker operators and by far Hong Kong's largest shipowner, which operated a fleet of around 70 vessels in the early 1990s. It is part of the business empire built by a man who has been described as the largest independent shipowner in the world: Hong Kong magnate Sir Yue-kong Pao. Since *Sir Y-K* resigned in 1986, his son-in-law, Austrian-born Dr Helmut Sohmen, took over as president of the group. Sohmen, who holds directorships with a range of other shipping, insurance, banking and property companies, became one of the leading men in international shipping. Among the positions he occupied were those of legislative councillor with the Hong Kong Government, chairman of the Hong Kong Shipowners' Association, council member of Intertanko (Oslo), and president of the Baltic and International Maritime Council (BIMCO). World-Wide's tanker business was and is conducted from offices in, e.g., Hong Kong, Bermuda, London, New York, Singapore, Tokyo, and the Cayman Islands.

In 1988, perhaps without having South Africa in mind, Sohmen declared that '...actual numbers of ships mean nothing. The essential factor is that they be operating successfully and that they are in demand.'[38] The company's vessels were certainly in demand from traders with South African contracts: between April 1979 and September 1993, World-Wide vessels transported at least *150* cargoes of oil to South Africa with a total volume estimated at 35.6 million tons. All except eight of these deliveries took place after October 1986; from that date until the lifting of the embargo, World-Wide transported more than three times as much as the largest Norwegian and Greek shipowners had done over a much longer period, or 34 per cent of South Africa's estimated crude oil imports. In fact, the company transported more than all its principal competitors, viz. the Greek shipowners, during the same period. During the first six months of 1991 – when South Africa was replenishing its strategic oil stockpile which it had drawn upon during the Gulf crisis – World-Wide supplies were equivalent to no less than *60 per cent* of the country's estimated average crude imports.

In its reports, the SRB criticised the arguments used by World-Wide executives such as Mr Allen[39] in support of their claim that owners were unable to influence the decisions of charterers: there was nothing to prevent shipowners from specifying in charter-parties that ships should not be used for carrying oil to South Africa; such restrictions were indeed often included in contracts. The Scandinavian examples showed that governments were even able to prescribe such a policy. But then, the government which had sovereignty over Hong Kong, the base of World-Wide Shipping, was the United Kingdom, a country which did not favour interference with the freedom of companies to deal with South Africa.

'London-based' and other Greek shipping companies

In the list of SRB findings, the Greeks closely follow the Norwegians. Until the mid-1980s, a relatively large number of Greek shipping companies were involved; almost half delivered a single cargo, and some only a few before they quit from this part of the trade. After 1985, these transports became much more concentrated in the hands of a few Greek shipping companies, and the volume of oil delivered to South Africa by Greek companies rose sharply. This coincided with the emergence of World-Wide Shipping and the banning of their Scandinavian competitors from further activity in this field. During the $2^1/_2$-year period between 1986 and mid-1988, Greek tankers transported a larger volume of oil than in the entire preceding seven-year period, and their involvement continued unabated until the lifting of the embargo.

The *G.P. Livanos/Carras Group* was the No. 1 Greek transporter until it was overtaken by *Embiricos Shipping*, which entered the field in 1989; yet, Livanos still heads the Greek list with 49 shipments, five more than Bergesen's 44, although the former ranks slightly lower in volume. Both the *Hadjipateras Group* and *C.M. Lemos* were involved during the entire period, the latter being most active during 1986–88. The tanker *Pacificos* of the *Kulukundis Group* was involved in a 'shuttle' to South Africa in 1988–89, *Peraticos* tankers were active from 1989 onwards, and from mid-1992, a new company named *Adriatic Tankers* soon skyrocketed into second place. As the oil embargo drew to a close, a number of Greek shipping companies which had until then remained aloof from this trade cautiously (re)entered the field.[40]

'We have noticed that your correspondence is addressed to an entity referred to as the Hadjipateras Group. We have no knowledge of a company or entity so entitled,' Peninsular Maritime Ltd (Shipbrokers) of London wrote, *'As Agents Only'*, to the Shipping Research Bureau in 1988. The major Greek shipping groups conduct much of their commercial business from offices in London and are generally referred to as 'the London Greek shipping community' or 'London-based Greek shipowners' in the trade and in trade journals (which, incidentally, have no qualms about calling a shipping group a 'group'). It took many years for the SRB to develop a more journalistic approach (and its possibilities to subscribe to trade journals were always restricted by the scarcity of its funds), so initially, it ran the risk of being intimidated by letters such as the one quoted. If Polembros Shipping replied 'as Agents only', the Bureau timidly described the shipowner in question as an 'unknown company c/o Polembros Shipping Ltd'. It was only after some time that it dawned upon the Bureau that it was common knowledge in the trade that Polembros was no more than shorthand for the Polemis brothers – who were shipowners not agents.

'We have always been proud to be able to trade everywhere in the world,' Peter G. Livanos said in 1994, in his first interview after taking over from his father, *George P. Livanos*, as the head of 'the vast Ceres Hellenic Shipping empire'.[41] Ceres Hellenic is the Piraeus-based operator of the Livanos fleet, the largest in Greece. No shipowner except World-Wide could pride himself on shipping so many cargoes to South Africa during the embargo as did Livanos. The shipping weekly *TradeWinds*, in which the interview appeared, added that 'Few shipowners seem so concerned about moral issues, but for Livanos, they seem to govern policy' – but what it was referring to was the company's involvement in environmental issues, another field in which it had more than cordial relations with South Africa.[42] The reference to the *morality* of shipowners involved in embargo-breaking transactions was a recurrent theme. When interviewed about his involvement with South Africa, Petter Sundt emphasised that Bergesen was one of the shipping companies which did not send its vessels into the war zone in the Persian Gulf because it was concerned about the crew's safety: 'That is a certain kind of morality.'[43] Remarkably, Livanos Jr. ended his statement which was quoted at the beginning of this paragraph by saying:

'...to trade everywhere in the world, *even in the Persian Gulf at the time the war was going on*'...

The lifting of the embargo did not lift the spirits of the Greek shipowner Panagis Zissimatos, owner and president of *Adriatic Tankers*, who had only entered the field of embargo busting towards the end. In 1994 *TradeWinds* interviewed him as well, and wrote: 'The market has not exactly been working in favour of Adriatic ... The *Lourdas [Bay]* was reported fixed last week for a South African cargo by Strategic Fuel Fund ... This market has been important for Zissimatos, but now as more players enter it, the competition becomes tougher and the profits get more squeezed. Furthermore, trading to South Africa is becoming more challenging as traffic increases, while capacity at the terminal is somewhat limited.'[44] In March 1993 *The Natal Mercury* became the first newspaper to publish a photograph of a tanker moored to the oil buoy off Durban. There was no sign of congestion at that time; a lonely tanker, the *Assos Bay*, was discharging her cargo of oil, one of eight deliveries made by two Adriatic tankers over a 12-month period.[45]

Embargo Politics

Legislation, Monitoring, Enforcement: the basic triplet of embargo politics. It appeared in the title of one of the papers published by the Shipping Research Bureau, but was an ongoing theme in all its publications. To make the oil embargo enforceable, legislation was essential; a mere policy statement or 'gentlemen's agreement' could too easily be ignored. Monitoring was needed to ensure that oil was not delivered to embargoed destinations. And to be sure that embargo regulations and destination clauses were being strictly adhered to, they had to be enforced by putting penalties on violations.

The same basic arguments were reflected in dozens of declarations and resolutions of organisations which supported the oil embargo, and could be found in the policies of some governments – if sometimes only on paper. The ANC's Frene Ginwala says: 'In the late 1970s, early 1980s the problem with the oil embargo wasn't to get support for it in principle. You could get resolutions easily. Enforcement was the problem.' Reports of the United Nations and the Shipping Research Bureau contained many examples of statements and policies which had been adopted on national and supranational levels. Successful attempts were presented as models worth following, but each and every example was seen as significant in view of the message it contained: that the support for the embargo was rising and the opposition was losing ground.

Unfortunately, it was not simply a matter of counting heads. Among the small number of adversaries of the oil embargo were some formidable opponents. Then again, verbal support or even formal legal measures were not always translated into effective action. But on the other side of the spectrum, there were those countries which, acting on their own or in unison with others, somehow managed to make it effectively impossible for their oil to reach South Africa or to prohibit their companies from getting involved in oil transports to the apartheid state. In between, there were shades of grey; it was hard to separate the sheep from the goats when looking at particular countries or supranational organisations. The proponents of the oil embargo had their favourite 'baddies' and ditto 'goodies' – or their love-hate relationship with a particular country.

Norway: Love-hate relationship

Throughout its existence the Shipping Research Bureau had what could be called a love-hate relationship with Norway.

For years, Norway refused to follow the example of its Nordic neighbour, Sweden, which supported the SRB financially; yet, the SRB's thoroughness and sponsorability was lauded even in the Norwegian parliament. A new government overnight became the SRB's biggest sponsor. But this funding was stopped prior to the lifting of the embargo, a decision viewed as a 'wrong political signal' at the time.

One had to concede that it was not only transporters that were involved in the flow of

'We find it hard to understand why Norwegian shipowners and seafarers continue to sail to South Africa ... We don't ask much. We only ask you to stop your shipments to South Africa, and we do so because they are very important to the South African regime. This goes, first of all, for the oil transports which are of vital importance to the South African army and police forces.'

– Don't you have any sympathy for the dilemma that such unilateral Norwegian initiatives could have a negative effect on employment in Norwegian shipping?

'No, that argument does not appeal to me ... I think that Norway, being one of the richest countries in the world, should be able to solve any problems that might arise as a result of a boycott of South African shipments. Moreover, such a line of thought is based on the belief that the apartheid state is here to stay. I can assure you: Apartheid in South Africa is not eternal ... My question is: Do Norwegian shipowners believe that a new, democratic South Africa will cling to Norwegian shipping for old times' sake? Don't they realise that it is possible for Norwegian shipping to now lay the foundation for a lasting access to the market in a free South Africa?'

From: 'Norwegian shipping stands much to gain by a boycott!' Interview with Thabo Mbeki in *Medlemsblad* (magazine of the Norwegian Seamen's Union), July–August 1986, 208-9

oil from the Middle East, yet Norway repeatedly used this argument in order to trivialise its responsibility, and its government and companies kept saying that the embargo lobby should direct its activities 'towards the Arabs'; however, as opposed to many Arab states, the country eventually adopted an effective boycott law.

Often the trade union federation and some of its member unions used the same argument, stressing the need for a policy aimed at stopping *sales* of oil to South Africa and making light of the country's major role in *shipping*.[1] The same trade union federation, though, became a loyal financial supporter of the SRB.

Norway adopted a legal ban on oil transports, which contained quite a few loopholes, and therefore came under criticism from the SRB's Norwegian allies; the SRB felt it had to support the latter, while at the same time 'promoting' the law internationally as an example worth following. For instance, Norway had shown that it was possible to include ships under foreign flags in national boycott legislation. In 1993, Norway delayed the lifting of its oil export ban until the date set by the UN; but it had in the meantime lifted the

The Citizen, South Africa, 17 March 1987

truly relevant ban – that on transport – prematurely, thus raising the suspicion that it had maintained the embargo on exports merely to show that *it* was determined that its oil would not reach South Africa.

During the second half of the 1980s, Norway was the only country which imposed a penalty in connection with a violation of the oil embargo – but the captain of the *Dagli* was fined only on the grounds that the identity of the ship had been concealed.

Norway was active on the international level and set an example for others to follow. Yet it said it abstained from voting in support of the oil embargo in 1983 'because' it had joined the UN Expert Group on the embargo. Alarming reports on its attitude in international consultations on the embargo sometimes reached the outside world. The SRB certainly agreed with the Norwegian argument that objections could be raised against the UN monitoring group submitting 'raw data'[2] on South African 'port calls' by small tankers to governments. Yet the country could not expect too much compassion from the SRB: its refusal to clarify the large number of port calls by Norwegian tankers certainly did not serve the aim of the embargo. Eventually, Norway resigned from the UN Group prior to a General Assembly decision to lift the embargo.

In Norway SRB researchers were received on the highest level with all due respect, even though on one occasion an angry minister had the accompanying representative of the Norwegian anti-apartheid movement thrown out of his office. On another occasion, at a meeting with a state secretary, it became evident to the SRB that governments do not make embargo politics during cordial discussions with visiting experts...[3]

At a certain stage Norway was the home of the SRB's favourite 'enemies' among the world's shipowners. Yet, some of these shipowners could expect a certain amount of sympathy from the SRB's researchers as they could always be counted upon to respond to queries in a straightforward manner. Among these was the biggest of all, who, soon after the implementation of the legal ban, got down to writing a last letter which could even be taken as a compliment: 'Looking back on your reports since 1981, we find them rather accurate, however not entirely perfect.'[4]

Norwegian media ate out of the palm of the SRB, be it that the Bureau was not always pleased when in their enthusiasm they broke press embargoes on its reports. Norway was also home to one of the SRB's favourite anti-apartheid movements, which treated oil as a focal point and worked on the issue even when the Bureau was not peering over its shoulder; its most prominent oil activist concedes one small self-critical remark when he says that he may sometimes have failed in drawing the *entire* organisation into the actual work.

Norway was the country with the biggest embargo-breaking shipowners, but at the same time the Norwegian example shows that something could be done about it. The Norwegian shipowners appeared to abide by the letter of the law which banned further crude oil transports. When they did not comply with the *spirit* of the law, the SRB could count on yet another spate of activities in the Norwegian media and by the anti-apartheid movement. Politicians spoke out in favour of closing the loophole regarding refined product shipments. However, words were no longer put into action at that stage.

Norway has a mixed record on the international oil embargo issue. The Norwegian experience shows that an answer to the question whether the country had a purely positive or negative influence can hardly be given; perhaps it is not an interesting question at all. What can be gleaned from the Norwegian example, however, is how things work in *prac-*

tice. Rather than drawing any further conclusions from this case history, we should take a closer look at a few more examples of 'baddies' and 'goodies'.

USA: Sabotaged oil sanctions

On 29 September 1986 and 2 October 1986, the United States Senate and House of Representatives, overruling a presidential veto, adopted the *Comprehensive Anti-Apartheid Act of 1986*. Section 321(a) of this Act prohibited exports of crude oil and petroleum products to South Africa:

> No crude oil or refined petroleum product which is subject to the jurisdiction of the United States or which is exported by a person subject to the jurisdiction of the United States may be exported to South Africa.

This was a country which did not have a record as an anti-apartheid champion, yet adopted a statutory oil embargo. The US president of the day, Ronald Reagan, kept the old flag flying when he exercised his veto and later refused to act in accordance with the explicit clause which stated that, failing significant progress toward ending apartheid in South Africa, additional measures should be implemented. Reagan continued to believe 'that the current punitive sanctions against South Africa are not the best way to bring freedom to that country.'[5] In her contribution, Donna Katzin recalls the 'Wise Bill' and the 'Dellums amendment' from 1987–88 which, if adopted, would have made the Act considerably more punitive. Among other things, the amendments imposed heavy penalties on the refusal of oil companies to disinvest in South Africa, and included a transport ban on oil to complement the export ban.[6] Another tightening of the law, the 'Rangel amendment' of 1988, meant that US companies in South Africa now faced double taxation, in South Africa as well as in the USA. 'The American oil company *Mobil Oil*, the biggest US investor in South Africa, will be severely hit by this new piece of legislation,' the SRB wrote at the time.[7]

The intended tightening of the US oil embargo did not materialise, and the enforcement of the existing legislation left much to be desired. In 1990 an investigation showed that US companies were able to continue shipping petroleum-based products to South Africa. While Congressional sponsors of the law had intended a broad ban on such exports, the Commerce Department determined that the law applied to just 49 of the hundreds of variations of petroleum products.[8]

On 10 July 1991 – at a stage when the liberation movements, the UN and others were calling for the continuation of the pressure, amongst others by maintaining the oil embargo – President Bush lifted the Anti-Apartheid Act, thus making the USA the first country in the world to lift its oil embargo. Four days later, the Israeli government followed suit and cancelled its largely symbolic 1987 ban on 'the sale and transfer to South Africa of oil and its products'. On 18 December 1992, during the last vote on the oil embargo taken by the UN General Assembly, the USA was the only country which persisted in its 'no' vote, even when the United Kingdom, its erstwhile partner in the old anti-oil-embargo alliance, no longer felt the need to do so and abstained.

The fact that there were a few very active members of Congress, a number of fairly stringent (oil) sanctions measures on state and local levels, and an active and effective anti-
apartheid movement which campaigned against companies such as Caltex, Mobil, Shell
and Fluor contributes towards a more balanced picture. In all probability, if an evaluation
is made of the contribution of the Comprehensive Anti-Apartheid Act towards the dismantling of apartheid, the balance will be more favourable than if the judgement is solely
based on the US position concerning oil sanctions. But the United States of America, the
home of some of the large multinational oil refiners in South Africa, of companies heavily
involved in assisting the country in its synthetic fuel and other import substitution programmes, and of a number of shipping companies that were identified as carriers of oil in
defiance of the boycott, and the country which was most consistent in its attempts to block
the implementation of a mandatory international embargo, stands an excellent chance of
appearing high on the black list of oil sanctions saboteurs.

The UK: Britannia waives the rules

'*Oil sanctions: heat turned on the British*' was the title of an article on the Shipping Research Bureau, which had 'begun a campaign against British-based oil sanctions busters,'[9]
according to the author who wrote this in January 1992. Although Britain had remained
cool under constant reproaches that it was one of the main collaborators of apartheid, it
was not the intention of the SRB to start a 'campaign' at that stage; all it wanted to do was
show the extent of the British involvement in violations of the oil embargo. In the list which
was published in January 1992 the UK was, '*in one way or another ... linked to 113 of the
122 deliveries, thus accounting for no less than 93 per cent of the total volume identified*'.[10]
   In the final list of SRB findings, which covers a longer period, the corresponding figures are lower. The exceptionally high percentage in later years was chiefly due to the
prominent role of World-Wide, the Hong Kong-based shipping company which rose to
prominence after the withdrawal of the Norwegians. According to a conservative estimate, the United Kingdom was nonetheless involved in approximately *two thirds* of all
the shipments identified by the SRB. A number of ships transported British North Sea oil
(or Norwegian oil transhipped in the UK); British major oil companies (Shell and government-controlled BP) sent tankers to South Africa; various British and London-based
Greek shipping companies were involved as owners and/or managers of tankers, some of
which sailed under the British flag, whereas others were registered in one of Britain's
dependencies such as Gibraltar, Hong Kong and Bermuda;[11] the major transporter of oil to
South Africa was based in Hong Kong; and one of the major oil traders was Bermuda-
based Transworld Oil. The role of the UK went even further: Shell and BP jointly owned
the Sapref refinery in Durban, which throughout the embargo period continued to process
imported crude oil; part of the oil came from sources controlled by these companies (for
Shell, notably Oman and Brunei); in Durban, all the larger tankers unloaded their oil at the
Sapref-operated oil buoy; British companies were involved in South African synfuel
projects, and South African companies had access to oil exploration in the British-con-
trolled areas of the North Sea.[12] Finally, London is a centre of the world oil trade, banking
and insurance, so 'it is in London that exporters, traders and shippers meet to stitch up the
deals.'[13] Was there ever a shipment which did not have any British connections?

The United Kingdom always resisted the implementation of oil sanctions by the United Nations. With regard to its own exports of crude oil from the North Sea, the British government had made it clear to oil companies in 1979 that it expected them to direct these to EC markets and to members of the International Energy Agency; theoretically speaking, British oil would, therefore, not reach South Africa, as it was not an IEA member. In 1985, when the joint EC oil embargo was implemented, Britain viewed this guideline as being adequate; this was also the case when later that year, the Commonwealth at its Nassau summit agreed upon a ban on the sale of oil to South Africa.

A perfect example of disimplementation of a presumed 'embargo' is offered by the story which was set in motion after the SRB discovered a transport of 77,860 tons of North Sea oil from the Sullom Voe terminal in the Shetlands in 1988. By applying the tried and tested method of collaborating with journalists – in this case Martin Bailey – the discovery was published in *The Observer*.[14] Shell UK, the seller, told Bailey that the contract had included 'the usual Shell clause prohibiting the supply of oil to South Africa', but that it was not able (or prepared?) to enforce this clause. Shell had sold the cargo to Sumitomo Corporation (U.K.) Ltd, a subsidiary of the Japanese trading house, which sold it on to the Austrian state-owned company Voest Alpine Intertrading GmbH. VAIT sold it to Tiger Petroleum, one of the companies of oil trader Mark Wolman (a former VAIT employee whose company Bonaire Trading had previously been found to be involved in supplying oil to South Africa). Wolman later told the SRB that he had sold the cargo to Intercontinental Transportation Corporation – a company known to be a Marc Rich front. This type of resale involving a chain of companies was often used in order to illustrate how difficult it was to monitor a particular shipment of oil once a tanker was on the high seas; however, all these transactions had taken place *before* 11 March 1986, the day the *Almare Terza* (which had been chartered by another Rich front, Rainbow Line Ltd of Hong Kong) departed from Sullom Voe 'for Lavera' (France). When the violation of the embargo surfaced two years later, British MPs and the Bureau requested the British government to launch an investigation. A few months later the government informed the Bureau that its enquiries were 'not yet complete'.[15] By that time the Italian government had submitted a lengthy summary of its conclusions to the UN Intergovernmental Group and had informed it that, 'Following the incidents regarding the chartering of the two ... ships, the management of Società Almare has arranged for the inclusion in all contracts of a clause excluding landings in South Africa.'[16] In January 1992, in a reply to yet another parliamentary question, the British government stated that the investigation 'has proved complex and time consuming ... No response has ... proved obtainable from the last identified owner, International Transportation Company [sic] ... and other inquiries have proved inconclusive.'[17]

Liberia: Africa's oldest republic

Liberia, the classic example of a flag of convenience nation, came under criticism from fellow African countries because of the fact that 'letterbox' companies operating on its territory and ships flying its flag were engaging in a massive number of oil embargo violations.

In 1981 it was reported that Liberia considered banning ships flying the Liberian flag from entering South African waters, after the OAU had requested it to introduce legislation that would ensure the effective monitoring of Liberian-flagged vessels. The requ⌣⌣ was made against the background of the SRB report presented to the OAU in Arusha, indicating that about one third of the tankers involved in oil transports to South Africa were registered in Liberia.[18] However, already in 1980, when asked if Liberia could expel ships carrying oil to South Africa from its register, the country's commissioner for maritime affairs said that 'If there was a conflict between business and political considerations, we will put business first. We want to keep the fleet free from politics.'[19] The politics of the Liberian Foc fleet are reflected in the SRB's findings which show that of the 865 identified oil deliveries to South Africa, 380 were made by ships flying the Liberian flag or whose registered owner was based in Liberia.

A greasy business

Greece is a prominent shipping nation and was also prominent in oil transports to South Africa during the embargo: 215 of the 865 shipments identified were made by tankers owned or managed by Greek companies, while many flew the Greek flag.

There were plenty of fine words. In 1988, Theodoros Pangalos, the Greek Alternate Minister of Foreign Affairs, denounced 'the hypocritical behaviour of certain countries or governments who may be very good in condemning apartheid with words but continue their economic relations with South Africa, and thereby continue to support South Africa in practice.'[20] He said this a few weeks after a press conference in Athens, at which the SRB had highlighted the role of Greek companies and stressed the responsibility of the Greek government. In a reaction to the SRB's revelations, the government claimed that alleged violations of the oil embargo had all been thoroughly investigated. According to a spokesman, the government had no knowledge of any deliveries by tankers flying the Greek flag; moreover, the 'few' Greek-flagged tankers investigated had all been chartered out to foreigners, and Greek companies could not control their movements. No investigations had been initiated with regard to movements of Greek-owned, foreign-flagged ships, as these would be 'beyond the competence of the Greek Government'. The spokesman said that the government had 'advised' Greek shipowners about the resolutions of the United Nations and had 'recommended' that they refrain from transporting oil to South Africa.[21] The inefficacy of this recommendation was guaranteed by the loophole indicated by the government's spokesman: probably in all cases, the ships had been chartered by foreign oil traders.

In fact, Greece always abstained when votes were cast at UN sessions on the oil embargo, and one example suffices to illustrate what its authorities meant by a 'thorough investigation' of cases brought to their attention: 'The Permanent Mission of Greece informed the Intergovernmental Group ... that the oil tanker *Monemvasia* called during December 1985 on the port of Mombasa, Kenya, to unload. It did not call on any South African port.'[22] This begs the question where the credulous Greek government had gotten its 'information' from. Under the secret code 'FG26', the *Monemvasia* arrived at the Durban SBM in the early morning hours of 26 December 1985, to unload 86,552.37 metric tons of crude which had been taken on board in Seria on 3–4 December under a scheme by which Brunei oil was channelled to South Africa via Marc Rich. Rich had appointed the British East Coast Group to handle the shipment. The discharge operation was completed before the end of the following day, and the ship sailed for Sri Lanka on the night of 29 December. It is not surprising that the records of the Kenya Ports Authority in Mombasa do not contain a single call by the vessel for the month of December 1985.

The Greek Shipowners' Association was more straightforward in its reaction to the SRB report in 1988, saying: 'There is no embargo, so neither are there violations of the embargo ... There is only a recommendation by the UN not to supply South Africa with oil. Some comply with this recommendation, others think that they don't need to ... Many ships sail to South Africa, which keeps ships and crews employed. We go wherever there is work. Blocking this would surely harm ships and seamen.'

The SRB report appeared after Denmark and Norway had introduced legislation which refuted the notion that it was 'beyond the competence' of governments to halt transports if companies 'had no control over the movements of their vessels'. Greek trade unions expressed their interest in the Scandinavian examples and said they would put pressure on their government. What in fact happened was that, from the mid-1980s, the involvement of a small group of Greek shipping companies increased rather than diminished.

Switzerland: A traders' paradise

In 1988, the German oil company Marimpex transferred its branch from the Swiss town of Zug to Rapperswil in the nearby canton of St. Gallen. Speaking to Swiss journalists, the South African head of the Swiss operation, Mr Jürgen Hasse, offered a neat explanation for the transfer. Traditionally, Zug has been the choice Swiss location for companies active in worldwide oil trading, including those supplying South Africa, such as Marc Rich & Co. AG. According to Hasse, *there were just too many of them in Zug*: 'When one is talking business with a partner during a meal in a restaurant, one has to be on the watch for unwanted listeners.'[23]

The history of Marc Rich serves as the clearest illustration of why it was so attractive for companies to channel their South African oil transactions via 'politically neutral'[24] Switzerland. Yet, the extent of the Swiss involvement is not to be gleaned from the presentation of the SRB's findings in the list of oil shipments. Some Swiss companies are listed, among others, African Middle East, Cast, Suisse-Outremer, Tradinaft, Vitol and, of course, Marc Rich. But many others, including companies with head offices in Germany, the Netherlands, Bermuda and elsewhere, profited greatly from the benefits offered by the country with its tradition in banking secrecy. In an address to parliament, a South African Minister of Mineral and Energy Affairs once quoted a business offer 'from what is probably one of the largest oil broker undertakings in the world': 'We would like to emphasize that because of the classified nature of these transactions a Swiss low-key operation stands by to immediately commence the activities related to this business.' According to the minister, suppliers 'established the company in Switzerland specifically in order to distance themselves from South Africa so that nobody should know that they were supplying this country with oil.'[25]

The Shipping Research Bureau regularly got information to the effect that a certain transaction involved a bank such as the Swiss Bank Corp., Paribas (Suisse), or the Banca della Svizzera Italiana, but due to its orientation towards oil-trading and shipping companies and its lack of expertise in this field, the Bureau did no more than conclude that the trader in question had an account with the bank. Swiss banks were targetted by the anti-apartheid movement; however, too little attention was given to research and actions in connection with their specific role in oil transactions.[26] Just before the SRB closed down, it obtained some information on the invaluable services that a limited number of Swiss and other banks had rendered to oil traders and their South African clients by providing finance for the latter's huge transactions (the value of one VLCC cargo of crude oil could easily amount to tens of millions of dollars). As the embargo period drew to a close and more banks started to offer their services, the margins became smaller[27] – even on this score, the embargo had added to South Africa's costs.

Egypt: Pipeline from Cairo to Cape Town

In 1980, the line adopted by OAU member state Egypt was crystal-clear. 'The competent authorities in Egypt have taken the necessary measures to ensure that all the sales contracts of Egyptian oil contain a standing provision prohibiting the reselling of its oil to the racist régime of South Africa. Egypt has also taken the necessary measures to enact legislation to ensure the applicability of an oil embargo against South Africa,' the Egyptian government wrote in a letter to the United Nations Special Committee against Apartheid on 3 April 1980.[28] When a single shipment of Egyptian oil was delivered to South Africa by the tanker *Mospoint* in 1986, the government announced that it would terminate its dealings with the ship's owner unless the company clarified what had happened to the cargo.[29]

In December 1986, the tanker *Mega Point* called at the same Egyptian oil terminal as the *Mospoint* had done 11 months earlier. Were the Egyptian authorities ignorant of the fact that the company had changed the name of its tanker in the meantime, or were they really satisfied with the reassurance that the *Mospoint* had sailed to the Persian Gulf? By the time the Egyptian government told the SRB about this last reassurance[30], it had become clear that something else had changed – something about which the government could no longer claim ignorance. 'Loading today, 22 December 1987, with an Egyptian shipment for South Africa is the *Captain John G.P. Livanos*. The company owning the cargo is called African Middle East. The minister knows where it is going...' was the tip given to the SRB. The shipment proved to be the first of an ongoing series of approximately one VLCC per month to South Africa.

From that moment on, neither the minister in question nor any other Egyptian official could be counted upon to provide serious answers in response to questions on embargo-breaking shipments. The UN was sent copies of Bills of Lading, but no discharge documentation. For the SRB, however, it was difficult to publish categorical allegations concerning connivance on the part of the Egyptian authorities on the basis of a single tip and a few indications about ostensible connections between high officials and African Middle East, a company which the Bureau had never come across before. The company had been incorporated in Panama in 1987, and was owned by two Egyptian brothers Abdelnour, who lived in Cairo; its day-to-day business was conducted from offices in Monaco and Switzerland. The SRB went so far as to write that various sources within the oil industry described the role of African Middle East as the major channel through which the Egyptian national oil company EGPC discreetly sold its surplus production of crude oil at market prices. 'Indeed, African Middle East has been described as "a sort of marketing arm for the Egyptian Government, but on an arm's-length basis". Apparently, quite a few of these spot cargoes of surplus Egyptian crude oil have found their way to South Africa, despite the official Egyptian embargo on oil deliveries to South Africa' – statements had to be worded carefully in an SRB report. Fortunately for the Bureau, in an update it was able to quote a public source, viz. a journal which claimed that foreign companies active in Egypt had reported that 'sizeable quantities of Egyptian crude oil are exported to South Africa, in contravention of the international boycott on that country, but earning a premium on the world price.'[31]

As time went by, the source of information which made it possible for the SRB to link specific cargoes to African Middle East dried up; that, and not the possible withdrawal of the company from deliveries to South Africa, is the reason why the company does not appear on the SRB's list of last-known owner(s) in connection with later shipments from Egypt. In three instances, the SRB established that *Marc Rich* was involved in the sale to South Africa; in two of these African Middle East had been the first buyer. The latter has always declined to reveal the identity of the company to which it had possibly resold the cargoes;[32] it is not difficult to venture a guess.

In July 1990, Egyptian president Mubarak's one-year term as OAU chairman expired. The South African press reported that the Egyptian embassy in Harare, where Mubarak had made a speech to the OAU summit, had issued a statement denying that the president was considering relaxing sanctions, saying he was a staunch supporter of the liberation movements in South Africa and had done as much as he could not only to maintain sanctions but also to increase pressure on the apartheid regime.[33]

Middle East: Business as usual

De Quaasteniet and Aarts deal extensively with the reasons why a number of countries in the Middle East failed to implement oil sanctions. First and foremost was the *United Arab Emirates*, which accounts for 213, or more than a quarter, of the 865 shipments identified by the Shipping Research Bureau. The UAE made one of the most remarkable statements ever to appear in a report of the UN Intergovernmental Group. In 1991 the Group submitted a copy of a model oil sanctions law to all member states. Discussing a proposed law at a time when Bush had already lifted the US oil embargo might seem like rearguard action, its author admitted during the 1991 oil embargo hearings of the Group, but he said it was still relevant for those who wished to maintain their embargoes and wanted to eliminate loopholes. In the briefest of reactions, the UAE said that *'the Government of the United Arab Emirates accepts the proposed model law'*.[34]

The earlier acceptance of strict destination clauses in oil-sales contracts and sometimes in legislation, and of a system for monitoring shipments by demanding discharge certificates, was not followed by effective enforcement in a number of oil-exporting countries. Just as shipping nations had their standard argument claiming that they were unable to monitor chartered vessels, so some of the oil-exporting countries used to ensconce themselves in a position exemplified by the following reply to the UN from the government of Oman: '...in all Oman's contracts for sale of oil, there is a specific clause restricting the destination. However, once the oil leaves the Sultanate, it becomes difficult to establish its final destination.'[35] The attempts by the ANC and the SRB to convince these countries to improve the enforcement of the embargo by showing them that it was possible to monitor violations, have been described in an earlier chapter. A letter to the SRB from the Iranian UN mission shows what 'enforcement' could be worth in practice: the Iranian ambassador had 'the honour to enclose herewith a copy of the certificate of discharge of the said ship which indicates Genova, Italy as the port of discharge, thus proving all allegations to the contrary baseless.'[36] The said ship was the *Beatrice*, which, as we have already seen, never went to Genoa.

The ANC's Frene Ginwala says she can't help concluding that 'at least some elements in the governments of those countries must have been fully aware of what was going on. They were benefiting in large amounts of money. Whether it was a government policy, or government closing its eyes, both, or just corruption...?' The same conclusion was arrived at by the opposition in the South African parliament in a debate on the secrecy legislation, when PFP spokesman Brian Goodall said that 'Those people [abroad] seem to have an awful lot of information. There are in fact published lists of companies and tankers that supply South Africa with oil. Overseas people know what is happening. If they wanted to take action, they could. The fact that they do not do so shows that people, particularly in a period of oil surpluses, are more concerned about finding buyers for their products than about who those buyers are.'[37]

The European Community: Half-hearted measures

Also on an intergovernmental level there were good and bad policies. The most important level was that of the United Nations, which is dealt with by Araim. On a lower level, a good example was offered by the Commonwealth, which included oil in its sanctions package of October 1985. A less laudable example was that of the *European Community*, which decided upon the introduction of, among others, a rather limited oil embargo in September 1985. In a resolution taken on 30 October 1987, the European Parliament urged stricter control on circumventions of the existing measures, to no avail. The resolution focussed, in particular, on the loopholes in the oil embargo, which had reduced it to a halfhearted sanction from the outset. The EC measure banned the sale of crude oil produced in EC countries to South Africa.[38] In practice, this applied to North Sea oil from the UK, Denmark and the Netherlands (Norway was not a member of the EC) – which was hardly important for South Africa. The example of the *Almare Terza* shows what the embargo was worth on the rare occasion it could have meant something. Not covered were (potentially) more important aspects, such as deliveries from bonded storage, refined products, the role of EC-based companies in selling and brokerage of oil, transfer of technology and capital for oil and gas exploration, and activities of South African subsidiaries of European oil companies.

All 28 crude oil shipments to South Africa from Rotterdam identified by the SRB were made from bonded storage. Although the channelling of oil to South Africa through Rotterdam had declined since 1980, the SRB warned the City of Rotterdam in its recommendations made in 1985 that 'The necessity of introducing measures arises from the fact that for South Africa a transhipment centre such as Rotterdam has acted and *could again act* as a "supplier of last resort".'[39] The attempts by the Dutch anti-apartheid organisations to

Marimpex: A German Oil Supplier to South Africa

According to Mr Lutter, the following points could have far-reaching consequences:

1. Regular supply to South Africa

At present, no one raises this issue, though those involved are known to all in the trade. In particular, downstream companies active in the South Africa trade have profited from the quiet on the market – reduction of risk premiums. At least for the time being, an official discussion is not regarded as opportune, neither by Iran (one knows that Iranian oil also goes to South Africa for a good price) and especially not by receivers in South Africa (the market is too transparent to protect the purchaser).

On 15 June 1985, a rather unfriendly conversation was held at the Hamburg offices of the oil-trading company Marimpex. Participants were a director of German BP, who took the above notes, and the head of Marimpex, Gert Lutter. Allegations had been aired by a subsidiary of German BP regarding the involvement of Marimpex in oil supplies to South Africa, arousing the irritation of Lutter. His visitor could not help observing that Lutter had outwitted his accusers.[1]

In 1985 Marimpex succeeded in effecting a large contract for Iranian oil via *German Oil*, a company set up by Marimpex (35, later 100 per cent) together with the Lower Saxon regional government with a view to reopening the shut-down Mobil refinery at Wilhelmshaven. The

```
Als Punkte, die sich kritisch entwickeln können, nannte
Herr Lutter:

1.   Belieferung Südafrika

     Dieses Thema wird zur Zeit von niemandem in die
     Diskussion gebracht, obgleich im Markt bekannt ist,
     wer in diesem Geschäft beteiligt ist. Insbesondere
     die im Südafrika-Geschäft vertretenen Downstream-
     Gesellschaften haben von Ruhe im Markt - Reduzierung
     der Risikoprämien - profitiert. Eine offizielle
     Diskussion wird zumindest z.Z. weder vom Iran (man
     weiß, daß auch iranisches Rohöl zu guten Preisen
     nach Südafrika geht) und schon gar nicht von den
     Empfängern in Südafrika (der Markt ist zu transparent,
     um den Endabnehmer schützen zu können) für opportun
     gehalten.
```

joint venture had brought about a good deal of political controversy regarding this cooperation by the government with a sanctions-busting company. For the time being, the oil was resold on lucrative contracts to German refining companies such as German Shell and BP – and to South Africa.

During the conversation on 15 June 1985, Lutter's rebuttal to the allegation that 'The first two ships from the processing contract NIOC–German Oil/Marimpex don't go to the FRG, but to South Africa' was that 'The first shipload was pumped through the pipeline to different purchasers, among them DBP [German BP] for Bavaria. The second ship also goes to the FRG and will be offloaded in Wilhelmshaven at the end of this month (possibly in the presence of an Iranian government representative).'[2] However, the presence of an Iranian official at the un-loading of 'the second ship' in Wilhelmshaven[3] could not prevent part of the oil aboard that ship from ending up in South Africa – *after* her call at Wilhelmshaven.

Berge King: Iranian crude to South Africa via Europe

On paper, the beneficiary of the Iranian oil cargo loaded by the tanker *Berge King* a few weeks before the above conversation took place was German Oil. When the BP memo which hinted at a sale to South Africa was leaked, the chief executive of German Oil said he was 'allergic' to that kind of allegation. He could 'indicate amount by amount' where the oil sold to his company went in the FRG. 'If Mr Lutter wants to do such a thing, he doesn't need German Oil for it.'[4]

Actually, the ship first went to Rotterdam/Europoort. As the agent of Marimpex, Cela Shipping, explained, the port of Wilhelmshaven was not deep enough for a fully laden supertanker of the size of the *Berge King*. Temporarily storing half of the cargo in Rotterdam would do the trick. After discharging some 100,000 tons, the vessel proceeded to Wilhelmshaven to deliver the first half of the original cargo. On 1 July, the empty ship returned to Rotterdam. If one has to believe the agent, there the remaining 100,000 tons were collected. Everyone, from shipping press to Dutch port authorities and curious journalists, was told that the ship again went to Wilhelmshaven. The ship's agent in the German port declared that the remainder of the cargo was indeed discharged there on 8 July. A statement which is all the more remarkable as, on the ship's earlier departure on 1 July, the port authorities of Wilhelmshaven had been informed that the *Berge King* was to sail directly to *Saudi Arabia*.

In reality, during her second call at Rotterdam, the *Berge King* had loaded far more Iranian crude oil, 194,903 tons, and she never returned to Wilhelmshaven. The ship headed south. On 8 July, she passed Dover Straits, on her way to South Africa, where the 'German' oil was discharged.

'If it is true that the Berge King of the Bergesen company has transported oil from Iran to South Africa, the Bergesen company will be boycotted by Iran,' said the Iranian *chargé d'affaires* in Norway, Mr Mohammed Hadi Ardebili, in October 1985.[5] In 1986, the *Berge King* was renamed *Khark 2*, after having been bought by ...the National Iranian Tanker Company.

1   The opening quotation is taken from a confidential memo by BP director Dr O. Schneider to BP board member Dr R. Stomberg, dated 18 June 1985, from a passage in which the author refers explicitly to Mr Lutter (original in German). The existence of the memo was first revealed by the West German weekly *Die Zeit*, 17 January 1986.
2   Memo Dr Schneider. NIOC = National Iranian Oil Company.
3   In a reply to a telex sent by the SRB on 19 June 1985 regarding possible deliveries to South Africa of oil loaded in Iran during that month, the government of Iran informed the Bureau that Marimpex had invited a representative of NIOC or the Iranian embassy in Bonn to be present at the unloading of 'the Marimpex tankers' in Wilhelmshaven (letter to SRB, 21 August 1985).
4   *Die Zeit*, 17 January 1986; *Wirtschaftswoche*, 24 January 1986.
5   *Aftenposten*, 19 October 1985.

tighten the EC embargo by taking measures on a local level failed when local authorities said that they were powerless to intervene in matters of 'government policy'. The same happened in 1989–90 when it was discovered that large quantities of refined products were being shipped via Amsterdam.

In June 1987, Ms Barbara Simons, member of the European Parliament, produced a report[40] in which she pointed at another weakness of the embargo. Simons concluded, *inter alia*, that a lack of uniformity in the implementation was undermining the effectiveness of the measures. As the EC oil embargo did not provide for a common implementation, member states had implemented it in different ways, varying from a ministerial decree or a regulation, compulsory licensing (in which case licenses for South Africa were not issued), 'monitoring' of oil exports, 'guidelines', no specific oil embargo measures at all (but 'adoption of the EC measures as a whole'), to incorporation in a law (which had only been done by Denmark).

The EC oil embargo had a very limited impact, but inasmuch as its adoption at least had a warning function, its lifting on 6 April 1992 was seen as the wrong signal by many observers. According to an EC press release, the embargo was lifted in order to 'encourage positive developments in South Africa'. The UN Special Committee against Apartheid immediately reacted by criticising decisions such as this which contravened General Assembly resolutions, since they 'would undermine the negotiations to peacefully end apartheid by eroding the leverage that the international community has so effectively used to help advance the political process in South Africa.' The chairman of the UN Intergovernmental Group, Tanzanian ambassador Anthony Nyakyi, said that 'this decision, as any premature decision on sanctions at this time tends to support one party only – the South African Government – in the negotiations ... rather than the ... process as a whole.' Two days after the EC decision, the South African Council of Churches expressed its concern 'that the European Community looks at events in South Africa from a White perspective, and not from those who have been, and still are, victims of the minority government of South Africa.' The president of the Anti-Apartheid Movement in Britain, Archbishop Trevor Huddleston, said he had sought the assurance of the Labour Party that it would not immediately relax UK guidelines enforcing the oil embargo in the event that it came to power in Britain's forthcoming election: 'The UK is the only major oil exporter in the EC and if a Labour government were to take this action it would effectively nullify the EC decision.'[41]

The abovementioned unwillingness or inability of local authorities in the Netherlands to assume a responsibility of their own was repeated on the national level. The policy of the Netherlands concerning the oil embargo can serve to illustrate a mechanism which could be discerned in the behaviour of many countries. For the Shipping Research Bureau (which never got financial assistance from the Dutch government, nor any serious answers when it presented cases of embargo violations to the authorities) it was odd having time and again to discover, on travels abroad, that the Netherlands had an image of being in the forefront of the anti-apartheid struggle. This was the country of Shell, of Transworld Oil, of Rotterdam, which since the mid-1980s refused to vote in favour of the oil embargo in the UN... At the same time the Netherlands had become a master of the art of passing the buck: unilateral measures were never considered, sanctions could perhaps be effective if only our neighbours, the Scandinavian countries, the EC, the Security Council...[42] Nabeela Al-Mulla must have had examples such as this one in mind when, in a speech made in her capacity as acting chairperson of the UN Intergovernmental Group in 1990, she referred to 'the public support in the West for a cause that had been somewhat lagging on the official level'.[43]

Kuwait: An effective embargo

Oil went to South Africa from a relatively small group of countries. Other oil-exporting countries were able to enforce a stringent policy; Kuwait was one of these. At most, six oil cargoes originating from Kuwait appear in the findings of the SRB over the entire period. In addition, the Bureau knows of one case in which a tanker had collected a part cargo of Kuwaiti oil, which had been previously discharged in Rotterdam. The Bureau is aware that it has overlooked the odd cargo (a South African document in its possession, in which the names of vessels have been erased, shows that John Deuss loaded Kuwaiti oil for South Africa twice in 1981).[44]

Thus, Kuwait was the 'cleanest' exporter amongst the world's top oil producers.[45] In the Netherlands, motorists who wished to avoid the *faux pas* of buying products from Shell, Total and other supporters of apartheid, could safely be advised, in an *Alternative Tanking Guide*, to use Kuwait's 'Q8' brand of petrol. But the judgement was not merely based on quantitative criteria. In the case of Kuwait, there were never any rumours which suggested that the government had been aware of a transport and had turned a blind eye. The cases which the SRB submitted to Kuwait were seriously investigated, and the Bureau was kept informed of the outcome, as in the case when it received a letter which stated that the contracts in question clearly stipulated that the final destinations of the oil were refineries in Rotterdam and Singapore, and that this left no doubt that the terms of the contracts signed with Kuwait as well as the rules governing Kuwaiti exports had been violated. The Kuwaiti authorities were continuing investigations concerning the transactions 'and shall decide on the measures to be adopted'.[46] After the scuttling of the *Salem*, Kuwait suspended and subsequently terminated its contract with Pontoil, the buyer of the Kuwaiti oil that had ended up in South Africa. The Kuwaiti Ministry of Oil tightened its oil sales terms following the incident. The active role of Kuwait in promoting the oil embargo on an international level has repeatedly been referred to in this book.

Nigeria: Trail-blazing actions

Nigeria has provided many of the chairmen of the UN Special Committee against Apartheid and was one of the oil-producing countries which participated in the Intergovernmental Group. A number of much-publicised actions taken by Nigeria during the embargo years struck fear into the hearts of the oil companies, and were used in publications by the proponents of the embargo as shining examples. In May 1979 Nigeria seized the *Kulu*, a Panamanian-registered tanker which had been sent by BP to collect Nigerian oil for Rotterdam, after the ship's South African ownership had been discovered; the vessel was only released after the oil cargo had been confiscated. That same month, the Nigerian government proclaimed a prohibition on entering Nigerian waters for ships that had been in 'contact' with South Africa, Rhodesia or Israel over the previous three months; 'contact' included refuelling, picking up post, having nationals of those countries as crew members, or being owned or chartered by any of the three countries.[47] The Nigerian government's most dramatic move came when it completely nationalised British Petroleum's substantial holdings in Nigeria because of Britain's decision to allow BP to supply oil to its South African subsidiary through a 'swap deal', one in which BP was to provide North Sea oil to the US oil company Conoco, and in return Conoco was to supply oil for BP South Africa. BP was only welcomed back in Nigeria in May 1991. In 1981 Shell Nigeria's MD Peter Holmes thought it sensible to make a categorical statement that 'Not a drop of Shell's Nigerian crude oil reaches South Africa, directly or indirectly' after a Nigerian newspaper had deduced from the January 1981 report of the Shipping Research Bureau that some of the company's oil was being shipped to South Africa through the Netherlands Antilles.[48] Later in 1981, the press reported that Nigeria had foiled an attempt by South African agents to buy large quantities of Nigerian crude oil from the country's Bonny terminal, when 'a disguised South African vessel' capable of carrying more than 2 million barrels of oil was intercepted by a naval patrol after a tip-off from the Nigerian security forces.[49]

In 1985 the Nigerian government informed the SRB that the Nigerian National Petroleum Corporation had boycotted the oil trader Marimpex since July 1984. Marimpex had been told that it did not qualify to purchase crude oil, and the Corporation had 'blacklisted all vessels owned or chartered by the company and any company associated or subsidiary to it'.[50] The Bureau immediately circulated the report through its publications – the magic of the good example had lost nothing of its cogency.

Reports on growing oil links between South Africa and a number of African states mounted from late-1990 onwards. Initially, Nigeria was not among these countries, but during 1991 a report stated that South African president F.W. de Klerk had been invited for an official visit to Nigeria (which at the time chaired the OAU); when the visit took place in April 1992, there were speculations about 'oily diplomacy'.[51] The UN Intergovernmental Group asked the SRB to provide it with an overview of this type of contact and – in a diplomatically worded statement – expressed its concern in its 1992 report. The most far-reaching report involved *Angola*, which had negotiated a contract with the SFF whereby the latter would sell Angolan crude on the international market; however, Angolan sources indicated that the agreement would be subject to satisfactory political change in South Africa. The ANC's Thabo Mbeki told an SRB representative, whom he met in Switzerland in late-1991, that Nigerian officials had given him the assurance that this type of deal would only come into effect in two to three years time; according to Mbeki one could not blame Nigeria and Angola for not wanting to miss the boat.

Algeria: A staunch ally

From the same censored document which showed that 'Lucina' (John Deuss) had been able to pick up a few Kuwaiti oil cargoes, it was possible to deduce that Deuss had smuggled a cargo of 'Hassl' crude to South Africa in August–October 1981. This was the missing link proving that the Greek tanker *Kyrnicos E.* had been used to violate the embargo of Algeria, a country which had since its independence manifested itself as an ally of the South African liberation movement (its liberation army put Nelson Mandela through a military training course in 1962). As an OPEC member, Algeria matched Kuwait and Nigeria in its efforts to campaign for an international oil embargo. The dedicated Algerian diplomat Mohamed Sahnoun chaired the Amsterdam oil embargo seminar held in 1980; his colleagues at the UN participated in the Intergovernmental Group. Algeria was one of the countries which soon fell out of favour with the embargo-busting oil companies as a source of oil. The SRB has identified fewer than five full shipments of oil from Algeria to South Africa, all of which took place before mid-1982.

Of Algeria's neighbour *Libya* it is known that a tanker, the *Atlantic Courage*, could not pick up a load of oil there in 1981 because the ship was known to have been in South African waters a year before. 'A new tanker had to be sent for and the charter firm ended up well over a million dollars out of pocket. It is this sort of thing that can make contact with South Africa an expensive business,' a 'UN source' was quoted as saying by the South African *Star*.[52]

Stringent embargo: A viable option

Were there 'good' and 'bad' countries as far as the oil embargo was concerned? One conclusion that can be drawn from an evaluation of the experiences gained during the years of the South African embargo is that there were good and bad *embargo policies*. De Quaasteniet and Aarts have made an attempt to map the background for differences between the various oil-producing nations in the Middle East. It is also possible to arrive at a number of conclusions which do not specifically apply to this group of countries.

The introduction to this chapter presented a basic scheme – legislation, monitoring, enforcement – which, as events have shown, did not represent a law of the Medes and Persians in practice. Some governments were able to act effectively without a statutory framework, and even at the United Nations much was achieved despite the voluntary nature of the embargo. On the other hand, the presence of stringent legislation did not necessarily go hand in hand with strict monitoring and enforcement.

Furthermore, it was possible for a country to have an impeccable record as far as the oil embargo was concerned – perhaps it did not cost much – whilst at the same time it had a rather objectionable record regarding other sanctions (Italy, which never halted its large imports of South African coal, is a plausible candidate; to a certain degree, the USA was an example of the reverse: a distinctly bad record on oil, but its Anti-Apartheid Act was instrumental in putting pressure on the apartheid government). In the case of Norway we saw that the fact that it had a more stringent legislation than many other countries did not mean that it willingly cooperated with the UN Intergovernmental Group on the oil embargo (of which it was itself a prominent member) when the interests of its companies in a branch of the oil trade which was not covered by the legislation were at stake. Countries were neither 'good' nor 'bad'; a country's dedication to the good cause was always kept in check by its never losing sight of its perceived self-interest.

Changes in the national political spectrum could affect the embargo policies of a specific country. When Denmark – which had preceded Norway in banning its shipping companies from the South African oil trade and imposed the strictest oil embargo of all the EC member states – lifted its oil sanctions after the South African whites-only referendum of March 1992 ahead of a joint European decision, this step was taken by the conservative

---

Attempts to conceal breaches of the oil embargo

• Late 1983, the Finnish company Neste sold a consignment of Qatar crude oil to Derby, UK. The *Manhattan Viscount* (a Sanko tanker on time charter to Fearnley & Eger) was hired to load the oil, which had meanwhile been resold to Intercontinental Transportation Corp., i.e. Marc Rich. The oil was destined for Singapore, the Japanese captain was told, but he was ordered to sail to Ras Tanura (Saudi Arabia) first. Neither call was reported in the shipping press. The captain received a telex message, saying that the Ras Tanura agents had been informed that

> *Vessel is calling for bunkers only. No cargo to be mentioned under any circumstances. Barbers* [Ras Tanura agents] *have already been advised that vessel will contact them. Vessel's VHF to be used for navigational matters only and no cargo business to be mentioned.*

After his departure from Ras Tanura the captain was ordered by the ship's operator to change course. When the shipowner objected to getting involved in an infringement of Qatar's embargo and the captain refused to discharge at Durban and to sign forged documents, a costly solution had to be found. The Persian Gulf/South Africa 'shuttle' tanker *Thorsholm* happened to be in South Africa, and was directed to international waters to take over the cargo by ship-to-ship transfer.

• All tankers were given instructions to conceal their involvement in breaches of the embargo, but the Shipping Research Bureau was only able to obtain a few examples. In January 1987 the *Licorne Océane* took over Iranian oil from a giant tanker used as a floating storage depot outside the war zone (several years later, information leaked out showing that the oil – destined 'for Singapore' – had been sold to the Marimpex front company German Oil). The operating company, Seatramp, transmitted detailed directions to the ship while she steamed off East Africa:

> *It is most important that the vessel's name is not displayed at the dis[charge] port ... If it is possible the vessel's name must be covered with canvas securely fitted in place on the bow, the stern and the bridge. The owners' identification on the funnel should also be removed. On leaving the dis[charge] port there should be nothing on board the vessel which would indicate where the vessel has actually been. This must include the disposal of all newspapers or magazines or calendars from the dis[charge] port. If any stores are taken then any packages or documents relating to them which would show where they were purchased must also be disposed of.*

As was usual with tankers deployed in breaches of the oil embargo, the ship was given a codename. Two weeks after the departure of the *Licorne Océane* from the Persian Gulf, tanker *'M49'* arrived at Durban to discharge her cargo at the offshore oil buoy. On the assumption that the crew of a ship not normally engaged in trading shrouded in secretiveness would be a little taken aback by the outlined procedure, Seatramp had reassuringly added to its instructions: *'We understand that the above requests may seem unusual but rest assured it is in the best interests of the vessel and her owners.'*

• In September 1988, the Norwegian tanker *Dagli* sailed from Odessa, loaded with Soviet fuel oil owned by Marc Rich. Still in the Mediterranean, the captain received orders to set course for *Cape Town*. An extensive camouflage operation was set up by the charterer's South African agent. First, the captain was requested to contact the agent via Cape Town radio solely using the secret code *'MF1'*. Next, a message was received from the charterer and passed on to the captain requesting that 'VESSEL PROCEED RELEVANT TERMINAL AT CAPETOWN ... IDENTIFYING AT ALL TIMES EXCLUSIVELY BY CALL SIGN MFI. ANY ALL COMMUNICATIONS ARE TO REFER ONLY TO BUNKERING OPERATION WITH NO REFERENCE WHATSOEVER TO CARGODISCHARGE VESSELS NAME OR LOADPORT ... VESSEL AT ALL TIMES ONLY USE CALL SIGN MFI AND UNDER NO CIRCUMSTANCES SHOULD VESSEL USE USUAL CALL SIGN.' One thing the master refused: *'under no circumstances will the name be painted over under my command stop but i will cover the name with canvas if the weather permits. regards mfi.'* Iver Bugge, the ship's operator, cabled that the company agreed, adding: 'BUT ALSO REMEMBER NOT TO SHOW THE FLAG OF NATIONALITY.'

On 15 October 1988, the *Dagli*, her name covered by tarpaulins, discharged her cargo in Cape Town. When the transport was revealed by the Norwegian television, chairman Jan Bugge admitted that his company had 'sailed close to the wind' by agreeing to hide the vessel's identity (the captain was later fined for this breach of the law). Bugge said he regretted that the oil had ended up in South Africa; however, 'it is not up to us to be concerned with the Russian policies in this respect.'

government of the day, thereby flying in the face of the majority of the Danish parliament.[53]

There were a lot of half-hearted measures – countries which did nothing to prevent companies active in shipping and trading from dealing with South Africa, nor took steps when violations occurred, or reluctantly adopted a verbal policy; supranational organisations which accepted irrelevant prohibitory measures; countries which prevented the United Nations from implementing a mandatory embargo; and oil-exporting countries which did not take any concrete steps to ensure that a nominal embargo was adhered to. However, the oil which, despite the embargo, went to South Africa came from a relatively small group of suppliers and was shipped by a relatively small group of companies. Shipping nations were able to take effective steps, thus refuting the argument that it was impossible to control their ships when they were chartered by foreign companies. Similarly, the weakness of the arguments used by a number of oil-exporting countries – such as the impossibility of establishing the final destination of oil cargoes – was demonstrated by the fact that other countries were able to enforce a stringent policy.

The Impact of the Oil Embargo

Have all the efforts which went into the oil embargo against South Africa been worthwhile? What has been the impact? In his contribution to this book, Van Bergeijk makes a distinction between the *effectiveness* of a sanction in inflicting damage upon the target and its *success* in achieving a change in the latter's behaviour. A preliminary question, which more directly concerns those who were campaigning for oil sanctions, is to what extent they succeeded in getting really effective oil sanctions implemented and enforced.

The question whether a research bureau whose primary aim was to monitor violations of the oil embargo can be said to have justified its existence is a relatively easy one to answer, the primary yardstick being the quality of its research findings. The Shipping Research Bureau has shown that monitoring the flow of oil to an embargoed country is feasible, even in a situation in which there is no or hardly any official monitoring nor physically enforced control. The Bureau was successful in achieving its primary goal; during the embargo years its publications usually covered between 50 and 60 per cent of estimated average oil imports, with an occasional peak exceeding 80 per cent. Moreover, the rate of success in keeping a close watch on companies and countries which were involved in embargo violations was higher than appeared in the publications; many suspected deliveries for which conclusive evidence was lacking were nonetheless presented to companies and governments,[1] which made them fully aware that they were 'being watched 24 hours a day and 365 days a year'. The success rate in linking shipments to specific *oil companies* was always lower than that in identifying the shipping companies involved and the countries of origin of the oil; yet, the Bureau has been able to identify the major oil traders involved in oil supplies to South Africa. However, the key question was not related to the quality of the SRB's research. The Bureau's monitoring activities were but one element in a global movement for oil sanctions.

Tightening oil sanctions

The first question to be answered in an attempt to assess the impact of the movement for oil sanctions is whether it was successful in getting measures adopted or in influencing the behaviour of companies; whether this in turn had any effect on South Africa is a question which will be dealt with later.

A number of successes – some of which could be directly attributed to the work of the Shipping Research Bureau – have been discussed in this book. The movement for oil sanctions has, however, a mixed record. Two contributions which appear in the second half of this book concern a campaign which had as its primary objective the withdrawal of Shell from South Africa – an objective it failed to attain, although it certainly succeeded in influencing Shell's behaviour. In the early 1980s the SRB's publications contributed towards the adverse publicity regarding the oil majors' open defiance of the embargo, under pressure of which these companies brought their direct and visible involvement to an end; in 1981 they stopped sending their own tankers to South Africa.[2]

An example often referred to by the SRB was that pertaining to the oil-trading company *Vitol*. When its involvement was exposed, the company's director said his company deplored the fact that those supplies had taken place and added: 'But immediately after this became known as a result of the [SRB] report, we took measures to prevent, once and for all, the possibility that this would happen again ... As you can imagine, a company like ours, which trades with COMECON countries, and also trades with OPEC – it would be suicide to do business with South Africa.'[3] The message was clear: publicity broke secrecy; oil deliveries to South Africa could not bear the light of day. Publicising information and stimulating public and political debate on the involvement of companies had a deterring effect in themselves and thus served to tighten the embargo. It was a message which was hoped would appeal to those who were reluctant or felt unable to take far-reaching measures. Meanwhile, there was a nagging suspicion that companies making such statements had in fact found new ways to continue their involvement in a less visible manner (a prime example was the statement made by *Transworld Oil*, cited on page 147, in which TWO's withdrawal from the oil trade with South Africa was announced). Yet it was remarkable that companies thought it would enhance their image if they were to distance themselves from the trade publicly.[4]

In other cases in which companies informed the Shipping Research Bureau that they had ceased their involvement, there was no doubt as to the integrity of their replies. A reply of a more vexed nature was one which the Bureau received in 1983, whereby a shipping company informed the Bureau that 'for your guidance our vessels have not called at South African ports since the publishing of your last report, but have been in lay-up. The reason for this is purely commercial and partly due to your activity. However, if you continue to publish our previous calls our commercial reason to discontinue our trade will cease to exist, and we will be free to break lay-up and trade world wide within lawful trading limits.'[5] Quite often companies found it opportune to inform the Bureau about their strict policy of not supplying embargoed oil directly or indirectly to South Africa. One company didn't have such a policy; even so, it informed the Bureau that 'whilst the Group is not philosophically opposed to doing business with South Africa, we have had no reason to fall under your scrutiny.'[6] The example of the Italian state-owned shipping company Almare, which until 1988 did not have an embargo policy but after disclosures by the SRB told charterers that company vessels could no longer dock at South African ports to deliver oil, has been referred to earlier. By mid-1989, when South Africa increasingly needed supplies of refined products and Norwegian companies were wilfully exploiting the loophole in their country's oil transport ban, Almare took another line. The Norwegian time charterers of three of Almare's OBO vessels requested the company to amend the clause in its charter-parties which read *'Vessel not to be employed in illegal trading such as oil to South Africa'* to apply to crude oil only; however, after consulting the SRB, Almare refused both this request and that of a number of brokers asking it to accept charters on three other vessels for oil product shipments to South Africa from the Netherlands. In the years that followed, the company stuck to this line. In April 1994 – the first ever democratic elections in South Africa had just started – the SRB got one last telephone call from Genoa, in which Almare said that there was now an opportunity for one of its vessels to be fixed for South Africa but that it wanted to check whether the embargo had indeed been lifted.[7]

Investigations by the *United Nations oil embargo monitoring group* had played a part in prompting the Italian government to ask Almare to change its policy; once again it was the SRB's information which had led to these investigations. When Singapore issued a ban on exports and transports of oil by its tankers as from 15 September 1989, this was also due to increasing pressure on governments from the UN Group.[8] *Anti-apartheid organisations* and their allies were also applying pressure (sometimes making use of SRB data), which on several occasions led to successes in the field of oil embargo legislation. Denmark and Norway are obvious examples, whilst in the United States anti-apartheid legislation attained a major success when in April 1989 the biggest US investor in South Africa, Mobil Oil, announced its withdrawal from South Africa.

One of the countries which took measures on the basis of a report by the Shipping Research Bureau was *Indonesia*, whose Mining and Energy Minister, Subroto, issued a circular to all oil companies operating in Indonesia in August 1981, which prohibited them from doing business with Galaxy Oil and Stardust International, after both companies had failed to provide clarification as to where the cargo of crude oil which the tanker *Cherry Vesta* had loaded in Indonesia in March 1979 had been discharged.[9]

Brunei was the only oil-exporting country which openly supplied crude oil to South Africa until 1982. But even after it had joined the embargo, Brunei oil continued to reach South Africa. In late 1986 Martin Bailey wrote in *The Observer* that at least 25 cargoes of Brunei oil had found their way to South Africa despite the embargo. The SRB subsequently published a survey listing even more shipments, in which it was able to reveal part of the scheme whereby Brunei oil reached South Africa, and in which Marc Rich was the main mover. The ensuing publicity induced the Brunei government to keep a closer watch on the application of its embargo regulations.[10] 'No oil transported by tankers sailing from Brunei has reached South Africa anymore since then. Thus, another source of oil for South Africa has dried up,' the Bureau wrote in its 1990 report under the heading 'Publicity and Action Are Effective'.[11]

A leaking tap is a nuisance

It was clear that in a number of cases the material impact of government or company action with regard to oil supplies to South Africa was negligible. The EC oil embargo of 1985 is a prime example, and the time-worn argument used by shipping companies 'if we don't do it, ten others are queuing to take over' all too often reflected reality. However, measures which at first appeared to be ineffectual often had a psychological effect. And even of the wishy-washy EC policy one could say that although North Sea oil was of no importance to South Africa by the time the measure was taken, the North Sea – from which a considerable number of cargoes *had* originated in the early 1980s – was, in principle, no longer available in cases of emergency. Secondly, with every country or company that was no longer prepared (or allowed) to cooperate in oil supplies to South Africa, a smaller group remained. Losing a source for a specific type of crude oil could result in higher production or procurement costs because refineries are often geared towards the processing of certain types of oil. As far as shipping was concerned, the Scandinavian bans led to South Africa's being effectively cut off from a major section of the world's tanker fleet which it had relied upon for many years. Generally speaking, embargo busters were able to demand a suitable remuneration for their continued willingness to assist South Africa in the face of world opinion. Although much depended on market circumstances, to be dependent upon a limited number of suppliers clearly made a difference. SFF chairman Danie Vorster told *The Executive* in 1991 that lifting the embargo would bring savings as it would make greater oil tanker tonnage available should countries like Norway allow their shipowners to ship to South Africa again;[12] it was this effect which, as we have seen earlier, was felt by Adriatic Tankers after the lifting of the embargo. On the oil-trading side of the business, it is even more evident that in the first years after the halt on supplies from Iran, a small group of traders were able to charge high premiums. South Africa's oil buyers in the SFF were indeed concerned that they were putting too many eggs in one basket (read: John Deuss).[13] UN consultant Paul Conlon wrote in 1984: '...on international oil markets, if you are a racist pariah, you automatically must pay more for equivalent amounts of oil. Since they lack important options, it is always easy to hoist the price on them. And it is this, rather than any solidarity with South Africa's long-range objectives, that leads large parts of the Western business world to help them run the embargo.'[14] As we have seen, even when it came to the financing of oil transports, it was not a problem to find a small group of banks which were both willing and able to offer their services, but the fact that it was a small group did have an effect on the rates.

A lesson to be learnt from the oil embargo against South Africa is that the effects referred to above occurred, *despite* the fact that the embargo was not mandatory nor universally applied. Contrary to what some opponents of the oil embargo maintained, it was possibile for unilateral measures to be effective. This seemed to contradict the intention of the embargo, insofar as it was interpreted as *cutting off the supply*. If that would have been the aim of oil sanctions against South Africa, they obviously were a failure, a conclusion also drawn by some who told the Shipping Research Bureau that its own lists of embargo violations were the ultimate advertisement for the bankruptcy of the embargo.

The question whether economic sanctions had to be comprehensive in order to 'bite' was already being debated in the early 1960s.[15] At the time, the oil embargo was still formulated in terms of 'blockading' the shores of South Africa; that idea was abandoned in the years since, as it became clear that the powers capable of implementing such a measure could not be expected to do so. 'The professionalisation of this embargo campaign is illustrated by the fact that the aims are not exclusively couched in terms of all or nothing,' a Dutch weekly wrote on the occasion of the March 1980 seminar which led to the founding of the Shipping Research Bureau.[16] The effectiveness of the campaign was no longer seen in terms of its ability to completely cut off the oil supply, although the notion continued to serve as a point of reference in the eyes of the chairman of the Special Committee against Apartheid, who in his address to the Amsterdam seminar said: 'Our task is to prevent any oil from reaching South Africa, not merely to make South Africa pay premium for its oil supplies.'

Sometimes an awkward opening sentence inadvertently showed up in a publication of the SRB: 'Despite the embargo, South Africa still imports all the oil it needs.' Whoever let that slip was assured of a response: in view of the country's huge efforts to reduce its fuel import needs, it reflected an all too static appraisal. But more importantly, it went counter to what the Bureau wanted to stress as its principal message: that even if it were not possible to shut off the flow of oil *completely* and South Africa continued to get fuel from abroad or from its oil-from-coal plants, the country got that fuel at an *increased cost* which made itself felt as a result of the embargo.

Costs of the oil embargo

Just as everything which had to do with energy was an 'official secret', so too was most information needed for attempts to quantify the burden placed on the South African economy by the oil embargo. This had the peculiar effect that very few experts made the attempt and that a bureau which did not consider this its primary responsibility was expected to speak authoritatively on the matter – to the extent that it was no longer possible for the SRB to base its 'guesstimates' on other publications which neglected to state that their information was based on ...the Bureau's guesstimates. *'Oil embargo has cost SA $2bn a year – economist'* was the title of an article in the South African *Business Day* of 6 May 1992, in which 'a senior visiting US economist ... who wants to remain anonymous' was quoted as saying that 'Most Western economists estimated SA's measures to get around the oil embargo had cost government $2bn a year for the past decade.' This figure was remarkably close to the estimates of the Bureau, which was left in the dark as to the identities of these 'Western economists'.

Table 1 lists the annual estimated costs of the oil embargo as calculated by the Bureau from 1979 to 1993. The Bureau used various types of data; however imprecise some of these may have been, each provided a partial basis for the calculations. Known figures on energy consumption, imports, etc. from the period before South Africa declared these figures a state secret were a basis for extrapolations. The SRB's own findings on oil imports offered some clues, as did the 'classified' item in the South African import statistics (which was often assumed to cover mainly oil). Guesstimates by some experts and international oil trade journals served as a basis for making comparisons. Statements of ministers in parliament gave some indications, e.g., on the amounts involved in payments to middlemen, while the revenues from the various levies on the price of petroleum products were used to estimate the volumes sold at the pump.

Official secrecy in South Africa has been largely lifted; an attempt can now be made to calculate the impact of the oil embargo on the South African economy and the costs of the apartheid government's energy policies more precisely. According to a statement made on 17 August 1994 in the South African parliament by the Minister of Mineral and Energy Affairs, all historical statistical data on the oil trade are now available on request. Other information will probably come to the surface less easily. For this book, Kevin Davie explored some of the costs; he wrote his contribution just before the new South African government took office in 1994. Davie, working as an economic journalist within South Africa, was closer to the fire than were overseas observers, but he was just as much restricted in his ability to find out details and publish on what was happening, as was shown when his trail-blazing article entitled 'Inside Sasol' of November 1991 sparked off a vigorous debate on apartheid's energy policies but landed the author in trouble. Davie's magazine was forced to capitulate when Sasol referred the matter to the South African

Table 1 Costs of the oil embargo

	estimated cost of crude oil ($ mln)	estimated additional cost of embargo* ($ mln)
1979	3,800	2,360
1980	3,800	2,360
1981	3,000	2,000
1982	3,000	2,000
1983	3,000	2,300
1984	3,000	2,300
1985	3,000	2,300
1986	1,300	2,200
1987	1,730	2,460
1988	1,400	2,410
1989	1,600	2,410
1990	2,300	2,500
1991	1,600	2,300
1992	1,500	2,500
1993	2,200	2,200
Total	**36,230**	**34,600**

* Estimated expenditure for: the onshore and offshore search for crude oil and gas; premiums paid to middlemen and traders on imported oil; the development and construction of the Sasol plants, and subsidies on their output and on the subsequent under-utilisation of the crude oil refineries; the Mossgas project; the construction and operation of storage facilities and loss of interest ensuing from the maintenance of the strategic oil stockpile. *Not included*, among others: cost of security measures by oil companies and the state; cost of repairs due to sabotage; ecological damage by Sasol and Mossgas; loss of potential export earnings on coal consumed by Sasol; impact on agriculture of excessive water consumption by Sasol; other synfuel projects; above-average costs of financing oil imports.

Media Council and to express its regret for 'any inference in its articles that Sasol would not be financially viable without support from government'. An open debate appeared impossible, and notwithstanding the fact that each and every point raised in his November 1991 article have become commonplace since, the author lost all public support except that which was expressed in the Newsletter of the Shipping Research Bureau. The latter, of course, was in a comfortable position to give that support, being outside the grasp of Sasol, the Media Council and the South African authorities.[17]

In his contribution, Davie deals extensively with the costs of the *synthetic fuel industry* (Sasol and Mossgas), the *stockpiling programme*, the effects of the *centralisation and regulation* of the energy sector imposed by the apartheid government in addition to the *premiums* which were paid to the middlemen in order to guarantee that oil imports were kept up. The latter issue is elaborated upon by Clive Scholtz in his contribution – unique because it is written by a South African who for the first time tells about his own involvement in a notorious legal wrangle (concerning Marino Chiavelli) and an equally notorious investigation (that of the South African Advocate-General) in the early 1980s. Scholtz gives examples of overpayment which were far in excess of figures given by the government at the time (the government spoke of premiums not exceeding $8 a barrel in 1980; this in itself would have meant an additional burden of several hundreds of millions of dollars annually, if this premium applied to all the imported oil[18]). In 1994 an oil broker, who owed a considerable portion of his fortune to multimillion dollar commissions from the SFF in the early 1980s, was asked how much the premium paid by South Africa for its oil had cost its economy? 'Mr Clingman wouldn't hazard a guess. "You could ask the same question for everything. For example, how much did SA Airways lose by having to fly round the bulge of Africa? How much did we lose by not being able to get high technology or software, or having to sell coal at a discount of one or two dollars a ton? It was a tremendous price South Africa paid for apartheid".'[19]

One of the items on the embargo bill was South Africa's desperate *quest for oil* on its own territory by Soekor, the state exploration company. In November 1993 the South African press quoted ANC president Nelson Mandela as saying, in his address to an oil conference in Cape Town, that Soekor 'had spent billions in state revenue searching for oil to reduce dependence on imports. After 30 years, all it had come up with was a small gas deposit off Mossel Bay which resulted in the R15 billion Mossgas "financial disaster".'[20] The only deposit with a larger potential which 'the world's leading dry hole expert'[21] ever came up with was the Kudu gas field off Namibia, which Soekor's Namibian offshoot, Swakor, intended to develop in the 1980s; Namibian independence dashed all hopes that this would contribute towards reducing the burden of the oil embargo.[22]

The size, the locations and the cost of South Africa's strategic *stockpile of oil* were, as shown by Davie's article, a closely guarded secret for many years. In October 1983, in a speech before a National Party congress, Prime Minister P.W. Botha listed what he believed were his government's achievements over the past five years, one of them being the fact that the strategic reserves were now large enough to enable South Africa to survive a total oil boycott almost indefinitely. It was thought that Botha based his statement on the assumption that the reserves would enable the country to tide over the period needed for a switch-over to domestic fuel production and a rigorous fuel-saving policy. 'It is the first time the Government has claimed in such confident and defiant terms that SA is invulnerable to an oil embargo,' wrote the *Rand Daily Mail*, adding that it came as a 'sudden and, in view of the authorities' moves to restrict oil supply information, unexpected declaration'.[23] During the 1980s, Paul Conlon, the Shipping Research Bureau and others went to great lengths in order to obtain information on the oil stocks, with partial success. Whether the reserves were equivalent to three years, 15 months or just six months of imports or consumption, having to keep a stockpile of such dimensions imposed a burden on the economy. The SRB liked to quote the more eloquent statements made by South African politicians and journalists condemning the waste. Democratic Party MP Roger Hulley never tired of repeating that Mossgas was a *gold-plated white elephant*, a product of the *siege mentality* of the P.W. Botha era.[24] Already in 1987 Minister Barend du Plessis had denounced the millions of rands 'squandered on building up the country's strategic reserves of oil'. Three years later he told *Le Figaro* that 'when the oil boycott against us is

STOCKPILED SECRETS

Government has
begun selling the
billions of rands worth
of oil it has buried
underground. But just
how vast is the
strategic oil reserve?

The first attempt to stockpile crude in a coal mine was unfortunate, the story goes. *Glub, glub, glub* and the entire load sunk irretrievably into the earth.

The story was probably apocryphal, but it was one of many which circulated about the strategic reserve built to keep South Africa going if the world did its worst and cut off the oil.

Some pundits say much of the crude has solidified, one version being that a front-end loader will be needed to get it out. Another story claims the oil can be refined, but only at great expense because of its thick consistency.

Some officials say the oil is being eaten by microbes. The mind boggles – here we've kept the oil all this time only to have it consumed by microbes. They say AECI was called in to ward off the oil-eating microbes.

Then there was the great battle of the coal mines in the 1970s, when government was intent on using a disused coal mine to house oil, while Lonrho was unenthusiastic as it was its coal mine.

Lonrho does not like governments pushing it around, so it took its case to court and won. Government got to use the mine, but paid Lonrho more than it was initially prepared to offer. The eastern Transvaal mine was chosen by the storage authority because of the coherent rock formation in the area.

The strategic reserve once served a useful purpose. Remember the sniffer plane scandal in France when a plane was supposed to be able to fly over oil fields and locate oil? It cost the French dearly. South Africa spent R5 million on the project before trying the plane out in the vicinity of stored oil supplies. The plane could not sniff the supplies and was sent packing.

The previous Mineral and Energy Affairs Minister, Dawie de Villiers, said in November that the high costs of recovering oil from the reserve meant a saving of only about five or six cents a litre compared to imported oil. The oil had to be pumped out of the ground and transported to the refineries.

The Minister's estimate was surprising: oil was then about $35 a barrel; it is about $18 now. Much of the stockpile was bought at ridiculously low prices. Is the stockpile an asset or a liability?

The man who can answer these questions is Danie Vorster, the keeper of the strategic oil reserve. Vorster is chairman of the Central Energy Fund (CEF), which looks after the oil stockpile. He is also chairman of the Strategic Fuel Fund (SFF), which buys South Africa's oil.

Vorster is enormously powerful in South Africa's oil business – the Ministry even directs questions on policy matters to him. The CEF has assets of R10 billion under its control, including a 50% stake in Mossgas, and this excludes the oil stockpile.

Vorster's CEF staff work over the road from his office at the Industrial Development Corporation (IDC), where he is a senior GM. Vorster does not grant interviews, but is happy to respond to faxed questions.

First the microbes. Vorster confirms the problem, but says it was localised to the pipes used to move the oil. He says microbes are a problem in corroded pipes. The problem has been solved by special treatment of the pipes using "certain chemicals from AECI". The corporation is "in no other way involved in maintaining the stockpile".

Vorster indicates that the balance of payments will benefit by R1 billion from the decision to tap the strategic reserve: "Part of the local refining requirement will come from the stockpile which means that imports will be reduced," he says.

But he rejects suggestions that a front-end loader will be needed to access underground stores. "The stockpile is in a condition to be refined on a cost-effective basis. There is no truth in the statement that some crude has solidified and cannot be tapped. The only crude that cannot be recovered from underground containers will be a small percentage remaining in crevices and uneven floor formations."

Vorster confirms, however, that "a relatively small part of the reserve consists of a heavy residue from previous refining operations", but says this does not present a refining problem.

"Oil from the stockpile is sold to local refineries at international prices and there is no saving for them compared to imported oil." says Vorster.

Asked how the oil will be accessed, specifically if pumps and road tankers are used, Vorster's answer suggests just how extensive South Africa's strategic reserve infrastructure is: "Oil is moved to the refineries in the same way that it was put there – by pipeline."

But while detailed maps are available overseas for anti-apartheid activists to peruse, Vorster will not disclose the location of the reserve. The Shipping Research Bureau says the underground stores are at Kendal and Ferrobank in the Transvaal, Vrede in the Free State and Saldanha Bay in the Cape.

Vorster says this is classified information and cannot be commented upon. He also won't say how vast the reserve is. It is estimated at between six months' and two years' supply. The Shipping Research Bureau believes South Africa has stockpiled about six months' supply or seven to eight million tons.

But *Petroleum Intelligence Weekly* says South Africa had two years' supply stockpiled at the end of 1987. Split the difference and assume South Africa has a year's supply stocked underground. This is about $2 billion or R5,7 billion at current prices. About R1 billion is to be sold to increase social spending, but government will be able to raise several billion more as it reduces the stockpile to the 30 to 90 days most western countries keep as a reserve.

The keeper of the strategic reserve will not throw more light on the size of the stockpile under his control: "This information is classified and cannot be commented upon." [E]

Kevin Davie in *The Executive*, August 1991, 26-27

> *Might the elimination of apartheid not have opened up world oil supplies at a far lower price, allowing the country to develop more viable resources? It is no accident that the huge SASOL plants haven't been matched in other countries. They had no need to tie up huge sums of development capital in such projects when cheaper fuel sources were available. Mossel Bay's degree of viability is related to the country's isolation.*
>
> From: *The Star*, 20 February 1987

lifted, we will begin to reduce these reserves down to a more normal level for a country like ours. That could immediately bring in foreign currency, so necessary for our economy',[25] a statement which drew criticism from the economic affairs spokesman for the Conservative Party, Daan Nolte, who condemned 'the irresponsible manner in which the Minister of Finance bandies about the existence of our sizeable strategic oil reserves. It is against our law for an ordinary citizen to make an irresponsible statement like this and I ask whether Mr F.W. de Klerk intends taking action against Mr Barend du Plessis for his indiscretion.'[26]

To a certain degree, South Africa could derive consolation from benefits it was able to reap from the strategic stockpile at hand. The government was able to manipulate the stockpile in its efforts to counter its economic and political problems, such as in 1984–85, when it drew upon the stocks in order to reduce expensive imports and save foreign currency; in 1986 the stocks were replenished after a drastic fall in the price of oil.[27] During the Gulf crisis of 1990 South Africa went even further. In October 1990, the *South African Shipping News & Fishing Industry Review* reported that 'Ship watchers on the west coast are furious. They see large tankers loading at Saldanha Bay and believe South Africa is exporting crude oil from its strategic reserves.' The magazine offered a different explanation: 'Oil is being back hauled to Durban for refining and use domestically, a process that has been going on since 1983'; but readers told the editors that their explanation 'was nonsense. They said they knew of at least one large tanker that had sailed laden from Saldanha Bay for Europe a few months ago.' This time the stocks were taken advantage of by selling a few VLCC cargoes of Iranian heavy crude to Europe when prices were around $30 a barrel; when prices had dropped to $20 in early 1991, South Africa replenished its stockpile with lighter crudes, thus drawing a nice profit.[28]

The statement made by Minister Du Plessis proved that the South African government was beginning to acknowledge that oil sanctions were having a negative effect on the economy. In fact, P.W. Botha had done so at an earlier stage when he addressed a meeting in Vereeniging on 24 April 1986, saying:

> *Between 1973 and 1984 the Republic of South Africa had to pay R 22 billion more for oil than it would normally have spent. There were times when it was reported to me that we had enough oil for only a week. Just think what we could have done if we had that R 22 billion today ... what could be done in other areas? But we had to spend it because we couldn't bring our motor cars and our diesel locomotives to a standstill as our economic life would have collapsed. We paid a price, which we are still suffering from today.*[29]

Botha repeated this statement on several occasions[30] – he saw it as useful election propaganda for his National Party. Frene Ginwala recalls that when she, together with the SRB, had worked out a figure on the cost of the oil embargo for the first time and published it with the ANC/SWAPO oil embargo statement of March 1985, 'everybody laughed, even in the ANC... But then Botha came out with his statement, boasting that "we spent 22 billion rands to make sure you got your oil!" He didn't realise that he was saying they *wasted* 22 billion rands... And it was exactly the figure we had come up with.'

In April 1991, President F.W. de Klerk echoed the earlier 'indiscretion' of his Minister of Finance – as well as his evaluation of the negative effects of the embargo – when he said: 'Sanctions and the threat of sanctions have obliged South Africa to invest a portion of its savings in strategic reserves, including oil.' He admitted: 'Obviously this is a very unproductive form of investment that has contributed to the unfavourable course of economic growth and job creation.' De Klerk announced: 'South Africa's relations with the rest of the world have improved to such an extent ... that it has now been decided to lower the strategic reserves as far as oil is concerned.'[31] The decision was prompted as much by financial necessity as it was by the consequence of 'improved relations'. Part of the proceeds were earmarked for covering the spiralling capital requirement of the Mossel Bay project. The remainder was to be used for housing and various other socio-economic projects and for addressing 'security problems'.

The success of the oil embargo

July 1991: *'Sanctions worked'* was the heading on the front page of the South African *Weekly Mail* in the week that the US Comprehensive Anti-Apartheid Act was lifted. The weekly said that in 1986, when the CAAA was introduced, President P.W. Botha warned that sanctions, boycotts and embargoes had never worked anywhere; but within months the argument against sanctions had switched from their lack of effectiveness to their damaging consequences: 'Sanctions were blamed for every ill in the economy and the pro-sanctioneers were accused of creating hunger and unemployment for the black people ... Anyone doubting the importance of the international community in De Klerk's deliberations need only note the euphoria of the lifting of the bans this week.'[32]

At the end of 1989 *Southern Africa Report*, followed by the SRB Newsletter on the oil embargo, had signalled a change in the tune of the South African government when it quoted a South African radio programme 'Comment', regarded as a government mouthpiece. Minister Du Plessis had admitted that sanctions were hurting; the radio broadcast was the first to be candid about the remedy: one of the ways of dealing with sanctions was to embark on 'positive and dynamic ... social and constitutional reform'.[33]

During a parliamentary debate in February 1991, the Deputy Minister of Mineral and Energy Affairs showed how a direct connection was slowly emerging between the pressure of the oil embargo and other sanctions, and the attempts made by the South African government to get rid of that pressure: 'What people ... tend to lose sight of ... is the fact South Africa is still subject to a crude oil embargo. *Despite everything that has already been done*, the old pressure groups ... are trying to withhold crude oil from South Africa from a dated point of view.'[34] ('The old pressure groups, that's probably you and us,' said the SRB director when he quoted the minister's statement during a speech made at a hearing of the UN oil monitoring group in August 1991, raising chuckles at an otherwise solemn occasion.) The connection was also apparent in March 1992 when the apartheid government in its whites-only referendum asked the electorate for permission to pursue a policy of reform using the bogey of sanctions in its attempt to get the 'yes' vote. Just before the referendum, Foreign Minister Pik Botha announced in a public meeting that France had lifted its ban on the importation of South African coal. He said the effect of economic sanctions on South Africa could not be underestimated, and he went on to warn that if the 'no' vote won, the country would face the most severe sanctions in its history.[35]

'Severe' was *Business Day*'s rating of the effect of the oil embargo; the paper based this on the above-mentioned interview with a US economist. The effect of the other sanctions which still remained at the time (May 1992) – financial sanctions, US state and local sanctions, IMF and World Bank measures and the arms embargo – was in each case rated 'moderate'.[36] Sometimes there was a certain amount of 'competition' between the proponents of various types of sanctions (*my sanction is better than yours*), leading to futile discussions such as whether the primary focus should be on the sports boycott or financial sanctions, or which sanction had been the decisive one. Many commentators have ascribed a triggering role to the *financial* sanctions of the mid-1980s, arguing that the refusal in 1985 of the international banks to renew their short-term credits to South Africa was the final blow to the system of apartheid. In this connection, a remarkable proposition is advanced in this book by Van Bergeijk, who argues that had it not been for the costs imposed by the oil embargo over a lengthy period, the 1985 debt crisis would probably not have emerged. Joe Hanlon expressed the same thought in some of his earlier publications. In a report for the Commonwealth, he wrote that part of South Africa's heavy borrowing abroad had been for the sake of major electrification schemes, nuclear power and Sasol plants, all of which were needed to reduce the impact of the oil embargo; in *The Sanctions Handbook* of 1987 he pointed out that at the time of the 1985 debt crisis, 'That debt was $24 billion, almost exactly the cost of breaking the oil embargo!'[37]

In 1993, four years after he had edited *Sanctions Against Apartheid*, a rare book published in South Africa which argued the case in favour of sanctions, Mark Orkin reviewed the role sanctions had played in bringing apartheid to its knees. According to Orkin, sanctions on their own would not have done the job. But nor would mass mobilisation, underground activity or diplomatic pressure. 'They all amounted to a successful mix,' he said, but he pointed out that during the second half of the 1980s, 'sanctions became a leading partner in the struggle. De Klerk was literally dancing to the tunes of sanctions deadlines after he took office in 1989 ... By late 1989 and early 1990, sanctions were a conspicuous ingredient in the mix that forced reformist moves on the part of the government.'[38]

In an interview with *Time* in June 1993, the last president of white South Africa, F.W. de Klerk, stressed how desperate he was to be relieved of sanctions: 'The sooner the few remaining sanctions, and especially the economic and financial sanctions, are lifted, the sooner we will be able to address the heartrending problems many of our people have.'[39]

The liberal opposition party in the white parliament, the Progressive Federal Party (later the Democratic Party), had never been in favour of sanctions, says its former energy affairs spokesman, John Malcomess: 'We said they would never do any more but lose jobs for black people, and we were never of the opinion that any embargo would bring down apartheid, because there is always a way around sanctions. However, if the poor economic situation in South Africa was primarily a result of sanctions, and if it was the economic situation that was one of the triggering mechanisms in De Klerk's mind, then I think our long-held opinion was wrong; I think that, yes, sanctions probably played a role in ending apartheid.'

On 30 November 1993, South African Foreign Minister Pik Botha seemed determined to prove that the last white government definitely wanted to have the oil embargo lifted as soon as possible. He instructed the Director-General of Foreign Affairs to send a telegram to UN Secretary-General Boutros-Ghali to point out that the Transitional Executive Council would begin its work on 7 December. 'Remind the Secretary-General that the United Nations itself set the installation of the TEC as the trigger for the lifting of the oil embargo,' the Minister told his Director-General. The latter said he would tell Boutros-Ghali 'We anticipate an early announcement on the lifting of the oil embargo.'[40] Or was Pik Botha anticipating his surprising appointment as Minister of Mineral and Energy Affairs after the elections of 1994?

On 9 December 1993 the president of the UN General Assembly, Ambassador S.R. Insanally of Guyana, announced that *'the embargo related to the supply of petroleum and petroleum products to South Africa and investments in the petroleum industry there is now lifted.'*[41]

Annex

Fifteen Years of Oil Embargo Violations[1]

Total 1979–1993: 865 vessels – 195,040,437 deadweight tons[2]

ship's name[3]	dwt tonnage	month in S. Africa	sailed to South Africa from	main shipping company[4]	owners of oil cargo
Bergehus	205,807	Jan 79	Iraq	Bergesen	–
Havdrott	240,259	Jan/Feb 79	Middle East	Havtor	Transworld Oil
Capt. John G.P. Livanos	259,657	Feb 79	Qatar	G.P. Livanos	Ionian Transport
Energy Evolution	216,796	Feb 79	Iran/UAE	C.Y. Tung	BP
Erviken	82,824	Feb 79	UK/Netherlands	Wallem Steckmest	–
Esso Portland	50,967	Feb 79	USA	Exxon	Exxon
Philippine Star	70,145	Feb 79	Brunei	United Philippine Lines	Royal Dutch/Shell
Cherry Vesta	44,066	Mar 79	Indonesia	Norse Management	Galaxy/Stardust
Energy Progress	281,864	Mar 79	Brunei	C.Y. Tung	Royal Dutch/Shell
Mobil Progress	215,002	Mar 79	Netherlands	Mobil	Mobil
Myrtea	212,998	Mar 79	Netherlands Antilles	Royal Dutch/Shell	Royal Dutch/Shell
South Sun	213,928	Mar 79	Saudi Arabia	Salén	Marc Rich
Berge Septimus	284,512	Mar/Apr 79	Netherlands Antilles	Bergesen	Royal Dutch/Shell
Champlain b/o	121,989	Apr 79	Netherlands	Cie Générale Maritime	–
Maasrix	318,754	Apr 79	Persian Gulf/Saudi Arabia	SHV & RSV	Marc Rich
Neptune World	237,366	Apr 79	Iran	NOL & World-Wide Shipping	Transworld Oil
Havdrott	240,259	May 79	Iran	Havtor	Transworld Oil
Maasrix	318,754	May 79	Saudi Arabia	SHV & RSV	Transworld Oil/Marc Rich
Nicos I. Vardinoyannis	136,861	May 79	Saudi Arabia/UAE	Varnima Corp.	Marc Rich
Olympic Archer	218,496	May 79	Netherlands Antilles	Onassis	BP
St. Nicolas	55,908	May/Jne 79	Qatar	Anchor Shipping & Trading	–
Berge Septimus	284,512	Jne 79	Netherlands Antilles	Bergesen	Royal Dutch/Shell
Energy Progress	281,864	Jne 79	Brunei	C.Y. Tung	Royal Dutch/Shell
Havdrott	240,259	Jne 79	Saudi Arabia	Havtor	Transworld Oil
Litiopa	310,991	Jne 79	Netherlands Antilles	Royal Dutch/Shell	Royal Dutch/Shell
Mobil Petroleum	215,205	Jne 79	Gabon	Mobil	Mobil
Santa Cristina Prima	80,945	Jly 79	Australia +	Italnavi	–
Berge Brioni o/o	227,557	Jly 79	Oman	Bergesen	Royal Dutch/Shell
Havdrott	240,259	Jly 79	Saudi Arabia	Havtor	Transworld Oil
Polyscandia	224,850	Jly 79	Netherlands Antilles	Einar Rasmussen	Royal Dutch/Shell
Santa Augusta	80,945	Aug 79	Netherlands Antilles	Italnavi	
Staland	254,892	Aug 79	UAE/Iran	Helmer Staubo	Transworld Oil
Alva Sea o/o	225,010	Sep 79	Brunei	Silver Navigation	Royal Dutch/Shell
Berge Septimus	284,512	Sep 79	Netherlands Antilles	Bergesen	Royal Dutch/Shell
Oro Chief o/o	125,173	Sep 79	Netherlands	Sigurd Herlofson	Vitol
Prijan I	99,911	Sep 79	Saudi Arabia	United Philippine Lines	Marc Rich
Schelderix	230,673	Sep 79	Saudi Arabia	SHV & RSV	Marc Rich
Litiopa	310,991	Sep/Oct 79	Oman	Royal Dutch/Shell	Royal Dutch/Shell
Maasbree	276,045	Sep/Oct 79	Netherlands	Nedlloyd	Marc Rich
Maasrix	318,754	Sep/Oct 79	Netherlands	SHV & RSV	Marc Rich
Alva Sea o/o	225,010	Oct 79	Oman	Silver Navigation	Royal Dutch/Shell
Dirch Mærsk	208,899	Oct 79	Oman	A.P. Møller	Hestonie
Havdrott	240,259	Oct/Nov 79	Saudi Arabia	Havtor	Transworld Oil
Laura Prima o/o	139,401	Oct/Nov 79	Saudi Arabia	Achille Lauro	Marc Rich
Karama Mærsk	337,733	Nov 79	Netherlands	A.P. Møller	Vitol

ship's name[3]	dwt tonnage	month in S. Africa	sailed to South Africa from	main shipping company[4]	owners of oil cargo
Maasrix	318,754	Nov 79	Saudi Arabia	SHV & RSV	Marc Rich
Dirch Mærsk	208,899	Dec 79	Oman	A.P. Møller	Hestonie
Havdrott	240,259	Dec 79	Saudi Arabia	Havtor	Transworld Oil
Ras Mærsk	289,166	Dec 79	Netherlands	A.P. Møller	–
Robert Mærsk	289,166	Dec 79	Saudi Arabia	A.P. Møller	Marc Rich
Humboldt	222,592	Dec 79/Jan 80	Greece	Schlüssel Reederei	Transworld Oil
Limatula	315,695	Dec 79/Jan 80	Brunei	Royal Dutch/Shell	Royal Dutch/Shell
Salem	213,928	Dec 79/Jan 80	Kuwait	Mitakis/Soudan/Reidel	Mitakis et al. [stolen oil]
Dirch Mærsk	208,899	Jan 80	Iraq/Oman	A.P. Møller	Hestonie
Mytilus	210,292	Jan 80	Oman	Royal Dutch/Shell	Royal Dutch/Shell
Staland	254,892	Jan 80	Greece	Helmer Staubo	Transworld Oil
Marakanda	217,520	Jan/Feb 80	Netherlands	N.J. Goulandris	Vitol
Elbe Maru o/o	158,591	Feb 80	Brunei	Sanko	–
Humboldt/Fleurtje	222,592	Feb 80	Saudi Arabia	Transworld Oil	Transworld Oil
Havdrott	240,259	Feb 80	Saudi Arabia/Persian Gulf	Havtor	Transworld Oil
Mytilus	210,292	Feb 80	Oman	Royal Dutch/Shell	Royal Dutch/Shell
I.D. Sinclair	254,735	Feb/Mar 80	Saudi Arabia/UAE	Canadian Pacific	Transworld Oil/Marc Rich
Albahaa B.	239,410	Mar 80	Saudi Arabia	Palm Shipping	Marc Rich
Kimberly	209,407	Mar 80	Saudi Arabia/Oman	Palm Shipping	Transworld Oil
Latirus	278,220	Mar 80	Netherlands Antilles	Royal Dutch/Shell	Royal Dutch/Shell
Havdrott	240,259	Mar/Apr 80	Oman/PG/Saudi Arabia	Havtor	Transworld Oil
Karoline Mærsk	339,308	Mar/Apr 80	Netherlands	A.P. Møller	Vitol
Berge Septimus	284,512	Apr 80	Netherlands Antilles	Bergesen	Royal Dutch/Shell
Dirch Mærsk	208,899	Apr 80	Persian Gulf/Oman	A.P. Møller	–
Fleurtje [ex-Humboldt]	222,592	Apr 80	Oman/Saudi Arabia	Transworld Oil	Transworld Oil
Kristine Mærsk	336,107	Apr 80	Saudi Arabia	A.P. Møller	Transworld Oil
Macoma	209,995	Apr 80	Brunei	Royal Dutch/Shell	Royal Dutch/Shell
Ogden Nelson	270,378	Apr 80	Saudi Arabia/Iran	Ogden Corp.	Marc Rich
Schelderix	230,673	Apr 80	Iran	SHV & RSV	Euravia
Staland	254,892	Apr 80	Iran/Saudi Arabia	Helmer Staubo	Transworld Oil
Flying Cloud	228,541	Apr/May 80	Iran	Palm Shipping	–
Höegh Rover b/o	95,361	Apr/May 80	Brunei	Leif Höegh	BP
Havdrott	240,259	May 80	Saudi Arabia/UAE/PG/Oman	Havtor	Transworld Oil
Jeppesen Mærsk	59,650	May 80	Canada +	A.P. Møller	–
Karoline Mærsk	339,308	May 80	Saudi Arabia/transhipment PG	A.P. Møller	Transworld Oil
Kate Mærsk	339,206	May 80	PG/Saudi Arabia/Oman	A.P. Møller	Marc Rich
Latirus	278,220	May 80	Oman	Royal Dutch/Shell	Royal Dutch/Shell
Liparus	315,700	May 80	Netherlands Antilles	Royal Dutch/Shell	Royal Dutch/Shell
Norse King	231,759	May 80	Netherlands Antilles	Odd Godager	–
Regina	233,009	May 80	Netherlands Antilles	Hansen-Tangen	NEEP
Fleurtje	222,592	May/Jne 80	Iran	Transworld Oil	Transworld Oil
Staland	254,892	May/Jly 80	Oman/Iran	Helmer Staubo	Transworld Oil
Dagmar Mærsk	212,759	Jne 80	Saudi Arabia/Iran	A.P. Møller	Euravia
Norse Queen	232,368	Jne 80	Iran	Odd Godager	Euravia
Rømø Mærsk	290,588	Jne 80	Netherlands Antilles	A.P. Møller	–
Ras Mærsk	289,166	Jne/Jly 80	Netherlands	A.P. Møller	Vitol
Havdrott	240,259	Jly 80	Saudi Arabia/Oman	Havtor	Transworld Oil
Macoma	209,995	Jly 80	Oman	Royal Dutch/Shell	Royal Dutch/Shell
Mytilus	210,292	Jly 80	Netherlands Antilles	Royal Dutch/Shell	Royal Dutch/Shell
Sangstad	152,399	Jly 80	Iran	A.F. Klaveness	–
Flying Cloud	228,541	Jly/Aug 80	Iran	Palm Shipping	–
Eastern Mobility	89,095	Aug 80	Brunei	World-Wide Shipping	Royal Dutch/Shell
Havdrott	240,259	Aug 80	Saudi Arabia/transhipment PG	Havtor	Transworld Oil
Jakob Mærsk	59,650	Aug 80	Canada +	A.P. Møller	–
Liparus	315,700	Aug 80	Oman	Royal Dutch/Shell	Royal Dutch/Shell
Robert Mærsk	289,166	Aug 80	Saudi Arabia	A.P. Møller	Marc Rich
Karen Mærsk	337,816	Aug/Sep 80	Iran/transhipment PG	A.P. Møller	Transworld Oil

ship's name[3]	dwt tonnage	month in S. Africa	sailed to South Africa from	main shipping company[4]	owners of oil cargo
Karoline Mærsk	339,308	Aug/Sep 80	Netherlands	A.P. Møller	–
Berge Septimus	284,512	Sep 80	Netherlands Antilles	Bergesen	Royal Dutch/Shell
Fleurtje	222,592	Sep 80	Persian Gulf/Oman	Transworld Oil	Transworld Oil
Ogden Sungari	275,932	Sep 80	Iran/Saudi Arabia/UAE	Ogden Corp.	Marc Rich
Regina	233,009	Sep 80	Saudi Arabia	Hansen-Tangen	Marc Rich
Tripharos o/o	164,990	Sep 80	Brunei	North Am. Ship Ag./Sanko	BP
Liparus	315,700	Sep/Oct 80	Netherlands Antilles	Royal Dutch/Shell	Royal Dutch/Shell
Argyle	74,055	Oct 80	Netherlands	Allied Shipping Int.	Vitol
Cast Puffin b/o	145,015	Oct 80	UK [Norwegian oil]	Cast Eurocanadian	Transworld Oil
Havdrott	240,259	Oct 80	Persian Gulf/Oman	Havtor	Transworld Oil
Kimberly	209,407	Oct 80	Saudi Arabia	Palm Shipping	Marc Rich
Norse King	231,759	Oct 80	UAE/Saudi Arabia/Iran	Odd Godager	–
Staland	254,892	Oct 80	Persian Gulf	Helmer Staubo	Transworld Oil
Cast Petrel b/o	145,052	Nov 80	t/s Singapore [Saudi Arabia]	Cast Eurocanadian	Marc Rich/Transworld Oil
Cast Skua b/o	104,749	Nov 80	Netherlands Antilles	Cast Eurocanadian	–
Skyros o/o	100,124	Nov 80	Tunisia [Algerian oil]	Eletson Corp.	–
Northern Star	130,318	Nov 80	UK [Norwegian oil]	York Shipping	Transworld Oil
Garden Green o/o	169,147	Nov 80	Netherlands	North Am. Ship Agencies	Kaiser Corp.
Macoma	209,995	Nov 80	Brunei	Royal Dutch/Shell	Royal Dutch/Shell
Robert Mærsk	289,166	Nov 80	Netherlands	A.P. Møller	Vitol
Tsushima Maru o/o	157,674	Nov 80	Brunei	Sanko	–
Norse King	231,759	Nov/Dec 80	Persian Gulf	Odd Godager	–
Staland	254,892	Nov/Dec 80	Oman	Helmer Staubo	Transworld Oil
Bralanta	155,211	Dec 80	Ecuador	Braathens Rederi	Marc Rich
Flying Cloud	228,541	Dec 80	Saudi Arabia	Palm Shipping	Marc Rich
Fleurtje	222,592	Dec 80/Jan 81	Saudi Arabia	Transworld Oil	Transworld Oil
Havdrott	240,259	Dec 80/Jan 81	Saudi Arabia/Persian Gulf	Havtor	Transworld Oil
Konkar Dinos o/o	234,752	Dec 80/Jan 81	Netherlands	Leif Höegh	Marimpex
Mytilus	210,292	Dec 80/Jan 81	Netherlands Antilles	Royal Dutch/Shell	Royal Dutch/Shell
Port Hawkesbury	257,028	Dec 80/Jan 81	Netherlands Antilles	Canadian Pacific	–
Cherry Nes	51,793	Jan 81	Saudi Arabia +	Norse Management	NEEP
Eastern Mobility	89,095	Jan 81	Brunei	World-Wide Shipping	Royal Dutch/Shell
Nai Rocco Piaggio	254,116	Jan 81	Saudi Arabia	Navigazione Alta Italia	Transworld Oil
Spey Bridge b/o	115,280	Jan 81	UK [Norwegian oil]	Silver Navigation	Transworld Oil
Cast Puffin b/o	145,015	Jan/Feb 81	Algeria	Cast Eurocanadian	Swiss company
Tripharos o/o	164,990	Jan/Feb 81	Brunei	North Am. Ship Ag./Sanko	–
Dagmar Mærsk	212,759	Feb 81	Netherlands [p.c. t/s UK +]	A.P. Møller	Vitol
Latirus	278,220	Feb 81	Netherlands Antilles	Royal Dutch/Shell	Royal Dutch/Shell
Nai Rocco Piaggio	254,116	Feb 81	Saudi Arabia/UAE	Navigazione Alta Italia	Marc Rich
Staland	254,892	Feb/Mar 81	Persian Gulf/Oman	Helmer Staubo	Transworld Oil
Liparus	315,700	Mar 81	Netherlands Antilles	Royal Dutch/Shell	Royal Dutch/Shell
Wilhelmine Essberger	244,694	Mar 81	Spain	John T. Essberger	–
Havdrott	240,259	Mar 81	Iran	Havtor	Transworld Oil
Jamunda	262,901	Mar 81	UAE/Persian Gulf	John Fredriksen	–
Port Hawkesbury	257,028	Mar 81	Saudi Arabia	Canadian Pacific	Marc Rich
Fleurtje	222,592	Mar/Apr 81	Saudi Arabia	Transworld Oil	Transworld Oil
Kimberly	209,407	Mar/Apr 81	Saudi Arabia	Palm Shipping	NEEP
World Premier	233,931	Apr 81	t/s France [unknown]	World-Wide Shipping	–
Regina	233,009	Apr 81	UAE	Hansen-Tangen	–
Nai Rocco Piaggio	254,116	Apr/May 81	Saudi Arabia	Navigazione Alta Italia	NEEP
I.D. Sinclair	254,735	May 81	t/s Spain [UK/Algeria/Norway]	Canadian Pacific	Transworld Oil
Jamunda	262,901	May 81	UAE/Saudi Arabia	John Fredriksen	Transworld Oil
Staland	254,892	May 81	Saudi Arabia	Helmer Staubo	Transworld Oil
Cast Fulmar b/o	161,805	May/Jne 81	Netherlands	Cast Eurocanadian	Vitol
Norse King	231,759	May/Jne 81	Saudi Arabia	Odd Godager	Transworld Oil
Oder Maru o/o	172,278	May/Jne 81	Brunei	Sanko	–
Cast Cormorant b/o	155,106	Jne 81	United Kingdom	Cast Eurocanadian	–

ship's name[3]	dwt tonnage	month in S. Africa	sailed to South Africa from	main shipping company[4]	owners of oil cargo
Cast Osprey b/o	104,749	Jne 81	United Kingdom/Spain	Cast Eurocanadian	–
Fleurtje	222,592	Jne 81	Saudi Arabia/UAE	Transworld Oil	Transworld Oil
Lake Mendocino b/o	145,092	Jne 81	Saudi Arabia	Cast Eurocanadian	Rakono Oil & Gas A.G.
Myrtea	212,998	Jne 81	Netherlands Antilles	Royal Dutch/Shell	Royal Dutch/Shell
Philip of Macedon	220,050	Jne 81	Saudi Arabia	P.M. Nomikos	Transworld Oil
Sibosix b/o	77,300	Jne 81	Persian Gulf	Tschudi & Eitzen	–
Jamunda	262,901	Jne/Jly 81	Iran	John Fredriksen	
Flying Cloud	228,541	Jly 81	Iran/PG/Saudi Arabia	Palm Shipping	Transworld Oil
Gorgona	150,977	Jly 81	Saudi Arabia	Kulukundis	–
Port Hawkesbury	257,028	Jly 81	United Kingdom	Canadian Pacific	–
Regina	233,009	Jly 81	Saudi Arabia	Hansen-Tangen	Latourag S.A.
Staland	254,892	Jly 81	Qatar/UAE	Helmer Staubo	Transworld Oil
Castleton	228,342	Jly/Aug 81	Oman	GATX/Marine Transport L.	Transworld Oil
Fleurtje	222,592	Jly/Aug 81	Saudi Arabia	Transworld Oil	Transworld Oil
Norse King	231,759	Jly/Aug 81	Qatar/Saudi Arabia	Odd Godager	Transworld Oil
Jane Stove	141,754	Aug 81	Saudi Arabia/UAE	Lorentzens Rederi	–
St. Marcos	92,100	Aug 81	Netherlands	Marimpex	Marimpex
Staland	254,892	Aug 81	Saudi Arabia	Helmer Staubo	Transworld Oil
Cast Narwhal o/o	268,728	Aug/Sep 81	Saudi Arabia/Iran	Cast Eurocanadian	NEEP
Castleton	228,342	Sep 81	Middle East [?]	GATX/Marine Transport L.	Transworld Oil
Eirama	104,447	Sep 81	Saudi Arabia	Thor Dahl	
Fleurtje	222,592	Sep 81	Saudi Arabia	Transworld Oil	Transworld Oil
Höegh Hill o/o	245,323	Sep 81	Netherlands	Leif Höegh	Marimpex
Montana	102,827	Sep 81	UAE/Saudi Arabia	Hadjipateras	NEEP
Norse King	231,759	Sep 81	UAE/Iran	Odd Godager	–
Regina	233,009	Sep 81	Saudi Arabia	Hansen-Tangen	Transworld Oil
World Splendour o/o	164,190	Sep 81	Brunei	World-Wide Shipping	–
Adna	233,011	Oct 81	Saudi Arabia	Hansen-Tangen	–
Cast Cormorant b/o	155,106	Oct 81	Iran/Oman	Cast Eurocanadian	Transworld Oil
Kyrnicos E.	122,233	Oct 81	Algeria	Tsakos Shipping & Trading	Transworld Oil
Norse Falcon	88,725	Oct 81	Saudi Arabia	Odd Godager	Tradinaft/Marcotrade
Wangli	126,999	Oct 81	Gabon	Jørgen P. Jensen	–
Recife b/o	152,396	Oct/Nov 81	Netherlands	Thyssen-Bornemisza	Marimpex
Regina	233,009	Oct/Nov 81	Oman	Hansen-Tangen	Transworld Oil
Staland	254,892	Oct/Nov 81	Oman	Helmer Staubo	Transworld Oil
Cast Cormorant b/o	155,106	Nov 81	unknown	Cast Eurocanadian	–
Cast Puffin b/o	145,015	Nov 81	Brunei	Cast Eurocanadian	–
Castleton	228,342	Nov 81	Oman	GATX/Marine Transport L.	Transworld Oil
Dona Margaro	144,148	Nov 81	Saudi Arabia	Eddie Hsu/John Essberger	NEEP
Moscliff	274,938	Nov 81	Oman/PG/Saudi Arabia	Mosvold Shipping	–
Norborn	289,574	Nov 81	Saudi Arabia	Sigurd Sverdrup	Montfort Trading S.A.
Thorsholm	284,299	Nov 81	Saudi Arabia	Thor Dahl	Transworld Oil
Adna	233,011	Dec 81	Saudi Arabia	Hansen-Tangen	–
Evita	133,760	Dec 81	Saudi Arabia	Uglands Rederi	Montfort Trading S.A.
Fleurtje	222,592	Dec 81	Saudi Arabia	Transworld Oil	Transworld Oil
I.D. Sinclair	254,735	Dec 81	Saudi Arabia	Canadian Pacific	Transworld Oil
Jalna o/o	158,694	Dec 81	Saudi Arabia	Anders Jahre	NEEP
Johs. Stove	135,900	Dec 81	Brunei	Lorentzens Rederi	–
St. Marcos	92,100	Dec 81	Netherlands	Marimpex	Marimpex
Northern Victory	90,855	Dec 81/Mar 83	Brunei	Palm Shipping	
Washington Enterprise [ex-Wilh. Essberger]	244,694	Dec 81/Jan 82	Iran	John Essberger	–
Berge King	284,919	Jan 82	Saudi Arabia	Bergesen	NEEP
Castleton	228,342	Jan 82	Oman	GATX/Marine Transport L.	Transworld Oil
Jane Stove	141,754	Jan 82	Saudi Arabia	Lorentzens Rederi	Montfort Trading S.A.
Johs. Stove	135,900	Jan 82	Saudi Arabia	Lorentzens Rederi	–
Moscliff	274,938	Jan 82	Persian Gulf	Mosvold Shipping	–

ship's name[3]	dwt tonnage	month in S. Africa	sailed to South Africa from	main shipping company[4]	owners of oil cargo
Ogden Nelson	270,378	Jan 82	Saudi Arabia	Ogden Corp.	NEEP
Staland	254,892	Jan 82	Saudi Arabia/Iran	Helmer Staubo	Transworld Oil
I.D. Sinclair	254,735	Jan/Feb 82	Oman	Canadian Pacific	Transworld Oil
Sirenia	228,670	Jan/Feb 82	Saudi Arabia	Alpaca Shipping	Transworld Oil
Thorsaga	284,299	Feb 82	Persian Gulf	Thor Dahl	–
Viking Harrier	81,279	Feb 82	Brunei	Norse Management	Marc Rich
Vinga	138,344	Feb 82	Brunei	Mowinckels Rederi	Marc Rich
Cast Narwhal o/o	268,728	Mar 82	Oman	Cast Eurocanadian	Transworld Oil
Fleurtje	222,592	Mar 82	Persian Gulf	Transworld Oil	Transworld Oil
Johs. Stove	135,900	Mar 82	UAE	Lorentzens Rederi	–
Norborn	289,574	Mar 82	Saudi Arabia/UAE	Sigurd Sverdrup	Montfort Trading S.A.
Ogden Sungari	275,932	Mar 82	UAE	Ogden Corp.	–
Regina	233,009	Mar 82	Saudi Arabia	Hansen-Tangen	–
Thorsholm	284,299	Mar 82	Saudi Arabia	Thor Dahl	Transworld Oil
Viking Falcon	81,279	Mar 82	Brunei	Norse Management	Marc Rich
Archontas	155,499	Mar/Apr 82	UK/unknown country?	Diamantis Pateras	–
Cast Razorbill b/o	103,078	Apr 82	Algeria	Cast Eurocanadian	–
Castleton	228,342	Apr 82	Oman	GATX/Marine Transport L.	Transworld Oil
Ogden Nelson	270,378	Apr 82	Persian Gulf	Ogden Corp.	–
Pericles Halcoussis b/o	84,141	Apr 82	Brunei	A. Halcoussis	Marc Rich
Staland	254,892	Apr 82	Iran	Helmer Staubo	Transworld Oil
Fleurtje	222,592	May 82	Iran/Oman	Transworld Oil	Transworld Oil
Höegh Fountain b/o	78,488	May 82	Brunei	Leif Höegh	Marc Rich
Johs. Stove	135,900	May 82	Brunei	Lorentzens Rederi	Marc Rich
Lancer Lion [ex-Jamunda]	262,901	May 82	Oman/Saudi Arabia/PG	John Fredriksen	–
Thorsholm	284,299	May 82	Iran/UAE/Oman	Thor Dahl	–
Berge King	284,919	Jne 82	UAE	Bergesen	–
Fleurtje	222,592	Jne 82	Saudi Arabia/Oman/PG	Transworld Oil	Transworld Oil
Sea Breeze	136,100	Jne 82	Libya	T.S. Bendixen	Coastal
Staland	254,892	Jne 82	Iran/Oman/UAE	Helmer Staubo	Transworld Oil
Ypatia Halcoussi b/o	84,137	Jne 82	Brunei	A. Halcoussis	Marc Rich
Cast Narwhal o/o	268,728	Jne/Jly 82	Persian Gulf	Cast Eurocanadian	–
Siljestad	152,398	Jly 82	Middle East or Far East	A.F. Klaveness	–
Staland	254,892	Jly 82	UAE/Saudi Arabia/PG	Helmer Staubo	Transworld Oil
Thorsholm	284,299	Jly 82	Persian Gulf	Thor Dahl	–
Johs. Stove	135,900	Jly/Aug 82	Brunei	Lorentzens Rederi	Marc Rich
St. Marcos	92,100	Jly/Aug 82	Netherlands	Marimpex	Marimpex
Castleton	228,342	Aug 82	Oman/UAE/Saudi Arabia	GATX/Marine Transport L.	Transworld Oil
Fleurtje	222,592	Aug 82	Oman	Transworld Oil	Transworld Oil
Thanassis M. o/o	70,341	Aug 82	Brunei	Thenamaris	Marc Rich
Platonic b/o	83,876	Aug/Sep 82	Brunei	C.M. Lemos	Marc Rich
St. Tobias	254,520	Aug/Sep 82	Netherlands	Marimpex	Marimpex
Staland	254,892	Aug/Sep 82	Oman	Helmer Staubo	Transworld Oil
Berge King	284,919	Sep 82	Iran	Bergesen	–
Berge Queen	284,976	Sep 82	Oman/Persian Gulf	Bergesen	Transworld Oil
Melpo Lemos	253,985	Sep 82	Iran	C.M. Lemos	–
Ogden Sungari	275,932	Sep 82	UAE/Iran	Ogden Corp.	–
Archontissa Katingo b/o	85,414	Sep/Oct 82	Brunei	Diamantis Pateras	Marc Rich
I.D. Sinclair	254,735	Sep/Oct 82	Persian Gulf	Canadian Pacific	–
Astraea	91,130	Oct 82	UAE	G.P. Livanos	–
Berge King	284,919	Oct 82	Qatar/Persian Gulf	Bergesen	–
Cast Narwhal o/o	268,728	Oct 82	Iran/Saudi Arabia	Cast Eurocanadian	–
Castleton	228,342	Oct 82	Oman	GATX/Marine Transport L.	Transworld Oil
Elmina o/o	94,464	Oct 82	Brunei	Thenamaris	Marc Rich
Hervang	127,004	Oct 82	Brunei	Olaf Vabøen	Marc Rich
St. Marcos	92,100	Oct/Nov 82	Soviet Union/Spain	Marimpex	Marimpex
Berge Queen	284,976	Nov 82	UAE	Bergesen	–
Castleton	228,342	Nov 82	Oman	GATX/Marine Transport L.	Transworld Oil

ship's name[3]	dwt tonnage	month in S. Africa	sailed to South Africa from	main shipping company[4]	owners of oil cargo
Mobil Weser	102,504	Nov 82	Netherlands	Leif Höegh	Marimpex
Ogden Nelson	270,378	Nov 82	Persian Gulf	Ogden Corp.	–
Staland	254,892	Nov 82	Oman	Helmer Staubo	Transworld Oil
Fleurtje	222,592	Dec 82	Persian Gulf	Transworld Oil	Transworld Oil
Berge King	284,919	Dec 82	Iran/Oman	Bergesen	Transworld Oil
Filikon L.	85,126	Dec 82	Brunei	G.P. Livanos	Marc Rich
Ogden Sungari	275,932	Dec 82	Iran	Ogden Corp.	–
St. Benedict	236,807	Dec 82	Netherlands	Marimpex	Marimpex
Kaszony b/o	75,470	Dec 82/Jan 83	Malaysia	Thyssen-Bornemisza	Transworld Oil
Berge Prince	284,522	Jan 83	UAE/Oman/Persian Gulf	Bergesen	–
Berge Queen	284,976	Jan 83	Iran	Bergesen	–
Bergebonde b/o	155,048	Jan 83	Brunei	Bergesen	Marc Rich
Castleton	228,342	Jan 83	Oman	GATX/Marine Transport L.	Transworld Oil
Eirama	104,447	Jan 83	Iran	Thor Dahl	–
Moscliff	274,938	Jan 83	Iran	Mosvold Shipping	–
Staland	254,892	Jan 83	Oman/Persian Gulf	Helmer Staubo	Transworld Oil
Neptune Pegasus	86,408	Feb 83	Brunei	Neptune Orient Lines	Marc Rich
St. Marcos	92,100	Feb 83	Oman	Marimpex	Marimpex
Thanassis M. o/o	70,341	Feb 83	Brunei	Thenamaris	Marc Rich
Alexander the Great	325,645	Feb/Mar 83	Persian Gulf	P.M. Nomikos	–
Moscliff	274,938	Feb/Mar 83	Persian Gulf	Mosvold Shipping	Marimpex
Berge Prince	284,522	Mar 83	Persian Gulf	Bergesen	–
Eirama	104,447	Mar 83	UAE/Persian Gulf	Thor Dahl	–
Fleurtje	222,592	Mar 83	Persian Gulf	Transworld Oil	Transworld Oil
Jane Stove	141,754	Mar 83	Persian Gulf	Lorentzens Rederi	–
Neptune Pavo	86,417	Mar 83	Brunei	Neptune Orient Lines	Marc Rich
Thorsholm	284,299	Mar/Apr 83	Persian Gulf	Thor Dahl	–
Fortuneship L.	268,081	Apr 83	Middle East	G.P. Livanos	–
Johs. Stove	135,900	Apr 83	Saudi Arabia	Lorentzens Rederi	–
Berge King	284,919	Apr/May 83	Persian Gulf	Bergesen	–
Castleton	228,342	Apr/May 83	Oman	Marine Transport Lines	Transworld Oil
Berge Prince	284,522	May 83	Persian Gulf	Bergesen	–
Filikon L.	85,126	May 83	Brunei	G.P. Livanos	Marc Rich
Fleurtje	222,592	May 83	Oman	Transworld Oil	Transworld Oil
Puma	240,270	May 83	Netherlands	John Fredriksen	Marimpex
Thorsholm	284,299	May/Jne 83	Oman	Thor Dahl	–
Jane Stove	141,754	Jne 83	Saudi Arabia	Lorentzens Rederi	Marimpex
Liberator	155,499	Jne 83	Oman/UAE	Diamantis Pateras	–
Berge King	284,919	Jne/Jly 83	Saudi Arabia	Bergesen	–
Fleurtje	222,592	Jne/Jly 83	Oman	Transworld Oil	Transworld Oil
Höegh Foam b/o	78,571	Jne/Jly 83	Brunei	Leif Höegh	Marc Rich
Archontissa Katingo b/o	85,414	Jly 83	Brunei	Diamantis Pateras	Marc Rich
Long Phoenix	51,361	Jly 83	Oman	Einar Lange	–
St. Tobias	254,520	Jly 83	Persian Gulf [?]	Marimpex	Marimpex
Ogden Nelson	270,378	Jly/Aug 83	UAE	Ogden Corp.	–
Thorsholm	284,299	Jly/Aug 83	Saudi Arabia	Thor Dahl	Marimpex
Alexander the Great	325,645	Aug 83	Saudi Arabia	P.M. Nomikos	–
Fleurtje	222,592	Aug 83	Oman	Transworld Oil	Transworld Oil
Jaguar	239,600	Aug 83	Iran	John Fredriksen	Marimpex
Palmstar Cherry	96,530	Aug/Sep 83	Brunei	Palm Shipping	Marc Rich
Kona b/o	169,080	Sep 83	Saudi Arabia	Fairwind Enterprises	–
Lorenzo Halcoussi b/o	71,143	Sep 83	Brunei	A. Halcoussis	Marc Rich
Manhattan Viscount	87,076	Sep 83	Brunei	Fearnley & Eger	Marc Rich
Moscliff	274,938	Sep 83	Iran/UAE	Mosvold Shipping	–
St. Tobias	254,520	Sep 83	Saudi Arabia	Marimpex	Marimpex
Virginia	240,597	Sep/Oct 83	Saudi Arabia/Kuwait	Hadjipateras	Marimpex
Alexander the Great	325,645	Oct 83	Persian Gulf	P.M. Nomikos	–

ship's name[3]	dwt tonnage	month in S. Africa	sailed to South Africa from	main shipping company[4]	owners of oil cargo
Fabian	285,700	Oct 83	Oman	Johan Reksten	Transworld Oil
Fleurtje	222,592	Oct 83	Oman	Transworld Oil	Transworld Oil
St. Benedict	236,807	Oct 83	Saudi Arabia	Marimpex	Marimpex
Thorsaga	284,299	Oct 83	Saudi Arabia	Thor Dahl	Marimpex
Johs. Stove	135,900	Oct/Nov 83	Persian Gulf	Lorentzens Rderi	–
Neptune Pegasus	86,408	Oct/Nov 83	Brunei	Neptune Orient Lines	Marc Rich
Ogden Nelson	270,378	Oct/Nov 83	Iran	Ogden Corp.	–
Fleurtje	222,592	Nov 83	Saudi Arabia/Oman	Transworld Oil	Transworld Oil
Heron	123,597	Nov 83	UAE	Soc.d'Etudes & de Gestion	–
Matterhorn [ex-Robert Mærsk]	289,166	Nov 83	Iran	A.P. Møller	Bonaire Trading [Wolman]
Höegh Fortuna b/o	78,531	Nov/Dec 83	Brunei	Leif Höegh	Marc Rich
Thorsaga	284,299	Nov/Dec 83	Qatar/UAE	Thor Dahl	–
Berge King	284,919	Dec 83	Saudi Arabia	Bergesen	–
Cougar	290,739	Dec 83	Saudi Arabia/Kuwait	John Fredriksen	Marimpex
Liberator	155,499	Dec 83	Brunei	Diamantis Pateras	Marc Rich
Moscliff	274,938	Dec 83	Persian Gulf	Mosvold Shipping	Marimpex
St. Tobias	254,520	Dec 83	Saudi Arabia/Persian Gulf	Marimpex	Marimpex
Virginia	240,597	Dec 83	Iran/Saudi Arabia/Oman	Hadjipateras	Bonaire Trading [Wolman]
Ogden Nelson	270,378	Dec 83/Jan 84	UAE	Ogden Corp.	–
Moscliff	274,938	Jan 84	Persian Gulf	Mosvold Shipping	–
St. Tobias	254,520	Jan 84	Persian Gulf ?	Marimpex	Marimpex
Thorsaga	284,299	Jan 84	Persian Gulf	Thor Dahl	–
Thorsholm	284,299	Jan 84	Qatar/UAE/Persian Gulf	Thor Dahl	–
Fleurtje	222,592	Feb 84	Oman	Transworld Oil	Transworld Oil
Medusa	333,000	Feb 84	Netherl. Antilles/St. Lucia	Kulukundis	–
Neptune Pavo	86,417	Feb 84	Brunei	Neptune Orient Lines	Marc Rich
Thorsholm[5]	87,076	Feb 84	t/s off South Africa [Qatar]	Thor Dahl	Derby/Marc Rich
Höegh Fulmar b/o	78,500	Mar 84	Turkey/unknown Middle East?	Leif Höegh	Marimpex
Matterhorn	289,166	Mar 84	Kuwait/Saudi Arabia	A.P. Møller	Marimpex
Ohio	117,909	Mar 84	Brunei	Hadjipateras	Marc Rich
Port Hawkesbury	257,028	Mar 84	Saudi Arabia/Oman	Canadian Pacific	–
St. Tobias	254,520	Mar 84	Persian Gulf	Marimpex	Marimpex
Tropic	85,469	Mar 84	Saudi Arabia	C.M. Lemos	–
Thorsaga	284,299	Mar/Apr 84	UAE/Iran/Persian Gulf	Thor Dahl	–
Johs. Stove	135,900	Apr 84	Brunei	Lorentzens Rederi	Marc Rich
Moscliff	274,938	Apr 84	Persian Gulf [?]	Mosvold Shipping	Marimpex
St. Tobias	254,520	Apr 84	Persian Gulf ?	Marimpex	Marimpex
Berge Princess	284,507	Apr/May 84	Persian Gulf	Bergesen	–
Aghia Marina b/o	85,461	May 84	Persian Gulf	Tsakos Shipping & Trading	–
Eirama	104,447	May 84	Persian Gulf	Thor Dahl	–
Friendship L.	267,590	May 84	Iran	G.P. Livanos	P.S.C.
Gorgona	150,977	May 84	Brunei	Kulukundis	Marc Rich
Moscliff	274,938	May 84	Persian Gulf	Mosvold Shipping	–
Thorsholm	284,299	May 84	Persian Gulf	Thor Dahl	–
Castor o/o	268,728	May/Jne 84	Iran	John Fredriksen	Marimpex/Mark Wolman
Alexander the Great	325,645	Jne 84	Iran	P.M. Nomikos	–
Jane Stove	141,754	Jne 84	Brunei	Lorentzens Rederi	Marc Rich
Medusa	333,000	Jly 84	Persian Gulf [?]	Kulukundis	–
Moscliff	274,938	Jly 84	Persian Gulf	Mosvold Shipping	Mark Wolman
Sungari [ex-Ogden S.]	275,932	Jly 84	Persian Gulf	OMI Corp.	–
Thorsholm	284,299	Jly 84	Oman	Thor Dahl	–
Eirama	104,447	Aug 84	Persian Gulf	Thor Dahl	–
Good News	240,260	Aug 84	Iran	Polembros	–
Neptune Pavo	86,417	Aug 84	Brunei	Neptune Orient Lines	Marc Rich
St. Tobias	254,520	Aug 84	Persian Gulf ?	Marimpex	Marimpex
Michael C.	123,511	Aug/Sep 84	Brunei	Laurel Sea Transport	Marc Rich

ship's name[3]	dwt tonnage	month in S. Africa	sailed to South Africa from	main shipping company[4]	owners of oil cargo
Jane Stove	141,754	Sep 84	Brunei	Lorentzens Rederi	Marc Rich
Sungari	275,932	Sep 84	Persian Gulf	OMI Corp.	–
Thorshavet	233,000	Sep 84	Iran/Persian Gulf	Thor Dahl	Marc Rich
Thorsholm	284,299	Sep 84	UAE/Saudi Arabia	Thor Dahl	–
Moscliff	274,938	Sep/Oct 84	Saudi Arabia	Mosvold Shipping	–
Akarita	230,683	Oct 84	Saudi Arabia/UAE	Uglands Rederi	–
Neptune Pegasus	86,408	Oct 84	Brunei	Neptune Orient Lines	Marc Rich
Berge Bragd [ex-Berge Queen]	280,476	Nov 84	Saudi Arabia/UAE	Bergesen	Transworld Oil
Capt. John G.P. Livanos	259,657	Nov 84	Iran/Persian Gulf	G.P. Livanos	Marc Rich
Mirafiori	290,271	Nov 84	Persian Gulf	Marimpex	Marimpex
Monemvasia	128,366	Nov 84	Brunei	Metropolitan Shipping	Marc Rich
Moscliff	274,938	Nov 84	Persian Gulf	Mosvold Shipping	–
Filikon L.	85,126	Nov/Dec 84	UAE	G.P. Livanos	Marc Rich
Good News	240,260	Dec 84	Saudi Arabia/UAE	Polembros	–
Mirafiori	290,271	Dec 84	Persian Gulf	Marimpex	Marimpex
Atlanticos	259,955	Jan 85	Iran/UAE	Kulukundis	–
Berge Prince	284,522	Jan 85	Saudi Arabia/UAE	Bergesen	–
Mirafiori	290,271	Jan 85	Persian Gulf	Marimpex	Marimpex
Thorsholm	284,299	Jan 85	Oman/Persian Gulf	Thor Dahl	–
Vardaas b/o	53,640	Jan 85	South Yemen	Arnt J. Mørland	–
Berge Prince	284,522	Feb 85	t/s Egypt [Iran]	Bergesen	–
Mirafiori	290,271	Feb 85	unknown	Marimpex	Marimpex
Volere	254,891	Feb 85	Persian Gulf	Achille Lauro/Lelakis	Magnum
Berge Lord	284,500	Mar 85	UAE	Bergesen	–
Fellowship L.	264,108	Mar 85	Iran/Persian Gulf	G.P. Livanos	Marc Rich
Fortuneship L.	268,081	Mar 85	Iran	G.P. Livanos	–
Thorsholm	284,299	Mar 85	Saudi Arabia/Persian Gulf	Thor Dahl	–
Neptune Pegasus	86,408	Mar/Apr 85	Singapore +	Neptune Orient Lines	Marc Rich
Evita	135,900	Apr 85	Saudi Arabia	Uglands Rederi	–
Moscliff	274,938	Apr 85	Persian Gulf	Mosvold Shipping	Marc Rich
Serifos	97,693	Apr 85	Persian Gulf	Eletson Corp.	Marc Rich
Thorsaga	284,299	Apr 85	Saudi Arabia	Thor Dahl	Marc Rich
Mistra	259,617	Apr/May 85	Persian Gulf	Coulouthros	–
Berge Pioneer	355,020	May 85	Oman	Bergesen	–
Hawaiian Sea	97,286	May 85	Middle East	Groton Pacific Carriers	Mark Wolman
Liberator	155,499	May 85	Brunei	Diamantis Pateras	Marc Rich
Mirafiori	290,271	May 85	Persian Gulf	Marimpex	Marimpex
Neptune Pavo	86,417	May 85	Brunei	Neptune Orient Lines	Marc Rich
Philippine Obo 3 b/o	54,500	May 85	South Yemen +	Andreas Ugland	–
Serifos	97,693	May/Jne 85	Oman/Bahrain	Eletson Corp.	Marc Rich
Berge Bragd	280,476	Jne 85	UAE/Iran	Bergesen	Marimpex
Jahre Transporter o/o	158,694	Jne 85	Brunei	Anders Jahre	Marc Rich
Liberator	155,499	Jne 85	Saudi Arabia	Diamantis Pateras	Mark Wolman
Meteora	86,754	Jne 85	Persian Gulf [?]	Metropolitan Shipping	Marc Rich
Moscliff	274,938	Jne/Jly 85	Iran	Mosvold Shipping	Transworld Oil
Capt. John G.P. Livanos	259,657	Jly 85	Brunei	G.P. Livanos	Marc Rich
Johs. Stove	135,900	Jly 85	Saudi Arabia	Lorentzens Rederi	–
Mirafiori	290,271	Jly 85	Iran	Marimpex	Marimpex
Thorsholm	284,299	Jly 85	UAE	Thor Dahl	–
World Truth o/o	249,223	Jly 85	Far East	World-Wide Shipping	–
Berge King	284,919	Jly/Aug 85	Netherlands	Bergesen	German Oil/Marimpex
Actor [ex-Moscliff]	274,938	Aug 85	Iran	Mosvold Shipping	Marimpex
Berge Bragd	280,476	Aug 85	Persian Gulf	Bergesen	–
Liberator	155,499	Aug 85	Iran	Diamantis Pateras	–
Neptune Pegasus	86,408	Aug 85	Brunei	Neptune Orient Lines	Marc Rich
Chase Venture	284,632	Aug/Sep 85	Iran	Wah Kwong	Derby Resources A.G.
Actor	274,938	Sep 85	UAE	Mosvold Shipping	Cit International

ship's name[3]	dwt tonnage	month in S. Africa	sailed to South Africa from	main shipping company[4]	owners of oil cargo
Harmony Venture	231,990	Sep 85	Iran	Wah Kwong	Marc Rich
Mirafiori	290,271	Sep 85	Iran	Marimpex	Marimpex
Skopelos	123,449	Sep 85	UAE	Eletson Corp.	Marc Rich
Actor	274,938	Oct 85	Middle East [?]	Mosvold Shipping	–
Lauberhorn	138,538	Oct 85	Brunei	Brokerage & Management	Marc Rich
Morning Cloud b/o	114,865	Oct 85	Oman	Reliance Pacific Shipping	–
Philippine Obo 3 b/o	54,500	Oct 85	South Yemen +	Andreas Ugland	Anglo Pacific
Berge Bragd	280,476	Nov 85	Saudi Arabia	Bergesen	–
Monemvasia	128,366	Nov 85	Persian Gulf	Metropolitan Shipping	–
W. Eagle	357,647	Nov 85	UAE/Saudi Arabia	John Fredriksen	–
W. Enterprise	357,430	Nov/Dec 85	UAE/Saudi Arabia	John Fredriksen	Marc Rich
Actor	274,938	Dec 85	unknown	Mosvold Shipping	–
Monemvasia	128,366	Dec 85	Brunei	Metropolitan Shipping	Marc Rich
Port Hawkesbury	257,028	Dec 85	Oman/UAE	Canadian Pacific	–
Almare Settima b/o	101,590	Dec 85/Jan 86	Saudi Arabia +	Almare	Marc Rich
Thorsholm	284,299	Dec 85/Jan 86	Oman/UAE	Thor Dahl	–
Capt. John G.P. Livanos	259,657	Jan 86	Iran	G.P. Livanos	–
Mospoint	138,780	Jan 86	Egypt	Mosvolds Rederi	–
Neptune Pegasus	86,408	Jan 86	Brunei	Neptune Orient Lines	Marc Rich
Tantra o/o	218,035	Jan 86	Persian Gulf	John Fredriksen	Mark Wolman
Hawaiian Sun	98,932	Feb 86	Persian Gulf +	Groton Pacific Carriers	Marc Rich
Johs. Stove	135,900	Feb 86	UAE	Lorentzens Rederi	–
I.D. Sinclair	254,735	Feb/Mar 86	Saudi Arabia	Canadian Pacific	Marc Rich
Port Hawkesbury	257,028	Feb/Mar 86	Qatar	Canadian Pacific	Marc Rich
Gentle Breeze b/o	102,799	Mar 86	Bahrain/Kuwait +	Wallem Shipmanagement	Marimpex
Jane Stove	141,754	Mar 86	UAE	Lorentzens Rederi	–
Neptune Pavo	86,417	Mar 86	Brunei	Neptune Orient Lines	Marc Rich
World Eminence	261,729	Mar 86	France	World-Wide Shipping	Marimpex
Almare Terza b/o	104,824	Mar/Apr 86	United Kingdom	Almare	Mark Wolman/Marc Rich
Janniche	224,607	Mar/Apr 86	Qatar/UAE/Persian Gulf	Periscopus/Norman Intern.	–
Liberator	155,499	Mar/Apr 86	Persian Gulf	Diamantis Pateras	Marc Rich
Actor	274,938	Apr 86	UAE/Oman	Mosvold Shipping	–
Akarita	230,683	Apr 86	Persian Gulf	Uglands Rederi	–
Archontissa Katingo b/o	85,414	Apr 86	Ecuador	Diamantis Pateras	–
Berge Prince	284,522	Apr 86	Iran/UAE	Bergesen	Marimpex
Berge King	284,919	May 86	Saudi Arabia/Persian Gulf	Bergesen	–
Berge Prince	284,522	May 86	UAE/Oman	Bergesen	–
Biscaya b/o	103,332	May 86	Bahrain +	John Fredriksen	Marimpex
Ethnic	274,629	May 86	Qatar/Oman	C.M. Lemos	–
Flagship L.	310,991	May 86	UAE/Oman	G.P. Livanos	–
Beatrice	54,626	May/Jne 86	South Yemen +	Uglands Rederi	–
Hawaiian Monarch	90,992	Jne 86	Brunei	Groton Pacific Carriers	Marc Rich
Janniche	224,607	Jne 86	UAE	Periscopus/Norman Intern.	–
Rafio [ex-Mirafiori]	290,271	Jne 86	Qatar/UAE	Marimpex	Marimpex/Mark Wolman
World Nisseki	268,467	Jne 86	UAE	World-Wide Shipping	–
Actor	274,938	Jne/Jly 86	UAE	Mosvold Shipping	Marc Rich
Berge Chief	289,981	Jly 86	Oman/UAE	Bergesen	Marimpex
Berge Prince	284,522	Jly 86	Persian Gulf	Bergesen	Marc Rich
Ethnic	274,629	Jly 86	Qatar/UAE	C.M. Lemos	Marc Rich
Faroship L.	268,951	Jly 86	Oman	G.P. Livanos	–
Neptune Subaru	87,768	Jly 86	Brunei	Neptune Orient Lines	Marc Rich
Fortuneship L.	268,081	Jly/Aug 86	Qatar/Persian Gulf	G.P. Livanos	Marc Rich
Freedomship L.	278,798	Jly/Aug 86	UAE	G.P. Livanos	Marimpex
Capt. John G.P. Livanos	259,657	Aug 86	UAE	G.P. Livanos	Marc Rich
Rafio	290,271	Aug 86	Persian Gulf	Marimpex	Marimpex
Tantra o/o	218,035	Aug/Sep 86	Persian Gulf	John Fredriksen	Marc Rich
Capt. John G.P. Livanos	259,657	Sep 86	Saudi Arabia	G.P. Livanos	–

ship's name[3]	dwt tonnage	month in S. Africa	sailed to South Africa from	main shipping company[4]	owners of oil cargo
Elmina o/o	94,464	Sep 86	Brunei	Thenamaris	Marc Rich
Louisiana	315,713	Sep 86	Qatar/UAE	Hadjipateras	Marc Rich
Rafio	290,271	Sep 86	UAE	Marimpex	Marimpex
Friendship L.	267,590	Sep/Oct 86	UAE	G.P. Livanos	–
Singa Star	87,281	Sep/Oct 86	Bahrain/Kuwait +	Singa Ship Management	Mosco
Berge Prince	284,522	Oct 86	UAE	Bergesen	–
Capt. John G.P. Livanos	259,657	Oct 86	UAE	G.P. Livanos	Marc Rich
Faroship L.	268,951	Oct 86	Iran	G.P. Livanos	Marimpex
Neptune Otome	87,768	Oct 86	Brunei	Neptune Orient Lines	Marc Rich
World Symphony	356,324	Oct/Nov 86	UAE/Qatar	World-Wide Shipping	Euravia/Marc Rich
Louisiana	315,713	Nov 86	UAE/Persian Gulf	Hadjipateras	Cit International
Neptune Pegasus	86,408	Nov 86	Brunei	Neptune Orient Lines	Marc Rich
Tactic	237,085	Nov 86	UAE/Qatar	C.M. Lemos	–
World Brasilia	283,761	Nov 86	UAE/Qatar	World-Wide Shipping	African Middle East Petr.
World Xanadu	264,170	Nov 86	UAE/Oman	World-Wide Shipping	–
Actor	274,938	Dec 86	UAE	Mosvold Shipping	–
Capt. John G.P. Livanos	259,657	Dec 86	Iran	G.P. Livanos	Mark Wolman
Patriotic	269,500	Dec 86	Persian Gulf	C.M. Lemos	Mark Wolman
World NKK	266,169	Dec 86	Persian Gulf	World-Wide Shipping	–
World Progress	237,285	Dec 86	UAE	World-Wide Shipping	Marc Rich
Friendship L.	267,590	Jan 87	Persian Gulf/Oman	G.P. Livanos	Transworld Oil
Patriotic	269,500	Jan 87	UAE/Qatar	C.M. Lemos	–
World Brasilia	283,761	Jan 87	Saudi Arabia	World-Wide Shipping	–
World Progress	237,285	Jan 87	UAE/Persian Gulf	World-Wide Shipping	Transworld Oil
Licorne Océane	290,767	Feb 87	Iran	Cie Gén. Marit. & Fin.	German Oil/Marimpex
Louisiana	315,713	Feb/Mar 87	Saudi Arabia	Hadjipateras	Mark Wolman
Berge Princess	284,507	Mar 87	Iran	Bergesen	Marc Rich
Fellowship L.	264,108	Mar 87	Oman/UAE	G.P. Livanos	Mosco
Fidius [ex-I.D. Sinclair]	254,691	Mar 87	Persian Gulf	Canadian Pacific	Marc Rich/Mark Wolman
Patriotic	269,500	Mar 87	Persian Gulf	C.M. Lemos	–
World Symphony	356,324	Mar 87	Iran/UAE	World-Wide Shipping	Marc Rich
Obo Baron b/o	103,230	Mar/Apr 87	Saudi Arabia/Persian Gulf	Sigurd Herlofson/B+H	–
Berge Chief	289,981	Apr 87	Oman	Bergesen	Transworld Oil
Berge Enterprise	360,700	Apr 87	Saudi Arabia/Qatar/UAE	Bergesen	Marimpex/Mark Wolman
Berge Prince	284,522	Apr 87	Iran	Bergesen	Marimpex
Ugland Obo-One b/o	54,500	Apr 87	France +	Andreas Ugland	AOT Ltd
World Nisseki	268,467	Apr 87	UAE	World-Wide Shipping	–
World Renown	262,267	Apr 87	Saudi Arabia	World-Wide Shipping	–
Patriotic	269,500	Apr/May 87	UAE	C.M. Lemos	Marc Rich/Mark Wolman
Actor	274,938	May 87	Iran/Persian Gulf	Mosvold Shipping	Marimpex
Neptune Pavo	86,417	May 87	Indonesia	Neptune Orient Lines	Mark Wolman
World Renown	262,267	May/Jne 87	Persian Gulf	World-Wide Shipping	–
Berge Enterprise	360,700	Jne 87	UAE/Oman	Bergesen	Transworld Oil
Berge Prince	284,522	Jne 87	Saudi Arabia/Persian Gulf	Bergesen	–
World Truth o/o	249,223	Jne 87	Persian Gulf	World-Wide Shipping	–
Fidius	254,691	Jly 87	Iran	Canadian Pacific	Marc Rich
Louisiana	315,713	Jly 87	UAE	Hadjipateras	Marc Rich
World Progress	237,285	Jly 87	UAE	World-Wide Shipping	Transworld Oil
World Truth o/o	249,223	Jly 87	UAE	World-Wide Shipping	Mark Wolman
Fellowship L.	268,255	Aug 87	Iran	G.P. Livanos	German Oil/Marimpex
Louisiana	315,713	Aug 87	UAE	Hadjipateras	Transworld Oil
Pacificos	268,467	Aug 87	Qatar/UAE	Kulukundis	–
World Progress	237,285	Aug/Sep 87	UAE/Saudi Arabia	World-Wide Shipping	Mark Wolman
Fellowship L.	268,255	Sep 87	UAE	G.P. Livanos	Transworld Oil
World Victory	237,011	Sep 87	Iran	World-Wide Shipping	Derby Resources A.G.
World Xanadu	264,170	Sep/Oct 87	Qatar/UAE	World-Wide Shipping	Marc Rich

ship's name[3]	dwt tonnage	month in S. Africa	sailed to South Africa from	main shipping company[4]	owners of oil cargo
Faroship L.	268,951	Oct 87	UAE/Saudi Arabia	G.P. Livanos	Transworld Oil
Louisiana	315,713	Oct 87	Iran	Hadjipateras	Mark Wolman
World Bermuda	271,580	Oct 87	Iran	World-Wide Shipping	Mark Wolman
Ambronia	249,953	Nov 87	Iran/Persian Gulf	Navigazione Alta Italia	Marimpex
Freedomship L.	283,271	Nov 87	Persian Gulf	G.P. Livanos	Marc Rich
Musashi Spirit o/o	258,268	Nov 87	Iran	Teekay Shipping	–
World Eminence	261,729	Nov 87	Persian Gulf	World-Wide Shipping	Marc Rich
World Xanadu	264,170	Nov 87	Iran	World-Wide Shipping	Mark Wolman
Eastern Promise	268,038	Nov/Dec 87	Iran	World-Wide Shipping	Marimpex
Obo Engin b/o	78,075	Nov/Dec 87	Tunisia +	Martı Shipping & Trading	Marc Rich
Dorian	260,158	Dec 87	Persian Gulf	Marimpex	Marimpex
Musashi Spirit o/o	258,268	Dec 87	Persian Gulf [?]	Teekay Shipping	–
World Eminence	261,729	Dec 87	UAE/Persian Gulf	World-Wide Shipping	Transworld Oil
World Progress	237,285	Dec 87	Iran/UAE	World-Wide Shipping	–
Friendship L.	267,590	Dec 87/Jan 88	Persian Gulf	G.P. Livanos	Marc Rich
World Xanadu	264,170	Dec 87/Jan 88	UAE	World-Wide Shipping	Marc Rich/Mark Wolman
Azuro	268,863	Jan 88	Iran	Marimpex	Marimpex
Capt. John G.P. Livanos	259,657	Jan 88	Egypt/Saudi Arabia	G.P. Livanos	Afr.Middle East/Marc Rich
Dorian	260,158	Jan 88	Persian Gulf	Marimpex	Marimpex
Rafio	290,271	Jan 88	Iran/Persian Gulf	Marimpex	Marimpex
World Renown	262,267	Feb 88	UAE/Oman	World-Wide Shipping	Melantos
Azuro	268,863	Feb/Mar 88	Persian Gulf	Marimpex	Marimpex
Boni	254,681	Mar 88	UAE/Iran	Thenamaris	Marc Rich
Ethnic	274,629	Mar 88	Oman	C.M. Lemos	–
Friendship L.	267,590	Mar 88	Middle East [?]	G.P. Livanos	Marc Rich
World Ambassador	237,474	Mar 88	Egypt	World-Wide Shipping	African Middle East Petr.
World Renown	262,267	Mar 88	Middle East [?]	World-Wide Shipping	–
Patriotic	269,500	Mar/Apr 88	UAE	C.M. Lemos	Marc Rich
Azuro	268,863	Apr 88	Iran	Marimpex	Marimpex
Friendship L.	267,590	Apr 88	Iran	G.P. Livanos	Marc Rich
World Eminence	261,729	Apr 88	Qatar/Oman	World-Wide Shipping	–
World Harmony	259,596	Apr 88	UAE/Qatar	World-Wide Shipping	Mark Wolman
World Bermuda	271,580	Apr/May 88	Persian Gulf	World-Wide Shipping	–
Capt. John G.P. Livanos	259,657	May 88	Qatar/UAE	G.P. Livanos	–
Louisiana	315,713	May 88	Saudi Arabia	Hadjipateras	Marc Rich
World Eminence	261,729	May 88	Persian Gulf ?	World-Wide Shipping	–
World Harmony	259,596	May 88	Oman	World-Wide Shipping	–
World Renown	262,267	May 88	Egypt	World-Wide Shipping	Afr.Middle East/Marc Rich
World Progress	237,285	Jne 88	Egypt	World-Wide Shipping	African Middle East Petr.
Alki	232,600	Jly 88	UAE	Seaarland	–
Azuro	268,863	Jly 88	Persian Gulf	Marimpex	Marimpex
Ethnic	274,629	Jly 88	UAE	C.M. Lemos	–
World Hitachi Zosen	268,904	Jly 88	Egypt	World-Wide Shipping	African Middle East Petr.
Indiana	300,029	Jly/Aug 88	Qatar	Hadjipateras	Marc Rich
Ethnic	274,629	Aug 88	UAE	C.M. Lemos	–
Patriotic	269,500	Aug 88	UAE/Qatar	C.M. Lemos	–
World Champion	273,117	Aug 88	Iran	World-Wide Shipping	Marc Rich
World Progress	237,285	Aug 88	Egypt	World-Wide Shipping	African Middle East Petr.
Alki	232,600	Sep 88	UAE	Seaarland	–
Aspra	249,992	Sep 88	Persian Gulf	Navigazione Alta Italia	–
Eastern Strength	267,577	Sep 88	UAE	World-Wide Shipping	–
Ethnic	274,616	Sep 88	UAE	C.M. Lemos	–
Rafio	290,271	Sep 88	Iran	Marimpex	Marimpex
World Harmony	259,596	Sep 88	Oman	World-Wide Shipping	–
World Victory	237,011	Sep/Oct 88	Middle East or Far East	World-Wide Shipping	Marimpex
Dagli	57,372	Oct 88	Soviet Union +	Iver Bugge	Marc Rich
Dorian	260,158	Oct 88	Persian Gulf	Marimpex	Marimpex

ship's name[3]	dwt tonnage	month in S. Africa	sailed to South Africa from	main shipping company[4]	owners of oil cargo
Eastern Strength	267,577	Oct 88	UAE	World-Wide Shipping	Marc Rich
Rafio	290,271	Oct 88	Iran	Marimpex	Marimpex
World Summit	260,064	Oct 88	Iran	World-Wide Shipping	Marc Rich
Ethnic	274,616	Oct/Nov 88	UAE/Qatar	C.M. Lemos	Marc Rich
Alki	232,600	Nov 88	Egypt	Seaarland	African Middle East Petr.
Pacificos	268,467	Nov 88	Egypt	Kulukundis	African Middle East Petr.
World Summit	260,064	Nov 88	Persian Gulf	World-Wide Shipping	–
World Xanadu	264,170	Nov 88	UAE	World-Wide Shipping	–
Rafio	290,271	Nov/Dec 88	Iran	Marimpex	Marimpex
Indiana	300,029	Dec 88	UAE	Hadjipateras	Marc Rich
World Progress	237,285	Dec 88	UAE	World-Wide Shipping	–
World Xanadu	264,170	Dec 88	Middle East	World-Wide Shipping	–
Alki	232,600	Jan 89	UAE	Seaarland	–
Pacificos	268,467	Jan 89	Middle East	Kulukundis	Marc Rich
Ocean Carrier b/o	123,999	Jan 89	Malaysia	John Fredriksen	Kuo International Oil Ltd
Eastern Promise	268,038	Jan 89	UAE	World-Wide Shipping	Euravia/Marc Rich
World Bermuda	271,580	Jan 89	Persian Gulf	World-Wide Shipping	–
Faroship L.	268,951	Jan 89	UAE	G.P. Livanos	–
World Hitachi Zosen	268,904	Feb 89	Egypt	World-Wide Shipping	African Middle East Petr.
Indiana	300,029	Feb/Mar 89	UAE	Hadjipateras	–
World Eminence	261,729	Mar 89	Persian Gulf	World-Wide Shipping	Marc Rich
World Hitachi Zosen	268,904	Mar 89	UAE	World-Wide Shipping	–
Ethnic	274,616	Mar 89	UAE	C.M. Lemos	–
World Summit	260,064	Mar 89	UAE	World-Wide Shipping	Marc Rich
Faroship L.	268,951	Mar 89	Persian Gulf	G.P. Livanos	–
Eastern Promise	268,038	Apr 89	Persian Gulf	World-Wide Shipping	–
Rafio	290,271	Apr 89	Persian Gulf	Marimpex	Marimpex
Anax	259,449	Apr 89	UAE	Peraticos	–
Batis o/o	155,089	Apr 89	Egypt	Embiricos	African Middle East Petr.
Dorian	260,158	Apr 89	Iran	Marimpex	Marimpex
Pacificos	268,467	Apr 89	Middle East	Kulukundis	–
World Xanadu	264,170	May 89	Persian Gulf	World-Wide Shipping	Marc Rich
World Champion	273,117	May 89	Egypt	World-Wide Shipping	African Middle East Petr.
Alki	232,600	May 89	UAE	Seaarland	–
Cali	236,425	May 89	UAE	World-Wide Shipping	–
Fortuneship L.	268,081	May 89	Persian Gulf	G.P. Livanos	–
World Champion	273,117	Jne 89	Middle East ?	World-Wide Shipping	–
Axon	219,287	Jne 89	UAE	Peraticos	–
Cali	236,425	Jne 89	UAE	World-Wide Shipping	–
Pacificos	268,467	Jne/Jly 89	Egypt	Kulukundis	African Middle East Petr.
Griparion b/o	70,247	Jne/Jly 89	Netherlands +	Thalassic SS	–
Batis o/o	155,089	Jly 89	Persian Gulf	Embiricos	–
Alki	232,600	Jly 89	Persian Gulf	Seaarland	–
Obo Vega b/o	97,947	Jly 89	Netherlands +	Martı Shipping & Trading	Cargo Trade/Orbit
World Renown	262,267	Jly 89	UAE/Oman	World-Wide Shipping	–
World Harmony	259,596	Jly 89	Persian Gulf	World-Wide Shipping	Marc Rich
Cali	236,425	Jly 89	UAE	World-Wide Shipping	Marc Rich
Afthoros b/o	77,727	Jly/Aug 89	Bahrain +	Polembros	B.B. Naft
Fortuneship L.	268,081	Aug 89 (1)	Iran	G.P. Livanos	–
Fortuneship L.	268,081	Aug 89 (2)	unknown	G.P. Livanos	–
Alki	232,600	Aug 89	UAE	Seaarland	–
Jarama b/o	77,673	Aug/Sep 89	Netherlands/Portugal +	Leif Höegh	–
World Admiral	237,311	Sep 89	Middle East [?]	World-Wide Shipping	–
World Harmony	259,596	Sep 89	Middle East ?	World-Wide Shipping	–
Illinois	290,753	Sep 89	Iran	Hadjipateras	–
Aurora Borealis	237,183	Sep 89	UAE	Embiricos	–
Alki	232,600	Oct 89 (1)	UAE/Oman	Seaarland	–

ship's name[3]	dwt tonnage	month in S. Africa	sailed to South Africa from	main shipping company[4]	owners of oil cargo
Höegh Fountain b/o	78,488	Oct 89	Sweden/Netherlands +	Leif Höegh	Inter-Med
Höegh Foam b/o	78,571	Oct 89	Romania +	Leif Höegh	Marc Rich
World Ambassador	237,474	Oct 89	UAE	World-Wide Shipping	–
Alki	232,600	Oct 89 (2)	unknown	Seaarland	–
Ambia Fair b/o	78,434	Oct 89	Greece +	Leif Höegh	–
World Renown	262,267	Nov 89	Egypt	World-Wide Shipping	African Middle East Petr.
Fortuneship L.	268,081	Nov 89	UAE	G.P. Livanos	–
World Ambassador	237,474	Nov 89	UAE	World-Wide Shipping	–
Höegh Foam b/o	78,571	Nov/Dec 89	Netherlands +	Leif Höegh	Marc Rich
Aurora Borealis	237,183	Dec 89	Persian Gulf	Embiricos	–
World Renown	262,267	Dec 89	Middle East ?	World-Wide Shipping	–
Batis o/o	155,089	Dec 89	UAE	Embiricos	–
Brittany	233,348	Dec 89	Egypt	World-Wide Shipping	African Middle East Petr.
Rafio	290,271	Dec 89/Jan 90	Persian Gulf	Marimpex	Marimpex
Aurora Borealis	237,183	Jan 90	UAE/Oman	Embiricos	–
Argos	219,175	Jan 90	UAE	Peraticos	–
Griparion b/o	70,247	Jan 90	Netherlands +	Thalassic SS	Marc Rich
World Bermuda	271,580	Jan/Feb 90	Egypt	World-Wide Shipping	–
World Champion	273,117	Feb 90	UAE	World-Wide Shipping	–
Aias	259,442	Feb 90	UAE	Peraticos	Marimpex
Batis o/o	155,089	Mar 90	Egypt	Embiricos	–
Pacificos	268,467	Mar 90	UAE/Oman	Kulukundis	–
World Ambassador	237,474	Mar 90	UAE	World-Wide Shipping	–
World Renown	262,267	Mar 90	Persian Gulf	World-Wide Shipping	–
Arrow Combiner b/o	116,281	Mar/Apr 90	Netherlands +	K.G. Jebsen	–
Eastern Promise	268,038	Apr 90	Persian Gulf	World-Wide Shipping	–
Aurora Borealis	237,183	Apr 90	UAE	Embiricos	–
Höegh Falcon b/o	81,158	Apr 90	Netherlands +	Leif Höegh	–
Indiana	300,029	Apr 90	Persian Gulf	Hadjipateras	–
World Admiral	237,311	May 90	UAE	World-Wide Shipping	–
Pacificos	268,467	May 90	Egypt	Kulukundis	Marc Rich
Lima	234,090	May 90	UAE	World-Wide Shipping	–
Aurora Borealis	237,183	May 90	Middle East ?	Embiricos	–
Freedomship L.	283,271	Jne 90	UAE	G.P. Livanos	–
World Ambassador	237,474	Jne 90	Middle East ?	World-Wide Shipping	–
Eastern Promise	268,038	Jne 90	UAE	World-Wide Shipping	–
Pacificos	268,467	Jne 90	UAE	Kulukundis	–
Fellowship L.	268,255	Jly 90	Iran/UAE	G.P. Livanos	Derby Resources A.G.
Obo Engin b/o	78,075	Jly 90	Netherlands +	Martı Shipping & Trading	–
Batis o/o	155,089	Jly 90	Egypt	Embiricos	–
Aurora Australis	227,440	Jly 90	UAE	Embiricos	–
Friendship L.	267,590	Jly 90	Persian Gulf	G.P. Livanos	–
Graz	233,335	Jly 90	Egypt	World-Wide Shipping	–
Aurora Borealis	237,183	Aug 90	UAE/Persian Gulf	Embiricos	–
Aurora Australis	227,440	Aug 90	UAE	Embiricos	–
Lima	234,090	Aug 90	Egypt	World-Wide Shipping	–
Aurora Borealis	237,183	Sep 90	UAE	Embiricos	–
Höegh Favour b/o	79,999	Sep 90	Netherlands +	Leif Höegh	Marc Rich
Brittany	233,348	Sep 90	UAE	World-Wide Shipping	–
World Ambassador	237,474	Sep/Oct 90	UAE	World-Wide Shipping	–
Aspra	249,992	Oct/Nov 90	Persian Gulf	Navigazione Alta Italia	–
Aurora Borealis	237,183	Nov 90	Egypt	Embiricos	–
Eastern Promise	268,038	Nov 90	UAE	World-Wide Shipping	–
Connecticut	227,355	Nov 90	UAE	Hadjipateras	–
Aurora Australis	227,440	Dec 90	UAE	Embiricos	–
Fortuneship L.	268,081	Dec 90	Egypt	G.P. Livanos	–
Aurora Borealis	237,183	Dec 90	UAE	Embiricos	–

ship's name[3]	dwt tonnage	month in S. Africa	sailed to South Africa from	main shipping company[4]	owners of oil cargo
Ethnic	274,616	Dec 90/Jan 91	UAE	C.M. Lemos	–
Obo Engin b/o	78,075	Jan 91	Netherlands +	Martı Shipping & Trading	Inter-Med
Graz	233,335	Jan 91	UAE	World-Wide Shipping	–
World Prelude	265,243	Jan 91	Persian Gulf	World-Wide Shipping	–
Aurora Borealis	237,183	Jan 91	UAE/Iran	Embiricos	–
World Brasilia	283,761	Jan 91	UAE	World-Wide Shipping	–
World Harmony	259,596	Feb 91	Egypt	World-Wide Shipping	–
Pisa	276,422	Feb 91	UAE	World-Wide Shipping	–
Obo Deniz b/o	103,312	Feb/Mar 91	t/s France [Soviet Union] +	Martı Shipping & Trading	–
Obo Başak b/o	103,312	Mar 91	Netherlands +	Martı Shipping & Trading	–
Pacificos	268,467	Mar 91	Middle East	Kulukundis	–
World Prelude	265,243	Mar 91	Egypt	World-Wide Shipping	–
World Brasilia	283,761	Mar 91	UAE	World-Wide Shipping	–
Graz	233,335	Mar 91	UAE	World-Wide Shipping	–
Batis o/o	155,089	Apr 91	Yemen	Embiricos	Texaco
World Brasilia	283,761	Apr 91	UAE	World-Wide Shipping	–
Alki	232,600	Apr 91	UAE	Seaarland	–
Eastern Power	275,553	Apr 91	Egypt	World-Wide Shipping	–
World Xanadu	264,170	Apr 91	UAE	World-Wide Shipping	–
Rome	274,531	May 91	Iran/UAE	World-Wide Shipping	–
World Harmony	259,596	May 91	UAE	World-Wide Shipping	–
World Pendant	265,316	May 91	Egypt	World-Wide Shipping	–
Brittany	233,348	May 91	UAE	World-Wide Shipping	–
Eastern Trust	270,985	May 91	UAE	World-Wide Shipping	–
World Brasilia	283,761	Jne 91	UAE	World-Wide Shipping	–
World Summit	260,064	Jne 91	Iran	World-Wide Shipping	–
World Harmony	259,596	Jly 91	UAE	World-Wide Shipping	–
Batis o/o	155,089	Jly 91	Egypt	Embiricos	–
World Brasilia	283,761	Jly/Aug 91	UAE	World-Wide Shipping	–
World Renown	262,267	Aug 91	Persian Gulf	World-Wide Shipping	–
Crete [ex-Aurora B.]	237,183	Aug 91	UAE	Embiricos	–
World Champion	273,117	Aug 91	Middle East or Far East	World-Wide Shipping	–
Obo Vega b/o	97,947	Aug/Sep 91	Netherlands +	Martı Shipping & Trading	–
Alki	232,600	Aug/Sep 91	UAE	Seaarland	–
Indiana	300,029	Aug/Sep 91	Persian Gulf	Hadjipateras	–
Eastern Courage	267,807	Sep 91	UAE	World-Wide Shipping	–
World Champion	273,117	Oct 91	Egypt	World-Wide Shipping	–
Chryssi [ex-Aurora A.]	227,440	Oct 91	UAE	Embiricos	–
World Hitachi Zosen	268,904	Nov 91	UAE	World-Wide Shipping	–
Friendship L.	267,590	Nov 91	Persian Gulf	G.P. Livanos	–
Sailor	232,397	Nov 91	Egypt	Coulouthros	–
Eastern Courage	267,807	Nov/Dec 91	Egypt	World-Wide Shipping	–
World Hitachi Zosen	268,904	Dec 91	Middle East [?]	World-Wide Shipping	–
Friendship L.	267,590	Dec 91	UAE	G.P. Livanos	–
Doha	275,396	Jan 92	UAE	World-Wide Shipping	–
Crete	237,183	Jan 92	UAE	Embiricos	–
Indiana	300,029	Feb 92	Persian Gulf	Hadjipateras	–
Hellespont Orpheum	315,700	Feb 92	UAE/Iran	Papachristidis	–
Pisa	276,422	Mar 92	UAE	World-Wide Shipping	–
Hellespont Orpheum	315,700	Mar 92	UAE	Papachristidis	–
World Admiral	237,311	Mar 92	Middle East or Far East	World-Wide Shipping	–
Ariel b/o	75,590	Mar/Apr 92	Netherlands +	Sørensen & Sønner	–
World Renown	262,267	Apr 92	Persian Gulf	World-Wide Shipping	–
World Ambassador	237,474	Apr 92	UAE	World-Wide Shipping	–
Chrisholm	59,999	Apr 92	Netherlands +	Torvald Klaveness	–
Ethnic	246,051	Apr/May 92	Persian Gulf	C.M. Lemos	–

ship's name[3]	dwt tonnage	month in S. Africa	sailed to South Africa from	main shipping company[4]	owners of oil cargo
World Admiral	237,311	May 92	Qatar/UAE	World-Wide Shipping	–
World Champion	273,117	May 92	Middle East [?]	World-Wide Shipping	–
World Ambassador	237,474	May 92	UAE	World-Wide Shipping	–
Alki	232,600	May/Jne 92	Egypt	Seaarland	–
Chryssi	227,440	Jne 92	Iran/UAE	Embiricos	–
Emerald b/o	64,289	Jne 92	Malta +	Seabulk/V.Ships	–
World Xanadu	264,170	Jne/Jly 92	Oman/Iran	World-Wide Shipping	Marc Rich
Crete	237,183	Jne 92	UAE	Embiricos	–
World Ambassador	237,474	Jly 92	Iran	World-Wide Shipping	–
BT Venture	215,925	Jly/Aug 92	Persian Gulf	BT Shipping	–
Anax	259,449	Jly/Aug 92	Qatar/UAE	Peraticos	–
Lini [ex-Lima]	234,090	Jly/Aug 92	UAE	World-Wide Shipping	–
Crete	237,183	Aug 92	Egypt	Embiricos	–
Summerrain b/o	84,573	Aug 92	Netherlands Antilles +	Alcyon Shipping	–
Assos Bay	275,333	Aug 92	Middle East	Adriatic Tankers	–
Myrtos Bay	257,073	Sep 92	UAE	Adriatic Tankers	–
World Pendant	265,316	Sep 92	Middle East ?	World-Wide Shipping	–
Baleares b/o	75,714	Sep 92	Malta/Italy +	Sørensen & Sønner	–
Crete	237,183	Sep 92	UAE	Embiricos	–
Connecticut	227,355	Sep/Oct 92	Qatar/UAE	Hadjipateras	–
Höegh Fountain b/o	78,488	Oct 92	Italy/Malta +	Leif Höegh	–
Cali	236,425	Oct 92	UAE	World-Wide Shipping	–
Myrtos Bay	257,073	Oct 92	Persian Gulf	Adriatic Tankers	Marc Rich
Graz	233,335	Oct 92	UAE	World-Wide Shipping	–
Ambia Fair b/o	78,434	Oct/Nov 92	Finland +	Leif Höegh	Marc Rich
World Ambassador	237,474	Oct 92	UAE	World-Wide Shipping	–
World Bermuda	271,580	Nov 92	Persian Gulf	World-Wide Shipping	–
Burwain Nordic	83,970	Nov 92	Italy +	BurWain	–
Chryssi	227,440	Nov 92	Egypt	Embiricos	–
Brittany	233,348	Nov 92	UAE	World-Wide Shipping	–
Graz	233,335	Nov 92	Middle East [?]	World-Wide Shipping	–
Pisa	276,422	Dec 92	Iran	World-Wide Shipping	–
Tinos [ex-Batis] o/o	155,089	Dec 92	Middle East [?]	Embiricos	–
SKS Breeze b/o	95,000	Dec 92	Finland +	Orient Ship Management	–
Lini	234,090	Dec 92	UAE	World-Wide Shipping	–
Assimina	254,735	Dec 92	Persian Gulf	Polembros	–
Mountain Cloud	285,468	Dec 92/Jan 93	Persian Gulf	Norbulk Shipping	–
Assos Bay	275,333	Jan 93	Iran	Adriatic Tankers	–
Crete	237,183	Jan 93	Middle East [?]	Embiricos	–
Skyros	328,285	Jan 93	UAE	Embiricos	–
Myrtos Bay	257,073	Jan 93	Persian Gulf [?]	Adriatic Tankers	–
Chryssi	227,440	Feb 93	UAE	Embiricos	–
Wyoming	356,324	Feb 93	Iran	Hadjipateras	Marc Rich
Cali	236,425	Feb 93	Middle East [?]	World-Wide Shipping	–
Crete	237,183	Feb/Mar 93	UAE	Embiricos	–
Obo Başak b/o	103,325	Mar 93	Greece +	Martı Shipping & Trading	–
Myrtos Bay	257,073	Mar 93	UAE	Adriatic Tankers	–
Assos Bay	275,333	Mar 93	Egypt	Adriatic Tankers	–
Sala	282,540	Mar 93	UAE	World-Wide Shipping	–
Eastern Promise	268,038	Mar 93	Persian Gulf	World-Wide Shipping	–
World Champion	273,117	Mar/Apr 93	Persian Gulf	World-Wide Shipping	–
Rome	274,528	Apr 93	Iran	World-Wide Shipping	–
Hikari Orient	232,413	Apr 93	UAE	Tanker Pacific Management	–
South Breeze	231,490	Apr 93	Persian Gulf	Mosvold-Farsund	–
Aias	259,442	Apr/May 93	Egypt	Peraticos	–
Sahara	356,400	May 93	Iran	P.M. Nomikos	Marc Rich
Hellespont Paradise	315,700	May 93	Persian Gulf	Papachristidis	–

ship's name[3]	dwt tonnage	month in S. Africa	sailed to South Africa from	main shipping company[4]	owners of oil cargo
Kirsten	339,300	May 93	Iran/Persian Gulf	Angelicoussis	Marc Rich
World Prince	265,322	Jne 93	Persian Gulf	World-Wide Shipping	–
World Prelude	265,243	Jne 93	Persian Gulf [?]	World-Wide Shipping	–
Sala	282,540	Jne 93	Persian Gulf	World-Wide Shipping	–
World Victory	237,011	Jne/Jly 93	UAE	World-Wide Shipping	–
Assos Bay	275,333	Jly 93	Iran/Persian Gulf	Adriatic Tankers	Scanports Shipping Ltd
Mariner	267,038	Jly 93	Persian Gulf	Coulouthros	–
Hikari Orient	232,413	Jly 93	UAE	Tanker Pacific Management	–
Sea Duchess	284,480	Jly 93	Iran	John Fredriksen	–
Sala	282,540	Aug 93	Iran	World-Wide Shipping	–
Delos	277,747	Aug 93	Persian Gulf	Embiricos	–
Soro	300,000	Aug 93	Persian Gulf	World-Wide Shipping	–
Sea Duchess	284,480	Aug/Sep 93	Iran	John Fredriksen	–
Indiana	300,029	Sep 93	Persian Gulf	Hadjipateras	–
Faroship L.	268,951	Sep 93	Iran/Persian Gulf	G.P. Livanos	–
Graz	233,335	Sep 93	Persian Gulf [?]	World-Wide Shipping	–
World Champion	273,117	Sep 93	Persian Gulf	World-Wide Shipping	–
Symi	269,349	Sep 93	Persian Gulf	Embiricos	–
Eriskay	226,314	Oct 93	UAE	John Swire	–
Freedomship L.	283,271	Oct 93	Persian Gulf	G.P. Livanos	–
Zante	252,741	Oct 93	Persian Gulf [?]	Embiricos	–
Faroship L.	268,951	Oct 93	Middle East [?]	G.P. Livanos	–
Sea Duchess	284,480	Nov 93	Iran	John Fredriksen	–
Bloom Lake	281,794	Nov 93	Iran	John Fredriksen	–
Faroship L.	268,951	Dec 93	Middle East [?]	G.P. Livanos	–

+   The SRB has information to the effect that the cargo of this ship was not crude oil, but refined petroleum products or intermediate products for further refining.

t/s   Board/board transhipment between vessels; the origin of the transhipped cargo is indicated between square brackets. In 1980, a number of such ship-to-ship transfers took also place in the Persian Gulf, mostly off Bahrain; oil from various Persian Gulf countries was mixed so as to conceal its origins.

1.   All vessels of 50,000 tons dwt and over identified by the Shipping Research Bureau as having called at South Africa and apparently delivered oil during their visits, 1979–93. For the *Cherry Vesta* (44,066 dwt, March 1979), see page 196.

2.   For a breakdown by year, see Table 2 on page 93; by countries/regions of sailing, see Table 1 on pp. 90-1.

3.   Changes of names are indicated for those ships which continued their sailings to South Africa for the same (shipping) company, albeit under a new name.

4.   The shipping companies whose names appear are those which, to the best of the SRB's knowledge, can be regarded as most directly responsible for the vessels' use in deliveries to South Africa and not necessarily the shipowners. It cannot be gleaned from this list, for instance, that a tanker, the *Bloom Lake*, which transported oil to South Africa shortly before the lifting of the embargo, was ultimately owned by the government of the People's Republic of China via a Hong Kong-based subsidiary of the state shipping company Cosco (t/c to Fredriksen).

5.   Deadweight of *Manhattan Viscount* (see pp. 191-2).

PART B

Enforcing Oil Sanctions
A Comparison of the Rhodesian and South African Embargoes

DR MARTIN BAILEY *

Rhodesia and South Africa have been two of the most important cases where the international community has used sanctions to enforce political change. In both examples the oil embargo lay at the heart of sanctions, because modern economies cannot function without this essential fuel. But oil continued to flow, supplied in clandestine sanctions-busting operations. Although the Rhodesian and South African embargoes were circumvented, this was only done at a substantial cost. These additional costs, plus the threat of intensified sanctions, exerted considerable pressure on the white regimes. Sanctions, along with other political, military and diplomatic factors, played a significant role in achieving majority rule in both countries. A comparison of the Rhodesian and South African experiences highlights the extent to which oil sanctions can be an effective instrument of international pressure.

Rhodesia

Oil sanctions were imposed in 1965 to quell the rebellion by Rhodesia's white minority. Southern Rhodesia had become a self-governing British colony in 1923, administered in the interests of European settlers who controlled the country's mineral and agricultural wealth. By the early 1960s, when Britain was giving independence to its many of African colonies, the Southern Rhodesian whites were increasingly worried about the 'winds of change' which were sweeping south. Prime Minister Ian Smith found himself on a collision course with Britain. On 11 November 1965 he proclaimed the Unilateral Declaration of Independence (UDI), breaking away from British rule and setting up an independent white-ruled state.

Britain's Labour Government was sympathetic towards African demands for majority rule but concerned about the backlash that would follow if it used armed force against fellow 'kith and kin' in Rhodesia. Sanctions seemed the pragmatic course. On 20 Novem-

* Dr Martin Bailey is a British journalist who has written extensively on oil sanctions. He is the author of *Oilgate: The Sanctions Scandal* (1979; on Rhodesia). Dr Bailey served as consultant to the Commonwealth Secretariat and in 1989–90 was a member of the Commonwealth's Expert Study Group on sanctions against South Africa. He has also served as a consultant to the UN Special Committee against Apartheid and is the (co-)author of four of its studies on oil sanctions. Until 1993 he was a news reporter on the London *Observer*.

ber 1965, nine days after UDI, the UN Security Council called for non-mandatory selective sanctions, including an oil embargo, to end the rebellion. Britain then introduced oil sanctions, making it illegal for UK-registered companies or UK citizens to supply oil to Rhodesia, or to intermediaries thought to be involved in supplying Rhodesia.[1] Similar legislation was introduced by virtually all other UN members, with the crucial exceptions of South Africa and Portugal (which administered Mozambique).

At the time of UDI Rhodesia consumed about 9,000 b/d of oil. Most supplies were imported as crude oil, shipped to the Mozambican port of Beira and sent by pipeline to the newly completed Rhodesian refinery at Umtali (now Mutare). Smaller quantities of specialised oil products were imported in refined form, usually by rail through Mozambique. The Umtali oil refinery and the internal Rhodesian distribution network were controlled by locally registered subsidiaries of five international oil companies. These were Shell (UK/Netherlands), BP (UK), Mobil (USA), Caltex (USA) and Total (France). Although Rhodesia had built up its stockpile in the weeks leading up to UDI, these were equivalent to only three months' consumption. As long as further supplies were cut off, the economy could not survive, and it was this assumption which led to Prime Minister Harold Wilson's prediction in January 1966 that sanctions would topple Smith 'within weeks, not months'.

The international oil companies immediately cut off crude oil to Beira, leading to the shut-down of the Umtali refinery on 15 January 1966. Rhodesia then sought alternative sources of crude oil elsewhere and on 5 April 1966 the Greek-registered 'pirate' tanker *Joanna V* arrived at Beira with a sanctions-busting cargo. Three days later Britain went to the UN Security Council to press for action, and a resolution was approved authorising a naval blockade off Beira. This blockade successfully ensured that no crude oil reached Rhodesia during the 14 years of sanctions.

But despite the effectiveness of the ban on crude oil, refined oil products continued to flow. Emergency supplies were initially sent by road tanker from South Africa, taken across to Rhodesia at Beit Bridge. This transport route was expensive and could only handle relatively small quantities. The only economic method of moving the oil was by rail. From February 1966 oil was railed to Rhodesia via the Mozambican capital of Lourenço Marques (now Maputo). Wilson pressed both South Africa and Portugal to prevent this trade, but he was unwilling to confront the Pretoria government because of fears of endangering relations with one of Britain's major trading partners. However, in an attempt to increase pressure on Rhodesia, the UN Security Council made the oil embargo mandatory on 16 December 1966, while a further resolution imposing comprehensive sanctions was approved on 29 May 1968.

Although refined oil products continued to be railed into Rhodesia from Mozambique, little was publicly known about this clandestine trade, and it was generally assumed that the international oil companies were not involved. It was not until a decade later that the true story began to emerge. In June 1976 a report on *The Oil Conspiracy* reproduced secret Mobil documents which revealed that the American-owned oil company was using a clandestine 'paper-chase' to supply its Rhodesian subsidiary. Imports went via the secret Rhodesian government procurement agency Genta (a play on the word 'agent'), but they were arranged by Mobil's Mozambican subsidiary. Similar information about the role of the British oil companies was published in March 1977 in a report on *Shell and BP in South Africa*.[2] By this time separate investigations were also being conducted by Lonrho,

ANNEX III

EVIDENCE OF CRIMINAL OFFENCES

This Annex gives references to evidence which may
be relevant when considering whether offences against the
Sanctions Orders have been committed.

NOTE: The remainder of this Annex is, at the request of
the Director of Public Prosecutions, not being·
published while matters covered by the report are
under consideration by him.

EVIDENCE OF CRIMINAL OFFENCES

This Annex gives references to evidence which may be relevant when
considering whether offences against the Sanctions Orders have been committed.
We review the position of the more important companies which feature either in
the organisation charts referred to in Chapter I, paragraph 1.45 or in the
chain of supply to Southern Africa described in Chapter I, Section C.

In respect of these companies we have appended lists of Directors.
The names of some of these Directors will be familiar from the narrative
Chapters, but we have not interviewed all those listed: some are dead; some,
now resident in South Africa and Rhodesia, are not free to speak to us; some
are foreign nationals not employed by the Shell and BP Groups. There are
some, either working in distant countries abroad or (in a few cases) at home
whose likely factual contribution we have not felt to be such as to justify
our asking for their evidence. We have concentrated on establishing the facts
and we have not examined witnesses simply in order to show whether or not they
have or may have committed criminal offences.

In the case of those companies incorporated and resident in the United
Kingdom, there is in our opinion no evidence that they supplied or delivered
or agreed to supply or deliver any petroleum or petroleum products to or to
the order of any person in Rhodesia. Any criminal liability on the part of
these companies would accordingly arise under Article 5(1)(b) or (c) of the
Sanctions Order or the corresponding provisions of its predecessors or not
at all. (See Chapter II, paragraphs 2.2 and 2.14).

CONFIDENTIAL: From the unpublished Annex of the Bingham report

the British-based company which owned the Beira-Umtali pipeline and had lost millions
of pounds from its closure.

Allegations that Shell and BP (in which the British government then had a 68 per cent
shareholding) were involved in sanctions busting caused great embarrassment for Labour
Prime Minister James Callaghan. On 8 April 1977 an official investigation was set up,
which was headed by Thomas Bingham, a distinguished lawyer. His report, published on
19 September 1978, confirmed that the Mozambican subsidiaries of the British oil companies had indeed supplied Rhodesia for most of the period since UDI. During 1966–68 and
1971–76 London-registered Shell Mozambique Ltd, jointly owned by Shell and BP, had
provided half of Rhodesia's oil. From 1968 to 1971 Shell Mozambique Ltd had participated in a swap arrangement with the French company Total to supply Rhodesia. Information on these arrangements was known to directors and senior executives of the oil companies in London, some of whom may well have committed offences under the UK
sanctions legislation.[3]

The Bingham Report also confirmed that the British government had known about the involvement of Shell and BP and had secretly condoned this trade. These revelations caused a political storm in Britain, and anger mounted when in December 1979 the Attorney General announced that no legal proceedings would be taken against Shell and BP or their directors. Foreign Secretary David Owen later described the affair as 'one of the biggest scandals in British post-war history'.[4] Energy Secretary Tony Benn admitted his own government's reaction to the revelations represented 'the biggest cover-up attempt I have ever come across'.[5] In the United States investigations by the Treasury confirmed that Mobil and Caltex had also been involved in sanctions busting.[6]

The Bingham revelations occurred at a time when Smith was facing increasing pressure, both internally and internationally. Rhodesia was then in the midst of an escalating guerrilla war led by the Zimbabwe African National Union and the Zimbabwe African People's Union. This armed action was eventually to claim 20,000 lives. Developments in neighbouring Mozambique were putting additional pressure on the Smith regime. Mozambique had attained independence from Portugal on 25 June 1975, and on 3 March 1976 the FRELIMO-led government cut off rail links to Rhodesia. From then on Rhodesia's oil supplies had to be sent on the recently opened direct rail link from South Africa at Beit Bridge. Smith became totally dependent on South Africa, and this led to the international community exerting further pressure on Pretoria to withdraw its support.

Sanctions were finally beginning to bite. On 12 June 1979 the head of Rhodesian intelligence, Ken Flower, privately warned Smith's cabinet that 'with every month that goes by, sanctions become more debilitating'.[7] Smith was forced to the negotiating table, and talks with the Zimbabwe liberation movements began in London in September 1979, culminating in the agreement which was signed at Lancaster House on 21 December. Elections in February 1980 led to a Patriotic Front victory. Robert Mugabe, leader of the Zimbabwe African National Union, was invited to form a government, and Zimbabwe achieved independence on 18 April 1980.

South Africa

Oil sanctions against South Africa were first proposed in the early 1960s over the government's policy of apartheid. After UDI in 1965, and Pretoria's subsequent support for the Smith regime, pressure developed to extend Rhodesian sanctions to include South Africa. South Africa's refusal to recognise UN authority in South West Africa/Namibia also led to calls for sanctions. There were therefore three separate issues which were invoked as a justification for sanctions against South Africa – its internal policy of apartheid, its support for Rhodesian UDI and its occupation of Namibia.

During the 1970s the UN General Assembly passed a series of resolutions calling for widespread sanctions, but although they received overwhelming support they failed to win the votes of the major Western powers. Since 1979 the General Assembly also approved an annual resolution calling specifically for an oil embargo. These General Assembly resolutions were recommendations and lacked the mandatory nature of Security Council decisions.

By the late 1970s South Africa's oil consumption was about 300,000 b/d, most of which was imported in crude form. South Africa was then supplied directly by the international oil companies, which shipped crude oil and then processed it at their refineries in South Africa. Specialised oil products were supplied in refined form.

South Africa initially had little difficulty in obtaining oil, but the situation changed after the 1973 oil crisis when Arab producers cut off exports to South Africa. Iran then became South Africa's major source of oil. Supplies were assured while the Shah was in power, but when he was overthrown, Ayatollah Khomeini introduced an embargo on South Africa. With the exception of Brunei, then a British protectorate, no significant oil-producing country openly supplied South Africa. The Iranian crisis led to a global oil shortage and pushed up prices, adding to South Africa's difficulties. The South Africans were so desperate that they had to buy cargoes from 'cowboy' companies, as was illustrated by the notorious *Salem* incident of January 1980.

In 1979–80 the international oil companies began to distance themselves from direct supply arrangements. From then on most crude oil went through the government procurement agency SFF (Strategic Fuel Fund), before being passed on to the South African subsidiaries of the international oil companies. The traders who were most deeply involved in supplying SFF were John Deuss and Marc Rich; other trading companies who supplied cargoes included Vitol, Marimpex, Tradinaft and African Middle East Petroleum.

The traders often bought embargoed oil direct from the oil-producing states, sometimes stating false destinations or inducing officials to turn a blind eye to this illegal trade. On other occasions oil consignments were bought by traders on the high seas and shipped to South Africa. Although the oil-producing countries usually required discharge certificates to ensure their oil was not sent to prohibited destinations, in many cases these documents were either falsified or never supplied. Investigations by the Shipping Research Bureau revealed that the original sources of South Africa's crude oil during the 1980s included many countries which officially embargoed South Africa.

By the early 1990s pressure to enforce the oil embargo began to fall away, mainly because of political developments. Zimbabwe had become independent under the Patriotic Front on 18 April 1980. Agreement was reached over the future of Namibia in 1989, and independence was achieved on 21 March 1990. Progress towards the dismantling of apartheid accompanied by negotiations between the ANC and the South African government led to the lifting of many bilateral sanctions in 1992–93. The ANC insisted that the UN oil embargo should be one of the last sanctions to be retained, and it was not lifted until 9 December 1993.

The South African oil embargo never came anywhere near cutting off supplies, although it did add a 'political premium' to procurement costs. South Africa was unable to scour the international market for the cheapest oil, and when supplies were obtained, there were additional costs involved in clandestine trade. During periods of international shortage, particularly in 1979–80, the political premium added substantially to South Africa's oil bill. With oil imports costing up to $4 billion a year and representing up to a third of total imports, even a small premium on every barrel added millions of dollars to the total bill.

South Africa also had to pay the very expensive costs of other protective measures against sanctions, including an intensive (but ultimately unsuccessful) search for commercially viable domestic oil deposits, oil stockpiling, Sasol's oil-from-coal production, and the Mossel Bay oil-from-gas project. These projects cost many billions of dollars.

President Botha himself admitted that between 1973 and 1984 South Africa had to pay R22 billion more than it would normally have spent on oil imports.[8]

These costs were a form of pressure on the South African government. The government also feared that if progress was not made over issues like Rhodesian UDI, Namibian independence and apartheid, then there would be increasing international demands for tightening the oil embargo. Although this might well have failed to cut off supplies, it would probably have added further costs. The oil embargo was therefore one of the most effective forms of sanctions against South Africa.

Comparisons

Rhodesia and South Africa provide an unusual opportunity to compare two cases of oil sanctions. Both countries lie adjacent to each other in southern Africa, their governments faced sanctions primarily because of their resistance to majority rule, the same international companies controlled their oil industries, and the two embargoes took place within a similar time frame. There were, of course, also important differences between the two cases, particularly the fact that Rhodesia had a friendly neighbour, but the embargoes highlight important issues about the efficacy of oil sanctions.

Target states

No modern economy can survive without oil. Neither Rhodesia nor South Africa had their own commercially exploitable oil deposits, and as the threat of sanctions loomed, both governments introduced contingency measures. Stockpiles were built up, representing several months' consumption in Rhodesia and over a year in South Africa, but these could never provide more than a short-term cushion. Both countries took steps to reduce oil consumption, although the impact could only be marginal without causing major disruption to their economies. In South Africa (but not Rhodesia), the government embarked on producing alternative sources of oil. Sasol's oil-from-coal production was expanded and by the mid-1980s it was providing about 30 per cent of South Africa's requirements. The Mossel Bay oil-from-gas project accounted for a further 5–10 per cent of the country's needs after it eventually came on stream in January 1993.

Despite these measures, Rhodesia and South Africa remained dependent on imported oil. Both governments took control of imports by setting up procurement agencies (Genta and SFF). As the embargoes were tightened by the outside world, so the two states successfully introduced new methods of evading sanctions. Supplies were obtained, but at a greater cost, and a 'political premium' had to be paid.

International oil companies

Rhodesia and South Africa were assisted by the international oil companies which controlled the local markets (Shell, BP, Mobil, Caltex and Total). After UDI the head offices of the oil companies lost formal control over their Rhodesian subsidiaries on the orders of the Smith regime. Profits generated inside Rhodesia were retained, and sanctions meant that no external investment could be provided. But despite this formal severing of ties, some informal contacts between the Rhodesian subsidiaries and their head offices abroad continued. The South African subsidiaries of the international oil companies remained under the formal control of their head offices in Europe and the United States, although in practice they too operated with considerable autonomy.

A key difference between the two embargoes was the role played by the international oil companies in supply arrangements. After UDI, the oil companies continued to send refined products to Rhodesia from South Africa and Mozambique, using a series of 'paper-chases' involving intermediaries and swap arrangements. These clandestine deals caused great embarrassment to the oil companies when they were exposed in 1976–79.

In the case of South Africa, until 1978 the international oil companies had no problem in supplying South Africa with crude oil from Iran. But in 1979–80, after the fall of the Shah, these companies gradually stopped shipping directly (although for a short time some tankers were sent from Brunei, Oman and the Netherlands Antilles). Since 1981, there appear to have been no cases of the oil companies shipping crude oil to South Africa in their own tankers or tankers openly chartered by them, although the companies participated in less direct arrangements. The international oil companies were embarrassed by the Rhodesian revelations and concerned about possible retaliation by the oil-producing countries. After the international oil companies had withdrawn from direct supply, crude oil was obtained via the government procurement agency SFF, although the local subsidiaries of the oil companies played some role in the supply.

The handling of the South African embargo shows the way in which multinational oil companies were able to take advantage of their complex structure of subsidiaries. When necessary, local subsidiaries in South Africa could undertake sensitive business, keeping their head offices at a distance. Profits from this trade still flowed back to international oil companies.

Traders

Oil-trading companies played a key role in the evasion of South African (but not Rhodesian) sanctions. Unlike the international oil companies – which are involved in all aspects of the oil industry – traders generally engage in buying and selling oil, attempting to make a cut on each deal. Oil traders are global concerns which can frequently evade national controls by funnelling profits into tax havens where they can operate under conditions of secrecy. Several trading companies made huge profits on South African sanctions busting.

Western governments

Western governments were guilty of great duplicity over Rhodesia. The British Government went to the UN to propose sanctions and then condoned the involvement of its own oil companies in supplying half of Rhodesia's oil.

In the case of South Africa, the major Western powers opposed mandatory oil sanctions, blocking action by the UN Security Council. Britain and the United States also voted against General Assembly resolutions on a voluntary oil embargo (only in 1992 did Britain abstain). However, both countries adopted a contradictory position in that they embargoed the supply of domestically produced crude oil. Britain's embargo was introduced in 1980, and the United States ban was part of a package of sanctions in force from 1986 to 1991. Despite these unilateral embargoes on their own oil, it was the major Western states which blocked tough mandatory sanctions against South Africa.

Oil producers

The oil-producing states played a relatively minor role over the Rhodesian embargo. Kuwait, which had a 5 per cent shareholding in the Umtali refinery, supported sanctions. The oil supplied to Rhodesia during UDI was despatched in refined form from South Africa and Mozambique, giving oil-producing states little leverage.

The situation was quite different over South Africa, where the attitude of the oil-producing states was crucial. After the cut-off of Iranian supplies, no oil-producing countries officially allowed exports to South Africa (except Brunei until 1982). Many oil-producing states made serious efforts to enforce the embargo, but others were lax and did little to interfere with this profitable traffic. Much more could have been done by the oil-producing states, such as the verification of discharge certificates or even action against tankers which had recently delivered cargoes to South African ports.

The oil-producing countries could wield considerable power over the international oil companies, as Nigeria demonstrated when its authorities seized the South African-owned tanker *Kulu* and confiscated its £30 million cargo in May 1979. In August 1979 BP's investments in Nigeria were nationalised after revelations about the company's swap arrangement to supply South Africa, making BP lose access to an important source of crude oil. Nigeria's determined stand was evidence of the growing power of the oil-producing countries over the world oil trade.

Enforcement

The Rhodesian embargo was a mandatory one, approved by the UN Security Council. In theory, there should have been no legal loopholes, although in practice the refusal of South Africa and Portugal to accept sanctions meant that the oil continued to flow. The South African embargo approved by the UN General Assembly was voluntary, although most UN members introduced some restrictions on oil exports to South Africa. However, there were widely differing interpretations of the scope of sanctions. Although sanctions usually covered exports of domestically produced crude oil, they often excluded refined products or crude oil obtained from a third state. Most major shipping states also allowed their companies to continue to transport oil to South Africa.

There were too many loopholes for the sanctions busters to exploit. Commercial enterprises were able to choose bases to operate from where restrictions were loose or enforcement lax. Sanctions busting became a truly multinational operation. In the case of the *Salem* fraud, for example, there were no less than 25 national jurisdictions involved, making it extremely difficult to take legal action against those involved in what was probably the world's largest maritime fraud.

Although both the Rhodesian and South African embargoes were supported by the United Nations, organisationally it had little impact on enforcement. The Rhodesian Sanctions Committee (known as the Security Council Committee Established in Pursuance of Resolution 253 Concerning the Question of Southern Rhodesia) played virtually no role in investigating the oil embargo, concentrating instead on many minor violations of sanctions. In the case of South Africa, the Intergovernmental Group to Monitor the Supply and Shipping of Oil and Petroleum Products to South Africa, established by the UN General Assembly in 1986, did little original investigation. However, the Intergovernmental Group was successful in raising questions about shipments which had been reported by other organisations, particularly the Shipping Research Bureau.

Rhodesia and South Africa both demonstrated the importance of factual evidence. General calls for sanctions could be brushed aside with equally vague rebuttals. Only when specific allegations were made did governments and companies come under pressure. Over Rhodesia, the combination of information from anti-apartheid groups, investigative journalists, and Lonrho forced the British government to set up the Bingham Inquiry, which confirmed allegations of duplicity.

In the case of South Africa, much more systematic research was conducted by the Shipping Research Bureau, set up in 1980 as a non-governmental organisation. The Bureau, which developed a reputation for publishing accurate data, regularly circulated its findings to international organisations, governments, anti-apartheid groups and the oil industry. The cost of this enforcement action was relatively small. The Bureau's total budget during its 14 years was under $2 million, while the additional costs of the oil embargo which South Africa paid may well have exceeded $50,000 million.

Conclusion

The embargoes against both Rhodesia and South Africa failed, in the sense that oil was obtained. But both countries faced high additional costs, and this represented a substantial form of pressure. Sanctions, particularly the oil embargo, therefore played an important role in encouraging political change. Sanctions may well have shortened both conflicts, reducing the incidence of violence.

The experience of the Rhodesian and South African embargoes can be summarised:

1 Political will is essential to make oil sanctions effective. The targeted state will do all it can to evade an embargo and commercial interests will seek to exploit any opportunities.

2 An oil embargo needs to be approved by the UN Security Council and made mandatory. Voluntary embargoes are unlikely to be successful because of the loopholes they provide. In the case of landlocked states, it is particularly important that an embargo is accepted by all governments which share a land border.

3 When a targeted state receives its oil supply by sea it is essential that enforcement action covers shipping. Action against tankers which have recently delivered oil to the targeted state should discourage shipowners from becoming involved in sanctions busting.

4 The oil-producing states have a vital role to play in enforcing sanctions. They can monitor end-user certificates to prevent their oil being supplied to the targeted state.

5 Monitoring of an oil embargo is essential. Non-governmental organisations have the flexibility to monitor efficiently, but their findings need to be taken up by governments and intergovernmental organisations.

6 Even if an oil embargo fails to cut off supplies, the financial costs for targeted states may be heavy. Partially effective sanctions can still be a major form of pressure.

The United Nations and the
Oil Embargo against South Africa

DR AMER SALIH ARAIM*

The international community became concerned when the National Party seized power in South Africa in 1948. The outrage at the policies of apartheid became more apparent after the Sharpeville massacre of 21 March 1960. The United Nations proclaimed 21 March the International Day for the Elimination of Racial Discrimination, and it has since been annually observed.

The General Assembly acted by adopting resolution 1761 (XVII) on 6 November 1962. Although the Assembly had adopted other resolutions on South Africa and apartheid before, for the first time it requested member states to take punitive measures against the government of South Africa. It also decided to establish a Special Committee against Apartheid. Earlier, the Security Council had adopted resolution 134 (1960) on 1 April 1960 which deplored the policies and actions which led to the Sharpeville massacre. The Council also adopted resolution 181 (1963) which imposed a voluntary arms embargo against South Africa. The Security Council approved other measures including the condemnation of the policies of apartheid and support for the struggle of the people of South Africa. These measures culminated in the adoption of resolution 418 (1977) on 4 November 1977 which imposed a mandatory arms embargo against South Africa. The Council subsequently adopted resolutions to impose a voluntary embargo on the import of arms from South Africa, to ensure the implementation of the arms embargo and to condemn the repressive policies of the government of South Africa. Despite the fact that South Africa featured prominently on the agenda of the Security Council, which determined 'that the acquisition by South Africa of arms and related materiel constitutes a threat to the maintenance of international peace and security', there was no consensus in the Council to adopt measures regarding the oil embargo against South Africa. The suggestion that an embargo be placed on the export of petroleum and petroleum products to South Africa had been made by an Expert Committee established pursuant to Security Council resolution 191 (1964).

---

* Dr Araim is Senior Political Affairs Officer in the Department of Political Affairs at the United Nations, New York. He was responsible for sanctions against South Africa since joining the UN Centre against Apartheid in 1978. In the 1980s, the oil embargo became an area of special attention in the UN. Dr Araim became the Secretary of the UN Intergovernmental Group to Monitor the Supply and Shipping of Oil and Petroleum Products to South Africa in 1986. He is the author of *Intergovernmental Commodity Organizations and the New International Economic Order* (Westport, CT: Praeger, 1991).

The views expressed in this article are those of the author and do not necessarily reflect the position of the United Nations.

There had been attempts to include provisions to impose an embargo on the supply of oil to South Africa in the resolutions of the General Assembly. For example, in a resolution taken on 13 November 1963 regarding the illegal occupation of Namibia by South Africa, reference was made to an oil embargo, but it was not until the 1970s that important developments took place in this regard. In 1973 the Summit Conference of Arab States agreed to an embargo on the supply of oil and petroleum products to South Africa. This embargo did not succeed in cutting off the flow of oil to South Africa because during the Shah's reign, Iran was supplying 90 per cent of South Africa's crude oil needs. Moreover, the transnational oil companies were in control of the oil industry and had vested interests in South Africa. They were therefore determined that there would be no interruption of oil supplies to South Africa. For the first time in resolution 3411 (XXX) G of 10 December 1975, the General Assembly appealed to all member states to take the necessary measures to impose an effective embargo on the supply of petroleum and petroleum products to South Africa.

In 1979 the General Assembly adopted resolution 33/183E which dealt exclusively with the question of the oil embargo against South Africa. Since then the Assembly, except for a few years in the mid-1980s, annually adopted a separate resolution calling for the imposition of an embargo on the supply and shipping of oil and petroleum products to South Africa.

The oil embargo adopted by the Arab Summit in 1973 failed to become really effective, due to the lack of mechanisms to ensure its full implementation. Therefore, the Organization of Arab Petroleum Exporting Countries (OAPEC) attempted to assist its member states with the implementation of policies regarding the oil embargo by adopting a detailed plan in May 1981, to put into effect the oil embargo which had been adopted in 1973. In 1989 the Secretary-General of OAPEC chaired the Hearings on the Oil Embargo against South Africa organised at the United Nations.

In the meantime, the revolutionary regime which came to power in Iran after the fall of the Shah gave a boost to the oil embargo when it decided to cut all links with apartheid South Africa in February 1979. Nevertheless, the apartheid regime continued to secure its needs for imported oil and petroleum products.

Role of the Special Committee against Apartheid

The Special Committee has been the catalyst with regard to initiating action on the oil embargo against South Africa. Since its inception, it has concluded that the struggle of the people of South Africa for the elimination of apartheid required that the international community impose punitive measures on the white minority regime in order to convince it that an abnormal society cannot have normal relations with the outside world.

In addition to repressing the black majority in South Africa, the apartheid regime was occupying Namibia and engaging in subversive campaigns against neighbouring states based on brutal force and an expansion of its army. The Special Committee therefore concluded that the oil embargo was complementary to the arms embargo imposed by Security Council resolution 418 (1977).

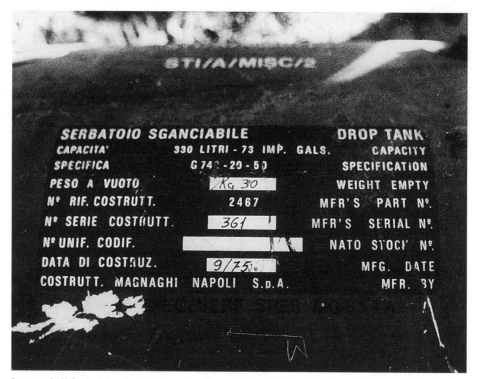

Imported oil fuelled South African aggression against neighbouring states. Fuel tank of South African plane shot down over Cunene province, Angola (photo: April 1981)

After the General Assembly adopted resolution 33/183E (1979) on the recommendation of the Special Committee, the latter devoted particular attention to this question. In 1980 the Committee convened the International Seminar on an Oil Embargo against South Africa in Amsterdam in the Netherlands, in cooperation with the Holland Committee on Southern Africa and the Working Group Kairos, two non-governmental organisations active in the struggle against apartheid. As a result of the work achieved during the Seminar, the Shipping Research Bureau was established with the active support of the Special Committee. Besides actively encouraging activities by non-governmental organisations, the Special Committee established contacts with oil-exporting and oil-shipping states. The Special Committee transmitted the results of the research done by non-governmental organisations concerning violations of the oil embargo against South Africa to those states. The Committee faced tremendous difficulties in its efforts to ensure the effective implementation of the oil embargo, because oil-exporting states considered the enforcement of the oil embargo to be the responsibility of the shipping states, while the latter emphasised the responsibility of the former. In 1980 the Special Committee therefore decided to initiate contacts with the permanent representatives of oil-exporting and oil-shipping states. It subsequently established an informal group to pursue the issue of the oil embargo against South Africa. In 1982 the General Assembly adopted resolution 37/69J, which authorised the Special Committee to appoint a group of experts, nominated by oil-exporting and oil-shipping states, to prepare a study on all aspects of the question of the oil embargo against South Africa. The group of experts met in 1983, and though it was able to tentatively agree on a draft report on its work, that report was shelved because there was no agreement on the final version. The failure of the group of experts to adopt its report once again underlined the complexities of the question of the oil embargo. Nevertheless, the Special Committee continued its efforts particularly to bring about an agreement between the various groups. The endeavours of the Committee culminated in convening, in cooperation with the Government of Norway, the United Nations Seminar on the Oil Embargo against South Africa in Oslo in June 1986, in which both oil-exporting and oil-shipping states participated.

General Assembly action

Since 1979, when the first separate resolution was adopted on the oil embargo, the General Assembly has supported the work of the Special Committee and later on the Intergovernmental Group to Monitor the Supply and Shipping of Oil and Petroleum Products to South Africa with large majorities.

It should be noted that since the establishment of the Intergovernmental Group (1986), many Western states have supported its work on the oil embargo. During the 47th session of the General Assembly (1992) there was only one negative vote against the resolution on the oil embargo, which was sponsored by all the members of the Intergovernmental Group. Most Third World countries supported the resolution year after year. Some Western states supported the aforesaid resolution; New Zealand and Norway were among its sponsors from 1987 onwards. There was some unease amongst certain Western states regarding the oil embargo. In addition to misgivings about the utility of sanctions in general, there was always a legal issue concerning the differentiation between the roles of the General Assembly and the Security Council. In accordance with the provisions of the Charter of the United Nations, it is the prerogative of the Security Council to impose sanctions and other punitive measures in order to ensure the maintenance of international peace and security.

Since the adoption of the 'Uniting for Peace' resolution on 3 November 1950, the General Assembly has become more and more involved in imposing measures (although not mandatory) on recalcitrant states which flagrantly violate the provisions of the Charter of the United Nations and rules of international law. This situation came about as a result of the Cold War and the lack of consensus in the Security Council. However, the Assembly's resolutions on the oil embargo and other sanctions against South Africa not only manifested a severe condemnation of the despicable policies of apartheid, but also represented the will of the larger international community to take action in the face of the inability of the Security Council to deal with a situation which the majority considered a threat to international peace and security. The Assembly's action stimulated the adoption by the United States of the Comprehensive Anti-Apartheid Act of 1986 which included an embargo on the supply of crude oil and refined petroleum products to South Africa. In 1985 the European Community took measures, which only included an embargo on the supply of crude oil to South Africa.

The role of non-governmental organisations

The oil embargo against South Africa is among the measures which drew the attention of the media and non-governmental organisations. The British journalist Martin Bailey, in his book *Oilgate: The Sanctions Scandal* about the role of the government of the United Kingdom in breaking the oil embargo against Southern Rhodesia, exposed the weakness of the mandatory oil embargo against the Smith regime despite the fact that it had been imposed by the Security Council. Bailey and others became also actively involved in the issue of the oil embargo against South Africa. The Special Committee published papers by Martin Bailey, Bernard Rivers, Paul Conlon and others on this subject.

Besides the significant contribution of the Shipping Research Bureau anti-apartheid movements all over the world, particularly the British Anti-Apartheid Movement, anti-apartheid groups in the Nordic states, the London-based organisations 'End Loans to South Africa' and 'Embargo', and academics and activists in the United States contributed to the success of the campaign. It may be recalled that in the 1980s there was a worldwide campaign against Shell. Shell credit cards were returned to the company in great numbers in protest against its involvement in the violation of the oil embargo against South Africa. Similar action was taken in Britain against British Petroleum, and in the United States against Mobil.

While the oil embargo against South Africa was initiated by governments and supported by the United Nations, it could not have gained such attention internationally without the persistent efforts of anti-apartheid groups, particularly the Shipping Research Bureau. As a matter of fact, this fruitful cooperation between the United Nations and anti-apartheid groups had further dividends because it gave publicity to the contribution of the United Nations in the field of human rights and the elimination of apartheid. Furthermore, it enriched the experience of the United Nations in following up on the compliance with sanctions.

The establishment of the Intergovernmental Group to Monitor the Supply and Shipping of Oil and Petroleum Products to South Africa

The campaign for the effective enforcement of the oil embargo against South Africa gained momentum in the 1980s. In the meantime, the Special Committee was determined to move forward, despite the difference between oil-exporting and oil-shipping states about the responsibility for enforcing the oil embargo which emerged during the meetings of the group of experts established in 1983. In the three years which followed, the Special Committee convened informal meetings of oil-exporting and oil-shipping states to consider action on the oil embargo against South Africa. At the above-mentioned Oslo seminar of June 1986, representatives of oil-exporting and oil-shipping states reached a consensus that the United Nations should establish an intergovernmental body to monitor the implementation of the oil embargo. Later that year, the General Assembly decided to establish the Intergovernmental Group to Monitor the Supply and Shipping of Oil and Petroleum Products to South Africa (General Assembly resolution 41/35F of 10 November 1986). Unlike the Special Committee against Apartheid and the Commission against Apartheid in Sports, the Intergovernmental Group comprised the five 'regional groups' in the United Nations (African, Asian, East European, Latin American and Caribbean, and Western and other states). The participation of New Zealand and Norway (the latter withdrew from the Intergovernmental Group in early 1993) enhanced the ability of the Group in its appeals to Western governments. The latter realised that the Intergovernmental Group was seriously interested in assisting governments to implement their policies concerning the oil embargo against South Africa rather than in assigning blame for their failure to do so. Members of the Intergovernmental Group included Algeria, Cuba, the German Democratic Republic (until 1990), Indonesia, Kuwait, New Zealand, Nicaragua, Nigeria, Norway (until early 1993), Ukraine and the United Republic of Tanzania.

The Intergovernmental Group began its work by encouraging governments to enact legislation or comparable measures to impose an embargo on the supply and shipping of oil and petroleum products to South Africa. With a view to assisting governments in this regard, it gathered and published measures concerning the oil embargo enacted by some governments; however, it also exposed the lack of legislation in many member states. After studying such legislation, the Group sought the assistance of academics with legal expertise in the United States. It was decided that the Group could assist governments by preparing a draft *model law* for the effective enforcement of the oil embargo against South Africa. For this purpose, the Centre against Apartheid contracted Professor Richard Lillich of the University of Virginia in Charlottesville (USA). Paragraph 3 of General Assembly resolution 46/79E of 13 December 1991 reads: 'Commends to Member States for their consideration the draft model law ... and recommends that they strive for an effective oil embargo by adopting the general principle of the model law within the framework of their own legal practices.'

While the Intergovernmental Group put emphasis on assisting states to enact legislation or comparable measures concerning the oil embargo, its main task was to *monitor* the supply and shipping of oil and petroleum products to South Africa. The Group depended to a large extent on the assistance provided by the Shipping Research Bureau. Notwithstanding the fact that the latter had been the main source of information on what the Group's reports called 'alleged violations' of the oil embargo, the Group requested the Secretariat to establish its own independent database in 1989. The purpose was to verify the information provided by the Shipping Research Bureau and to expand its research to include all ships capable of carrying oil and/or petroleum products which called at South African ports. These cases were known in the Group's work as 'port calls'. On balance, it can be fairly stated that the research of the Shipping Research Bureau, in addition to that of the Secretariat, has enabled the Intergovernmental Group to have a full exposé of South Africa's trade in oil and petroleum products. While the Intergovernmental Group was successful in ensuring the cooperation of many states, there were, nevertheless, a number of states which persistently refused to answer its queries.

The work of the Intergovernmental Group helped to expose the weak links in the oil embargo and contributed to a deepened feeling of isolation by the apartheid regime. It should also be noted that in 1979, the latter decided to enact legislation imposing severe penalties on anyone revealing the secrets of its illicit oil trade. The regime was also reported to have spent between $25 to $30 billion more for its oil imports during the 1980s than it would otherwise have done. Furthermore, it also depended on its oil-from-coal industry, which is a very expensive and environmentally unsound policy.

Conclusion

A question which is often raised is: 'What has been the impact of the voluntary oil embargo against South Africa?' It has been said that South Africa was able to import all of its oil requirements, despite the action of the international community.

However, a valid question is to what extent the oil embargo and other sanctions have been factors in bringing about a change in the policies of the government of South Africa, which led to the release of Nelson Mandela and other political prisoners, the abrogation of the legislation which had been used to impose the abhorrent system of apartheid for almost half a century, and the commencement of negotiations.

It must be emphasised that the positive changes in South Africa were brought about, first of all, by the hard and determined struggle of the black majority in South Africa under the leadership of the liberation movements. It was recognised all along that the role of the international community in general, and the United Nations in particular, could only be a complement to the struggle of the people of South Africa, through isolating the apartheid regime and rendering the continuation of the system of apartheid more costly politically, economically and morally. The United Nations has succeeded in achieving that goal.

Moreover, from the beginning, the Special Committee, the Intergovernmental Group and all other anti-apartheid forces realised that in order to have a really effective embargo on the supply and shipping of oil and petroleum products to South Africa, there must be a *mandatory* decision by the Security Council to impose such an embargo. There was none in this regard. Therefore, those who supported the embargo hoped that it would be rendered more effective through the resolutions of the General Assembly. Furthermore, the later experiments of the Security Council in imposing oil embargoes against Haiti and Yugoslavia have proven that for an oil embargo to be effective, active cooperation between all states concerned is required in order to ensure its implementation. And even in such cases where there is cooperation, greed and profiteering render the implementation of an oil embargo less than perfect.

The uniqueness of South Africa's strategic location and its being a major centre for bunkering, repairs and supplies for oil tankers using the important sea route around the Cape complicated the task of any investigating agency to verify whether porting ships had delivered oil or petroleum products to South Africa or whether they had stopped for other purposes.

In spite of all the obstacles which prevented a total embargo on the supply of oil and petroleum products to South Africa, the United Nations' efforts, from the early 1980s to the end of 1993 when the oil embargo was lifted, have been successful in isolating the apartheid government in South Africa and by forcing it to pay premium prices for its oil imports. In the meantime, it must be emphasised that for a *voluntary* oil embargo to be an effective instrument, the cooperation of all states concerned is absolutely essential. In the case of South Africa, the voluntary oil embargo was a component of a wider strategy to ensure the total isolation of the apartheid regime and to force it to agree to the elimination of apartheid and the establishment of a democratic and non-racial society. With the agreement to hold the first democratic, free and non-racial elections on 27 April 1994, and the agreement on the establishment of a Transitional Executive Council in the beginning of December 1993, the efforts of the United Nations, the Organization of African Unity (OAU), the League of Arab States and many other governmental and non-governmental organisations, particularly the Shipping Research Bureau and anti-apartheid groups, reached their successful conclusion. The President of the African National Congress of South Africa, Mr Nelson Mandela, in a historic statement before the Special Committee against Apartheid on 24 September 1993, called for the lifting of economic sanctions. As far as the oil embargo was concerned, Mr Mandela said,

> This Organisation also imposed special sanctions relating to arms, nuclear matters and oil. In this regard, we would like to urge that the mandatory sanctions [the arms embargo – AA] be maintained until the new government has been formed. We would leave the issue of the oil embargo to the discretion of the Committee of the General Assembly responsible for the enforcement of this particular sanction [the Intergovernmental Group – AA].

Mandela's words clearly indicated that the liberation movements of South Africa had viewed the oil embargo as being of particular importance. On 29 September 1993 an extraordinary ministerial meeting of the OAU Committee on Southern Africa issued a statement calling for a positive response to Mr Mandela's appeal. With respect to the oil embargo the Committee urged that it be lifted after the establishment of the Transitional Executive Council, the first body with executive powers in which all the political parties participating in the negotiations process were represented. On 8 October 1993, the General Assembly of the United Nations adopted resolution No. 48/1 to lift the oil embargo once the Transitional Executive Council was installed. Following the first meeting of the Council, the United Nations lifted the oil embargo on 9 December 1993.

At that moment of triumph, the people of South Africa were preparing for their first democratic and non-racial election. The oil embargo, financial, trade and investment sanctions and other measures had helped in bringing about the change, a change which was overdue and had demanded great sacrifices. Had the Security Council adopted a mandatory oil embargo and mandatory economic sanctions against apartheid South Africa, positive changes would probably have come much earlier and with less cost in terms of suffering of the people of South Africa and the whole southern African region. It is now up to the international community to generously help by providing moral and material support to the people of South Africa in order to ensure a peaceful transformation into a non-racial and democratic society as well as a prosperous and better future for all South Africans.

Apartheid and the Cost of Energy Self-Sufficiency

When the definitive history of apartheid is written, at least one chapter should be devoted to the economics of apartheid, including the attempts to buy energy self-sufficiency in the face of oil sanctions. This represented government intervention in the economy on a grand scale as vast resources were diverted to stockpile oil, pay front men and make synthetic fuel from coal and gas.

While the jury is still out on the cost of this exercise, expert estimates suggest it could have been sufficient in itself to bring the entire economy to its knees.

Some of these costs survive at the time of writing in the form of an overly regulated and subsidised energy sector which vested interests appear determined to preserve as South Africa leaves the age of sanctions which this system was designed to counter.

The issue of the structure of the South African energy sector, government regulation and fuel pricing remains very much on the boil. This contribution was written just before the first democratic South African government took office in May 1994. The system described is a product of apartheid economics inherited by the new government.

The synfuel dream: Sasol and Mossgas

Synthetic fuels today are synonymous with the R11 billion, 30,000 barrels-a-day (b/d) Mossgas fuel-from-gas project which has doubtful viability even if its entire capital cost is written off, and the much larger 100,000 b/d Sasol 2 and 3 synthetic fuel plants at Secunda which have a replacement value in excess of R40 billion.

Sasol's finances remain a source of ongoing speculation, with some analysts arguing that, stripped of all its protection, South Africa's highest-profit industrial group (with taxed profits of R1.48 billion in 1992/93), could actually show a loss. Sasol, for its part, sees itself as a private sector company with relatively moderate levels of protection.

Auditors Deloitte & Touche, who produced a report in August 1993 for the Auditor-General on Mossgas, estimated that Mossgas's break-even level was in excess of $75 a barrel.

In preparing this article, I asked for Sasol's break-evens, which have never been disclosed. Sasol said its 'latest grassroots synfuel plants, using low-cost natural gas as

* Kevin Davie is editor of the South African *Sunday Times, Business Times*. He has written extensively on the South African fuel industry and exposed many of its secrets, both during the sanctions and the post-sanctions age.

feedstock, are economically viable at crude oil prices of $20 a barrel. For the existing Sasol plants the investments were made ten years ago at significantly lower capital costs and profit break-even is therefore lower than in the case of new plants.'

In 1985, Paul Conlon, an energy expert at the United Nations, estimated Sasol's break-even to be the same as that of Mossgas: $75 a barrel. Elsewhere, Brian Levy writes in an informal World Bank paper (1992) that Sasol's break-even was probably about $45 a barrel.

In their report, Deloitte & Touche disclose that neither the National Party (NP) government nor the Central Energy Fund, which controlled the finances, expected to be able to repay the capital invested in Mossgas.

This appears to have been the reasoning behind synthetic fuels; to write off the capital cost of the project as quickly as possible so that the capital was sunk and the project could then meet its working costs on an ongoing basis.

Sasol: A giant on feet of clay

Sasol and the NP government maintained that the government's investment in Sasol was productive and that government had realised a good return. But how could this have been possible with a break-even above $45 while crude oil prices, with rare exceptions during the worst months of the oil crises, have traded in a band between $25 and $15?

This question is central to understanding the economics of synthetic fuels. Sasol provided some clues, when in 1993 it said that if the full extent of its 'tariff protection' – the amount of direct support the government has paid to ensure its profitability – had been extended, then Sasol would have gotten 38 c/l from the government for every litre of synthetic fuel it produced. This was about 40 per cent of the wholesale price of petrol at the time, excluding taxes and levies.

The decision to proceed with Sasol 2 (50,000 b/d), which began operations in 1980, and later Sasol 3 (50,000 b/d; on stream in 1982) followed jumps in the price of crude oil. The go-ahead for Sasol 2 came in 1974, shortly after the Yom Kippur War pushed crude prices from $3 to $12 a barrel. But, says Conlon, 'the entire project dragged on slowly for lack of financing or perhaps willpower until 1979, when the revolutionary Iranian government cut off oil supplies to the racists.' Sasol 3 got the green light in February 1979, shortly after the fall of the Shah of Iran at the end of 1978. Spot oil prices jumped to $40 a barrel and suggested a future for synthetic fuels. Prices remained high during 1979, traded at about $25 a barrel during the early 1980s before falling to well below $20 in the late 1980s. Prices jumped above $30 during the next oil crisis, precipitated by the invasion of Kuwait by Saddam Hussein in 1990, but settled at around $15 in 1993 before falling to $12 in late 1993.

Sasol remained in the black during the 1980s and emerged in the 1990s as South Africa's highest-profit industrial company with net profits in excess of R1 billion. It has also for some years been ranked as the most profitable company in its sector in the world by *Fortune* and in the top 20 of all *Fortune 500* industrial corporations.

According to Conlon in 1985, the Fischer-Tropsch-Synthol process used at the Sasol plants was an antiquated first-generation technology even when it was selected: 'Its thermal efficiency is low and its capital intensity is too high'. He said once the strategic reason for the Sasol plants had gone, 'they will emburden the national economy as unprofitable white elephants of appalling magnitude.'

How can a company which has to make its fuel from coal compete and outperform those which refine their fuel from crude? It mines the coal using some 10,000 miners, uses vast coal supplies to heat coal to turn it into gas and then converts the gas into fuel. Conventional refiners source their raw material much more cheaply from oil wells.

Conlon wrote that the economics of the operation was only possible through a hidden subsidy which the government had made available to Sasol, and which he was unable to identify.

Sasol and the crude oil refiners: The benefits of regulation

There is in fact more than subsidy involved in the regulated structure of the South African fuel industry which has helped ensure Sasol's survival and profitability. Industry regulation dates back to the 1930s, but was adapted during the 1980s to ensure the profitability of not only the conventional refiners but also synthetic refining. This regulation affects every aspect of the industry. Government allows cartel behaviour, chairs the cartel and sanctions restrictive practices such as market-sharing and price-fixing. Government also sets the formulas which set profitability levels for the industry.

These restrictive practices have been slammed in a Competition Board report released in March 1994. The report called for the restrictive practices which govern the industry to be speedily phased out. The key ingredients which regulate the industry are the In-Bond Landed Cost (IBLC), the pricing system on which South African domestic fuel prices are based; the supply agreement between Sasol and the oil companies which market its fuel; the wholesale and retail margin formulas; the Sasol $23 a barrel floor price payment called 'tariff protection' from the Equalisation Fund, based on providing Sasol with a 10 per cent return on investment whether oil prices are high or low (if the oil price falls below $23, this subsidy comes in); and the service station rationalisation plan (the Ratplan), which controls fuel distribution and limits the number of new market entrants. There is more: import control on fuel; resale price maintenance which outlaws offering any incentive linked to fuel sales; payments of hundreds of millions of rands to the oil companies because of loss of capacity when Sasol 2 and 3 came on stream; and a government-administered rate for pipeline costs which is worth hundreds of millions annually to the pipeline operator, state-owned Transnet. The pipeline charge also allows Sasol, which produces its fuel on the Reef, to charge substantially more for its fuel despite the fact that it hardly pays any pipeline costs.

It has also been argued by some industrial analysts that Sasol cross-subsidises its uneconomic synthetic fuel centre by setting higher prices for other products. Industry sources say that liquefied petroleum gas (LPG) and industrial gases supplied by Sasol are well above import parity partly because the government has put restrictions on imports. Sasol rejects this charge, saying it has to compete with alternative energy sources in this market, and that it has been pushing up demand for its industrial gas for many years.

Prices of feedstocks for the plastics industry paid by local producers are well above export prices. A World Bank paper says the difference is 50 per cent. This explains why

South Africa exports only 2 per cent of its plastic products. Sasol says the reason for local prices being higher than export prices is international dumping, which is depressing world prices. South Africa's non-competitive plastic prices have serious implications for jobs as the job creation potential in upstream, capital-intensive plants is limited, while access to cheap inputs can generate much labour-intensive, downstream production. This is the formula which countries such as Taiwan have used to underpin their economic miracles.

The IBLC: The benefits of administered pricing

The In-Bond Landed Cost is a complex subject. In the days before South Africa had its own oil refineries, government determined that the selling price in South Africa would be the price of the refined product in the Middle East plus the cost of shipping to South Africa. Following the nationalisation of refineries in the Middle East during the early 1970s, 'it was deemed essential to switch to another refining centre obtaining its crude oil from the same area as South Africa and which was situated at more or less the same distance from South Africa as the Gulf refineries,' the government said in its May 1993 report on its involvement in the oil industry. Since the 1970s, prices from three Singapore refineries owned by Shell, BP and Mobil and one in Bahrain owned by Caltex came to be used for calculating the IBLC. Several controversies arise:

1. Singapore prices are higher than those in Northwest Europe. Why not use Northwest European prices?

2. 'Posted prices' are used. These are offer prices or what the refinery hopes to get rather than the actual traded prices, which are usually lower.

3. Singapore is an oil-importing centre, some distance from the Middle East. Its prices therefore already reflect costs of shipping, wharfage and insurance. In a competitive market South African refinery prices could be expected to approximate those of Singapore, it is argued. Yet the IBLC adds to Singapore prices the notional cost of transporting the product to Durban. This is a 10 per cent difference or six cents a litre, worth about R900 million a year in additional income to the South African oil industry.

4. South Africa is well-served with six domestic refineries (including Sasol and Mossgas). Competition could actually lead prices to fall below the cost of importing the refined product.

5. Also controversial is the history of the IBLC in the early 1980s. Between 1980 and 1985 the IBLC showed very little relation to market prices. It was at times up to $11 a barrel higher than Northwest European prices during these years. This was the period in which Sasol 2 and 3 came on stream, between them supplying 40 per cent of South Africa's fuel needs. The conventional refiners mothballed the equivalent capacity and received 'synthetic element' payments to compensate for the shortfall. The extent of these payments for the early 1980s has not yet been disclosed, but totalled R1 billion between 1985 and 1992. They continue to this day (R100 million in 1992) and are scheduled to expire in 1996.

If one compares the IBLC with Rotterdam prices during the 1980s, the conclusion is that the IBLC was on average $5.80 a barrel higher during the 1980s (1991 prices). This difference has been calculated at about R2.2 billion a year in 1991 money. In money-of-the-day terms the IBLC was on average $4.70 a barrel higher than the Rotterdam price.

Figures made available by government show a less marked average difference of $2.40 a barrel between South African and European prices.

I have not been able to get to the bottom of the difference between the IBLC and market prices, but at least one analyst told me that it must have given Sasol substantially increased cash flow and partly compensated the oil refiners for the massive loss of capacity brought about by Sasol coming on stream.

Sasol: Billions of rands given away

Sasol says the government's investment there has been sound. The total cash invested by the state was R4.9 billion, and the return received was R14 billion, or an internal rate of return of 12 per cent. This argument neglects the fact that the government had protected its investment from competition at the expense of the rest of the economy.

It also neglects to take account of other payments designed to ensure Sasol's profitability, such as the synthetic levy payments of R1 billion to the oil industry. And, as noted by analyst Jacques Pickard, the 12 per cent return should be compared with the annual rate of inflation during this period of 14.7 per cent, giving the state a negative real return of 2.7 per cent on its investment.

Also controversial is the price Sasol Limited, the entity established when the state embarked upon the privatisation of the Sasol plants, paid for the Secunda plants. A downpayment of R50 million ensured that Sasol got 50 per cent of the equity of Sasol 3. The remaining 50 per cent was sold by the Central Energy Fund in November 1991 for R2.9 billion (compare this with Sasol 3's replacement cost which is estimated at about R15 billion). An upfront payment of R750 million was agreed, and five further instalments were spread out over five years.

Not disclosed at the time of the R750 million payment was cash of R800 million on Sasol 3's books. This has been likened to buying a house for a R10,000 deposit and on taking possession finding R12,000 in one of the kitchen drawers.

The four remaining annual payments of R400 million and a fifth of R550 million are conditional on Sasol getting the $23 floor price which during 1992/3 was worth R650 million in payments to Sasol from the Equalisation Fund. If the subsidised price is set below $23 a barrel, the payments are at the same time reduced. So there is the pretence of Sasol paying for the asset, but not all are convinced.

But the NP government always intended that Sasol would take transfer of these assets without affecting its profitability. The 1979 prospectus which set out the terms for Sasol's privatisation said the acquisitions of Sasol 2 and 3 by Sasol Limited would take place 'at a price and on terms which as far as possible will not result in a decrease in the attributable earnings per Sasol share and will not unreasonably affect the dividend growth prospects for shareholders in Sasol'. In essence, this amounts to saying that Sasol would not be asked to pay for the transfer of the assets.

The IBLC, which has been consistently higher than market prices, has been one form of subsidy to Sasol. Another has been the tariff revenue which the government has paid to top up Sasol's income. As we have seen above, the *pipeline* has also acted to boost Sasol revenues by hundreds of millions of rands annually. The pipeline tariff, which oil industry spokesmen say is three times higher than anywhere else in the world, charges 10.9 cents to move one litre of fuel from the coast to the Reef. Reef motorists are forced to pay the 'transport cost' despite the fact that very little refined oil actually moves from the coast. Instead it is moved by pipeline from Secunda in the Transvaal. Sasol picks up the full 10.9 cents yet incurs relatively low transport costs. Assuming the actual cost to Sasol is three cents a litre, the pipeline tariff boosts its operating income annually by R424 million. This is almost one-third of the 1991/92 operating income.

Add about R450 million from the IBLC (half of the industry's total of R900 million), R538 million from 'tariff protection', several hundred million from the sale of LPG and industrial gas and from loading the domestic market with plastic prices, and Sasol, South Africa's most profitable industrial company, will have sunk into the red if all its protection is removed.

And this is *before* competition is introduced into the market. With deregulation would come competition and the end of the supply agreements which have to date given Sasol volume protection.

It would in all probability have to cut prices to be able to sell its products, suggesting that the cartel structure acts as a further subsidy to Sasol. By one estimate Sasol would lose as much of 30 per cent of its volume protection in a competitive market.

Are synfuels viable after sanctions?

The above-mentioned break-even point of over $75 per barrel for Mossgas, as estimated by Deloitte & Touche, takes all capital costs into account; if all its capital costs are written off, the break-even will be $16 per barrel. Brian Levy speculated that Sasol would break even at $10 a barrel. The South African Automobile Association has written that it believes Sasol breaks even at $13.

Sasol has declined comment, but the analysis above suggests that its break-even in a competitive market could well be above that of Mossgas. Conlon's suggestion of a white elephant of some magnitude appears prophetic.

In 1993, Deloitte & Touche suggested that no more public funds should be put into Mossgas, as there were much more important areas such as socio-economic development which would give a better return. If Sasol does indeed break even at the above prevailing world prices, this suggests that Deloitte & Touche's recommendation with regard to Mossgas contained a message for the new government's policy with regard to Sasol as well.

In 1993 Sasol moved to counter its critics. It commissioned research to show the employment (26,000), foreign exchange (R4 billion a year), value-added (R4 billion a year) and technology benefits it brought to the economy. It also applied to the government to be able to run its own retail chain of service stations (it was limited to 8 per cent of the national market through 'blue pump' sales on the forecourts of other service stations). It also intended applying to the Board on Tariffs and Trade for an import duty to be placed on crude oil. The idea is that this duty will replace the 'tariff protection' from the Equalisation Fund.

Johannesburg September 1994 – Oil companies were compelled to have Sasol 'Blue Pumps' along-side their own brands at their filling stations in the Transvaal, the Free State and Northern Cape

The restructuring of Sasol started prior to the end of sanctions. The aim is to reduce its reliance on synthetic fuels and to make sure that its profitable businesses have separate identities. Some senior industry sources suggest that Sasol will sell or give its uneconomic synfuel core back to the state, retaining its profitable chemical and other businesses; Sasol denies this.

The restructuring brought opposition from the conventional refiners, who see Sasol as a subsidised competitor moving into their markets. In 1993, Engen chief executive Rob Angel proposed that Sasol's synthetic fuel core should be converted into a utility-type public enterprise 'to save the country R670 million a year'. Critics such as Angel say that Sasol, if converted into a utility, would still save foreign exchange and bring other benefits, but that the need to artificially inflate its profits by hundreds of millions of rands annually would have been removed.

The oil industry: Just how profitable?

The cost of synthetic fuels has not been the total cost of combating the oil embargo.

The costs of regulating the South African fuel industry also extended to the conventional refiners who for years have benefited from the IBLC, the fixed wholesale margin and the plethora of other controls such as market-sharing agreements.

The conventional refiners have argued that they operate worldwide in regulated and deregulated markets and that it should be understood that deregulation in South Africa would have the effect of job losses, service station closures and price increases in rural areas. Behind the public position is the fact that regulation holds major benefits for the industry such as virtually guaranteed, attractive returns.

I compared oil companies listed by *Fortune 500* and *Petroleum Intelligence Weekly* in 1993. Those showed that South African oil companies had profitability ratios several times those of private companies overseas. While multinationals Shell, BP and Caltex are not listed on the stock exchange in South Africa and do not disclose their accounts, Sasol emerged from this comparison with the highest profits as a percentage of sales and Engen with the largest profits as a percentage of assets. Their returns were more than three times the international average on the two key ratios of taxed profit as a percentage of sales and assets. Sasol recorded taxed income of 13.9 per cent as a percentage of sales in 1991, more than four times higher than the international average of 3.15 per cent. Sasol explained the difference by saying its capital intensity was much higher than that of conventional refiners: 'As a result Sasol's profits as a percentage of revenue have to be almost twice as high as that of a conventional oil company to give the same return on capital'.

Some of the formulas the industry benefits from can also be used to turn on the flow of hundreds of millions of rands when needed. In mid-1991, the government decided that the average 15 per cent return on assets which it allows the industry would in future apply only to marketing assets (until then it applied to both refining and marketing assets). This led to an increase in the wholesale margin from 5.5 cents a litre to 13.5 cents during a 14-month period in 1992/93, a difference of R1.2 billion annualised. But oil industry executives complained that even with this margin increase, they still battled to keep up with inflation and continued to petition the government for further increases.

The cost of stockpiling

Two other costs, that of stockpiling oil and paying premiums to middlemen, have also added billions to South Africa's fuel bill.

Sasol proposed a strategic crude oil storage programme in the 1960s after deciding against a synthetic fuels programme because of low oil prices of only $2 a barrel. The cost of the stockpile has been identified by Conlon as one the key components of the price which was paid in order to ensure that the apartheid regime secured ample fuel supplies.

The Strategic Fuel Fund gave details in November 1992 of one of its huge stockpile facilities, six underground concrete bunkers at Saldanha Bay near Cape Town, which could hold 45 million barrels of oil. This was enough to replace nearly six months of oil imports in 1992. Details of the stockpile at Saldanha Bay were released by the SFF as it was then offering part of the facility for rental. The bunkers, each the equivalent size of a giant supertanker, would cost R500 million to replace. Of concern is the fact that the stockpile at this facility, which first housed oil in January 1980, was built up during the early 1980s, when according to a document – claimed to be official – South Africa was paying between $8 and $20 a barrel premium on contracts of 120,000 b/d.

Some of the stockpiled oil has been sold from 1991 onwards, partly to help fund development spending.

Conlon said he did not believe the South African authorities' estimates of the stockpile under its control, 'but if what they say is true, then it would mean that they have purchased a relative degree of protection from the oil embargo with a financial bloodletting of appalling dimensions'. Conlon said the total amount of oil in storage according to official claims would be 127.5 million barrels with a market value of $3,832 million (in 1985). His own estimate from 1987 (first published through the Newsletter of the Shipping Research Bureau, No. 10, January 1988) was that the total volume stored probably did not exceed 60 million barrels. The actual amount could have been greater than this. Details disclosed by the SFF in early 1994 show that South Africa's oil storage facility could store 180 million barrels, although it was never more than 80 per cent (144 million barrels) full.

Conlon said in 1985 that his estimate 'would have to be adjusted upwards by an additional $640 million in order to allow for the pariah penalty averaging $5 a barrel'. He said the storage facilities could have cost $500 million (government disclosed in 1994 that the replacement value of the facilities was R1.2 billion). 'A further ramification, not immediately obvious to the layman, is that an enormous opportunity cost is being incurred on tied-up inventory. At a reasonable interest rate, say 1.5 per cent above Libor [the London inter-bank offered rate, an international benchmark rate] this opportunity loss would come to $480 million at present'.

Chiavelli and friends: Rich pickings

The premiums paid to middlemen such as Marino Chiavelli, Marc Rich and John Deuss were also never officially confirmed by the former government. Two court cases, one in which Johannesburg businessman Taki Xenopoulos claimed R140 million from Chiavelli and another in which several parties brought an action against the Strategic Fuel Fund, were classified in terms of the Petroleum Products Act until late 1993.

But enough information has leaked over the years to put together a picture of SFF's operations after the 1979 oil crisis.

Chiavelli, a flambloyant Italian with a desire for publicity and a criminal record and controversial past, was involved in the trade of animal hides and skins when asked by Xenopoulos whether he could supply oil. Chiavelli claimed he could, and indeed it turned out that he had some very good Saudi Arabian oil contacts. Chiavelli met government and SFF officials in Cape Town on 15 March 1979. He told the officials that Abdulhady Taher, governor of Petromin, the state-owned Saudi oil company, had asked him to contact the South African government while in South Africa. 'Taher & Co worried about high oil prices on spot market. They realise we [are] also operating in this market and in view of their objective to keep oil prices down [presumably because the Saudis are a low-cost producer], they might be interested in starting negotiations with us,' the minutes of the meeting say.

A set of negotiations followed, which included Botswana officials, who were to front as the stated destination for the oil. The Botswana company would get 40 US cents a barrel, while Chiavelli would get $3 a barrel for 100,000 b/d over the three-year contract. A note on the draft agreement says: 'Dr Chiavelli made these arrangements possible. The Saudis know the story – they just don't want to deal with us openly. The $3.00 is premium.

Dr C will pay a premium to Petromin. We will arrange with Dr C for $2.50 premium for Petromin (Dr Taher) for 12 months. Thereafter it will be reviewed'.

The $3 appears cheap as the Advocate-General, Mr Justice van der Walt, who investigated South Africa's oil affairs in 1984, said the SFF was paying $8 a barrel during 1980. But a document said to be official shows that in June 1979 under one of the SFF contracts the premium was $20. The price paid was $33 a barrel for oil while the official government selling price was only $13.

Chiavelli's deal seemed set to go. The South African Volkskas bank sent a letter to Citibank in Geneva saying it held $358 million on behalf of SFF for Chiavelli, the $358 million to be paid in instalments over the three-year period. But the deal never got off the ground, and Chiavelli wrote a cheerful note saying perhaps a later deal might be possible.

In the meantime, Xenopoulos, who had introduced Chiavelli to the government, had initiated a R90 million (plus interest) Supreme Court action, claiming 2 per cent commission which he said Chiavelli had agreed would be his.

An analysis of documentation held by the Department of Mineral and Energy Affairs shows that while details of shipper and consignee had been erased in most cases, 63 tankerloads or 68 million barrels could have been delivered from Petromin between 1979 and 1982. Almost all the oil was delivered by companies owned by Marc Rich or John Deuss. Whereas Chiavelli was said to have 'never moved a barrel of oil in his life', these traders had moved many barrels, specialising in boycott markets.

The Xenopoulos/Chiavelli case never went to trial, but was settled for a sum of tens of millions. Payment, I was told, did not come from Chiavelli, but from the Arabs for whom he had fronted. Chiavelli died in 1993. Even in death he remains a controversial, enigmatic figure, symbolising the worst excesses of the apartheid era.[1]

Allegations surfaced in Parliament during 1984 that SFF had overpaid by hundreds of millions on contracted amounts. In those days, SFF was staffed by senior Sasol officials (control switched to the Industrial Development Corporation in 1984). The Advocate-General investigated these allegations and concluded there was no evidence of wrongdoing on the part of officials or middlemen. The investigation remains controversial in view of the fact that key people who had information were not called to give evidence.

Clive Scholtz, who had acted as Xenopoulos's investigator, produced an analysis of the Advocate-General's report, saying that notwithstanding its conclusions, the allegation of overpayment stands. But in the repressive days of the mid-1980s, issues surrounding South Africa's oil supplies did not get an airing, and as we have seen above, public examination of the issue until 1993 was thwarted as key information was withheld from scrutiny.

Abolishing the legacy of apartheid

There should be no doubt, though, that the costs of attempting to achieve energy self-sufficiency have been horrendous and that some of these costs have survived the passing-away of apartheid in ongoing excessive protection and subsidies akin to state enterprises in former socialist economies of Eastern Europe and the Soviet Union.

Engen chief executive Rob Angel estimated in April 1994 that deregulation of the fuel

industry would save R2.5 billion to R4 billion a year. This compares with total net savings
for the country of just R6 billion during 1993. The R4 billion figure coincides with an
analysis of the industry done by an industry source and made available to me in 1992. In
the paper, entitled 'A study in the abuse of power', the author concludes that but for
synthetic fuels, South Africa could have housed 14 million people over a ten-year period.

For all the enormous cost of Sasol and Mossgas, both projects needn't have happened. If
government had set up two teams, one to buy embargoed oil as cheaply as possible and
one to make synthetic fuel, the economics of the latter would have been impossible to
justify. But the same team which was building Sasol (at a cost of $75 a barrel, according to
Conlon) was also buying oil from crooks such as Marino Chiavelli at inflated premiums.

This point has been noted by Alan Clingman, a New York-based South African commodity broker who got his break as a 21-year-old when he began broking oil deals for the
Strategic Fuel Fund at the height of the embargo. Simon Barber, who interviewed Mr
Clingman for *Business Times* in 1994, reported that the premiums 'did not bother the SFF,
which was, after all, virtually synonymous with Sasol, which in turn depended on high oil
prices to make economic sense in a world where, as the trader himself concedes, crude
was never that difficult to obtain'.

Sasol and Mossgas represent massive investments, and debate will no doubt rage on
how to turn this investment to good account. There are parties both on the Left and Right
who argue that significant parts of the operations should be state-owned to produce for the
public good as the plants save foreign exchange, create employment and could be used to

'On the other hand, with a few modifications, we could flog it to the AVU as a volkstaat.'
The Natal Mercury, 21 September 1993

provide competitive inputs into the economy. But Sasol is resisting this option, insisting that its protection is moderate and no different to that enjoyed by other manufacturing industries. It claims that its protective regime should be reduced over time in line with South Africa's overall commitment to GATT to reduce protection.

Two images have recurred during the period while I have been researching South Africa's tragic attempts to buy energy self-sufficiency. It is some time in the future, and competition rather than bureaucracy rules: Mossgas rusts in the sea; Sasol, with enough pipes to go completely around the world, is windswept and desolate.

References

Anon., 1992, *The transport fuels industry: A study in the abuse of power.* [South Africa].
Barber, S., 1994, 'A fortune built on the apartheid premium', *Sunday Times*, 25 September 1994.
Conlon, P., 1985, *The SASOL liquefaction plants: Economic implications and impact on South Africa's ability to withstand an oil cut-off.* New York: UN Centre against Apartheid, October 1985.
Davie, K., 1991a, 'How South Africa gets its oil', *The Executive*, August 1991.
Davie, K., 1991b, 'Inside Sasol', *The Executive*, November 1991.
Davie, K., 1992, 'Secrets of Marino Chiavelli', *The Executive*, April 1992.
Davie, K., 1992–1994, Reports in *Business Times, Sunday Times*.
Department of Mineral and Energy Affairs, 1993, *Government's Involvement in the Oil Industry*, May 1993.
Levy, B., 1992, *How Can SA Manufacturing Efficiently Create Employment? An Analysis of the Impact of Trade and Industrial Policy.* Informal World Bank paper, January 1992.
Pickard, J., 1993, *Current developments in the oil industry in SA.* Johannesburg: Davis, Borkum and Hare, 11 June 1993.
Sasol information session. Mabula Game Lodge, August 1993.
Special Report of the Auditor-General on the Independent Expert Evaluation of the Economic Viability of the Mossgas Project, 1993.

Drive Now and Pay Forever – The Apartheid Way

CLIVE SCHOLTZ[*]

It was the 1970s. The reign of the Shah of Iran was rapidly drawing to a close. When it finally ended, the South African Government found itself without a reliable supply of oil. International sanctions were in operation, and with the exception of the Shah of Iran, most oil-producing countries had already implemented them. It is believed that international oil companies then conveyed a message to the South African Government to the effect that they could not be seen, either directly or indirectly, to be supplying oil to South Africa. The Government, in defiance of the world, decided to form its own procurement arm in order to ensure that South Africa would not run out of oil. It was for this purpose that the Strategic Fuel Fund (SFF) was created. It was financed by the Industrial Development Corporation, a government agency, but was manned by officials from Sasol, another parastatal. Since that time Sasol has been involved, not only in producing synthetic oil and other products from coal, but also in the purchasing of South Africa's crude oil.

This obviously suited Sasol and, whether by accident or design, the South African motorist paid most dearly for oil. The higher the price of oil, the higher the profits for Sasol. Article ii,4 of the contract by which Sasol Limited managed the SFF authorised Sasol 'to purchase crude oil on behalf of SFF/SASOL at such prices and under such conditions that SASOL Limited or its nominees considers to be fair and reasonable'.

By the nature of its operation, Sasol was a manufacturer and had very little or no experience of international trade of the magnitude that was to follow. SFF/Sasol was therefore dumped overnight into the shady world of international traders and soon found itself among the circle of thieves and international con men.

The Salem Affair

One of the first encounters which SFF/Sasol had with shrewd con men was the purchase of the *Salem* oil, which made headlines worldwide – except of course in South Africa, where it was forbidden to publish any details regarding it. This episode in the early history of SFF/Sasol began one day when two so-called international oil traders knocked on the

---

[*] The author of this document was commissioned by Fontana Holdings (Pty) Ltd in May 1981 to investigate the Fontana/Chiavelli case. After four and a half years of investigations a settlement was negotiated between Fontana and Chiavelli. At present the author is an investigator, specialising in investigating third-party claims in South Africa.

   The editors wish to thank the author for his permission to include the document, which was written in August–September 1994, in this book.

doors of SFF/Sasol in Sasolburg. These men convinced the Manager, Mr Wiggett, and his colleagues, Mr Naudé and Mr Bredenkamp, that they could supply South Africa on a fairly regular basis, although on a small scale. They had managed to procure a number of Saudi oil cargoes and were prepared to ship these to South Africa. But before the plan materialised, they came up with a second offer involving inexpensive, 'safe' oil, which would be delivered in the interim.

One can imagine the glint in the eyes of these officials when the scheme was explained to them by the two men. According to Mr Reidel and Mr Soudan, they had a contact who was the 'captain of the oil farm' in Mina al Ahmadi in Kuwait. Billions of barrels of crude oil were being pumped from the various oil fields into this large tank farm, and from these huge tanks the oil was loaded onto tankers. As a great deal of evaporation, spillage and wastage was inevitable, it was accepted that a certain percentage would have to be written off on the inlet side of the tanks. According to SFF/Sasol's new-found friends, this farm manager was prepared to write off more oil to evaporation and spillage than was actually the case, and the oil thus 'saved' would be made available to them. He was therefore quite prepared to let this oil 'evaporate at a very special price' as a favour to South Africa.

The beauty of it all was that no record of this oil would be kept, nor would a Bill of Lading be signed by a ship's captain. This oil would also not have to be insured through Lloyd's. They would be buying 'non-existent' oil, so to speak. SFF/Sasol would only need to pay after the oil had been offloaded and would not even run the risk of losing it in a storm. At a time when the rest of the world was boycotting them, this must have sounded like the answer to their prayers, and they immediately made use of this opportunity to procure oil for South Africa at low prices. It must have given them great satisfaction to outsmart the whole world. In the final paragraph, the contract stipulated that payment would be made on delivery.

After having concluded the deal and on preparing to leave, the two traders divulged that they had one minor problem. They did not have any means of conveying the oil to South Africa. They suggested that it would be most helpful if they could have their own ship and crew. This would thwart efforts of South Africa's enemies to identify the movement of oil to South Africa.

The only problem was that these two traders had not built up enough capital to buy their own ship. 'No problem,' was the answer from SFF/Sasol, 'we will arrange finance and we will give you guarantees.' Very shortly afterwards, one of their friends, Mr J.C.J. van Vuuren, who had negotiated the deal, walked away with R220,000 as commission. SFF/Sasol had given a guarantee to Mercabank, who had financed the purchase of the *South Sun*, for $12,000,000. (This ship was in such a shocking state that the manager of the oil buoy off Durban refused to allow her access to the buoy again after her first call.)

The ship, renamed *Salem*, docked at the port of Mina al Ahmadi, and after loading set off for the high seas. *En route*, a signwriter could be seen hanging over the bow of the ship while changing the ship's name once again. To SFF/Sasol, the call of the tanker *Lema* which anchored off Durban on 27 December 1979 must have been in perfect accordance with their expectations: the Certificate of Analysis from the Surveyors checking the cargo on their behalf seemed to prove that here was the first of the promised cargoes of 'non-existent' Kuwaiti oil, ready to be delivered to them. The ship offloaded her cargo, and

Excerpts from communication dated 9 January 1980 from SASOLKOR, Johannesburg (J.F. Bredenkamp) to Beets Trading AG, Zug, Switzerland, attention: Mr A. Reidel. [NB. 'V35' was the tanker 'Lema' or *Salem* – Editors]

RE OUR TELECONS AND YOUR TELEXES OF 8/1 AND 9/1/80.

1) WE GIVE BELOW THE DETAILS OF OUR $305 411 TRANSFER TODAY:

QUANTITY DELIVERED

1 310 381 BBLS AT $34,50
PER BARREL $45 208 144

[...]

2) [...] FOR YOUR INFORMATION WE QUOTE A TELEX RECEIVED FROM THE S B M MANAGER RE YOUR VESSEL:

QUOTE:

SUBSTANDARD SHIPS

PLEASE BE ADVISED THAT V35 WHICH DISCHARGED AT THE SBM FROM 28/12/79 TO 02/01/80 SHOULD BE CONSIDERED SUBSTANDARD FOR THE UNDER-MENTIONED REASONS AND WILL NOT AGAIN BE ALLOWED TO DISCHARGE THROUGH THE SBM SYSTEM.

1) WINDLESS NOT CAPABLE OF LIFTING SLACK MOORINGS WITHOUT ASSIST-ANCE OF SECOND WINCH.

2) FORECASTLE LAYOUT NOT SUITABLE FOR SBM OPERATIONS [...].

[...]

4) MASTER LEFT VESSEL FOR THREE DAYS, OFFICERS AND CREW UNRELI-ABLE.

5) POOR HOUSEKEEPING, DIRTY ACCOMODATION.

6) NO INERT GAS SYSTEM.

ANY OTHER VESSEL WITH SIMILAR LOW STANDARDS OF SAFETY AND OPERA-TIONAL CAPABILITIES CANNOT BE ALLOWED TO DISCHARGE THROUGH THE SBM.

UNQUOTE.

REGARDS

BREDENKAMP

SFF/Sasol issued a cheque to the traders and celebrated the first successful shipment of the 'non-existent oil' which they had managed to obtain against such great odds.

SFF/Sasol had swallowed one of the biggest con operations in modern maritime history hook, line and sinker. The first basic prerequisite for a 'sting' or a 'con' operation is that of extreme secrecy. Secondly, it must be quasi-illegal or immoral. Greed and gullibility on the part of the victim seem to be further prerequisites. SFF/Sasol was the perfect target for these clever crooks.

Their enthusiasm, however, turned to incredulity when Shell instituted a claim with their insurers for the loss of an oil cargo which had sunken off the African coast opposite Senegal. Lloyd's had, as a routine procedure, instructed their Assessors to investigate and assess the claim. What made the Assessors suspicious was the fact that, although the ship, a tanker by the name of *Salem*, had sunken extremely fast, the crew had found time to pack all their belongings. A remarkable oversight was the ship's logbook. The Assessors' suspicions were confirmed when they discovered that this cargo of oil, which Shell had bought on the high seas from Pontoil – which had actually purchased the crude from Kuwait in a perfectly legal transaction and had hired the *Salem* to lift the cargo – was identical to the cargo which had been delivered in Durban by the *'Lema'* and which had been purchased by SFF/Sasol.

Lloyd's repudiated Shell's claim, as fraud was evident. After delivering the oil in Durban, the ship had sailed off, filled with a fake 'cargo' of seawater. As she sailed past Senegal and reached a very deep ravine in the seabed, she was scuttled – on the instructions of Soudan and Reidel.

Upon receiving the repudiation of the claim, as well as Lloyds' reasons for doing so, Shell immediately instructed their lawyers to take action against SFF/Sasol, who was in possession of their oil. SFF/Sasol was caught by surprise. It called in its legal adviser, Dr Dirk Mostert, the former Dean of the Faculty of Law at the University of Pretoria. This eminent person launched a personal investigation into the *Salem* affair. At the same time, SFF/Sasol, wherever possible, thwarted the efforts of Shell and the international shipping community to bring the crooks to book. It gave instructions to everyone involved, including its London office, not to divulge any information whatsoever to any person. This included Scotland Yard, who, at the insistence of Shell, had started with an investigation into charges of fraud against Mr Soudan and Mr Reidel.

On 8 February 1980 SFF/Sasol was taken to court. A request was lodged for an interdict to seize the oil in SFF/Sasol's tanks belonging to Shell.

Certain documents reveal some rather interesting actions on the part of SFF/Sasol. According to a copy of a letter kept in SFF/Sasol's *Salem* file, Dr Mostert was, on that very same day, to hand over a letter to the two oil traders concerned, who were in South Africa at the time. The letter notified them that it had come to the notice of SFF/Sasol that a dispute had arisen regarding the ownership of the oil. The letter further notified Mr Soudan that, if SFF/Sasol was to suffer any damages, it would hold Mr Soudan and/or Mr Reidel responsible.

What is amazing is that SFF/Sasol failed to report to the South African Police that SFF/Sasol had been defrauded out of $45,000,000 and that the crooks were booked in at the Carlton Hotel in Johannesburg, South Africa. It is believed that they had lunch with them instead. In fact, SFF/Sasol never lodged an official complaint with the police nor requested them to investigate the matter. At the same time, SFF/Sasol advised the Cabinet that South Africa had no choice but to come to an agreement with Shell to split their losses on a 50/50 basis and that South Africa would have to pay Shell $31,000,000 in compensation. (SFF/Sasol later boasted that it had paid less for the oil than Shell, as Shell had paid $57,000,000 while SFF/Sasol had paid $45,000,000...)

It would also appear from a note in SFF/Sasol's *Salem* file that information received prior to the delivery and payment of the oil, but after SFF/Sasol had already bought it, hinted that the traders were offering the *Lema* oil for sale to others as well. The note says that Mr Bredenkamp and Mr Naudé were to be informed of the situation. They obviously paid no attention; the South African motorist had to pay $31,000,000 for this oversight.

During a press conference in March 1983, Dr Mostert, with the permission of the then Minister of Mineral and Energy Affairs, opened the *Salem* file and informed his audience that he had tried everything in his power to lure these two gentlemen back to South Africa so that they could be arrested by the South African Police. In actual fact, SFF/Sasol had from the start refused to cooperate with the international community, who hunted these two crooks down and brought them to justice in the USA and elsewhere. They had refused to divulge any information and had even refused to give evidence during the international hearing on the matter. Having flown from South Africa to London (at the expense of the motorist), Mr Naudé and Mr Bredenkamp decided that it would not be in their interests to give evidence after all.

The Marc Rich Connection

During April 1979 SFF/Sasol entered into a contract for the delivery of oil with the trader Marc Rich (under the guise of Minoil Inc.). They agreed on a price of $22 per barrel, which at that stage was at a premium of $7.50 per barrel. Paragraph 3.3 of the contract, however, made provision for a possible change in the oil price during the duration of this contract. It said that a new price could be renegotiated and that if a new price for further cargoes had been agreed on by both parties, the *old* price of $22 would be applicable for all shipments of oil a) which had been delivered; b) which had been loaded; and c) for which ships had already been commissioned.

On 5 May 1979 the first shipment of oil was loaded. Not much later, Marc Rich informed SFF/Sasol that he felt that the price should be readjusted. On 21 May 1979, after negotiations, a new price of $33 per barrel was agreed upon, which again was thought to be a good price under the circumstances, in spite of the fact that the official government selling price (OGSP) of the oil in question was $14.55. This new price was thus at a premium of $18.45 per barrel. In June, the OGSP was fixed at an even lower level, namely $13.00. Nevertheless, further shipments arrived, and payment was made according to the new price ruling – that is, for all shipments, including those loaded before the new price ruling. SFF/Sasol signed cheques for $33 per barrel for approximately seven shipments of oil which had originally been priced at $22. The result is that SFF/Sasol overpaid by approximately $64,000,000! Even when this 'error' was brought to the attention of the

South African Government a few years later, and the Advocate-General was appointed to investigate the matter, SFF/Sasol was able to 'prove' to the judge that it had paid according to the contract.

Who Are the Goodies, Who Are the Baddies?

More traders arrived on the scene. SFF/Sasol was presented with a term contract in which a trading company called Semafor was to deliver 40,000 barrels of Omani oil per day over a period of three years. The contract was signed on 12 June 1979 for delivery of the oil at a price of $18.30 per barrel. The amount of oil delivered under this contract is not known. There was supposed to be one shipment per month. It would appear, however, that by December 1979 only one or two shipments had in fact been delivered. Furthermore, Semafor had apparently not been able to deliver on time. This made it possible for SFF/Sasol to cancel the contract during February 1980.

In putting the pieces of this jigsaw puzzle together, it is interesting to note that *John Deuss* – whom we will meet later – had presented to SFF/Sasol a Sale/Purchase Agreement between his company Transworld Oil and the Sultanate of Oman, dated 2 January 1980. In this agreement Oman undertook to 'assign HESTONIE'S Agreement Volume (40,000 barrels per day) [the Semafor contract] to TRANSWORLD OIL'. On 30 January 1980, Deuss made an offer to SFF/Sasol to sell 40,000 barrels of Oman oil per day as from 1 January 1980 at a price of $36.50. SFF/Sasol accepted this offer even before the Semafor contract was cancelled.

Due to the actions of SFF/Sasol and John Deuss, the South African motorist unknowingly paid an additional $3,250,000 for a breach of contract, which SFF/Sasol had to pay out because of this escapade.

Years later, Mr Helge Storch-Nielsen, who had negotiated the Semafor/Stonie contract, was sued together with SFF/Sasol by some disgruntled foreign middlemen who missed out on their commission. The claim was based on the alleged collusion between SFF/Sasol, John Deuss and the Sultanate of Oman to cancel the deal.

At that stage, I was in the possession of certain documents, including the aforementioned letter of 2 January 1980. This letter and other documents clearly indicate that there had been collusion between SFF/Sasol and John Deuss. I was very tempted to present this document to the legal team of the claimants. However, I discovered that it would once again have been the South African motorist who would have had to come up with the commission, as Sasol had indemnity cover and would therefore never be held responsible for the actions of SFF/Sasol. SFF/Sasol had a certificate of indemnity from the Industrial Development Corporation (IDC) that none of its officials nor SFF/Sasol would be held responsible for their actions. And, believe it or not, the IDC also had in its safe a letter from Minister Van der Merwe, the Minister of Planning and Environment from 1976 to 1978, indemnifying the IDC of any claims or damages suffered by any person. The end result would be that the South African taxpayer would have to foot the bill for the actions of the officials of SFF/Sasol.

The Rising Star on the Horizon

SFF/Sasol was looking for a long-term contract from a 'reliable source'. Its good friend John Deuss was able to supply it with a few shipments of oil which he was able to procure on the spot market. Ironically enough, Deuss had been a bankrupt second-hand car dealer who had moved on to become an oil trader working for the Russians until they cancelled the contract after a dispute had arisen. After the cancellation of the contract, the Russian bureaucracy – which seems to operate much like its South African counterpart – failed to notify the loading port that no oil should be loaded onto Deuss' ships. Deuss had a few ships loaded with oil which he decided he was not going to pay for, as the Russians had cancelled the contract. It was at this stage that John Deuss set his sights on South Africa.

He managed to impress on the officials of SFF/Sasol that he was the reliable partner for whom they had been waiting, and they eagerly made use of his services. However, having run out of Russian supplies, Deuss perhaps had no ready alternatives; it is not clear whether the Arab countries – for instance, the Saudis – were loath to enter into dealings with him because of his former association with the Russians.

The Doctor to the Rescue!

If there was such a problem, the solution arrived in the form of Marino Chiavelli, who was introduced to SFF/Sasol in May 1979 by a South African businessman. Mr Chiavelli, who had bestowed upon himself the Italian title of 'dottore', had a very close relationship with the Arabs. His introduction to the Arab world apparently took place one evening when he

---

1981: SFF/Sasol starts to learn the trade

> 2.4 Paragraaf 2.3 maak voorsiening daarvoor dat SFF 'n verteenwoordiger voltyds of deeltyds in die kantore van Marimpex kan plaas en dat hulle onderneem om alle ter saaklike dokumente, kontrakte ens aan hom te toon; trouens hy word 'n deel van hulle bedryfspan. 'n Voordeel hiervan is dat daar 'n direkte, deur-lopende kontrole uitgeoefen kan word deur SFF, wat ook terselfdertyd eerstehandse ondervinding in eie geledere kan opdoen van die internasionale olie-handel.

From letter of D.F. Mostert (Sasol Ltd) to the Director General, Ministry of Mineral and Energy Affairs, 15 May 1981 ('VERTROULIK EN PERSOONLIK' – Private and Confidential). *Translation*: Section 2.3 [of draft agreement on the purchase of Russian crude from Marimpex] provides for the posting of an SFF representative, part-time or full-time, to the offices of Marimpex and an undertaking from their side to show him all relevant documents, contracts, etc.; he will in fact become one of their employees. This has the advantage that it will enable SFF to exercise direct and continuous supervision, while simultaneously offering people from within its ranks the possibility to acquire first-hand experience in the international oil trade.

had been sitting alone in a hotel in Geneva. He spotted two lonely Arab boys who were far from home, and very generously sought their companionship. When their families, who are believed to have been oil sheikhs in Saudi Arabia, heard of this fine gentleman who had looked after their boys in the Western world, they opened their doors of hospitality to him. He then obtained a three-year contract of 150,000 barrels of Saudi Arabian oil per day.

After acquiring this contract, Mr Chiavelli mentioned it in passing to his import/export agent in South Africa. This businessman immediately saw an opportunity to acquire oil for South Africa, as it had become evident that the Shah's oil had dried up. Chiavelli was introduced to SFF/Sasol during 1979, and a scheme was designed during 1980 by which a front organisation would be formed in a neighbouring African country. Saudi Arabia would enter into a three-year contract with this country to deliver 150,000 b/d, two thirds of which were destined for South Africa.

Over the next few years a legal battle ensued between Chiavelli and his erstwhile business partner regarding an amount of $90,000,000, which was the commission on the deal. Chiavelli denied that he had ever made such an agreement, and he denied that he had delivered any oil to South Africa. He was strongly supported by SFF/Sasol officials who later called the Department of Mineral and Energy Affairs and its Minister to their aid. The latter supported them all the way.

It was on 24 May 1981 that I was commissioned to investigate the oil deals and to establish whether Mr Chiavelli had in fact delivered oil to South Africa, either directly or indirectly, so that my client could calculate and claim his estimated $90,000,000 in commission allegedly owed to him by Mr Chiavelli.

The Rising Star is Shining

On 18 August 1980, seemingly out of the blue, John Deuss offered SFF/Sasol 80,000 barrels of Saudi Arabian oil per day on a three-year contract (the 'Lucina' contract). The volume was later increased to 120,000 b/d. Thereafter, Chiavelli received $7,500,000 per month for oil that had found its way to the South African ports. SFF/Sasol was able, with a smile of satisfaction, to assure the Minister that South Africa would have enough oil to keep the wheels moving.

What on Earth Is Going On?

Towards the end of 1981, I stumbled across information which seemed to indicate that South Africa was paying exorbitant amounts for oil; much higher, in fact, than the prices stipulated in two contracts.

During that time, a new minister was appointed for Mineral and Energy Affairs, namely Mr Piet du Plessis. We had already approached his predecessor, Mr F.W. de Klerk, and had presented him with certain facts in our possession which indicated that South Africa had received oil from Mr Chiavelli. We had urged the Minister to ensure that SFF/Sasol officials supplied the statistics of oil delivered by Mr Chiavelli so that my client's commission could be calculated. Mr De Klerk presented this information to SFF/ Sasol and finally received its answer. SFF/Sasol denied that Chiavelli had been involved in oil deliveries and urged the Minister to stop us from making further enquiries or investigations into the oil deals, as 'this was jeopardising the flow of oil to South Africa'.

After the appointment of Mr Du Plessis, I thought it worthwhile approaching him, as he might choose to be the proverbial 'new broom which sweeps clean'. After our discussions, he decided to launch a thorough investigation. Two senior officers of the National Intelligence Service (NIS) were commissioned to investigate the SFF/Sasol files in order to establish the truth.

Within the first hour or so, Mr Pieter Swanepoel of the NIS came across certain contracts and other documentation which seemed to indicate that something was being covered up. As a result of this information, certain documents were presented which aided the plaintiff in Mr Chiavelli's case tremendously.

It was also pointed out to Minister Du Plessis that South Africa was paying too much for oil and that there were reputable oil merchants who were quite willing and able to supply oil at very reasonable prices. Minister Du Plessis challenged these allegations, and a reputable South African businessman met the challenge by delivering a tanker of oil from a reputable merchant with the offer of a term contract, thereby proving that this was in fact possible.

SFF/Sasol was legally bound to the term contract it had made with John Deuss. The Minister, however, insisted that it should renegotiate both the price and the quantity in order to reduce the price. The Minister began to realise that something was wrong, but once again he had to rely on 'the SFF/Sasol experts' for his information.

Had the Minister seriously investigated the contract and the prices being paid, he would have discovered that SFF/Sasol had overpaid by $4 per barrel on the Deuss contract. This information was obviously not revealed to the Minister.

However, as a result of the Minister's efforts, the Deuss contract price eventually came down to the agreed price, namely $2.50 premium over the so-called 'marker price'.[1] This was during October 1981. It resulted in a saving to the South African motorist of $480,000 per day. As a result, the Minister was able to announce a reduction of 1.5 cents per litre in the price of petrol in February 1982. A historic moment for the fuel industry!

The ray of hope was soon extinguished, as Minister Du Plessis was replaced by Minister Danie Steyn. For some reason or another, Minister Steyn fell into line with the SFF/ Sasol bureaucracy, and the lid was once again placed on the secret and shady dealings of the oil world.

However, at the beginning of 1984, I gathered substantial evidence regarding various oil deals. While sifting through these documents, I discovered to my amazement that, according to my calculations, overpayments had been made on two contracts amounting to $200,000,000. I double-checked the figures, consulted various oil journals, and came to the conclusion that the South African motorist was being taken for a costly ride.

My first inclination was to inform the relevant authorities. However, I knew how the system operates and that such a step would prove futile. I realised that it would even jeopardise my own position, as I had information in my possession which, under the Petroleum Products Act, would classify me as a criminal. After some deliberation, I decided on a course of action which would allow me to achieve my objective.

Shortly after this, the Leader of the Opposition, Mr Van Zyl Slabbert, received a registered parcel consisting of a memorandum as well as other documents which had emanated from the files of SFF/Sasol, indicating that overpayments had been made. The memorandum requested that Van Zyl Slabbert use this information, not for party political means, but in the interests of the country and bring it to the attention of the Government.

Being a good South African, Dr Van Zyl Slabbert decided to act accordingly. He brought the matter to the attention of Prime Minister P.W. Botha, who immediately instructed the newly appointed Advocate-General, whose function it was to look into corruption and maladministration, to investigate the allegations.

My knowledge of the inner workings and work culture of the bureaucracy was once again confirmed. Although a commission of enquiry was appointed, ostensibly to get to the bottom of these alleged overpayments, the behind-the-scenes manoeuvres were of a totally different nature.

Both the NIS and the South African Police were instructed – at the highest level – to find out who the unpatriotic culprit was who had passed the classified information on to the Leader of the Opposition. There were two suspects, Brigadier Jan Blaauw and myself. The former had at one stage been part of the military establishment, but had subsequently started his own business as a wheeler-dealer and investigator. Both of the suspects' telephones were tapped and their contacts and activities monitored.

A Minister Accidentally Slides Out of the Gravy Train

General Jan Grobler, the then head of the Detective Branch of the South African Police, was in charge of the police investigation. Based on the information which they had gathered through the tapping of Brig. Blaauw's telephone, they were able to arrest a policeman in Krugersdorp. The latter was eventually charged with corruption and found guilty. They also discovered that the private secretary of Minister Fanie Botha, a man by the name of Frans Whelpton, had been working with Brig. Blaauw and that they had allegedly been blackmailing Minister Fanie Botha to give them certain diamond concessions on the West Coast. As a result of this, Minister Fanie Botha suddenly developed an ailment, resigned from the Cabinet and lived happily and healthily ever after on the public's pension payroll. Brig. Jan Blaauw and Mr Whelpton were eventually charged with extortion.

In retaliation, Brig. Blaauw laid charges of illegal tapping of his telephones against the South African Police and, in particular, against General Grobler. The notorious Captain Dirk Coetzee, who fled South Africa and joined the ANC after 'baring his soul' regarding the 'dirty tricks department' of the South African Police, had informed his friend Blaauw that the SAP were tapping his phones.

A Judge Does His Utmost

In my naiveté, I thought that a man of the stature of Judge Piet van der Walt, the Advocate-General at the time, would surely get to the bottom of the mismanagement of oil. After all, it was a clear-cut case! Whether one wishes to call it maladministration or corruption, $200,000,000 had been overpaid and could now be recouped from the two traders. Both traders were still transacting a high volume of deals with SFF/Sasol. As far as John Deuss was concerned, the disputed deals still fell within the prescription period in which SFF/Sasol could reclaim approximately $144,000,000 from him. All that SFF/Sasol had to do was to realise that it had been defrauded of $144,000,000 and that it could institute claims against Deuss in order to recoup this money on behalf of the South African motorist – as the Russians had done upon discovering that Deuss had stolen their oil.

At that stage Mr Pieter Swanepoel of the NIS was seconded to Judge Van der Walt's office to assist him with the investigation. Pieter Swanepoel knew me very well. He was also aware that I had been involved with the investigations into the Chiavelli matter.

He assured me that Prime Minister Botha had instructed that this mess be cleaned up. However, approximately two or three weeks into the investigation, I became aware that something was wrong. Judge Van der Walt was aware that I was sitting on very valuable information. Yet I was not approached by him to assist in his investigation or to give evidence. I decided to make an appointment to see him. On my arrival I was met by the Judge and his personal assistant and was asked what he could do for me. I told him that for the past three years I had been involved in an investigation in the oil industry and that I had very valuable information which could assist him in his investigation, upon which he informed me that he had finalised his investigation and that his secretary was busy typing his report.

The case being such a clear-cut one, he, as an eminent judge, had probably made a wise decision.

Chiavelli, the Dutiful Taxpayer

At approximately the same time, it came to my attention that Mr Marino Chiavelli had found a beautiful tax-free haven in sunny South Africa.

I looked into the matter and discovered that he had closed all his bank accounts in Italy and had notified the Italian Receiver of Revenue that he was a permanent resident in South Africa and that he was paying tax there. At the beginning of 1981, the Receiver of Revenue in London became aware of this extremely wealthy gentleman living on their doorstep (he had a house in London, too). They checked their records and discovered that he had not been paying all his taxes to them. They approached him, and he informed them that he was not resident in London, but that he was in fact resident in South Africa, where he was paying all his taxes. The Department of Revenue in England felt it their duty to inform the South African authorities accordingly. They asked the South African authorities to look into the matter and to notify them as to whether this was the case indeed.

The South African tax authorities checked their records and discovered that there was no such taxpayer registered in South Africa. They approached Mr Chiavelli, who apologised, saying that he would love to be a South African taxpayer and that he would henceforth declare his income and pay his dues. Finally, after two years of being granted permanent residence in South Africa, he registered as a taxpayer.

Subsequently, the Receiver of Revenue in Johannesburg received a letter with a cheque to the amount of R1,906 as his contribution for the previous two fiscal years during which he had been resident in South Africa. He declared his only income in South Africa to be interest earned on an investment in Nedbank, to the value of R190,000.

Digging deeper into the tax liabilities of Mr Chiavelli, I discovered that during 1979 he had tried to obtain tax-free citizenship in Ghana by bribing the contending political party in Ghana with $1,000,000. This party won the election, but was soon replaced by Sgt Rawlings in his second coup attempt. As a result, Mr Chiavelli lost that chance. Apart from suing the beneficiaries, in an effort to recoup the unproductive bribe, he then turned his eyes to South Africa. During April 1980 he successfully applied for permanent residence. One of the conditions was that, in keeping with South African exchange control regulations, he had to declare all his overseas assets. These he declared at $250,000,000 at the time; he also declared his annual income to be $250,000. He further undertook, in exchange for permanent residence in South Africa, to bring all his overseas income into the country. This income would obviously have to be used or invested. He would hence-forth have to pay taxes on any income derived from investments of this income. But Mr Chiavelli simply omitted to register as a taxpayer in South Africa.

During my investigation, I discovered that during 1981 Mr Chiavelli had been receiv-ing a monthly income of $7,500,000 from the oil deals with South Africa. None of this income was even declared or brought into South Africa, and in my opinion this must have been one of the biggest tax cons in South Africa, if not in the world. Mr Chiavelli had informed the Italians as well as the British that he was a permanent resident in South Africa and that he was paying tax here, and the South African taxman was quite happy that he was paying annual tax in the region of R1,000.

What followed sounds like a fairy tale. During 1983, I approached the Reserve Bank, where I personally spoke to the present governor, Dr Chris Stals. I provided him with my information regarding Mr Chiavelli's non-compliance with the exchange control regula-tions, his undertakings in exchange for his permanent residence in the country, as well as the fact that at that stage he must have been owing the South African Government millions of rands in taxes. I was assured that they would look into the matter.

However, in March 1984 I again checked and discovered that nothing had been done to ask Mr Chiavelli to pay his taxes. I then compiled a memorandum in which I pointed out that, based on the available evidence, Mr Chiavelli owed South Africa between R30,000,000 and R60,000,000 in taxes. To add insult to injury, these were profits which he had made on oil deals with SFF/Sasol, and for which SFF/Sasol had overpaid, once again at the expense of the South African motorist.

In order to ensure that this was brought to the attention of the South African Govern-ment, I addressed it to four separate ministers, namely Minister F.W. de Klerk, then Min-ister of Internal Affairs, who was dealing with the application of Mr Chiavelli's perma-nent residence; Minister Danie Steyn as the Minister of Mineral and Energy Affairs; Minister Piet du Plessis, as he had inside knowledge regarding Mr Chiavelli and was the former Minister of Mineral and Energy Affairs; and Deputy Minister Louis Nel, who also had personal knowledge of this matter. Each of the ministers personally acknowledged the receipt of the memorandum on 2 April 1984. I received information that Minister Steyn had passed his copy on to the Advocate-General.

Thus, during my visit to the Advocate-General, and after he had assured me that he had successfully completed his investigation, I asked him about the allegations contained in my report that Mr Chiavelli had not been paying his taxes. He explained that this was not part of his brief, which was limited to the allegation of overpayments on the oil contracts.

He commented that he was quite sure that the officials would, in the normal course of business, look into this matter and that he did not feel it his duty to bring it to the attention of the tax authorities.

South Africa, George Orwell's 1984

It was a great shock to me when the Advocate-General's report was rushed through Parliament and received the rubber stamp of approval. The report stated that there had been no overpayment on the oil contracts whatsoever and that it would appear that the allegations had been based on incorrect information and circulated with malicious intent.

Later, when I tried to reveal the fact that the Advocate-General had been given false information upon which he based his report, I was told by the NIS that, as far as they were concerned, the case was closed and that they no longer needed this information. I was told – off the record – that the Government could not afford such a scandal and that I should, for my own sake, let sleeping dogs lie; or, to put it differently, let lying dogs sleep.

This was in *1984* – Judge Van der Walt and the Nationalist Government very effectively fulfilled Orwell's prophesy in the Republic of South Africa. Orwell's vision was that of a country being ruled by a powerful bureaucracy which was able to construct the 'truth' of the past, the present, and therefore also the future. I, however, believe that no one, not even the South African Government, can alter a mathematical fact. I set out to prove that two plus two, even in 1984 is still four; in an 11-page analysis of the Advocate-General's report, I came to the conclusion that it was another one of those whitewash jobs by a 'commission of enquiry' to which the South African taxpayer had been subjected over the past decade or three.

In my analysis of the Advocate-General's report[2] I focussed on SFF/Sasol's contracts with Marc Rich and John Deuss. With detailed references to contract clauses I pointed out errors in the Advocate-General's conclusions. In the case of the Marc Rich contract, these errors were related to the 'old' and 'new' prices for shipments under the contract. In the case of the John Deuss contracts, the prices SFF/Sasol had to pay before and after these prices were renegotiated at the request of the Minister, were linked to the development of the 'marker price' and the open market prices of certain Middle East oils. With extensive references to the *Petroleum Economist* and other oil industry publications, I was able to show that the version of the 'marker' as purported by SFF/Sasol, which had been swallowed by the Advocate-General and which was consistently higher than the true OPEC marker during the period in question, had no basis in actual fact. I showed that as a consequence the Advocate-General had overlooked the fact that SFF/Sasol could have saved large amounts if it had paid the prices as assured to the Minister and the Advocate-General and had adhered to the price calculation as laid down in the contract. From the figures and arguments given in my analysis, it appeared as if the complaint lodged by the Progressive Federal Party (as set out in the Advocate-General's report), that SFF/Sasol paid in excess of the contract and/or without the permission of the Minister, was still valid, in spite of the findings of the Advocate-General.

On studying the report and comparing it with facts, it seemed obvious to me that the Advocate-General had either decided on his own, or had been influenced by someone else, or had been instructed by the Government to bring out such a report. According to my calculations, the South African motorist had overpaid approximately $200,000,000 on the two contracts. In the case of the John Deuss contract, the South African motorist had overpaid $480,000 *per day for a period of ten months*.

There, however, appears to have been some lone voices crying in the wilderness, even within the Establishment; people who tried to reveal the truth.

The General Should Mind His Own Business

After the Advocate-General presented his report, General Jan Grobler must have realised through listening to all the conversations which I had with friends, foes and business associates alike, that I was not such a bad boy after all.

I believe that the Minister of Police had instructed General Grobler to conduct a thorough investigation into the various oil deals, regardless of the Advocate-General's findings. The General approached me for certain information. Although the General did not divulge any details, it became quite clear to me during my liaison with him that he was making progress. He had gathered all the information regarding the offloading of the various shipments of oil at the various harbours and had checked this with Volkskas Bank, through which all the payments had been made. He had then come across certain discrepancies relating to overpayments on certain shipments. This information was also discovered by Mr Swanepoel during his investigation. What, however, intrigued the General was that certain monies had been paid to numbered Swiss accounts which had clearly not been made out to the oil trader in question. General Grobler therefore approached the Department of Mineral and Energy Affairs and SFF/Sasol to declare the various contracts and payments as well as the persons by whom and to whom these payments had been made.

I happened to be in his office on 9 September 1984 when he received a telephone call from a certain Mr Van der Berg from the Department of Mineral and Energy Affairs. I could obviously only hear one side of the conversation, but based on subsequent comments added to what I had heard, it seemed obvious to me that the Department had informed the General that they would not divulge any information to him, as they regarded their files as secret and that not even the Police would have access to it. General Grobler's comment was that he was acting on the instructions of his Minister and that, as far as he was concerned, it had been a Cabinet decision that he should investigate the matter. He further informed Mr Van der Berg that he would relay the message to his Minister with the request that it be sorted out at Cabinet level. The Minister in turn would have to inform the Minister of Mineral and Energy Affairs, Minister Steyn, to open their files for his investigation.

The General replaced the receiver and commented, 'You see, now they're all running for cover.' He then told me that he was going to approach his Minister for a clarification of the situation. Later he told me that the matter was being discussed at Cabinet level and that he was waiting for the green light to continue with his investigation. Needless to say, General Grobler went on pension without ever getting this 'green light'.

The 'Groot Krokodil' Does His Thing!

During 1986 I brought it to the attention of the National Intelligence Service that the government administration was not as clean as President P.W. Botha had assured the taxpayers. President Botha's nickname was *Die Groot Krokodil* (the Big Crocodile) because he was abrupt and used to snap at his underlings. The President was in charge of the NIS.

I therefore submitted all the relevant facts to Dr N. Barnard, the Director-General of the NIS, with the request that it be brought to the attention of the President that certain officials had provided the Advocate-General with false information. I pointed out that it was obvious that the Advocate-General had not verified the information, with the result that the sovereign Parliament of South Africa had put a stamp of approval on a fraudulent report. I begged the honourable doctor, in the interests of clean administration, to wash the dirty linen in the scullery. His reply was that according to him the file was closed, and that if I had any further complaints, I should address them to the South African Police. Strangely enough, the Police were anxiously awaiting a green light from the Cabinet – which of course never materialised.

The Advocate-General was subsequently promoted and is presently the ombudsman, to whom all South Africans are to address their suspicions concerning corruption among government officials as well as abuse of their positions and squandering of the taxpayer's money. Perhaps the prominent Judge Pieter van der Walt did bring out a report in the interests of the Government and its bureaucracies. Makes one think, does it not? The King is dead, long live the King.

Putting Money over Mouth, Profit over Principle
Arab and Iranian Oil Sales to South Africa, 1973–1993

TOM DE QUAASTENIET AND PAUL AARTS*

The oil embargo against South Africa has never been watertight. Year after year 15 million tons of crude 'disappeared' from the world market, and ended up in South African hands. The embargo policy of many oil-exporting countries in the Middle East was violated more often than it was observed.

From 1973 to 1979 the embargo was only a minor irritation to South Africa because the country could rely completely on its ally, Iran. After the fall of the Shah in 1979, the situation changed, and the oil trade with South Africa became one of the most closely guarded secrets of recent history.

In the words of Klinghoffer: 'Governments, oil companies, and shipping lines routinely [took] the moral high road in public, condemning apartheid and even endorsing the oil embargo and claiming adherence to its principles. Clandestinely, however, they [took] the low road of pecuniary interest.'[1]

Many states in the Middle East[2] decided to fill the gap and secretly accelerated their deliveries of oil to South Africa. They placed themselves in the unique situation of being able to condemn apartheid while, at the same time, lubricating its wheels. These states were not merely turning a blind eye when their oil was sold to South Africa; they were deeply and actively involved in the trade.

Since part of this trade took place during a period of high oil prices on the world market, economic necessity cannot be the sole argument for those states' failure to honour their declared policies. Other reasons were of importance as well.

This article gives an overview of Arab and Iranian oil deliveries to South Africa and tries to explore some of the motives behind the behaviour of the oil states.

A diplomatic deal

On 6 October 1973, Arab states entered into another war with Israel. This war was different from the previous ones for several reasons. Firstly, the war was not expected by the Israelis and therefore brought them close to defeat. Secondly, the tightening of the oil

* Tom de Quaasteniet is a political scientist, affiliated to the Amsterdam-based Middle East Research Associates (MERA). Paul Aarts is a lecturer at the Department of International Relations and Public International Law, University of Amsterdam, Netherlands, and a member of RECIPE (Research Center for International Political Economy and Foreign Policy Analysis), University of Amsterdam.

market made the oil weapon more potent than before. Once 'the United States hit 100 percent in terms of production rates, that old warrior, American production, could not rise up again to defend against the oil weapon.'[3]

But most important was the international dimension of this war. While Israel was supported by most of the Western states, the Arab states sought African backing against Israel. At the Council of Ministers' meeting of the Organization of African Unity (OAU), held at Addis Ababa from 19–22 November 1973, a trade-off emerged, linking African support for the Arab cause against Israel with the struggle against minority rule in southern Africa. OAU Secretary General Nzo Ekangaki pointed out that 90 per cent of South Africa's oil came from the Persian Gulf and that 'the time has come for our Arab brothers to use the oil embargo as a weapon against the white regimes' in southern Africa.[4]

The subsequent Algiers Arab Summit of 26–28 November followed the OAU's lead. A decision was made to break all political, consular, economic and cultural ties with South Africa, and an oil embargo was imposed on South Africa, Rhodesia and Portugal. In a separate resolution an embargo was imposed against states supporting Israel. Furthermore, 'the heads of state decided to convey greetings and appreciation to the fraternal African states for their decisions to break off relations with Israel.'[5]

This concerted attempt to impose a complete Arab oil embargo against South Africa seemed very effective in its early stages. However, the Arab-African diplomatic deal soon gave way to resentment. According to the Africans, the Arab states were overly preoccupied with the Arab-Israeli conflict. Furthermore, the African states criticised Arab unwillingness to support them economically.[6] It became apparent that Arab states were not inclined to offer oil at preferential prices or to provide the degree of financial assistance anticipated. Most African states were therefore seriously affected by the 1973 oil crisis.

The Arab embargo against Israel's allies ended in March 1974, but the embargo on South Africa was not terminated. It was in fact strengthened by the OAU, OAPEC (the Organization of Arab Petroleum Exporting Countries) and members of OPEC (the Organization of the Petroleum Exporting Countries).[7] The OAU stepped up the pressure by establishing a committee of seven to gain the cooperation of OPEC. In 1977 all OPEC members, except Iran, individually endorsed the embargo and solemnly declared to adhere to it. OAPEC strengthened the embargo in 1981 with a resolution calling for the blacklisting of tankers that had visited South African ports and the refusal of oil to companies involved in deliveries.[8] Finally, the United Nations installed an Intergovernmental Group to Monitor the Supply and Shipping of Oil and Petroleum Products to South Africa, in which Kuwait figured prominently.

The Iranian factor

The oil embargo of November 1973 caused concern in South Africa, but the country continued to receive adequate supplies of oil for two main reasons. Firstly, the international oil companies helped to ensure that regular supplies continued to be delivered, and secondly, Iran was willing to provide most of the country's oil requirements.

Prior to the embargo, Iran had already been an important supplier to South Africa (see Table 1). South Africa now became extremely dependent on Iranian oil deliveries: Iran supplied around 90 per cent of South Africa's crude oil during the period 1973–78. The

Table 1 Major sources of South Africa's crude oil imports

	1972 quantity (b/d)	%	1974 quantity (b/d)	%	1977 quantity (b/d)	%
Iran	138,000	54	254,000	90	230,000	91
Iraq	50,000	19	15,000	5		
Saudi Arabia	41,000	16				
Qatar	28,000	11	13,000	5		
Kuwait	1,000					
Various countries					23,000	9
Total	**257,000**	**100**	**283,000**	**100**	**253,000**	**100**

Sources: OPEC, *Annual Statistics Bulletin 1976*, Vienna 1977; UN Department of Economic and Social Affairs, *World Energy Supplies 1971–1975*, New York 1977; M. Bailey and B. Rivers, *Oil Sanctions against South Africa*, 1978/1985, 23-24.

Iranian government did not accept the decision of the Arab countries to impose oil sanctions against South Africa. In 1977, in the United Nations General Assembly, an Iranian representative tried to explain his government's position by stating that Iran 'always considered oil as a commodity and not a political weapon'.[9]

The Iranian attitude can be largely explained by the special relationship the country had with South Africa. Shah Mohammed Reza Pahlevi's father, Reza Shah, sought refuge in South Africa after his abdication in 1941 and was buried in Johannesburg following his death in 1944. Iranians were granted the status of 'honorary whites' according to South Africa's racial categories.[10] Under a 1975 agreement Iran invested in South African uranium enrichment in return for supplies of uranium; the deal was seen as partly an effort on the part of South Africa to ensure friendly relations with a prominent oil supplier.[11]

In the oil sector, an important factor was the relationship between the National Iranian Oil Company (NIOC) and the refinery at Sasolburg near Johannesburg owned by National Petroleum Refineries of South Africa (Natref). Four hundred 'honorary white' skilled workers were brought in to construct this refinery, which was conditioned to process light crude imported from Iran. NIOC owned 17.5 per cent of the Natref refinery and had a contract to supply it for a 20-year period, from the start of operations in 1971. By the time of the Arab embargo, Iran was already providing almost 60 per cent of the oil processed by the Natref refinery.[12]

Iran clearly had no interest in curtailing deliveries to South Africa. It indicated that it would participate in an embargo only if all other countries did likewise and the Security Council mandated sanctions. The Shah's regime distrusted the sanctions behaviour of the Arab oil-producing countries. During the 1951–53 nationalisation dispute with the British, Arab states had moved into its markets while its oil was being embargoed.[13]

When South Africa was blacklisted, Iran's Minister of Finance, Jamshid Amouzegar, travelled to South Africa and assured the country that Iran saw no reason to halt or reduce supplies. Tehran more than fulfilled this commitment. By the end of 1978, South Africa's crude imports from Iran had risen to 96 per cent.[14]

Most of this oil was supplied by companies belonging to the Iranian Consortium, a group of foreign companies selling Iranian oil, rather than by the National Iranian Oil Company directly. Iran claimed that it had no control on the final destination of its oil exports, an argument also used by other countries which provided the rest of South Africa's oil.

In the early 1970s power had not yet shifted from the international oil companies to the oil-exporting countries. The international oil companies which operated in South Africa could therefore easily ensure that oil continued to flow. Sir Eric Drake, chairman of British Petroleum, openly said that the oil companies had intentionally set out to thwart Arab attempts at enforcing oil embargoes on countries like South Africa.[15] The South African *Financial Mail* commented that 'there can be no greater blessing for South Africa – apart from the fact that Iran is well-disposed – than that the oil business is still largely in the hands of international companies with no discernable leanings of excessive patriotism.'[16]

Table 1 shows that during the 1970s a small part of South Africa's crude oil imports originated from countries supporting the embargo. The oil majors, who bought the oil from these countries, most likely resold it to South Africa without the knowledge of the governments concerned.

Strikingly, the shifting of power from the oil companies to the producing countries had no immediate effect on the flow of oil to South Africa. It was the political events in Iran, at the end of the 1970s, which served to highlight South Africa's vulnerability and brought the country to the brink of despair.

Iran after 1978: A new era?

The Iranian Revolution gave rise to expectations that a dramatic change was to take place in the relationship between Iran and South Africa. The newly established Islamic regime vowed to boycott South Africa, and on 4 March 1979, Iran officially broke all relations with South Africa. The South African oil situation changed drastically.

Some South Africans had previously expressed their concerns about the dependence on Iranian oil,[17] but hardly any action was taken. The Iranian Revolution caught the South African government by surprise. It was only by turning to the spot market, where it had to pay exorbitant prices, and by offering lucrative premiums for cargoes of crude oil, that South Africa was able to survive the crisis.

However, the dramatic rise in oil import costs was largely offset by the jump in the price of gold. The booming prices of gold, platinum and diamond exports helped South Africa to pay the bill. In early 1979 there were reports that South African gold was actually bartered for oil from various sources, in order to fulfil Pretoria's oil needs.[18] Nevertheless, Pretoria's oil procurement had to be cast in a different mould as a result of the upheaval in Iran.

Despite public denial, some diplomatic and economic links continued to exist between Iran and South Africa. A South African consulate started to operate unofficially in Tehran in order to smooth trade relations. Trade was therefore not totally halted. South African steel, timber and maize were among the products shipped to Iran, as were industrial plastics, falsely listed as originating from Swaziland or Mozambique.[19] Furthermore, Tehran was stuck with its 17.5 per cent share in the Natref refinery and its contractual obligation to supply it with oil.

According to the Iranians the ownership of Natref was a legal nuisance. The Iranian regime said it had prohibited Iranian employees from attending the Natref board meetings and that it had tried to sell its shares in the refinery.[20] These attempts were blocked since it was in the interest of the apartheid regime that Iran kept its shares and its commitment to deliver oil. If Iran wanted to give up its multimillion dollar stake in Natref it would have to accept a considerable financial loss, which was unacceptable to the Iranian government. This situation lasted until 1989 when Iran suddenly declared that 'After certain legal maneuvers, the Islamic Republic of Iran was finally able to dissolve all these assets and thus put an end to the un-holy heritage of the previous regime.'[21]

It soon became clear that even under the new government, oil continued to flow to South Africa. This was largely based on self-interest. In 1980 Iran and Iraq entered into a vicious and bloody war. Iraq was supplied with sophisticated weaponry by its Western allies such as the United States, West Germany, France and the United Kingdom.[22] Iran, on the other hand, was pictured in the West as a pariah and an aggressor, and the country could therefore neither count on Western deliveries of weapons nor on spare parts. South Africa, which was not only plagued by an oil embargo but also by a ban on armaments, had developed the state-owned Armaments Corporation of South Africa (Armscor), which produced high-quality weaponry. Armscor produced heavy-calibre howitzers, ground-to-air and air-to-air missiles, artillery systems, the G-5 superguns and a wide range of ammunition. Iran desperately needed this weaponry after the losses in the first years of the war, and this resulted in a trade-off.

In one of the deals made, the government of Iran agreed in 1985 to purchase $750 million worth of South African weapons. In return, South Africa purchased Iranian crude oil of the same value. Although Iran repeatedly denied making barter deals with South Africa, various deals were exposed. In some cases weapons were directly shipped, in other cases deliveries were made via the Comoro Islands. Reportedly, the most ingenious case was through the Greek arms manufacturer, Hellenic Explosives and Ammunitions Industry (Elviemek); in 1985, South African businessman Taki Xenopoulos took over Elviemek and started to use the company as a front for the arms-for-oil barter deals with Tehran.[23]

Iran was not the only country in the Middle East to engage in barter deals with the apartheid regime. The government of Iraq signed an oil-for-arms deal with South Africa with a reported value of $1 billion in 1985.[24] Later deals with Iraq had a clause which forbade Armscor to sell weapons to Iran. Iraq was prepared to buy all unsold weaponry if Armscor accepted the clause.[25] After Iraq's occupation of Kuwait in 1990, South African president De Klerk, while visiting the United States, publicly admitted that South African arms had been sold to Iraq.[26]

Secret oil deliveries

Barter trade as described above was not the main source of oil for South Africa. From 1979 onwards, Pretoria developed a number of measures to persuade countries to sell oil

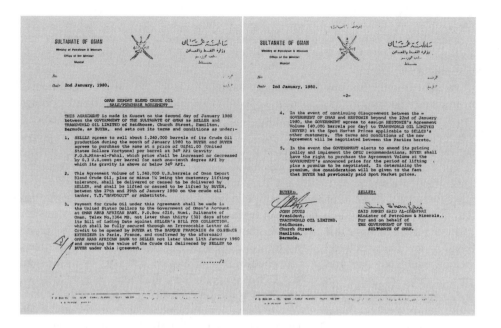

to South Africa, among them, secrecy legislation protecting the sources of imported oil from being exposed and the payment of large premiums to middlemen who were able to ensure access to oil.

In the 1980s and early 1990s, shipments of oil from the Middle East to South Africa formed a steady flow. Over 670 of the 865 tankers listed by the SRB in this book sailed to South Africa from the Middle East.[27] The cargo capacity of these tankers was about 150 million tons, or 85 per cent of the total volume identified. The research findings show that the United Arab Emirates, Saudi Arabia, Iran and Oman were the main violators of the Arab oil embargo against South Africa.[28]

During the embargo, the suppliers of South Africa's oil and the middlemen involved tried to cover their tracks, albeit with partial success. The role of John Deuss of the Transworld Oil company (TWO) in laying the groundwork for the extensive trade became internationally known during the 1980s as a result of the work of the Shipping Research Bureau and others. The publicity surrounding a number of court cases in South Africa and the leaking of Advocate-General Van der Walt's report in 1984 helped to unveil some details relating to contracts between South Africa and Oman, and South Africa and Saudi Arabia.[29]

The 1984 report of the South African Advocate-General failed to include information with regard to a deal concluded in June 1979 involving the purchase of 44 million barrels of crude from *Oman*. From January 1980 onwards, John Deuss acted as intermediary. The key Omani contact in this deal, Dr Omar Zawawi, a close advisor of Sultan Qaboos bin Said, has been considered by some to be the brains, if not the real power, behind the throne.[30] The contract included a surcharge of $4.50 a barrel, which Oman received in addition to the original price of the oil.

Much more could be found, despite the censor's efforts, in the Advocate-General's report on contacts between South Africa and *Saudi Arabia*.[31] The role played by Marino

Chiavelli in forging these contacts – a role which according to many was rather significant – was played down in the report. What the report made abundantly clear, however, was that the Saudi Arabian traders who dealt with John Deuss were fully aware that their oil was to be resold to South Africa. Deuss was not tricking them into trading with a pariah state, boycotted by their own government. Moreover, it was the Saudis who demanded that the deals be kept absolutely secret. They were eager to pocket as much as possible from the deals, both in the selling price of the oil and in their share of the premiums South Africa paid to Deuss.

In December 1980, the Saudis even tried to increase their gains from a contract which had been entered into four months earlier. They proposed to deliver an additional two million tons of oil over and above the original four million tons per year and wanted an extra premium of $5.50 per barrel (in the August 1980 contract the premium, shared between Deuss and the Saudis, was between $2 and 4.50 a barrel, depending on market fluctuations). This would have given the Saudi traders a premium of one million dollars per day. Pretoria accepted the offer for extra oil, but reacted strongly against a higher commission. After tough bargaining, South Africa succeeded in maintaining the old premium by threatening to look for 'a more "reliable" source'.[32]

Officially, the Saudi government claimed to adhere to the embargo, and repeatedly said it would punish violators. However, it also admitted that 'the government of the Kingdom of Saudi Arabia does not maintain a list of oil companies or tanker companies that have violated the contracts of sale or shipping by supplying or shipping oil and petroleum products to South Africa'.[33] The absence of a black list of offending companies made it easier for Saudi Arabia to turn a blind eye while its crude was being shipped to South Africa.

Another reason for Riyadh's attitude was the identity of the Saudi Arabian traders. Deuss had many acquaintances in the Saudi royal family and maintained a business partnership with Prince Muhammed bin Fahd, second eldest son of the King of Saudi Arabia and an important supplier of oil to South Africa. It is believed that he and John Deuss jointly chartered tankers owned by his elder brother, Prince Faisal bin Fahd. Prince Muhammed bin Abdul Aziz was another member of the Saudi royal family who sold oil to whomever he pleased. It has been argued that since the high-spirited Prince Muhammed was passed over for the throne in 1975, he was allocated a share of Petromin[34] oil which his younger brothers allowed him to sell at his own discretion and in a manner he saw fit.[35]

The names on the 'princely-oil' list are numerous.[36] Besides high-ranking Omani and Saudi officials, Deuss also had important contacts in other major oil-producing countries, including the United Arab Emirates. Its Minister of Petroleum, Mana bin Said al-Oteiba, has long been considered one of Deuss's closest associates.[37]

An interesting angle to Saudi-South African oil ties was provided by the Congressional hearings on the so-called Irangate scandal. Jerusalem-born US businessman Sam Bamieh testified that the Saudi Prince Bandar bin Sultan had approached him to participate in an arrangement whereby an offshore company would buy oil from Saudi Arabia, resell it to South Africa at a one-dollar profit a barrel and then direct the proceeds to Angola. South Africa could thus evade the oil embargo and covertly finance its intervention in Angola. Fearing he would be drawn into illegal activities, Bamieh refused to participate, but he believed that others stepped into the deal, furnishing South Africa with oil until February 1986.[38]

All in all, it does not come as a surprise that Saudi Arabia was South Africa's biggest supplier in the period from 1979 to mid-1985, probably providing at least thirty per cent of South Africa's oil imports. Saudi-South African oil relations were so cordial that Pretoria's Minister of Justice, Jimmy Kruger, became a broker of Saudi oil in the United States after he left office in 1982.[39]

Differences on the Peninsula

The predominant position of *Saudi Arabia* with regard to sanctions busting in the early 1980s can be partly explained by a combination of economic factors relating to domestic politics. At the time, Saudi Arabia sold its oil well below OPEC's official price. The Saudis, strongly supported by the US government, maintained that high oil prices might permanently damage the world economy and cause an undesirably large drop in the demand for OPEC crude.[40] From 1979 until the end of 1981, Saudi Arabia's oil price was fixed at between two and eight US dollars a barrel below the prices charged by other oil-producing countries. As a result, the demand for Saudi oil rose to unprecedented levels. Paying commissions for Saudi oil therefore became inevitable for all consumers (this did not only apply to South Africa).

Paying commissions for major economic transactions in Saudi Arabia is a time-honoured practice. It is part of the Arab tradition of giving and receiving among friends. Besides cultural-historical reasons, there was clearly a political motive involved. Ever since the Kingdom was unified in the 1920s by King Abdul Aziz, the royal family used money as a means of maintaining loyalty among its princes and among potential rival tribes.[41]

The Saud family has to take tribalism, sectarianism and regionalism into consideration as the three main destabilising forces.[42] The legitimacy of the regime is maintained with the help of threats, coercion, promises and rewards. In this stick-and-carrot policy all

---

> Mnr Hennie Bekker, LPR vir Jeppe, het bevestig dat hy 'n samespreking volgende week gereël het tussen Prins Fahed van Saoedi Arabië en ondergetekende in Malaga, Spanje. Die Saoedis is glo begerig om Arab Light 1,5 miljoen vate per maand aan ons te verkoop. Hoewel ek skepties is oor die realisering van so 'n samekoms, moet ek op sterkte van sy bevestiging dit opvolg. Tydens die gesprek, indien dit realiseer, sal ek poog om groter duidelikheid in verband met Deuss se posisie te verkry.

From letter of D.F. Mostert, Director of the SFF Association, to the Director General of Mineral and Energy Affairs, 13 April 1982 (headed 'GEHEIM', Secret). *Translation*: Mr Hennie Bekker, Provincial Councillor for Jeppe, confirmed that he has arranged an meeting between Prince Fahd of Saudi Arabia and the undersigned in Malaga, Spain, next week. The Saudis are keen to sell us 1.5 million barrels of Arabian Light per month. Although I am sceptical whether the meeting will take place, I have to follow this up on the basis of his confirmation. If the meeting takes place, I shall try to get a clearer picture of Deuss' position.

kinds of handouts are used. The huge oil income has enabled the government to refrain from installing a taxation system and to introduce a welfare system 'from the cradle to the grave'. Consequently, starting from the historical truism that there is 'no taxation without representation', the regime's reasoning is that the reverse holds true in the Kingdom, i.e. 'no representation without taxation'.

Politics in Saudi Arabia is thus incontestably controlled by the Saud family. The Kingdom is glued together by a royal family of over 4,000 princes. It has strong alliances with the major Western powers, strong modern means of repression, a firm grip on the armed forces, and a state-owned controlled press which ensures that the only Saudi news is good news. The elements of 'civil society' are almost non-existent: Saudi citizens are severely curtailed in their freedom to set up social, political, cultural or economic organisations.

The differences between Saudi Arabia and neighbouring *Kuwait* are striking and might provide a clue to their differences with regard to the oil embargo against South Africa. Kuwait has perhaps the most outspoken and independent press in the Arab world. Generally speaking, Kuwaiti civil society has a most lively character, unrivalled by any of the other Gulf states. The opulent Emirate has a parliamentary tradition, the foundation of which was laid two centuries ago. A crucial factor in this process was the alliance between the merchants in command of the financial resources and the sheikhs who controlled political and military matters.[43] Two years after independence (1961), elections were held for the National Assembly. Compared to Western standards, Kuwaiti 'democracy' is very immature, but its significance should not be underestimated. Even during non-parliamentary periods Kuwait has not been free of political turmoil. In particular, since the mid-1980s, the pro-democracy movement has gradually come into prominence, leading to its overwhelming victory during the October 1992 elections.[44]

Therefore, it is not surprising that hardly any Kuwaiti oil reached South Africa in the 1980s. The limited number of shipments that (partly) originated in Kuwait – the Shipping Research Bureau identified only six during the period 1979–93, including the notorious *Salem* shipment – must, by all accounts, have taken place unknown to the responsible authorities. Kuwait's prominent position in the United Nations Intergovernmental Group to Monitor the Supply and Shipping of Oil and Petroleum Products to South Africa – personified by Ms Nabeela al-Mulla from the Mission of Kuwait to the UN – underscores the country's tenacity in this matter.

In contrast, the political structure of Saudi Arabia made it almost inevitable that oil from that country would be delivered to South Africa. There was no controlling political body, and the people were left ignorant by a censored press. Furthermore, the allocation of Petromin oil to princes who in turn could sell it as they saw fit was part of a policy to guarantee political stability in the Kingdom. As for the other sanctions busters in the Persian Gulf region, they – with the exception of Iran – share the socio-political make-up of Saudi Arabia.

No longer taboo

In the 1980s the oil market gradually changed from a sellers' into a buyers' market. Conservation measures in Western countries, the relentless buildup of non-OPEC oil supply and the 'Great Inventory Dump' resulted in overcapacity, overproduction and low prices on the world market.[45]

The oil glut forced the oil-producing countries into a fierce competition. In order to ensure that they could keep their market share, they became less selective in the choice of their customers. They were happy as long as they could sell as much oil as possible.

As a result, it became easier for South Africa to find even less roundabout and less expensive ways in which to acquire oil. If one country refused to deliver, another would happily fill the gap. According to several sources, South Africa regularly turned to the spot market to buy surpluses of oil. In January 1987, Pretoria bought large stocks of oil from Dubai and Oman, and in July 1988 it bought 3.6 million barrels of oil from Dubai when Japanese refiners suddenly terminated their contract.[46] From 1986 onwards, the United Arab Emirates became South Africa's largest oil supplier.

The secret oil deliveries from Arab countries to South Africa were a thorny issue for the South African Muslim organisation 'The Call of Islam'. It regularly contacted its brethren in the Arab world in an attempt to convince them to stop the shipments. According to its former leader, Farid Esack, only the Palestinian Liberation Organization (PLO) was pre-pared to listen, but they finally decided not to interfere. 'There were two main reasons for this decision. Firstly, apartheid in South Africa already had more media coverage than the Palestinian issue. Secondly, it would have brought unnecessary friction between the PLO and its funding partners.'[47]

As the official dismantling of apartheid got underway in 1990, the Arab states started to openly develop political and economic ties with the South African regime.

The South African government stimulated these developments and prepared for an export offensive. The countries targeted in the first instance were the United Arab Emir-ates, Egypt, Turkey and Morocco. Their markets were flooded with South African prod-ucts. The UAE proved very eager to buy sophisticated South African weaponry.[48]

Pretoria was especially eyeing Cairo, because Egypt is a key member of the OAU and the Arab League and was therefore a possible advocate for the lifting of the remaining sanctions. Nevertheless, it came as a surprise when the state-owned Egyptian General Petroleum Corporation's oil allocations for 1993 appeared in print in an oil journal and were shown to include South Africa, which was allowed to import between 500,000 tons and 2 million tons of Egyptian oil. This was about a year before the official embargo was eventually lifted.[49]

South Africa's attempts to become a respectable partner during the final years of the embargo were very successful. Delivering oil to South Africa was clearly no longer taboo for most Arab countries.

As a result of the political events in South Africa, Kuwait officially decided to lift its economic boycott on 21 November 1993. Kuwait's Oil Minister, Ali Ahmed al-Baghli, stated that although there had been no oil or other trade between the two countries during the past 30 years, time had come for a change. Early December 1993, the first shipment of oil from Kuwait arrived in South Africa, accompanied by a Kuwaiti offer for the delivery of one million tons of crude in 1994.[50]

Conclusion

The key word describing Arab and Iranian behaviour regarding the oil embargo against South Africa is without any doubt 'self-interest'. The imposition of the embargo in 1973 was directly linked to the Arab-Israeli conflict.

The Iranian deliveries from 1973 to 1978 were a result of the special relationship between the Shah and Pretoria. Nevertheless, after the fall of the Shah, Iranian oil deliveries continued out of military self-interest. Iran desperately needed (South African) weapons in its war with Iraq. Furthermore, the Natref shares could only have been disposed of with an unacceptable loss.

The violation of the embargo after 1979 can be primarily explained by economic self-interest. South Africa paid premiums to greedy middlemen (like Deuss) and to the traders in the oil-producing countries (like the 'Z people' mentioned in the Advocate-General's 1984 report) in order to get its oil needs fulfilled. The governments of the oil-producing countries showed a clear lack of interest in the implementation of the embargo as long as the cash-flow continued. Administrative control was considered to be a nuisance. The idea of getting high prices for oil and of concluding profitable barter deals – oil for gold or weapons – proved to be irresistible.

The economic motive got a new ring in the period of the oil glut: 'If I don't sell oil to South Africa, my neighbour probably will.' This argument served to justify the role played by many oil-producing countries. During the last few years of the oil embargo, South Africa took advantage of the changing attitude by beginning a credibility offensive, whereby it offered trade and investment incentives.

In retrospect, it is our view that even a mandatory oil embargo would not have been able to prevent South Africa from securing an oil lifeline from the Middle East. The temptations were simply too strong.

A Defeat for the Shipping Lobby?

The Norwegian Experience

ØYSTEIN GUDIM[*]

Between 1980 and 1987 the question of oil sanctions against South Africa was a hot political issue in Norway. The Shipping Research Bureau, the anti-apartheid forces and the media revealed that the Norwegian shipping industry was heavily involved in secret crude oil deliveries to South Africa. Behind Norway's public anti-apartheid policies, the shipping interests were allowed to reap profits from the continued fuelling of the apartheid state. Successive governments, the Norwegian Shipowners' Association (NSA) and the Norwegian anti-apartheid umbrella organisation, the Norwegian Council for Southern Africa (NOCOSA), were the main actors on the political scene. NOCOSA provided information to the Shipping Research Bureau, while at the same time depending heavily on the research of the Bureau for its political campaign work.

Norway is a very small nation in international politics, but the country has some of the world's largest shipping companies and tanker fleets. The network spreads across the globe and includes shady companies in countries with 'flags of convenience'. After a long political battle Norway was the only major shipping nation to impose a legal ban on crude oil transports to South Africa, following the example set by Denmark. Clearly, this was a political defeat for one of Norway's strongest business lobbies. On the other hand, the remaining shipping links with South Africa were not affected. This could be seen as the outcome of a tacit agreement between the Shipowners' Association and the then Labour government.

How could the anti-apartheid forces of Norway, with limited resources, fight such an influential business group, which had enormous resources at its disposal? While doing research for this chapter, several classified documents and confidential memoranda became available, showing the shipping lobby's efforts behind the scenes to ward off a complete defeat.

An accidental start

On 10 October 1979, a Norwegian left wing weekly, *Ny Tid*, carried a story about two Norwegian oil tankers from the Bergesen Group which had delivered crude oil to South

---

[*] The author of this chapter has since 1975 held various positions in the Norwegian Council for Southern Africa (Fellesrådet for det sørlige Afrika), and he has in particular worked on the oil sanctions issue. In 1994 he was appointed programme coordinator for South Africa in Norwegian People's Aid, a humanitarian organisation linked to the labour and trade union movement in Norway.

Africa in June and July of that year. These calls had been briefly mentioned in a report from the Norwegian Consulate General in Cape Town to the Ministry of Foreign Affairs in Oslo. By accident, the document was seen by a researcher and anti-apartheid activist, who noted the details and gave the story to *Ny Tid*.

Other newspapers paid little attention to the story. As a NOCOSA activist I found the article interesting. Until then, the sanctions debate in Norway had mainly focussed on fruit and mineral imports from South Africa. Shipping services were never reflected in the Norwegian statistics on trade with South Africa. Shortly after the *Ny Tid* story, I attended the UN-sponsored International Seminar on the Role of Transnational Corporations in South Africa, held in London from 2–4 November 1979, and quoted the article on the two Bergesen vessels. I was contacted by Dr Martin Bailey, who had just published his book on Rhodesian oil sanctions busting. Some of the first informal contacts on the oil sanctions issue were made during the course of this meeting.

Alliance with the press

The real breakthrough came with a large front page article in the liberal newspaper, *Dagbladet*, on 12 April 1980. The tanker *Havdrott* had apparently run a shuttle service between the Persian Gulf and South Africa. This was to become the first of several press reports on the issue. While NOCOSA had no role in initiating the first articles, journalists and anti-apartheid activists subsequently developed a mutual cooperation.

Newspapers were eagerly competing with each other to publish more stories. On some occasions seamen told journalists that they had been involved in secret calls to South Africa. However, generally speaking, Norwegian seamen and their unions were seldom sources for the press. Some sailors revealed their trips to South Africa unintentionally, by signing the guest book of the Seamen's Mission in Durban, by participating in listeners' request programmes on Radio Norway International, or by mentioning calls in a trade union magazine. Most sailors, however, remained silent – partly out of loyalty to their employers and partly because they feared for their jobs.

One of the stories which appeared in the conservative tabloid, *Verdens Gang*, on 29 May 1980, was of particular interest. The ship, *Norse King*, had called at Cape Town under a false identity. The charterer had demanded that the ship's name and the company markings on the funnel be covered. The crew carried out the order by painting over the name and identification marks the day before the ship arrived in Cape Town. Subsequent stories on other tankers told about crew members ordered to cover the names with grey tarpaulins and lower the Norwegian flag when calling at South African ports.

Even though several shipowners vehemently denied such stories, public interest was aroused. Politicians of different persuasions and a number of newspapers began to comment that some people obviously had something to hide. The shipping industry was accused of oiling the apartheid war machine. The shipowners defended themselves by saying that their trade was not illegal but were asked by the Labour Foreign Minister, Knut Frydenlund, to stop oil shipments to South Africa voluntarily.

The shipowners became much more conscious about the need for secrecy with regard to their transports to South Africa. They began to censor the information they provided to the business newspaper *Norges Handels- og Sjøfartstidende*. In its weekly 'Shipping List' the paper, which traditionally had the best coverage of Norwegian shipping, published details of departures and planned calls of Norwegian ships as an information service to the business community and seamen's relatives. While it had previously been common practice to mention Cape Town or Durban as destinations for tankers, the information now became more sketchy. A tanker would be reported to have left a port in the Persian Gulf 'for orders' or 'for Europe', only to return soon thereafter in order to collect a new cargo. These 'gaps' in the list raised our suspicions, and in the end did not help much to camouflage secret trips to South Africa. Although the newspaper in question was one of the papers which were very strongly against shipping sanctions, it inadvertently helped our research and campaign work.

Soon after the establishment of the Shipping Research Bureau in 1980, we made contact and went on to enjoy a fruitful cooperation. My own recording of suspicious tankers was a part-time hobby, while the Bureau in Amsterdam was better equipped to do thorough investigations; soon the Bureau was also able to decipher the Norwegian 'Shipping List'.

We developed a 'division of labour', whereby NOCOSA would accuse shipowners of transporting oil to South Africa – often based on suspicion and without hard evidence. In some cases the shipowners were able to prove that their ships had not been to South Africa; some would refuse to comment; other companies would admit to their transports, saying that they were doing legal business. Others would simply lie.

The Shipping Research Bureau on the other hand had a more careful and scientific approach. The press coverage of the publication of each of its reports was very good, and joint NOCOSA/SRB press conferences in Norway were well attended. On at least two occasions, the press was so eager to cover the reports that they flouted the international press embargo in order to publish a scoop. After some time we often saw the Bureau described in the Norwegian press as a 'well-respected research institute'. Its thorough work really impressed many journalists. In the shipping industry it was widely believed that the Bureau had an advanced computer system keeping track of the movements of all tankers. We did nothing to dispel this belief.

The relations with the press were crucial for our campaign. In a small country such as Norway, there is always a good chance that a former fellow student is a journalist, and a number of former NOCOSA activists had also become journalists over the years. The close cooperation we managed to develop with the media probably surprised the shipowners. Even though the latter had influential contacts in the public TV news and in conservative and business-oriented newspapers, others set the agenda for the debate.

A moral issue

The Norwegian oil transports to South Africa became an important political and moral issue. This kind of political debate was not the home ground of the shipowners, who preferred legal and economic arguments. However, a distinct moralistic element prevails in Norwegian politics. A critique of apartheid as a moral and political issue formed the basis for the emergence of a broad alliance of anti-apartheid forces in the 1980s.

The Church of Norway, a Lutheran church representing more than 90 per cent of the population, together with some smaller churches, many trade unions and solidarity organisations, shared a common goal, namely to stop Norwegian oil transports to South Africa. Each of these groups had its own modus operandi.

Some people found it easier to engage themselves in the struggle for freedom in South Africa when there was a target within Norway to protest against. The shipowners transporting oil to South Africa became an ideal target for anti-apartheid activists from diverging backgrounds. NOCOSA's membership grew thanks to Bergesen, Mosvold and other shipowners. 'The enemy' was no longer only a white regime far away but its friends in Norway.

However, the whole process did not take place in isolation. It was part of the international build-up of pressure against apartheid in South Africa. The internal and the external struggle were two sides of the same coin. The increased oppression and aggression of the South African regime did much to mobilise people. From 1984 onwards, the political mood in Norway became increasingly in favour of sanctions.

From 22–24 March 1984 NOCOSA organised an international hearing in Oslo on South Africa and its aggression against neighbouring states. A key speaker was Bishop Desmond Tutu, who returned to Oslo later that year, when he was awarded the Nobel Peace Prize. While the hearing took place, the Shipping Research Bureau revealed that not only had Norwegian shipowners transported other countries' oil to South Africa, but there were examples of Norwegian oil from the North Sea being sold to South Africa. Even though the quantities had been small, we were given maximum press coverage, and the government was forced to act.

The Ministry of Oil and Energy had earlier notified national and foreign companies operating in the North Sea oil fields that it disapproved of the sale of Norwegian crude oil and oil products to South Africa. This was in effect only a weak gentlemen's agreement, and after years of intense pressure by representatives of six political parties, 11 trade unions and all the bishops of the Church of Norway, the Norwegian Parliament finally banned the sale of Norwegian crude oil and gas in a law which became effective on 20 June 1986. The ban was extended to include refined oil products on 15 July 1986. (This law was to remain in effect longer than any other piece of Norwegian boycott legislation, except for the arms embargo. When in December 1993 the South African Transitional Executive Council was installed – the condition set by the United Nations for the lifting of the oil embargo – the Norwegian government lost no time in announcing the scrapping of the oil export ban. By a remarkable coincidence, the cabinet meeting in question was held just hours before Nelson Mandela and Frederik de Klerk were to receive the Nobel Peace Prize in Oslo. The law was abolished on 1 February 1994.)

'Aristocrats'

The public debate was not confined to the sale of Norwegian oil to South Africa, but it also focussed on the role of Norwegian shipowners. Questions were being raised in Parliament. Yet, the government remained reluctant to impose a ban on the shipping industry.

Unlike many other European countries, Norway has never had a significant aristocracy. The closest one could get to 'aristocrats' were the shipowners. Before Norway became an oil nation, shipping was a major source of foreign exchange. To this day, it has

Sig Bergesen SA protest

ABOUT 100 people were arrested in Oslo after they tried to brick up the front door of a tanker owner involved in supplying oil to South Africa, police said yesterday.

The anti-apartheid demonstrators had filled in about half the doorway of Sig Bergesen's offices in Drammensveien

Sig Bergesen has been identified in a recent study as one of the two Norwegian tanker owners most heavily involved in shipping crude to South Africa. The republic has to import about 15 million tonnes a year. Norwegian ships are reckoned to carry as much as 35% of the total.

Lloyd's List, 30 August 1985, front page

remained an important industry. In some towns shipowners were far more powerful than politicians. Some of them owned local newspapers and sponsored cultural activities and municipal projects. To pick on them would often elicit a hostile response from the public.

A few journalists had gradually started to go behind the façade. They revealed stories of tax frauds and the secret foreign fortunes of some shipowners, a few of whom were brought to court. In the middle of the 1980s, shipowners were no longer protected by the glamorous picture they had created of themselves. A few emigrated to avoid Norwegian taxes and government interference.

The shipowners realised that they had to counter the public criticism of their role, but they were embroiled in a political debate that was difficult for them to handle. One of the key shipowners once tried to participate in a public meeting on sanctions. Petter C.G. Sundt, part-owner and managing director of Bergesen, Norway's largest shipping group and a leading company in oil transports to South Africa, defended his position. Mr Sundt, one of the toughest leaders of a very competitive business, saw the meeting turn out to be a disaster for him. He was known to be sympathetic towards a Norwegian right-wing party, ironically named the Progressive Party, which from its fledgling days maintained cordial relations with the apartheid government.[1] In the debate Mr Sundt was exposed as a defender of the apartheid regime. Mr Sundt was probably 'saved' by a low press turn-out at the meeting.

Politics

Ms Gro Harlem Brundtland of the Labour Party resigned as Prime Minister after she lost the general election in September 1981. She was succeeded by Kåre Willoch of the Conservative Party. He first led a minority government headed by his own party and from June 1983 to May 1986, a coalition with the Centre Party, which represents farmers' and other rural interests, and the Christian People's Party.

The Norwegian Shipowners' Association seldom participated in public meetings and preferred the traditional method of quiet lobbying of civil servants and politicians. They had easy access to the top levels. After Willoch became Prime Minister, it was revealed that while being a Member of Parliament, he had received an extra salary from the business lobby – including the NSA. Except for a break in the payments while he was Minister of Commerce and Shipping in a previous government, he had always been on their payroll until he became Prime Minister.

Most of the Conservative Party MPs were generally not in favour of sanctions, and the Foreign Minister, Svenn Stray, was clearly against. There were a few younger and relatively liberal MPs who had succeeded in convincing their party to accept limited measures. Between 1977 and 1980, when the debate on oil and shipping sanctions started, the Labour government banned imports of South African wine and liquor, as well as new investments in and bank loans to South Africa. None of these measures had a serious impact on Norwegian business interests.

When the Christian People's Party joined Willoch's coalition government in 1983, one of its members, Asbjørn Haugstvedt, became the new Minister of Commerce and Shipping. This was important, since the party has traditionally been a moral watchdog in Norwegian politics. It is far more 'Third World' oriented than the Conservative Party. Haugstvedt soon came under immense pressure, caught between the commercial interests of the shipping lobby and the moral and political interests of the churches and other anti-apartheid forces. Most likely this was the most controversial issue he ever handled as a minister, in addition to being a thorn in his relations with Foreign Minister Stray.

In 1984, acting on a NOCOSA initiative, a majority of local authorities in Norway decided to support sanctions. The shipowners became worried when local harbour authorities started to boycott ships that made trips to or from South Africa. In January 1985, the Norwegian Shipowners' Association wanted clarity on the government's position as to who was responsible for the Norwegian foreign trade policy, the national government or the local authorities.

In order to defuse the situation, an interdepartmental working group had been established in the spring of 1984 to review new measures to be taken by Norway. The intention was not to ban shipping and trade completely, but to consider more limited measures. Certain groups within the Ministry of Commerce and Shipping echoed the views of the NSA. Nobody expected much from the group's report, and it was hardly off the press in December 1984 before the recommendations were rejected in public debate as being 'too little, too late'.

Parliament demands registration

Most of the political battles on sanctions were fought out in public, but an important part remained invisible to outsiders. Information on informal, personal contacts between the Norwegian Shipowners' Association and the government is not readily available. Internal documents of government departments remain classified. However, several letters (including some confidential ones) exchanged between 1985 and 1987 in a hectic correspondence between the various shipping interests – shipowners, brokers, officers' associations – and the Norwegian authorities have now become available. In late 1993, I was able to get hold of copies, which provided an insight as to what had happened behind closed doors. The NSA opened its files more readily than the Ministry of Foreign Affairs.

In January 1985 discussions started between the Ministry of Commerce and Shipping and the shipowners on a proposal which had been submitted a few months earlier by NOCOSA. The proposal, which was supported by churches and trade unions, was to reg-

Registrering av skipsanløp

Handelsdepartementet har utarbeidet et lovutkast til en meget omfattende registrering av skipsanløp i Syd-Afrika, både med

Registration of ships' calls at South Africa

ister and publish information on Norwegian shipping links with South Africa. The idea behind it was to prevent the shipowners from claiming that figures on Norwegian oil transports were exaggerated by the Shipping Research Bureau and NOCOSA.

Two months later, on 27 March 1985, Mr Haugstvedt told Parliament that the government would cooperate with the NSA – on a voluntary basis – to register deliveries of oil to South Africa on tankers flying the Norwegian flag. The NSA was to provide statistics for each quarter showing the number of tankers and the quantity of oil delivered, without giving the names of the ships and the companies involved. No decision was made on publication of the expected findings. The NSA was very eager to have a voluntary arrangement instead of government regulations.

The foreign affairs committee of the Norwegian Parliament was not satisfied. NOCOSA had established a 'contact group' of MPs representing all parties except the right-wing Progressive Party. In principle, NOCOSA wanted total sanctions against South Africa, including a ban on all shipping services. Knowing that it was unrealistic to get a majority for this view, NOCOSA provided the members of the contact group with a list of possible steps that could be taken.

When the foreign affairs committee discussed the South Africa policy in June 1985, it asked for a comprehensive registration of all Norwegian-owned ships, including those flagged out to foreign registries. The registration would furthermore be carried out by a government body, and the lists of ships were to be made publicly available. The committee had fully accepted a NOCOSA proposal, and Mr Haugstvedt thereby received parliamentary backing for his relatively pro-sanctions position within the coalition.

The shipping lobby was caught by surprise, and the reactions were vehement. The Norwegian Shipbrokers' Association objected to unilateral Norwegian actions and said that a complete ban on trade combined with government compensation to the industry would have been better. The Norwegian Shipmasters' Association warned that national interference in the shipping industry's freedom of movement could be the end of Norway's role in international shipping. They were worried that this would lead to unemployment among Norwegian officers and seamen. The Norwegian Mates' Association, representing senior officers, raised the same concerns, but insisted that all Norwegian-owned ships had to be treated in the same way to prevent ships from being flagged out.

The most comprehensive reaction came from the NSA, where the alarm bells had really started to ring. In a 10-page memorandum, dated 2 September 1985, the Association warned the Ministry of Commerce and Shipping that Norway would violate important policy principles on free trade, and that the legal implications of putting demands on ships sailing under foreign flags could threaten Norwegian shipping interests. Public registration of calls could violate confidentiality clauses in contracts, thereby resulting in their cancellation. The shipowners feared that Norwegian ships would be boycotted by their business partners. This could be far more dangerous than the loss of the South African contracts. The NSA feared that Parliament's recommendation could have a 'serious and lasting' effect on Norwegian shipping.

The NSA document estimated that Norwegian-registered oil tankers had made 20 calls to South Africa in 1984, earning a gross income of between 50 and 80 million Norwegian kroner (NOK). This amount would in itself not be a great loss to the shipowners, but the Association warned that oil companies and traders would avoid Norwegian ships if they did not have maximum flexibility. Other Norwegian earnings from the South African trade were estimated at between NOK 200–300 million for bulk transports, NOK 230 million for general cargo and containers, and NOK 300 million for chemical tankers.[2]

These figures – not public at the time – show that crude oil was a small part of the total picture. It is only now that we are able to establish to what extent the Norwegian anti-apartheid forces focussed their attention on a small part of the business.

The Arthur D. Little report

Mr Haugstvedt and the Ministry of Commerce and Shipping were now in trouble. They had to carry out Parliament's recommendation but had the shipping industry on their back. A draft registration law was sent to the industry for comments. Once again, the reactions were strong.

The Norwegian Shipbrokers' Association had a meeting with Haugstvedt on 2 October 1985. The minister informed the Association that he considered contacting Greece and Liberia in an attempt to persuade the two shipping nations to take joint action with Norway on the registration issue. It later appeared that neither of the countries were interested, which gave rise to speculations that this may have been just another part of a delaying tactic against sanctions.

The industry also started to send letters to politicians and no longer only to the civil service. In a letter to the Ministry of Commerce and Shipping dated 8 October 1985, a copy of which was sent to the Prime Minister's deputy, State Secretary Arne Skauge, the Norwegian Shipowners' Association called Parliament's proposals 'unacceptable'. The NSA argued that, if the proposals were adopted, this would 'put political pressure on the shipowners' and would have 'very serious consequences' for Norwegian shipping. One source indicates that the director of the NSA, Mr David Vikøren, was very selective in his political contacts. By sending a copy of this letter to Mr Skauge, the NSA obviously wanted the PM's office and the Conservative Party to influence Mr Haugstvedt. They probably feared that he would give in to pressure from the public and from Parliament. In its letter, the NSA stated that the Ministry of Commerce and Shipping generally agreed with the view that a voluntary arrangement was preferable to one introduced by law. Nevertheless, it seems that the Ministry was prepared to proceed with the proposed law unless the NSA agreed to extend the voluntary registration to include the additional data wanted by Parliament.

The NSA wrote that the registration (a) should not include Norwegian-owned ships under foreign flag, and (b) that the names of ships should not be published. Legal arguments were brought forward to support these points. Once again, the NSA indicated that it was willing to provide statistical information only.

Knowing that its arguments had a fairly slim chance of being accepted, the NSA already had an extra card up its sleeve. It had ordered an independent report on the issue from the international consultancy company, Arthur D. Little in Boston, USA.

At the same time, the Association adopted a higher media profile in the newspaper debate on sanctions. The Little report was presented in a letter of 4 November 1985 to Prime Minister Kåre Willoch, but simultaneously made public by the NSA. It was widely used by the shipping lobby in the public debate. The report was based on interviews with key representatives of the business partners of the Norwegian shipping industry in September and October 1985. The Little report, and the NSA, emphasised that the *indirect* consequences of sanctions against South Africa were by far the most important. The NSA warned that Norwegian shipping could lose between 5 and 10 per cent of the world's shipping markets (and even up to 20 per cent of the bulk shipping market) if public registration was introduced. It said that the very existence of Norwegian shipping was at stake. Some more balanced and less dramatic comments from the Little report were not highlighted by the NSA, which also urged the government not to present proposals to Parliament other than the limited, voluntary registration it had itself suggested.

To some extent, the pressure worked. By crying 'wolf' very loudly and spending an unknown amount to pay Arthur D. Little, the shipowners forced the government to reconsider its position. The Norwegian Parliament's original recommendation was not carried out, and a law on registration was never introduced.

Public reaction and political compromise

Still the Norwegian Shipowners' Association was faced with mounting public pressure for registration. The whole process took place at time when South Africa featured prominently in the media. The South African aggression against neighbouring states underlined the argument that oil deliveries fuelled apartheid's wars. The declaration of the state of emergency in South Africa and the sanctions debate in other countries, in particular the USA, influenced the Norwegian process.

The primate of the Church of Norway, Bishop Aarflot of Oslo, criticised the government and the shipowners at a reception on 1 January 1986. He probably had an enormous moral impact in the debate within the Christian community and the Christian People's Party. Aarflot's statement was printed in several newspapers, and it resulted in a strong public reaction from NSA director Vikøren. In a letter to the bishop, he claimed that the Association had 'not engaged itself in the debate whether South Africa should be isolated economically' but merely sought to protect the business community from the effects of unilateral Norwegian action. Vikøren did not fail to send copies to Minister Haugstvedt and State Secretary Skauge.

An apparently 'leftist' position was held by the president of the Norwegian Seamen's Union, Henrik Aasarød. In an interview with the Labour-oriented newspaper *Arbeiderbladet*, he said that Norway should give arms to the ANC rather than ban oil transports to South Africa. This peculiar view was countered by NOCOSA which argued that it would probably have more effect on the military situation in southern Africa if the South African military forces ran out of fuel. Unlike many other unions in the Norwegian trade union confederation (LO), the Seamen's Union was not very supportive of oil sanctions. It supported comprehensive sanctions, in principle, but was against separate shipping sanctions. Unlike its British and Danish counterparts, the Norwegian Seamen's Union had not joined the Maritime Unions Against Apartheid when it was formed in 1983. Generally speaking, it was on the defensive, its main concern being the sharp decline in the number of jobs for Norwegian seamen, caused by shipowners busily flagging out their ships.

To avoid internal problems in the government coalition, a debate took place behind closed doors. In a confidential letter of 23 January 1986 from NSA director Vikøren to Mr Haugstvedt, he referred to a new agreement reached between the three coalition parties in Parliament, according to which the Association would register all Norwegian-owned tankers calling at South African ports. Only quarterly statistics on the numbers of calls and the volume of oil would be made public. Although the NSA protested against having to register Norwegian-owned tankers under foreign flag, it had to reluctantly reconcile itself with the political reality. The guidelines were made public by the government on 31 January 1986.

The government expected the shipowners to contribute to a gradual reduction of Norwegian oil transports to South Africa. The threat of a legal ban, if this did not happen, was kept in reserve. The NSA later claimed that as a part of this secret agreement, they discouraged their members from transporting oil to South Africa. However, Haugstvedt's State Secretary, Mr Arne Synnes, today says that the Association was not in a position to instruct its members to take any action. Members were not necessarily loyal to the NSA, and some shipowners were not members. In an interview with the author on 26 July 1994,

Table 1   Official figures on deliveries by Norwegian-owned tankers under the voluntary registration system

quarter	number of deliveries	flag: Norwegian	other	tons of crude oil
1986 Apr–Jne	4	2	2	926,438
1986 Jly–Sep	2	1	1	527,466
1986 Oct–Dec	1	–	1	250,000
1987 Jan–Mar	0	–	–	0
1987 Apr–Jne	4	3	1	1,200,000

Source: Press statements Norwegian Ministry of Commerce and Shipping

Synnes said that some shipowners officially declared that they wanted to do business wherever they preferred, and that they considered moral constraints to be irrelevant.

From 1 April 1986 to 30 June 1987, the NSA provided the Ministry of Commerce and Shipping with information under the registration system. The figures were made public in quarterly press releases. Table 1 provides an overview of the information as submitted by the Shipowners' Association to the Ministry of Commerce and Shipping. The sharp increase during the second quarter of 1987 elicited a sharp comment from Minister Haugstvedt's successor, Shipping Minister Mosbakk, who said that the government strongly regretted the shipments 'as it was the intention of Parliament that we stop the transport of oil to South Africa'.

The NSA hoped to use the registration as an argument for the postponement of all other actions against the oil trade. In a letter of 14 October 1986 to the Ministers of Foreign Affairs and Commerce and Shipping, the Association suggested that no proposal for a law against oil transports to South Africa should be brought into discussion until the end of 1987. Unfortunately for them, this suggestion fell on deaf ears. By mid-1987 registration was no longer on the agenda. It had been replaced by a law which banned oil transports.

The sanctions law

After having instituted the registration system in early 1986, Minister Haugstvedt still faced more public pressure. A license system was introduced for imports from and exports to South Africa. Nobody was allowed to trade with the country unless it could be proved that there was no clear alternative to the South African market. This did not directly affect shipping, but it effectively ended the fruit imports which had already declined sharply due to sanctions campaigns. Popular campaigning had achieved a minor victory, while the major goal on oil transports remained.

The demand for a proper sanctions law became even stronger after the state of emergency was extended in South Africa in June 1986. In April of that year, the coalition government of Willoch resigned over a budget issue, and Ms Brundtland of the Labour Party became Prime Minister once again. The new Minister of Commerce and Shipping, Kurt Mosbakk, inherited the 'hot potato' of sanctions. Whilst in opposition, the Labour Party had criticised Willoch's South Africa policy, and many Labour MPs had supported oil sanctions. The new government had to go further. The Christian People's Party, no longer constrained by its role in the government coalition, was able to pursue a policy more in line with its moral heart.

The government issued a white paper (No. 26, 1985–86) on Norwegian measures against South Africa, and in July 1986, the Ministry of Commerce and Shipping asked the shipping industry to comment on the possible consequences of a *total* ban of all economic links with South Africa and South African-occupied Namibia. A new round of political debate followed, in which old arguments were repeated and new ones were conjured up where the old ones had become obsolete.

The Shipbrokers' Association argued that, in order for economic sanctions to have any effect, countries which were the main importers of South African goods should take part. The Association warned that its member companies would move to London if a law was introduced. If the government, for political reasons, still found unilateral sanctions necessary, the shipbrokers wanted them to involve only crude oil.

Table 2 NSA estimates of shipowners' gross earnings from SA trade

type of transport	income Norwegian flag	income foreign flag
crude oil	NOK 30 million	NOK 30 million
other tank/chemicals	NOK 80 million	NOK 130 million
bulk/OBOs	NOK 140 million	NOK 370 million
general cargo/containers	NOK 230 million	NOK 20 million
Total	**NOK 480 million**	**NOK 550 million**

The NSA reiterated its arguments, but in August 1986 presented new estimates of the gross earnings of Norwegian shipowners from their trade with South Africa (Table 2). The figures were more detailed than those previously provided (page 287), and for the first time made an interesting distinction between vessels under the Norwegian flag and those under a foreign flag. The number of ships registered under the Norwegian flag was lower than in the past; according to the NSA this was partly due to the sanctions threats. The Association also introduced a new argument; it expressed the fear that sanctions could undermine efforts to establish a second registry of ships called Norwegian International Ship Register (NIS), which was to compete with registration under a flag of convenience. It is questionable, however, whether this was very important, since the work towards the establishment of the NIS continued anyway despite the sanctions law.

According to the NSA, the total direct and indirect annual loss of gross income for the shipowners would amount to NOK 4 billion. The NSA realised that there was very little chance of getting economic compensation for these losses, since it would be very difficult to substantiate the claims. The main demand of the shipping industry was to be able to compete under the same conditions as its competitors.

Two days before the law was eventually passed in Parliament, the Bergesen Group, which had been heavily involved in the oil transports to South Africa, wrote a letter to the Ministry asking for economic compensation. In the letter, signed by Petter C.G. Sundt, Bergesen claimed that the company had gross incomes from South Africa of approximately NOK 60 million in 1985 and NOK 70 million in 1986. Sundt did not specify whether this included both oil and bulk transports. Bergesen claimed that ships representing 3,030,000 tons deadweight were affected by the sanctions. Asked by the Ministry to comment on Bergesen's request, the NSA supported the company's demand in principle. In a document to Parliament, the government clearly said that no compensation was envisaged for shipopwners losing income due to sanctions. In its letter, the NSA asked the Ministry to review its position on the issue.

'Swiss cheese'

A bill was introduced on 14 November 1986, and in spite of all the shipping interests' lobbying, they did not manage to stop it. On 16 March 1987 Parliament approved the Sanctions Law, which was to come into effect on 20 July 1987.

Many remained critical of the law, particularly trade unions and NOCOSA. The president of NOCOSA, Reidar Andestad, a former chairperson of the Christian People's Party's youth league, compared the law with a 'Swiss cheese', full of holes. It had only banned the transport of crude oil; refined oil products could still be shipped to South Africa. However, a further loophole remained regarding crude oil shipments to South Africa; if the Norwegian company could not reasonably have known beforehand that an oil cargo was destined for South Africa, a delivery would not qualify as a violation of the law. Services such as general cargo, bulk and chemicals transport in cross-trading for other countries were not banned either.

In an interview with the author on 10 October 1994, former Minister Kurt Mosbakk confirms that there were different opinions within the Labour Party on the sanctions issue. Some asked for comprehensive sanctions, while those who wanted to allow exemptions won the day. All the same, Mosbakk believes that the job of forging a law was easier for the Labour government, being a one-party government, than it had been for the previous coalition.

The shipowners had protested all along, but looking at the figures involved in the different types of shipping, the law was probably acceptable to them. As far as crude oil was concerned, the law was effective. Apparently, no use was made of the escape clause that had been challenged by the law's anti-apartheid critics. Between March 1987 and 15 March 1993, when the Sanctions Law was revoked, no further crude oil transports were detected by either the Shipping Research Bureau or the press.

Transports of refined oil products did, however, take place and caused major headlines when revealed in 1989 and 1990. The SRB, NOCOSA, some Labour and Socialist Left Party MPs, representatives of LO and even the Young Conservatives asked for this loophole to be closed, but still nothing came of the idea. The sanctions debate had started to lose momentum, after the release of Nelson Mandela and with negotiations in the offing.

Defeat, compromise or victory?

Legal and economic arguments were unable to stop the political pressure on the Norwegian government. It is remarkable that at a time of 'Thatcherism', the most free market-oriented Norwegian industry was forced to accept limitations on its freedom to engage in business transactions. On the other hand, crude oil transports were sacrificed in order to be able to maintain the other shipping links with South Africa. The shipping industry managed to protect most of its interests and probably the most profitable part of the trade.

Director Arild Wegener of the Norwegian Shipowners' Association today admits that it is impossible to calculate how large the losses of the shipping industry were due to the ban on crude oil transports. It is, however, questionable whether there were any significant losses in the end. Due to the boom in the shipping business, shipowners were less worried about South Africa. In an article which appeared in the Norwegian business magazine *Økonomisk Rapport* No. 18/1988, Eivind Grønstad concluded: 'The Norwegian ban on oil transports to South Africa came at an opportune moment, both for the Norwegian authorities and for the shipping business. With a booming international tanker market, the consequences of being locked out from South Africa are limited.' His story was to a large extent based on an interview with Mr Sundt of Bergesen, who agreed with him:

'Sundt thinks that the consequences would have been very unfortunate if the sanctions law had come about while the market was down.' Sundt also thought that it was impossible to say what the financial impact of the law would be, since there was little to compare it with. But he said that he did not know of any concrete cases of Bergesen ships losing cargoes to other destinations on account of the law.

Is it fair to conclude that the NSA lost the political struggle on the crude oil issue? Many would be inclined to agree, while Wegener now says that this would depend on when the question was raised. 'When it became clear that the restrictions were limited to crude oil, there was a common feeling that it was a victory, and we were generally satisfied. Ship-owners who primarily did business with ULCCs were uncomfortable,' Mr Wegener said in an interview on 3 June 1994, adding that 'a general ban on shipping links with South Africa would have been worse.' Wegener admits that at times the NSA feared such a general ban, and that the political discussion was not easy for the Association to handle, since feelings on South Africa and sanctions ran high. He said that the anti-apartheid forces and the NSA had completely different perspectives: 'Our job was to argue for what was economical and rational in order to protect our business interests.'

From the correspondence between the shipping industry and the government, we are led to conclude that a tacit agreement was reached between the NSA and the government. The documents we unearthed create the impression that the NSA reluctantly accepted that some of its members were affected by sanctions, now that other profitable branches of shipping were left intact. Mr Wegener strongly rejects this. He says that there was no agreement with the government, since the NSA was against *all* unilateral Norwegian restrictions on business links with South Africa.

However, according to Mr Mosbakk, the shipowners had accepted a compromise. They had a firm position on principles until the very end but were certainly not oblivious to political realities. The former minister went on to state that there had not been any major complaints from the NSA, when the decision was taken. His view is that the Association 'could live with the Sanctions Law'. Other shipping questions, such as the establishment of the NIS, were more important to the NSA, according to Mosbakk.

Politicians are reluctant to admit a defeat; if they lose, they tend to say that the loss was less than what they feared. Wegener's comment fits this picture. Previously, the various governments had lent an ear to the arguments put forward by the NSA. However, on this occasion, the NSA lost political sympathies to a large extent and met with political arguments and situations which were not easy to handle. One can therefore conclude that the NSA lost the political struggle, but still managed to protect most of the shipowners' economic interests. The NSA was able to live with the final outcome, even though it had had to concede a defeat with regard to some important principles.

What can be learnt?

A number of lessons can be learnt from the Norwegian experience.

• Events in South Africa were a major factor in the process. The sanctions movement that had started in the early 1960s did not take off until after the Soweto uprising in 1976.

The main argument used for the implementation of sanctions was to put an end to the oppressive policies of apartheid and to end South African aggression against the neighbouring states. Our experience in pro-sanctions activities have taught us that organisations are unable to achieve their goals unless there are important political events which create media coverage and public interest.

• It is important to assist the media in digging up stories, since the campaign work is strengthened by media coverage. Personal contacts with selected journalists of major media can be very fruitful. One exclusive full-page story in a large paper is better than 15 small reports hidden in several papers.

• The information provided to the media should be as accurate as possible. The Shipping Research Bureau managed to enhance its credibility by not exaggerating figures and accusations. NOCOSA's political and moral arguments were well balanced by the SRB's more thoroughly researched work.

• It is important to be well informed about the kind of business campaigns are directed at. Neither NOCOSA nor the SRB knew much about shipping when we started. We would have been better equipped to deal with the legal and formal arguments used by the shipowners if our access to business information and to sources within companies had been better at an early stage.

• When adversaries see their old arguments failing, be prepared for a list of new ones. For example, in the beginning, the Norwegian Shipowners' Association argued in favour of free trade and against government interference in lawful business. Legal arguments were extensively used against any Norwegian action against Norwegian-owned interests abroad. When it became morally impossible to argue in favour of continued fuelling of the apartheid regime, the arguments focussed on the negative effects sanctions would have on their own businesses. In the end, the shipowners demanded compensation.

• If David is to beat Goliath, it is important to create strategic alliances. Both public campaigning and lobbying activities directed towards a broad group of politicians were important. In public, the general demand was for total sanctions. In NOCOSA's contact with politicians, a more pragmatic 'step-by-step' sanctions policy was suggested. This made it easier for the politicians to start moving.

• The change of government in Norway in 1986 benefited the campaign. Even though the differences between successive governments were relatively small, the Labour Party had to do 'a little more' than its predecessors, the conservative coalition, which it had criticised while in opposition.

• The campaign for sanctions was partly successful. In Norway, the oil export and crude oil transport bans were probably the only important sanctions to be implemented. Some have concluded that 'what is banned is not important and what is important is not banned'. To a large extent this maxim also applied to Norway. The early sanctions only had an effect on marginal areas, such as the import of wines, bank loans and new investments.

While some of these areas were important in other countries, Norwegian loans and investments were negligible. The areas in which Norway had an important role to play, such as shipping services and manganese ore imports, were not affected by the Sanctions Law. Norway did, however, introduce sanctions in a strategically important area: crude oil. In this case 'what was important *was* banned'.

We are left with some unanswered questions from our experiences in anti-apartheid work. If the idea was to stop all commercial links with South Africa, did we not focus too narrowly on a small range of sanctions in our campaigns? Were other shipping links not just as important as oil, or maybe even a more significant target, quantitively speaking? Were refined oil products not just as strategically important for the South African military forces as was crude oil? The figures in Table 2 suggest that these questions can be answered in the affirmative. On the other hand, it can also be argued that in view of the limited resources at our disposal, the decision to concentrate on certain areas was both inevitable and sensible. Crude oil transports were easier to monitor than other shipping links, and there were strong arguments for viewing the former as of greater strategic importance to South Africa.

The choice of Shell as the main target among the oil companies involved in South Africa was another contentious issue in Norway and to a certain degree also among anti-apartheid activists. We decided to focus on Shell as the largest transnational oil company. We did not have the capacity nor the resources to hit at the other oil companies with the same force.

Questions regarding such tactical choices are bound to remain controversial among those who have been active in the sanctions campaign against apartheid South Africa.

Maritime Unions Against Apartheid

HENRIK BERLAU*

All seafarers know the characteristic silhouette of the mountains when passing the Cape of Good Hope. Thousands of ships pass every year on voyages between the Atlantic and the Indian Ocean. Most simply pass by, whilst others call for a short visit to restock provisions.

During the 1970s until the early 1990s, these visits meant more than just a short stop for those seafarers who were hired on oil tankers carrying oil to South Africa. Without any say in the matter, they were forced to participate in the violation of the United Nations oil ban and thereby indirectly prolong the survival of the apartheid regime.

Moreover, all seafarers who participated in those transportations were subjected to restrictions on their personal freedom during their stay in South Africa. They were not allowed to send letters to families or friends nor use the ship's radio for private phone calls. Only official communications from ship to shore were allowed via South African coastal radio stations. This secrecy was intended to hide the position of the ships. Both the ships' masters and their owners were well aware that their activities could create problems: problems with the United Nations, problems with their own authorities, and problems with the trade unions.

Trade unions, particularly the seafarers' organisations, had an obligation to take a clear position on apartheid as a political system and on UN sanctions.

Sanctions

The first official call for international trade union sanctions against apartheid came from the South African Congress of Trade Unions, in the aftermath of the Sharpeville massacre. While some national federations, particularly those of the then socialist countries, responded immediately, in the Western world trade union federations were slow to act. The response was more or less left to individual unions, some of whom reacted by taking action against South African imports and exports.

It took many years to get apartheid firmly on the agenda of the international trade union movement. As the struggle escalated inside South Africa, the Western world was entering the recession of the 1980s. It was difficult to get many trade unions in the industrialised countries to see past the possibility of redundancies at home rather than direct their efforts against the horrendous effects of apartheid on their fellow workers in South Africa.

---

* President, Danish Seamen's Union.

However, a substantial change in approach was looming concerning the United Nations oil and arms embargoes.

Oil and arms embargoes

The arms embargo against South Africa preceded the oil embargo. A voluntary arms embargo was adopted by the UN Security Council in 1963; the embargo became mandatory in 1977. The oil embargo was first introduced in a UN General Assembly resolution on apartheid in 1975. Although there had been occasional initiatives by workers and trade unions on the oil issue before, real trade union interest in the oil embargo only arose when it became the topic of discussion at a meeting of the International Labour Organisation (ILO) in Geneva in June 1983.

In the trade union world the issue of the oil and arms embargoes had been steadily approaching a flashpoint. The action taken by the Danish Seamen's Union against Trigon and other Danish shipping companies involved in large-scale arms smuggling to South Africa became the catalyst for a broad international campaign. When the Danish Seamen's Union first revealed, in 1978, that ships flying the Danish flag were supplying Pretoria with arms, there was no official response. These illegal arms transportations took place from ports in virtually all European countries. Regardless of the political system or official politics, arms dealers could freely buy any weapon system that Pretoria requested. The need for hard currency and technological innovations which resulted from arms deals

A Danish ship against the skyline of Durban's harbour, the Danish and South African flags as well as the red *'Beware: Explosives On Board'* sign hoisted. Years after this souvenir picture had been taken, it turned up among one of the crew members' papers, and began a new life as documentary evidence for an illegal arms shipment to South Africa, providing a suitable illustration of the ways seamen could help in identifying violations of embargoes

made governments turn a blind eye, while at the same time voting in favour of mandatory sanctions in the United Nations.

Danish ships played a crucial role in these transactions. No one would suspect *them* of violating the embargo. The Danish flag was as well respected as the Red Cross flag, and Danish merchant vessels were suitable for this purpose. The ships were rather small, and they were able to load and unload very discreetly. Once out at sea the crew were ordered to rename the ship and remove all company markings. The ship's log was forged so as to show that the ship had officially called at other ports, such as Maputo in Mozambique.

Despite all these precautions, it was the shipowners' greed that resulted in their exposure. When the crew went ashore in South Africa, the company always remembered to deduct the seafarers' wages for currency paid to them *in rands*. It was the crew members' pay slips, showing these mysterious payments in South African rands during calls 'at Mozambique', which eventually enabled the Danish Seamen's Union to expose this illicit trade.

Cooperation with dockworkers and others helped with quick identification. Countries such as Romania, Bulgaria, Italy, Belgium, France and Portugal were all found to be willing suppliers. Governments of all the aforementioned countries were well aware of but secretly condoned the violations. Others such as Yugoslavia, Greece, England, Poland and Czechoslovakia – in fact, any country with a weapons industry – queued up to make an arms deal. All shipments were organised by the South African agents Michael Jordaan, who profited from diplomatic immunity provided by the South African embassy in Paris, and Charles Canfield.

From 1978 onwards, Danish ships participated in at least 60 illegal shipments. The Danish Seamen's Union established a network which monitored arms shipments to South Africa. As if in direct response, shipowners transferred ships to 'flags of convenience' and refrained from employing Danish seafarers. The cost of principle and solidarity was high for the union and its members.

Sixteen owners were eventually convicted in the Danish courts for their activities, and Danish legislation was tightened up. The major supplier, shipowner Anders Jensen of the Danish company Trigon, escaped to South Africa where, according to Interpol, he still resides at the time of writing.

The 'Maritime Unions Against Apartheid' initiative

The existing network was shown to be very valuable when after preliminary discussions in 1983, the Danish Seamen's Union together with two British unions, the National Union of Seamen (NUS) and the Transport and General Workers Union (TGWU), and the Seamen's Union of Australia (SUA), in cooperation with the Shipping Research Bureau, established *Maritime Unions Against Apartheid* (MUAA) in February 1984. The aim was to generate support for the implementation of United Nations resolutions, mainly regarding the arms and oil embargoes.

The Danish Seamen's Union had earlier entered into a unique cooperation with the Shipping Research Bureau, which had undertaken specific investigations into the role of Dan-

Radiotelegram fra/from DURBAN   Nr./No. 1655   65/61 ord. indleveret den 20/ 6 19 80 Kl./Time 1230
Wds. handling in date

	Gfr.	Cts.	dkr.	Øre	MASTER			Tj. bemærkn./Service instructions
afgift charge					OWJC			Skibsstationens navn/Name of vessel
~fgifter rge								
I alt Total					ZSD			Dato/Date

Modtaget fra/Received from ZSD   Kl./Time 1400z   Af/By h.a.   Sendt til/Sent to   Dato/Date   Kl./Time   Af/By

= contrary previous instructions you are now required berth sbm daylight
sunday 22/6 pls arrange arrive 2 miles east of sbm 22/6 o6oo hrs when
pilot boarding stop maersktank advise freight guarantee still not received
expect revert later this evening reverting stop receivers require now order
of discharge urgently understand two parcels 147000 ts and 56300 ts
respectively =
        maerskline

Radiotelegram fra/from KØBENHAVN   Nr./No. 3o66 103/91 ord. indleveret den 20/ 6 19 8o Kl./Time 17o4
Wds. handling in date

	Gfr.	Cts.	dkr.	Øre	KAPTAJNEN			Tj. bemærkn./Service instructions
Skibsafgift ship's charge					DAGMAR MÆRSK/OWJC			Skibsstationens navn/Name of vessel
~fgifter rge								
I alt Total					LYNGBYRADIO			Dato/Date

Modtaget fra/Received from LYRA   Kl./Time   Af/By   Sendt til/Sent to   Dato/Date   Kl./Time   Af/By

km 10558/41 befragterne meddeler berthing nu 22/6 am hvorfor afgå fra
nuvrende position således at eta off durban bliver 21/6 pm stop skibet må gå
til lossebøjen men losning må ikke påbegyndes før tilladelse modtaget fra enten
rederiet eller maerskline durban grundet stadig udestående fragt/bankgaranti
stop hvis tilladelse er givet påbegyndes med losning crude olie spuling må ikke
gentager ikke påbegyndes før overstyrmand thau fra rederiet kommer ombord stop
overstyrmand thau forventes at ombordkomme 22/6 1500 stop såfremt instruktioner
ikke modtaget når skibet går til bøjen da kontaktes rederiet ++++

O'stmd

R 2 (DRA)   STK. NO. 331643

Leaked radio telegrams from the Mærsk agency in Durban (No. 1655) and the head office of A.P. Møller in Copenhagen (No. 3066) to the master of the *Dagmar Mærsk* (call sign OWJC), instructing him to sail to the oil buoy ('sbm') off Durban, and to prepare for discharge of the cargo (June 1980)

ish tankers in oil supplies to South Africa. When it began to dawn upon the Bureau that Mærsk-Møller, the major Danish tanker-owning company, had been deeply involved in breaking the embargo, it took advantage of information provided to the Union by its member seafarers employed on Mærsk tankers during trips to South Africa. At the same time, the Bureau assisted the Union in detecting the movements of Danish ships involved in arms smuggling. The cooperation served as a model for MUAA in its efforts to set up a flow of information between unions and the Shipping Research Bureau on clandestine oil shipments.

The four unions which had played an active role in establishing MUAA represented both seafarers and dockworkers. The activities of MUAA involved affiliates from both the World Federation of Trade Unions (WFTU) and the International Confederation of Free Trade Unions (ICFTU). Any successful action had to come from a united front of the world's maritime unions. However, united action by unions from both affiliations was hardly common practice during the period when Cold War-related splits prevailed in the international trade union movement.

The objectives of MUAA were:
- to involve the seafarers in the oil embargo adopted by the United Nations,
- to force owners to refrain from shipping oil to South Africa,
- to take action against companies which violated the embargo, and
- to press for national legislation prohibiting all transports to South Africa.

The road to the implementation of these objectives was not an easy one. The workings of the international trade union bodies were found to be as complex and full of intrigue as the world of government diplomacy. At the ILO meeting in Geneva in 1983, Denis Akumu, General Secretary of the Organization of African Trade Union Unity (OATUU), opened the conversation with the words: 'I have been requested not to meet you.' The same evening the hotel informed the delegation of the Danish and Australian unions, which would later become the co-founders of MUAA, that it no longer had rooms available, and the delegates were unceremoniously kicked out of their rooms. Fortunately, Geneva had more than one hotel, and Denis Akumu and the OATUU went on to play a fundamental role in establishing the trade union oil embargo.

It was these negative attitudes and hindrances that were aptly summed up by Archbishop Trevor Huddleston: 'I am sick,' he told those present at the major MUAA conference held in London in October 1985, 'of governments and other people saying that of course they are opposed to apartheid, that they consider it a crime against humanity ... saying these things and then, by their inaction, supporting the continuance of the system.' In the international trade union movement, many unfortunately still looked on the apartheid issue with reluctance and waited for a substantial development to arise by itself.

The formation of MUAA was the result of endless meetings and discussions until finally, in 1985, MUAA arranged the Conference of Maritime Trade Unions on Oil Supplies to South Africa, with the participation of dockers' and seafarers' unions from all over the world. The conference, held in London on 30–31 October 1985, was co-sponsored by the United Nations Special Committee against Apartheid. Participants included ANC President Oliver Tambo, South African Congress of Trade Unions (SACTU) Secretary John Nkadimeng and Major-General Joseph Garba, Nigerian ambassador to the United Nations and chairman of the UN Special Committee against Apartheid. The conference was opened by the British Labour leader Neil Kinnock.

The state-controlled South African Broadcasting Corporation TV recorded the whole conference – 'for private screenings only'...

NUS General Secretary Jim Slater opened the debate with the following remarks:

In coming together today we have been able to show that whatever other issues may be contentious between us, we are united in our opposition to apartheid and in our determination to join with the black people of South Africa in their struggle.

We bring to our activities against apartheid no ideology and no affiliation other than a deep-rooted hatred of continued segregation, the homeland system, forced resettlement, the destruction of families and homes, slave wages, the persecution of trade unionists, detentions, torture and murder.

There have been many resolutions from individual trade unions and international trade union organisations condemning apartheid, but what we are here to do now is to go beyond this and translate all the verbal support into positive action, and to commit ourselves to tightening the embargo on oil supplies to South Africa.

Representatives from all important maritime nations attended the conference. For the first time ever, the conference brought together the two international trade union organisations ICFTU and WFTU, through their respective transport affiliates International Transport Workers' Federation (ITF) and Trade Union International of Transport Workers (TUI). After vigorous debate over two days, a declaration and plan of action were unanimously agreed to, and this allowed the net to be drawn even tighter around oil transports to South Africa (see Annex: Declaration).

Prior to the conference, more than 10,000 posters in five languages and questionnaires (along the lines of the ones distributed by the ITF among its affiliated unions in January 1984) were globally distributed to seafarers, trade unions, seamen's clubs, seamen's churches, seamen's houses and other places frequented by seamen. Seafarers who had participated in any transportation to South Africa were requested to give the name of the ship and company they had worked for and information on the countries and ports of loading.

Shipping companies were requested to voluntarily inform MUAA whether their ships had been or would be involved in oil transportation to South Africa. They were requested to include clauses in their contracts that their ships would not be allowed to go to South Africa.

Companies which were exposed for continuing their activities were pointed out in public and demonstrations arranged at their headquarters. Ships which had been in contact with South Africa became liable to industrial action, and the companies were warned of the consequences. Several ships were diverted, and the cargo sold somewhere else; enormous costs were passed on to the apartheid regime.

In Denmark the Danish Seamen's Union closely participated in the campaign to prohibit all oil transportation to South Africa by law. The owners threatened to flag out their ships and refrain from building new ones. It was for that reason that many trade union leaders failed to support the embargo. The persistence of the dedicated, however, finally convinced the Danish parliament that they were willing to bear the consequences of an embargo, which was introduced in 1986.

MUAA turned out to play the role it was destined for and joined in the overall campaign with many other forces, in particular the Shipping Research Bureau, to make it much more difficult and certainly much more expensive for Pretoria to buy oil.

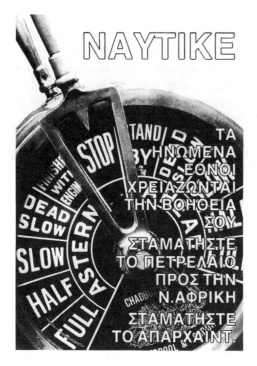

Greek sailors are called upon to support the oil embargo. Posters in Greek as well as English, Spanish, Danish and Arabic were distributed by the Maritime Unions Against Apartheid

On account of its size and diversity, the international trade union movement can be slow to act. The trade union movement is often restricted and strongly connected to governments and parties whose politics are contrary to the interests of the unions and their members.

Sometimes it is left to individual trade unions and even individual trade unionists to overcome the structural deficiencies in order to gain the objective. MUAA showed that this could nevertheless be achieved, and the memory of having participated has its own reward.

That memory includes working with many dedicated people such as those involved in the activities of the Shipping Research Bureau, civil servants and, of course, seafarers. However, the major source of inspiration for all the MUAA participants was working with the South African people, who after such a tortuous path are at last envisaging freedom, justice and democracy.

Annex

DECLARATION OF MARITIME UNIONS ON THE IMPLEMENTATION OF THE UNITED NATIONS OIL EMBARGO AGAINST SOUTH AFRICA, 30/31 OCTOBER 1985

This international conference on the United Nations (UN) oil embargo against South Africa convened on the initiative of seafarers' and dockers' unions, and co-sponsored by the UN Special Committee Against Apartheid,

RECALLING that Apartheid has been declared a crime against humanity, and that the Security Council of the United Nations since its unanimously adopted resolution 182/1963 has affirmed the conviction that the situation in South Africa is seriously endangering international peace and security;

RECOGNISING that apart from the mandatory arms embargo (resolution 418c/1977), the oil embargo is considered the most effective peaceful means for those outside South Africa to assist in the ending of apartheid;

SHARING the growing concern of the international community of workers and their trade union organisations at the deterioration of the situation in South Africa under apartheid and the need for action, as shown in the programme of action adopted by the UN General Assembly and in subsequent resolutions and instruments adopted by that assembly, in the Declaration Concerning the Policy of Apartheid in South Africa adopted by the International Labour Conference of the ILO in 1981, and in the declaration from the International Conference of Trade Unions on Sanctions and Other Actions Against the Apartheid Regime in South Africa (Geneva, June 1983);

RECALLING the UN resolutions 32/105 of 1977 and 37/69 of 1982, and resolutions of 1983 and 1984 on the oil embargo against South Africa;

COMMENDS the action of those governments which have supported the UN oil embargo, in particular the member governments of the Organisation of Petroleum Exporting Countries and the Organisation of Arab Petroleum Exporting Countries which have applied the embargo scrupulously;

CONDᴱMNS the South African minority apartheid regime for totally ignoring world opinion as expressed by the above-mentioned resolutions, and for consistently refusing to abide by international standards as enshrined in the UN Charter;

WARNS that South Africa's systematic violation of human and trade union rights in South Africa and the rapid escalation in the tightening and application of apartheid policies, constitute an imminent threat to world peace and security;

REJECTS AND CONDEMNS so-called constitutional changes which totally exclude the black majority people from all political rights and are designed to consolidate apartheid further, and which have been strongly condemned by the trade union movement;

DENOUNCES AND CONDEMNS continuing murders, arrests, bannings, psychological and physical torture leading to death in detention, harassment and victimisation of black trade unionists and those assisting black workers to organise themselves;

DEPLORES AND CONDEMNS continuing raids and incursions on sovereign neighbouring countries and the apartheid regime's efforts to destabilise the frontline states;

VIGOROUSLY CONDEMNS the South African white minority racist regime for the illegal occupation of the territory of Namibia, its persistent refusal to agree to the implementation of UN Security Council resolution 435/1978, and the imposition of the apartheid system in that country;

SALUTES the black workers of South Africa for the courage and determination they have shown in the face of imprisonment, torture and death to organise themselves into trade unions, which have become a strong expression of the aspirations of the majority peoples of South Africa;

RESOLUTELY CONDEMNS all shipowners and shipping management companies (including flag of convenience operators), shipping agents and the oil companies, involved in violating the UN resolutions on the oil embargo against South Africa;

DEPLORES the failure of some states to fully implement UN resolutions and decisions on South Africa;

CALLS ON governments throughout the world to:

–   endorse and implement the UN resolutions on apartheid in particular those on the oil embargo, and

–   immediately lift any legislation which restricts trade union solidarity action with the black people of South Africa;

CALLS ON employers' organisations and companies to comply with all UN resolutions on apartheid, in particular on the oil embargo;

WARNS all shipowners, shipping management companies, shipping agents, and the oil companies that until assurance is received that they are not involved, or their involvement in the delivery of oil has ceased, the vessels under their jurisdiction are liable to trade union action including boycott;

RESOLVES that all seafarers, port, dock and other transport workers represented at this conference will:

–   press on governments, including those offering flag of convenience facilities, to pass national legislation and regulations to make it illegal to supply or transport oil to the South African apartheid regime; the legislation to include the imposition of severe penalties on violators of the laws arising from the legislation,

–   exchange information on ships violating the UN oil embargo on South Africa, including those discharging oil in Namibia,

–   take direct action against the vessels of any companies involved in supplying oil to South Africa in order to tighten the UN oil embargo and to increase the risks and costs of supplying South Africa with oil,

–   co-ordinate their activity in these areas to facilitate the speediest and fullest implementation of the UN oil embargo on South Africa;

STRONGLY URGES all trade union organisations representing seafarers port, dock and other transport, oil and chemical workers throughout the world to:

–   join in action against companies involved in the supply of oil to South Africa,

–   exchange information on ships violating the UN oil embargo on South Africa,

–   campaign among their members for solidarity action with the black people of South Africa,

– publicise, including through the ILO, all legislative and administrative measures which restrict trade union solidarity action with the black people of South Africa;

REQUESTS the UN to organise a full-scale conference of oil producers and transporters, with participation of governments, shipowners and trade unions, to lay down very specific mandatory procedures to make the oil embargo really effective.

The Dutch Campaign against Shell

ERIK VAN DEN BERGH*

The *outcome* was certainly unexpected. A few years before, this scenario would have been difficult to predict: Shell South Africa urges that sanctions not be given up too quickly, while anti-apartheid organisations call for companies to invest heavily in South Africa. From 'Shell House' in Johannesburg, the ANC transforms itself from a liberation movement into a government party.

The *beginning* was just as remarkable. In 1973 Kairos spokesman Cor Groenendijk attended the shareholders' meeting of the Royal Dutch Petroleum Company. His appeal to top Dutch Shell officials and shareholders to choose for black South Africa and to break the ties with the apartheid regime received much attention and formed the start of an international campaign that was to continue until 1991. This contribution focuses on the Dutch campaign and Shell's reaction to it. The campaign in the US is dealt with by Donna Katzin (see the appendix to this chapter for a review of other international actions).

The Netherlands and South Africa

Because of the extensive historic, cultural and religious ties between the two countries, interest in South Africa has remained high in the Netherlands throughout the last decades. Few international issues have challenged the minds of the Dutch government as intensely as the struggle against apartheid. Foreign Affairs Minister Van der Klaauw (1977–81) sighed at the end of his term: 'I will not try to conceal the fact that South African policy probably caused me the most difficulty.'[1] In the Dutch parliament during the 1970s, ten times as many questions were posed on South Africa than on Cambodia and Uganda combined, two regions which could certainly not be called conflict-free.[2] Emotions ran high. Several times a Dutch cabinet was nearly brought to collapse over a South African issue. A number of factors tended to reinforce each other:

• The Dutch have not yet come to terms with their colonial past. The difficult recent decolonisation processes of Indonesia, New Guinea/Irian Jaya and Surinam, as well as the forms Dutch colonisation took in the past, have left their mark on debates on Third World issues. In addition, the kinship which many apartheid ideologists felt for the Netherlands and the views which they (perhaps unjustly) based on Calvinist doctrine have brought about a large share of guilt.

• An equally sensitive issue in the multicultural Dutch society is racism. The trau-

---

* Senior staff member, Kairos, Ecumenical Advice and Information Centre on South Africa, Utrecht (the Netherlands).

mas of the Second World War are in many respects still alive. Guilt over the lack of massive support for the Dutch Jews – 82 per cent were unable to escape from deportation and worse – go a long way towards explaining why the vast majority of the Dutch found apartheid laws unacceptable. The struggle for freedom in South Africa was often compared to the struggle against Nazi Germany. The murder of Martin Luther King and the struggle for the emancipation of black Americans also stirred up emotions and confronted the Dutch with their own attitudes regarding racism.

• Since the mid-1970s, repression in South Africa had increased sharply. The township revolts in 1976, the murder of Steve Biko and the banning of the Christian Institute and black consciousness movements a year later showed that the minority government would have to go to great lengths to maintain its position.

• Reporting on developments in South Africa underwent a noticeable change. Television became an increasingly important medium, bringing shocking images of the horrors of apartheid into the living room of every Dutch citizen.

• Political developments in the Netherlands (in 1973 Labour became a coalition partner for the first time in years) also found their way into foreign policy. The notion that the Netherlands should provide moral 'guidance' in international politics gained popularity. Third World issues received much attention, and the struggle against apartheid became an important touchstone; few politicians and opinion-formers escaped passing judgement on the regime in Pretoria. A Dutch historian describes the direct connection with the democratisation movement: 'The attack on internal power structures, in the eyes of many progressives, made the Netherlands pre-eminently suited to help liquidate suspect power structures elsewhere ... It is easier to launch protest actions against corrupt practices in distant places in the world than to fully consider the imperfections of the democratisation process at home. Seldom did idealism involve so little risk or cost as it did in the Netherlands of the 1960s and 1970s.'[3]

The emigration of Dutch to South Africa, numbering in the tens of thousands after the Second World War, is in itself a factor explaining why developments in that part of the world were followed with more than just normal curiosity.

The special relationship between the two countries was aptly summed up by G.A. Wagner, former chairman of the Shell Group, who stated in 1989: 'There can be no doubt that the Netherlands has a special and extraordinarily uncomfortable tie with South Africa. In this lie the roots of pre-eminent Dutch resistance. We have a bond with South Africa, but we want to deny that. We want to break free, but cannot.'[4]

In the 1970s the Dutch Third World movement had grown into an influential network with many branches. When the government began to give financial support to organisations active on Third World issues, participation in an even greater number of activities became possible. Anti-apartheid organisations were among the strongest movements in this sector, measured by membership, employees and financial means. Following Dutch tradition, a few large and many small organisations had come to coexist over the years which concerned themselves with southern African issues, often acting independently from each other, sometimes in unexpected harmony. At times there were so many actions that some irritation was inevitable. The Surinam-born writer Ellen Ombre, now residing in the Netherlands, expressed her scepticism: 'It strikes me how much interest my new countrymen have in the suffering of the coloured man, the more so if he's far away: the distant black man is always dearer than their own.'[5]

Shell in South Africa

The title sounds neither exciting nor dynamic: *Shell in South Africa*. Yet the content of this report, published in 1976 by OSACI (Ecumenical Study and Action Centre on Investments) and Working Group Kairos (Christians Against Apartheid), was decisive in the many years of pressure on Shell. The English translation of this study, submitted to Shell before its publication, played an important role in the rise of the campaign in the United Kingdom and elsewhere. The report drew the following conclusions:[6]

(a) Wages at Shell South Africa (Shell SA) were comparatively high and discrimination relatively mild. Yet the company paid a minimal wage below the effective minimum level for African families. It profited from the extremely low level of black wages, but for Shell this factor was less important than the growing demand for oil products which ensured high profits in certain sectors. Shell had, in proportion to invested capital, few manual labourers and could easily afford to pay them better wages; however, 'The fact that Shell pays better wages to perhaps a thousand blacks is commendable, but it does not make the racial laws any easier, the trade unions any freer or the bayonets of the police any blunter.'

(b) Shell injected billions into the country, announced in cheerful advertisements, and thereby did its bit for the image building of the apartheid government: 'We are backing South Africa'. Shell's growing involvement in South Africa did not make it any easier for the Dutch and British governments to dissociate themselves from the apartheid regime.

(c) Shell's principal role was, however, 'not that of foreign investor or employer, but that of an oil company'. Oil was indispensable, also for the military and police; the oil majors brought new technologies into the South African economy. Shell was also preparing for its role as an exporter of South African coal.

Shell in South Africa was followed by hundreds of reports, brochures, pamphlets and articles exposing the troublesome aspects of Shell's activities in the apartheid republic. Shell, too, kept its end up, especially after 1985: social reports, brochures and leaflets were produced in large quantities. In the Netherlands, the moral integrity of the company was expanded upon: by remaining in South Africa Shell would be able to make a contribution to change. In South Africa, Shell SA stressed its economic contribution, which it summarised in an advertisement headed 'Two is a company – eight is a commitment' (1986), which told the readers that Shell was active 'in no fewer than eight vital industries'. Besides the extensive oil division, in the 1980s Shell also operated coal, metals, chemicals and forestry divisions.

Criticism of the Anglo-Dutch multinational was primarily based on moral grounds. A number of central themes concerning the position of Shell in South Africa came up again and again during the debates:

South African legislation
Shell's general business principles were put clearly forward by former chairman Wagner: 'A strict loyalty to the laws of the land must be the constitution of every company; also in

all branches of an international company. If one does not hold true to these laws, one will lose, in fact, one's right to exist. The most scrupulous observance of the local regulations is demanded, and the entrepreneur must, in my opinion, take care never to give anyone the idea that his operations in the host country are balancing on the borderline.'[7] Thus, in South Africa strict apartheid legislation determined the framework for Shell. This position was never abandoned, despite all the pressure from, for example, Dr C.F. Beyers Naudé, who in a speech to shareholders in 1989 emphatically urged Shell's policy to be changed on precisely this point. When Mobil withdrew from South Africa, Shell stated: 'Shell listens to the voice of black South Africa'; it should have added: '...and responds as far as apartheid legislation permits.'

Supplies for the military and police
Shell sometimes went quite a bit further. In his book, *Oilgate*, Martin Bailey describes in detail how the Group Managing Director responsible for Africa, Frank McFadzean, pressed for an end to the British arms embargo against South Africa in 1968.[8] Later Chemico – a company in which Shell SA held an interest – also appeared to have interpreted its duty rather liberally. The *South African Defence Force Yearbook* eagerly accepted advertisements in which Chemico presented itself as a military supplier. In 1991 the South African *Weekly Mail* published an overview which showed that Shell had violated the UN arms embargo by shipping 5.7 tons of isopropyl alcohol from the Netherlands to a South African company which produced missiles and missile fuels for the military.[9] Thus, Shell was considerably more involved than was demanded on the basis of legal duty.

Shell and the South African government
When in 1985 the situation in South Africa escalated and a state of emergency was proclaimed, a remarkable turnabout took place at Shell SA. The *Financial Times* reported as front page news in 1986 that the Royal Dutch/Shell Group had emphatically rejected apartheid for the first time. In numerous speeches and interviews, Shell SA chairman John Wilson, also the chairman of the Federated Chamber of Industries, expounded the new course. He was clear about the motivation: 'The business of business is business and not politics. Yet the business community now realises that there is an enormous threat to its very existence, which can only be removed if fundamental political reforms are made in the structure of South Africa'.[10] Wilson pleaded for negotiations with the true leaders of South Africa. In a later speech Wilson was even clearer: 'The calls for the unbanning of the ANC, the release of political prisoners and the reprieve of political exiles are growing in volume daily both nationally and internationally. Business, various organisations and politicians are pressing for this as the only remaining option for resolving the black power struggle in South Africa through bargaining and negotiation.'[11] In response, the South African *Financial Mail* used the phrase: *'Shell's day of awakening'*.

But there was also a relative side to this awakening, as appeared from an interview with Wilson, printed in the *Financial Mail* a few years later: 'Are you in conflict with government? Do you perceive a tension between yourselves and the authorities? "No I don't see us as being in conflict with government. One's got to remember first of all that government is the voice of the electorate. In the case of the current government, it's the voice of the white electorate of SA. There are those who will say it's a minority voice, but be that as it may, the government is the voice that people democratically elected".'[12]

Shell and South African society

For Wilson, verbal action was no longer enough. Shell was 'committed to doing all it can, including by way of its social responsibility programme, to eradicate apartheid and to ensure a free and equal society for all'.[13] The company decided to increase its social responsibility programmes by no less than 70 per cent in 1987. Educational projects received the most attention. Shell's profile was radically adjusted, for example, by the placing of full-page advertisements in progressive weeklies calling for a democratic and non-racial South Africa. Shell SA also tried to make its sense of social responsibility more conspicuous through organisations such as the Urban Foundation. This changing company profile was not only the result of changing political insight, as shown in a Shell SA Public Affairs internal communication which stated: 'Due to the increased pressure on Shell SA in respect of the Shell boycott and disinvestment it has been necessary to step up on our corporate advertising'.

Although exact data on the social projects which Shell supported and the ways in which these were selected are not known, a clear shift was unmistakable: considerably more funds were made available for projects that reflected the needs of a growing number of South Africans. Naturally, any insinuation was denied that the increase in funding came from external pressures: 'It's not done to gain brownie points overseas but because we have a genuine commitment to social change within the country.'[14] In his thorough study on Shell in South Africa, however, the English researcher M.S. Adams put the changes into perspective: 'The changes should not be overstated ... For its outlay Shell gains itself an enhanced corporate image, aiding its sales drive among black consumers ... The company increases the skills base of the country, addressing its own skills shortages; distances itself and the business community from apartheid and disarms the disinvestment campaign, legitimising the presence of multinational corporations in South Africa and the "free enterprise system". The increase in the company's social responsibility spending reflected wider trends both in South Africa and abroad, and dovetailed with P.W. Botha's need for increased private sector welfare spending to take the burden from the state in the late 1970s and early 1980s. The company's expenditure is furthermore relatively cheap. While in 1987 its Corporate Social Responsibility budget was around R12 m, the company spent R90 m opening the first motorway service station in South Africa. Compared with a turnover of R4 bn, R12 m is not too great an outlay. However, as a strategy to end apartheid, CSR programmes have only limited impact.'[15]

Shell, employees and unions

Opinions also varied widely as regards Shell SA's personnel policy and its relationship to trade unions. The upper echelons were completely white. The six-fold increase in the number of blacks in management functions between 1977 and 1987 must also be seen in perspective: it was partly due to a general increase in personnel, while the total number of blacks remained extremely low. Shell SA established an internal programme to see to it that the personnel composition better reflected the society as a whole. The salaries paid by Shell were reasonable, although not out of the ordinary. In general, salaries in the oil industry were above the South African average. Shell, therefore, scarcely differed from other comparable companies. Adams concluded: 'Shell South Africa is neither the trendsetter, nor the impeccable employer, that it likes to portray itself as. There are employers who offer better wages and conditions, and those of the employees that do not work for companies bearing the Shell name [but for Shell subsidiaries bearing other names] receive lower wages and according to the Chemical Workers Industrial Union (CWIU), work in poorer conditions.'[16]

A comparable difference in opinion existed regarding Shell's relationship with trade unions. Shell was proud of the large contribution multinationals had made to the changes in labour legislation and their pressure on the government to allow unions to operate. Wilson called the 'growth of labour the greatest contribution of multinationals in South Africa'.[17] With regard to opportunities for union activities at Shell's companies, the unions did not exhibit such optimism. 'In an opinion poll conducted by CWIU amongst its shop stewards and organisers in the petroleum sector, Shell ranked lowest in terms of labour relations practices.'[18]

Shell appeared to be prepared and able, *when put under pressure*, to adjust its policies on various levels. It exerted pressure on the apartheid government, more money became available for social projects, personnel policy underwent changes. But the fundamental problems remained, and critics remained unconvinced. After Sean McBride, winner of the Nobel Peace Prize, spoke to shareholders of Royal Dutch in 1983 and consequently had the positive aspects of Shell's policy pointed out to him, he replied: 'That is what we call the "Uncle Tom" syndrome: attempting to make the unacceptable acceptable, through the payment of higher salaries.'[19]

Shell in the Netherlands

For many of the Dutch the Shell trademark was the symbol of national pride. The Royal Dutch/Shell Group was, after all, a surprisingly successful company, active in more than 100 countries. No other company holds so much economic power in the Netherlands as Royal Dutch, representing about 30 per cent of all stock traded on the Amsterdam stock exchange.[20]

In a speech to Royal Dutch shareholders in 1990, the historian Prof. Ger Harmsen reflected upon the company's 100-year past, quoting F.C. Gerretson, who had been commissioned by the company to write the history of its first decades: Royal Dutch was a daughter of Freedom, born and raised in a world that considered political borders as detrimental, as barriers which hindered the development of the natural order of the world economy. Free world movement of persons, goods and capital was a requirement of its existence and flourishing. Its native country was the world market; God's Earth, which was created for all, belonged to all. For Gerretson Shell's duty was 'to provide the widest field of potential consumers, without distinction of state or rank, race or colour, with the primary necessaries of life: light, warmth, power'. A difficult task, Harmsen concluded, for a company that can rightfully be called a product of bloodstained Dutch colonialism.[21]

Other historians also present a less positive picture of Royal Dutch. In a letter to his colleague Gerretson, the Dutch historian Pieter Geyl referred to the leadership of the Group as 'filthy paraffin traffickers'.

The past of the Royal Dutch/Shell Group has influenced its current image. The British researcher and publicist Anthony Sampson demonstrated how the British branch of the

Group, Shell Transport and Trading Company, lacking control over extensive oil stocks, was forced to assume a cosmopolitan pose. Royal Dutch has also exhibited a strong international orientation throughout its history. In the literature on the Group, among the many positive descriptions – solid, self-assured, efficient – one also finds quite a few less noble qualifications – hierarchical, authoritarian, arrogant. Formerly, many Shell employees remained with the company for the duration of their careers. Partly thanks to favourable social conditions, the degree of organisation among Shell employees in the Netherlands was relatively low.

Campaign against Shell

The decision to target Shell was not taken lightly. In the first discussions that took place in 1970 at Kairos, it was quickly decided that activities should be directed toward severing economic ties between South Africa and the Netherlands. The thinking within the World Council of Churches – which started the Programme to Combat Racism in 1970 – had a strong influence on the discussion. When in 1972 the World Council went a step further and called for disinvestment from South Africa, Kairos decided to act upon this appeal and was quickly led to Shell, because of the strategic nature of the latter's investments as well as the scope of its involvement. Another consideration was that the oil industry was not extremely labour-intensive, and the effect on South African unemployment would therefore be limited if Shell withdrew from the apartheid economy.

The *objective* of the campaign never changed; the credo remained: Shell must completely, and preferably as quickly as possible, withdraw from South Africa and sever all ties with the apartheid regime. The withdrawal must take place – and this was increasingly emphasised – in close collaboration with South African trade unions.

In the *first phase* of the campaign (1973–77), the accent lay in large measure on research and dialogue. After a prolonged period of talks between the management and its critics, in 1976 it became clear that further talks were of little use. The standpoints on both sides were clearly incompatible. In the *second phase* (1977–85), the campaign was broadly expanded. The demand for Shell's withdrawal became a component of the actions to realise an oil embargo. Political aspects were at the centre of the campaign, but, at the same time, social pressure on Shell took on strong aspects. The *third and last phase* (1985–91) was characterised by radicalisation and internationalisation. New elements in the Netherlands, Scandinavia and elsewhere included hard forms of action such as sabotage of filling stations. An important impetus came from the US campaign.

In the first phase, *Rhodesia* occupied a central place. The involvement of Shell in breaches of the Security Council embargo against Rhodesia brought increasing questions. The way in which Shell denied and, when that was no longer possible, trivialised its role caused increasing scepticism. The supply of false information by the company management led to a deep-seated distrust. The publication of the English Bingham Report and a parliamentary investigation in the Netherlands led more than 120 Dutch jurists in 1982 to sign a declaration in which it was regretted that Dirk de Bruyne, the responsible Shell executive, and others involved had not been taken to court to answer for their part in illegal oil deliveries to Rhodesia.

The activities of the Group in *Namibia* and the supply of oil to the occupation army also received harsh criticism. Sean McBride, former UN Commissioner for Namibia, stated in 1983: 'The United Nations should take the Royal Dutch/Shell Group before the International Court of Justice on charges of sanctions busting. The occupation of Namibia is illegal and Shell must simply abide the law.'[22]

Shell's role in *South Africa* remained the focal point. Oil was the central issue, but Shell's involvement in undermining the coal boycott was also expounded in detail.

At the start of the campaign, *Shell management* formed the most important target group. After talks failed to bring accord, shareholder meetings were chosen as the forum best suited to exert pressure on the responsible Shell directors and commissioners.

The second group were the *employees*. Efforts to reach them via works councils and unions had little result at first. Their identification with the management seemed strong, but later – under influence from much criticism from society – the attitude of many employees changed.

Politicians were the third group at which the campaign was aimed. Politicians were quick to respond; a substantial parliamentary majority advocated an oil boycott. An official oil embargo would form the framework which could limit or even end the involvement of Shell and other companies in the apartheid economy. However, the actual implementation of the wishes of the House majority proved unattainable. The oil embargo had become such a sensitive political subject that in 1980 the Dutch government nearly collapsed due to its refusal 'to institute an oil boycott against South Africa now'. The Christian-Democratic Party became an important target for lobbying, since its position in the parliamentary debates was decisive. In some instances, communication with Christian-Democrat politicians was quite direct, but especially after the forced departure in 1983 of the party's spokesman on South Africa, Jan Nico Scholten, more indirect methods had to be sought. These included efforts to exert influence via church and trade union contacts.

Four Dutch organisations carried the campaign through the years. After Kairos had initiated the action, Pax Christi quickly offered its support. Later, the Holland Committee on Southern Africa and the Netherlands Organization for International Development Cooperation (Novib) joined in. The ensuing close cooperation among four quite diverse groups was remarkable by Dutch standards.

Kairos was a modest group, started in 1970 as a support group for Dr C.F. Beyers Naudé's Christian Institute for Southern Africa. The drive behind the Shell campaign was Kairos chairman Cor Groenendijk. The group received – also in the campaign against Shell – financial support from Dutch churches and worked closely with church bureaus. *Pax Christi Nederland* was part of the international Roman Catholic peace movement and had an authoritative Dutch bishop as its chairman. The *Holland Committee on Southern Africa* (HCSA, Komitee Zuidelijk Afrika) was founded in 1975 as a continuation of the Angola Comittee, set up in 1961, and became one of the most powerful Third World lobbies in the Netherlands. Finally, *Novib* is a large donor organisation which supports many projects in developing countries and serves the interests of the Third World in the Netherlands.

A strong coalition was created which was difficult to ignore politically and which had broad access to other social organisations and the media. Cooperation on the content of the activities and organisational preparations flowed in a supple manner. Research and operations were handled mostly through the HCSA and Kairos; the involvement of Novib and Pax Christi served to broaden the basis, as shown, for example, by a letter signed by Cardinal Willebrands in which the 1979 shareholder action was praised: 'The Diocesan Pastoral Council of the Archbishopric Utrecht is extremely pleased with the manner of presentation in a milieu where your ideals and proposals are not experienced as self-evident'.[23]

Five characteristics of the campaign can be distinguished:

1 *The objectives were fixed; the strategy was extremely flexible.* No one expected that Shell would immediately withdraw from South Africa. Yet the goal of the campaign remained firm, which gave the advantage of clarity, while at the same time allowing for some leeway. The organisations remained in negotiation with Shell on how sections of policy might be modified, but held on to the conviction that only the actual breaking of all ties between the Group and South Africa would be effective. The strategy, however, was frequently adjusted; the emphasis was on feasibility and effectiveness. When, for example, after several years the debates in parliament continued to lead nowhere, the campaign concentrated itself on lower government bodies.

2 *Opinion from South Africa: Growing enthusiasm for economic pressure.* In the 1970s it was no simple matter to obtain a true picture of South(ern) African opinion concerning sanctions and disinvestment. The liberation movements, ANC and SWAPO, had spoken out sharply, calling for comprehensive economic pressure, but this did not mean that this pressure was of the highest priority. Partly due to the influence of contacts with solidarity groups such as the HCSA and Kairos, and later due to the work of the Shipping Research Bureau, the conviction grew within the liberation movements that the oil embargo was an important weapon in the struggle against the apartheid regime. Intensive talks which started at the end of the 1970s with, among others, ANC president Oliver R. Tambo and the ANC's sanctions specialist in London, Dr Frene Ginwala, were a powerful stimulant for the solidarity groups to direct all their available energy to the campaign for an oil embargo and to exert pressure on Shell. The extent to which sanctions were valued by the ANC can be gleaned from a description of the first contacts between Oliver Tambo in exile and Nelson Mandela in prison. Tambo supported Mandela's plea for negotiations with Pretoria, but also added a warning: 'Look, there is only one problem: don't manoeuvre yourself into a situation where we have to abandon sanctions. That's the key problem. We are very concerned that we should not get stripped of our weapons of struggle, and the most important of these is sanctions. That is the trump card with which we can mobilize international opinion and pull governments over to our side.'[24]

Contacts in South Africa were a problem. Open debates over sanctions were out of the question; legislation was stringent, and pronouncements in favour of boycotts could lead to long prison sentences. In the first years of the campaign, individual contacts were cautiously pursued. In church circles criticism of apartheid became more sharply formulated, and especially after 1985, calls to exert economic pressure on the government were made by the South African Council of Churches, the Southern African Catholic Bishops' Conference and others. The trade unions, too, came to support the call for sanctions.

3   *Thorough investigations formed the basis for action.* Following the first report of OSACI, both HCSA and Kairos invested a great deal of energy in research. In 1980, the two organisations established the Shipping Research Bureau, which supplied much information on oil deliveries to South Africa by Shell. In later years the Bureau played an important role in the shareholder actions and especially in the internationalising of the campaign.

4   *Multifaceted action led to maximum participation.* The social basis of the campaign broadened as appeals were made to many people and organisations, each on their own level. For trade unions, international solidarity was a strong motivation to action. As the campaign received more support from the South African unions, support in the Netherlands also increased. The opinions of their South African partners provided a starting point for church organisations. Orders and congregations were confronted regarding their holdings, and many were prepared to sell their shares or to authorise activists to attend shareholders' meetings. Within universities Shell-affiliated scholarships, prizes, etc. were no longer accepted as a matter of course. A pattern was established in which nearly everyone could, in one way or another, contribute to the pressure on Shell. On a grassroots level, too, the strength of the campaign was made visible by divergent methods of support. Local action groups demonstrated at Shell filling stations; more that 100 Protestant church councils endorsed an appeal for the withdrawal of Shell from South Africa. Clergymen, mayors and city councillors let their voices be heard, as did scientists and artists.

5   *Internationalisation needed to tackle a multinational.* In 1975 Kairos started working closely with other, especially British, like-minded organisations. In addition, shareholder resolutions and the like were placed as advertisements in prominent European newspapers. In the campaign much emphasis was laid on United Nations declarations. Campaigners continued to reproach the Shell Group for its violations of the Rhodesian embargo and its refusal to follow the UN call for an oil embargo against South Africa. The UN Centre against Apartheid supported the campaign morally and, to a limited extent, financially. With the start of American actions in 1985, Shell's difficulties increased sharply, and the pressure took on a strong international character.

Shell isolated

For Shell the campaign was a new experience. Initially, it seemed that it wouldn't be too bad. Polite talks between gentlemen were not insuperable. Pressure exerted at shareholders' meetings, however, entailed much negative publicity. When the activists began to make use of shareholder rights as well, a change of the company's by-laws seemed necessary to severely limit the influence of small shareholders. When the campaign started to acquire a mass character, HCSA and Kairos were threatened by telex with legal action as the 'nature and composition of the campaign material are in considerable measure contrary to the care which is due in society'. The organisations distributed more than a million leaflets which resembled Shell material – in design only – but no legal steps were taken.

In 1980, in an effort to neutralise the work of the anti-apartheid organisations, Shell's European PR head advocated equal governmental support for pro-apartheid organisations in the Netherlands: 'The existing imbalance has the disadvantage that certain problems – such as the treatment of multinational companies – only receive broad public attention from an extremely one-sided minority viewpoint'.[25]

Not until 1985 did Shell realise that it could no longer keep up its reticent role, expressing little reaction in public to the campaign. The leaking of the *Pagan report*, which set forth a strategy intended to break the boycott, and had been commissioned by Shell Oil in the US, was a serious set-back. From this report – of which Shell Nederland denied all knowledge – and a multitude of talks between the company and social organisations, Shell's strategy after 1985 can be reconstructed as follows: (a) Acknowledge cautiously that in the past Shell was indeed too reticent with respect to apartheid and give the assurance that it is now doing everything in its power to make a contribution to peaceful change; (b) say that Shell does not disagree with its critics in their opinion of the inhumane system of apartheid, but is convinced that not running away from the problem will be more effective in the long term than disinvestment; the message that sanctions and boycotts are no solution must be clearly conveyed; (c) isolate radical critics as much as possible, but carry on talks with more moderate organisations. 'If religious groups join [the campaign], critical mass will be achieved making resolution of the boycott difficult,' Pagan warned.

It was a painful experience, however. Executives, shareholders and employees were beginning to feel uncomfortable. Consumers, too, were becoming increasingly reluctant to buy Shell products. Above all, the cost was great in time and energy, especially for management.

Shell top management was personally affected. In their personal contacts, they suffered as a result of the pressure on their company. Three examples: In an extensive interview in 1986, Wagner, then chairman of the supervisory board of Royal Dutch, described how the question of South Africa had led to painful estrangement from some of his cherished political friends. A year later Delft Technical University – which maintains close ties with Shell – withheld an honorary degree from Royal Dutch's president L.C. van Wachem. And in 1989 the city of Delft refused to allow one of its historic buildings to be rented for the farewell dinner of the president of Shell Nederland.

Shareholders were provoked. Year after year, dozens of speakers from the United States, Africa and Europe attended the shareholders' meetings to sharply criticise the company. On one occasion, the number of 'protest shareholders' totalled half of those with voting rights. Often one to two hours were spent addressing apartheid issues. Media coverage focussed on the protest. The address of Dr Beyers Naudé in 1989 made a big impression. His dignified speech was also printed in Shell publications. From their entrance, through drummers, banners and demonstrators, until the moment that the numerous 'protest shareholders' (accompanied by the media) left the hall singing, the ordinary shareholders, interested in little except dividend earnings, were irritated to distraction.

Shell employees were put on the defensive. During the first years of the campaign, it was taboo in the company to speak about the relationship between Shell and South Africa. Later on, more and more often employees were questioned on Shell's role. Confrontations occurred at work as critics distributed leaflets during company sporting events, organised massive 'Telephone Shell' actions (in the words of Bertolt Brecht, 'Evil has an address; it has a telephone number'), or set up blockades. In their private lives, too, employees were called upon to account for their employer's South African activities; they were confronted with posters and slogans along the motorways, statements by churches, unions, etc. and lots of publicity. The employees that took the courage to express their criticism of the South African policy of the Shell management within the company and even during the shareholders' meetings grew in number; Beyers Naudé commended them in his speech to the shareholders.

None so deaf as those who do not wish to hear: Dr Beyers Naudé addressing Royal Dutch shareholders at their annual meeting, 11 May 1989

Consumers were informed. Even though no formal consumer boycott was ever organised against Shell, motorists driving in for a fill-up were on occasion met by demonstrations. A 'Tanking Guide' was produced listing untainted brands and filling stations. From confidential surveys by Shell Nederland, it appeared that 'the general impression of respondents towards Shell has become less favourable since 1986 than towards other companies'. There was 'a (possibly increasing) critical group that has a well-founded negative opinion of Shell'.

Shell was tarnished. The 'shell' emblem suffered quite a few blows. Some large consumers such as municipalities refused to renew contracts. Shares held by churches, orders and congregations were sold. Trade unions and their affiliated banks revised their portfolio criteria. Actors refused to appear in Shell commercials or became objects of ridicule if they did. University newspapers cancelled their Shell advertisements. Sponsorships became the subject of painful debates, and museums, artists, educational institutions and others increasingly declined Shell funding. The degree of pressure felt by Shell from local governments was illustrated in 1989 by the lengthy letter of H. Hooykaas, president of Shell Nederland, to mayor and aldermen in The Hague, where Royal Dutch has its headquarters. The municipality was sternly warned about the consequences of a strict anti-apartheid – or anti-Shell – policy. Shell was further provoked when more than 60 municipalities decided on a preferential treatment of companies which had no ties with South Africa.

There was no significant support for the increasingly isolated company. Pro-apartheid groups offered their help, which was not warmly received by the management. The publication of the Pagan report strengthened distrust of Shell. In an analysis of the report, the magazine of the research bureau of the Christian-Democratic Party stated: 'What is so troublesome about such a report is that it allows no actual dialogue or opportunity to test company ethics against that of another group. Its point is not to find a morally responsible direction for Shell in regard to South Africa. The Pagan report is purely based on economic company interests which are in no way relativised with respect to other considerations, for example, those of a social or moral nature'.[26] Characteristic of Shell's isolation was that the magazine proved unwilling to print a response from Shell Nederland's Public Affairs director, M.J. van Rooijen – former State Secretary for the Christian-Democratic Party.

Political failures led to grim resistance

Despite the increase of both repression and resistance in South Africa, politicians in the Netherlands were seeking ways to soften the call for an oil embargo. The majority in parliament which supported an embargo failed to get legislation passed. The section on South Africa in the 1985 election programme of the Christian-Democrats, who were the strongest party in government, looked extremely weak. Even Shell's Wagner seemed to endorse the activist view on South Africa: 'The situation there is completely out of hand; they have gone berserk,' but Dutch politicians were unresponsive.

Then the fat caught fire. In September 1985 arson was committed at a Makro retail store, owned by SHV, a company with extensive holdings in South Africa. Responsibility for the attack, which caused about $16 million damage, was claimed by the group 'RaRa' (Revolutionary Anti-Racist Action). Extensive investigation by the Internal Security Service and the police failed to prevent new attacks. In the years that followed, eight more RaRa-claimed attacks struck South Africa-related targets. In addition, hoses were cut at a large number of Shell filling stations, not necessarily by the same group. RaRa left little doubt about its ideological stand in the struggle against world imperialism. At the same time it made clear that its struggle was an alternative, not a complement, to the existing forms of pressure exerted on Dutch businesses to break their ties with South Africa. Organisations which were active in the campaign against Shell had little sympathy for these grim strategies, which they feared would be counter-productive. Anti-apartheid supporters certainly had their reservations about the fact that these attacks had prompted SHV to withdraw from South Africa. Would a hard-line approach yet be more effective than legal means?

The attacks, which later also occurred in other places such as Scandinavia, attracted much public attention. Exact numbers are not available, but a Shell publication reported that the number of worldwide attacks on Shell service stations had fallen to 76 in 1991. 'At their peak, attacks were running at around 10 a week'.[27]

The 'Shell out of South Africa' committee (SuZa), which was started in October 1988 as a cooperation effort among various trade union groups, anti-apartheid activists, peace groups and radical movements, tried to bridge the gap between 'established' Shell critics and RaRa. New forms of action were sought that balanced on the edge of what was legally permitted. RaRa's actions were rejected, but the effectiveness of the anti-apartheid organisations was questioned; they were perhaps too civilised. SuZa organised an international day of action at Shell filling stations, fashioned its own 'celebration' of Shell's centennial at headquarters in The Hague and managed to temporarily obstruct a ship carrying South African coal in Rotterdam. Its most important effort was a large-scale blockade of the Shell laboratory in Amsterdam, in which an estimated 7500 activists took part. The 'blockade spectacle', which included many playful elements but also acquired a more serious character when police took action, was primarily intended to harm Shell's image. Shell attempted in vain to get a court order to require the 14 politicians who signed their support for the blockade to take another position. The event succeeded in stirring up discussion on South Africa at the laboratory, where many employees were disturbed by the blockade. Nevertheless, no less than 123 of them signed a letter to Group director Van Wachem requesting the withdrawal of Shell from South Africa.

On Shell's side, irritation had, not surprisingly, reached a high point. H. Hooykaas, the president of Shell Nederland, said in interviews that the pressure had become 'indecent'. 'The goal is not "Shell out of South Africa", but rather, "Break Shell",' he stated.

Judgement against the violent RaRa actions was widespread, and spokespersons for the ANC, too, left no doubt that these kinds of actions definitely brought South Africa no closer to freedom. For Shell, however, it seemed scarcely possible – or at least undesirable – to make a distinction between hard action such as that taken by RaRa and legal forms of protest. Directly and indirectly, Shell seized on the attacks as an opportunity to put their critics on the defensive. One indirect way was through Pagan International, which (on its own initiative?) had sent a letter to Dr Emilio Castro, the secretary-general of the World Council of Churches. In August 1988 this organisation – much to the regret of Shell – called on churches to support the campaign. In October 1987 Pagan had written to Castro concerning his leaked report, stating: 'Most regrettable of all is that the stolen document has also been placed in the hands of Dutch activists that have a sorry track record for violent behavior. If violence and personal injury result from this ill-gotten and carelessly shared information, the responsibility will have to rest with those who sent it.' The reaction of the World Council was unequivocal: 'You are accusing the bona fide anti-apartheid groups in the Netherlands of violent behaviour whereas you should know that they have denied their involvement and have clearly distanced themselves from violent acts against Shell petrol stations ... The second possibility is that you know of other activists who have received the document and who are responsible for the damage done to several Shell service stations. In this case you have done more thorough research than the police who have never been able to identify the perpetrators. If you know more than the police in the Netherlands, I would advise you to share this information with them.'[28]

When questioned, Shell declared in 1988 that it 'never had directed accusations toward the Working Group Kairos, the Holland Committee on Southern Africa or the Shipping Research Bureau concerning involvement in or responsibility for physical attacks and violence directed at Shell'.[29] One year later, however, John Kilroe, chairman of Shell SA and a former director of Shell Netherlands Refinery, stated on Dutch television: 'I think that the average Dutch citizen is probably appalled that taxpayers' money is sometimes used, through subsidies, by groups who end up burning down service stations and create a system where violence and terrorism is, if one is not careful, something which becomes acceptable'.[30]

Dilemmas for Shell

Two questions seemed to comprise Shell's biggest dilemmas.

Who is responsible? 'Is the water company responsible if I drown my mother-in-law in the bathtub?' exclaimed a Shell spokesman during a public debate. The public's reaction was a counter-question: 'Wasn't the gas supplier in Auschwitz partly responsible for the mass murders?' The public debates were decidedly not devoid of emotion; talks behind closed doors, however, often went further than just an exchange of accusations by both sides. Questions regarding the social responsibility of a company with global operations are difficult to answer. It is noteworthy that in the Netherlands only few ethicists pursued this theme; the first substantial ethical study on Shell and South Africa was not published until 1991.[31]

Shell grappled much more with internal communications and patterns of responsibility than with the question of external social responsibility. The autonomy of operating companies was a cornerstone of the Shell philosophy. However, the Pagan report observed that 'Critics do not accept Shell statements concerning operational autonomy. They link all affiliates together as sources of profit for and potential pressure points against Royal Dutch/Shell.' For three reasons many critics indeed did not seem inclined to accept Shell's argument: (1) Adams concluded that 'decentralisation can be useful for a host of reasons related to industrial relations, pressure groups, governments and markets. However, studies have shown that in reality there are powerful centralising forces in the MNCs. Thus, while executives often state publicly (and perhaps believe) their companies are decentralised, the reverse is often closer to the truth; "an ideology of decentralisation ... marks a reality of centralisation." The centralisation of research, the standardisation of financial and management techniques, ethics and attitudes all help to produce a centralisa-

Selling Botha his pumpernickel

Shell Oil Company's involvement in South Africa appears to be generating increased pressure on it both in Europe and the United States. Issue No. 11 of the newsletter, Oil Embargo Against South Africa, of April 1988, published by the Shipping Research Bureau in Amsterdam, reports that Congressman Bob Wise of West Virginia has presented to Congress a bill requiring U.S. based oil companies to disinvest from South Africa within 12 months or be prohibited from acquiring U.S. federal coal, oil or gas leases.

Shell Oil U.S.A., the multinational's American subsidiary, is said to make heavy use of federal leases and would be seriously affected by the bill. A senior spokesman of Shell Nederland told a public meeting in the Netherlands that if the Wise bill (The Anti-Apartheid Petroleum Sanctions Act) becomes law, Shell will seriously consider withdrawing from South Africa.

On the European front, the faculty of medicine of the University of Tromso in Norway declined to accept funds from

Shell Norway to support a medical research project. The reason for rejecting the grant of about one million Norwegian crowns (US$160 000) was the activities of the Royal Dutch/Shell Group in South Africa.

In Britain, Shell U.K. lost a contract to supply oil products to the Sheffield municipality early this year because of its activities in South Africa. The contract was worth £1.8 million.

Shell also had trouble in the Netherlands in March when 35 of its petrol stations were vandalised causing damage estimated at U.S.$160 000. An anonymous press release claimed that the petrol stations were attacked because of Shell's activities in South Africa.

More municipal pressure was brought to bear in March when 23 mayors of major cities in the United States and 83 mayors of major cities in Europe released a statement calling on Royal Dutch/Shell to withdraw from South Africa. The General Board of the United States Methodist Church endorsed a boycott of Shell in February, stating that "only

through the support of international oil corporations to the apartheid regime can that oppressive system survive."

The newsletter quotes a spokesman of Shell Norway, Mr. Carl Johan Sverdrup, as saying in an interview with the Norwegian weekly *Dag og Tid:* "Shell feels the effects of the boycott in Norway, Sweden, Denmark, the Netherlands, and partly in the U.S.A. In other countries we are not affected, and it is only in Norway, Sweden and Denmark that the boycott has an economic effect worth mentioning."

Asked whether Shell had no scruples in selling its products to the South African military and police, he said this was just the consequence of being present in a country. "Neither politically, nor in a practical way, are our petroleum products to be blamed for the policies of the South African government. To put it in a demagogic way; from the fact that Hitler ate pumpernickel, it does not follow that there is anything wrong with pumpernickel".

Yes – but would it have been right to keep him happy by selling him his favourite food? ∎

The Southern African Economist, June/July 1988

tion of control. Royal Dutch/Shell is no exception.'[32] (2) A more specific criticism was based on Shell's record with regard to the embargo against Rhodesia. In spite of strong denials by the company, it appeared that at headquarters both in London and The Hague, much more was known of the embargo violations than was ever admitted. (3) Finally, it was recognised that the company sometimes encountered problems over differences in company culture between Cape Town, London and The Hague. Yet, partly because of the systematic circulation of executives, there was, especially in London but also in The Hague, much knowledge available on the working methods of Shell South Africa. A noticeable paradox exists in the way in which Shell spokespersons, on the one hand, laid the full responsibility for South African policy on the South African subsidiary but, on the other, did not hesitate to hold organisations such as HCSA and Kairos responsible for violent actions not undertaken by them.

To stay or to go? Should the interests of 2500 local Shell employees be placed before the fate of South Africa's black majority? In 1986 Group chairman Van Wachem said there was no dilemma, since the presence of Shell in South Africa served the interests of all residents.

Three factors seemed essential for Shell. The first was the *economic motive*: southern Africa was an important market; Shell SA, which served large parts of that market, was a healthy and very profitable business. Only if serious economic damage would be inflicted upon the company by its remaining in South Africa, could this force its withdrawal. At a certain stage, pressure in the US forced the company to consider disinvestment as a real possibility.

A second motive to stay was to avoid a *precedent*. What consequences would a withdrawal from South Africa have for the company's presence in other countries? What would be the next conflict, and who would be the next special interest group to interfere with the company's activities? The environmental movement? Moreover, the fear was expressed that once Shell withdrew from South Africa the way back might not be so easy, and the market might be lost forever.

A third motive concerned Shell's own *personnel* and its *corporate image*. Much valuable management time was taken up by the issue of South Africa. At the time of the laboratory blockade, the president of Shell Nederland stated in an interview that he spent one third of his time on the issue. Unrest among the company's personnel was also a matter of concern. Yet, the two motives first mentioned seemed to be decisive in strengthening Shell's determination to stay.

The results of the campaign

What was achieved in 18 years of campaigning? A provisional tally gives the following picture.

Shell remained, but it was prepared to accept a new policy in South Africa. The public and political profile was changed radically; personnel policy was also changed. Never before had the company spent so much time and energy on extending information on a similar political problem.

Other companies were not particularly envious of the Royal Dutch/Shell Group: the avoidance of similar pressure was worth a lot. Decisions made by other companies to withdraw, or not to invest in South Africa and do no business there, were strongly influenced by the nature and scope of the pressure on Shell. Although other oil companies were also pressurised to break their ties with South Africa, no other company came under as much fire as the Royal Dutch/Shell Group.

Trade unions faced an often difficult choice between international solidarity and protecting the interests of their own members. Verbally, the choice was fairly simple; yet the reality proved recalcitrant, for example, when it came to the question of whether employment in Rotterdam harbour could be maintained. The unionists – in consultation with their South African colleagues – certainly exerted pressure, but they also became aware of their limitations. For example, unionists had great hesitation in applying their economic power to influence portfolio decisions of pension funds.

Churches and church bodies had largely the same problems as trade unions. They, too, were placed in a dilemma. They wanted to follow the calls from South Africa for sanctions but were confronted with the views of their members, for instance those who worked for Shell. It wasn't until the campaign was already in an advanced stage that the position of church-affiliated Shell employees was recognised as a problem, and meetings were organised to discuss existing tensions. The biggest dilemma for the churches, however, was turning pronouncements into policy. The campaign 'Does you money support apartheid?' (1986), intended to increase the awareness of the economic aspects of apartheid and Dutch involvement in it, brought up difficult aspects when the question was put as 'Are our church funds used to support apartheid or businesses with interests in apartheid?' In the Reformed ('Gereformeerde') Churches in the Netherlands, stock portfolios were purged; in the Netherlands Reformed ('Nederlands Hervormde') Church, intense debates led to a stalemate between supporters and opponents, and to frustration.

Most Dutch politicians have little reason to look back with pride on the time of the campaign for an oil embargo and against Shell. The inability of the parliament to pass adequate embargo legislation against Rhodesia and South Africa offered an unedifying spectacle. The organisations which had campaigned for an oil embargo found little satisfaction in what had (or had not) happened on the political level. Trust in politics was seriously undermined. For politicians, too, it was a difficult experience. Former Foreign Affairs Minister Hans van den Broek is not noted for his tendency to look back with regret at views he has taken. On his own role in the parliamentary discussions on the oil and coal boycott, however, he is critical: 'In the House I said that the Dutch government would welcome voluntary measures taken by business and industry. I find that now an extraordinarily gratuitous remark. What was the consequence? That I stimulated business concerns to stop doing business with South Africa. I don't believe you can do that as minister. If the government refuses to economically isolate South Africa, you cannot say to business and industry: you do it then. Because that in fact means that you leave business at the mercy of campaigners. And I would not want business to become a sort of plaything of the campaigners.'[33]

The *campaigning organisations* can look back on a long period in which a lot happened but the objective (Shell out of South Africa) was not realised. There are, however, some compensations. In part because of these kinds of campaigns, the economic pressure on the apartheid regime was extremely strong. The call of the liberation movements and other South African organisations for disinvestment and boycotts found much sympathy in the Netherlands. The rift in the Dutch government policy between strong denouncements of apartheid and the unwillingness to take radical measures became visible for more and more people. For the activists, too, the Shell campaign was a learning process, in which many received more insight into the interweaving of racism and economic power. Although many elements of the campaign, such as the shareholder actions, inspired other organisations, for example those campaigning on environmental issues or the Third World debt issue, too little attention was given to the response of the larger South African public, in spite of good contacts with South African partners.

Between the Royal Dutch/Shell Group and many of its critics, communications remained open. Too much of the communication, however, consisted of the repetition of identical moves. There was no shortage of clarity. As Kairos chairman Cor Groenendijk put it in 1986 in a conversation with Van Wachem: 'I'll say it straight to your face – you are a collaborator.' Neither was there a shortage of initiatives by Shell to improve policies in several smaller issues. But the fundamentals stayed solid. On both sides.

Answers in the future

It will take some time before the balance can be drawn up. South Africa's oil secrets have by far not all been revealed. Details are still surfacing. In December 1993, the South African Energy Minister, George Bartlett, revealed that Shell and Total had purchased their own crude oil during the sanction years, while the South African government provided oil 'for companies that no longer could get supplies from their parent companies'.[34] The explanation was rather at odds with the picture that had been created by statements made by Shell spokesmen in London and The Hague over the years.

An interview that Albert Nothnagel, South African ambassador in The Hague, gave on his departure from the Netherlands in 1994 showed that the years of pressure on the Royal Dutch/Shell Group had not been without effect. Nothnagel told how in January 1990 he reported to his government that Shell topman Van Wachem wanted to see 'visible results', 'so that the pressure on Shell would ease off a bit'. Whereupon Foreign Minister Pik Botha phoned and told the ambassador: 'Albert, just say that a big announcement is coming.'[35] On 2 February 1990, De Klerk announced in parliament that Mandela would be freed and that the ban on the ANC and all other parties would be abolished.

Annex: Twelve forms of international pressure on Royal Dutch/Shell[36]

• May 1986: The Methodist Church (UK) disposes of its 220,000 shares in the Shell Transport and Trading Co., worth £1.5 m. The British Council of Churches and the United Reformed Church take similar decisions.

• September 1986: ANC and SWAPO make a joint declaration in which the campaign against Shell is strongly supported.

• November 1986: Negotiations between the Isolate South Africa Committee and the Shell Dealers Association of Sweden lead to a joint delegation being sent to London to plea for the withdrawal of Shell from South Africa and Namibia.

• March 1987: The British Anti-Apartheid Movement launches its 'Year against Shell' campaign. Referring to the withdrawal of Barclays Bank, a spokesman of the AAM says: 'In 1986 it was the year of Barclays, this year will be the year of Shell. Within a year they will have to reconsider their decision to keep dealing with apartheid'.

• May 1987: The United Mine Workers of America and 25 other trade unions place an advertisement in the British *Independent* and the European edition of the *Wall Street Journal*.

• June 1987: The Danish South Africa Committee reports the results of their eight-month action: The municipality of Aalborg has broken a one-year contract with Shell worth £357,000, just as eight other town councils have also decided to boycott Shell. The public transport company in Copenhagen also changed its oil supplier. One of the largest Danish newspapers, *Politiken*, accepts no more advertisements from Shell.

• August 1987: The Danish association of cooperative housing companies stops buying Shell products. The amount of money involved, 200 million Danish crowns (about $25 m), is the largest amount so far lost by Shell in Denmark from a single consumer.

• March 1988: The United Church in Australia adopts a resolution 'to encourage the councils and members of the church to write to the Royal Dutch/Shell Group or take other peaceful action to register their disapproval of the operations of the company in the Republic of South Africa'.

• August 1988: The Central Committee of the World Council of Churches, meeting in Hanover, 'encourages the churches to support the International Campaign to boycott the Shell Oil Corporation' (i.e. the Royal Dutch/Shell Group).

• March 1989: At its congress in Harare, the Miners International Federation takes the decision 'to pressurise the Royal Dutch/Shell Group to disinvest from South Africa'.

• January 1989: An imminent three-year sponsoring agreement between Norske Shell and the Norwegian Football Association is foiled when in a last-minute decision the Association says no to the contract, following the policy adopted by other sports organisations. Under the agreement, the first division would be redubbed the 'Shell League'.

• September 1989: The United Nations World Health Organisation (WHO) will no longer supply its staff members with Shell petrol coupons.

Just before completing this book, the SRB laid its hands on copies of some highly 'Confidential and Personal' South African documents, which made it possible to uncover one of the closest guarded secrets of the sanctions era: the role of the international oil companies in supplying their South African branches with oil during the embargo years. From the early 1980s onwards, the oil majors repeatedly claimed that none of their companies outside South Africa were involved in supplies to their 'independent' South African subsidiaries and that they were not aware how the latter obtained their crude oil. These documents from within the country's energy bureaucracy – which were never intended for publication – provide conclusive evidence to the contrary. In December 1993, Minister Bartlett stated that Shell SA and Total SA had been allowed to import their own crude oil; we are now able to show that the parent companies were knowingly involved.

1. Part of a review of South Africa's 1981 long-term crude oil import contracts (Annex to a letter dated 2 October 1981 of D.F. Mostert, Director of SFF Association, Johannesburg, to the Director General at the Ministry of Mineral and Energy Affairs in Cape Town, in Afrikaans). *Overeenkomste*: contracts; *vate/dag*: barrels/day; *ton/jaar*: tons/year; *Kontrak termyn*: contract term; *Saoedi*: Saudi; *Termyn*: term contract; *Sê*: Say (this refers to columns with prices, not shown here). 1.1–1.4: SFF contracts; in section 2.2.3 of his letter, Mostert wrote that SFF bought oil from Brunei *through BP* ('Deur bemiddeling van BP word 300 000 ton Seria olie vanaf Brunei (2,2%) gekoop').

)eenkomste	Volume (vate/dag)	Massa (ton/jaar)	Kontrak termyn
SPF			
1.1 Deuss:			
1.1.1 Saoedi	120 000	6 000 000	1/1/81-31/12/83
1.1.2 Oman	40 000	2 000 000	1/2/80-31/1/83
1.2 Brunei/BP	6 000	300 000	1/1/81-31/12/82
1.3 Gabon	10 000	500 000	1/4/81-31/3/82
1.4 Harimpex	50 000	1 250 000	1/7/81-31/12/81
SHELL	44 000	2 200 000	Termyn Sê Arab Light
TOTAL	24 000	1 200 000	Termyn Sê Arab Light
CALTEX	10 000	500 000	1/1/81-31/12/81 Gabon
	304 000	13950 000	

2. From a letter which Mostert/SFF wrote to the Director General of Mineral and Energy Affairs, 13 April 1982 (headed 'GEHEIM', secret). *Translation*: 3. The Position of the Republic of South Africa. 3.1. Currents contracts. (a) Transworld Oil 120,000 b/d Arabian Light (renegotiable 31-12-1983). (b) Transworld Oil 40,000 b/d Oman Light (ren. 31-12-1984). (c) Marc Rich 10,000 b/d Seria (ren. 31-12-1982). (d) Marimpex 25,000 b/d Russian oil (ren. 31-12-1982). (e) Shell 46,000 b/d (indirectly from Shell International Trading Co.). During the first quarter of 1982, crude oil has been delivered to Shell SA from Brunei, Iran and the UAE. (f) Total 19,000 b/d (indirectly from Compagnie Française Pétrole [Total parent company]. During the first quarter of 1982 crude oil has been imported from Saudi Arabia and Brunei.

```
3    DIE RSA-POSISIE

     3.1  Huidige kontrakte

          (a)  Transworld Oil 120 000 vate per dag Arab Light.
               (Heronderhandelbaar 31.12.83).

          (b)  Transworld Oil 40 000 vate per dag Oman.
               (Heronderhandelbaar 31.12.84).

          (c)  Marc Rich 10 000 vate per dag Seria.  (Her-
               onderhandelbaar 31.12.82).

          (d)  Marimpex 25 000 vate per dag Russiese olie.
               (Heronderhandelbaar 31.12.82).

          (e)  Shell 46 000 vate per dag (indirek vanaf Sitco)
               Gedurende die eerste kwartaal van 1982 is ru-
               olie uit Brunei, Iran en Arabiese Emirate aan
               Shell SA gelewer.

          (f)  Total 19 000 vate per dag (indirek vanaf CFP).
               Gedurende die eerste kwartaal van 1982 is ru-
               olie uit Saoedi-Arabië en Brunei ingevoer.
```

3. From a document, ref. N27/6/3/2/2 GE, entitled 'Ru-olie benodigdhede van die S.A. raffinaderye' ('Crude Oil Requirements of SA Refineries') and signed by Mr F.K. Siebrits of the Ministry of Mineral and Energy Affairs on 3 November 1982. *Translation*: Two of the companies, Shell and Total, are still able to provide for themselves through the kind offices of their parent companies [in 1983]. On account of the pressure exerted on their parent companies in the form of sanctions threats, all the other companies prefer that SFF supplies them with crude oil through government purchases.

```
     3.  Twee van die maatskappye, te wete Shell en Total, kan

     nog daarin slaag om deur bemiddeling van hul moedermaatskappye

     in hulle eie behoeftes te voorsien.  Al die ander maatskappye

     het weens druk in die vorm van sanksie-dreigemente op hul

     moedermaatskappye verkies dat SFF deur middel van Staatsaankope

     in hulle ru-olie behoeftes voorsien.
```

Anatomy of a Boycott
The Royal Dutch/Shell Campaign in the US

DONNA KATZIN*

Royal Dutch/Shell did not withdraw from South Africa. And yet, after organisers waged a seven-year campaign against the company in 14 countries on three continents, they ended their boycott by declaring victory. Their triumph was the boycott's catalytic role in galvanising the anti-apartheid movement and focussing its effective economic and psychological pressure on Pretoria at the height of the anti-apartheid movement. As a result of such campaigns and the intense struggle waged by the South Africans themselves, legislated apartheid gave way to a democratisation of power, the announcement of the country's first multiracial elections, and the democratic movement's consequent call to lift sanctions. Moreover, the boycott helped strengthen international alliances which laid the foundation for ongoing work for economic justice and corporate responsibility in the emerging South Africa.

The Shell boycott in the United States was a multifaceted example of the broad range of strategies which were brought to bear on Royal Dutch/Shell (Royal Dutch/Shell is a Anglo-Dutch transnational corporation, owned 60 per cent by the Royal Dutch Petroleum Company, based in The Hague, and 40 per cent by Shell Transport and Trading Company, based in London). For that reason the US boycott is an instructive case study of the campaign – its strengths, weaknesses, and lessons for future efforts to influence the conduct of multinational corporations and to achieve democracy in South Africa, and elsewhere.

The boycott unfolds

> *One of our members died accidentally because of the carelessness of the [Shell-owned Rietspruit coal-mine] management, so our members desired to hold a memorial service. The company refused. Our members went ahead, they held a service. Then after that the company decided to fire 86 workers. They called the South African police to come and take out those workers through the barrel of the gun. Those who were on strike in solidarity with those who were fired were forced to go underground, were assaulted as well, were tear gassed. We tried to negotiate with Shell. It refused to negotiate with us.*
> James Motlatsi, President of the National Union of Mineworkers of South Africa[1]

* Director, Shared Interest (a fund for social investment in South Africa established by the FREESA Development Fund for South Africa), New York. Until September 1994, Donna Katzin was the director of South Africa Programs at the Interfaith Center on Corporate Responsibility.

Squatter family by their home outside Villiersdorp (1991)

The boycott was launched in the US in January 1986. The United Mine Workers of America (UMWA) was the first to respond to Shell's dismissal and intimidation of organised workers at its 50 per cent-owned Rietspruit coal-mine, which began in 1985. At the initiation of UMWA, the major United States labour federation, the AFL-CIO, threw its weight behind the struggle of the South African mine workers. Together with the African-American-led Free South Africa Movement (which had previously led civil disobedience actions at the South African consulate), UMWA followed the lead of the Dutch anti-apartheid movement by calling a press conference to launch the boycott against Shell Oil (Royal Dutch/Shell's wholly owned US subsidiary). The boycott soon grew to include major institutions in labour (such as the United Auto Workers) and the civil rights movement (including the National Association for the Advancement of Colored People and Southern Christian Leadership Council).

By the spring of 1987, the *Chicago Tribune* reported: 'At a time when consumer boycotts often prove impotent, a union-prodded boycott against Royal Dutch/Shell Group shows surprising vigor, calculation, and ability to nettle the opposition.'[2] It also spread, quickly and deliberately, to galvanise other constituencies which were key to the US anti-apartheid movement. The religious community responded rapidly to the campaign. Although boycotts have not traditionally been readily espoused by members of the US faith community, the Shell boycott was an exception.

The petroleum industry, after all, was highly strategic, given that oil is virtually the only critical natural resource South Africa lacks. A leader in that industry, Shell South

Africa was one of the largest international processors and retailers of petroleum products in the country, with a network of 853 petrol stations, or 18 per cent of South Africa's petrol retail market in 1986. Shell was also reported to be the only international oil company which had continued to supply oil to South Africa in large quantities, in defiance of the oil embargo imposed by the United Nations in 1979.[3] A mainstay of South Africa's petroleum, mining and chemical industries, Royal Dutch/Shell was considered a company whose withdrawal would send shock waves through the economic and political bedrock of South African society.

Moreover, as the largest transnational corporation in the world (in terms of assets), Royal Dutch/Shell symbolised the international exploitation of human and natural resources which had characterised first the colonial, then the apartheid political economy of South Africa. Its subsidiaries around the world provided a unique opportunity for a coordinated transnational campaign by labour, religious and anti-apartheid organisations to change the behaviour of the biggest transnational company on earth.

Several months after the launch of the boycott in the US, the Interfaith Center on Corporate Responsibility (ICCR) took up the campaign by adding Shell to its list of 12 corporate 'Partners in Apartheid' – ICCR's 'dirty dozen'. The ICCR, a coalition of some 250 religious institutional investors, worked with its member Protestant denominations, Roman Catholic communities and Jewish institutions to put pressure on Shell US, the ultimate goal being that it would in turn insist that its corporate parent withdraw operations from South Africa. That year several church groups sold their shares of stock in Shell Transport and Trading Company. These included the National Council of the Churches of Christ, whose holdings in the company at the time were valued at approximately $1 million.

Other institutions followed suit. The Los Angeles County Board of Investments divested $15 million in the company's stock, while Harvard University divested $31 million.

By 1988, endorsers of the Shell boycott included the World Council of Churches, the National Council of the Churches of Christ in the USA, and mainstream denominations such as the Episcopal Church in the USA, United Methodist Church, Unitarian Universalist Association of Congregations, the American Baptist Churches and United Church of Christ. A number of Roman Catholic communities, such as the Adrian Dominican Sisters and Sisters of Mercy of Brooklyn, also endorsed the boycott.

The strategy was clear and supported by South African leaders like Archbishop Desmond Tutu, who stated on 3 May 1988:

We applaud the actions by the U.S. religious community and others in support of full sanctions and complete corporate withdrawal from the land of apartheid. Such lobbying, investor initiatives, and consumer actions, like the Shell boycott, are sending a clear message to the Congress and those corporations with continuing ties to South Africa. Such economic pressures may be the international instrument to help bring Pretoria to its senses and justice to our land – without which there can be no genuine lasting peace.

Creative tactics

Having won an unprecedented and energising victory with the passage of the Comprehensive Anti-Apartheid Act of 1986 (over President Reagan's veto), the movement turned its
attention to implementing the new law and focussing on specific companies. Shell was a
prime target. In turn, the boycott's strategic alliance and ongoing coordination of labour,
religious and civil rights organisations captured the imagination of the movement and
precipitated a plethora of creative new anti-apartheid tactics.

Investors' strategies began along traditional lines. Activist labour and religious shareholders in the US met with Shell representatives in an attempt to convince them to press
their parent company to terminate its operations in South Africa. Those religious and
other institutional investors with South Africa divestment policies sold their shares in
Royal Dutch/Shell. In the case of the US this was significant, since most managers of
investment portfolios focussed on screening US companies. Royal Dutch/Shell was the
major foreign-based multinational divestment target as a result of the campaign.

A second shareholder initiative, led by the American Baptist Churches and New York
City's employee retirement funds, was the campaign for an 'extraordinary meeting' of the
Royal Dutch Petroleum stockholders on an 'issue of importance' – its operations in South
Africa. According to the company's by-laws, the owners of 10 per cent of the corpora-
tion's stock can call for such a convocation. The effort paralleled the Dutch anti-apart-
heid movement's attempts to be heard at Royal Dutch Petroleum's annual meetings in the
Netherlands, where shareholder concerns about the company's South African operations
were not placed on the agenda.

The 'extraordinary meeting' strategy succeeded in educating major institutional shareholders about the role of Royal Dutch/Shell in South Africa. Moreover, it demonstrated
the support for this initiative by owners of 6 per cent of the outstanding shares – including
major financial institutions such as Mellon and Wells Fargo Bank and State Street Boston
Corporation. This was a major feat, given the mammoth size of the corporation. Moreover, by raising the issue of shareholder rights to have their concerns placed on the agenda
of an annual meeting, it helped to raise the profile and increase the perceived legitimacy of
the boycott.

Legislative strategies also extended and deepened support for the boycott. On the national
level, anti-apartheid forces and the United Mine Workers of America campaigned for and
obtained an addition to Congressman Dellums' amendment to the Comprehensive Anti-
Apartheid Act of 1986. The resulting 'Anti-Apartheid Petroleum Sanctions Act' (H.R.
3317), which was approved by the US House of Representatives, was known as the 'Wise
amendment'; it was introduced by Congressman Bob Wise of West Virginia, a coal-pro-
ducing state, of which the legislative agenda reflects the concerns of its large population
of mine workers. The bill would have denied US federal oil, coal and natural gas leases to
companies which sold petroleum to South Africa.

In an interview shortly before he retired in 1989, Shell South Africa's Chairman John
Wilson noted:

Recently I was asked: "Can you never see Shell moving?" The answer to that is: No, I would not say that at all. There are factors beyond our control which could force us to leave. For example, if the Dellums Bill were promulgated in its original form, it would force out not only Shell, but the whole of the international oil business.[4]

Though there was never sufficient support in the Senate to pass the Dellums amendment, the oil companies paid dearly for their lobbying to defeat the Wise component. Shell's federal leases for exploration in states like Louisiana and California made the company particularly vulnerable to provisions of H.R. 3317 and determined to lobby against it.

At the same time there were a number of legislative victories on the local level. Mayors of 23 US cities and the National Black Caucus of State Legislators endorsed the Shell boycott. Eleven cities joined the ranks of more than 100 national organisations, as well as local academic, religious, labour and civic institutions, by declaring themselves 'Shell-Free Zones' and ending their purchase of Shell products. These municipalities included New York, Boston, Philadelphia, Seattle, Berkeley and New Haven.

These local victories were accelerated by diverse and creative grassroots tactics, which helped create the climate for legislative initiatives. One of the most successful organising tools was the *media campaign* waged in Boston with the help of the most popular disc jockey of the city's top-rated radio station, WBCN. Working closely with religious and anti-apartheid activists, D.J. Charles Laquidara introduced a hard-hitting daily sequence entitled 'Shell Shock'. Over a period of several months, he and guest experts supplied information about Shell's South Africa connections, answered callers' questions and encouraged listeners to boycott Shell. He specifically invited listeners to cut their Shell credit cards in half and send them in to the station (listeners without cards were encouraged to apply – and cut up their cards upon receiving them). Response to the programme was electric. Cards poured into the station, and special guests (including the city's mayor and the starting pitcher of the Boston Red Sox baseball team) came into the studio to cut up their cards on the air.

Other *activist strategies* spread the boycott into churches and synagogues, local unions, campuses and clubs. These included letter and postcard campaigns, individual and institutional 'no buy pledges', distribution of 'Shell *Dis*credit Cards'. Direct action abounded. There were prayer vigils, pickets and demonstrations at Shell stations and offices – some on a regular basis, others on special days such as Human Rights Day and the anniversaries of the Sharpeville and Soweto massacres in South Africa.

In dozens of cities, activists lobbied local managers of Shell service stations in an attempt to convince them to sell other companies' products instead of Shell's. In some cases dealers were convinced to change brands and even joined the campaign to get others to follow suit.

Perhaps the most successful local campaign took place in the state of New Jersey to move the governor not to renew Shell's $250 million five-year contract to operate service stations along the state's major highway. The campaign to 'Get the Shell off the Turnpike' succeeded. The Governor's decision in February 1991 to terminate the company's contract was the most significant financial penalty imposed to date on Shell as a result of its parent's South Africa ties.

Shell's counter-campaign

Early in 1987, ICCR received a leaked copy of a secret 254-page strategy document commissioned by Shell Oil to counter the US boycott. Though the plan was not fully implemented (partially due to the fact that it was publicly exposed before it could be put into effect), it provided a rare glimpse into those aspects of the boycott which Shell found most threatening – and the strategies it devised to deflect them.

The document (code-named the *Neptune strategy*) carefully outlined strategies to reduce the impact and control the spread of the boycott in the labour, religious, academic and civil rights communities, as well as in media, government and international circles. Though it appears that Shell did not 'buy' all components of the plan, it did attempt to carry out several – particularly those aimed at religious organisations. The faith community was viewed as the key to containment of the boycott.

This was not surprising, given the experience of Pagan International, the Washington-based consulting firm which produced the document. Its Chief Executive Officer, Rafael Pagan, himself the son of an Episcopal minister, had formerly headed the Nestlé Nutrition Center, where he was responsible for countering the boycott Nestlé faced in response to infant formula abuses. Mr Pagan had been instrumental in negotiating the settlement between religious and activist groups and Nestlé in 1984, which concluded the boycott.

In its 'Religious Groups Strategy' section, the Pagan report noted:

> Mobilized members of religious communions provide a "critical mass" of public opinion and economic leverage that should not be taken lightly.
> It can be assumed that as long as apartheid continues as the official policy of the Republic of South Africa, Shell South Africa's presence there will be offensive to and attacked by many religious and ethical persons in the U.S. The Royal Dutch Shell Group has taken the position that it plans to stay in South Africa. The churches represent the "critical mass" of opposition. If they join the boycott and pressure for disinvestment, it

will become a radically different and far more costly problem than it now is.[5]

The basic thrust of the Neptune strategy was to engage current and potential boycott supporters and turn their attention away from the campaign. The introduction to the religious groups section of the Neptune document concludes:

> To engage the ecumenical institution, churches and critical spokespersons in postapartheid planning should deflect their attention away from the boycott and disinvestment efforts and direct their vision and energy into productive channels.[6]

Though a number of meetings with religious 'targets' had been carried out by the time ICCR received a copy of the Neptune plan in 1987, the strategy backfired. When religious supporters learned about Shell's intentions to deter them from backing the boycott, they reacted instead by strengthening their support for the campaign. They distanced themselves from such groupings as the Council on Southern Africa (COSA) – a self-appointed and Pagan-encouraged group of religious leaders supposedly opposed to sanctions. They also shunned events focussing on 'post-apartheid South Africa', which reflected the anti-sanctions, anti-boycott agendas of Shell and other companies.

Shell's Neptune strategy exposed the company's fear of the legitimacy and catalytic role which religious institutions could lend to the boycott. Clearly, the company understood that faith-based organisations not only had the capacity to shape the attitudes, behaviour and consumption of their millions of members, but also to work collaboratively with other key constituencies, such as the labour and civil rights movements and academia. The company demonstrated its concern that such multisectoral, multidimensional support for the boycott could spread the campaign and increase its impact dramatically. The fact that Shell invested more than $100,000 in the project bears witness to the company's recognition that expanded and intensified support for the boycott had the potential to affect its bottom line.

The boycott: Strengths, weaknesses and implications

When organisers decided to lift the Shell boycott officially, following Nelson Mandela's call for the lifting of international sanctions against South Africa on 24 September 1993, Shell had not withdrawn from South Africa. And yet, though the boycott had begun to lose momentum several years before then, it had achieved a number of successful, in some cases unforeseen results.

Outcomes

The boycott had a decided impact on Royal Dutch/Shell – short of pulling it out of South Africa. First, the campaign caused Shell to incur substantial liabilities. In addition to the billions of dollars of business lost as a direct result of the boycott, Shell paid the 'apartheid premium' of its international public relations measures and strategic planning to circumvent and undermine the boycott.

The boycott also sullied Shell's image among socially concerned customers, including workers, students, anti-apartheid and religious activists, socially responsible investors and communities of colour. Though it is not possible to place a dollar value on this factor, it was sufficient to cause the company concern. 'Shell' even virtually became a dirty word in states like New Jersey, where people campaigned to 'Get the Shell off the Turnpike'.

To enhance its deteriorating image in the face of the Rietspruit crisis and ensuing boycott, Shell began to pump money into public relations and corporate responsibility programmes in South Africa. It published a series of costly advertisements declaring its support for democracy and human rights in South African newspapers such as the *Weekly Mail* and expanded its own programmes for employees and their communities. Moreover, it strengthened its relationships with the African National Congress and, in 1992, sold the organisation its Johannesburg building for a headquarters (which still goes by the name of 'Shell House').

The boycott also sent a strong signal to Pretoria that its apartheid policies would continue to generate sustained international opposition, coordination and penalties. In the case of a company such as Royal Dutch/Shell, a strategic mainstay of the South African economy, this message could not be overlooked. John R. Wilson, Chairman of Shell SA, noted in 1988:

> You have to respect the anti-apartheid lobbyists and their views. They are right in believing that South Africa can only change by attacking the economy. And of course it is true that the South African economy would suffer a severe blow if a company the size of Shell felt forced to pull out.[7]

The Shell boycott had an equally important effect on the US anti-apartheid movement. It strengthened the organisations' relationships with both South African counterparts (such as the National Union of Mineworkers) and with international partners (such as the Dutch, British and Australian anti-apartheid movements). Moreover, it reinforced collaboration and coordination between the labour, religious, civil rights and anti-apartheid organisations themselves. These relationships not only boosted and broadened the boycott; they also helped sustain momentum and support for sanctions at both the national and local levels.

Finally, by pinpointing a single transnational corporation, the boycott helped to focus the attention of the US anti-apartheid movement on the significance of multinational companies in the South African economy. Thus, the campaign provided an effective vehicle for popular education about *de facto* corporate contributions to apartheid. It also paved the way for labour, religious and anti-apartheid collaboration to follow sanctions on corporate responsibility in a democratic South Africa.

Strengths of the boycott
Keeping a boycott alive for seven years is no small task – especially when the campaign is directed against the largest corporation in the world. A number of factors contributed to this strategic accomplishment. First, the coordination and leadership of the United Mine Workers of America cannot be overemphasised. The union devoted substantial resources to the boycott, which in turn multiplied the impact of other catalytic organisations such as ICCR and the National Council of Churches within the religious community, and TransAfrica in civil rights and anti-apartheid circles.

The strong intersectoral ties reinforced each other. Support in union circles was magnified by the blessings of the faith community. Religious organisations in turn were empowered by the recognition of workplace and community support for the boycott. Anti-apartheid and campus groups, in turn, worked with labour and religious advocates, building on the strength and breadth of both constituencies. This dynamic made its greatest contribution to coalition-building at the height of the US anti-apartheid movement between 1986 and 1990.

The campaign's greatest asset may have been the grassroots 'ownership' of the boycott. Miners, for example, understood in concrete terms that the same company which was laying off US workers in the coalfields was attempting to control and bust unions in South Africa – thereby reducing their overseas wage bill and creating incentives to move US jobs out of the country. Religious leaders felt that they had been personally and institutionally targeted by the company's Neptune strategy and were determined to demonstrate that they had not been confused or compromised by Shell's counter-campaign. Finally, Shell's vast network of retail operations gave communities across the country hundreds of convenient focal points for local organising and direct action.

The result was the wide variety of creative approaches developed at the grassroots level. In this context the role of national organisations was not only to initiate strategies, but to distribute reams of information to local groups about each other's activities and victories, which in turn sparked new and innovative tactics.

Weaknesses
The boycott was eventually undermined by a number of dynamics. First, there were the tremendous historical and economic odds against sustaining any boycott for seven years – much less one directed at the largest multinational in the world.

Second, since Royal Dutch/Shell had operations around the globe, and its two parent companies were structurally based in the Netherlands and England, the boycott would have required simultaneous and escalating strength in these home countries, as well as others (like the US) where the company had substantial operations. Though this was the case at the beginning of the boycott, it became increasingly difficult to maintain.

Third, since the boycott was a response to the struggle in South Africa, the sustained support of counterparts there was needed to continue to fuel the boycott. Despite strong statements by South African labour and religious leaders, there was little organisational momentum for the campaign inside the country. The boycott, for example, was never carried out inside South Africa. This may have been due largely to the logical internal dilemma of workers who sought to pressure their employer without jeopardising their own jobs, despite the unions' support for disinvestment. Another contributing factor may have been the fact that as the South African unions achieved some of their own goals – reduced repression and better contracts for the NUM and recognition for the Chemical Workers Industrial Union (CWIU) – they had less incentive to call for the boycott. It was also due to the fact that, while the democratic movement in South Africa supported the boycott of multinationals overseas as an economic tactic to isolate Pretoria, its leading organisations did not target individual companies inside the country. Thus, Shell was not squeezed from within the country and did not experience maximum pressure to disinvest.

The fourth, and perhaps most important, factor was the declining momentum of the movement in the United States. While the boycott continued to build at the peak of the anti-apartheid movement between 1986 and 1990, Nelson Mandela's release from prison and the unbanning of the major South African democratic movements in 1990 began to remove some of the impetus for anti-apartheid organising. Though all but two of the cities, counties and states with anti-apartheid laws managed to hold the line and prevent their repeal after President Bush lifted sanctions in 1991, there were few places in the country where the anti-apartheid movement of the boycott gathered speed after that time (New Jersey being one notable exception). In this environment it was possible for the boycott to continue, but not to escalate. History argues that increasing momentum is necessary for success. Boycotts must grow – or die.

Why did Shell remain in South Africa, while Mobil left?

Though both oil giants were targets of prolonged US campaigns for their withdrawal from South Africa, and Royal Dutch/Shell was the focus of a 14-country boycott, *Mobil Oil* was more vulnerable to US pressure than Shell. First, it was a US-based company, operating in an environment in which more than two thirds of companies with South African operations disinvested during the sanctions movement. Royal Dutch/Shell, on the other hand, was based in two countries where historical colonial ties helped sustain relationships with South Africa and where few companies (particularly those with century-long histories in South Africa) had actually sold their assets there.

Second, Mobil was the subject of an intense campaign which combined shareholder, community and consumer initiatives with dramatic direct action (including a series of demonstrations and arrests) both at its New York headquarters and at public events it sponsored to enhance its corporate image. More than any law or other rationale the company supplied to explain its withdrawal, the 'hassle factor' appears to have played a major role. Mobil may have also been influenced by the example of Shell and sought to avoid becoming the target of a similar boycott.

Finally, Royal Dutch/Shell and Mobil differed in their perspectives on South Africa. Though Shell is estimated to have lost billions of dollars as a result of the boycott, it took a longer-term view of its operations and markets in the region than did Mobil. Shell's Durban refinery – where it imported crude oil, refined, and in turn supplied the company's operations in Botswana, Zimbabwe and Zambia as well as South Africa – was the key to Shell's sub-Saharan operations. Unlike Mobil, Royal Dutch/Shell appears to have calculated that the losses it sustained as a result of the boycott were less than its actual and potential profits in the region. In this context, the company decided to ride out the boycott.

The challenge of corporate responsibility

The Shell boycott demonstrated that it is possible to take on one of the world's biggest companies through a coordinated multinational, multisectoral boycott. It advanced international understandings of the dynamics of domestic and international solidarity and supplied important lessons for building corporate campaigns.

Ironically, though the Neptune strategy boomeranged, one of the major legacies of the Shell boycott is the challenge of promoting corporate responsibility in an emerging South

Africa. As companies are invited to play a role in the country's democratic reconstruction, the ways in which they do so are likely to gather increasing attention and importance. The same labour, religious and anti-apartheid organisations which put the Shell boycott together are now responding to their South African counterparts' concerns that companies do business in South Africa within the parameters set by the country's own democratic organisations.

Between 1991 and 1993, the South African labour movement, ANC and South African Council of Churches and Southern African Catholic Bishops' Conference produced similar sets of principles to inform responsible corporate behaviour. These include common priorities such as affirmative action, labour rights, social programmes to redress the legacy of apartheid, environmental protection, and accountability to local stakeholders. Though the ANC has focussed on developing policy and laws on corporate conduct for the country's first democratic government while the religious community has concentrated on working with other non-governmental organisations to write and implement a voluntary code, there remains substantial agreement about the objectives and standards for corporate responsibility in the emerging South Africa.

Shell campaigners are uniquely positioned to support the call for responsible reinvestment – according to the criteria established on the ground. After accelerating the end of apartheid and enhancing international solidarity, the greatest victory of the Shell boycott may be the unprecedented international foundations it has established for promoting economic justice and corporate responsibility in a new South Africa. That chapter remains to be written.

The Oil Embargo and the Intellectual
The Academic Debate on Economic Sanctions against South Africa

DR PETER A.G. VAN BERGEIJK[*]

High hopes often breed disappointment. It will be very difficult to find a case that more convincingly shows the validity of this conventional wisdom than the oil embargo against South Africa. The prospects for this particular diplomatic instrument were considered to be very promising from the start, and consequently, disappointment reigned during the 1980s when sanctions did not appear to succeed in ending apartheid.

The pessimism of the 1980s, however, turned out to be misplaced. This chapter sketches – with hindsight – the academic debate amongst economists on economic sanctions against South Africa. It starts with a warning about the unreliability of economic observations. The Shipping Research Bureau has provided ample evidence of the poor quality of statistics regarding the trade between South Africa and its partners and has done much to improve our knowledge about actual oil deliveries that have been kept out of the books. In Section 2 the arguments for and against the potential efficacy of the sanction instrument are highlighted. Section 3 argues that success is not the same as effectiveness: a change of policy does not exclusively depend on the damage that is caused by the implementation of the sanction. Section 4 deals with the actual economic impact of the oil embargo and with the question of how to improve the effectiveness of sanctions.

1 Lies, Damned Lies and Statistics

Our observations are not necessarily accurate. Official trade statistics cannot be expected to provide a sufficient empirical basis, especially in the case of South Africa. For example, Hayes (1988, 271) points to the fact that even before the South African authorities suspended publication of detailed trade statistics in 1986 'considerable aggregation in the statistics of the figures for certain "sensitive" items and trading partners' prevented detailed analysis of the effects of sanctions on the South African economy. A recent study asserts that

> artificially-engineered data paucities have generated problems facing researchers. Quite apart from the suppression of disaggregated trade and investment statistics by

* Ministry of Economic Affairs, Research Unit, Economic Policy Directorate (AEP), The Hague. Comments by Robert Haffner, Richard Hengeveld, Ruud de Mooij, Jarig van Sinderen and Pieter Waasdorp were very useful. The views expressed in this article should not be contributed to the government of the Netherlands.

the South African authorities, nations, firms and individuals engaging in economic relationships with South Africa tend to disguise or understate the extent of their transactions.[1]

During the period 1979–93 the Shipping Research Bureau provided a much needed empirical basis on which to judge the potential effectiveness of trade-related political measures in the future. The Shipping Research Bureau revealed that distorted statistics are not typical for South Africa. Authorities that are supposed to enforce economic sanctions seldom check the stated destination of goods. Hence, the data on specific bilateral transactions may be very inaccurate. Sometimes governments even dictate the official trade statistics. In April 1989, for example, Saudi Arabia reported that it was fully complying with the UN oil embargo against South Africa. This official view was reflected in the Saudi trade figures. The Shipping Research Bureau, however, established that at least 134 oil tankers had sailed from Saudi Arabia to South Africa between 1979 and mid-1988, many of which delivered Saudi oil.

Between 1979 and 1993 the Shipping Research Bureau identified 865 oil deliveries to South Africa, estimated at 1.3 billion barrels. This suggests that during this period international commercial transactions equal to at least two years of total South African imports of goods and services – if valued at world market prices – have been kept out of the books. It is quite probable that the holes in the official trade statistics are much larger. Firstly, one must admit it is unlikely that all secret oil deliveries were uncovered by the Shipping Research Bureau. Secondly, actual South African oil import prices substantially exceeded world market prices. All in all it is quite possible that official statistics over this period have underestimated total South African imports by an amount equivalent to the cumulated import bill for several years.

Keeping these uncertainties in mind, we are still able to assess the effectiveness of the oil embargo. We may use economic theory and empirical lessons from other cases to understand how sanctions work and which variables are important. From the development of such variables, we may learn something about the phenomena that cannot readily be observed (such as the damage resulting from sanctions). Furthermore, we now have access to data on South Africa's present energy supplies, which have started to become available since the lifting of the oil embargo.

2 Thinking about sanctions

Many economists have argued against the potential utility of economic sanctions in general and against economic sanctions against South Africa in particular. In 1987, for example, Prof. Duncan Reekie from the University of Witwatersrand in Johannesburg went as far as to deny that sanctions against South Africa could ever work. In his view the apartheid regime was quite invulnerable, at least in an economic sense.

The protagonists of economic sanctions, however, stressed that many characteristics of the South African economy made it rather vulnerable to foreign economic pressure.[2] Trade linkage with the countries of the OECD was substantial, while South Africa's political stability and economic health in the 1980s deteriorated. In addition, several specific features of the South African import and export structures, such as the country's dependence on a limited number of suppliers for capital goods (machinery, trucks, intermediate inputs, spare parts, etcetera) and the apparent rigidity of South African production and consumption patterns, pointed to substantial vulnerability for international economic pressure. The oil embargo looked very promising, especially when after the demise of the Shah, the new Iranian government decided to join the campaign in 1979. Even after the launching of large-scale oil-from-coal projects, South Africa still had to import about 70 per cent of its requirements. The African National Congress regarded sanctions and the isolation of the apartheid regime as a weapon which could complement the armed struggle. In an address to the international business community in London in 1987, Oliver R. Tambo stated that the efficacy of the economic weapon followed from the fact that

> South African society to a considerable extent [has] been the product of foreign influence and that, to a significant degree, its political and socio-economic character has been determined by outside interests ... Over the years ... international connections helped sustain, and continue to sustain, the very system we seek to abolish.[3]

Still, many economists did not consider sanctions against South Africa a viable case. Indeed, oil is not found in exploitable quantities in South Africa, but the country is a major producer of most other strategic raw materials. Therefore, its dependence on other countries – with the exception of energy – is low. Moreover, its position as a supplier of strategic materials meant that South Africa could effectively retaliate against economic sanctions by OECD countries, while the income from its gold export reduced South Africa's vulnerability to foreign economic pressure.[4] All in all, according to economists, the weight of evidence suggested that sanctions against South Africa would not work. Indeed, one of the most outstanding characteristics of the debate on economic sanctions against South Africa has been the scepticism among economists of the potential merits of economic coercion in ending or mitigating apartheid.

The economist's attitude has not been typical for the case of economic sanctions against South Africa only. Many academic articles and books deal with the case of South Africa, but the economist's negative verdict also pertains to other cases such as the COCOM sanctions against the former Eastern bloc or sanctions against human rights violations in Latin America. The economic profession's scepticism of economic sanctions as an instrument against apartheid should mainly be seen as a result of the academic, neo-classical outlook on the world. Since the eighteenth century, when classical economists argued that trade generates mutual economic benefits and that this will create the basis for political cooperation, economic advisors and policymakers have claimed that the cessation of economic exchange could never help to solve political conflicts.

Many arguments for this distrust of the economic sanctions instrument have been put forward. Failure was considered to be evident in some widely publicised and discussed cases such as sanctions against Israel and Rhodesia. The practical usefulness of economic sanctions was generally considered to be rather low. The urge for free trade was considered to be too strong, implying that sanctions busting and trade diversion were the most probable outcomes of economic sanctions. Some have argued that it would hardly be possible to create the necessary political unity for punitive boycotts or embargoes and – if established at all – sanctions would be easy to circumvent. Others have questioned the plausibility of a change in behaviour resulting from economic damage. Sanctions are public measures; if the target is susceptible to the ensuing pressure, this may damage the target leadership's world prestige or diminish its domestic support. Hence, the leaders of the target country will offset the economic loss resulting from sanctions against the loss of political standing they will suffer if they give in to foreign pressure. Others pointed out that the lapse of time between the decision to apply economic sanctions and their actual implementation offers the target country the possibility to adjust its economy, thus reducing the potential damage of the sanction. Moreover, a long-lasting total embargo appears hardly possible, both on economic grounds (for example, cartel theory) as well as on political grounds. This led many economists to believe that sanctions could not become a useful instrument of diplomacy. Consequently, they considered economic sanctions to be mere symbolic gestures.

Most academic economists just did not consider economic sanctions a topic worthy of investigation. The academic input to the debate on sanctions against South Africa was based upon an *a priori* negative view of the potential of sanctions to change the country's domestic policies. Research efforts mainly aimed at developing new theories explaining why sanctions had to fail (as they appeared to be doing). A lack of command of the facts about South Africa was a noteworthy feature of most academic investigations. Professional literature hardly discussed ways of improving the effectiveness of sanctions. Furthermore, academics did not appear to be very interested in the empirical side of the problems at hand. All in all, economic contributions to sanctions theory were rather limited, while the empirical question of the efficacy of economic sanctions was left to journalists, civil servants and other 'non-economists'. According to one observer,

> the gulf between policy significance and theoretical and empirical development is probably wider in the area of economic sanctions than in any other region at the confluence of economic and political streams of thought.[5]

In the early 1990s the mood began to change, both because theoretical economists, developing game-theoretic concepts, started to treat economic sanctions as a serious topic, and because policy experience with the sanction instrument contradicted the traditional economic arguments against economic sanctions. Sanctions appeared to be a potentially useful instrument in foreign policy. Boycotts and embargoes were shown to be effective in terms of economic damage done and successful in terms of political impact. The clearest example is supplied by South Africa, which showed that sanctions implemented by the international community started to have a positive political pay-off.

Since the Shipping Research Bureau has discontinued its activities because of the end of apartheid, this is perhaps the right moment to take a fresh look at some of the questions related to the impact of the oil embargo on South Africa.

3 *Effectiveness and success*

It is important to distinguish between the effectiveness and the success of economic sanctions. Effectiveness relates to the (potential) economic damage of an economic sanction –

the economic loss that sanctions impose on, in this case, South Africa. Success relates to the desired change in political behaviour – i.e. the ending of apartheid (Losman 1972). Many observers have commented that the link between economic damage (effectiveness) and the desired policy change is not obvious and strict.[6] It is by no means obvious that effective sanctions will succeed.[7] Conversely, in order for sanctions to be successful, they do not necessarily have to be effective: it is simply not necessary for them to do a lot of damage. Indeed, even ineffective sanctions may be successful, as argued by Kaempfer and Lowenberg (1986, 1988). They showed that sanctions which cause little or no economic hardship to South Africa could still generate political change and argued (1988, 768) that

> sanctions can communicate signals or threats, not necessarily entailing severe economic damage, which in turn produce policy changes.

The *effectiveness* of economic sanctions is probably the natural line of approach for economists. Their tool of analysis is the traditional trade model. Trade liberalisation and the associated gains from trade are useful concepts for two reasons. Firstly, comprehensive embargoes and boycotts are the mirror images of the movement from the no-trade situation of autarky to a state of the world in which free trade prevails. The welfare gains from this movement are one of the topics of the international trade model. Secondly, all countries benefit from international specialisation according to their respective comparative advantage. Leaving the political aspects aside, this is the economist's realm *par excellence*. It is, however, only one part of the picture. For example, it may not have been that sanctions were deemed effective or particularly efficient, but that other instruments were even less promising to end apartheid. In the *International Herald Tribune* of 14 July 1986, Malcolm Fraser, former Australian prime minister and co-chairman of the Commonwealth Eminent Persons Group (a body set up in 1985 to mediate between the South African government and the black opposition), argued that only pressure will persuade the Afrikaners:

> The Afrikaner is stubborn, he is determined. He will not be dissuaded from his course by reasoned argument or quiet diplomacy, even if it is called "constructive engagement". He will only be dissuaded by pressure, often extreme pressure.

4 The impact of the oil embargo

Oil is generally considered to be a strategic commodity. To an economist this means that oil is essential for the proper functioning of the economy, i.e. to support economic growth. In an economic sense, the demand for strategic goods is rather inelastic: only very substantial increases in price will negatively affect the demand for such a commodity. To the soldier, 'strategic' means that oil is essential for national defence, most often simply to keep the tanks running. Also, the police force will find it difficult to function properly if oil supplies diminish. To the politician, 'strategic' means that oil should not be in short supply if he wants to be re-elected. Although economists, soldiers and politicians often disagree on the specific usefulness of this commodity, this is one of those rare situations in which they would seem to agree that the strategic value of oil is substantial indeed. Accordingly, many observers argued that an oil embargo against South Africa would have the greatest potential for success of all possible trade sanctions.[8] Indeed, many believed that oil was the soft spot of South Africa and that turning off the oil tap would force Pretoria to its knees.

It is true that the more essential – or strategic – a commodity is for the target economy, the more inelastic the target's demand for that commodity and hence the higher the welfare loss will be if the foreign supply of such goods is decreased by means of an embargo. However, the elasticity of the target's demand for the goods that are hit by sanctions is not the only thing that matters. Even if the target's demand is quite inelastic, one needs to consider the possibilities of increased supply by countries that do not impose sanctions and of sanctions busting and import substitution.

It is simply a matter of supply and demand: if the country which imposes sanctions refuses to supply the target with the essential commodity, it thereby artificially raises the price of the commodity to the target. Other suppliers will be tempted to refrain from taking part in the embargo and supply the target economy with the much wanted product. Indeed, any sanction could ultimately be ineffective in economic terms if sufficient new suppliers come to the rescue of the target and old suppliers act as sanction busters. This is even true when the target's demand for the product was rightly considered to be very inelastic.

In the case of the oil embargo, the fact that a country can get the right type of oil almost anywhere implies an almost infinite elasticity of substitution. Secondly, the supply elasticity from import substitution – that is, local production replacing imports – appears to have been rather large. In 1992 about 30 per cent of South Africa's demand for fuel was covered by synthetic oil production by the Sasol plants. The Mossgas project was expected to reduce the dependence on foreign supplies by an additional 5 to 10 percentage points. Obviously, this would still leave between 60 and 65 per cent of South Africa's oil requirements uncovered. The point, however, is that it can be shown that domestic production (import substitution) of 30 per cent increases the elasticity of South Africa's *import* demand for oil by more than 40 per cent, implying much lower economic losses resulting from the oil embargo.[9]

Nevertheless, the availability of foreign oil and synthetic oil substitutes inside South Africa did not stop the embargo from imposing costs on the South African economy; the country's growth perspectives were definitely hurt by the economic sanctions. Measurements of damage that focus on trade flows and possibilities of substitution fail to take account of this indirect loss. Such estimates only cover the direct costs and neglect the indirect costs of an economic sanction. Let us consider these costs.

Direct costs
The direct costs entail additional financial and real outlays immediately related to the sanctions. In the case of the oil embargo, these direct costs consist of premiums paid to middlemen, transporters and traders (approximately $8 a barrel in the early 1980s), import substitution facilities, storage facilities for strategic oil reserves and obsolescence of specific parts of the capital stock (for example in the refinery sector). In general terms, the direct costs have more than doubled South Africa's oil import bill. Substantial amounts of money were involved; the direct costs of the oil embargo in the 1980s equalled South Africa's gross foreign debt, which by the end of decade was estimated at between $15 to 20 billion. Indeed, had the oil embargo not been imposed, the 1985 South African debt crisis would probably not have emerged.

Indirect costs

In addition to these direct costs, economic activity in South Africa suffered from spill-over effects to other markets and opportunity costs, while the country's long-term development potential was hurt. Undoubtedly, the oil embargo's indirect spill-over effects to other sectors of the South African economy, possibly reflected in an anti-export bias, have been important. In her 1992 presidential address to the Economic Society of South Africa, Merle Holden pointed out:

> Although South Africa is emerging from many years of international isolation, it still carries the burden of the past reflected in a state-controlled economy structured to maintain independence from the rest of the world. The SASOLs, MOSSGAS and Atlantis Diesel remain as edifices to this state of semi-autarky. Protectionism, exchange controls and dual exchange rates formed part of the arsenal which was used to insulate the economy.[10]

Economic activity in South Africa has also been hampered by the fact that fewer new technologies became available to the country during the implementation of sanctions. Inferior technology and suboptimal investment decisions were absorbed in the capital stock, thus reducing the effectiveness of subsequent investment. Sanctions may have prevented qualified international contractors from participating in projects, thus reducing the availability of modern technology, which may also have affected the potential for import substitution. For example, in the early 1990s reports on the Mossgas project suggested that budgets were exceeded by more than 100 per cent, basically because both the latest technology and international expertise were not available.[11] In addition, large parts of the capital stock were tied to unproductive ends, such as the synthetic oil production facilities and the strategic oil stock (which at the average world oil price and the average world interest rate in the 1970s and the 1980s carried an annual opportunity cost of about $2 per barrel in depot). Finally, even small income losses may reduce both the efficiency for the economy as a whole and the rate of economic growth, which in the long run imposes a substantial burden on the economy. So even when the direct costs of a sanction appear to be small, the indirect costs may put a considerable strain on the embargoed economy.

During the 1980s several attempts were made to increase economic pressure on South Africa. One method used was to extend the number of goods and services covered by the sanctions: the cumulative impact of partial sanctions may impose costs that at the level of individual measures seem negligible (Hermele and Odén 1988). Another was to investigate sanctions busting and to provide information about companies that played important roles in the violation of the embargo. This has helped to put pressure on countries and officials that were involved in the enforcement of sanctions. For example, the reports and the newsletters of the Shipping Research Bureau have played a very useful role in generating public awareness of the leaks in the oil embargo. Indeed, the Bureau's *raison d'être* has been its firm conviction that the oil embargo can only be effective if the necessary information is available, if adopted policies are duly implemented, and if legislation and contract clauses are enforced.

Another intensification of economic pressure came in the second half of the 1980s, when both banks and multinational corporations considered the political risks of lending to and investing in South Africa too large. Consequently, substantial amounts of capital were withdrawn from the country in the wake of the South African debt crisis. This disinvestment wave not only hit the economy in a direct manner (less capital means less production), but also indirectly. Disinvestment limited South Africa's access to international markets even further, while at the same time the country was much less able to benefit from the modern technologies and management techniques that are the invisible components of international capital flows.

All these factors helped to put economic pressure on Pretoria. At the end of the 1980s the economic impact of economic sanctions was substantial. It is quite likely that this pressure contributed to the policy changes that led to the end of apartheid in the early 1990s, thus contradicting the views which economists have held on this topic for several decades.

References

Baldry, Jonathan C. and Brian E. Dollery, 1992, 'Investment and trade sanctions against South Africa in a model of apartheid', *UNE Working papers in economics* 1. Armidale.

Hanlon, Joseph and Roger Osmond, 1987, *The Sanctions Handbook*. Harmondsworth: Penguin.

Hayes, J.P., 1987, *Economic Effects of Sanctions on Southern Africa*. London: Trade Policy Research Centre.

Hayes, J.P., 1988, 'Divided Opinions on Sanctions Against South Africa', *The World Economy* 11, 267-280.

Hermele, Kenneth and Bertil Odén, 1988, *Sanctions Dilemmas. Some Implications of Economic Sanctions against South Africa*, Discussion Paper 1. Uppsala: Scandinavian Institute of African Studies.

Kaempfer, William H. and Anton D. Lowenberg, 1986, 'A Model of the Political Economy of International Investment Sanctions: The Case of South Africa', *Kyklos* 39, 377-396.

Kaempfer, William H. and Anton D. Lowenberg, 1988, 'The Theory of International Economic Sanctions: A Public Choice Approach', *American Economic Review* 78, 786-793.

Kaempfer, William H., Anton D. Lowenberg, H. Naci Mocan and Kudret Topyan, 1993, 'International Sanctions and Anti-Apartheid Politics in South Africa'. Paper for the OCFEB workshop on economic sanctions, Erasmus University, Rotterdam 13 August 1993.

Lipton, Merle, 1988, *Sanctions and South Africa: The Dynamics of Economic Isolation*, Economist Intelligence Unit Special Report 1119. London: EIU.

Losman, Donald L., 1972, 'The Effects of Economic Boycotts', *Lloyds Bank Review* 106, 27-41.

Lundahl, Mats, 'Economic Effects of a Trade and Investment Boycott against South Africa', *Scandinavian Journal of Economics* 86, 68-83.

Porter, Richard C., 1979, 'International Trade and Investment Sanctions: Potential Impact on the South African Economy', *Journal of Conflict Resolution* 23, 579-612.

Reekie, Duncan, 1987, 'The Economics of Apartheid Politics', *Economic Affairs* 7, 10-13.

Shipping Research Bureau, 1982, *Oil Tankers to South Africa 1980–1981*. Amsterdam.

Smeets, Maarten, 1990, 'Economic Sanctions Against Iraq: The Ideal Case?', *Journal of World Trade* 24(6), 105-120.

Van Bergeijk, Peter A.G., 1994, *Economic Diplomacy, Trade and Commercial Policy: Positive and Negative Sanctions in a New World Order*. Aldershot: Edward Elgar.

Notes

Introduction

1 R. First et al., *The South African Connection: Western Investment in Apartheid*. London: Temple Smith, 1972, 103.
2 Letter to the Editor, *Financial Mail*, 21 January 1994.
3 The qualification is from the South African Energy Minister Steyn, Hansard 9 July 1984, col. 11033.

PART A

'The Last Peaceful Weapon'

1 Peter Calvocoressi, 'The politics of sanctions: The League and the United Nations', in: R. Segal (ed.), *Sanctions against South Africa*. Harmondsworth: Penguin, 1964, 48.
2 Ibid., 52. Also Vincent Cronin, *A Concise History of Italy*. London: Cassell & Co. Ltd, 1973; Martin Blinkhorn, *Mussolini and Fascist Italy*. London & New York: Methuen, 1984; and Mervyn Frost, 'Collective sanctions in international relations: An historical overview of the theory and practice', in: D. Willers and S. Begg (eds), *South Africa and Sanctions: Genesis and Prospects. A Symposium*. Johannesburg: South African Institute of Race Relations and South African Institute of International Affairs, 1979, 1-25.
3 Cronin, op. cit., 210.
4 Calvocoressi, op. cit., 52.
5 K.N. Raj, 'Sanctions and the Indian experience', in: Segal (ed.), op. cit., 197; D.N.H. Johnson, 'Sanctions against South Africa? The legal aspect', in: ibid., 62ff.
6 Johnson, op. cit., 70.
7 Appeal by leaders of the ANC, the SA Indian Congress and the Liberal Party of SA for a boycott of South African produce by the British people, December 1959. Printed as Document 13 in: United Nations, *The United Nations and Apartheid, 1948–1994*, UN Blue Books Series Vol. 1. New York: UN Department of Public Information, 1994, 243.
8 Quoted in: Martin Bailey and Bernard Rivers, *Oil Sanctions against South Africa*. New York: UN Centre against Apartheid, 1978, 74.
9 Resolution 6 adopted at Cairo, 21 July 1964; quoted by Bailey and Rivers, ibid.
10 See E.S. Reddy, *A Review of United Nations Action for an Oil Embargo against South Africa*. New York: UN Centre against Apartheid, 1980, 2n.
11 Brian Lapping, 'Oil sanctions against South Africa', in: Segal (ed.), op. cit., 147-148.
12 Amer Araim, pp. 234-5.
13 Reddy, op. cit., 2.
14 'Introduction', in: Segal (ed.), op. cit., 7 and 8-9.
15 Ibid., 9 and 14.
16 Lapping, op. cit., 135.
17 W.F. Gutteridge, 'Strategic implications of sanctions against South Africa', in: Segal (ed.), op. cit., 113-114.
18 A. Maizels, 'Economic sanctions and South Africa's trade', in: Segal (ed.), op. cit., 129; Lapping, op. cit., 148; for Iran's attitude in 1973 and later, see De Quaasteniet and Aarts.

19 Gutteridge, op. cit., 144.
20 Lapping, op. cit., 136.
21 Ibid., 142.
22 'Reports of Commissions I and II', in: Segal (ed.), op. cit., 249.
23 Lapping, op. cit., 149.
24 Ibid., 148.
25 'Introduction', in Segal (ed.), op. cit., 12; see also ibid., 265.
26 See the figures in Table 1 on page 271.
27 *Sunday Express* (Johannesburg), 25 December 1966; quoted in: Bailey and Rivers, op. cit., 57. A lot of what follows in this section is based on Bailey and Rivers.
28 Bailey and Rivers, op. cit., 75; A.J. Klinghoffer, *Oiling the Wheels of Apartheid*. Boulder & London: Lynne Rienner, 1989, 26.
29 *Far Eastern Economic Review*, 15 April 1977; quoted in: Bailey and Rivers, op. cit., 23n.
30 *Financial Times*, 10 November 1977; quoted in: Bailey and Rivers, op. cit., 48.
31 See De Quaasteniet and Aarts, page 272.
32 M. Spring, 'Calendar 1973: Energy', in: *South Africa 1974: Official Yearbook of the Republic of South Africa*. Johannesburg: Department of Information, 1974, 32.
33 See Amer Araim's contribution. For additional details: E.S. Reddy, op. cit., 2-4. A lot of what follows in this section is based on Reddy.
34 Resolution on South Africa, Non-Aligned Summit, Colombo, 16-19 August 1976; quoted in: M. Bailey, *Shell and BP in South Africa*. London: Anti-Apartheid Movement/Haslemere Group, 1977, 6. In October 1977, the Commonwealth Committee on Southern Rhodesia proposed an oil embargo against South Africa. Ecosoc resolutions 1978/73 of 4 August 1978; 1979/75 of 3 August 1979; 1980/59 of 24 July 1980; quoted in: United Nations, *Activities of Transnational Corporations in South Africa and Namibia and the Responsibilities of Home Countries with Respect to their Operations in this Area*. ST/CTC/84. New York: UN Centre on Transnational Corporations, 1986, 24.
35 See, e.g., M. Tanzer et al., *Oil – A Weapon Against Apartheid*. New York: Sanctions Working Group, March 1980, 42-48.
36 The story is taken from M. Bailey, *Oilgate: The Sanctions Scandal*. Sevenoaks: Coronet, 1979, 19ff.
37 Bailey, *Shell and BP in South Africa*, op. cit., 7 and 35.
38 Bailey and Rivers, op. cit., 86.
39 Ibid., 54 (Chairman's statement quoted from *Financial Mail*, 4 November 1977).
40 Ibid., 7.
41 Ibid., 15. Their source was B. Rogers, *White Wealth and Black Poverty*. Westport CT: Greenwood, 1976, 262; Rogers had mentioned the same example in her article entitled 'Southern Africa and The Oil Embargo', which was published as long ago as the spring of 1974 in *Africa Today* 21(8), 3-8.
42 Bailey and Rivers, op. cit., 55 and 57 (quote from *The Star*, 11 February 1978).
43 Ibid., 62 and 80.
44 Pik Botha related the story on his visit to the Shah and other secret visits to oil-exporting countries in Africa and the Middle East to the Afrikaans newspaper *Beeld*: 'Pik Botha se verhale van sy eie Arabiese nagte op soek na olie' ('Pik Botha's stories on his Arabian Nights in search of oil'), 4 June 1994. The paper reported that Botha was soon to start writing his memoirs, especially those concerning what took place behind the scenes during the 'dark days' of sanctions. Klinghoffer (op. cit., 37) writes that Botha also visited Iran in October 1978 and was told that Iran would embargo deliveries if South Africa imposed a unilateral settlement in Namibia.
45 Tanzer et al., op. cit., 30-32; Klinghoffer, op. cit., 37.
46 M. Bailey, *The Impact on South Africa of the Cut-Off of Iranian Oil*, Notes and Documents 16/79. New York: UN Centre against Apartheid, 1979.
47 Interview 1994; the interviewee prefers to remain anonymous.
48 SRB Newsletter No. 33, 3-4.

49 *The Executive*, August 1991, 30.
50 *Lloyd's List*, 24 February 1979.
51 Quoted in Tanzer et al., op. cit., 32.
52 Heunis statement from 1983; both were quoted by Martin Bailey in *The Observer*, 3 June 1984.
53 E.g.: Tanzer et al., op. cit., 38-41; D. Taylor, 'Oily intrigue ... bungled invasion', *New African*, July 1979, 10-14.
54 *Financial Mail*, 18 May 1979; quoted by M. Bailey in: *Oil and Apartheid: Churches' Challenge to Shell and BP*. London: Christian Concern for Southern Africa, 1982, 20.
55 Quoted in: Tanzer et al., op. cit., 17.
56 *Report of the Seminar...*, UN General Assembly A/AC.115/L.521, 18 April 1980, Annex III, 5. The Rotterdam spot market, allegedly a source of crude oil to South Africa, was mentioned by many speakers, and the Dutch government was called upon to investigate its role. Misconceptions regarding the 'Rotterdam market' (i.e. the NW European section of the world spot trade in refined products) were widespread at the time. South Africa was indeed forced by the difficult situation in which it found itself to turn to spot supplies of *crude* oil (i.e. costly single cargoes not covered by long-term contracts), but that did not involve Rotterdam. It gradually managed to lessen its dependence on spot purchases, and interest in the spot market soon fizzled out.
57 E. Ellen and D. Campbell, *International Maritime Fraud*. London: Sweet & Maxwell, 1981, 53.
58 A.J. Klinghoffer, *Fraud of the Century: The Case of the Mysterious Supertanker Salem*. London: Routledge, 1988.
59 B. Conway, *The Piracy Business*. Middlesex: Hamlyn, 1981; idem, *Maritime Fraud*. London: Lloyd's, 1990; E. Ellen and D. Campbell, op. cit. – The IMB has been renamed ICC Commercial Crime Services since; it is based in Barking, Essex, UK.

The Spear of the Nation

1 This chapter is mainly based on interviews held in 1993–94 with Frene Ginwala, Aboobaker Ismail (Rashid), John Malcomess, David Moisi, the late Joe Slovo and Jacob Zuma. In addition, contemporary newspaper reports were consulted, among others from *The Star*, *Rand Daily Mail*, *Post* (Transvaal), *The Citizen*, and *de Volkskrant* (Netherlands). Useful sources were the clipping compilation *Facts and Reports* (Holland Committee on Southern Africa, various years 1980–86); *Focus on Political Repression* (IDAF, various issues, 1981–86); *Survey of Race Relations in South Africa/Race Relations Survey* (SA Institute of Race Relations, various years). Some information on attacks on oil installations was extracted from SRB's *Newsletter on the Oil Embargo against South Africa*.
Other publications used:
Stephen M. Davis, *Apartheid's Rebels: Inside South Africa's Hidden War*. New Haven & London: Yale University Press, 1987 (Mobil attack: 148).
Stephen Ellis and Tsepo Sechaba, *Comrades against Apartheid: The ANC & the South African Communist Party in Exile*. London: James Currey, 1992 (Obadi arrest Swaziland: 106).
Evelien Groenink and Bart Luirink, *Zuid-Afrika: Van township tot Tafelberg*. Amsterdam: Odyssee, 1992 (Merebank activist: 172).
Joseph Hanlon, *Beggar Your Neighbours*. London: CIIR/James Currey, 1986.
Hans Hoffmann, 'Het ware gezicht van Shell in Zuid-Afrika', *FNV Magazine*, Amsterdam, 8 November 1986 (Shell/BP refinery: 6)
Ronnie Kasrils, *'Armed and Dangerous': My Undercover Struggle Against Apartheid*. Oxford: Heinemann, 1993 (commissar: 151-2; toyi-toyi: 192; Matola raid: 207)
John Pampallis, *Foundations of the New South Africa*. London & New Jersey/Cape Town: Zed Books/Maskew Miller Longman, 1991 (Barney: 266)
Jacques Pauw, *In the Heart of the Whore*. Halfway House: Southern Book Publishers, 1991 (Dirk Coetzee: 1ff, 45-6, 271-2)
Oliver R. Tambo, 'South Africa: Strategic Options for International Companies', Address Business International Conference, London, 27 May 1987 (Key Points Act: 4)

First Steps of the Shipping Research Bureau

1   The March 1980 seminar 'took note with appreciation of the intention of the Holland Commit-
     tee on Southern Africa and Work Group KAIROS to establish in co-operation with the Special
     Committee against Apartheid and the national liberation movements of South Africa and Na-
     mibia an office for research and investigation on all aspects of the supply of oil to South Africa.
     It expressed the hope that the office would be set up soon, after full consultations with Govern-
     ments, liberation movements and anti-apartheid movements, as well as the United Nations and
     the Organization of African Unity' (from the Declaration of the Seminar). Consultations were
     held, although not with all of the bodies named.
2   Jan Stoof, 'Olieboycot van Zuid-Africa gebroken vanuit de Nederlandse Antillen', *Vrij
     Nederland*, 30 June 1979; see also *Amigoe* (Curaçao), 3, 10 and 13 July 1979. Martin Bailey, in
     the *Toronto Star* of 26 July 1979, cited 'informants from within the oil industry' who 'also
     confirmed that Bonaire is now the main source of South Africa's oil' (Bonaire is one of the oil
     transhipment centres in the Netherlands Antilles).
3   The plans were set forth in a paper presented by the Group to the OAU, 20 June 1979, and in *Oil
     – A Weapon Against Apartheid*, a paper presented to the Amsterdam seminar, March 1980.
4   In the article that the Sanctions Working Group wrote in *Arab Oil & Gas*, Paris, 1 December
     1980, it still gave much attention to the methodology of monitoring tanker movements using the
     concrete examples of a 'Tanker X' and a 'Tanker Y'. In a friendly letter of February 1981 which
     was sent to the Sanctions Working Group, Bernard Rivers ventured to guess the identities of the
     tankers that had been referred to as 'X' and 'Y' and referred to the unfortunate lack of commu-
     nication between the two groups. – A Statement of Purpose put out in 1982 also stated that
     'research on tanker movements to detect the companies fueling South Africa', along with,
     among other things, 'research in the field of the Israel-South Africa connection, particularly in
     the energy field', were still activities of the IOWG, the Sanctions Working Group's successor
     (in discussions that the SRB had with the group, the linkage between the Palestine question and
     oil for apartheid had already proven itself to be a problematic factor).
5   A brochure by Terisa Turner entitled *Trade Union Action to Stop Oil to South Africa* (published
     by OATUU) was disseminated in that year and proved to be the only concrete result of the
     handbook project. The brochure, containing the 1982 list of 'tankers and companies thought
     most likely to have delivered oil', consisted of an undigested list of 21 vessels about which it
     had been reported that they had called at or passed by South Africa in 1982. Among the vessels
     listed were gas tankers, specialised chemical carriers, small product tankers, and only a few
     crude carriers. Only one of the vessels listed in the IOWG brochure can be found in the SRB list
     of embargo violations.
6   The SRB properly informed the IOWG that it had taken the liberty of providing both OATUU
     and the Maritime Unions with a copy of the updated version of the IOWG list, which it also
     included in its letter to the IOWG itself. (Admittedly, the updated version was not new. When
     the Bureau had, two years earlier, received a request to check the accuracy of the IOWG list
     from an unspecified source, the internal paper containing the results of this critical analysis had
     not been shown to the IOWG at that stage.)
7   See pp. 142ff.
8   Bernard Rivers complained in a letter to the board of the SRB, when its name had been finally
     decided on, that it perhaps was not quite the best name; the Bureau did, indeed, concentrate on
     the shipping aspect of the oil embargo, but 'what if we later do a report on, say, oil sales by
     certain countries which we suspect or know were for South Africa? Ships may not feature at all
     in such a report'. The Bureau's later history doesn't seem to indicate that its name ever became
     problematic in this regard, also not when, for example, reports were devoted to the subject of oil
     traders rather than shipowners. What remained true is that even such reports were primarily
     based on findings regarding *tanker voyages*; until its very end, that would always be the SRB's
     strongest suit.
9   On 12 April 1980 the Norwegian newspaper *Dagbladet* had already exposed a similar series of

shuttle voyages undertaken by the *Havdrott* during a more limited period, namely four trips that were made between February and August 1979.

10 From an internal memorandum. As of the third main report that was published in 1984, the principal tables only showed those tankers which 'apparently delivered crude oil cargoes' during their calls at South Africa, and of these, only those of 50,000 tons dwt and over were actually considered. In the first report the cut-off point had still been set at 25,000 tons, and the explicit qualification had been laid down that the report did not contain proof that all tankers listed had actually delivered oil; these two factors account for the greater number of Norwegian tankers in the SRB's first publication. Of the 32 cases in the Norway report, only 11 can be found in the list of this book (though the names of seven gap tankers that were only later identified were also added).

11 See Bailey on pp. 226-8.

12 Wellen was asked by phone if the Antillean government would be willing to tell the Bureau which of the 19 tankers had not, in their opinion, been to the Antilles. That request was repeated more formally to Don Martina by telex. But they refused.

13 For 18 of the 19 tankers, the agent in the Netherlands Antilles certainly possessed information concerning the exact dates during which they had been in the Antilles; in some cases, however, the dates differed slightly from those which the SRB had given to the government. The 19th ship had apparently given 'Aruba' as her previous port when arriving in Cape Town.

14 'Fleet of supertankers is busting Arab oil embargo on South Africa', *The Observer*, 18 January 1981; see also Martin Bailey, 'De geheimzinnige tankers van Transworld uit Berg en Dal' ('The Secretive Tankers of Transworld from Berg en Dal'), *Vrij Nederland*, 7 March 1981, 3. More on Transworld Oil on pp. 146 and 147-9.

Bailey got his article labelled 'Exclusive' on 'Shell tankers break ban' *after* the publication of the SRB Dutch report, in *The Observer* of 22 February 1981.

15 UN Special Committee against Apartheid, *Oil Tankers to South Africa: Replies received from Member States*, 3 April 1981, A/AC.115/L.538.

16 This one time the vessel did not dock at a South African port. But together with the *Johs. Stove*, it was responsible for 17 SRB-identified deliveries of oil to South Africa between the years 1981 and 1986. The ships' owner, the Norwegian Lorentzens Rederi Co., once replied to a letter of the SRB requesting information concerning some suspected deliveries with the statement that the company operated 'strictly ... in accordance with Norwegian law and practice ... Thus we are not prepared to accept the spirit of illegality implicitly contained in your letter and have no further comments in this matter' (letter to the SRB, 29 February 1984).

17 *How Britain Fuels the Apartheid War Machine*. Five days later the AAM caused more of a stir with a subsequent report not only in the UK, but also via a press release of the Dutch anti-apartheid committees in the Netherlands. In its report, *South African Mining Interests Move into North Sea Oil!*, the AAM attacked the UK government for granting two South African companies a stake in the latest round of North Sea oil exploration licenses. The companies were the Anglo American daughter company Charter Consolidated and Federale Mynbou daughter Unilon Oil Exploration Ltd. The row in the Netherlands had to do with the fact that the Dutch state-owned company DSM worked in two consortia with the South African companies.

18 The SRB was especially pleased that its report was ordered by a number of oil and shipping companies on account of publicity that appeared in the specialised oil trade journal *Platt's Oilgram*.

19 Some of the examples are also interesting enough to be named in this book, see pp. 194-6.

20 Quoted in *Daily News* (Tanzania), 22 May 1980.

21 Resolution on Sanctions, CM/Res. 817 (XXXV).

22 Section Two, 'Provisions relative to oil', of the 'General Principles for the Boycott against Israel' of the Principal Bureau for the Boycott against Israel (League of Arab States, Damascus) listed in detail a considerable number of steps which the member states were supposed to enforce in order to prohibit the passage of their oil to Israel (Article 50:1-7) and in order to impose penalties upon those apprehended for smuggling (51:1-7). Each Boycott Office was required to

subscribe to *Lloyd's Shipping Index* 'in order to keep close watch on the movements of tankers, especially those which frequent Israel ports' (51:5). (Produced in an undated publication by the OAU, apparently as material for the March 1981 meeting in Arusha.)

23 Resolution UNGA 36/172G of 17 December 1981. At Kuwait's request the OAPEC resolution was also publicised and disseminated by the UN (A/36/665 S/14750, 12 November 1981). The SRB reprinted the resolution in several of its publications, e.g., in its second and third main reports.

24 The OAPEC had written to the UN Special Committee against Apartheid on 19 April 1980, after receiving the Declaration of the Amsterdam seminar on the oil embargo, that 'since it [was] not a supra-national organization it would be beyond its scope to take mandatory decisions regarding any oil embargo. However, we are fortunate, as far as the issue of an oil embargo against South Africa is concerned, in that all our member States have adopted the entire body of United Nations' resolutions regarding this matter, and have shown both willingness and enthusiasm for their implementation' (reproduced in: UN Special Committee against Apartheid, *Replies to the letter...*, 6 August 1980, A/AC.115/L.530). See also the contribution of De Quaasteniet and Aarts.

25 The Namibia question remained another basis for abortive attempts to implement a mandatory oil embargo, as when Niger, Tunisia and Uganda submitted a draft resolution to that effect in the Security Council in April 1981 (Ref. S/14461, 27 April 1981).

26 Ref. A/AC.115/L.538 and addenda.

27 With the OAU and SWAPO as secondants, both of which were kept well-informed during all subsequent years with respect to preliminary findings and mailings to both companies and governments.

Secrecy Is Essential

1 Minister D. Steyn, Hansard 20 May 1985, col. 5864.
2 Ibid., col. 5863-4.
3 *The Star*, 14 June 1980.
4 Hansard 21 March 1985, col. 2587, 2586.
5 Hansard 21 March 1985, col. 2589.
6 Hansard 9 March 1983, col. 2631.
7 Stephen M. Davis, *Apartheid's Rebels*. New Haven & London: Yale University Press, 1987, 168.
8 Hansard 20 May 1985, col. 5864.
9 *Financial Times*, 13 July 1982.
10 *The Star*, 17 October 1983.
11 Such as when the *Sunday Tribune* was warned by the authorities in a lengthy fax that it was not allowed to disclose any detailed information on the delivery by a tanker 'Apatite' which had caught fire while offloading her cargo at the oil buoy off Durban on 23 June 1992 (*Sunday Tribune*, 28 June 1992). The SRB Newsletter No. 28, 1, revealed that there was no tanker bearing the name 'Apatite', which must have been a code-name assigned by the South African authorities. The crew of the tanker had been requested to paint over her real name, *World Xanadu*.
12 *The Citizen*, 9 September 1991; *The Natal Mercury*, 9 September 1991.
13 'SA's oil "secrets" spotlighted by Dutch group', *Southern Africa Report* (Johannesburg), 13 July 1984. The illustration on page 76 is from *The Star*, 13 September 1988.
14 'Wraps lifted off top secret SA oil deals', *Rand Daily Mail*, 27 October 1984.
15 Hansard 3 February 1984, col. 44; *Rand Daily Mail*, 4 February 1984.
16 *Rand Daily Mail*, 19 August, 3 and 4 September 1982.
17 *The Observer*, 31 October 1982.
18 Hansard 3 May 1984, col. 5690.

19 For more information on both cases, see Davie and especially Scholtz. The quote from *Financial Mail* is from its issue of 11 May 1984.
20 Much more can be found in the contribution written by Scholtz.
21 James McClurg in the *Rand Daily Mail*, 27 August 1984.
22 Hansard 14 February 1989, col. 692-3. The minister referred to was Pietie du Plessis.
23 *Weekly Mail*, 2–8 November 1990, 3.

South Africa's Lifeline

1 L. Runderkamp and F. Salverda, 'De geheime olieleverancier van Zuid-Afrika: Saoedi-Arabië' ('The secret oil supplier of South Africa: Saudi Arabia'), *Vrij Nederland*, 6 April 1985; SRB Newsletter No. 2, June 1985, 1. The qualification is from an author in *Mideast Markets* (UK), 13(7), 31 March 1986, 9, who neglects to mention his sources.
2 These cases are indicated 't/s' in the large list of shipments included in this book. N.B. The SRB was not able to ascertain in all known cases of ship-to-ship transfer which type(s) of oil ended up in the ship which sailed to South Africa; concealing the origin of an oil cargo could be the very reason for stage-managing such transhipments.
    Also in some instances in which oil was routed to South Africa via *storage* in a third country, the SRB managed to discover the origin of the oil (especially if it had been stored in nearby Rotterdam). None of these cases are indicated in the tables; however, some information can be found in various chapters.
3 Some of the tankers listed carried refined products, not crude oil. Excluding these deliveries from the calculation hardly affects the outcome.
4 The first shipments investigated by the SRB took place in January 1979. The Bureau never tested the findings of Bailey and Rivers and the belief held generally by the press and by trade journals at the time that *Iran* used to supply 90–95 per cent of South Africa's oil, or in other words, that hardly any oil reached the country from the Arab oil-exporting countries *prior to 1979* (Brunei accounted for a few per cent as well). The relatively simple research method used by Bailey and Rivers differed from the one later developed by the SRB. Indeed, *Petroleum Intelligence Weekly* of 2 April 1979 quoted a Lloyd's of London shipping publication which said 'there were "reports" in 1978 of vessels moving to South Africa from Iraq, Saudi Arabia, Venezuela and Brunei, with smaller tankers also moving from Brazil and Curacao.'
5 With a peak of almost 10 per cent during 1982–84, after Marc Rich had taken over the supply of Brunei crude to South Africa.
6 All 20 ships loaded in Amsterdam; three of them also loaded part cargoes at refineries elsewhere (Sweden, Portugal, Rotterdam). All oil collected in Amsterdam had previously been brought there from other sources. Other countries drawn on by Marc Rich and other traders as sources for oil products for South Africa between 1987 and 1993 included Bulgaria, Finland, France, Greece, Italy, Kenya, Malta, Romania, the Soviet Union, Tunisia, the UK and the USA.

The ANC, the Oil Embargo and the SRB

1 Statement reprinted in N. Mandela, *The struggle is my life*. London: IDAF Publications, 1990, 160.
2 F. Ginwala, 'The Case for Sanctions', in: J. Lonsdale (ed.), *South Africa in Question*. Cambridge/London/Portsmouth, N.H.: African Studies Centre, University of Cambridge/J. Currey/Heinemann, 1988, 97-8 and 102.
3 *The Guardian*, 20 April 1982.
4 Making use of a draft paper entitled *Oil Supplies to South Africa: The Role of Tankers of Open-Registry Fleets*, draft version, written by the Shipping Research Bureau, Amsterdam, May 1981.

5 Press conference with Tambo in Dubai; *Gulf News*, 30 April 1982 (quoted in *ANC Weekly Newsbriefings*, 2 May 1982).

6 This did not refer to all the oil-exporting countries. *Oman* was not a 'diplomatic' target in the contact between the ANC and OAPEC, as it was not a member state. Therefore, when the first SRB preliminary report (in which many shipments involving Shell and Oman were summarised) appeared in January 1980, the ANC had no qualms about 'naming names'.

7 SRB, *Oil Tankers to South Africa 1980–1981*, 1982, 7.

8 Letter to the secretary of the SRB, 10 August 1983.

9 For a case in point concerning ship-to-ship transfer practices in the Persian Gulf, see the photographs on page 92.

10 See box on pp. 191-2.

11 Page 88.

12 R. Kasrils, *'Armed and Dangerous'*. Oxford: Heinemann, 1993, 82.

13 It should also be borne in mind that, to the extent that there were various political tendencies within the ranks of the Dutch anti-apartheid movement, the historical affiliation of the SRB was not to circles in which a healthy distrust of the socialist motherland would have been seen as 'not done'.

14 Letter of AFL-CIO International Affairs Department to the SRB, 28 July 1987. The Bureau only found out about the article several months after its appearance (*Reformatorisch Dagblad*, 11 October 1986), when a Norwegian right-wing paper quoted an obscure Swiss press agency, which had based its version on the Dutch paper. In the process the distinction between purely hypothetical reasoning (the Dutch original) and statements of 'fact' (the Norwegian 'translation') had completely disappeared.

15 The author was even able to indicate with reasonable accuracy the whereabouts of the secret location of the SRB in Amsterdam. The surprised SRB staff couldn't help having a similar feeling about the journalist as he had towards them: that the Bureau had access to 'a gigantic intelligence organisation which by using the most advanced hi-tech products is able to discover the most highly classified information'.

16 In 1984, the SRB was informed by the Soviet delegation that after the authorities had obtained the Bureau's research findings, Marimpex was told that violation of contract clauses would not be tolerated (Marimpex had, of course, responded by saying that it always complied).

17 *Winston-Salem Journal* (USA), 17 August 1984.

18 BBC Summary of World Broadcasts, 5 September 1984.

19 Address by Ambassador Benjamin Netanyahu (Israel), UNGA Plenary Session 31 October 1985, A/40/PV.54, 46.

20 Meir Joffe (Israel), Statement in the Fourth Committee, New York, 1 October 1986; and Statement by Benjamin Netanyahu at the UN General Assembly, 6 November 1986, issued by the Israeli Ministry of Foreign Affairs, Information Division, Jerusalem.

21 Ms Nabeela Al-Mulla (Kuwait), UNGA 5 December 1988, A/43/PV.68, 87. The resolution referred to was the one on the oil embargo.

22 SRB Newsletter No. 8, July 1987, 1-2; No. 11, April 1988, 8; No. 15/16, July 1989, 1-2. Quotes and sources regarding Saudi statements can be found in the various issues.

23 See Berlau's contribution.

24 The statement 'Oil Fuels Apartheid' partly appeared in *Sechaba*, the official organ of the ANC, May 1985, 21-25 (page 18 lists the examples of international action referred to in the text, plus a few others).

25 E.g., in 1987 *Sechaba* published a contribution 'by a Special Correspondent' (read: Ginwala) entitled 'Shell Fuels Apartheid' (March 1987, 24-27), in addition to a Statement of 10 September 1986 ('...SWAPO of Namibia and the African National Congress welcome and support the international campaign to persuade Royal Dutch Shell to break all economic and other links with apartheid').

26 One wonders for instance what brought Lo van Wachem, chairman of the Royal Dutch/Shell Group, to the official dinner which followed the presentation of the Nobel Peace Prize to Nelson

Mandela in Oslo in December 1993. But then, Mandela's co-laureate was F.W. de Klerk; according to a Norwegian press report, it was the latter's embassy which had put Van Wachem on the list of invitees (*Klassekampen*, Norway, 21 December 1993).

27 *International Herald Tribune*, 23 October 1989.

28 *Aftenposten*, 10 December 1993.

Monitoring Invisible Trade

1 *Telegraph* (MNAOA newspaper), December 1983; see also the July 1984 issue in which it was said that the December appeal for members to provide information to the union was the result of a request by the SRB.

2 *Århus Folkeblad*, 23 October 1980.

3 The first to do so was *Dagbladet*, 16 July 1985; see also SRB Newsletter No. 3, 14.

4 *Arbetaren* (Sweden), 9 December 1983; former crew members of the tankers *Athene* and *Regina*.

5 Reporter Mikael Wenger, Radio Väst, Uddevalla.

6 'The best source of information on shipping movements ... are the great powers' satellites ... In an interview ... a Sheribu [sic] staff member has already expressed the wish to have access to data from these satellites. It would be interesting to see whether this is already being done and also whether, for example, the Soviet Union is among the regular suppliers of information' (*Reformatorisch Dagblad*, 11 October 1986). Dr David Owen, then British MP, wrote in the *Guardian* dated 29 August 1988 that satellite monitoring of 'the movements of all ships entering or leaving South African ports' was 'now technically perfectly possible to do', but in a letter to the Holland Committee on Southern Africa, written soon afterwards, he said he was 'sorry not to be of more help' on this issue (letter dated 22 November 1988). The staff of *Shirebu* once investigated the possibility of using satellites as a source of information, only to conclude that the only satellite within the Bureau's reach was able to photograph Durban and its surroundings once every 16 days at a cost of over $4,000 per photograph; the scale would allow – that is, provided the sky was cloudless – a tanker to be recognised ...*as a ship*.

7 See pp. 18-20.

8 Once, in a commendable action, the crew of a tanker en route to South Africa with a cargo of oil transmitted the following message prior to its arrival: 'THE CREW OF THE "INTREPIDO" CONDEMNS THE POLICY OF APARTHEID EFFECTING A WORK STOPPAGE OF SOLIDARITY FOR FOUR HOURS' (*Transport Workers of the World*, No. 4/1986, 10). Just before it would have included the story in its *Newsletter on the Oil Embargo against South Africa*, the SRB discovered that the vessel was a very small vegetable oil carrier.

9 A special problem was posed by instances in which the SRB had an eyewitness report of a discharge operation in Durban that appeared 100 per cent reliable, involving a ship which had not long before also discharged a cargo of oil. Once it had been established that the second cargo most probably came from the storage tanks in Saldanha Bay on the South African West Coast, the shipment could *not* be included in the list of deliveries. See page 202.

10 Another problem was that in some ports where Lloyd's had agents (South Africa!), the authorities did not allow them to report details on tanker calls.

11 On 4 November 1994, *SouthScan* reported that Iran had 'become SA's main oil supplier, providing more than 60% of its import requirements.' In October, Alfred Nzo had once again visited Tehran, now as South Africa's Foreign Minister.

12 Statements by company spokespersons in the media, sometimes in reaction to SRB reports, served as an additional source of information.

13 An obvious possibility was to assume that the company's reply contained a lie in disguise ('Our company was not involved' – All right, but perhaps your Swiss branch was?). The SRB has documented a sufficient number of cases in which companies 'spoke the truth' in this manner. However, suspicion could not replace evidence.

14 It was indeed possible to prove that there were a number of links between the company in question, Comet Oil, and Deuss.

15 Third (extensive) letter from the Nigerian Embassy in The Hague to the SRB, 23 July 1986.

16 Conversation with Terry Macalister, Durban, May 1993. In the article based on the interview (*TradeWinds*, 21 May 1993) Hitchman was quoted as stating that his company was 'never aware of who the traders or the shippers are'; the SRB also claims accuracy when disputing that statement.

17 Of course, mentioning such cases chiefly served to demonstrate that the Bureau had traced more suspicious shipments than it had dared to 'identify' as confirmed shipments.

18 For an example, see page 142.

19 John Oakes, 'S.Africa oil-embargo busters hit back at research bureau', *Seatrade*, July 1984, 43. When Oakes wrote about the contents of previous reports, he was mainly referring to the lists of tankers in the *first* SRB report, which were based on calls reported by Lloyd's, which indeed 'inevitably' resulted in a longer list than one which was limited to cases which involved the suspicion of an oil delivery.

20 The Bureau, or others. On one occasion the World Council of Churches consulted the SRB on a detail concerning a pipeline supposedly operated by Shell together with the government-run South African Railways. The claim, which could be traced to a book by Peter Odell, had appeared in various publications used in the Shell boycott, and finally in a WCC leaflet which was highly contested by Shell in discussions with the churches. The WCC assumed that the SRB was the source. Thus, many people came to be involved in a minor matter. In cases such as this, Shell was fond of requesting those concerned to 'undertake steps' to prevent the dissemination of further 'damaging innuendos', whereby the fundamental issue – Shell's support of apartheid – was kept out of harm's way.

21 An amusing error in the main report from 1988 concerns the attempt of the SRB to get its findings to coincide with the published figures of the official registration of oil deliveries by Norwegian tankers, i.e. to find the names of anonymously registered cases. On page 27 of its report, the SRB stated that deliveries identified by the Bureau 'supported' the Norwegian figures. In the first quarters this had required some Procrustean labour, though. It was decided to attribute an extra voyage to the 'shuttle tanker' *Actor* (Liberian flag) – highly likely, but the evidence was lacking; it was assumed that the *Akarita* had been in South Africa shortly before rather than after the starting date of the registration; one voyage for the *Janniche* was quite rightly included, albeit the wrong one (it was only years later that the SRB laid its hands on evidence regarding the real dates of call of the ship). For those interested in a new attempt, for what it is worth: 1986-II *Akarita – Actor – Berge King – Janniche*; 1986-III *Actor – Berge Chief* (the figures appear in Table 1 in Gudim's contribution). – This was an unusual problem for the SRB; Norway was the only country which offered reliable figures with which to compare its findings, albeit for five quarters only.

22 Inasmuch as it is possible to define this demand in terms of *risks* for the researcher, the principal risk involved in the specific type of research done by the Bureau was probably not the usual one – that of damage being done to the reputation of the researcher – but the possibility of being *sued*. The only time someone actually threatened to take the SRB to court, this did not pertain to the Bureau's research findings. Alan Duncan MP, ex-employee of Marc Rich, and consultant to Vitol (*Private Eye*, 7 May 1993; on Vitol, see pp. 195 and 365), through his lawyer threatened to sue the SRB after the SRB Newsletter had reprinted a story from *Private Eye* regarding his alleged involvement in Rich's shipments of Brunei oil to South Africa. The attempt failed, if only because Duncan had not taken any steps against the British magazine itself. See SRB Newsletter No. 27, 4-5, No. 29, 6, and No. 32, 4; *Private Eye*, 8 May 1992, and 7 May, 10 September and 8 October 1993.

23 *De Volkskrant*, 17 October 1985.

24 See pp. 97ff.

25 Book review in SRB Newsletter No. 19, 8.

26 *De Volkskrant*, 16 August 1985, 1. The story of the tanker, the *Berge King*, appears on pp. 186-7.

27 A less consequential risk was attached to speedy publications (or reports to the United Nations monitoring group) regarding deliveries which *had* been confirmed: Lloyd's sometimes altered the published movement records of ships after months. Suddenly 'Iran' would appear in a record which had until then only listed UAE ports, but in SRB and UN publications the case would remain linked to the UAE only.

The workings of the laborious method can also be illustrated by the example of the company Beta, mentioned at the beginning of this chapter. It was only through this method that the SRB, after more than a year, came across a shipment by the Beta-operated tanker *White Excelsior*, which served as confirmation for the tip from the seamen's union. The tip had been given *while the ship was en route to South Africa with a cargo of petrol.*

28 The SRB was under the impression that each of the callers had rediscovered a lengthy story which appeared in *Africa Confidential*, 15 April and 13 May 1987. Martin Bailey wrote a shorter piece on Williamson and the Seychelles in *The Observer*, 26 April 1987 ('Spy hired to bust sanctions').

29 Quite often press reports reproduced in the SRB Newsletter would start a new life of their own, with other media quoting them as 'According to the Shipping Research Bureau...' An article published by *Noticias* (Mozambique) on 3 November 1989 spoke of 'the director of the bureau for maritime research in Amsterdam, who has declared that his organisation has been transporting Nigerian petroleum to South Africa since 1984'!

30 *Mail on Sunday* (UK), 24 November 1985.

31 *Platt's Week*, 23 May 1988; see also SRB Newsletter No. 12, 4.

32 When an SRB diskette listing 68 UAE shipments went to 'Embargo' in London, which processed the data in a well-written letter to the Group, one could in a way maintain that the latter had consulted an additional source. However, in a subsequent unofficial meeting in New York, the director of the SRB was able to gather that the Group's secretariat was not easy to fool.

33 This is also illustrated by the way cases of 'alleged violations' of the oil embargo were phrased in the Group's first report: 'Ship X delivered oil to South Africa, after allegedly having sailed from country Y.' In fact, the departure from, say, the UAE was in most cases well-documented; the *allegation* was that the ship did not go to Singapore or to Italy as reported, but to South Africa instead.

34 Mr Chagula (Tanzania), General Assembly, 28 November 1988, Provisional verbatim record, A/43/PV.60, 23.

35 SRB Newsletter No. 18, 1990-I, 7: review of the third report of the Intergovernental Group.

36 VPRO television (Netherlands), 10 September 1989 (programme on Transworld Oil and 'Iran-Contragate', researched by SRB staff member Jaap Rodenburg during his stint with Dutch television).

37 *Klassekampen* (Norway), 10 February 1990 – interview with former UN ambassador, Minister Vraalsen.

Marc Rich: Fuel for Apartheid

1 A senior executive of one of the companies of Marc Rich, quoted in: A. Craig Copetas, *Metal Men: Marc Rich and the 10-Billion-Dollar Scam*. New York and London: Putnam & Sons, 1985, 120.

2 Copetas, op. cit., 119. 'Chocolates' was the code word for dollars paid as bribes. The SRB fancied using such quotes in its publications. It once used this particular one, omitting the chocolates; this considerate act of self-censorship could be explained in several ways, one certainly being that it was not in the least unthinkable that the media would start parroting each other in writing that 'according to the SRB, Rich has bribed Nigeria in connection with oil shipments to South Africa.'

3 The next report appeared in September 1986. In the interim Rich had perhaps only gained in prominence, but with only one delivery attributed to Rich (the *Filikon L.*, late 1984), the SRB

had little to go by and therefore did not include him under the heading 'The Main Companies Involved'.
4　*Toronto Star*, 26 July 1979.
5　'Secret oil trail to S.Africa's billions', *The Observer*, 30 May 1982.
6　The Rich case is described, e.g., by Copetas, op cit., and Ingo Walter, *Secret Money: The Shadowy World of Tax Evasion, Capital Flight and Fraud*. London: Unwin, 1986, 53-58.
7　Copetas, op cit., 192-3.
8　Rich's excellent contacts with the former Soviet Union were confirmed by a leading article which appeared in *Izvestiya* when Rich was indicted in 1983. The article denounced the US for persecuting such a distinguished businessman. During the final days of the Soviet empire and subsequent to its demise, Rich succeeded in consolidating the position of his company in the former Eastern bloc countries; *Izvestiya* changed its tune and now referred to him as 'the wealthy, influential and dangerous' Rich, 'sought by the police the world over' (quoted from: *Bilanz*, 9/1992, 174).
9　Hansard 4 May 1984, col. 7-8.
10　Copetas, op. cit., 195.
11　Not to Marc Rich, who had over the years received enough letters to which he had not replied.
12　Kevin Davie, in *The Executive*, August 1991, 29, concluded from the SRB's reports that Deuss was the major middleman in the early 1980s, while Rich dominated the supply line at the time of writing his article. It was possible indeed to draw that conclusion from the Bureau's published data. In the 20 August 1986 issue of *Africa Confidential* the anonymous author (Martin Bailey) put Deuss at the top of the list and Rich as number two; Bailey partly based his statements on information other than that published by the SRB.
13　Advocate-General Van der Walt was not very forthcoming regarding the actual number of deliveries by Rich during the period covered in his report. According to Van der Walt, the Minoil contract could not be cancelled during the first year. It is therefore rather unclear how he could ever state that 17 cargoes *in all* were delivered under this contract, whereas the list which, in his own words, contained all except two of the Minoil cargoes under the contract, showed that as many as 15 cargoes had been delivered during the *three* months May–July 1979. The 15 deliveries amounted to approx. 1.4 million tons. The contract stipulated that 2.4 million tons would be delivered during the first *six* months, and an additional 1.6 million tons, ± 10 per cent, during the second half of the year, while the Advocate-General (who knew the contents of the Minoil contract) referred in his report to 'a rate of 4 000 000 tons (± 10 percent)' and '2 500 000 tons', respectively (figures which he had taken from a previous telex). – Are such inconsistencies and mistakes of an accidental nature?
14　In a letter to the SRB, the managing director of Eastco, Mr D.H. Cavendish-Pell, whose company's links to Hollywell could be traced through the companies' directors, confirmed that Eastco had chartered the *Fidius* in 1987 on behalf of Intercontinental Transportation Corp. (Grand Cayman), but he stated that 'we have no reason to suspect that the vessel ... discharged in South Africa.'
15　'If all identified deliveries in which the Eastco/Holywell group were involved were made in connection with Marc Rich sales, the number of crude oil deliveries [undertaken by Rich] would still be higher.'
16　Understandably, such countries are preferred as locations for 'brass-plate companies'. Yet the government of the Cayman Islands, when requested to look into the voyages of the *Fidius*, had a heartening word for the Shipping Research Bureau: '...the company is registered here. We have no means, however, of verifying the ownership of the cargo or taking any action in Cayman law against the company, or exerting pressure on it even if it [owned the cargo,] even while sympathizing with your general aims' (letter to the SRB, 21 June 1988).
17　Combinations between Rich and *Transworld Oil* are among the loose ends in the SRB's research. The *Maasrix* (May 79) and the *I.D. Sinclair* (Feb/Mar 80) delivered Minoil cargoes, but according to other sources, the ships had been chartered by TWO. A Rich cargo of Saudi oil 'for Thailand' was transhipped to the *Cast Petrel* in Singapore and was delivered to South Africa by

TWO. A few more deliveries could perhaps have been linked to both names, e.g., that by the *I.D. Sinclair* (TWO, May 81); her part cargo of Algerian crude had been transhipped from a tanker chartered by Rich. Most interestingly, the name of TWO appeared in the indictment in the case USA v. Marc Rich et al. The decoded documents on which the prosecution partly based its case showed that cargoes of Iranian oil had been sold by Rich to TWO during the US embargo. The names of several tankers appearing in the indictment also appear in the SRB list, around the dates mentioned in the Rich documents; this suggests that oil sold by Rich to TWO may have ended up in South Africa.

18 See page 180.

19 Only when it was established that a fixed pattern existed could it be taken for granted that the company at least *should have known*. In the case of Neste, the Bureau was able to uncover a few more cargoes which had gone from Neste via Rich to South Africa – sufficient evidence to conclude that it showed complicity? In 1991, some people in Finland were convinced that this was the case, and they avidly used the data from the Bureau to substantiate their claims in the media (see pp. 156-7).

20 If that were done in the case of all the AMP shipments and all unnamed Egyptian cargoes, in addition to all shipments linked to the names of Euravia and the presumably Rich-controlled companies Montfort and Latourag, then Marc Rich would rise in the list to *191* of the 865, or *20 per cent* of the total tonnage. Such a step would be more difficult to make in the case of Derby (and Scanports Shipping Ltd, to which it was linked – both also based in Zug), since the latter represented a major trading company in its own right (Phillip Brothers, or Phibro).

21 *Africa Confidential*, 22 March 1991.

22 Once the international oil embargo was lifted, the secrecy surrounding tanker charters to South Africa slowly started to disappear. At the end of March 1994 a charter report also listed a voyage *from* South Africa: a supertanker had been chartered to transport 260,000 tons of oil to 'UK/ Continent'. The charterer was *Masefield* – a typical Zug company with the appearance of a Marc Rich front.

23 *Fortune*, 1 August 1988.

24 *Business Day*, 6 December 1990.

25 *Business Times*, 1 December 1991; *International Coal Report*, 21 March 1994.

26 Various issues of SRB's *Coal Monitor*, 1990–92.

27 'How Rich got rich', *Forbes*, 22 June 1992, 43.

28 BRRI (Switzerland), 8 October 1990.

29 *Financial Times*, 12 March 1993.

30 Did nothing many others hadn't done...: In his 1985 book on Marc Rich, Craig Copetas quotes one of Rich's senior oil traders, who explained that 'The company was thriving at the time [1979], and we had no need to make money by buying domestic wells or daisy chaining oil. But Marc and Pinky [Green] saw others making a fortune out of daisy chaining and decided that they'd be able to get away with it ... We had recently finished an oil deal with South Africa that screwed them out of an extra $400 million on about three or four shipments. Marc said the South Africans didn't complain, so why should anyone else?' (Copetas, op. cit., 178-9).

31 See SRB Newsletter No. 2, June 1985, 7; *Forbes*, 12 June 1989; *Institutional Investor*, August 1992, 69.

32 On Jamaica (and a row involving Rich in Mexico), see SRB Newsletter No. 17, October 1989, 11, and A. Craig Copetas, 'The Sovereign Republic of Marc Rich', *Regardies*, February 1990; on Namibia: SRB Newsletter No. 27, 1992-II, 6; on Iraq: *Africa Confidential*, 28 August 1992.

33 His US attorney and Rich himself later said the offer had to be viewed as an 'expression of interest' and was made subject to the lifting of UN sanctions against Iraq. However, *Forbes* (22 June 1992, 43) quoted US government officials who said they were looking into charges that Rich had been lending money to Saddam Hussein's Iraq, in return for future deliveries of cheap oil. See *Wall Street Journal*, 16 January 1992; *The Observer*, 26 July 1992 (this paper was forced to publish a rectification afterwards); *Financial Times*, 12 March 1993. On US investigations, see also *Business Week*, 11 November 1991, 76. During a secret meeting which the SRB

had with a private investigator in a station buffet in September 1991 the latter promised to provide copies of the same highly confidential communications between Rich and Iraq. Unfortunately, this never materialised.

34 *Africa Confidential*, 18 February 1994 and 18 November 1994. Glencore International AG is the new name of Marc Rich & Co. AG (Zug) as per 1 September 1994.

35 *ARTnews* (USA), September 1989; *L'Hebdo* (Switzerland), 28 July 1988.

36 On one occasion the Swiss government said that it was aware of allegations regarding circumventions of the oil embargo by Marc Rich but that it was unable to obtain concrete evidence and that the circumventions had not taken place on Swiss territory. See, a.o., *Wochenzeitung*, 30 January 1987; *Zuger Nachrichten, Zuger Tagblatt* and *Luzerner Nachrichten*, January/February 1987, various issues; *Tagesanzeiger*, 22 December 1987.

37 SRB Newsletter No. 25, 1991-IV, 8; *Seatrade Week* (USA), 25 October-1 November 1991; *Iltalehti* (Finland), 2 July 1992.

38 *Institutional Investor*, August 1992, 67. Other quotations in this paragraph appeared in publications of the USWA and the AFL-CIO. Other sources include: *FNV Magazine* (Netherlands), 3 August 1991; Peter Martin, 'Rich pickings', *The Independent Magazine* (UK), 27 March 1993.

39 'South Africa: Rich pickings', *Africa Confidential*, 28 August 1992.

40 Quoted in: *Institutional Investor*, August 1992, 66-67.

41 Dieter Boettcher, quoted in: *Forbes*, 22 June 1992, 41. Interestingly, Metallgesellschaft had previously featured in publications of the USWA in the Ravenswood affair, under the heading 'Business Dealings with Marc Rich May Be Hazardous to Your Company's Financial Health – Join the Growing Movement to Ostracize Fugitive Marc Rich'. The USWA cited a Reuters wire report dated September 1991 which stated that a company in which Metallgesellschaft had a 59 per cent stake had submitted a copper contract with Clarendon for arbitration 'because it was unwilling to do business with a firm ... whose chief was under indictment in the US.' Another example used by the USWA was a quote from 1991 made by the chairman of *Salomon Brothers*, who had ordered his trading executives 'to sever all ties with Marc Rich & Co.': 'It's inappropriate for a Salomon affiliate to be doing business with a fugitive.' It should be noted that Lurgi, a subsidiary of Metallgesellschaft, played a major role in the construction of the Sasol oil-from-coal plants and in the Mossel Bay fuel-from-gas project, and that Salomon's affiliated company Phibro – partly South African-owned – has been involved in the South African oil trade.

Shipping Companies

1   Leaving aside the question of who may be the owners of *that* company: its shareholders (some of whom could be other companies), a government...

2   One example is the Norwegian J.P. Røed, and his Singapore-based company Norse Management, which appears in the list 4 times.

3   19 shipments by the Marimpex tankers *St. Benedict, St. Tobias* and *Mirafiori/Rafio*. Fearnley & Eger was also the time charterer of the *Manhattan Viscount*, and thus involved in the transhipment incident mentioned on pp. 191-2. The company is linked to shipments of more than 5 million tons of oil in all. On 12 May 1981, the Norwegian newspaper *Dagbladet* reported that Fearnley & Eger had been involved in a transport of 90 Centurion tanks (camouflaged as 'scrap') to South Africa in 1978, in contravention of the mandatory arms embargo.

    N.B. Fearnley & Eger merely has historical links with another company named Fearnleys A/S, which was the 100 per cent owner of the Thor Dahl-operated tanker *Thorshavet* (South Africa September 1984) and owned a 25 per cent share in the tanker *Moscliff* (information 31 December 1984).

4   E.g., managers of all Cast vessels which accounted for 16 identified deliveries in 1980–82; see the example of the *Cast Puffin* on page 125.

5   'S.Africa oil-embargo busters hit back at research bureau', *Seatrade*, July 1984.

6   Sørlandssendingen, Norwegian radio, 11 February 1982.

7   There were other vessels with similar Swedish links. The state became part-owner of ships which had been built in a Swedish state-owned dockyard, after the buyers were unable to pay.

8   *Verdens Gang*, 14 March 1986.

9   Hegnar was also the owner of Norwegian LPG tanker, *Osco Cecilia*, which delivered Norwegian LPG to South Africa in November 1985. In a reaction to questions in parliament, Minister Haugstvedt of Commerce and Shipping said that the bill which had been tabled concerning the prohibition of oil sales would also include Norwegian-produced gas (SRB Newsletter No. 4, 5f).

10 *Fædrelandsvennen*, 26 and 27 February 1986; *Norges Handels og Sjøfartstidende*, 6 March 1986; and SRB Newsletter No. 4, 6, for further references.

11 Refined product transports are extensively dealt with in: SRB, *Fuel for Apartheid*, 9-13 and 89-94; and SRB, *The Oil Embargo 1989–1991*.

12 Common address and directorship links between the two firms in Denmark. Regarding Jensen, see Berlau.

13 SRB, *South Africa's Lifeline*, 1986, 42.

14 Official statistics of the Danish government mention a figure of 4.75 million tons of oil shipped by Danish tankers during the same period. Report of 25 March 1985 to Parliamentary Committees on Foreign Affairs and Energy Policy; quoted in: Kirkernes Raceprogram, *Bricks to Apartheid. Denmark's Economic Links with South Africa.* Århus, 1987 (1985), 108. Two smaller Mærsk tankers delivered oil products from Canada in 1980.

15 Parliamentary debates, e.g., on 11 November 1980. Articles in, a.o., *Århus Folkeblad*, 23 October 1980; *Land og Folk*, 10 and 11 March 1981; telegrams: 'Her er beviset for Mærsks oliehandel med Sydafrika: Hemmelige telegrammer afslører A.P. Møller' ('Here is the proof of Mærsk's oil trade with South Africa: Secret telegrams unmask A.P. Møller'), *Ekstra Bladet*, 1 August 1983 (see page 299); North Sea oil to South Africa: *Aktuelt*, 24 January 1985.

16 Quoted in: *Bricks to Apartheid* (see note 14), 109.

17 As regards Møller-owned vessels, the Danish newspaper *Land og Folk* stated that 'the Kirsten Mærsk once was boycotted by Saudi Arabia for similar transactions, which is a possible explanation for A.P. Møller to presently transport oil to South Africa secretively' (11 March 1981).

18 See *Politiken*, 27 January 1985.

19 Letter from Mr Mærsk Mc-Kinney Møller to the SRB, 30 September 1983.

20 *Bricks to Apartheid* (see note 14), 8 and 67.

21 *Lloyd's List*, 17 September 1985, 1; the article was prompted by the publication of the SRB survey.

22 *Vårt Land*, 11 July 1986.

23 *Dagbladet*, 16 September 1986; NTB: *Fædrelandsvennen*, 17 September 1986. N.B. Mosvold Shipping should not be confused with Farsund-based Mosvolds Rederi.

24 Press conference 17 December 1984, Oslo, resulting in newspaper captions such as 'Haugstvedt badly informed in Parliament' (*Aftenposten*), 'Haugstvedt put on the carpet in Parliament: Get information right!' (*Arbeiderbladet*); on *Eirama*: *Dag og Tid*, 20 December 1984 (a typical case in which the press provided an outlet for 'raw' SRB findings – the Bureau was still awaiting a reply from the company).

    The day after Haugstvedt's statement, on 12 December, the Norwegian government said that North Sea oil from three companies had found its way to South Africa despite a gentlemen's agreement, adding that the three would be reprimanded. This announcement came after the government had investigated four shipments at the request of the SRB and the Oslo-based honorary secretary of the British AAM, Abdul Minty, and had discovered eight more cases in the course of the investigation. The companies, by sequence of the number of putative deliveries, were Petrofina (Belgium), Total (France) and Phillips (US) (*Dagbladet*, 14 and 21 December 1984).

25 *Aftenposten*, 18 December 1984.

26 *Dagbladet*, 16 June 1985 (information based on film lists).

27 *Lloyd's List*, 20 September 1986.

28 *Verdens Gang*, 16 December 1986. Decree Number One prohibited the exploitation of Na-

mibia's natural resources without the consent of the UN Council for Namibia.

29 *Skip & Sjø* 4/94, 15.

30 *Ukens Nytt* on 31 December 1985.

31 *Aftenposten*, 13 March and 19 May 1987.

32 *Berge Princess, Berge Prince* (on the transaction, see *Lloyd's List*, 12 November 1985, and *Seatrade Week*, 8–14 November 1985). The foreign company was General Ore International Corp. (Liechtenstein); Bergesen claimed that he did not have any ownership interests in the company. The companies had a long-standing relationship regarding the shipping of South African iron ore (see Alf R. Jacobsen, *Kværner, krig*. Oslo: Cappelens Forlag, 1987, 61-3).

33 See pp. 292-3.

34 Svein Erik Amundsen, in: *Arbeiderbladet*, 8 May 1991.

35 *South China Morning Post* (Hong Kong), 2 April 1989.

36 'World-Wide Shipping: The Major Oil Transporter to South Africa – Update', in: SRB Newsletter No. 23, 5-8.

37 *Skip & Sjø*, February 1988 (emphasis added).

38 *Lloyd's List*, 31 December 1988.

39 More examples in SRB Newsletter No. 23, 8.

40 The reader should bear in mind that conclusions regarding rankings refer to *the findings of the SRB*. If the SRB had been able to obtain a more comprehensive overview of *all* shipments, then the exact formulation might have been (slightly) adjusted. Although the Bureau always aimed at exact formulations ('The SRB has never identified shipments by this company', rather than 'this company has never been involved'), this was sometimes a tiresome affair.

41 *TradeWinds*, 16 September 1994.

42 In its 1992 annual report, the Hellenic Marine Environment Protection Association (founded by George Livanos) declared that it, together with the South African embassy in Athens, had taken the initiative towards the establishment of scholarships, named after George P. Livanos, for Greek students to pursue environmental studies in South Africa.

43 *Ukens Nytt*, 31 December 1985.

44 *TradeWinds*, 23 September 1994.

45 See photograph on page 85.

Embargo Politics

1 For example, see letter circulated by Thorvald Stoltenberg and Vesla Vetlesen, dated 4 November 1981, from LO, Oslo, to unions in oil-exporting countries canvassing support for a UN oil embargo conference.

2 The qualification is from the Norwegian Minister Vraalsen, former Chairman of the UN Intergovernmental Group, quoted in *Klassekampen*, 10 February 1990.

3 8 June 1984: Minister Asbjørn Haugstvedt of Commerce and Shipping (who subsequently apologised to his foreign guest, saying he wanted a frank talk 'without reports in the papers the next day'); 18 September 1986 and 20 May 1987: State Secretary Karin Stoltenberg of Commerce and Shipping (who in 1986 said, 'What could *we* do for you? You see, *your* work is of tremendous use for us...', while in 1987 she seemed mainly annoyed by having to listen to complaints about loopholes in the new law).

4 Letter Bergesen d.y. A/S to SRB, 4 March 1988.

5 *Progress Toward Ending the System of Apartheid. Communication from the President of the United States transmitting the first annual report on the extent to which significant progress has been made toward ending apartheid in South Africa, pursuant to 22 U.S.C. 5091(b)*. Washington, 6 October 1987, 4.

6 More details in SRB, *Oil to South Africa*, 1988, 28.

7 Ibid. – Mobil withdrew from South Africa in 1989, citing the Rangel Amendment as one of the reasons; Donna Katzin does not mention this in her article, because as she told the editors, she

'never believed that for a minute. Every other company with South African investments was affected in the same way, and only Mobil pulled out. I think this was the rationale they gave for being sick and tired of the hassle they were receiving as a result of their South African ties.' More on Mobil's withdrawal in: SRB, *Fuel for Apartheid*, 1990, 33f, and SRB Newsletter No. 15/16, 5ff.

8 The products shipped were largely vital lubricant additives. The prime US exporter was Lubrizol, followed by Caltex. Another big exporter, Mobil Corp., said it had stopped because of the passing of the law in 1986 (*The Philadelphia Inquirer*, 13 May 1990). The USA was not significant as a source of *crude* oil for South Africa; only one small shipment was identified by the SRB dating back to February 1979 (*Esso Portland*).

9 *Southern Africa Report* (South Africa), 31 January 1992.

10 SRB, *The Oil Embargo 1989–1991*, March 1992, 3.

11 On Britain's hold over the oil embargo policies of its dependencies, see SRB Newsletter No. 23, 7f.

12 If there were one place in the world where the 'heat was turned on the British', then it was most certainly in the UK itself. *Shell and BP in South Africa* (1977), *How Britain Fuels the Apartheid War Machine* (1981) and the *Embargo Newsletter* (1986ff) are but a few of the titles of the publications of the British Anti-Apartheid Movement and allied organisations which specifically dealt with British links with South Africa's oil.

13 Martin Bailey in *The Observer*, 3 June 1984. Bailey added that 'Sasol ... maintains only one overseas office – in Pall Mall.'

14 The SRB report which appeared soon afterwards quoted the standard phrase: 'Press reports confirm this oil delivery: *The Observer*, U.K., 31 July 1988' (*Oil to South Africa*, 35). The example of the *Almare Terza* was the subject of Bailey's testimony at the UN oil embargo hearings in New York in April 1989.

15 Letter Foreign and Commonwealth Office to SRB, 16 November 1988.

16 *Report of the Intergovernmental Group...*, 28 October 1988, 44f (quoted in SRB Newsletter No. 14, 16). The reply also referred to the *Almare Settima* (December 1985/January 1986). In the case of the *Almare Terza*, while the ship was en route, the charterer requested that the ship continue to Singapore via the Cape and, subsequently, that the oil be delivered to Cape Town.

17 Written Answers, Mr Wakeham, 23 January 1992, col. 284 (question by Mr Dobson).

18 ELWA, Liberian radio, in English, 13 May 1981. For the Arusha meeting, see page 69.

19 *Journal of Commerce*, 29 October 1980.

20 *Frontline States: How to Counter South African Destabilisation*, Report of the seminar in Athens, 20–23 October 1988. Amsterdam: African-European Institute, 1989, 6.

21 Statement quoted from the Greek press, in: SRB Newsletter No. 13, 4, where the sources can be found for these and other statements made subsequent to the SRB's 1988 report (which listed 17 tankers related to Greece, *15* of which flew the Greek flag). When visiting his Greek counterpart in October 1985, Norwegian Shipping Minister Haugstvedt was told that 'since 1980 no Greek oil tanker had called at South Africa' (*Aftenposten*, 19 October 1985).

    The argument concerning ships which had been chartered out was certainly not only used by Greece. In another example, in 1990 the Canadian government stated that 'Canada has a ban on the export of oil to South Africa *not* on the actual shipping of this commodity. In the case of the "Tenacity" ... the ship alleged to have transported the oil was under the Singapore flag, possibly chartered by a Bermuda-based company. My government, therefore, does not accept that this issue has a Canadian connection' (letter Permanent Representative of Canada to the UN to the SRB, 1 May 1990); the 'possible' charterer referred to was the Bermuda branch of ...Canadian Pacific.

22 *Report of the Intergovernmental Group...*, 1988 (November 1987), UNGA Supplement No.45 (A/42/45), 51.

23 *St. Galler Tagblatt* (Switzerland), 31 August 1988.

24 *Der Spiegel* (FRG), 14 November 1988, on Marimpex's oil trade with South Africa via Switzerland.

25 Minister Danie Steyn, Hansard 21 March 1985, col. 2587.

26 Nor to the potential, if not easily accessible, source of information which banks were. It is possible that the Bureau sometimes, unknowingly, tapped this source. The same can be said of insurance companies, likewise a sector to which the SRB paid too little attention.

27 Confidential information from the banking community.

28 *Replies to the letter dated 28 March 1980 from the Chairman of the Special Committee against* Apartheid *requesting comments or information on action taken with regard to an effective oil embargo against South Africa.* A/AC.115/L.530, 6 August 1980, 2.

29 *Dagbladet* (Norway), 17 September 1986; letter Egyptian Embassy in Oslo to Norwegian Council for Southern Africa, 28 August 1986; *Report of the Intergovernmental Group...*, 1988 (November 1987), op. cit., 51 and 48.

30 Letter from Egypt's UN Ambassador to the SRB, 16 June 1988.

31 SRB, *Fuel for Apartheid*, 20; *Petroleum Economist*, March 1991, 25.

32 Cf. SRB, *Fuel for Apartheid*, 88 note 7.

33 *Business Day*, *The Citizen*, 13 July 1990. Cf. De Quaasteniet and Aarts, page 278.

34 *Report of the Intergovernmental Group...*, 9 October 1991, A/46/44, S/23126, 14. On the model law: see Araim, page 239. The discussion on the model law (author: Prof. R. Lillich) took place during the Intergovernmental Group hearings on the status of the oil embargo, New York, 15 August 1991; UN Department of Information, Press Release SAF/125.

35 *Report of the Intergovernmental Group...*, 1990 (October 1989), A/44/44, 24. A number of examples of contract clauses and related measures regarding the prohibition of oil sales to South Africa have been named in SRB, *South Africa's Lifeline*, 1986, 41n, and in many other SRB and UN publications.

36 Letter of the Iranian UN mission to the SRB, 14 December 1988. N.B. The certificate has been reproduced and discussed on pp. 135-6. – Yet the Bureau somehow appreciated the cooperation of the government of Iran, if only because it enabled the Bureau to lay its hands on copies of forged certificates. Of course, in such cases, the Bureau's answer was phrased in terms such as 'assisting your Government' and 'continuing investigations'; it had learnt something about diplomatic parlance.

37 Hansard 14 May 1985, col. 5509.

38 The measure also banned the sale of crude oil brought into 'free circulation' within the common market, i.e. oil originating in non-EC countries, imported into the EC and traded via EC member states.

39 On the SRB's study commissioned by the City of Rotterdam, see pp. 123-4 and SRB, *South Africa's Lifeline*, 23-27 (a chapter based on the SRB's Rotterdam report). The South African *Star* overdid it in an article of 10 October 1985, in which it stated that 'Rotterdam, the world's busiest port, is about to impose a total ban on shipment of oil to South Africa. The Labour Party-dominated local authorities are drafting a letter to the Dutch Foreign Minister, Mr Hans van den Broek, informing him of the action. The action stems from a recent report by the Anti-Apartheid Movement, which keeps close tabs on shipping movements to and from South Africa.'

40 *Draft report on the implementation by member states of the Community of measures restricting trade with the Republic of South Africa*, Rapporteur B. Simons, June 1987.

41 Huddleston: *The Citizen*, 8 April 1992; the other statements (and more) were quoted in: SRB Newsletter No. 27, 2f.

42 On page 287, Øystein Gudim refers to another example involving Norway and Greece.

43 Speech at International Workshop on sanctions against South Africa, Norway, 8–11 March 1990.

44 All but one of the six cargoes (the *Salem* cargo being the exception) were shipped by tankers that had called at a second country in the Persian Gulf as well as at Kuwait ('multi-porting'). The shipment from Rotterdam was made by the tanker *Karoline Mærsk* in March–April 1980 (part cargoes of Saudi and Kuwaiti oil).

45 *Iraq* hardly ever appears in the list, but reports on large-scale arms deals involving this large oil producer and South Africa and rumours about a three-way deal in which Iraqi oil was not deliv-

ered to South Africa itself (SRB Newsletter No. 21, 5, and No. 22, 11) leave many questions unanswered.

46 Letter from the UN ambassador of Kuwait to the SRB, 29 July 1986.

47 The initial reason for the SRB to name the countries which vessels sailed to *after* calling at South Africa emanated from the wish that other countries would follow Nigeria's example.

48 *West Africa*, 26 January 1981. What the SRB report had in fact indicated was that 'a fair amount' of the oil stored in the Netherlands Antilles came from Nigeria; the Bureau had not implied that it had information in its possession which showed that oil which was transhipped to South Africa actually came from Nigeria.

49 E.g., *Africa Economic Digest*, 27 November 1981.

50 Letter of the Nigerian Embassy in the Netherlands to the SRB, 14 February 1985.

51 *Africa Confidential*, 17 April 1992. With regard to South Africa's oil contacts with various African states, see SRB Newsletter No. 22, 12; No. 23, 1f; No. 24, 2f; No. 27, 3. *Report of the Intergovernmental Group...*, 9 November 1992, A/47/43, S/24775, 4.

52 *The Star*, 30 March 1983. The newspaper obviously did not mention the name of the tanker. The SRB quoted the Libyan example in its report *Secret Oil Deliveries to South Africa*, 1984, 46, to indicate that it would be wise for charterers to check the previous movements of tankers they planned to use.

53 Danish anti-apartheid organisations, AWEPAA and SRB went to the assistance of opposition MPs in a vain attempt to prevent a decision from being taken which they saw as premature; the SRB sent a flood of faxes to political parties, the Danish Foreign Affairs Minister, and the UN oil embargo monitoring group, in what was to be the last of its lobbying activities.

The Impact of the Oil Embargo

1 Many such cases, as well as previously unknown shipments, were included in the final list, thereby boosting the *overall* score to 81 per cent (see page 89).

2 The last Shell shipment listed in SRB publications used to be the *Eastern Mobility* (t/c), January 1981; three more deliveries, by Shell-owned tankers, have emerged only recently, the last of which occurred in June 1981. The last BP shipment in the list is that by the *Tripharos*, September 1980. Mobil is only represented by two shipments which took place in the first half of 1979, and Exxon with only one in early-1979; both companies told the SRB that the oil in question was not embargoed. The first shipment of crude oil by a major oil company that emerged after many years was the one by the *Batis* for Texaco in April 1991.

(A lot of information on the involvement of the oil majors over the embargo years remains classified; this is why the text refers to 'direct and visible' involvement. If documents obtained by the SRB after the research for this book had already been concluded had been available at an earlier stage, the conclusions would have been phrased differently. – Note February 1995).

3 Vitol's Mr Detiger, VARA Radio (Netherlands), 13 March 1985. The SRB never came across subsequent crude oil shipments by Vitol, but the company continued its business in refined products, and it was the first foreign oil company which, in 1993, prior to the lifting of the oil embargo, signed a crude-processing agreement with a South African refinery (Caltex) (*Sunday Times, Business Times*, 14 March 1993; *Petroleum Intelligence Weekly*, 15 March 1993). By that time the idea that this was a 'no-go' area had not lost its power; in mid-1993 the SRB was contacted by a consultancy firm on behalf of a client who wanted to do a deal with Vitol and wanted to know to what extent the latest reports 'reflected badly on the organisation'; would it, for instance, lead to problems with the UN?

4 This may also serve to explain occasional threats from companies which indicated they considered taking legal measures against the SRB, which never materialised.

5 Telex from Hansen-Tangen (Kristiansand, Norway) to SRB, 4 August 1983.

6 Letter from Bulk Oil (U.K.) Ltd to SRB, 21 March 1984.

7 Various telephone conversations and correspondence between Captain Fanciulli, Operations

Manager, Almare di Navigazione SpA, and the SRB, 24 August 1989–27 April 1994. The Norwegian company was Arcade Shipping Co., Oslo.

8   See SRB Newsletter No. 17, 12, where some criticism is voiced regarding several loopholes in Singapore's measures.

9   The circular (No. 2577/M.521/DJM/1981) was reproduced in: UN General Assembly, *Question of Namibia, Action by Member States in support of Namibia, Report of the Secretary-General*, 28 April 1982. A/37/203, 4f. The history of this case offers an additional reason why it has been decided to maintain the *Cherry Vesta*, the only tanker of under 50,000 tons dwt, in the list of shipments in this book. – Martin Bailey commented that it is easier to blacklist a tanker than the companies behind the trade: '...there is little to stop the businessmen behind *Galaxy* or *Star Dust* from surfacing again under other astral names' (*Africa Confidential*, 5 January 1983, 4).

10 'Missing Brunei oil "in S Africa"', *The Observer*, 2 November 1986. 56 shipments (of which 38 since January 1982) were listed in the SRB's survey on Brunei of January 1987. See also SRB Newsletter No. 6, 1; No. 7, 5-8; No. 8, 2; No. 9, 8; No. 12, 4. Newsletter No. 14, 14, quotes the oil-sales contract clauses used by Brunei in order to implement its embargo (from: United Nations, *Report of the Intergovernmental Group...*, October 1988, 20).

11 SRB, *Fuel for Apartheid*, 1990, 43.

12 Kevin Davie, 'How South Africa gets its oil', *The Executive*, August 1991, 30.

13 Cf. Scholtz.

14 'How Profitable is Sasol Oil-from-Coal?', Euromart Research Consultants, 1 February 1984.

15 See page 13.

16 *De Groene Amsterdammer*, 19 March 1980.

17 *The Executive*, November 1991. On problems with the Media Council, see SRB Newsletter No. 26, 3ff and 27, 7f.

18 Energy Minister Steyn mentioned maximum premiums of $8 for 1980, $5+ for 1981, $3.50 for 1982, and $1.90 for 1984 (Hansard 4 May 1984, col. 102).

19 South African businessman Alan Clingman (New York), whom *Forbes* named successor to Marc Rich as 'king of that rare and special breed, the international commodity trader', interviewed by Simon Barber, *Business Times*, 25 September 1994.

20 *The Citizen*, 30 November 1993.

21 Democratic Party energy spokesman Roger Hulley in the South African parliament, 7 May 1992, quoted in SRB Newsletter No. 28, 2.

22 SRB, *Oil to South Africa*, September 1988, 23-4; SRB, *Kudu: South African Development of Namibia's Gas Deposits to Circumvent the Oil Embargo?*, March 1988.

23 *Rand Daily Mail*, 31 October 1983.

24 Once Hulley was given a lecturing in a parliamentary committee meeting by Energy Minister Dawie de Villiers: 'I have here a newsletter from one of the organisations that go out of their way to monitor oil supplies to South Africa, in order to intensify the oil embargo. It is called "Oil Embargo against South Africa Newsletter of October 1989" ... The newsletter is published quarterly by the Shipping Research Bureau, based in Amsterdam. On the front page, of course, they quote the hon member for Constantia ... in connection with Mossgas ... I can only hope that they misquoted him'. The minister accepted Hulley's word that he had 'never spoken to them', adding: 'This confirms, however, that we must proceed with caution when we discuss figures of this kind' (Extended Public Committee, Hansard 8 May 1990, col. 8322).

25 First quote from *The Natal Mercury*, 12 November 1987; second from *Le Figaro*, France, 20 September 1990, quoted in: *Business Day*, 21 September 1990.

26 Quoted in SRB Newsletter No. 21, 6.

27 Manipulations with the strategic stockpile were cited to explain fluctuations in the SRB's 'score'. For example, the SRB's 5th main report showed a total of 68 identified deliveries, unevenly spread: 27 cases in 1985, 41 cases in 1986 (*Oil to South Africa*, 4). See also page 89.

28 *South African Shipping News & Fishing Industry Review*, October 1990, 3; idem, December

1990, 18; on the late-1990 sales (in which *Marc Rich* was reportedly involved as an intermediary): *Africa Confidential*, 22 March 1991.

29 *Windhoek Advertiser*, 25 April 1986.

30 C. Hope (*White boy running*. London: Secker & Warburg, 1988) heard Botha saying the same during a meeting in May 1987.

31 Reuter, Cape Town, 29 April 1991; *The Citizen*, 30 April 1991.

32 *Weekly Mail*, 12–18 July 1991.

33 SABC radio, 6 November 1989; *Southern Africa Report*, 10 November 1989, 11; SRB Newsletter No. 18, 5.

34 Hansard 14 February 1991, col. 1014; emphasis added.

35 Radio report, 12 March 1992; quoted from *Facts and Reports*, 1992: F39.

36 *Business Day*, 6 May 1992.

37 Independent Expert Study Group, headed by Dr Joseph Hanlon, *South Africa: The Sanctions Report*. Prepared for the Commonwealth Committee of Foreign Ministers on Southern Africa. London: Penguin and James Currey, 1989, 108; Hanlon in: J. Hanlon and R. Omond, *The Sanctions Handbook*. Harmondsworth: Penguin, 1987, 210.

38 *Sunday Nation*, South Africa, 3 October 1993. M. Orkin (ed.), *Sanctions Against Apartheid*. Cape Town & Johannesburg/London: David Philip/CIIR, 1989.

39 *Time* (USA), 14 June 1993.

40 *The Citizen*, 1 December 1993.

41 In: United Nations, *The United Nations and Apartheid, 1948–1994*, The United Nations Blue Book Series, Volume I. New York: UN Department of Public Information, 1994, 484.

PART B

Martin Bailey

1   For a detailed account of the Rhodesian embargo see the official report of the Bingham Inquiry, *Report on the Supply of Petroleum and Petroleum Products to Rhodesia*. London: HMSO, 1978, and Martin Bailey, *Oilgate: The Sanctions Scandal*. Sevenoaks: Coronet Books, 1979. A Dutch edition of *Oilgate* was published as *Het olieschandaal 1965–1980*. Amsterdam: Komitee Zuidelijk Afrika and Werkgroep Kairos, 1981.

2   *The Oil Conspiracy* (written by Bernard Rivers). New York: United Church of Christ, 1976, and Martin Bailey, *Shell and BP in South Africa*. London: Haslemere Group/Anti-Apartheid Movement, 1977.

3   The unpublished Annex III of the Bingham Report, entitled 'Evidence of Criminal Offences', was withheld at the request of the Director of Public Prosecutions. The 23-page document lists hundreds of Shell and BP directors who may have committed criminal offences.

4   David Owen, *Time to Declare*. Michael Joseph, 1991, 291 (see also 292-97).

5   Tony Benn, *Conflicts of Interest: Diaries 1977–80*. Hutchinson, 1990, 366 (see also 333-5, 339, 344-5, 351-2 and 390).

6   'Report on Investigation into Alleged Violations of the Rhodesian Sanctions Regulations by the Mobil Oil and Caltex Petroleum Corporations'. US Treasury Office of Foreign Assets Control, 7 October 1985. This followed an earlier Treasury report, dated 12 May 1977.

7   Ken Flower, *Serving Secretly: An Intelligence Chief on Record*. John Murray, 1987, 227.

8   Speech P.W. Botha, quoted in *Windhoek Advertiser*, 25 April 1986.

Kevin Davie

1   *Editors' note*: For additional details, see the document by Clive Scholtz which is printed elsewhere in this book.

Clive Scholtz

1   The 'marker price' is the official selling price of OPEC's benchmark crude. A simple way to explain the concept is that if in the motorcar market, an Audi would for example be used as the 'marker car', the price of a BMW would therefore be the marker price, i.e., that of an Audi, plus 15 per cent; a Mercedes Benz would be the marker price (Audi price) plus, say, 30 per cent, and that of a Volkswagen would be the marker price minus 30 per cent.
2   *Editors' note:* Mr Scholtz's full analysis as contained in the original document was for the purpose of this book abbreviated at the request of the editors.

Tom de Quaasteniet and Paul Aarts

1   Arthur Jay Klinghoffer, *Oiling the Wheels of Apartheid: Exposing South Africa's Secret Oil Trade*. Boulder & London: Lynne Rienner Publishers, 1989, 3.
2   Throughout this article we will refer to the behaviour of 'states' or countries. However, we are well aware that Arab and Iranian oil deliveries were undertaken by individuals as well as state agencies. Our criticism extends to those governments which remained passive whilst individuals were engaging in sanctions-busting activities.
3   Daniel Yergin, *The Prize: The Epic Quest for Oil, Money and Power*. New York: Simon and Schuster, 1991, 593.
4   Martin Bailey and Bernard Rivers, *Oil Sanctions against South Africa*. New York: United Nations Centre against Apartheid, 1985 (1978), 75.
5   Klinghoffer, op. cit., 6.
6   Olusola Ojo, *Afro-Arab Relations*. London: Rex Collings, 1982, 129.
7   Members of OPEC are: Algeria, Ecuador (until 1992), Gabon, Indonesia, Iran, Iraq, Kuwait, Libya, Nigeria, Qatar, Saudi Arabia, the United Arab Emirates and Venezuela.
          Members of OAPEC are: Algeria, Bahrain, Egypt, Iraq, Kuwait, Libya, Qatar, Saudi Arabia, Syria and the United Arab Emirates.
8   See the Resolution of the Council of Ministers of the Arab Petroleum Exporting Countries on the strengthening of the oil embargo against the South African regime: Resolution 26/5 and Recommendations (reprinted as United Nations document A 36/665 S 14750, 12 November 1981).
9   Bailey and Rivers, op. cit., 79.
10 African National Congress (ANC), *Fuelling Apartheid*. New York: United Nations Centre against Apartheid, 1980, 7.
11 Dan Smith, *South Africa's nuclear capability*. London: World Campaign against Military and Nuclear Collaboration with South Africa, 1980, 15 and 22.
12 Fereidun Fesharaki, *Development of the Iranian Oil Industry*. New York: Praeger, 1976, 205; Klinghoffer, op. cit., 36; ANC, op. cit., 7.
13 Yergin, op. cit., 450-479.
14 Advocate-General of South Africa, Report in terms of section 5(1) of the Advocate-General Act, 1979 (Act 118 of 1979), as amended by Select Committee. Submitted to the House of Assembly of South Africa, 27 June 1984, 7.
15 *Rand Daily Mail* (South Africa), 5 March 1974; quoted in: Bailey and Rivers, op. cit., 76.
16 *Financial Mail* (South Africa), 7 December 1973.

17 *Financial Mail*, 19 July 1974.

18 *Lloyd's List* (United Kingdom), 29 January 1979; *Rand Daily Mail*, 8 February 1979; *Petroleum Economist* (United Kingdom), February 1979.

19 *Lloyd's List*, 29 January 1979; *Financial Mail*, 17 September 1979; Klinghoffer, op. cit., 39; *Star Weekly* (South Africa), 14 February 1981.

20 Letter of the Embassy of the Islamic Republic of Iran in Norway to the Shipping Research Bureau, 13 August 1986; quoted in: *SRB Newsletter* No. 5, 1986.

21 Letter of the Permanent Representative of the Islamic Republic of Iran to the United Nations to the Chairman of the Hearings on the Oil Embargo against South Africa, 13 April 1989. – It had already been reported in 1980 that according to Sasol, the Iranians had not delivered their share of crude for Natref and had in fact abandoned their interest in the venture; see the *Financial Times* (United Kingdom) of 12 February 1981. In March 1982, the *Petroleum Economist* wrote that after the fall of the Shah, Sasol had agreed with NIOC to assume the latter's share of capacity, giving Sasol an effective share of 70 per cent (page 104). See also *Financial Mail*, 19 March 1982, 1305.

22 See: Kenneth R. Timmerman, *The Death Lobby*. Houghton: Mifflin, 1991.

23 Middle East News Agency (Egypt), 12 January 1986; *The Independent* (United Kingdom), 27 November 1987; *The Observer* (United Kingdom), 18 October 1987; *Financial Times*, 13 November 1987; *International Herald Tribune*, 27 November 1987; *Africa Confidential*, 22 January 1988.

24 *Euromoney Trade Finance Report* (United Kingdom), February 1986; *International Defense Review* (Switzerland), No. 5, 1988.

25 Timmerman, op. cit., 173; *Lancaster Intelligence Journal* (USA), 14 January 1991; *Minneapolis Star Tribune* (USA), 19 January 1991.

26 *Amandla* (Netherlands), March 1991, 21-22; *SRB Newsletter* No. 21, 1990, 5.

27 This figure does not include cargoes of Middle East oil offloaded in other countries before being shipped to South Africa, e.g. via Rotterdam or the Caribbean.

28 See page 90.

29 This book provides much more evidence, not available at the time, pertaining to these contracts. See pp. 142ff, and the contributions by Davie and Scholtz.

30 Robert Whitehill, 'Apartheid's Oil: Arab Hypocrisy in South Africa', *The New Republic* (USA), 10 February 1986, 11.

31 The Shipping Research Bureau identified the 'Z country' referred to in the Advocate-General's report as Saudi Arabia; see pp. 87-8.

32 Advocate-General of South Africa, op. cit., 24-25.

33 Report of the Intergovernmental Group to Monitor the Supply and Shipping of Oil and Petroleum Products to South Africa, United Nations General Assembly official records; Forty-second session, Supplement No. 45 (A/42/45), S/19251, 5 November 1987, 41.

34 Petromin, the General Petroleum and Mineral Organisation, was founded in 1962 and handled the marketing of Saudi oil which was not allotted to the major oil companies.

35 David Ignatius, 'Royal Payoffs: Some Saudi Princes Pressure Oil Firms for Secret Payments', *Wall Street Journal* (USA), 1 May 1981; Martin Bailey, 'How a Saudi prince won the oil jackpot', *The Observer*, 23 August 1981; Stephen Ellis, 'South Africa's secret oil trade', unpublished draft, 1987.

36 Said K. Aburish, *The Rise, Corruption, and Coming Fall of the House of Saud*, London: Bloomsbury, 1994, 294-302.

37 *Business Week* (USA), 30 June 1986.

38 John and Janet Wallach, 'The Man Who Knew Too Much', *Regardie's* (USA), March 1987; J. Marshall, 'Saudi Arabia and the Reagan Doctrine', *Middle East Report* (USA), November–December 1988; M. Klein, 'U.S.-Saudi Deal Oils Apartheid Regime', *The National Alliance* (USA), 24 July 1987; M. Kranish, 'Oil May Be Key in Iran Dealings', *The Boston Globe* (USA), 22 March 1987.

39 *The Star* (South Africa), 16 October 1982.

40 Yergin, op. cit., 703.

41 Ignatius, op. cit.

42 G. Salamé, 'Political power and the Saudi state', in: B. Berberoglu (ed.), *Power and stability in the Middle East*. London: Zed Books, 1989, 87.

43 Paul Aarts, Gep Eisenloeffel and Arend Jan Termeulen, 'Oil, money, and participation: Kuwait's *Sonderweg* as a rentier state', *Orient* (Germany), Vol. 32 No. 2, 205.

44 Paul Aarts, 'Les limites du "tribalisme politique": le Koweit d'après-guerre et le processus de démocratisation', *Monde arabe, Maghreb-Machrek* (France), No. 142, October–December 1993, 61-79.

45 Yergin, op. cit., 718.

46 Reuter Press Agency, 22 January 1987; *Business Day* (South Africa), 23 January 1987; *Citizen* (South Africa), 27 January 1987; Reuter Press Agency, 8 June 1988.

47 Interview with Farid Esack, Amsterdam, 7 September 1993.

48 Mushtak Parker, 'South Africa's growing ties with the Middle East', *Middle East International* (United Kingdom), 17 April 1992, 20-21; 'South Africa and the Middle East: No longer taboo', *The Middle East* (United Kingdom), March 1993, 35-37; 'South Africa and the Middle East: Let's talk business', *The Middle East*, November 1991, 34-35.

49 *Middle East Economic Survey* (Cyprus), 11 January 1993, A9-A10.

50 Saudi Arabia had already decided to end the boycott a week earlier. *Citizen*, 22 November 1993; *Business Day*, 6 December 1993; *SouthScan* (United Kingdom), 28 January 1994.

Øystein Gudim

1 Source: the South African former State Secretary of Information Eschel Rhoodie, interviewed in 1979 by the Dutch *Elsevier's Magazine*, August 1979 (translation in: *Facts and Reports*, 1979, Q79, 28) (Rhoodie: 'In Norway ... we suddenly booked considerable progress ... [when] contacts were established with a group of conservative politicians ... [which] managed to obtain four seats in parliament'.)

2 The exchange rate between NOK and US dollars has fluctuated over the years, but NOK 7 is roughly equal to $1.

Erik van den Bergh

1 J.W. van der Meulen, 'Nederland en de apartheid', in: *Het woord is aan Nederland: Thema's van buitenlands beleid in de jaren 1966–1983*. The Hague, 1983, 73.

2 S. Rozemond, 'Buitenlandse politiek en Nederlands belang', *Acta Politica*, 1983/1, 5.

3 H.W. von der Dunk, 'Macht en moraal: De vereniging van het onverenigbare', in: *Dezer jaren: Buitenlands beleid en internationale werkelijkheid*. Baarn, 1982, 92.

4 Harry van Seumeren, *Gerrit A. Wagner. Een loopbaan bij de Koninklijke*. Utrecht/Antwerpen, 1989, 55.

5 Ellen Ombre, *Maalstroom*, Amsterdam, 1992, 22.

6 Sami Faltas, *Shell in South Africa*. Amsterdam/Utrecht: OSACI/Kairos, 1976, 76-77.

7 Van Seumeren, op. cit., 42-43.

8 Martin Bailey, *Oilgate: The Sanctions Scandal*. Sevenoaks, 1979, 264-265.

9 *De Volkskrant*, 9 November 1991.

10 J.R. Wilson, 'Business and the Reform Process in South Africa', FCI Annual Banquet, 29 October 1985, 3.

11 J.R. Wilson, 'Business as a catalyst in bringing about a government of national unity', 31 July 1986, 4.

12 'Shell, A corporate report', Supplement to *Financial Mail*, 22 April 1988, 10.

13 'Time to fight back', in: *Corporate social responsibility*, Supplement to *Financial Mail*, 30 January 1987, 46.

14 'Communication – The first step to social responsibility', *Interchange*, March 1989, 6-7.

15 Mark Stephen Adams, *Multinationals, Apartheid and Reform: The Case of Shell South Africa*, Thesis submitted in accordance with the requirements of the University of Liverpool for the degree of Master of Philosophy, 1990, 170-171.

16 Adams, op. cit., 209.

17 *Financial Mail* supplement, 22 April 1988, 6.

18 'Things don't go well with Shell', *South African Labour Bulletin* 14(5), November 1989, 12.

19 *Elseviers Weekblad*, 28 May 1983, 9.

20 *NRC Handelsblad*, 24 February 1994.

21 G. Harmsen, 'Toespraak tot de aandeelhoudersvergadering', 17 May 1990.

22 'UN is urged to sue "sanctions busting" Shell', *Rand Daily Mail*, 4 May 1983.

23 Letter from Cardinal Willebrands and M. Dierick-Van der Ven, on behalf of the Diocesane Pastorale Raad, Aartsbisdom Utrecht, to Pax Christi, 19 June 1979.

24 Allister Sparks, *Tomorrow Is Another Country: The Inside Story of South Africa's Negotiated Revolution*. Wynberg, Sandton: Struik Book Distributors, 1994, 65.

25 L. Wesseling, quoted in: *De Groene Amsterdammer*, 21 January 1981.

26 *Christen Democratische Verkenningen*, 1988/1.

27 *Interchange* 1992/1, 4.

28 Letter from Rob van Drimmelen, World Council of Churches, to Rafael D. Pagan Jr, 16 October 1987.

29 Letter from M.J. van Rooijen, Shell Nederland, to M.J. Faber, Interkerkelijk Vredesberaad, 11 May 1988.

30 When asked for concrete examples of these accusations, Shell refused to disclose further information on which group was meant. Letter from G.C. Westbroek, Shell Nederland, to E. van den Bergh, Werkgroep Kairos, 2 August 1989.

31 Rob van Es, *Een ethiek van belangen: Moreel handelen door onderhandelen over belangen*. Groningen: Wolters-Noordhoff, 1991.

32 Adams, op. cit., 47-48.

33 *Vrij Nederland*, 16 February 1985.

34 'Shell Zuid-Afrika ontdook sinds 1979 olieboykot VN', *Het Financieele Dagblad*, 16 December 1993; 'Het onbestrafte spel van Shell in Zuid-Afrika', ibid., 27 December 1993.

35 *De Volkskrant*, 25 November 1994.

36 More in various issues of the SRB Newsletter.

Donna Katzin

1 Interfaith Center on Corporate Responsibility, *U.S. Churches Denounce Shell Oil's South Africa Ties*. New York, September 1988.

2 *Chicago Tribune*, 17 May 1987.

3 Catherine M. Kovak, 'Fueling the Machines of Apartheid: Shell in South Africa', *ICCR Brief*, 15(5), 1986, 3A; the ultimate source for the statement was the SRB's findings on deliveries by Shell tankers in 1979–81.

4 *Boycott Shell Bulletin*, No. 14 (Summer 1989), 3.

5 Pagan International, *Shell U.S. South Africa Strategy*. Washington, DC, 1986.

6 *Ibid.*.

7 John R. Wilson, Chairman, Shell South Africa, 24 May 1988.

Peter van Bergeijk

1 Baldry and Dollery (1992, 1-2).
2 Indeed, the general economic requirements for potentially successful sanctions that have been identified by econometric research on more than 100 cases in which economic sanctions were applied during the period 1946–1989 seem to have been met in the South African case. See Van Bergeijk (1994, 71-97) for a detailed discussion.
3 Business International Conference 'South Africa: Strategic Options for International Companies', London 27 May 1987. I participated as a junior economist for ABN Bank in this first meeting between the international business community and the ANC. Friends of apartheid had organised an anti-ANC demonstration. The pro-apartheid demonstration was very provocative, and the atmosphere was hostile. This visibly provided a unique experience to the 'captains of industry' and the management of the Mayfair Inter-Continental Hotel in London. Accordingly, security was very strict, although the main speaker, Oliver R. Tambo, was quite relaxed and even took a walk.
4 Indeed, according to Lundahl (1984, 69), the investment funds amassed via gold mining have played a strategic role for the South African economy.
5 J. Leitzel's review of Hufbauer and Schott's *Economic Sanctions Reconsidered, Kyklos* 40(1), 1987, 286.
6 See for examples relating to South Africa: Porter (1979), Lipton (1988) and Kaempfer, Lowenberg, Mocan and Topyan (1993).
7 The episode of UN sanctions against the Iraqi occupation of Kuwait is an example of the failure of an effective sanction (Smeets, 1990).
8 See, for example, the introduction to the Shipping Research Bureau's 1982 research report, page 1: 'Of all the forms of trade embargo which could be imposed against South Africa beyond the mandatory arms embargo that was approved by the United Nations Security Council in 1977, there is little doubt that an oil embargo has the greatest potential for success'.
9 See Van Bergeijk (1994, 32-33) for a formal proof of this point.
10 65th Annual General Meeting, 1992. Atlantis Diesel Engines was another South African autarky project, aimed at the local production of diesel engines.
11 *Special Report of the Auditor-General Concerning the Independent Evaluation of the Mossgas Project*, Pretoria 1991.

Annex
Shipping Research Bureau 1980–1995

'From a secret address in Amsterdam an unknown number of people work for the low national legal minimal wage. They register and monitor the world's tanker fleet with a view to establishing which ships deliver oil to the apartheid regime in South Africa,' a Norwegian newspaper wrote in 1985.[1] When Norway was discussing the pros and cons of an embargo, the media discovered the institute which fuelled the debate with its revelations on the involvement of Norwegian tankers and companies. Journalists, photographers and TV reporters flew to Amsterdam to have a closer look at the nerve centre of the mysterious organisation. But media representatives didn't get very far if they were too curious about certain matters.

During most of the SRB's existence, its staff had a strict policy of not telling anybody about anything which was considered 'secret'. They were not even supposed to tell how many people were on the SRB's payroll, or who its funders were. In their attempts to discover the size of the staff, some callers seemed prepared to spend an amount of money which came close to the size of the Bureau's annual budget – which was not revealed to them either. Some people presenting themselves as journalists were so tenacious on such details that the staff became suspicious about their real motives.

Visitors were never welcomed into the lion's den. Photographers and camera people would be sent home with shots of SRB researchers working in a makeshift office on the premises of the Holland Committee on Southern Africa, a few canals away. A few piles of paper, a rattling telex spitting out 'confidential' messages, and an oil embargo poster glued to the wall worked wonders to satisfy the curiosity of visitors looking for 'authentic' pictures.

Banks have spacious marble halls in order to inspire confidence in their visitors. Thoroughly researched reports on violations of the oil embargo against South Africa required glossy covers and a 3-digit price tag and had to create the impression that a well-equipped and suitably accommodated staff had worked on them, in order to convince the readers of the reliability of their contents. Among the reasons why the exact location of the SRB at Prins Hendrikkade 48, opposite Amsterdam Central Station, was always kept hidden from outsiders, was the fact that the reality was so far removed from the above.

Many people who dealt with the 'Shipping Research Bureau' were under the impression that while they were in contact with the spokesperson engaged with oil sanctions against South Africa, numerous colleagues were busy at the same time preparing equally well-wrought reports on entirely different subjects. In fact, however, the Bureau started and ended its life as a one- to two-person operation, and never more than (during a limited period) four staff members at the same time, for years earning no more than their part-time share of the legal minimal wage, kept the Bureau running. Their small, file-cluttered office certainly did not resemble anything like what people could have imagined as being appropriate accommodation for an 'authoritative research institute'.

There were never indications that keeping the address of the SRB secret also served the safety of the staff and its informers – until a warning reached the Bureau after the London ANC office was bombed and burgled in 1982. Suspects were caught in Britain,[2] and documents in their possession indicated that a 'shipping' organisation in Amsterdam had also been targeted. Frene Ginwala, who passed on the warning to the Holland Committee, was convinced that the SRB was the intended target. An abortive attempt at bombing the office of the SRB's parent organisation, Kairos, was made in 1989; the device used would have reduced the building to a pile of rubble if it had detonated.

A constant threat was that posed by infiltrators. The SRB had its share of people passing themselves off as journalists (Mr Fuehrer, who worked for Pagan on the Shell anti-boycott strategy, came to interview the Bureau's staff for his 'magazine'). Then there were 'refugees'; never was there any-body as persistent as one South African 'conscientious objector' who demanded that he interview a staff member for the magazine of his organisation *in the SRB office*). A 'do-gooder' offered his services as a volunteer and was helpful in disposing of the Bureau's waste paper, which he gathered 'on behalf of a school'. The school certainly got the paper, not only from the SRB but also from various Third World solidarity organisations, and was able to buy a trampoline from the proceeds – only after it had been channelled through a private security firm. The SRB kept a watchful eye on the contents of its waste-paper bin, but its neighbours, AWEPAA, were unpleasantly surprised when information which could only have been taken from their disposed-of fax messages appeared in newspapers.

The SRB was a private foundation, parented by two anti-apartheid committees, the Holland Com-mittee on Southern Africa (KZA, HCSA) and the Working Group Kairos. In keeping with the compartmentalisation of Dutch society, many flowers were blooming in the Dutch anti-apartheid world. HCSA and Kairos cooperated in certain areas, including oil. The SRB had no institutional connections with the Dutch Anti-Apartheid Movement (AABN). Relations of its parent committees with the AABN were not always smooth, but the various committees were able to maintain a certain division of labour. The SRB nonetheless worked with the AABN on topics of mutual interest; the AABN was not directly involved in the oil campaign. Contacts with the PAC-oriented Azania Com-mittee were minimal. Members of the *board* of the SRB were nominated by both parent organisa-tions on a 50/50 basis:

Mr Cor Groenendijk	(chairman, 1980ff)
Mr Jan de Jong	(secretary, 1980–81)
Mr Peter Sluiter	(secretary, 1981–85)
Ms Marijke Smit	(secretary, 1985–87)
Mr Kees de Pater	(secretary, 1987–91)
Mr Frank Hendriks	(1989ff; secretary, 1991ff)
Mr Gerrit Schellingerhout	(treasurer, 1980ff)
Ms Adri Nieuwhof	(1980–83)
Mr Sietse Bosgra	(1983–89)
Mr John Franssen	(1986–89)
Mr Ruurd Huisman	(1989–94)
Mr Ruud Bosgraaf	(1992ff)

The SRB's by-laws of 1980 stipulated that its aims were to do research and related activities on oil transports and supplies, and to furnish the HCSA, Kairos and others with its research findings. In 1983 a public affairs officer was appointed to work alongside the director, who remained responsi-ble for the research.

Despite its neutral-sounding name, the Bureau basically focussed on the oil embargo against South Africa. The SRB's researcher also assisted Bernard Rivers in his research for the Scholten commission, a Dutch parliamentary inquiry into *Rhodesian* sanctions, which exposed shipments of Shell oil and by Dutch tankers to Rhodesia during the embargo.[3] A significant amount of attention was also given to *Namibia* in special reports and Newsletters; before and after its independence, the country was heavily dependent on petroleum supplies from South Africa. Journalists certainly knew how to find the SRB when they wanted expert comment on any embargo. From 1989 until 1992, the SRB had a separate *Coal Section*, which performed research related to the boycott of South African coal.

Mr Frank Janzen	(research director, 1980–81)
Mr Janwillem Rouweler	(research director, 1981–85)
Mr Jaap Woldendorp	(research director, 1985–91)
Mr Richard Hengeveld	(research co-director, 1985–91; director 1991ff)

Mr Jaap Rodenburg   (public affairs, 1983–87; coal section, 1990–92)
Ms Huguette Mackay   (public affairs, 1987–94)
Ms Natascha Verhaaren   (coal section, 1989–90)
Mr Bernard Rivers   (New York; consultant, 1980–84)

The bibliography lists the SRB's *publications*: main reports on the oil embargo, which were the Bureau's showpiece, topical surveys, conference papers and miscellaneous publications. The *Newsletter on the Oil Embargo against South Africa*, which came under the responsibility of the SRB's public affairs officer, was published from February 1985 (No. 1) until 1993-IV/1994-I (No. 33). The Coal Section published the *Coal Monitor* as a special section of the SRB Newsletter from October 1989 (No. 1) until 1992-III (No. 12). *Annual Reports* were not intended for general distribution, but given to journalists who wanted to gain an impression of the SRB's activities and produced chiefly for (potential) funders.

The SRB was only occasionally commissioned to do research (or rather, it would elicit a commission, if it considered the subject important, such as in the case of the port of Rotterdam). Standard practice for the SRB was to apply for grants in support of the ongoing work on the embargo, with no strings attached. Many organisations were willing to give that support, some on a once-only basis, while others were loyal supporters over a long period.

The Norwegian shipowner Sigurd Herlofson knew that the SRB was 'financed and controlled from Moscow', because cutting off South African imports would affect the standard of living of the black population, which was the Soviets' 'only possibility to create a seed-bed for revolution'.[4] Life would have been easier for the cash-starved SRB if these roubles had materialised. Other governments, however, were among the Bureau's funders. The Swedish International Development Authority was one of the pillars without which the SRB's fragile structure would have collapsed in the initial phase; Norway replaced Sweden as the SRB's main supporter after 1986. The UN Special Committee against Apartheid was hampered in its freedom to support the SRB until 1986–87, when the UN oil embargo monitoring group began its work; the UN Council for Namibia had preceded it with a considerable grant in 1984. A notably unresponsive category of potential funders was the trade union movement, which as a whole was also the most frustrating target to win over to an active pro-embargo stance. The few exceptions proved the rule; the Norwegian labour movement's solidarity committee (AIS), in which the trade union federation participated, was one of the SRB's important financial supporters. From the beginning, the churches were among the Bureau's loyal funders. A church-oriented solidarity group such as Kairos considered it important that the churches took the step to support this work, even if on a small scale, because the attendant internal discussion raised the awareness that economic sanctions were a necessary part of the fight against apartheid.

Broederlijk Delen, Entraide et Fraternité, ICFTU (Belgium); Interchurch Fund for Intern. Development, Min. of External Affairs (Canada); WFTU (Czechoslovakia); Danchurchaid (Denmark); Böll-Stiftung, Evang. Missionswerk, SPD, Ver. Evang.-Luth. Kirche (FRG); Adviescommissie Missionaire Aktiviteiten, Alg. Diakonaal Bureau/Zending en Werelddiakonaat (Geref. Kerken), Gen. Diakonale Raad/Commissie Werelddiakonaat (NH Kerk), Novib, Kommissie voor de Projekten in Nederland, Raad van Kerken, St. Oecumenische Hulp (Netherlands); AIS, Min. of Foreign Affairs, Norsk Kjemisk Industriarbeiderforbund (Norway); SIDA (Sweden); Lutheran World Federation, World Council of Churches (Switzerland); War on Want (UK); Council for Namibia, Special Committee against Apartheid (UN); Evang. Lutheran Church in America, Lutheran World Ministries, Tides Foundation, UMWA and private grant (USA).

Notes

1   *Stavanger Aftenblad*, 13 July 1985.
2   Master spy Craig Williamson managed to escape to Belgium immediately after the bomb attack in March 1982, he told *de Volkskrant* (20 February 1995).
3   See, e.g., *African Business*, April 1982, 7–8.
4   Letter to the Editor, *Morgenbladet*, 12 July 1985.

Select Bibliography
on the Oil Embargo against South Africa

Part I lists the publications of the Shipping Research Bureau. Part II contains a selection from an unpublished Bibliography on the Oil Embargo which will be available at the Institute for Southern Africa (Amsterdam), the Mayibuye Centre (Cape Town) and other libraries.

A number of specialised publications have reported extensively on matters relating to the embargo. These include *The Oil Daily, Oil & Gas Journal, Petroleum Argus, The Petroleum Economist, Petroleum Intelligence Weekly, Platt's Oilgram News, Lloyd's List, Financial Mail* (Energy supplements), *Amandla* and others. Useful clipping compilations are provided by *Facts and Reports* (Holland Committee on Southern Africa) and Stock Press (South Africa). The bibliography only offers a limited selection of the abundance of booklets, leaflets, etcetera from groups around the world which devoted themselves to the embargo and of publications by Shell and other companies reacting to boycott actions. For titles not included here, see references in this book.

Abbreviations

CAA   UN Centre against Apartheid, New York.
COL   Consultations of ANC/SWAPO and solidarity groups on the oil embargo, London, 10–11 March and 17–18 November 1984.
CSD   Conference of Seafarers' and Dockers' Trade Unions on the Supply of Oil to South Africa, London, 30–31 October 1985.
[D]   In Dutch.
FJM   First Joint Meeting of the OAU Sanctions Committee and Committee of 19, Arusha, Tanzania, 16–21 March 1981; papers issued by the OAU, Addis Ababa (also in Arabic and French).
HOE   UN Hearings on the Oil Embargo, New York, 12–13 April 1989.
ISA   International Seminar on an Oil Embargo against South Africa, Amsterdam, 14–16 March 1980.
N&D   Notes and Documents of the UN Centre against Apartheid.

Part I: Publications of the Shipping Research Bureau

Oil Supplies to South Africa: The Role of Norwegian Tankers, December 1980.
Oil Supplies to South Africa: The Role of Tankers Connected with the Netherlands and the Netherlands Antilles, January 1981 (Dutch version: *Oliebevoorrading van Zuid-Afrika: De rol van tankers verbonden met Nederland en de Nederlandse Antillen*, January 1981).

Oil Tankers to South Africa [1st main report], March 1981 (2nd printing; 1st unpublished printing: December 1980).

Some Evidence Regarding How South Africa Obtains Its Oil Imports, paper presented by B. Rivers at the FJM, March 1981.

Oil Supplies to South Africa: The Role of Tankers of Open-Registry Fleets [draft], 15 May 1981.

Annual Report 1980–1981, January 1982; subsequent reports on 1982–1983, 1984–1985, and annually until 1992, [1984...1993].

Oil Tankers to South Africa 1980–1981 [2nd main report], June 1982 (2 printings; ISBN 90-70331-05-5).

Het olie-embargo tegen Zuid-Afrika en de rol van Rotterdam: Informatie- en diskussiestuk [D], November 1982.

Oil Embargo against South Africa, and the Role of European Countries, paper presented by B. Rivers to the Conference of West European Parliamentarians for Sanctions against South Africa, The Hague, 26–27 November 1982 (also in French). English version published in: *Papers presented to the Conference...* CAA, December 1982, 9-16.

The Oil Embargo against South Africa, and the Role of Asian Countries, paper prepared for the Seminar on Asian Youth and Student Actions against Apartheid in South Africa, December 1982 (also published in *Asian Student News*, January 1983, 8-10).

De noodzaak van een Nederlands olie-embargo tegen Zuid-Afrika, document [D] prepared for parliamentary hearings on policies towards South Africa, The Hague, 6 June 1983.

Possible Contributions of Trade Unions to Promote and Implement an Effective Oil Embargo against South Africa, paper presented to the International Conference of Trade Unions on Sanctions and Other Actions against the Apartheid Regime in South Africa, Geneva, 10–11 June 1983.

Kairos, 1983, *Oilboycott against South Africa: Contributions of the churches*, discussion paper for the 6th Assembly of the WCC, Vancouver, 24 July–10 August 1983, prepared in cooperation with the SRB.

Eindbestemmings-certificaat en Het identificeren van in Rotterdam geladen tankers die die olie mogelijk hebben gelost in Zuid-Afrika, working paper [D], 14 September 1983.

Testimony, Holland Committee on Southern Africa and Working Group Kairos (Christians Against Apartheid), The Netherlands [on the oil embargo], General Assembly, United Nations, Thirty-eighth session, Special Political Committee, Agenda item 32: Policies of apartheid of the government of South Africa, 8 November 1983; presented by P. Sluiter (HCSA/SRB board) and J. Rodenburg (SRB).

Oil and Tanker Interests that Facilitate the Exploitation of Namibia's Natural Resources, SRB paper presented by D. de Beer at the Seminar on the Activities of Foreign Economic Interests in the Exploitation of Namibia's Natural and Human Resources, Ljubljana, 16–20 April 1984; also in: *Seminar on the Activities...*, report published by the UN Council for Namibia, New York, 1985, 21-32. 2nd updated ed. presented at UN Council for Namibia regional conference on the implementation of Decree No. 1, Geneva, 27–31 August 1984; also in French (ref. A/AC.131/GSY/CRP.5).

Secret Oil Deliveries to South Africa 1981–1982 [3rd main report], June 1984 (1st ed.), [September 1984] (2nd ed.) (ISBN 90-70331-15-2).

Rodenburg, J., 1984, 'Rapport toont ontduiking olie-embargo aan' [D], *Amandla* (ISSN 0166-0373), June–July, 20.

The Oil Embargo against South Africa: West European Involvement and Possible Actions, paper prepared for the founding conference of AWEPAA, Copenhagen, 2–3 November 1984 (also published as Information Note 57/84 of the CAA).

Oil Shipments to South Africa by the Tankers Thorsaga, Thorshavet & Thorsholm, Owned by A/S Thor Dahl of Norway (1981–1984), survey. Amsterdam/Oslo, December 1984 (2 printings).

Hidden Practices. How Oil and Shipping Companies Deceive Governments Which Have Imposed an Oil Embargo against South Africa, paper presented at the International Hearing on South African Aggression against the Neighbouring States, Oslo, 22–24 March 1984 (Dutch version:

Duistere daden: Hoe olie- en scheepvaartbedrijven de Rotterdamse haven misbruiken om het olie-embargo tegen Zuid-Afrika te ontduiken, 18 April 1984).

John Deuss – Transworld Oil. Zuid-Afrika's belangrijkste olieleverancier ('John Deuss/Transworld Oil: South Africa's Main Supplier of Crude Oil'), survey [D] with an English summary, January 1985 (2 printings).

Newsletter on the Oil Embargo against South Africa, (1) February 1985 – (33) 4th Quarter 1993/1st Quarter 1994; Nos. 17–28 included the *Coal Monitor*, (1) October 1989 – (12) 3rd Quarter 1992 (ISSN 0169-3956).

West European involvement in breaking the oil embargo against South Africa, paper prepared for the Workshop on Strategies towards economic isolation of South Africa of the Programme to Combat Racism, WCC, Frankfurt/M, 20–23 May 1985.

The Oil Embargo against South Africa, paper presented to the Conference 'The Struggle against Colonialism and Racism – 40 Years of United Nations Action' of the NGO Sub-Committee on Racism, Racial Discrimination, Apartheid and Decolonization, Geneva, 4-5 June 1985.

Oil Shipments to South Africa on Maersk Tankers: The Role of A.P. Møller of Denmark, survey, June 1985.

Oil Shipments to South Africa by Tankers Owned and Managed by Sig. Bergesen d.y. & Co. of Norway (Jan. 1979 – Jan. 1985), survey. Amsterdam/Oslo, July 1985 (1st ed.), 12 August 1985 (2nd ed.).

Olieleveranties aan Zuid-Afrika: De betrokkenheid van Rotterdam, report [D] commissioned by the City of Rotterdam, August 1985.

West European Companies Breaking the Oil Embargo against South Africa. Possibilities for a West European Response, paper prepared for the Conference 'Apartheid and Southern Africa: The West European Response', Amsterdam, 12–14 September 1985 (also in French).

Marimpex: A German Oil Supplier to South Africa, survey, October 1985 (2 printings); 3rd updated ed.: February 1989. German ed.: 'Umgehung des Ölembargos gegen Südafrika: Marimpex liefert Öl', *epd-Entwicklungspolitik: Materialien* IV/86 (ISSN 0177-5510). Frankfurt/M: Evangelische Pressedienst, 1986.

Companies Breaking the Oil Embargo against South Africa, paper prepared for the CSD, October 1985.

Rodenburg, J., 1985, 'Kooplieden in de olie' [D], *Amandla* (ISSN 0166-0373), November.

South Africa's Lifeline: Violations of the Oil Embargo [4th main report], September 1986 (ISBN 90-70331-13-6).

The International Campaign against Shell, prepared for Workshop on Namibia and on Sanctions against South Africa, Stockholm, 15–19 October 1986.

West European Loopholes in the Oil Embargo against South Africa: Actual Situation of Policies and Action Potential of Parliamentarians to Close the Loopholes, discussion paper prepared for Working Session on Economic Sanctions against South Africa, AWEPAA, Strasbourg, 23–24 October 1986.

Tightening the Oil Embargo against South Africa: Possible Actions to Close the Loopholes, paper prepared for the World Conference on Sanctions Against Racist South Africa, Paris, 16–20 June 1986.

Shell, Marubeni, Rich: Crude Oil Deliveries to South Africa from Brunei (Jan. 1979 – Oct. 1986), survey, January 1987.

Oil Embargo against South Africa: How to Close the Loopholes in Current West European Measures, paper prepared for AWEPAA Seminar on Support to SADCC and Action against Apartheid, Strasbourg, 13–15 May 1987.

The Commonwealth and the Oil Embargo against South Africa, paper, [September 1987].

Closing the Loopholes in the Oil Embargo against South Africa, paper prepared for the International Conference 'The World United against Apartheid for a Democratic South Africa', organised by the ANC, Arusha, 1–4 December 1987.

The European Community and the Oil Embargo against South Africa, paper (1st ed., November 1987) prepared for the NGO Initiative on EC and Apartheid, Copenhagen, 4–5 December 1987;

2nd revised and updated ed., prepared for the Consultative Meeting of Anti-Apartheid Movements from the EC Countries, Bonn, 13–14 February 1988.

Kudu: South African Development of Namibia's Gas Deposits to Circumvent the Oil Embargo?, paper prepared for the Seminar on the International Responsibility for Namibia's Independence, Istanbul, 21–25 March 1988 (2 printings).

Legislation, Monitoring and Enforcement: Tightening the Oil Embargo against South Africa, paper prepared for the AWEPAA/UN Twin Conference 'Southern Africa's Future – Europe's Role', Lusaka and Harare, 23–30 March 1988.

Royal Dutch/Shell: A summary of essential data regarding Shell's involvement in South Africa and Namibia, paper prepared for the meeting of the Central Committee of the WCC, Hanover, 10 August 1988.

Oil to South Africa: Apartheid's Friends and Partners [5th main report], September 1988 (ISBN 90-70331-19-5).

Oil: South Africa's Lifeline, paper prepared for the International Conference on Anti-Apartheid, organised by the Nigerian National Committee against Apartheid, Lagos, 7–9 November 1988, and the International Conference of the Afro-Asian People's Solidarity Organisation (AAPSO), New Delhi, 24–28 November 1988.

Hengeveld, R., 1989, 'Onder Griekse vlag' [D], *Lychnari* (ISSN 0921-3597) 3(1), 11-12.

World-Wide Shipping Group: A Hong Kong Oil Shipper Comes to South Africa's Rescue, survey, April 1989.

The Oil Embargo against South Africa: Past, Present and Future, statement by J.J. Woldendorp, UN Hearings on the Oil Embargo against South Africa, New York, 12–13 April 1989.

SOMO, 1989, *Broken Chains? Boycott of South African Coal in North-West Europe* (Dutch version: *De keten gebroken? Boycot van Zuidafrikaanse kolen in Noord-West Europa*), report commissioned by the Cities of Rotterdam and Amsterdam (research assistance by SRB Coal Section). Amsterdam: Stichting Onderzoek Multinationale Ondernemingen, 21 May.

No Fuel for Apartheid [working title], draft report for the International Confederation of Free Trade Unions (ICFTU), June 1989.

Boycott of South African Coal: An Effective Sanctions Weapon, [draft] report for the International Workshop on Sanctions, Oslo, 8–11 March 1990.

Coal Imports from South Africa: The Belgian Situation, etcetera: 10 country reports (Belgian, Danish, French, Greek, Italian, Luxembourg, in the Netherlands, Portuguese, Spanish, West German) commissioned by AWEPAA, March 1990.

Exports of South African Coal Worldwide, report for the International Labour Organisation, May 1990.

Woldendorp, J.J., 1990a/b, 'Some successes of the oil embargo' and 'Technology transfer to circumvent the oil embargo', in: J. Hanlon (ed.), *South Africa: The Sanctions Report: Documents and Statistics*, A report from the Independent Expert Study Group on the Evaluation of the Application and Impact of Sanctions against South Africa prepared for the Commonwealth Committee of Foreign Ministers on Southern Africa. London/Portsmouth, NH: James Currey (ISBN 0-85255-338-2) and Heinemann (ISBN 0-435-08049-0), 175-179 and 222-225.

Woldendorp, J.J., 1990c, 'The Oil Embargo against South Africa: Effects and Loopholes', in: R.E. Edgar (ed.), *Sanctioning Apartheid*. Trenton, NJ: Africa World Press, 165-180 (ISBN 0-86543-162-0/163-9) (revised version of paper prepared for the conference on 'Sanctions and South Africa', Howard University, Washington, DC, 30–31 October 1987, published by the SRB in October 1987).

Fuel for Apartheid. Oil Supplies to South Africa [6th main report], September 1990 (ISBN 90-70331-24-1).

'Shipping Research Bureau: "Why South Africa does not have to worry about the oil boycott", statement by Huguette Mackay', and 'Shipping Research Bureau: "Make coal an effective weapon against apartheid", statement by Natascha Verhaaren', in: *Transnational Corporations in South Africa: Second United Nations Public Hearings, 1989, Volume II, Statements and Submissions* [Geneva, 4–6 September 1989]. New York, 1990: UN Centre on Transnational Corporations, 113-116 and 117-118 (ISBN 92-1-104341-7).

'Mr Richard Hengeveld, Shipping Research Bureau', Excerpt from statement, in: *Hearings on the Oil Embargo against South Africa (New York, 15 August 1991)* (N&D 18/91), 7-9.

European Sanctions against South African Coal: Actual situation, information paper prepared for the meeting of the Liaison Group of the National Anti-Apartheid Movements in the EC Countries, Amsterdam, 27–29 September 1991.

The Oil Embargo against South Africa and Sanctions on South African Coal, information paper prepared for the CAA in support of consultations of anti-apartheid movements and non-governmental organisations, Geneva, 4–5 November 1991.

The Oil Embargo 1989–1991: Secrecy Still Rules, March 1992.

Information paper, presented to UN Consultations of anti-apartheid movements and NGOs, Geneva, 30 November–1 December 1992 (2 pp.).

Groenendijk, C., 1995, paper on the South African coal boycott prepared for the SRB symposium 'Sanctions in international policy: Lessons from the oil embargo against South Africa', Amsterdam, 16 October 1995.

Embargo: Apartheid's Oil Secrets Revealed, edited by R. Hengeveld and J. Rodenburg. Amsterdam: Amsterdam University Press (ISBN 90-5356-135-8), October 1995.

Report of the SRB symposium 'Sanctions in international policy: Lessons from the oil embargo against South Africa', Amsterdam, 16 October 1995 [forthcoming].

Part II: Select Bibliography on the Oil Embargo

Adams, M.S., 1990, *Multinationals, Apartheid and Reform: The Case of Shell South Africa*, thesis University of Liverpool, December.

Advocate-General [of South Africa], 1984, *Report to the Leader of the House of Assembly in Terms of Section 5(1) of the Advocate-General Act, 1979 (Act 118 of 1979)*, No. 7, 27 June.

Africa Bureau, 1975, *The Role of Iran in South Africa* (Fact Sheet 44). London, November–December.

Africa Fund/American Committee on Africa, 1979, *Fluor*. New York, August.

African National Congress, 1974, 'Oil Embargo Against South Africa', *Sechaba* 8(5), May, 11.

—, 1977, 'Oil and Apartheid', *Sechaba* (11)3, 3rd quarter, 46-56.

—, 1980a, *Fuelling Apartheid*, paper presented at the ISA and at the 3rd Session of the International Committee against Apartheid, Racism and Colonialism in Southern Africa, Stockholm, 11–13 April 1980 (N&D 13/80) (also in: *Development and Social Progress* (16), July–September 1981, 113ff).

—, 1980b, *Paper on military, nuclear collaboration and supply of oil*, presented at the International NGO Action Conference for Sanctions against South Africa, Geneva, 30 June–3 July 1980.

—, 1980c, *Mandatory Economic Sanctions and the Oil Embargo against South Africa*, document prepared for the International Conference on Namibia, Paris, 12–13 September 1980; with annex: ANC statement to UNCTAD, Geneva, 4 September 1980.

African National Congress and SWAPO of Namibia, 1984a/b, *Oil – The Regime's Vulnerability and Strategy and the Necessary Scope of an Oil Embargo*, document for the COL, March (8 pp.); *Feasibility and Options: Campaign for an Oil Embargo in Western Europe*, working paper for the COL, November (3 pp.). London. [Various papers and memorandums.]

—, 1985a/b, *Call for an Oil Embargo*. Lusaka, 7 March; with annex: *Oil Fuels Apartheid*, London, 7 March (partly reprinted in: *Sechaba*, May 1985, 21-25).

AGIS, [1984], *Sweden and the Oil Embargo*, memorandum by P. Wahren for the COL, [March(?)] (1 p.). [Stockholm:] Afrikagrupperna i Sverige.

Akumu, J.D., 1984, 'Towards an Effective Oil Embargo', *Bulletin of the International Oil Working Group* 1(1). New York, Spring.

Anti-Apartheid Movement, 1980a, *Shell Out of Namibia and South Africa*. London, August.

—, 1980b, *British Petroleum's Oil Deal with South Africa: A report by the Anti-Apartheid Movement on the take-over of Selection Trust from Anglo-American Corporation by British Petroleum*. London, September.

—, 1981a, *How Britain Fuels the Apartheid War Machine. A Report on Britain's Role in Supplying Oil to South Africa.* London, March.

—, 1981b, *South African Mining Interests Move into North Sea Oil!* London, March.

—, 1988, *The Mossel Bay Gas Project: British Involvement in South Africa's Offshore Gas Development* (2nd ed.). London, February.

Arbeitskreis Internationale Solidarität, 1990, *Shell raus aus Südafrika! Kill a Multi.* Amsterdam/ Berlin: Edition ID-Archiv im IISG und Verlag Diederich, Hoffmann, Schindowski (ISBN 3-89408-006-X).

Arthur D. Little, 1985, *Impact on Norwegian Shipowners' Charter Prospects of Possible Government Legislation on Calls to South African Ports*, Final report to the Norwegian Shipowners' Association. Cambridge MA, November.

Auditor-General, 1991, *Special Report of the Auditor-General Concerning the Independent Evaluation of the Mossgas Project* (incl. Brooks report). Pretoria: Government Printer (ISBN 0-621-14247-6).

—, 1993, *Special Report of the Auditor-General on the Independent Expert Evaluation of the Economic Viability of the Mossgas Project* (incl. Deloitte & Touche report). Pretoria: Government Printer (ISBN 0-621-15486-5).

Automobile Association of South Africa, 1992, *The South African Oil Industry.* Braamfontein, November.

AWEPAA, 1989, *Implementation of the Oil Embargo by Western Countries*, paper submitted to the HOE. Amsterdam: Association of West European Parliamentarians for Action against Apartheid.

Baars, H., et al., 1990, *Shell-werknemers tussen zwart en wit. Een handreiking voor een gesprek over Shell en Zuid-Afrika in kerk en bedrijf.* Amsterdam: Landelijk Bureau DISK.

Bailey, M., 1977, *Shell and BP in South Africa.* London: Haslemere Group and Anti-Apartheid Movement, March (2nd ed.: April 1978); summary published by UN, New York (A/AC.115/ L.459), 21 March 1977.

—, 1979a, *The Impact on South Africa of the Cut-Off of Iranian Oil* (N&D 16/79), July (also in French).

—, 1979b, *Oilgate: The Sanctions Scandal.* Sevenoaks: Coronet Books (ISBN 0-340-24488-7). Translation into Dutch, revised and updated by the author: *Het olieschandaal 1965–1980* (with an introduction by R. 't Hart). Amsterdam/Utrecht: Komitee Zuidelijk Afrika and Kairos, October 1980.

—, 1979c, 'Was mystery tanker bound for South Africa?', *Toronto Star*, 26 July.

—, 1980a, *Oil Sanctions: South Africa's Weak Link*, paper submitted to the ISA (N&D 15/80) (also in French). Also issued by the International University Exchange Fund as No. 5 of its series on *Economic sanctions against South Africa* (Geneva, 1980); reprint 1981 by the Africa Bureau, London. Reissued by the UN on the occasion of the CSD. Excerpts in: *Objective: Justice* 13(1), UN Department of Public Information, May 1981, 6-21; and in: *The Case for Sanctions against South Africa.* New York: United Nations, May 1982, 3-18. Translated into Norwegian as: *Oljesanksjoner: Sør-Afrikas Svake Punkt.* Copenhagen: Forente Nasjoner's Informasjonskontor for de nordiske land, 1982.

—, 1980b, 'Mauritius: Oil for Sale', *Africa Confidential*, 18 June.

—, 1981a, 'Fleet of supertankers is busting Arab oil embargo on South Africa', *The Observer*, 18 January.

—, 1981b, *Western Europe and the South African Oil Embargo*, paper prepared for the Conference of West European Parliamentarians on an Oil Embargo against South Africa, Brussels, 30–31 January 1981 (N&D 9/81) (also in French); reprinted in UN, 1981a. Reissued by the UN on the occasion of the CSD.

—, 1981c, 'Shell tankers break ban', *The Observer*, 22 February.

—, 1981d, *Sasol: Financing of South Africa's Oil-From-Coal Programme* (N&D 8/81) (also in French).

—, 1981e, *The Impact of Oil Sanctions on South Africa's Neighbours*, paper presented at the FJM.

—, 1981f, 'Secret oil deal with South Africa', *Africa Now*, April.

—, 1981g, 'Big Saudi oil deal breaks embargo', *The Observer*, 9 August.

—, 1982a, 'The Oil Companies Involvement in Southern Africa', in: Christian Concern..., 1982, 5-23.

—, 1982b, 'Secret oil trail to S.Africa's billions', *The Observer*, 30 May.

—, 1982c, *Britain's Role in South Africa's Oil Supply*, revised version (3 pp.), internal paper prepared for Labour Party, International Committee. London, November.

—, 1982d, 'Unmasking the traders who fuel apartheid', *South*, November; reprinted in *OPEC Bulletin* 13(11), December 1982/January 1983, 57-60.

—, 1983a, 'South Africa: Vital oil flows', *Africa Confidential* 24(1), 5 January, 1-4.

—, 1983b, 'Southern Africa: The oil weapon', *Africa Confidential* 24(7), 30 March, 1-3.

—, 1983c/d, 'Tanzania in secret oil deal with South Africa', *The Observer*, 13 November; 'Captain turned down oil bribe', ibid., 20 November.

—, 1984a, *The Oil Embargo against South Africa*, paper for International Hearing on South African Aggression against the Neighbouring States, Oslo, 22–24 March 1984. Oslo: Fellesrådet for det sørlige Afrika et al.

—, 1984b/c, 'Shell earns secret millions in sanction-busting deals' [with D. Leigh], *The Observer*, 5 August; 'Shell linked to new South Africa oil deal', ibid., 12 August.

—, 1984d, 'Lost oil cargo riddle ... the strange story of the Irenes Serenade', *The Observer*, 26 August.

—, 1985, 'Guinness cash link in S Africa oil deal', *The Observer*, 19 May.

—, 1986, 'Missing Brunei oil "in S Africa"', *The Observer*, 2 November.

—, 1989, *The 'Almare Terza': A Case Study of Sanctions-Busting*, Testimony to the HOE.

Bailey, M. and B. Rivers, 1977a, *Oil Sanctions against Rhodesia*, A paper prepared for the Working Group on Sanctions of the Commonwealth Committee on Southern Africa. London: Commonwealth Secretariat, 30 July.

—, 1977b, *Oil Supplies to South Africa: Memorandum to the OAU Ministerial Committee of Seven on Oil Sanctions*. London: Haslemere Group, 20 December.

—, 1978a, *Oil Sanctions against South Africa*, prepared at the request of the Special Committee against Apartheid (N&D 12/78), June (also in French). Reissued by the UN on the occasion of the CSD. Translation into Dutch: *Oliesancties tegen Zuid-Afrika*. Amsterdam/Utrecht: Komitee Zuidelijk Afrika and Kairos, February 1979.

—, 1978b, *Oil Sanctions against Rhodesia: Proposals for Action*, A paper prepared for the Commonwealth Secretariat. London: Commonwealth Secretariat, 2 October.

Bailey, M., et al., 1978, 'BP confesses it broke sanctions – and covered up', *The Sunday Times*, 27 August.

Beerthuizen, C.M.G., 1989, 'De Wereldraad van Kerken versus Shell in Zuid-Afrika', in: A.F. Brand et al. (eds), *Bedrijfsethiek in Nederland – Onderneming en verantwoordelijkheid*. Utrecht: Het Spectrum, 179-197 (ISBN 90-274-2351-2).

Bingham, T.H. and S.M. Gray, 1978, *Report on the Supply of Petroleum and Petroleum Products to Rhodesia*. London: HMSO, September.

Boycott Shell Campaign, [1986]–90, *Boycott Shell Bulletin*, (1) [1986] – (17) Summer 1990. Washington, DC: United Mine Workers of America et al.

Centre for Intergroup Studies, 1982, *Appraisal of Shell South Africa (Pty) Limited*. Rondebosch: University of Cape Town, May.

Checole, K., 1982a, *Oil and the Military Situation in Namibia*, paper presented at the Council for Namibia Seminar on the Military Situation in and Relating to Namibia, Vienna, 8–11 June 1982. New York: International Oil Working Group.

—, 1982b, 'The Oil Embargo, South Africa's Militarisation and Illegal Occupation of Namibia', *ICSA Bulletin* (ISSN 0260-7522), August, 15-17.

Chemical Workers Industrial Union, 1989, *Statement to the United Nations Intergovernmental Group...*, HOE. [Durban:] CWIU.

Christian Concern for Southern Africa, 1982, *Oil and Apartheid: Churches' Challenge to Shell and BP*. London, March.

[Conlon, P.], 1982, 'South Africa's New Offshore Drilling Rigs'. New York: Euromart Research Consultants, 1 December.

—, 1984, 'How Profitable is Sasol Oil-from-Coal?'. New York: Euromart Research Consultants, 1 February.

Conlon, P., 1985a, *South Africa's Offshore Oil Exploration* (N&D 8/85; revised ed. First version published by CAA, April 1983).

—, 1985b, *The SASOL Coal Liquefaction Plants: Economic Implications and Impact on South Africa's Ability to Withstand an Oil Cut-Off* (N&D 10/85).

—, 1985c, *South Africa's Attempts to Reduce Dependence on Imported Oil* (N&D 9/85) [summary of Conlon, 1985a and 1985b].

—, 1989, *International Oil Trade and South Africa's Energy Requirements*, paper prepared at the request of the Task Force on the HOE. New York: United Nations (Ref. A/AC.234.4).

Craine, D., 1989, *The United Kingdom and the Oil Embargo against South Africa*, Submission to the HOE (1990: *Update*, 2 pp., 19 July). London: Embargo.

Davie, K., 1991a, 'How South Africa gets its oil', *The Executive* (ISSN 1012-5280), August.

—, 1991b, 'Inside Sasol', *The Executive*, November.

Davis, J., 1980, *United States Participation in the Supply of Oil to South Africa*, paper presented to the ISA. New York: American Committee on Africa.

Dell, M.W., et al., 1985a, *Werkgelegenheidsaspecten van een Olieboycot tegen Zuid-Afrika*, report commissioned by the City of Rotterdam. Rotterdam: Erasmus University, July.

—, 1985b, 'Economische gevolgen van een olieboycot tegen Zuid-Afrika', *Economisch-Statistische Berichten* (ISSN 0013-0583), 1058f.

Didde, R., et al., 1989, *Als het tij keert: Shell en Nederland, macht en verbeelding*. Amsterdam: Ravijn (ISBN 90-72768-06-X).

Eilertsen, I.-L. and C.-E. Schulz, 1986, *Økonomiske sanksjoner mot Sør-Afrika: Virkninger av ensidig norsk boikott* (FAFO Rapport 61). Oslo: Fagbevegelsens senter for forskning, utredning og dokumentasjon.

El Bouri, W., 1981, paper submitted to the International Conference on Sanctions against South Africa, Paris, 20–27 May 1981. Kuwait: OAPEC.

—, 1983, *The Oil Embargo against South Africa*, Lecture at the 6th Program on the Fundamentals of the Oil and Gas Industry 1982 (in Arabic). Kuwait: OAPEC.

ELTSA, 1980, *Campaign against the Financing of Sasol*, paper presented at the ISA. London: End Loans to South Africa.

—, 1985, *Transworld Oil Lubricates Apartheid: International Day of Action – June 26th, 1985*, leaflet.

Embargo, 1986–89, *Newsletter of the Campaign against Apartheid's Oil Link*, (1) Autumn 1986 – (8) Winter 1989. London: Embargo.

Faltas, S., 1976, *Shell in Zuid-Afrika*, report prepared by the Ecumenical Study and Action Centre on Investments (OSACI) for the Working Group Kairos. Utrecht/Amsterdam: Kairos/OSACI, June (also in English: *Shell in South Africa*).

Federatie Nederlandse Vakbeweging, 1984, *Possible Trade Union Actions Towards an Oil Embargo against South Africa*, paper presented at the Evaluation Symposium on ICFTU Programme of Action in Support of Independent Black Trade Union Movement in South Africa, Agenda item 5: Oil, Transport and Science, Düsseldorf, 19–20 January 1984.

Göransson, P. and H. Wall, 1989, *Shell Smörjer Apartheid: Vad döljer sig bakom skalet?* (2nd revised ed., March). Stockholm: Isolera Sydafrika Kommittén (ISBN 91-87518-04-X).

[Hanlon, J.], 1989, 'Arms and Oil', in: *South Africa: The Sanctions Report*, prepared for the Commonwealth Committee of Foreign Ministers on Southern Africa. London: Penguin and James Currey, 140-147 (ISBN 0-14-052396-0).

Hendriks, F. (ed.), 1990, *Tankgids* (Series Consumenten tegen Apartheid No. 1), with annex: 'Apartheid-vrije benzinestations' (revised version of *Alternatieve tankgids Nederland*, published by the HCSA). Amsterdam/Utrecht/Den Haag: Komitee Zuidelijk Afrika, Anti-Apartheids Beweging Nederland, Federatie Nederlandse Vakbeweging; Kairos; Consumenten Kontakt (ISBN 90-70331-21-7).

Holland Committee on Southern Africa, 1979, *Shell en Zuid-Afrika: De rol van een Nederlandse olie-multinational*. Amsterdam: Komitee Zuidelijk Afrika, September (ISBN 90-70331-02-0).

Holland Committee on Southern Africa and Kairos, 1980, *The Dutch Campaign for an Oil Embargo against South Africa and the Withdrawal of Shell from South Africa*, paper presented at the ISA. Also presented at the 3rd Session of the International Committee against Apartheid, Racism and Colonialism in Southern Africa (ICSA), London, 11–13 April 1980 (also in French). Amsterdam: Komitee Zuidelijk Afrika and Kairos.

Holland Committee on Southern Africa et al., 1986, *Shell Schaduwrapport: Verslag van Shell's aktiviteiten in Zuid-Afrika en Namibië*. Amsterdam/Utrecht/Den Haag: Komitee Zuidelijk Afrika, Kairos and Pax Christi, 15 May. Edition in English by the publishers: *Shell Shadowreport: Report of Shell's Activities in South Africa and Namibia*. British edition, published by the Anti-Apartheid Movement and Embargo: *Shell Shadow Report*, July 1986; 2nd revised ed. March 1987.

Holtmann, B., 1990, *Das Verhalten und Handeln multinationaler Konzerne in der Republik Südafrika – eine soziologische Analyse am Beispiel Royal Dutch/Shell*, Hausarbeit im Rahmen der ersten Staatsprüfung für das Lehramt an der Sekundarstufe II. Münster, 23 September.

Interfaith Center on Corporate Responsibility, 1975a/b, *Caltex (in South Africa)*, draft; *The Shell Group (in South Africa)*, draft. New York: ICCR.

International Oil Working Group, 1982a, *Towards an Oil Embargo against South Africa: Historical Background and a Review of Embargo Resolutions*, AAPSO Seminar on Transnational Corporations and Development, Addis Ababa, 1982. New York: IOWG.

—, 1982b, *Enforcement of the Oil Embargo against South Africa*, Testimony, General Assembly United Nations, Thirty-Seventh Session, Special Political Committee, Agenda Item 33: Policies of Apartheid of the Government of South Africa, 8 November 1982 (Rev. 1).

Iversen, J. and O. Hove, 1987, *Bricks to Apartheid: Denmark's Economic Links with South Africa* (translation from Danish, chapter 4 of *Byggeklodser til Apartheid*, 1985). Århus: Kirkernes Raceprogram (ISBN 87-87967-07-3).

Kairos, 1982, 'The Dutch Campaign Against Shell For An Oil Embargo 1972–1981', in: *Christian Concern...*, 1982, 39-55.

Kairos et al., 1979, *Wat een Shell aandeelhouder mag weten*, published on the occasion of the shareholders' meeting of Royal Dutch, The Hague, 17 May 1979. Utrecht: Pax Christi Nederland and Kairos (a revised version for the shareholders' meeting of 20 May 1980 was published by Kairos, HCSA and Pax Christi).

—, 1980, *Shell – Smeer 'em uit Zuid Afrika*. Utrecht/Amsterdam: Kairos and Komitee Zuidelijk Afrika.

—, 1982, *Bruinboek bij het afscheid van drs Dirk de Bruyne als president-direkteur van de 'Koninklijke'*. Utrecht [etc.]: Kairos, Komitee Zuidelijk Afrika, Pax Christi and Novib, 19 May. English ed. by Christian Concern for Southern Africa: *Oil Supplies to Southern Africa: The De Bruyne Paper – A Report from Kairos in Holland*. London.

—, 1983, *De aan(deel)houder wint: 10 jaar protest tegen steun Shell aan Zuid Afrika*. Utrecht/The Hague: Kairos; Pax Christi and Novib (ISBN 90-6610-011-7).

Klinghoffer, A.J., 1988, *Fraud of the Century: The Case of the Mysterious Supertanker Salem*. London: Routledge (ISBN 0-415-00246-X).

—, 1989, *Oiling the Wheels of Apartheid: Exposing South Africa's Secret Oil Trade*. Boulder & London: Lynne Rienner (ISBN 1-55587-164-X).

Lapping, B., 1964, 'Oil sanctions against South Africa', in: R. Segal (ed.), *Sanctions against South Africa*. Harmondsworth: Penguin.

League of Arab States, 1982, *Arabs and Africans: The Common Struggle against Apartheid* (N&D 14/82).

Leonard, R.W., 1988, *British Petroleum and Its Record in Support of Apartheid in South Africa and Namibia: Opportunities for Action*. Lakewood/Denver, CO: Oil, Chemical & Atomic Workers International Union.

Liff, D.M., 1979, *The Oil Industry in South Africa*. Washington, DC: Investor Responsibility Research Center, January.

Lillich, R.B., 1991, *Model law on the Oil Embargo against South Africa* (N&D 10/91) (based on report presented to UN Intergovernmental Group, 31 August 1990).

Manaças, F., 1984, 'Political factors involved in an oil embargo against South Africa', *SADCC Energy* 2(5), June/August, 6-8.

Minty, A., 1985, *Oil as a Strategic Commodity*, discussion paper for the CSD.

Movimiento Anti-Apartheid Español, 1984, paper for the COL, November (4 pp.). Madrid, 22 October.

Namibia Support Committee, 1984, *Oil and Namibia*, paper for the COL, November (3 pp.). London.

National Labor Boycott Shell Committee, 1987, *The Royal Dutch/Shell Group of Companies: Alternative Corporate Report 1987*. Washington, DC, May.

NOCOSA, 1979, *Report on Norwegian and Multinational Companies and Their Role in Norwegian Collaboration with South Africa*, preliminary report prepared for the International Seminar on the Role of Transnational Corporations in South Africa, London, 2–4 November 1979. Oslo: Fellesrådet for det sørlige Afrika.

—, 1984, *Norway's Role in the Struggle for Oil Embargo against South Africa*, background document for the COL, March (2 pp.).

NOCOSA and Namibia Association, 1986, *Norway's Role in Oil Deliveries to Apartheid South Africa; Norway and the Struggle for Oil Embargo against Apartheid South Africa*, Information document. Oslo/Elverum: Fellesrådet for det sørlige Africa and Namibia Foreningen, 3 June.

Oilfields Workers Trade Union, 1980, 'Trinidad and Tobago Oilworkers' Statement Against Texaco Worldwide', in: Turner and Nore (eds) (see: Turner, 1980), with Appendix: 'Texaco and South Africa', 99-118 (reprint of OWTU pamphlet, 1978).

Organization of African Trade Union Unity, 1983, *Trade Union Action to Stop Oil to South Africa*, paper presented at the International Conference of Trade Unions on Sanctions and Other Actions against the Apartheid Regime in South Africa, Geneva, 10–11 June 1983; prepared on behalf of OATUU by the International Oil Working Group. Accra: OATUU. (Reissued as Turner, 1985.)

Organization of African Unity, 1978, *Report of the Mission of the OAU Committee of Seven to Major Oil Exporting Countries*, Council of Ministers, 31st Ordinary Session, Khartoum, 7–15 July 1978. Addis Ababa: OAU, ref. CM/886(XXXI)Rev.I.

—, 1980, *Report of the Secretary-General on the Impact of an Oil Embargo on Botswana, Lesotho, Swaziland, Zimbabwe and Namibia*, Council of Ministers 35th Ordinary Session, Freetown, Sierra Leone, 18–28 June 1980. Addis Ababa: OAU, ref. CM/1043(XXXV).

Osterrieth, C., 1994, *Het olie-embargo tegen de Republiek van Zuid-Afrika: Kritische analyse met vergelijkende gevolgtrekking naar het embargo in stand gehouden tegen Servië-Montenegro*, Undergraduate thesis. Louvain: Catholic University of Louvain, Faculteit der Economische Wetenschappen.

Pagan International, 1986, *Shell U.S. South Africa Strategy*, report prepared for the Shell Oil Company [Neptune report]. Washington, DC, June.

Paschlau, H., 1984, *Towards an oil and energy embargo against apartheid South Africa: Report on activities of solidarity and anti-apartheid groups in the Federal Republic of Germany*, paper for COL, November (8 pp.).

Passebois, S., 1986, 'Total: Le carburant de l'apartheid', *Apartheid Non!* (Numéro spécial 64; ISSN 0369-8262), November.

Reddy, E.S., 1980, *A Review of United Nations Action for an Oil Embargo against South Africa*, paper presented at the ISA. CAA, March. Reprinted in UN, 1981a.

Riishøj, S., 1984, *Danish policies of sanctions against South Africa, including measures regarding transport and sale of oil*, paper for the COL, November (3 pp.). [Copenhagen,] October.

Ritsema, G. (ed.), 1990, *De Shell-connectie: Shell, Zuid-Afrika en de Nederlandse universiteiten*. Amsterdam: Ravijn (ISBN 90-72768-11-6).

[Rivers, B.], 1976, *The Oil Conspiracy: An investigation into how multinational oil companies provide Rhodesia's oil needs*. New York: Center for Social Action of the United Church of Christ, 21 June.

Rivers, B., 1978, 'Fuelling Apartheid: American Oil Interests in South Africa', *Newsletter* of the Council on Economic Priorities (New York), 4 December.

Rivers, B., 1981a, *Violations of the Oil Embargo against South Africa: Some Thoughts on Possible Improved Forms of Legislation, Monitoring and Enforcement*, paper presented at the FJM (also presented as an SRB paper at the International Conference of Trade Unions in Solidarity with the Workers and Peoples of Palestine, South Africa and Namibia, Tripoli, Libya, 24–27 March 1982).

—, 1981b, *Evidence regarding the involvement of Dutch tankers in transporting oil destined for Rhodesia*, report commissioned by the Rhodesia Boycott Working Party of the Second Chamber of the Dutch Parliament, October.

Rivers, B. and M. Bailey, 1981, *South Africa's Oil Supply: its importance, how it is obtained, and how the existing embargo could be made more effective*, paper commissioned by the CAA for presentation to the UN/OAU International Conference on Sanctions against South Africa, Paris, 20–27 May 1981. CAA.

Rogers, B., 1974, 'Southern Africa and The Oil Embargo', *Africa Today* 21(2), Spring, 3-8.

[Rogers, B.], 1976, *The Expansion of Foreign Oil Companies in South Africa*. New York: Interfaith Center on Corporate Responsibility, March.

Rowe, D.M., 1993, 'Slippery Business: Oil Sanctions Against Rhodesia', Chapter Six (242-298) of *Surviving Economic Coercion: Rhodesia's Response to International Economic Sanctions*, Ph.D. Dissertation. Durham, NC: Duke University, Department of Political Science.

Rozenburg, R., 1986, 'Olieboycot', chapter 3 (57-74) of *De bloedband Den Haag–Pretoria: Het Nederlandse Zuid-Afrikabeleid sinds 1945*. Amsterdam: Komitee Zuidelijk Afrika, Anti-Apartheids Beweging Nederland and Uitgeverij Jan Mets (ISBN 90-70331-12-8).

SACTU, 1984, *The Oil Embargo and International Trade Unions Role*, paper for the COL, November (3 pp.). London: South African Congress of Trade Unions.

Sanctions Working Group, 1979, *Implementation of an Effective Oil Embargo Against South Africa: A Proposal for Capitalising on the Withdrawal of Iran as South Africa's Principal Supplier of Oil*, paper commissioned by the OAU and circulated at its Ministerial and Heads of State Conferences, Monrovia, July 1979. New York, 20 June.

—, 1980a, *Towards Stopping the Supply of Oil to South Africa: Proposals for Collective Action for an Effective Oil Embargo Against South Africa*, paper presented at the Oil Workers' World Antimonopolist Conference, Tripoli, Lybia, 26–30 March 1980. New York, February.

—, 1980b, *Oil – A Weapon against Apartheid: Proposals for Action to Cut Off South Africa's Supply of Oil*, paper presented at the ISA. New York, March.

—, 1980c/h, *Methods for Implementing an Oil Embargo Against South Africa, Methods of Detecting Illegal Supplies of Oil to South Africa* and *Penalties for Embargo Breakers*, 4 June; *How South Africa Obtains Illegal Supplies of Oil. A Case Study: s.s. Salem*, June (updated version included in 1980l, 22-26); *Oil Embargo Resolutions and Proposals: A Chronology, 1960–1980*, June (later ed. updated until December 1980; ed. by IOWG updated until 1983); *Fact Sheet: Oil Sanctions Against South Africa*, June (rev. 1, August 1980). Submissions to the 57th Conference of OPEC, Algiers, June 1980.

—, 1980i, *Implementing an Effective Oil Embargo Against South Africa: The Current Situation*, paper presented at the International NGO Action Conference for Sanctions against South Africa, Geneva, 30 June–3 July 1980 (N&D 21/80).

—, 1980j, *Excerpt from 'Tanker Monitoring: Enforcement of the Oil Embargo against South Africa and the Elimination of Flags of Convenience'*, note prepared by the SWG as background information for the ANC and WCC delegations to UNCTAD's Committee on Shipping, Geneva, 1 September 1980.

—, 1980k, *Control of the Oil Market: OPEC Initiatives to Embargo South Africa – A Case Study of the Exercise of National Sovereignty*, paper presented to the International Association of Democratic Lawyers, 11th Congress, Malta, 13–17 November 1980 (also in *Development and Socio-Economic Progress* 4(17), October–December 1981, AAPSO).

—, 1980l, 'Tracking Oil to South Africa', *Arab Oil & Gas*, 1 December, 18-26 (also in French and Arabic).

—, 1980m, 'Toward an Effective Oil Embargo of South Africa', *Monthly Review* (ISSN 0027-0520) 32(7), 58-62.

—, 1981a/b, *Enforcing the Oil Embargo Against South Africa* and *Towards a New Energy Order in Southern Africa: Strategies for Energy Independence from South Africa*, presented at the Union For Radical Political Economics Conference on Energy – What Is To Be Done, New York, 6–7 March 1981.

—, 1981c, *Testimony presented before The United Nations Special Committee against Apartheid and Preparatory Committee for the International Conference on Sanctions against South Africa*, New York, 11 March 1981 (also published by the CAA under the title *Means for the Implementation of an Effective Oil Embargo against South Africa*, March 1981, ref. Pa-81-019).

SFF, 1983, *Memorandum on the Salem Tanker* [confidential]. [Sasolburg:] Strategic Fuel Fund Association.

Shell International Petroleum Company, 1985ff, *South Africa. Summary of developments* (Management Brief), December 1985, and various other internal memorandums, leaflets, etc. London: SIPC/Group Public Affairs.

Shell Internationale Petroleum Maatschappij, 1988, *Shell en Zuid-Afrika*. The Hague, April.

Shell Nederland, 1981, *Enig commentaar van Shell op het rapport 'Shell en Zuid-Afrika: De rol van een Nederlandse Olie-Multinational'*. Rotterdam, 30 January.

—, 1987ff, *Shell in Zuid-Afrika*, December 1987, and other leaflets, etc.

Shott, T., 1982, 'The Role of the Churches in Britain', in: Christian Concern..., 1982, 25-37.

Sindab, J., 1989, *Shell Shock: The Churches and the Oil Embargo*. Geneva: WCC (also in German).

Sjollema, B., 1982, 'Oil and Coal', in: *Isolating Apartheid: Western collaboration with South Africa – Policy decisions by the World Council of Churches and church responses*. Geneva: WCC, Programme to Combat Racism, 46-56 (ISBN 2-8254-0696-1).

Smit, M., 1986, *The oil embargo against South Africa and the international campaign against Shell*, paper delivered to the NGO Workshop on Namibia and Sanctions Against South Africa, Stockholm, 15–19 October 1986. Amsterdam: Komitee Zuidelijk Afrika.

—, 1987, 'Shell in Zuid-Afrika', in: F. Hendriks (ed.), *Shell*. Amsterdam/Utrecht: Stichting Onderzoek Multinationale Ondernemingen and Uitgeverij Jan van Arkel, 163-190 (ISBN 90-6224-151-4).

SuZa, 1989–90, *Nieuwsbrief SuZa*, [0] [1989] – (2) February 1990. Amsterdam: Committee 'Shell uit Zuid-Afrika'.

Swanepoel, P.C., 1983, *Report on the Circumstances Surrounding the Sale of the Cargo of Crude Oil on Board the Vessel SALEM to South Africa in 1979* [confidential]. [South Africa,] 18 November.

Sydafrikakomiteen i Århus, 1984, *Denmark's role in the struggle for an oil embargo against South Africa*, background document by E. Søndergård for the COL, November (4 pp.). Århus.

Tanzer, M., et al.: see Sanctions Working Group.

Turner, T., 1980, 'Iranian Oilworkers in the 1978–79 Revolution', in: T. Turner and P. Nore (eds), 1990, *Oil and Class Struggle*. London: Zed Press, 272ff (ISBN 0-905762-38-X/27-4).

—, 1983, *Namibian Independence and the Oil Embargo against South Africa*, paper prepared for the International Conference in Support of the Struggle of the Namibian People, Paris, 25–29 April 1983 (also distributed as Miscellaneous Paper No. 186, UN Council for Namibia, Standing Committee III). New York: International Oil Working Group.

—, 1985, *Trade Union Action to Stop Oil to South Africa* [reprint of OATUU, 1983]. Port Harcourt: Publication Committee, University of Port Harcourt.

—, 1987, *Control of the Oil Market: Class Dimensions of the Oil Embargo against South Africa*, paper presented at the Conference on Sanctions and South Africa, Howard University, Washington, DC, 30–31 October 1987.

Turner, T., and A. Baker, 1985, 'Fuelling Apartheid', *International Labour Reports*, May–June, 16-19 and 28.

United Mine Workers of America, [1986a...], *Boycott Shell: A Guide to the Shell Boycott Campaign*; *Protect Our Jobs: How the Shell campaign helps preserve coal jobs in the U.S.*; and other material. Washington, DC: Boycott Shell Campaign c/o UMWA.

United Nations, 1980a, *Shareholders Call on Royal Dutch Shell Group to Withdraw from South Africa* (Information Note 15/80). CAA, 24 March.

—, 1980b/c, *Report of the International Seminar on Oil Embargo against South Africa Held in Amsterdam, from 14 to 16 March 1980.* New York: UN Special Committee against Apartheid, 18 April (Ref. A/AC.115/L.521). The *Declaration* of the Seminar was issued as document A/35/160-S/13869 and reprinted in N&D 18/80 and UN, 1981a. Excerpts from the statement by B.A. Clark, Chairman of the Special Committee, were also published under the title 'The Case for a Mandatory Oil Embargo against South Africa', in: *Objective: Justice* (ISSN 0029-7593) 13(1), May 1981, 2-5. [Various unpublished background papers and statements.]

—, 1981a/b, *Conference of West European Parliamentarians on an Oil Embargo against South Africa,* Brussels, 30–31 January 1981: (a) collection of papers (Bailey, 1981b; ANC; SWAPO; Reddy, 1980), February; (b) report (also in French), April. CAA. Declaration also in UN Press Release GA/AP/1167 and N&D 5/81.

—, 1981c, *Oil Tankers to South Africa: Replies received from Member States.* CAA, 3 April (Ref. A/AC.115/L.538) and addenda.

—, 1982, *Report by His Excellency Alhaji Yusuff Maitama-Sule, Chairman of the Special Committee against* Apartheid, *on His Mission to Kuwait, United Arab Emirates, Saudi Arabia, Netherlands, Denmark, Sweden, Norway and Finland, 5–29 April 1982.* CAA, 11 May.

—, 1986, *Declaration of the Seminar on Oil Embargo against South Africa,* held at Oslo, 4–6 June 1986 (N&D 12/86).

—, 1987–1994, *Report[s] of the Intergovernmental Group to Monitor the Supply and Shipping of Oil and Petroleum Products to South Africa* (also in French and Spanish); Official Records of the General Assembly, Supplements [full list in UN, 1994, 182]; Addendum, 1994. New York: UN General Assembly/UN Security Council.

—, 1989a, *Resolutions Adopted by the United Nations General Assembly on the Oil Embargo against South Africa, 1979–1988.* CAA, 27 March.

—, 1989b, *Report of the Panel on the Hearings on the Oil Embargo against South Africa, United Nations Headquarters, 12 and 13 April 1989.* New York, 16 May (Ref. A/44/279-S/20634). [Various unpublished statements and testimonies.]

—, 1991, *Hearings on the Oil Embargo against South Africa (New York, 15 August 1991)* (N&D 18/91).

—, 1993, *United Nations Ends Oil Embargo against South Africa* (N&D 11/93).

—, 1994, *The United Nations and Apartheid, 1948–1994* (The United Nations Blue Book Series, Vol. 1); section entitled 'Oil embargo' (53-56), bibliography and reprints of various resolutions, documents, etc. New York: UN Department of Public Information (ISBN 92-1-100546-9).

Van Haalen, W.C.I.M., 1984, *De kwestie van een olie-embargo tegen Zuid-Afrika,* Project Binnenlandse beïnvloeding van het buitenlands beleid (Deelstudie 2). Leiden: University of Leiden, Instituut voor Internationale Studiën.

—, 1985, 'An oil embargo against South Africa?', in: P.P. Everts (ed.), *Controversies at home: Domestic factors in the foreign policy of the Netherlands.* Dordrecht: Nijhoff, 215-229 (ISBN 90-247-3227-1).

Van Riemsdijk, M.J., 1994, *Actie of dialoog: Over de betrekkingen tussen maatschappij en onderneming,* Ph.D. thesis; Chapter 5: 'Case III: Shell', 63-97. Enschede: Universiteit Twente (ISBN 90-9007302-7).

Van Schaik, J., 1993a/b, 'Shell Zuid-Afrika ontdook sinds 1979 olieboykot VN', *Het Financieele Dagblad,* 16 December; 'Het onbestrafte spel van Shell in Zuid-Afrika', ibid., 27 December.

Verheugen, G., 1986, 'Alles in Butter, Herr Lutter? Wie das Öl nach Durban kommt', Chapter 11 of *Apartheid: Südafrika und die deutschen Interessen am Kap.* Cologne: Kiepenheuer & Witsch, 144-150 (ISBN 3-462-01800-0).

Vetlesen, V., 1984, Comments [LO Norway] (5 pp.) on Agenda item 5: Oil, Transport and Science, Evaluation Symposium on ICFTU Programme of Action in Support of Independent Black Trade Union Movement in South Africa, Düsseldorf, 19–20 January 1984.

Wellmer, G., 1979(?), *Oiling Apartheid: The role of West German loans for South Africa's Strategic Oil Fund.* Bonn: Informationsstelle Südliches Afrika.

Whitehill, R., 1986, 'The Sanctions That Never Were: Arab and Iranian Oil Sales to South Africa', *The Middle East Review* (ISSN 0305-3210) 19(1), Fall.

Wiggers, G., 1983, *De kwetsbaarheid van Zuid-Afrika voor een olie-embargo* (Ontwikkeling & Veiligheid 7). Groningen: University of Groningen.

Wilson, J.R., 1985ff, *Business and the Reform Process in South Africa*, Presidential Address at the FCI Annual Banquet, 29 October 1985. Johannesburg: Federated Chamber of Industries; and various other addresses.

World Council of Churches et al., 1984, *Fuelling apartheid: Shell and the Military* [based on research by M. Bailey]. Geneva/London/Utrecht: WCC, Programme to Combat Racism; Christian Concern for Southern Africa and Catholic Institute for International Relations; Kairos.

Index